Future of Business and Finance

The Future of Business and Finance book series features professional works aimed at defining, describing and charting the future trends in these fields. The focus is mainly on strategic directions, technological advances, challenges and solutions which may affect the way we do business tomorrow, including the future of sustainability and governance practices. Mainly written by practitioners, consultants and academic thinkers, the books are intended to spark and inform further discussions and developments.

Sepehr Ehsani • Patrick Glauner • Philipp
Plugmann • Florian M. Thieringer
Editors

The Future Circle of Healthcare

AI, 3D Printing, Longevity, Ethics, and Uncertainty Mitigation

Editors
Sepehr Ehsani
Department of Philosophy
University College London
London, UK

Ronin Institute for Independent
Scholarship, Montclair, NJ, USA

Philipp Plugmann
SRH University of Applied Health Sciences
Campus Rheinland, Leverkusen
Rhine-Westphalia, Germany

Woxsen University, Hyderabad, India

Patrick Glauner
Applied Computer Science
Deggendorf Institute of Technology
Deggendorf, Bayern, Germany

Woxsen University, Hyderabad, India

Florian M. Thieringer
Cranio-Maxillo-Facial Surgery
and 3D Print Lab, University Hospital Basel
Basel, Basel-Stadt, Switzerland

Swiss MAM Research Group
Smart Implants - MIRACLE II
Department of Biomedical Engineering
University of Basel, Allschwil
Basel-Landschaft, Switzerland

ISSN 2662-2467   ISSN 2662-2475   (electronic)
Future of Business and Finance
ISBN 978-3-030-99840-0   ISBN 978-3-030-99838-7   (eBook)
https://doi.org/10.1007/978-3-030-99838-7

This Springer imprint is published by the registered company Springer Nature Switzerland AG
The registered company address is: Gewerbestrasse 11, 6330 Cham, Switzerland

Contents

About the Editors

Sepehr Ehsani (https://ehsani.info/) studied laboratory medicine and pathobiology at the University of Toronto at the BSc and PhD levels. While completing his undergraduate degree, he was part of a neuropathology research group. During his postgraduate study, he worked in a protein biology lab with a focus on the prion protein implicated in a number of neurodegenerative diseases. Ehsani was a postdoctoral fellow at the Whitehead Institute for Biomedical Research and the MIT Computer Science and AI Lab, both in Cambridge, Massachusetts, from 2013 to 2016. There, he worked mainly on the alpha-synuclein protein—another neurodegenerative disease-linked protein. In 2015 and 2016, he was a Teaching Fellow at Harvard College's Program in General Education. He has been studying analytic philosophy at University College London since 2017 and is researching the augmentation of mechanistic explanations of disease with *ceteris paribus* laws and cell biological principles.

Patrick Glauner (https://www.linkedin.com/in/glauner/) is a Full Professor of Artificial Intelligence at Deggendorf Institute of Technology (Germany) since age 30 and the Ramon O'Callaghan Professor of Technology Management and Innovation at Woxsen University (India). He has been ranked by CDO Magazine and Global AI Hub among the worldwide academic data leaders. In parallel to his academic roles, he is the Founder and CEO of skyrocket.ai GmbH, an AI consulting firm. As an expert witness, he advised the parliaments of France, Germany, and Luxembourg. He also regularly advises politicians on the European, federal, state, and local levels. He has published four books: *"Creating Innovation Spaces"* (Springer, 2021), *"Digitalisierungskompetenzen: Rolle der Hochschulen"* (Hanser, 2021), *"Digitalization in Healthcare"* (Springer, 2021), and *"Innovative Technologies for Market Leadership"* (Springer, 2020). His works on AI were featured by New Scientist, McKinsey, Imperial College London, Times Higher Education, Coursera, Udacity, the Luxembourg National Research Fund, Towards Data Science, Süddeutsche Zeitung, Tagesspiegel, Deutsche Welle, Bayerischer Rundfunk, Westdeutscher Rundfunk, Wehrtechnik, Konstruktionspraxis, and others. He was previously Head of Data Academy at Alexander Thamm GmbH, Innovation Manager for Artificial Intelligence at Krones Group, a Fellow at the European Organization for Nuclear Research (CERN), and a visiting researcher at the University of Quebec in Montreal (UQAM). He graduated as valedictorian from

Karlsruhe University of Applied Sciences with a BSc in Computer Science. He subsequently received an MSc in Machine Learning from Imperial College London, an MBA from Quantic School of Business and Technology, and a PhD in Computer Science from the University of Luxembourg. He is an alumnus of the German National Academic Foundation (Studienstiftung des deutschen Volkes).

Philipp Plugmann (https://www.linkedin.com/in/prof-dr-dr-plugmann/) has been doing multidisciplinary work for the last 22 years in parallel to practicing as a dentist in his own clinic in Leverkusen, Germany. He is also a Full Professor of Interdisciplinary Periodontology and Prevention at the SRH University of Applied Health Sciences (Germany) and Professor of Practice at Woxsen University (India). His first book on innovation in medical technology, published in 2011, was reviewed by Cisco. His second book on innovation, published with Springer in 2018, had more than 135,000 chapter downloads during the first 48 months after its release. Previously, he held multiple adjunct faculty appointments for over seventeen years, winning multiple teaching awards. He also holds an MBA in Health Care Management, an MSc in Business Innovation (both from the EBS University of Business and Law, Germany), and an MSc in Periodontology and Implant Therapy (DGParo, German Society for Periodontology); he is currently pursuing his third doctorate. Prof. Plugmann has given research talks in the field of innovation at conferences at Harvard Business School (USA), Berkeley Haas School of Business (USA), Max Planck Institute for Innovation and Competition (Germany), Max Planck Institute for Social Law and Social Policy (Germany), and Nanyang Technological University (Singapore). He is a serial entrepreneur and advisor to several companies, including a global technology consultancy as a Senior Advisor for Life Science and Health Care. Since 2020, he is a reviewer for the Federal Health Bulletin (*Bundesgesundheitsblatt*).

Florian M. Thieringer (https://www.linkedin.com/in/thieringer/) studied medicine at the TU Munich, dentistry at the LMU Munich, and health business administration at the FAU Erlangen-Nuremberg. He is an oral- and cranio-maxillofacial surgeon as well as a medical 3D expert with a focus on tumor, trauma, reconstructive, and orthognathic surgery. Located at the University Hospital Basel and University of Basel, Switzerland, FMT is currently senior surgeon and *Privatdozent* for oral and cranio-maxillofacial surgery. He is also a Head of the Medical Additive Manufacturing Research Group at the University of Basel's Department of Biomedical Engineering. He has earned international recognition for his expertise in computer assisted surgery and medical additive manufacturing, extensively exploring and promoting the integration of virtual surgical planning, 3D printing, and other innovative technologies at the point-of-care (such as additive manufacturing of patient-specific implants in various biomaterials, including bioprinting and regenerative surgery). Since 2016, he has acted as a Co-Director of the multidisciplinary 3D Print Lab at the University Hospital of Basel. Since 2020, he has been a Co-Principal Investigator of the innovative MIRACLE 2 project (Minimally Invasive Robot-Assisted Computer-guided LaserosteotomE). Funded by the Werner Siemens Foundation, the 12m Swiss Franc research project aims to develop a robotic endoscope to perform contact-free bone surgery with laser light. Perfectly fitting patient-specific implants will be designed in AR/VR for production through intra- and extra-corporeal 3D printing.

Abbreviations (Future Circle of Healthcare)

AAOS	American Academy of Orthopaedic Surgeons
ABG	autologous bone graft
AD	Alzheimer's disease
ADMET	absorption, distribution, metabolism, excretion, and toxicity
AI	artificial intelligence
AM	additive manufacturing
AMR	antimicrobial resistance
APP	amyloid precursor protein
BCI	brain-computer interface
CAD	computer-aided design
CAD/CAM	computer-aided design and computer-aided manufacturing
CAR-T	chimeric antigen receptor T-cell
CASP	critical assessment of structure prediction
CBCT	cone beam computed tomography
CCM	collaborative care model
CDC	Centers for Disease Control and Prevention (U.S.)
CII	computer-implemented invention
CIRC	COVID inpatient risk calculator
CPATH	computational pathology
CT	computed tomography
DBE	Department of Biomedical Engineering (University of Basel, Switzerland)
DBM	demineralized bone matrix
DICOM	Digital Imaging and Communications in Medicine
DMTA	design-make-test-analyze
DN	deductive-nomological model
DP	digital pathology
EBD	evidence-based design
ECG	electrocardiogram
EEG	electroencephalography
e-Health	electronic health
EHR	electronic health record
ELSA (E.U.)	ethical, legal, and social aspects
ELSI (U.S.)	ethical, legal, and social implications

EMA	European Medicines Agency
EMPAIA	Ecosystem for Pathology Diagnostics with AI Assistance
ENT	ear, nose, and throat
EPC	European Patent Convention
EPO	European Patent Office
EU	European Union
FDA	Food and Drug Administration (U.S.)
FFF	fused filament fabrication
GAD	generalized anxiety disorder
GHI	green hospital initiative
GIS	geographic information system
GMP	good manufacturing practice
gnomAD	genome aggregation database
GWAS	genome-wide association study
hDPSC	human dental pulp stem cell
HPV	human papillomavirus
HTS	high-throughput screening
IP	intellectual property
LIS	laboratory information system
MBC	measurement-based care
MDD	major depressive disorder
MDE	model-driven engineering
m-Health	mobile health
ML	machine learning
MRI	magnetic resonance imaging
NAPLS	North American Prodrome Longitudinal Study
NCD	non-communicable disease
NCE	new chemical entity
NCS-R	National Comorbidity Survey Replication
NFT	neurofibrillary tangle
NICE	National Institute for Health and Care Excellence (U.K.)
NIH	National Institutes of Health (U.S.)
NIMH	National Institute of Mental Health (U.S.)
NLP	natural language processing
NM	new mechanism
NSAID	nonsteroidal anti-inflammatory drug
OCL	object constraint language
OCR	optical character recognition
OECD	Organisation for Economic Co-operation and Development
OSCC	oral squamous cell carcinoma
PCR	polymerase chain reaction
PEEK	polyether ether ketone
PEMF	pulsed electromagnetic field
PIcc	Pathology Innovation Collaborative Community
PLGA	poly(lactic-*co*-glycolic acid)

PM	principled mechanism
PMMA	poly(methyl methacrylate)
POS	parts of speech
PrEP	pre-exposure prophylaxis
PRP	platelet-rich plasma
QSAR	quantitative structure–activity relationship
QTL	quantitative trait locus
RAISE	Recovery After an Initial Schizophrenia Episode
RAP	Research Analysis Platform
RB	regular behavior
RCT	randomized controlled trial
R&D	research and development
RE	requirements engineering
RF	random forest
RF-SLAM	random forests for survival, longitudinal, and multivariate (data analysis)
rhBMP-2	recombinant human bone morphogenetic protein-2
RIC	reverse integrated care
RNN	recurrent neural network
RRI	responsible research and innovation
SCARP	severe COVID-19 adaptive risk predictor
SCC	squamous cell carcinoma
SDG	sustainable development goal (U.N.)
SLA	stereolithography apparatus
SLR	systematic literature review
SLS	selective laser sintering
SMILY	Similar Medical Images Like Yours
STL	standard tessellation language
STS	science and technology studies
SVM	support vector machine
TCP	tricalcium phosphate
3GL	third-generation language (programming)
TMJ	temporomandibular joint
UI	user interface
UML	unified modeling language
WHO	World Health Organization
WIPO	World Intellectual Property Organization
WSI	whole slide imaging
xAI	explainable artificial intelligence
XML	extensible markup language

Introduction: Trends, Puzzles, and Hopes for the Future of Healthcare

Sepehr Ehsani, Patrick Glauner, Philipp Plugmann, and Florian M. Thieringer

Abstract

This book is being published at a time when the collective attention of the world has been focused, for more than 2 years, on the coronavirus pandemic. The interrelatedness of various facets of biomedicine (whether scientific, societal, political, legal, or cultural) has been vividly illustrated to health practitioners, researchers, and the public at large—often on a very personal level. It is now manifestly obvious to many that planning for the future of clinical and experimental medicine is a must. Although the task of predicting the exact trajectory of any profession might be in vain, it is essential that one at least looks at past and current trends in order to envision future scenarios and plan for them.

S. Ehsani (✉)
Theoretical and Philosophical Biology, Department of Philosophy, University College London, Bloomsbury, London, UK

Ronin Institute for Independent Scholarship, Montclair, NJ, USA
e-mail: ehsani@uclmail.net

P. Glauner
Deggendorf Institute of Technology, Deggendorf, Germany

Woxsen University, Hyderabad, India

P. Plugmann
SRH University of Applied Health Sciences, Campus Rheinland, Leverkusen, North Rhine-Westphalia, Germany

Woxsen University, Hyderabad, India

F. M. Thieringer
Cranio-Maxillo-Facial Surgery and 3D Print Lab, University Hospital Basel, Basel, Basel-Stadt, Switzerland

Swiss MAM Research Group, Smart Implants – MIRACLE II, Department of Biomedical Engineering, University of Basel, Allschwil, Basel-Landschaft, Switzerland

S. Ehsani et al. (eds.), *The Future Circle of Healthcare*, Future of Business and Finance, https://doi.org/10.1007/978-3-030-99838-7_1

We can thus shape our *expectations* about how the various threads of biomedicine could develop; these could then inform our preparedness.

The chapters in this volume each cover one or more of four general themes. First, there is the rapid pace and ubiquity of technological advances in areas such as artificial intelligence (AI), machine learning, additive manufacturing, and wearable electronics. Second, there is the theme of healthy aging, longevity, and the management of chronic diseases. Third, there are the ethical dimensions of medical decisions. And fourth, there is the notion of uncertainty in various domains of medical knowledge and its mitigation and translation into clinical practice. This introductory chapter is meant to provide a broader context for the book, providing an up-to-date analysis of current trends and areas that deserve our attention over the next several years.

1   The Essentials

A commentary on the future of healthcare cannot begin without stating the obvious: the essentials of life must first be in place. These essentials include access to safe drinking water and nutrition of suitable quantity and quality. The essentials also include the broader topics of climate change, air pollution, and environmental damage (Bernstein et al., 2022; Chase et al., 2022; Lin et al., 2021a). On this topic, *Thomas Spittler* and *Helana Lutfi* write about "Innovations for Sustainable Healthcare" in Chap. "Innovations for Sustainable Healthcare".

Other layers of healthcare essentials pertain to improving child health and ending preventable deaths in the very young (Perin et al., 2021), addressing inequities in birth registrations around the globe (Bhatia et al., 2019), and providing widespread, inclusive, and affordable access to healthcare and medicine, such as ready access to insulin (Sharma & Kaplan, 2021). This is why an underlying theme of discussions about future trajectories in biomedicine should always be health equity, understood as the "absence of unfair, avoidable and remediable differences in health status among groups of people" (WHO, 2021, p. 2).[1]

Medically, perhaps one of the most (if not the most) pressing dangers over the coming years is the threat from antimicrobial resistance or AMR (Kirchhelle, 2018; Kwon & Powderly, 2021). The most recent comprehensive analysis based on data from 2019 paints an alarming picture: "there were an estimated 4.95 million (3.62–6.57) deaths associated with bacterial AMR in 2019, including 1.27 million (95% [uncertainty interval] 0.911–1.71) deaths attributable to bacterial AMR" (Antimicrobial Resistance Collaborators, 2022). Although various novel solutions are being explored (Ardell & Kryazhimskiy, 2021; Atanasov et al., 2021; Brives & Pourraz, 2020; Deghelt & Collet, 2022; Durand-Reville et al., 2021; Huynh &

---

[1] For the topic of universal health coverage, see The Lancet (2021).

Wood, 2021; Kaplan et al., 2021; Larsen et al., 2022; Leimer et al., 2021; Miethke et al., 2021; Mitcheltree et al., 2021; Vandenbroucke-Grauls & Kluytmans, 2022; Tibbits et al., 2022; Wang et al., 2022), much more urgent and widespread attention needs to be directed at the global problem of AMR. Parallel to AMR, antifungal drug resistance also poses a global challenge in need of serious research and policy investment (MacAlpine et al., 2021; Revie et al., 2018; Rocheleau, 2022).

2   Longevity and Aging

Notwithstanding variations in local patterns and projections (Finkelstein et al., 2021; Janssen et al., 2021; Livingston et al., 2020), humans now generally live longer than in the past. This could be due to many factors, such as public health campaigns, increased hygiene, antibiotics, and so on. As Steven Johnson (2021) points out, "during the century since the end of the Great Influenza outbreak [1918–1920], the average human life span has doubled." Increased longevity has brought about changes in the leading causes of mortality around the world. For example, the ten leading causes of death in 2020 in the United States comprised the following proportions of the total number of deaths attributed to those ten causes (2,506,540): heart disease (28%), cancer (24%), COVID-19 (14%), accidents (unintentional injuries) (8%), stroke (cerebrovascular diseases) (6%), chronic lower respiratory diseases (6%), Alzheimer's disease (5%), diabetes (4%), influenza and pneumonia (2%), and nephritis, nephrotic syndrome, and nephrosis (2%) (CDC National Center for Health Statistics, 2020). A decade earlier, the ten leading causes and their proportions (out of a total of 1,852,349 cases) were as follows: heart disease (32%); cancer (31%); chronic lower respiratory diseases (7%); stroke (cerebrovascular diseases) (7%); accidents (unintentional injuries) (7%); Alzheimer's disease (5%); diabetes (4%); nephritis, nephrotic syndrome, and nephrosis (3%); influenza and pneumonia (3%); and intentional self-harm (suicide) (2%) (Heron, 2013, p. 9).

Each one of these categories has seen impressive research advances in the past few years. For instance, one could point to cancer immunotherapy (Ochoa de Olza, 2021; Ravaud, 2021; Sriram et al., 2021) and the strides toward understanding the mechanisms of tumor immune evasion (Baldwin & Gattinoni, 2022; Kaufman, 2021; Saha et al., 2022; Zhang et al., 2021). There have also been substantial reductions in cervical cancer rates due to human papillomavirus vaccinations (Falcaro et al., 2021). For type 1 diabetes (100 years after the discovery of insulin), stem cell-based islet replacement therapy is progressing (de Koning & Carlotti, 2021; Ramzy et al., 2021), and there have been successful gene therapies for monogenic conditions, such as sickle cell disease and β-thalassemia (Esrick et al., 2021; Frangoul et al., 2021) or rare liver disease (Kaiser, 2021a). However, this success has been checkered in the case of conditions such as Huntington's disease (Kwon, 2021a). Highly targeted gene delivery techniques are also advancing rapidly (Tabebordbar et al., 2021). *Maryam Parhizkar* and *Dimitrios Tsaoulidis* describe these and other approaches in depth in "The Outlook for Novel Pharmaceutics" (Chap. "The Outlook for Novel Pharmaceutics").

The topic of aging and longevity is itself a very active area. Researchers are learning about the biology of lifespan by studying bats, whales, naked mole rats, elephants, and albatrosses, among other species (Austad & Finch, 2022; Belzile et al., 2022; da Silva et al., 2022; Eisenstein, 2022; Holmes, 2021; Kaya et al., 2021; Kolora et al., 2021; Lu et al., 2021a; Reinke et al., 2022). A Seychelles giant tortoise (called "Jonathan," hatched c. 1832) is currently the oldest known living land animal. The microscopic multicellular animals, bdelloid rotifers, have been reported to survive for extremely long periods in an Arctic permafrost environment (Shmakova et al., 2021). There are also studies of the ability of tardigrades to withstand conditions that are otherwise too extreme for other living things (Hashimoto et al., 2016; Neves et al., 2020) and the extreme longevity of the plant species *Welwitschia mirabilis* (Wan et al., 2021).

There are now different biotech start-ups focused on antiaging therapies (Dolgin, 2021; Regalado, 2021). In the laboratory and beyond, the underlying biology of aging in humans and other species is under intense scrutiny (Augustin & Kipnis, 2021; Fan et al., 2017; Garcia et al., 2021b; Gorbunova et al., 2021; Grunewald et al., 2021; Hägg & Jylhävä, 2021; Lengefeld et al., 2021; Lin et al., 2021b; Lu et al., 2021c; Martinez-Miguel et al., 2021; Sato et al., 2022; Stein et al., 2022; Vidal-Pineiro et al., 2021; Wang & Blau, 2021; Wiley & Campisi, 2021). These projects pursue many different exciting threads, including the so-called "senotherapeutics" (Robbins et al., 2021); the relationship between aging and the microbiome (Rimal & Patterson, 2021; Sato et al., 2021; Shukla et al., 2021); biological constraints on the rate of human aging (Colchero et al., 2021); the effects of physical activity on aging (Horowitz et al., 2020; Lieberman et al., 2021); the effect of dietary polyamines (Schroeder et al., 2021), fasting (Helfand & de Cabo, 2021; Ulgherait et al., 2021), and the efficacy of supposed "antiaging diets" in general (Lee et al., 2021; Longo & Anderson, 2022); the role of the immune system (Yousefzadeh et al., 2021); the social aspects of healthy aging (Charles et al., 2021; Hanc, 2021; Savage, 2022); and the economics of treatments that target aging (Scott et al., 2021).

Within the context of longevity and aging research, there is also intense focus on understanding conditions that are all grouped on the spectrum of dementias and Alzheimer's-like presentations (Mesulam et al., 2021). *Sepehr Ehsani* delves into the theoretical aspects of Alzheimer's disease research in "New Horizons in Studying the Cellular Mechanisms of Alzheimer's Disease" (Chap. "New Horizons in Studying the Cellular Mechanisms of Alzheimer's Disease").

The leading causes of death vary widely across both local and global regions. As an important case in point, it is estimated that neglected tropical diseases "affect more than one billion people globally" (Ackley et al., 2021). Tuberculosis continues to pose a significant burden, particularly in low- and middle-income countries (Jesus et al., 2022; Wang et al., 2021). Dengue fever, a neglected tropical disease, has recently seen advances on the therapeutic front (Biering & Harris, 2021; Kaptein et al., 2021). But in the case of malaria, we may be facing the prospect of artemisinin-resistant *Plasmodium falciparum* (Balikagala et al., 2021; White, 2021).

3 The Technological Turn

There is a dizzying pace to the addition of new technological tools in both the laboratory and the clinic. Various AI and related approaches are being used in medicinal chemistry and for drug repurposing (Carvalho et al., 2022; Fang et al., 2021), in structural biology to help with predicting protein and RNA folds (Baek et al., 2021; Berg, 2021; Nature Editors, 2021a; Weeks, 2021), in analysis of electronic health records (Ehsani et al., 2008; Murray et al., 2021), in the field of pathology (Lu et al., 2021b), and in the diagnosis of Alzheimer's disease (Sohn, 2022). In this volume, *Amir Feizi* and *Jahir M. Gutierrez* write on "Harnessing AI and Genomics to Accelerate Drug Discovery" (Chap. "Harnessing AI and Genomics to Accelerate Drug Discovery"), *Tim-Rasmus Kiehl* discusses "Digital and Computational Pathology: A Specialty Reimagined" (Chap. "Digital and Computational Pathology: A Specialty Reimagined"), and *Kevin Lano, Sobhan Y. Tehrani, Mohammad Umar,* and *Lyan Alwakeel* expound on "Using Artificial Intelligence for the Specification of m-Health and e-Health Systems" (Chap. "Using Artificial Intelligence for the Specification").

What exactly is AI? And what can the various tools categorized under the "AI" label (e.g., machine learning, deep learning, and artificial neural networks) actually do? This is an important issue. For instance, the machine learning pioneer Michael I. Jordan cautions that "while the science-fiction discussions about AI and super intelligence are fun, they are a distraction", and that "there's not been enough focus on the real problem, which is building planetary-scale machine learning–based systems that actually work, deliver value to humans, and do not amplify inequities" (quoted in Pretz, 2021b). In "An Assessment of the AI Regulation Proposed by the European Commission" (Chap. "An Assessment of the AI Regulation Proposed by the European Commission"), *Patrick Glauner* discusses the usual conflation that occurs between AI and software that performs statistical tasks.

AI approaches, such as deep learning, face some basic obstacles. For instance, "it has been claimed that deep learning is untrustworthy because it is not explainable—and unsuitable for some applications because it can experience catastrophic forgetting," and hence it might be "risky to use deep learning on any life-or-death application, such as a medical one" (Pretz, 2021a). Commentators have also noted the questionable utility of many AI tools built to deal with the COVID-19 pandemic (Heaven, 2021; Roberts et al., 2021). For these and other reasons, a subfield within AI research has emerged that tries to move toward "explainable AI" (see, for example, Lauritsen et al., 2020 and Lundberg et al., 2020). At the same time, concerns remain about how explainable "black box" algorithms can ultimately be (Babic et al., 2021).

Moving beyond the realm of AI, the expanded technological toolbox that has been in the spotlight in recent years includes additive manufacturing (Gu et al., 2021), robotic surgery (Metz, 2021), robotic manufacturing platforms for cell therapies (Winn, 2021), exoskeletons that can remove "kinetic energy during the swing period of the gait cycle [and reduce] the metabolic cost of walking" (Shepertycky et al., 2021, p. 957), the application of optogenetics in vision restoration (Sahel et al., 2021), artificial kidneys and miniaturized dialysis (Gura et al., 2016; Huff, 2020), artificial pancreas systems (Ware et al., 2022), functional human organoids (Eicher et al., 2022), modern microscopy techniques such as cryo-electron tomography (D. Kwon, 2021b), organ-on-chip systems for novel compound screenings (Roth & MPS-WS Berlin 2019, 2021), ultrasound-on-chip platforms for medical imaging (Rothberg et al., 2021), inertial microfluidic platforms for sepsis monitoring (Jeon et al., 2021), wearable optically pumped magnetometers (Tierney et al., 2019), wearable sensors for physiological monitoring (Dunn et al., 2021), and DNA-hydrogel-based wound infection sensors (Xiong et al., 2021).

In relation to these novel technological areas, *Jens Eckstein* writes about "Mobile Sensors in Healthcare: Technical, Ethical, and Medical Aspects" (Chap. "Mobile Sensors in Healthcare: Technical, Ethical, and Medical Aspects"); *Anna Kasparbauer, Veronika Reisner, Cosima Schenk, Anna Glas, Helana Lutfi, Oscar Blanco*, and *Thomas Spittler* on "Sensor Devices, the Source of Innovative Therapy and Prevention" (Chap. "Sensor Devices, the Source of Innovative Therapy and Prevention"); *Estefanía Lang, Alice Martin,* and *Elien Wallaeys* on "Teledermatology: Current Indications and Future Perspectives" (Chap. "Teledermatology: Current Indications and Future Perspectives"); *Florian M. Thieringer, Philipp Honigmann* and *Neha Sharma* on "Medical Additive Manufacturing in Surgery – Translating Innovation to the Point-of-Care" (Chap. "Medical Additive Manufacturing in Surgery: Translating Innovation to the Point-of-Care"); and *Andy W. K. Yeung* and *Michael M. Bornstein* on "Personalized Dental Medicine with Specific Focus on the Use of Data from Diagnostic Dental Imaging" (Chap. "Personalized Dental Medicine with Specific Focus on the Use of Data fromDiagnostic Dental Imaging").

It is essential that we carefully consider the responsibilities and ethical questions that arise when specific technologies are put into actual practice (Chiang et al., 2021). *Hannah Howland, Vadim Keyser,* and *Farzad Mahootian* meticulously analyze the web of such responsibilities and considerations in "Redesigning Relations: Coordinating Machine Learning Variables and Sociobuilt Contexts in COVID-19 and Beyond" (Chap. "Redesigning Relations: Coordinating Machine Learning Variables and Sociobuilt Contexts in COVID-19 and Beyond"). *Masoud Ghalambor* explains the context of "Ethical Challenges in Applying New Technologies in Orthopedic Surgery" (Chap. "Ethical Challenges in Applying New Technologies in Orthopedic Surgery"). In doing so, he reminds us to ask the following questions: Does a new technology solve a problem that cannot be solved with our available tools? And are we solving a problem more effectively?

The technological turn and the involvement of myriad corporations, companies, and start-ups in biomedicine is so significant that commentators now talk of the "commercial determinants of health" (Kickbusch et al., 2016). The pitfalls associated with the long-term consequences of monetized user-generated personal (health) data require discussions among all stakeholders (see, for example, Sharon & Lucivero, 2019). So, too, does the question of the ethics of patents and their effects on creativity in different areas of biomedicine (Moser, 2016; Nature Editors, 2021b, c). *Anna Katharina Heide* provides a detailed outline of "Patents on Inventions

Involving AI in the Life Sciences and Healthcare" in Chap. "Patents on Inventions Involving AI in the Life Sciences and Healthcare". Furthermore, as healthcare technologies evolve, the concomitant adaptation of robust, timely, and efficient regulations that protect patients' health and privacy is vital (Avin et al., 2021; Marks, 2021; McGraw & Mandl, 2021).

4   Uncertainty Everywhere

"Progress" in biomedicine and healthcare can be defined using several components. Two of these components could be the *augmentation of our understanding* of the underlying biology of medical diagnoses and phenomena and the *implementation* of this augmented understanding. Bearing these two prongs of "progress" in mind, we can see how progress ebbs and flows. For example, understanding a new facet of cancer metastasis can lead to both new questions and new unappreciated unknowns. Similarly, implementing a new treatment program can lead to unexpected consequences. As such, the twin tasks of dealing with uncertainty and mitigating its effects are crucial in biomedicine and healthcare.

Uncertainty can come in different shapes and forms. For example, there are "different types of uncertainty involved in diagnostic and prognostic judgments" (Chiffi & Zanotti, 2017, p. 928). There is also the uncertainty that results when implementing the outcomes of clinical trials, such as in the case of cancer screening programs (Menon et al., 2021) (see also Couzin-Frankel, 2021). Crucially, uncertainty also lies in the nature of the evidence, confirmation, reproducibility, and robustness of laboratory and clinical results (Bird, 2021; Errington et al., 2021a, b; Guttinger & Love, 2019; Kaiser, 2021b; Nature Editors, 2021d; Schupbach, 2018). At a more theoretical level, researchers often encounter uncertainty when making claims of causality and have to navigate between differing conceptions of correlation, association, causation, and so on (e.g., for recent studies on the association of the Epstein–Barr virus with multiple sclerosis, see Bjornevik et al., 2022; for causal claims concerning obesity, energy balance and fat storage, see Ludwig et al., 2021). Finally, more general types of uncertainty can arise at a system level, such as in relation to how hospital systems are funded under different governance models for healthcare (Colmers & Glied, 2021).

In the present volume, *Erman Sozudogru* provides a philosophical analysis of these issues in "Uncertainty in Medicine: An Active Definition" (Chap. "Uncertainty in Medicine: An Active Definition"). *Aaron James Goldman* writes on the "Post-Truth Implications for COVID-Era Healthcare: Verification, Trust, and Vaccine Skepticism" (Chap. "Post-Truth Implications for COVID-Era Healthcare: Verification, Trust, and Vaccine Skepticism"). Given the importance of medical education systems in introducing students to conceptualizations of uncertainty (Steele & Stefánsson, 2021) and heuristics under conditions of limited information and time (Chopra et al., 2021; Li & Colby, 2021; Singh, 2021), *Mark H. Wan* and *Qiu Ning Lee* delve into "The Future of Medical Education" in Chap. "The Future of Medical Education".

5   Puzzles and Paradoxes

Related to the topic of uncertainty is the fact that future healthcare professionals and researchers will have to deal with the various puzzles, paradoxes, and unresolved projects that are handed down to them. These range from issues at the subcellular level all the way up to the anatomical and population-wide levels. Examples of such issues are provided below:

1. Deciphering the nuances of the array of non-protein-coding segments in the genome (Leypold & Speicher, 2021), mapping the spectrum of sequence variations relative to reference human genomes (Aganezov et al., 2022; Pennisi, 2022; Vollger et al., 2022), and completing the full sequence of the Y chromosome (Nurk et al., 2022; Reardon, 2021).
2. Studying the "nongenetic" functions of the genome (Bustin & Misteli, 2016).
3. Better understanding the basics of protein biochemistry (including its interactions with water molecules) and protein–protein interaction at the amino-acid level (Fass & Semenov, 2021; Hosseinizadeh et al., 2021; Ourmazd, 2019; Pullanchery et al., 2021; Wensien et al., 2021).
4. Better understanding the intricate interactions of genes and the environment (e.g., see Garcia et al., 2021a).
5. Better understanding the nature of transcriptional noise in gene expression (Ham et al., 2021).
6. Studying extant puzzles in evolutionary biology (Lucas et al., 2020).
7. Studying species-wide mechanisms of organ and tissue repair and regeneration (Griffin et al., 2021; Murugan et al., 2022).
8. Shedding light on "idiopathic" conditions (see Richeldi et al., 2017) and conditions such as sporadic Creutzfeldt-Jakob disease (Mead, 2021).
9. Augmenting efforts at systematizing correct diagnoses and disease classifications (Liu et al., 2021; Nassiri et al., 2021) and better understanding the spectrum of rare diseases (Genomes Project Pilot Investigators et al., 2021). Indeed, many "rarer" conditions may often get diagnosed as a more common disease, which means the patient never receives the right kind of care and treatment. The "Undiagnosed Diseases Program" at the US National Institutes of Health (Macnamara et al., 2020) is an example of a creative approach to systematically tackling this issue.
10. Better understanding the cellular mechanisms of metastasis (Dai et al., 2022; Diamantopoulou et al., 2022; Fares et al., 2020; Pascual et al., 2021), the spontaneous regression of cancer (Brodeur, 2018; Colom et al., 2021; Diede, 2014; Riedmeier et al., 2021), natural cancer resistance (Vincze et al., 2022), and seasonal patterns of presentation of cancers and other diseases (Ehsani et al., 2009).
11. Akin to AMR, deciphering resistance mechanisms toward novel cancer treatments (Awad et al., 2021) and further exploring creative treatment modalities such as oncolytic virotherapy (Melcher et al., 2021).

12. Finding the means to analytically determine drug–drug interactions and what one might call the "polymechanisms" of action of novel compounds (Abolhassani et al., 2021; Wolff et al., 2021; Zhang et al., 2016). In this context, consider that 50 new drugs were approved by the FDA in 2021; indeed, the "5-year average sits at 51 drugs per year [and] a decade ago, it was 24 drugs per year" (Mullard, 2022).
13. Better understanding placebo and nocebo effects (Crawford et al., 2021; Haas et al., 2022; Resnick, 2021).
14. In the context of neurotrauma (traumatic spinal cord injury), studying what is called the neuroanatomical–functional paradox (Fouad et al., 2021).
15. Deeply exploring the fields of neuroscience, cognitive science, and perception, which are rife with puzzles (Ekroll et al., 2016; Gallistel, 2021; Hulse et al., 2021; Langille & Gallistel, 2020; Potrich et al., 2022; Robinson & Brandon, 2021). Let us take one example: when writing on motor planning, Emilio Bizzi and Robert Ajemian pose the following question: "how is an evanescent wish to move translated into a concrete action? This simple question and puzzling miracle remains a focal point of motor systems neuroscience" (Bizzi & Ajemian, 2020, p. 1815). They further note that "nature needed millions of years to achieve the sublime level of performance of a tennis player or a gymnast, a level of adroitness that far surpasses state-of-the-art robotics capabilities. Somehow, nature has generated a system that, with variations (a cerebral cortex is not present in all vertebrates), works for the entire universe of species" (Bizzi & Ajemian, 2020, p. 1821).
16. Finally, bridging "alternative" approaches to healthcare with what may be considered "mainstream" disciplines. These approaches could include the effects of different nutritional components and regimens (Guasch-Ferre et al., 2022; Neal et al., 2021), neurofeedback methods for psychiatric conditions (Dudek & Dodell-Feder, 2021), and studying the modes of action of traditional medicines (Lin et al., 2021c; Molimau-Samasoni et al., 2021; Shi et al., 2021).

While tackling puzzles such as these and finding innovative solutions, it may help to remember that, in the words of Chuck Hull, "when you're trying to do something new, very few people see the wisdom of it" (quoted in Brooks, 2016, p. 41). Taking this reality in stride, innovation also requires risk-taking and persistence. Francis Collins, the former director of the US National Institutes of Health (NIH), noted that "hypothesis-driven research is the bedrock of NIH's success. Thus, one should prioritize support of risk-taking research and pay less attention to preliminary data and more to the potential importance of a premise" (Collins, 2022, p. 123).

6 Hopes

More than a century ago, before the advent of the new relativistic physics, a prevailing thought in the physical sciences was that most fundamental issues in the field had been resolved. For example, the physicist Albert A. Michelson remarked the following:

> While it is never safe to affirm that the future of Physical Science has no marvels in store even more astonishing than those of the past, it seems probable that most of the grand underlying principles have been firmly established and that further advances are to be sought chiefly in the rigorous application of these principles to all the phenomena which come under our notice. It is here that the science of measurement shows its importance— where quantitative work is more to be desired than qualitative work. An eminent physicist remarked that the future truths of physical science are to be looked for in the sixth place of decimals. (Michelson, 1896, p. 159)

We should not make the same mistake in the realm of biomedicine, thinking that all the fundamental cellular and molecular "principles" have been discovered. Moreover, qualitative and quantitative work in biomedicine should go hand in hand. This is why much effort should now be devoted to theoretical and philosophical biology and to the re-amalgamation of theory and experiment in the life sciences (Ehsani, 2020; Gershman et al., 2021). Different areas of philosophy could have widespread and/or specific applications to biomedical research. There are too many cases to enumerate, but examples range from studies around the idea of a "universal genome" in evolutionary biology (Sherman, 2007) and "genomically minimal" cells (Pelletier et al., 2021) to generating diagnostic hypotheses at the clinical level (Stanley & Nyrup, 2020), applying Kant's "non-pathological definition of mental illness" to mental health research (Thomason, 2021, p. 189), and determining what the so-called "ends of medicine" could and/or should be (MacDougall, 2020).

Realizing the above path is a major hope. Another hope—one of no lesser significance—is that areas traditionally relegated somewhat to the periphery of attention in both the laboratory and the clinic are integrated more fully into future research paradigms. The first such area could be that of palliative care (Mathews & Zimmermann, 2020). The second is the management of chronic pain (Donnelly et al., 2020). For the third, we need a greater focus in medical schools on the "medical philosophy" of physician-/surgeon-trainees (akin to how teachers and lecturers are asked to provide a "teaching philosophy" statement when applying for a job). This is of importance because a physician's personal philosophy toward their job manifests itself in all domains of their profession. Finally, we need to pay equal attention to what patients expect from the healthcare system along with their own roles in the diagnoses and treatments they receive and the medical research in which they participate (Feinsinger et al., 2022; Servick, 2022).

A further hope to mention here is greater emphasis on the question of "medicalization." "Is old age, for example, a medical condition? Should it be?," asks Julian Sheather (2019, p. 88). Moreover, for various mental health conditions, what should be the first line of treatment in each case, and why (Callesen et al., 2020; Nakao et al., 2021)?

In relation to some of these areas, *Julia Plugmann* and *Philipp Plugmann* write about "The Future Open Innovation Approach in Health Care Needs Patients' Support" (Chap. "The Future Open Innovation Approach in Health Care Needs Patients' Support"), *Horst Kunhardt* on "Modern Home Care: A Glimpse into the

Future of Patient-Centered Healthcare Systems" (Chap. "Modern Home Care: A Glimpse into the Future of Patient-Cen-tered Healthcare Systems"), and *Kristin Beizai, Ashley Stone,* and *Yash Joshi* on "Innovations in Psychiatric Care Models: Lessons from the Past to inform the Future" (Chap. "Innovations in Psychiatric Care Models: Lessons from the Past to Inform the Future").

In closing, we should note that the road to progress in biomedicine does not have to be convoluted and challenging. Practicable solutions often require the initial step of a simple and theoretically sound enunciation of the problem at hand, followed by rational inquiry. It is helpful to always remain cognizant of puzzles posed by seemingly mundane and at-first unrelated observations. Take, for example, the intriguing question of whether understanding the physiology behind the very high blood pressure of giraffes could aid our understanding of hypertension and cardiovascular problems in people (Aalkjær & Wang, 2021).[2] In all, the adage about the "optimism of the will and pessimism of the intellect" may be the right framework for hoping to build on past successes and to confront the challenges facing biomedicine and healthcare over the next decade.

References

Aalkjær, C., & Wang, T. (2021). The remarkable cardiovascular system of giraffes. *Annual Review of Physiology, 83,* 1–15.

Abolhassani, N., Castioni, J., Santschi, V., Waeber, G., & Marques-Vidal, P. (2021). Trends and determinants of polypharmacy and potential drug-drug interactions at discharge from hospital between 2009-2015. *Journal of Patient Safety, 17*(8), e1171–e1178.

Ackley, C., Elsheikh, M., & Zaman, S. (2021). Scoping review of neglected tropical disease interventions and health promotion: A framework for successful NTD interventions as evidenced by the literature. *PLoS Neglected Tropical Diseases, 15*(7), e0009278.

Aganezov, S., Yan, S. M., Soto, D. C., Kirsche, M., Zarate, S., Avdeyev, P., . . . Schatz, M. C. (2022). A complete reference genome improves analysis of human genetic variation. *Science, 376*(6588), eabl3533.

Antimicrobial Resistance Collaborators. (2022). Global burden of bacterial antimicrobial resistance in 2019: A systematic analysis. *Lancet, 399*(10325), 629–655.

Ardell, S. M., & Kryazhimskiy, S. (2021). The population genetics of collateral resistance and sensitivity. *Elife, 10,* e73250.

Atanasov, A. G., Zotchev, S. B., Dirsch, V. M., Supuran, C. T., & International Natural Product Sciences Taskforce. (2021). Natural products in drug discovery: Advances and opportunities. *Nature Reviews Drug Discovery, 20*(3), 200–216.

Augustin, H. G., & Kipnis, J. (2021). Vascular rejuvenation is geroprotective. *Science, 373*(6554), 490–491.

Austad, S. N., & Finch, C. E. (2022). How ubiquitous is aging in vertebrates? *Science, 376*(6600), 1384–1385.

Avin, S., Belfield, H., Brundage, M., Krueger, G., Wang, J., Weller, A., Anderljung, M., Krawczuk, I., Krueger, D., Lebensold, J., Maharaj, T., & Zilberman, N. (2021). Filling gaps in trustworthy development of AI. *Science, 374*(6573), 1327–1329.

---

[2] See also Gil et al. (2022) for an analogous and intriguing area of investigation with the potential of impacting our understanding of human physiology.

Awad, M. M., Liu, S., Rybkin, I. I., Arbour, K. C., Dilly, J., Zhu, V. W., Awad, M. M., Liu, S., Rybkin, I. I., Arbour, K. C., Dilly, J., Zhu, V. W., Johnson, M. L., Heist, R. S., Patil, T., Riely, G. J., Jacobson, J. O., Yang, X., Persky, N. S., … Aguirre, A. J. (2021). Acquired resistance to KRAS(G12C) inhibition in cancer. *The New England Journal of Medicine, 384*(25), 2382–2393.

Babic, B., Gerke, S., Evgeniou, T., & Cohen, I. G. (2021). Beware explanations from AI in health care. *Science, 373*(6552), 284–286.

Baek, M., DiMaio, F., Anishchenko, I., Dauparas, J., Ovchinnikov, S., Lee, G. R., Wang, J., Cong, Q., Kinch, L. N., Schaeffer, R. D. B., & D. (2021). Accurate prediction of protein structures and interactions using a three-track neural network. *Science, 373*(6557), 871–876.

Baldwin, J. G., & Gattinoni, L. (2022). Cancer cells hijack T-cell mitochondria. *Nature Nanotechnology, 17*(1), 3–4.

Balikagala, B., Fukuda, N., Ikeda, M., Katuro, O. T., Tachibana, S. I., Yamauchi, M., Opio, W., Emoto, S., Anywar, D. A., Kimura, E., & Mita, T. (2021). Evidence of artemisinin-resistant malaria in Africa. *The New England Journal of Medicine, 385*(13), 1163–1171.

Belzile, L. R., Davison, A. C., Gampe, J., Rootzén, H., & Zholud, D. (2022). Is there a cap on longevity? A statistical review. *Annual Review of Statistics and Its Application, 9*(1), 21–45.

Berg, J. (2021). Banking on protein structural data. *Science, 373*(6557), 835.

Bernstein, A. S., Sun, S., Weinberger, K. R., Spangler, K. R., Sheffield, P. E., & Wellenius, G. A. (2022). Warm season and emergency department visits to U.S. children's hospitals. *Environmental Health Perspectives, 130*(1), 17001.

Bhatia, A., Krieger, N., Beckfield, J., Barros, A. J. D., & Victora, C. (2019). Are inequities decreasing? Birth registration for children under five in low-income and middle-income countries, 1999-2016. *BMJ Global Health, 4*(6), e001926.

Biering, S. B., & Harris, E. (2021). A step towards therapeutics for dengue. *Nature, 598*(7881), 420–421.

Bird, A. (2021). Understanding the replication crisis as a base rate fallacy. *The British Journal for the Philosophy of Science, 72*(4), 965–993.

Bizzi, E., & Ajemian, R. (2020). From motor planning to execution: A sensorimotor loop perspective. *Journal of Neurophysiology, 124*(6), 1815–1823.

Bjornevik, K., Cortese, M., Healy, B. C., Kuhle, J., Mina, M. J., Leng, Y., Elledge, S. J., Niebuhr, D. W., Scher, A. I., Munger, K. L., & Ascherio, A. (2022). Longitudinal analysis reveals high prevalence of Epstein-Barr virus associated with multiple sclerosis. *Science, 375*(6578), 296–301.

Brives, C., & Pourraz, J. (2020). Phage therapy as a potential solution in the fight against AMR: Obstacles and possible futures. *Palgrave Communications, 6*, 100.

Brodeur, G. M. (2018). Spontaneous regression of neuroblastoma. *Cell and Tissue Research, 372*(2), 277–286.

Brooks, M. (2016). The day the world became 3D. *New Scientist, 232*(3096), 40–41.

Bustin, M., & Misteli, T. (2016). Nongenetic functions of the genome. *Science, 352*(6286), aad6933.

Callesen, P., Reeves, D., Heal, C., & Wells, A. (2020). Metacognitive therapy versus cognitive behaviour therapy in adults with major depression: A parallel single-blind randomised trial. *Scientific Reports, 10*(1), 7878.

Carvalho, D. M., Richardson, P. J., Olaciregui, N., Stankunaite, R., Lavarino, C., Molinari, V., Corley, E. A., Smith, D. P., Ruddle, R., Donovan, A., & Jones, C. (2022). Repurposing Vandetanib plus everolimus for the treatment of ACVR1-mutant diffuse intrinsic pontine glioma. *Cancer Discovery, 12*(2), 416–431.

CDC National Center for Health Statistics. (2020). *Leading causes of death (Mortality in the United States, 2020, data table for figure 4)*. Retrieved from https://www.cdc.gov/nchs/fastats/leading-causes-of-death.htm

Charles, S. T., Rocke, C., Sagha Zadeh, R., Martin, M., Boker, S., & Scholz, U. (2021). Leveraging daily social experiences to motivate healthy aging. *The Journals of Gerontology: Series B, 76*(Suppl 2), S157–S166.

Chase, H., Hampshire, K., & Tun, S. (2022). Improving the medical curriculum on planetary health and sustainable healthcare. *BMJ, 376*, o209.

Chiang, S., Picard, R. W., Chiong, W., Moss, R., Worrell, G. A., Rao, V. R., & Goldenholz, D. M. (2021). Guidelines for conducting ethical artificial intelligence research in neurology: A systematic approach for clinicians and researchers. *Neurology, 97*(13), 632–640.

Chiffi, D., & Zanotti, R. (2017). Fear of knowledge: Clinical hypotheses in diagnostic and prognostic reasoning. *Journal of Evaluation in Clinical Practice, 23*(5), 928–934.

Chopra, R., Patel, K., & Rich, M. W. (2021). Preoperative stress testing before elective arthroplasty: A teachable moment. *JAMA Internal Medicine, 181*(12), 1633–1634.

Colchero, F., Aburto, J. M., Archie, E. A., Boesch, C., Breuer, T., Campos, F. A., Collins, A., Conde, D. A., Cords, M., Crockford, C., & Alberts, S. C. (2021). The long lives of primates and the 'invariant rate of ageing' hypothesis. *Nature Communications, 12*(1), 3666.

Collins, F. S. (2022). Lessons learned from leading NIH. *Science, 375*(6577), 123.

Colmers, J., & Glied, S. (2021). Let's change how we pay for hospitals. *Knowable Magazine*. Retrieved from https://knowablemagazine.org/article/society/2021/lets-change-how-we-pay-hospitals

Colom, B., Herms, A., Hall, M. W. J., Dentro, S. C., King, C., Sood, R. K., Alcolea, M. P., Piedrafita, G., Fernandez-Antoran, D., Ong, S. H., Fowler, J. C., Mahbubani, K. T., Saeb-Parsy, K., Gerstung, M., Hall, B. A., & Jones, P. H. (2021). Mutant clones in normal epithelium outcompete and eliminate emerging tumours. *Nature, 598*(7881), 510–514.

Couzin-Frankel, J. (2021). How pandemic pressure is re-engineering clinical trials. *Science, 374*(6573), 1308–1309.

Crawford, L. S., Mills, E. P., Hanson, T., Macey, P. M., Glarin, R., Macefield, V. G., Keay, K. A., & Henderson, L. A. (2021). Brainstem mechanisms of pain modulation: A within-subjects 7T fMRI study of placebo analgesic and nocebo hyperalgesic responses. *The Journal of Neuroscience, 41*(47), 9794–9806.

Dai, J., Cimino, P. J., Gouin, K. H., Grzelak, C. A., Barrett, A., Lim, A. R., Long, A., Weaver, S., Saldin, L. T., Uzamere, A., Schulte, V., Schulte, V., Clegg, N., Pisarsky, L., Lyden, D., Bissell, M. J., Knott, S., Welm, A. L., Bielas, J. H., ... Ghajar, C. M. (2022). Astrocytic laminin-211 drives disseminated breast tumor cell dormancy in brain. *Nature Cancer, 3*(1), 25–42.

da Silva, R., Conde, D. A., Baudisch, A., & Colchero, F. (2022). Slow and negligible senescence among testudines challenges evolutionary theories of senescence. *Science, 376*(6600), 1466–1470.

de Koning, E. J. P., & Carlotti, F. (2021). Stem cell-based islet replacement therapy in diabetes: A road trip that reached the clinic. *Cell Stem Cell, 28*(12), 2044–2046.

Deghelt, M., & Collet, J. F. (2022). Bacterial envelope built to a peptidoglycan tune. *Nature, 606* (7916), 866–867.

Diamantopoulou, Z., Castro-Giner, F., Schwab, F. D., Foerster, C., Saini, M., Budinjas, S., ... Aceto, N. (2022). The metastatic spread of breast cancer accelerates during sleep. *Nature, 607*(7917), 156–162.

Diede, S. J. (2014). Spontaneous regression of metastatic cancer: Learning from neuroblastoma. *Nature Reviews Cancer, 14*(2), 71–72.

Dolgin, E. (2021). Out for blood in the search to stall aging. *Knowable Magazine*. Retrieved from https://knowablemagazine.org/article/living-world/2021/out-blood-search-stall-aging

Donnelly, C. R., Andriessen, A. S., Chen, G., Wang, K., Jiang, C., Maixner, W., & Ji, R. R. (2020). Central nervous system targets: Glial cell mechanisms in chronic pain. *Neurotherapeutics, 17*(3), 846–860.

Dudek, E., & Dodell-Feder, D. (2021). The efficacy of real-time functional magnetic resonance imaging neurofeedback for psychiatric illness: A meta-analysis of brain and behavioral outcomes. *Neuroscience and Biobehavioral Reviews, 121*, 291–306.

Dunn, J., Kidzinski, L., Runge, R., Witt, D., Hicks, J. L., Schussler-Fiorenza Rose, S. M., Li, X., Bahmani, A., Delp, S. L., Hastie, T., & Snyder, M. P. (2021). Wearable sensors enable personalized predictions of clinical laboratory measurements. *Nature Medicine, 27*(6), 1105–1112.

Durand-Reville, T. F., Miller, A. A., O'Donnell, J. P., Wu, X., Sylvester, M. A., Guler, S., Iyer, R., Shapiro, A. B., Carter, N. M., Velez-Vega, C., Moussa, S. H., McLeod, S. M., Chen, A., Tanudra, A. M., Zhang, J., Comita-Prevoir, J., Romero, J. A., Huynh, H., Ferguson, A. D., ... Tommasi, R. A. (2021). Rational design of a new antibiotic class for drug-resistant infections. *Nature, 597*(7878), 698–702.

Ehsani, S. (2020). Analytic philosophy for biomedical research: The imperative of applying yesterday's timeless messages to today's impasses. In P. Glauner & P. Plugmann (Eds.), *Innovative technologies for market leadership: Investing in the future* (pp. 167–200). Springer.

Ehsani, S., Kiehl, T.-R., Bernstein, A., Gentili, F., Asa, S. L., & Croul, S. E. (2008). Creation of a retrospective searchable neuropathologic database from print archives at Toronto's University Health Network. *Laboratory Investigation, 88*(1), 89–93.

Ehsani, S., Croul, S. E., Knight, K., & Kiehl, T.-R. (2009). Seasonal patterns of presentation in primary malignant brain tumors and metastases based on a retrospective neuropathologic database. *Nature Precedings, 2009*, 1–1.

Eicher, A. K., Kechele, D. O., Sundaram, N., Berns, H. M., Poling, H. M., Haines, L. E., Sanchez, J. G., Kishimoto, K., Krishnamurthy, M., Han, L., Zorn, A. M., Helmrath, M. A., & Wells, J. M. (2022). Functional human gastrointestinal organoids can be engineered from three primary germ layers derived separately from pluripotent stem cells. *Cell Stem Cell, 29*(1), 36–51.

Eisenstein, M. (2022). Does the human lifespan have a limit? *Nature, 601*(7893), S2–S4.

Ekroll, V., Sayim, B., Van der Hallen, R., & Wagemans, J. (2016). Illusory visual completion of an object's invisible backside can make your finger feel shorter. *Current Biology, 26*(8), 1029–1033.

Errington, T. M., Denis, A., Perfito, N., Iorns, E., & Nosek, B. A. (2021a). Challenges for assessing replicability in preclinical cancer biology. *Elife, 10*, e67995.

Errington, T. M., Mathur, M., Soderberg, C. K., Denis, A., Perfito, N., Iorns, E., & Nosek, B. A. (2021b). Investigating the replicability of preclinical cancer biology. *Elife, 10*, e71601.

Esrick, E. B., Lehmann, L. E., Biffi, A., Achebe, M., Brendel, C., Ciuculescu, M. F., Daley, H., MacKinnon, B., Morris, E., Federico, A., Abriss, D., Boardman, K., Khelladi, R., Shaw, K., Negre, H., Negre, O., Nikiforow, S., Ritz, J., Pai, S.-Y., ... Williams, D. A. (2021). Post-transcriptional genetic silencing of BCL11A to treat sickle cell disease. *The New England Journal of Medicine, 384*(3), 205–215.

Falcaro, M., Castanon, A., Ndlela, B., Checchi, M., Soldan, K., Lopez-Bernal, J., Elliss-Brookes, L., & Sasieni, P. (2021). The effects of the national HPV vaccination programme in England, UK, on cervical cancer and grade 3 cervical intraepithelial neoplasia incidence: A register-based observational study. *Lancet, 398*(10316), 2084–2092.

Fan, X., Wheatley, E. G., & Villeda, S. A. (2017). Mechanisms of hippocampal aging and the potential for rejuvenation. *Annual Review of Neuroscience, 40*, 251–272.

Fang, J., Zhang, P., Zhou, Y., Chiang, C.-W., Tan, J., Hou, Y., Stauffer, S., Li, L., Pieper, A. A., Cummings, J., & Cheng, F. (2021). Endophenotype-based in silico network medicine discovery combined with insurance record data mining identifies sildenafil as a candidate drug for Alzheimer's disease. *Nature Aging, 1*(12), 1175–1188.

Fares, J., Fares, M. Y., Khachfe, H. H., Salhab, H. A., & Fares, Y. (2020). Molecular principles of metastasis: A hallmark of cancer revisited. *Signal Transduction and Targeted Therapy, 5*(1), 28.

Fass, D., & Semenov, S. N. (2021). Previously unknown type of protein crosslink discovered. *Nature, 593*(7859), 343–344.

Feinsinger, A., Pouratian, N., Ebadi, H., Adolphs, R., Andersen, R., Beauchamp, M. S., Chang, E. F., Crone, N. E., Collinger, J. L., Fried, I., Mamelak, A., Richardson, M., Rutishauser, U., Sheth, S. A., Suthana, N., Tandon, N., Yoshor, D., & NIH Research Opportunities in Humans Consortium. (2022). Ethical commitments, principles, and practices guiding intracranial neuro-scientific research in humans. *Neuron, 110*(2), 188–194.

Finkelstein, A., Gentzkow, M., & Williams, H. (2021). Place-based drivers of mortality: Evidence from migration. *American Economic Review, 111*(8), 2697–2735.

Fouad, K., Popovich, P. G., Kopp, M. A., & Schwab, J. M. (2021). The neuroanatomical-functional paradox in spinal cord injury. *Nature Reviews Neurology, 17*(1), 53–62.

Frangoul, H., Altshuler, D., Cappellini, M. D., Chen, Y. S., Domm, J., Eustace, B. K., Foell, J., de la Fuente, J., Grupp, S., Handgretinger, R., Ho, T. W., Kattamis, A., Kernytsky, A., Lekstrom-Himes, J., Li, A. M., Locatelli, F., Mapara, M. Y., de Montalembert, M., Rondelli, D., ... Corbacioglu, S. (2021). CRISPR-Cas 9 gene editing for sickle cell disease and beta-thalassemia. *The New England Journal of Medicine, 384*(3), 252–260.

Gallistel, C. R. (2021). The physical basis of memory. *Cognition, 213*, 104533.

Garcia, A. R., Finch, C., Gatz, M., Kraft, T., Eid Rodriguez, D., Cummings, D., Charifson, M., Buetow, K., Beheim, B. A., Allayee, H., Thomas, G. S., Stieglitz, J., Gurven, M. D., Kaplan, H., & Trumble, B. C. (2021a). APOE4 is associated with elevated blood lipids and lower levels of innate immune biomarkers in a tropical Amerindian subsistence population. *Elife, 10*, e68231.

Garcia, D. M., Campbell, E. A., Jakobson, C. M., Tsuchiya, M., Shaw, E. A., DiNardo, A. L., Kaeberlein, M., & Jarosz, D. F. (2021b). A prion accelerates proliferation at the expense of lifespan. *Elife, 10*, e60917.

Genomes Project Pilot Investigators, Smedley, D., Smith, K. R., Martin, A., Thomas, E. A., McDonagh, E. M., Cipriani, V., Ellingford, J. M., Arno, G., Tucci, A., Vandrovcova, J., Chan, G., Williams, H. J., Ratnaike, T., Wei, W., Stirrups, K., Ibanez, K., Moutsianas, L., Wielscher, M., ... Caulfield, M. (2021). 100,000 genomes pilot on rare-disease diagnosis in health care - Preliminary report. *The New England Journal of Medicine, 385*(20), 1868–1880.

Gershman, S. J., Balbi, P. E., Gallistel, C. R., & Gunawardena, J. (2021). Reconsidering the evidence for learning in single cells. *Elife, 10*, e61907.

Gil, K. N., Vogl, A. W., & Shadwick, R. E. (2022). Anatomical mechanism for protecting the airway in the largest animals on earth. *Current Biology, 32*(4), 898–903.e1.

Gorbunova, V., Seluanov, A., Mita, P., McKerrow, W., Fenyo, D., Boeke, J. D., Linker, S. B., Gage, F. H., Kreiling, J. A., Petrashen, A. P., Woodham, T. A., Taylor, J. R., Helfand, S. L., & Sedivy, J. M. (2021). The role of retrotransposable elements in ageing and age-associated diseases. *Nature, 596*(7870), 43–53.

Griffin, D. R., Archang, M. M., Kuan, C. H., Weaver, W. M., Weinstein, J. S., Feng, A. C., Ruccia, A., Sideris, E., Ragkousis, V., Koh, J., Plikus, M. V., Di Carlo, D., Segura, T., & Scumpia, P. O. (2021). Activating an adaptive immune response from a hydrogel scaffold imparts regenerative wound healing. *Nature Materials, 20*(4), 560–569.

Grunewald, M., Kumar, S., Sharife, H., Volinsky, E., Gileles-Hillel, A., Licht, T., Permyakova, A., Hinden, L., Azar, S., Friedmann, Y., Kupetz, P., Tzuberi, R., Anisimov, A., Alitalo, K., Horwitz, M., Leebhoff, S., Khoma, O. Z., Hlushchuk, R., Djonov, V., ... Keshet, E. (2021). Counteracting age-related VEGF signaling insufficiency promotes healthy aging and extends life span. *Science, 373*(6554).

Gu, D., Shi, X., Poprawe, R., Bourell, D. L., Setchi, R., & Zhu, J. (2021). Material-structure-performance integrated laser-metal additive manufacturing. *Science, 372*(6545), eabg1487.

Guasch-Ferre, M., Li, Y., Willett, W. C., Sun, Q., Sampson, L., Salas-Salvado, J., Martínez-González, M. A., Stampfer, M. J., & Hu, F. B. (2022). Consumption of olive oil and risk of total and cause-specific mortality among U.S. *Adults. Journal of the American College of Cardiology, 79*(2), 101–112.

Gura, V., Rivara, M. B., Bieber, S., Munshi, R., Smith, N. C., Linke, L., Kundzins, J., Beizai, M., Ezon, C., Kessler, L., & Himmelfarb, J. (2016). A wearable artificial kidney for patients with end-stage renal disease. *JCI Insight, 1*(8), e86397.

Guttinger, S., & Love, A. C. (2019). Characterizing scientific failure: Putting the replication crisis in context. *EMBO Reports, 20*(9), e48765.

Haas, J. W., Bender, F. L., Ballou, S., Kelley, J. M., Wilhelm, M., Miller, F. G., Rief, W., & Kaptchuk, T. J. (2022). Frequency of adverse events in the placebo arms of COVID-19 vaccine trials: A systematic review and meta-analysis. *JAMA Network Open, 5*(1), e2143955.

Hägg, S., & Jylhävä, J. (2021). Sex differences in biological aging with a focus on human studies. *Elife, 10*, e63425.

Ham, L., Jackson, M., & Stumpf, M. P. (2021). Pathway dynamics can delineate the sources of transcriptional noise in gene expression. *Elife, 10*, e69324.

Hanc, J. (2021). Doctors harness the power of human connections. *The New York Times.* Retrieved from https://www.nytimes.com/2021/04/28/health/social-medicine-programs.html

Hashimoto, T., Horikawa, D. D., Saito, Y., Kuwahara, H., Kozuka-Hata, H., Shin, I. T., Minakuchi, Y., Ohishi, K., Motoyama, A., Aizu, T., Enomoto, A., Kondo, K., Tanaka, S., Hara, Y., Koshikawa, S., Sagara, H., Miura, T., Yokobori, S.-I., Miyagawa, K., ... Kunieda, T. (2016). Extremotolerant tardigrade genome and improved radiotolerance of human cultured cells by tardigrade-unique protein. *Nature Communications, 7*, 12808.

Heaven, W. D. (2021). Hundreds of AI tools have been built to catch covid. None of them helped. *MIT Technology Review.* Retrieved from https://www.technologyreview.com/2021/07/30/1030329/machine-learning-ai-failed-covid-hospital-diagnosis-pandemic/

Helfand, S. L., & de Cabo, R. (2021). Evidence that overnight fasting could extend healthy lifespan. *Nature, 598*(7880), 265–266.

Heron, M. (2013). Deaths: Leading causes for 2010. *National Vital Statistics Reports, 62*(6), 1–96.

Holmes, B. (2021). Genetic tricks of the longest-lived animals. *Knowable Magazine.* Retrieved from https://knowablemagazine.org/article/health-disease/2021/genetic-tricks-longest-lived-animals

Horowitz, A. M., Fan, X., Bieri, G., Smith, L. K., Sanchez-Diaz, C. I., Schroer, A. B., Gontier, G., Casaletto, K. B., Kramer, J. H., Williams, K. E., & Villeda, S. A. (2020). Blood factors transfer beneficial effects of exercise on neurogenesis and cognition to the aged brain. *Science, 369*(6500), 167–173.

Hosseinizadeh, A., Breckwoldt, N., Fung, R., Sepehr, R., Schmidt, M., Schwander, P., Santra, R., & Ourmazd, A. (2021). Few-fs resolution of a photoactive protein traversing a conical intersection. *Nature, 599*(7886), 697–701.

Huff, C. (2020). How artificial kidneys and miniaturized dialysis could save millions of lives. *Nature, 579*(7798), 186–188.

Hulse, B. K., Haberkern, H., Franconville, R., Turner-Evans, D. B., Takemura, S. Y., Wolff, T., Noorman, M., Dreher, M., Dan, C., Parekh, R., Hermundstad, A. M., Rubin, G. M., & Jayaraman, V. (2021). A connectome of the Drosophila central complex reveals network motifs suitable for flexible navigation and context-dependent action selection. *Elife, 10*, e66039.

Huynh, A., & Wood, K. B. (2021). Finding the right sequence of drugs. *Elife, 10*, e72562.

Janssen, F., Bardoutsos, A., El Gewily, S., & De Beer, J. (2021). Future life expectancy in Europe taking into account the impact of smoking, obesity, and alcohol. *Elife, 10*, e66590.

Jeon, H., Lee, D. H., Jundi, B., Pinilla-Vera, M., Baron, R. M., Levy, B. D., Voldman, J., & Han, J. (2021). Fully automated, sample-to-answer leukocyte functional assessment platform for continuous sepsis monitoring via microliters of blood. *ACS Sensors, 6*(7), 2747–2756.

Jesus, G. S., Pescarini, J. M., Silva, A. F., Torrens, A., Carvalho, W. M., Junior, E. P. P., Ichihara, M. Y., Barreto, M. L., Rebouças, P., Macinko, J., Sanchez, M., & Rasella, D. (2022). The effect of primary health care on tuberculosis in a nationwide cohort of 7.3 million Brazilian people: A quasi-experimental study. *The Lancet Global Health., 10*(3), e390–e397.

Johnson, S. (2021). How humanity gave itself an extra life. *The New York Times Magazine.* Retrieved from https://www.nytimes.com/2021/04/27/magazine/global-life-span.html

Kaiser, J. (2021a). Gene therapy that once led to tragedy scores success. *Science, 372*(6544), 776.

Kaiser, J. (2021b). Key cancer results failed to be reproduced. *Science, 374*(6573), 1311.

Kaplan, Y., Reich, S., Oster, E., Maoz, S., Levin-Reisman, I., Ronin, I., Gefen, O., Agam, O., & Balaban, N. Q. (2021). Observation of universal ageing dynamics in antibiotic persistence. *Nature, 600*(7888), 290–294.

Kaptein, S. J. F., Goethals, O., Kiemel, D., Marchand, A., Kesteleyn, B., Bonfanti, J. F., Bardiot, D., Stoops, B., Jonckers, T. H., Dallmeier, K., Geluykens, P., Thys, K., Crabbe, M., Chatel-Chaix, L., Münster, M., Querat, G., Touret, F., de Lamballerie, X., Raboisson, P., ... Neyts, J. (2021). A pan-serotype dengue virus inhibitor targeting the NS3-NS4B interaction. *Nature, 598*(7881), 504–509.

Kaufman, D. L. (2021). GABA molecules made by B cells can dampen antitumour responses. *Nature, 599*(7885), 374–376.

Kaya, A., Phua, C. Z. J., Lee, M., Wang, L., Tyshkovskiy, A., Ma, S., Barre, B., Liu, W., Harrison, B. R., Zhao, X., Zhou, X., Wasko, B. M., Bammler, T. K., El Promislow, D., Kaeberlein, M., & Gladyshev, V. N. (2021). Evolution of natural lifespan variation and molecular strategies of extended lifespan in yeast. *Elife, 10*, e64860.

Kickbusch, I., Allen, L., & Franz, C. (2016). The commercial determinants of health. *The Lancet Global Health, 4*(12), e895–e896.

Kirchhelle, C. (2018). Pharming animals: A global history of antibiotics in food production (1935–2017). *Palgrave Communications, 4*, 96.

Kolora, S. R. R., Owens, G. L., Vazquez, J. M., Stubbs, A., Chatla, K., Jainese, C., Seeto, K., McCrea, M., Sandel, M. W., Vianna, J. A., Maslenikov, K., Bachtrog, D., Orr, J. W., Love, M., & Sudmant, P. H. (2021). Origins and evolution of extreme life span in Pacific Ocean rockfishes. *Science, 374*(6569), 842–847.

Kwon, D. (2021a). Failure of genetic therapies for Huntington's devastates community. *Nature, 593*(7858), 180.

Kwon, D. (2021b). The secret lives of cells—As never seen before. *Nature, 598*(7882), 558–560.

Kwon, J. H., & Powderly, W. G. (2021). The post-antibiotic era is here. *Science, 373*(6554), 471.

Langille, J. J., & Gallistel, C. R. (2020). Locating the engram: Should we look for plastic synapses or information-storing molecules? *Neurobiology of Learning and Memory, 169*, 107164.

Larsen, J., Raisen, C. L., Ba, X., Sadgrove, N. J., Padilla-Gonzalez, G. F., Simmonds, M. S. J., . . . Larsen, A. R. (2022). Emergence of methicillin resistance predates the clinical use of antibiotics. *Nature, 602*(7895), 135–141.

Lauritsen, S. M., Kristensen, M., Olsen, M. V., Larsen, M. S., Lauritsen, K. M., Jorgensen, M. J., Lange, J., & Thiesson, B. (2020). Explainable artificial intelligence model to predict acute critical illness from electronic health records. *Nature Communications, 11*(1), 3852.

Lee, M. B., Hill, C. M., Bitto, A., & Kaeberlein, M. (2021). Antiaging diets: Separating fact from fiction. *Science, 374*(6570), eabe7365.

Leimer, N., Wu, X., Imai, Y., Morrissette, M., Pitt, N., Favre-Godal, Q., Iinishi, A., Jain, S., Caboni, M., Leus, I. V., Bonifay, V., Niles, S., Bargabos, R., Ghiglieri, M., Corsetti, R., Krumpoch, M., Fox, G., Son, S., Klepacki, D., . . . Lewis, K. (2021). A selective antibiotic for Lyme disease. *Cell, 184*(21), 5405–5418.

Lengefeld, J., Cheng, C. W., Maretich, P., Blair, M., Hagen, H., McReynolds, M. R., Sullivan, E., Majors, K., Roberts, C., Kang, J. H., Steiner, J. D., Miettinen, T. P., Manalis, S. R., Antebi, A., Morrison, S. J., Lees, J. A., Boyer, L. A., Yilmaz, Ö. H., & Amon, A. (2021). Cell size is a determinant of stem cell potential during aging. *Science Advances, 7*(46), eabk0271.

Leypold, N. A., & Speicher, M. R. (2021). Evolutionary conservation in noncoding genomic regions. *Trends in Genetics, 37*(10), 903–918.

Li, M., & Colby, H. (2021). Physicians' flawed heuristics in the delivery room. *Science, 374*(6565), 260–261.

Lieberman, D. E., Kistner, T. M., Richard, D., Lee, I. M., & Baggish, A. L. (2021). The active grandparent hypothesis: Physical activity and the evolution of extended human healthspans and lifespans. *Proceedings of the National Academy of Sciences of the United States of America, 118*(50), e2107621118.

Lin, B. B., Ossola, A., Alberti, M., Andersson, E., Bai, X., Dobbs, C., Elmqvist, T., Evans, K. L., Frantzeskaki, N., Fuller, R. A., Gaston, K. J., Haase, D., Jim, C. Y., Konijnendijk, C., Nagendra, H., Niemelä, J., McPhearson, T., Moomaw, W. R., Parnell, S., . . . Tan, P. Y. (2021a). Integrating solutions to adapt cities for climate change. *The Lancet Planetary Health, 5*(7), e479–e486.

Lin, J.-R., Sin-Chan, P., Napolioni, V., Torres, G. G., Mitra, J., Zhang, Q., Jabalameli, M. R., Wang, Z., Nguyen, N., Gao, T., Laudes, M., Regeneron Genetics Center, Görg, S., Franke, A., Nebel, A., Greicius, M. D., Atzmon, G., Ye, K., Gorbunova, V., . . . Barzilai, N. (2021b). Rare genetic coding variants associated with human longevity and protection against age-related diseases. *Nature Aging, 1*(9), 783–794.

Lin, Y. E., Lin, C. H., Ho, E. P., Ke, Y. C., Petridi, S., Elliott, C. J., Sheen, L. Y., & Chien, C. T. (2021c). Glial Nrf2 signaling mediates the neuroprotection exerted by Gastrodia elata Blume in Lrrk2-G2019S Parkinson's disease. *Elife, 10*, e73753.

Liu, P., Quinn, R. R., Lam, N. N., Elliott, M. J., Xu, Y., James, M. T., Manns, B., & Ravani, P. (2021). Accounting for age in the definition of chronic kidney disease. *JAMA Internal Medicine, 181*(10), 1359–1366.

Livingston, G., Huntley, J., Sommerlad, A., Ames, D., Ballard, C., Banerjee, S., Brayne, C., Burns, A., Cohen-Mansfield, J., Cooper, C., Costafreda, S. G., Dias, A., Fox, N., Gitlin, L. N., Howard, R., Kales, H. C., Kivimäki, M., Larson, E. B., Ogunniyi, A., ... Mukadam, N. (2020). Dementia prevention, intervention, and care: 2020 report of the Lancet Commission. *Lancet, 396*(10248), 413–446.

Longo, V. D., & Anderson, R. M. (2022). Nutrition, longevity and disease: From molecular mechanisms to interventions. *Cell, 185*(9), 1455–1470.

Lu, J. Y., Seluanov, A., & Gorbunova, V. (2021a). Long-lived fish in a big pond. *Science, 374*(6569), 824–825.

Lu, M. Y., Chen, T. Y., Williamson, D. F. K., Zhao, M., Shady, M., Lipkova, J., & Mahmood, F. (2021b). AI-based pathology predicts origins for cancers of unknown primary. *Nature, 594*(7861), 106–110.

Lu, Y. X., Regan, J. C., Esser, J., Drews, L. F., Weinseis, T., Stinn, J., Hahn, O., Miller, R. A., Grönke, S., & Partridge, L. (2021c). A TORC1-histone axis regulates chromatin organisation and non-canonical induction of autophagy to ameliorate ageing. *Elife, 10*, e62233.

Lucas, T., Kumaratilake, J., & Henneberg, M. (2020). Recently increased prevalence of the human median artery of the forearm: A microevolutionary change. *Journal of Anatomy, 237*(4), 623–631.

Ludwig, D. S., Aronne, L. J., Astrup, A., de Cabo, R., Cantley, L. C., Friedman, M. I., Heymsfield, S. B., Johnson, J. D., King, J. C., Krauss, R. M., Lieberman, D. E., Taubes, G., Volek, J. S., Westman, E. C., Willett, W. C., Yancy, W. S., & Ebbeling, C. B. (2021). The carbohydrate-insulin model: A physiological perspective on the obesity pandemic. *The American Journal of Clinical Nutrition, 114*(6), 1873–1885.

Lundberg, S. M., Erion, G., Chen, H., DeGrave, A., Prutkin, J. M., Nair, B., Katz, R., Himmelfarb, J., Bansal, L., & S.-I. (2020). From local explanations to global understanding with explainable AI for trees. *Nature Machine Intelligence, 2*(1), 56–67.

MacAlpine, J., Daniel-Ivad, M., Liu, Z., Yano, J., Revie, N. M., Todd, R. T., Stogios, P. J., Sanchez, H., O'Meara, T. R., Tompkins, T. A., Savchenko, A., Selmecki, A., Veri, A. O., Andes, D. R., Fidel Jr, P. L., Robbins, N., Nodwell, J., Whitesell, L., & Cowen, L. E. (2021). A small molecule produced by Lactobacillus species blocks Candida albicans filamentation by inhibiting a DYRK1-family kinase. *Nature Communications, 12*(1), 6151.

MacDougall, D. R. (2020). The ends of medicine and the experience of patients. *The Journal of Medicine and Philosophy, 45*(2), 129–144.

Macnamara, E. F., D'Souza, P., Network, U. D., & Tifft, C. J. (2020). The undiagnosed diseases program: Approach to diagnosis. *Translational Science of Rare Diseases, 4*(3–4), 179–188.

Marks, P. (2021). What regulators must learn from COVID-19. *Nature Medicine, 27*(11), 1858.

Martinez-Miguel, V. E., Lujan, C., Espie-Caullet, T., Martinez-Martinez, D., Moore, S., Backes, C., Gonzalez, S., Galimov, E. R., Brown, A. E., Halic, M., Tomita, K., Rallis, C., von der Haar, T., Cabreiro, F., & Bjedov, I. (2021). Increased fidelity of protein synthesis extends lifespan. *Cell Metabolism, 33*(11), 2288–2300.

Mathews, J., & Zimmermann, C. (2020). Palliative care services at cancer centres - room for improvement. *Nature Reviews Clinical Oncology, 17*(6), 339–340.

McGraw, D., & Mandl, K. D. (2021). Privacy protections to encourage use of health-relevant digital data in a learning health system. *npj Digital Medicine, 4*(1), 2.

Mead, S. (2021). The intractable puzzle of sporadic Creutzfeldt-Jakob disease in very young people. *Neurology, 97*(17), 801–802.

Melcher, A., Harrington, K., & Vile, R. (2021). Oncolytic virotherapy as immunotherapy. *Science, 374*(6573), 1325–1326.

Menon, U., Gentry-Maharaj, A., Burnell, M., Singh, N., Ryan, A., Karpinskyj, C., Carlino, G., Taylor, J., Massingham, S. K., Raikou, M., Kalsi, J. K., Woolas, R., Manchanda, R., Arora, R., Casey, L., Dawnay, A., Dobbs, S., Leeson, S., Mould, T., ... Parmar, M. (2021). Ovarian cancer population screening and mortality after long-term follow-up in the UK Collaborative Trial of Ovarian Cancer Screening (UKCTOCS): A randomised controlled trial. *Lancet, 397*(10290), 2182–2193.

Mesulam, M. M., Coventry, C., Kuang, A., Bigio, E. H., Mao, Q., Flanagan, M. E., Gefen, T., Sridhar, J., Geula, C., Zhang, H., Weintraub, S., & Rogalski, E. J. (2021). Memory resilience in Alzheimer disease with primary progressive aphasia. *Neurology, 96*(6), e916–e925.

Metz, C. (2021). The robot surgeon will see you now. *The New York Times*. Retrieved from https://www.nytimes.com/2021/04/30/technology/robot-surgery-surgeon.html

Michelson, A. A. (1896). *Annual register*. The University of Chicago.

Miethke, M., Pieroni, M., Weber, T., Bronstrup, M., Hammann, P., Halby, L., Arimondo, P. B., Glaser, P., Aigle, B., Bode, H. B., Moreira, R., Li, Y., Luzhetskyy, A., Medema, M. H., Pernodet, J.-L., Stadler, M., Tormo, J. R., Genilloud, O., Truman, A. W., ... Muller, R. (2021). Towards the sustainable discovery and development of new antibiotics. *Nature Reviews Chemistry, 5*(10), 726–749.

Mitcheltree, M. J., Pisipati, A., Syroegin, E. A., Silvestre, K. J., Klepacki, D., Mason, J. D., Terwilliger, D. W., Testolin, G., Pote, A. R., Wu, K. J., Ladley, R. P., Chatman, K., Mankin, A. S., Polikanov, Y. S., & Myers, A. G. (2021). A synthetic antibiotic class overcoming bacterial multidrug resistance. *Nature, 599*(7885), 507–512.

Molimau-Samasoni, S., Woolner, V. H., Foliga, S. T., Robichon, K., Patel, V., Andreassend, S. K., Sheridan, J. P., Te Kawa, T., Gresham, D., Miller, D., Sinclair, D. J., La Flamme, A. C., Melnik, A. V., Aron, A., Dorrestein, P. C., Atkinson, P. H., Keyzers, R. A., & Munkacsi, A. B. (2021). Functional genomics and metabolomics advance the ethnobotany of the Samoan traditional medicine "matalafi". *Proceedings of the National Academy of Sciences of the United States of America, 118*(45), e2100880118.

Moser, P. (2016). Patents and innovation in economic history. *Annual Review of Economics, 8*, 241–258.

Mullard, A. (2022). 2021 FDA approvals. *Nature Reviews Drug Discovery, 21*(2), 83–88.

Murray, L., Gopinath, D., Agrawal, M., Horng, S., Sontag, D., & Karger, D. R. (2021). MedKnowts: Unified documentation and information retrieval for electronic health records. In *The 34th Annual ACM Symposium on User Interface Software and Technology* (pp. 1169–1183). Association for Computing Machinery.

Murugan, N. J., Vigran, H. J., Miller, K. A., Golding, A., Pham, Q. L., Sperry, M. M., Rasmussen-Ivey, C., Kane, A. W., Kaplan, D. L., & Levin, M. (2022). Acute multidrug delivery via a wearable bioreactor facilitates long-term limb regeneration and functional recovery in adult Xenopus laevis. *Science Advances, 8*(4), eabj2164.

Nakao, M., Shirotsuki, K., & Sugaya, N. (2021). Cognitive-behavioral therapy for management of mental health and stress-related disorders: Recent advances in techniques and technologies. *BioPsychoSocial Medicine, 15*(1), 16.

Nassiri, F., Liu, J., Patil, V., Mamatjan, Y., Wang, J. Z., Hugh-White, R., Macklin, A. M., Khan, S., Singh, O., Karimi, S., Corona, R. I., Liu, L. Y., Chen, C. Y., Chakravarthy, A., Wei, Q., Mehani, B., Suppiah, S., Gao, A., Workewych, A. M., ... Zadeh, G. (2021). A clinically applicable integrative molecular classification of meningiomas. *Nature, 597*(7874), 119–125.

Nature Editors. (2021a). Artificial intelligence in structural biology is here to stay. *Nature, 595*(7869), 625–626.

Nature Editors. (2021b). License CRISPR patents for free to share gene editing globally. *Nature, 597*(7875), 152.

Nature Editors. (2021c). A patent waiver on COVID vaccines is right and fair. *Nature, 593*(7860), 478.

Nature Editors. (2021d). Replicating scientific results is tough - but essential. *Nature, 600*(7889), 359–360.

Neal, B., Wu, Y., Feng, X., Zhang, R., Zhang, Y., Shi, J., Zhang, J., Tian, M., Huang, L., Li, Z., Yu, Y., Zhao, Y., Zhou, B., Sun, J., Liu, Y., Yin, X., Hao, Z., Jie, Y., & Elliott, P. (2021). Effect of salt substitution on cardiovascular events and death. *The New England Journal of Medicine, 385*(12), 1067–1077.

Neves, R. C., Hvidepil, L. K. B., Sorensen-Hygum, T. L., Stuart, R. M., & Mobjerg, N. (2020). Thermotolerance experiments on active and desiccated states of Ramazzottius varieornatus emphasize that tardigrades are sensitive to high temperatures. *Scientific Reports, 10*(1), 94.

Nurk, S., Koren, S., Rhie, A., Rautiainen, M., Bzikadze, A. V., Mikheenko, A., ... Phillippy, A. M. (2022). The complete sequence of a human genome. *Science, 376*(6588), 44–53.

Ochoa de Olza, M. (2021). A promising platform for predicting toxicity. *Elife, 10*, e73191.

Ourmazd, A. (2019). Cryo-EM, XFELs and the structure conundrum in structural biology. *Nature Methods, 16*(10), 941–944.

Pascual, G., Dominguez, D., Elosua-Bayes, M., Beckedorff, F., Laudanna, C., Bigas, C., Douillet, D., Greco, C., Symeonidi, A., Hernández, I., Gil, S. R., Prats, N., Bescós, C., Shiekhattar, R., Amit, M., Heyn, H., Shilatifard, A., & Benitah, S. A. (2021). Dietary palmitic acid promotes a prometastatic memory via Schwann cells. *Nature, 599*(7885), 485–490.

Pelletier, J. F., Sun, L., Wise, K. S., Assad-Garcia, N., Karas, B. J., Deerinck, T. J., Ellisman, M. H., Mershin, A., Gershenfeld, N., Chuang, R. Y., Glass, J. I., & Strychalski, E. A. (2021). Genetic requirements for cell division in a genomically minimal cell. *Cell, 184*(9), 2430–2440.

Pennisi, E. (2022). Upstart DNA sequencers could be a 'game changer'. *Science, 376*(6599), 1257–1258.

Perin, J., Mulick, A., Yeung, D., Villavicencio, F., Lopez, G., Strong, K. L., Prieto-Merino, D., Cousens, S., Black, R. E., & Liu, L. (2021). Global, regional, and national causes of under-5 mortality in 2000-19: An updated systematic analysis with implications for the sustainable development goals. *The Lancet Child & Adolescent Health., 6*(2), 106–115.

Potrich, D., Zanon, M., & Vallortigara, G. (2022). Archerfish number discrimination. *Elife, 11*, e74057.

Pretz, K. (2021a). Deep learning can't be trusted, brain modeling pioneer says. *IEEE Spectrum.* Retrieved from https://spectrum.ieee.org/deep-learning-cant-be-trusted

Pretz, K. (2021b). Stop calling everything AI, machine-learning pioneer says. *IEEE Spectrum.* Retrieved from https://spectrum.ieee.org/stop-calling-everything-ai-machinelearning-pioneer-says

Pullanchery, S., Kulik, S., Rehl, B., Hassanali, A., & Roke, S. (2021). Charge transfer across C-HO hydrogen bonds stabilizes oil droplets in water. *Science, 374*(6573), 1366–1370.

Ramzy, A., Thompson, D. M., Ward-Hartstonge, K. A., Ivison, S., Cook, L., Garcia, R. V., Loyal, J., Kim, P. T., Warnock, G. L., Levings, M. K., & Kieffer, T. J. (2021). Implanted pluripotent stem-cell-derived pancreatic endoderm cells secrete glucose-responsive C-peptide in patients with type 1 diabetes. *Cell Stem Cell, 28*(12), 2047–2061.

Ravaud, A. (2021). A step ahead in metastatic renal cell carcinoma. *The New England Journal of Medicine, 384*(14), 1360–1361.

Reardon, S. (2021). A complete human genome sequence is close: How scientists filled in the gaps. *Nature, 594*(7862), 158–159.

Regalado, A. (2021). Meet Altos Labs, Silicon Valley's latest wild bet on living forever. *MIT Technology Review.* Retrieved from https://www.technologyreview.com/2021/09/04/1034364/altos-labs-silicon-valleys-jeff-bezos-milner-bet-living-forever/

Reinke, B. A., Cayuela, H., Janzen, F. J., Lemaitre, J. F., Gaillard, J. M., Lawing, A. M., ... Miller, D. A. W. (2022). Diverse aging rates in ectothermic tetrapods provide insights for the evolution of aging and longevity. *Science, 376*(6600), 1459–1466.

Resnick, B. (2021). The weird science of the placebo effect keeps getting more interesting. *Vox.* Retrieved from https://www.vox.com/unexplainable/22405880/placebo-mystery-open-label-pain-medicine

Revie, N. M., Iyer, K. R., Robbins, N., & Cowen, L. E. (2018). Antifungal drug resistance: Evolution, mechanisms and impact. *Current Opinion in Microbiology, 45*, 70–76.

Richeldi, L., Collard, H. R., & Jones, M. G. (2017). Idiopathic pulmonary fibrosis. *Lancet, 389*(10082), 1941–1952.

Riedmeier, M., Stock, A., Krauss, J., Sahm, F., Jones, D. T. W., Sturm, D., Kramm, C. M., Eyrich, M., Härtel, C., Schlegel, S., Schlegel, P. G., Monoranu, C.-M., & Wiegering, V. (2021). Spontaneous regression of a congenital high-grade glioma-a case report. *Neuro-Oncology Advances, 3*(1), vdab120.

Rimal, B., & Patterson, A. D. (2021). Role of bile acids and gut bacteria in healthy ageing of centenarians. *Nature, 599*(7885), 380–381.

Robbins, P. D., Jurk, D., Khosla, S., Kirkland, J. L., LeBrasseur, N. K., Miller, J. D., Passos, J. F., Pignolo, R. J., Tchkonia, T., & Niedernhofer, L. J. (2021). Senolytic drugs: Reducing senescent cell viability to extend health span. *Annual Review of Pharmacology and Toxicology, 61*, 779–803.

Roberts, M., Driggs, D., Thorpe, M., Gilbey, J., Yeung, M., Ursprung, S., Aviles-Rivero, A. I., Etmann, C., McCague, C., Beer, L., Weir-McCall, J. R., Teng, Z., Gkrania-Klotsas, E., Aix, C., Rudd, J. H. F., Sala, E., & Schönlieb, C.-B. (2021). Common pitfalls and recommendations for using machine learning to detect and prognosticate for COVID-19 using chest radiographs and CT scans. *Nature Machine Intelligence, 3*(3), 199–217.

Robinson, J. C., & Brandon, M. P. (2021). Skipping ahead: A circuit for representing the past, present, and future. *Elife, 10*. https://doi.org/10.7554/eLife.68795

Rocheleau, J. (2022). New antifungal medications are sorely needed. *Knowable Magazine*. Retrieved from https://knowablemagazine.org/article/health-disease/2022/new-antifungal-medications-sorely-needed

Roth, A., & MPS-WS Berlin 2019. (2021). Human microphysiological systems for drug development. *Science, 373*(6561), 1304–1306.

Rothberg, J. M., Ralston, T. S., Rothberg, A. G., Martin, J., Zahorian, J. S., Alie, S. A., Sanchez, N. J., Chen, K., Chen, C., Thiele, K., Grosjean, D., Yang, J., Bao, L., Schneider, R., Schaetz, S., Meyer, C., Neben, A., Bob Ryan, J. R., Petrus, J. L., . . . Fife, K. G. (2021). Ultrasound-on-chip platform for medical imaging, analysis, and collective intelligence. *Proceedings of the National Academy of Sciences of the United States of America, 118*(27), e2019339118.

Saha, T., Dash, C., Jayabalan, R., Khiste, S., Kulkarni, A., Kurmi, K., Mondal, J., Majumder, P. K., Bardia, A., Jang, H. L., & Sengupta, S. (2022). Intercellular nanotubes mediate mitochondrial trafficking between cancer and immune cells. *Nature Nanotechnology, 17*(1), 98–106.

Sahel, J. A., Boulanger-Scemama, E., Pagot, C., Arleo, A., Galluppi, F., Martel, J. N., Esposti, S. D., Delaux, A., de Saint Aubert, J. B., de Montleau, C., Gutman, E., Audo, I., Duebel, J., Picaud, S., Dalkara, D., Blouin, L., Taiel, M., & Roska, B. (2021). Partial recovery of visual function in a blind patient after optogenetic therapy. *Nature Medicine, 27*(7), 1223–1229.

Sato, Y., Atarashi, K., Plichta, D. R., Arai, Y., Sasajima, S., Kearney, S. M., Suda, W., Takeshita, K., Sasaki, T., Okamoto, S., Skelly, A. N., Okamura, Y., Vlamakis, H., Li, Y., Tanoue, T., Takei, H., Nittono, H., Narushima, S., Irie, J., . . . Honda, K. (2021). Novel bile acid biosynthetic pathways are enriched in the microbiome of centenarians. *Nature, 599*(7885), 458–464.

Sato, T., Shapiro, J. S., Chang, H. C., Miller, R. A., & Ardehali, H. (2022). Aging is associated with increased brain iron through cortex-derived hepcidin expression. *Elife, 11*, e73456.

Savage, N. (2022). Robots rise to meet the challenge of caring for old people. *Nature, 601*(7893), S8–S10.

Schroeder, S., Hofer, S. J., Zimmermann, A., Pechlaner, R., Dammbrueck, C., Pendl, T., Marcello, G. M., Pogatschnigg, V., Bergmann, M., Müller, M., Gschiel, V., Ristic, S., Tadic, J., Iwata, K., Richter, G., Farzi, A., Üçal, M., Schäfer, U., Poglitsch, M., . . . Madeo, F. (2021). Dietary spermidine improves cognitive function. *Cell Reports, 35*(2), 108985.

Schupbach, J. N. (2018). Robustness analysis as explanatory reasoning. *The British Journal for the Philosophy of Science, 69*(1), 275–300.

Scott, A. J., Ellison, M., & Sinclair, D. A. (2021). The economic value of targeting aging. *Nature Aging, 1*, 616–623.

Servick, K. (2022). Window of opportunity. *Science, 375*(6578), 256–259.

Sharma, A., & Kaplan, W. A. (2021). Insulin imports fail to meet many countries' needs. *Science, 373*(6554), 494–497.

Sharon, T., & Lucivero, F. (2019). Introduction to the special theme: The expansion of the health data ecosystem – Rethinking data ethics and governance. *Big Data & Society, 6*(2), 2053951719852969.

Sheather, J. (2019). *Is medicine still good for us?* Thames & Hudson.

Shepertycky, M., Burton, S., Dickson, A., Liu, Y. F., & Li, Q. (2021). Removing energy with an exoskeleton reduces the metabolic cost of walking. *Science, 372*(6545), 957–960.

Sherman, M. (2007). Universal genome in the origin of metazoa: Thoughts about evolution. *Cell Cycle, 6*(15), 1873–1877.

Shi, J., Weng, J. H., & Mitchison, T. J. (2021). Immunomodulatory drug discovery from herbal medicines: Insights from organ-specific activity and xenobiotic defenses. *Elife, 10*, e73673.

Shmakova, L., Malavin, S., Iakovenko, N., Vishnivetskaya, T., Shain, D., Plewka, M., & Rivkina, E. (2021). A living bdelloid rotifer from 24,000-year-old Arctic permafrost. *Current Biology, 31*(11), R712–R713.

Shukla, A. K., Johnson, K., & Giniger, E. (2021). Common features of aging fail to occur in Drosophila raised without a bacterial microbiome. *iScience, 24*(7), 102703.

Singh, M. (2021). Heuristics in the delivery room. *Science, 374*(6565), 324–329.

Sohn, R. (2022). AI could analyze speech to help diagnose Alzheimer's. *IEEE Spectrum*. Retrieved from https://spectrum.ieee.org/ai-to-detect-alzheimers

Sriram, G., Milling, L. E., Chen, J. K., Kong, Y. W., Joughin, B. A., Abraham, W., Swartwout, S., Handly, E. D., Irvine, D. J., & Yaffe, M. B. (2021). The injury response to DNA damage in live tumor cells promotes antitumor immunity. *Science Signaling, 14*(705), eabc4764.

Stanley, D. E., & Nyrup, R. (2020). Strategies in abduction: Generating and selecting diagnostic hypotheses. *The Journal of Medicine and Philosophy, 45*(2), 159–178.

Steele, K., & Stefánsson, H. O. (2021). *Beyond uncertainty: Reasoning with unknown possibilities*. Cambridge University Press.

Stein, K. C., Morales-Polanco, F., van der Lienden, J., Rainbolt, T. K., & Frydman, J. (2022). Ageing exacerbates ribosome pausing to disrupt cotranslational proteostasis. *Nature, 601*(7894), 637–642.

Tabebordbar, M., Lagerborg, K. A., Stanton, A., King, E. M., Ye, S., Tellez, L., Krunnfusz, A., Tavakoli, S., Widrick, J. J., Messemer, K. A., Troiano, E. C., Moghadaszadeh, B., Peacker, B. L., Leacock, K. A., Horwitz, N., Beggs, A. H., Wagers, A. J., & Sabeti, P. C. (2021). Directed evolution of a family of AAV capsid variants enabling potent muscle-directed gene delivery across species. *Cell, 184*(19), 4919–4938.

The Lancet. (2021). Reinstating universal health coverage on the global agenda. *Lancet, 398*(10316), 2051.

Thomason, K. K. (2021). The philosopher's medicine of the mind: Kant's account of mental illness and the normativity of thinking. In A. Lyssy & C. Yeomans (Eds.), *Kant on morality, humanity, and legality: Practical dimensions of normativity* (pp. 189–206). Palgrave Macmillan.

Tibbits, G., Mohamed, A., Call, D. R., & Beyenal, H. (2022). Rapid differentiation of antibiotic-susceptible and -resistant bacteria through mediated extracellular electron transfer. *Biosensors and Bioelectronics, 197*, 113754.

Tierney, T. M., Holmes, N., Mellor, S., Lopez, J. D., Roberts, G., Hill, R. M., Boto, E., Leggett, J., Shah, V., Brookes, M. J., Bowtell, R., & Barnes, G. R. (2019). Optically pumped magnetometers: From quantum origins to multi-channel magnetoencephalography. *NeuroImage, 199*, 598–608.

Ulgherait, M., Midoun, A. M., Park, S. J., Gatto, J. A., Tener, S. J., Siewert, J., Klickstein, N., Canman, J. C., Ja, W. W., & Shirasu-Hiza, M. (2021). Circadian autophagy drives iTRF-mediated longevity. *Nature, 598*(7880), 353–358.

Vandenbroucke-Grauls, C., & Kluytmans, J. (2022). Tracing the origins of antibiotic resistance. *Nature Medicine, 28*(4), 638–640.

Vidal-Pineiro, D., Wang, Y., Krogsrud, S. K., Amlien, I. K., Baare, W. F., Bartres-Faz, D., Bertram, L., Brandmaier, A. M., Drevon, C. A., Düzel, S., Ebmeier, K., Henson, R. N., Junqué, C., Kievit,

R. A., Kühn, S., Leonardsen, E., Lindenberger, U., Madsen, K. S., Magnussen, F., . . . Fjell, A. (2021). Individual variations in 'brain age' relate to early-life factors more than to longitudinal brain change. *Elife, 10*, e69995.

Vincze, O., Colchero, F., Lemaitre, J. F., Conde, D. A., Pavard, S., Bieuville, M., Urrutia, A. O., Ujvari, B., Boddy, A. M., Maley, C. C., Thomas, F., & Giraudeau, M. (2022). Cancer risk across mammals. *Nature, 601*(7892), 263–267.

Vollger, M. R., Guitart, X., Dishuck, P. C., Mercuri, L., Harvey, W. T., Gershman, A., . . . Eichler, E. E. (2022). Segmental duplications and their variation in a complete human genome. *Science, 376*(6588), eabj6965.

Wan, T., Liu, Z., Leitch, I. J., Xin, H., Maggs-Kolling, G., Gong, Y., Li, Z., Marais, E., Liao, Y., Dai, C., Liu, F., Qijia, W., Song, C., Zhou, Y., Huang, W., Jiang, K., Wang, Q., Yang, Y., Zhong, Z., . . . Wang, Q. (2021). The Welwitschia genome reveals a unique biology underpinning extreme longevity in deserts. *Nature Communications, 12*(1), 4247.

Wang, Y. X., & Blau, H. M. (2021). Reversing aging for heart repair. *Science, 373*(6562), 1439–1440.

Wang, A., MacNeil, A., & Maloney, S. (2021). Comparison and lessons learned from neglected tropical diseases and tuberculosis. *PLOS Global Public Health, 1*(10), e0000027.

Wang, Z., Koirala, B., Hernandez, Y., Zimmerman, M., Park, S., Perlin, D. S., & Brady, S. F. (2022). A naturally inspired antibiotic to target multidrug-resistant pathogens. *Nature, 601*(7894), 606–611.

Ware, J., Allen, J. M., Boughton, C. K., Wilinska, M. E., Hartnell, S., Thankamony, A., de Beaufort, C., Schierloh, U., Fröhlich-Reiterer, E., Mader, J. K., Kapellen, T. M., Rami-Merhar, B., Tauschmann, M., Nagl, K., Hofer, S. E., Campbell, F. M., Yong, J., Hood, K. K., Lawton, J., . . . Kids AP Consortium. (2022). Randomized trial of closed-loop control in very young children with type 1 diabetes. *The New England Journal of Medicine, 386*(3), 209–219.

Weeks, K. M. (2021). Piercing the fog of the RNA structure-ome. *Science, 373*(6558), 964–965.

Wensien, M., von Pappenheim, F. R., Funk, L. M., Kloskowski, P., Curth, U., Diederichsen, U., Uranga, J., Ye, J., Fang, P., Pan, K. T., Urlaub, H., Mata, R. A., Sautner, V., & Tittmann, K. (2021). A lysine-cysteine redox switch with an NOS bridge regulates enzyme function. *Nature, 593*(7859), 460–464.

White, N. J. (2021). Emergence of artemisinin-resistant plasmodium falciparum in East Africa. *The New England Journal of Medicine, 385*(13), 1231–1232.

WHO. (2021). *Health equity and its determinants*, pp. 1–9. Retrieved from https://www.who.int/publications/m/item/health-equity-and-its-determinants

Wiley, C. D., & Campisi, J. (2021). The metabolic roots of senescence: mechanisms and opportunities for intervention. *Nature Metabolism, 3*(10), 1290–1301.

Winn, Z. (2021). Building robots to expand access to cell therapies. *MIT News*. Retrieved from https://news.mit.edu/2021/multiply-labs-cell-therapy-0512

Wolff, J., Hefner, G., Normann, C., Kaier, K., Binder, H., Hiemke, C., Toto, S., Domschke, K., Marschollek, M., & Klimke, A. (2021). Polypharmacy and the risk of drug-drug interactions and potentially inappropriate medications in hospital psychiatry. *Pharmacoepidemiology and Drug Safety, 30*(9), 1258–1268.

Xiong, Z., Achavananthadith, S., Lian, S., Madden, L. E., Ong, Z. X., Chua, W., Kalidasan, V., Li, Z., Liu, Z., Singh, P., Yang, H., Heussler, S. P., Kalaiselvi, S. M. P., Breese, M. B. H., Yao, H., Gao, Y., Sanmugam, K., Tee, B. C. K., Chen, P.-Y., . . . Ho, J. S. (2021). A wireless and battery-free wound infection sensor based on DNA hydrogel. *Science Advances, 7*(47), eabj1617.

Yousefzadeh, M. J., Flores, R. R., Zhu, Y., Schmiechen, Z. C., Brooks, R. W., Trussoni, C. E., Cui, Y., Angelini, L., Lee, K. A., McGowan, S. J., Burrack, A. L., Wang, D., Dong, Q., Lu, A., Sano, T., O'Kelly, R. D., McGuckian, C. A., Kato, J. I., Bank, M. P., . . . Niedernhofer, L. J. (2021). An aged immune system drives senescence and ageing of solid organs. *Nature, 594*(7861), 100–105.

Zhang, F., Mamtani, R., Scott, F. I., Goldberg, D. S., Haynes, K., & Lewis, J. D. (2016). Increasing use of prescription drugs in the United Kingdom. *Pharmacoepidemiology and Drug Safety, 25*(6), 628–636.

Zhang, B., Vogelzang, A., Miyajima, M., Sugiura, Y., Wu, Y., Chamoto, K., Nakano, R., Hatae, R., Menzies, R. J., Sonomura, K., Hojo, N., Ogawa, T., Kobayashi, W., Tsutsui, Y., Yamamoto, S., Maruya, M., Narushima, S., Suzuki, K., Sugiya, H., . . . Fagarasan, S. (2021). B cell-derived GABA elicits IL-10(+) macrophages to limit anti-tumour immunity. *Nature, 599*(7885), 471–476.

Innovations in Psychiatric Care Models: Lessons from the Past to Inform the Future

Kristin Beizai, Ashley Stone, and Yash Joshi

Abstract

With the progressive transformation of healthcare delivery systems, innovative psychiatric care models are on the cusp of implementation. We will discuss the history of the chronic care model in nonpsychiatric medical care models and the application to psychiatric care models such as the collaborative care model. We will describe a complementary model of reverse integrated care and imagine the future model of care for our patients, considering the care of individuals with initial onset of psychosis as a case study. These models reflect the range of possibilities being translated into effective clinical care for the management of chronic psychiatric disease.

1 Introduction

Over the last several decades, the corpus of basic science that informs psychiatric treatment has exploded. Advances in genetics, pharmacology, neuroimaging, and emerging interventions have led to a staggering range of innovations in clinical treatments. However, psychiatry has lagged behind nonpsychiatric medical fields in outcomes, in part because of difficulties with bridging the gap between clinical knowledge and clinical care.

Major depressive disorder illustrates some of the current challenges. Many clinical trials of novel treatments for major depressive disorder (MDD) recruit homogeneous patient populations, often at academic medical centers, to determine

K. Beizai (✉) · A. Stone · Y. Joshi
Department of Psychiatry, University of California San Diego, San Diego, CA, USA

U.S. Department of Veterans Affairs (VA San Diego Healthcare System), San Diego, CA, USA
e-mail: kbeizai@health.ucsd.edu; als081@health.ucsd.edu; yajoshi@health.ucsd.edu

whether the putative treatment is better than a placebo or the usual care. However, once approved, these treatments or methods must be implemented in heterogeneous populations across multiple contexts. How should novel individual treatments be implemented in real-world clinics and health systems? Which models of care delivery provide the best clinical outcomes at the individual level? At the population level? What are the current practice patterns at the levels of systems, regions, and nations? What resources must be mustered to support the implementation of new models of care delivery? Psychiatric disorders accounted for 27% of all health-related disabilities in the United States (Vos et al., 2012), and there is a shortage of psychiatrists in the United States and globally. Answers to these questions loom large for the future of psychiatry and for the recovery of our patients.

In this chapter, we will discuss these topics in a cross-historical context as we consider the delivery of psychiatric care in the future. We first provide an overview of the chronic care model in medicine and how that has led to the development of the collaborative care model for the treatment of depression and anxiety. We then explore the reverse integrated model for psychiatric care. Finally, we will imagine the future model of care for patients living with psychiatric illness using the initial onset of psychosis as an example. The overarching theme of this chapter is the transformation of psychiatric models of care prompted by the uncertain impact of past models on healthcare outcomes.

2   The Chronic Care Model: Applicability to Psychiatric Care

Wagner and colleagues developed the chronic care model in the 1990s in response to the significant global burden of chronic diseases in terms of death and disability. Evidence at that time revealed that the usual standard of care was not adequate to manage chronic conditions for most patients. At the time, only 27% of patients with hypertension were adequately treated and only 14% of patients with coronary heart disease reached the low levels of low-density lipoprotein cholesterol recommended by national standards (Grumbach & Bodenheimer, 2002). The majority (80%) of visits for common chronic conditions such as hypertension, cardiac disease, and diabetes took place in primary care clinics, an environment that was strained at the time (Grumbach & Bodenheimer, 2002). Challenges included inadequate patient access to healthcare, the increasing accountability and administrative burdens that accompanied advances in medical care, inefficient workflow patterns, and decreasing physician satisfaction. The drive to provide effective, longitudinal, coordinated care for patients led to the transformation of the ambulatory care delivery system. The proposed model recommended six interrelated changes in the design of clinical systems for ambulatory patients, including increasing the expertise and enhancing the skills of providers, educating and supporting patients within their community, providing team-based planned care, and making better use of registry-based information via clinical informatics (Wagner, 1998; Wagner et al., 1996).

The chronic care model emphasized population-based care, measurement-based care, and stepped care to ensure that the delivery of clinical care would be proactive rather than reactive, that self-management skills and resources would empower patients, and that care would be consolidated through team-based care. Evidence suggests that redesigning practices in accordance with these suggested principles generally improved the quality of care and outcomes for patients, particularly in clinics with a specialty focus on a single chronic condition. For example, compared to patients in control practices, patients of providers who actively participated in the Institute of Healthcare Improvement's Breakthrough Series (Congestive Heart Failure Collaborative) were more knowledgeable, used recommended therapies more often, visited the emergency department less often, and experienced 35% fewer days in the hospital (Coleman et al., 2009). Despite this encouraging data, challenges remain related to implementing this design across a wide range of organizational contexts and the associated costs (Coleman et al., 2009). Multiple reimbursement structures further complicate the transformation of services.

The US Institute of Medicine reports "Crossing the Quality Chasm" (2001) and "Improving the Quality of Health Care for Mental and Substance Use Conditions" (2006) called for further improvement in quality of care and identified the underlying reasons for inadequate quality as the growing complexity of science and technology, the increase in chronic conditions, and poorly organized delivery systems (Institute of Medicine, 2001, 2006). Since 2008, the triple aim of improving population health, improving how patients experience care, and reducing the cost of healthcare has been adopted as a framework and widely used metric for the development of quality healthcare. However, applying these principles to psychiatric care delivery models remains a key challenge to the implementation of these goals (Berwick et al., 2008; Pincus et al., 2016).

3   Psychiatry and Measurement-Based Care

Psychiatric disorders have a long history of being underrecognized and undertreated and result in significant cost to individuals, communities, and populations. The National Comorbidity Survey Replication (NCS-R), which was completed in 2004, was an effort to capture epidemiologic data related to mental health diagnoses, mental health services, and treatment adequacy (based on available evidence-based guidelines). Most patients with psychiatric disorders (60%) had not received any care in the previous 12 months. Of those who did, over half received care in a general medical setting, and only one-third of those received treatment that met minimal treatment standards of adequacy (Raney, 2017; Wang et al., 2005). Indeed, primary care physicians are sole physician managers for one-third of all psychiatric disorders, including over one-third of children with attention deficit/hyperactivity disorder (Anderson et al., 2015).

While many fields of US healthcare have made progress in meeting the challenge of system redesign, psychiatry has lagged behind. The National Committee for Quality Assurance's Healthcare Effectiveness Data and Information Set has reported improvement in measures that assess changes in diabetes and hypertension care in the period 2006–2014, but average quality declined for behavioral health measures for two out of three payers (Pincus et al., 2016). Applying the principles of the chronic care model and the triple aim framework to psychiatric models of care is a needed innovation.

One principle of the chronic care model, the implementation of measurement-based care (MBC), provides an example of the challenges with redesigning psychiatric care delivery models. MBC is the practice of routinely administering standardized measures to support clinical decision-making and monitor treatment response and progress. MBC-derived data aims to inform effectiveness of treatments when integrated with the clinical encounter in a timely and systematic way. Standardized and clinically meaningful tools that can be used regularly to measure symptoms such as depression and anxiety have been developed but have been incorporated into standard practices slowly. The barriers include how to measure outcomes related to psychosocial functionality and recovery and how to engage psychiatric clinicians to accept and implement these tools. MBC is typically underutilized in general psychiatric care, including treatment for substance use disorders. Typically, less than 20% of practitioners integrate it into their general practice, and as few as 5% use it according to an empirically informed schedule (Kroenke & Unutzer, 2017; Lewis et al., 2019).

There is a substantial need for MBC implementation. Providers of psychiatric care detect deterioration or increased symptomatology in only 21.4% of their patients based on clinical judgment alone. The detection rates are even worse for patients who are not improving as expected. Clinical inertia is described as the failure to appropriately modify treatment and has been found to be prevalent particularly for conditions with less acute symptoms, such as persistent depression. One study found that only one-third of the less severely depressed patients, with less than a full response, were offered treatment adjustments. This under recognition of deterioration or lack of improvement and the resultant clinical inertia can be countered by the systematic implementation of MBC (Fortney et al., 2018; Henke et al., 2009). MBC has been associated with better treatment outcomes, improved quality of care, better detection of clinical improvement and decline, improved therapeutic alliance, more accurate clinical assessments, and improved individualization of care (Aboraya et al., 2018).

However, there are still questions about how MBC can be best implemented. What measures are relevant and where do they fit in clinical guidelines and algorithms? And how can we leverage increasingly rich and voluminous sources of information for the future of psychiatric care?

4   Current Innovative Psychiatric Care Models

4.1   Collaborative Care

As noted above, the care of psychiatric disorders—many of which are chronic diseases—stands to benefit from care delivery within the MBC frame. Development of the collaborative care model (CCM) pioneered at the University of Washington provides evidence of such a framework in action.

This innovative integrated population-based model of care was based on understanding recurrent major depressive disorder as a chronic medical disease, bringing the care to where the patients were seeking treatment (the primary care clinic), and applying the principles of MBC, population-based, and stepped care. The treatment of depression with this model, which emphasizes team-based care and provides evidence-based treatments, led to improved healthcare outcomes for patients with depression as well as for the comorbid medical conditions, specifically diabetes and cardiovascular disease. The Improving Mood-Promoting Access to Collaborative Treatment trial led by Unützer and colleagues was based on elements of the chronic care model. The large randomized controlled trial of over 1800 patients assigned the patients to receive either the usual care for depression within the primary care clinic, or the collaborative care model within the primary care clinic. The results demonstrated that the CCM more than doubled the effectiveness of depression treatment for patients in the primary care setting. In addition to significant improvement in outcomes, the CCM also showed increased patient satisfaction and a reduction in healthcare costs. These results met the goals of the triple aim in quality health care (Katon, 2012; Unützer et al., 2002). The implementation of this model across delivery systems has accelerated now that multiple trials have demonstrated the effectiveness of collaborative care treatment for depression and since the passage of the Affordable Care Act.

The practice of the CCM includes a patient-centered team that includes the primary care and mental health team (typically a nurse care manager, a psychologist, and a psychiatrist). Goals of the team include rapid access and treatment without referral to the specialty clinic and communication between team members to promote teamwork and enhance patient care. A stepped care approach is utilized in which the mental health team function as consultants, educators, and facilitators to the primary care team, always with the patient at the center of care.

For example, the primary care clinician may prescribe an antidepressant for a patient with major depressive disorder, and the psychiatric nurse care manager concurrently provides health education and self-management strategies (such as behavioral activation). As this care is initiated, MBC is implemented, using standardized assessment tools for depression such as the PHQ-9 (Kroenke et al., 2001). The patient's response is tracked in databases called registries and systematically reviewed by the mental health team. Response to treatment, adherence, and indications for further recommendations or interventions are the areas of focus. Subsequent to registry review, interventions may include input to and education for primary care teams or direct consultations by mental health providers for brief evidence-based psychotherapies or pharmacotherapy consultation. Thus, depending on clinical need, patient care is stepped and patient-centric (Raney, 2017). Further standardized assessment tools may be used to supplement primary measures including the GAD-7 (which screens for generalized anxiety disorder) and AUDIT-C (which screens for alcohol use), with the goal of improved healthcare outcomes across the clinic population (Bush et al., 1998; Spitzer et al., 2006).

Current areas of research include the applicability and effectiveness of the collaborative care model within other clinical settings (e.g., a pediatric or geriatric practice) and the management of other psychiatric diagnoses (such as bipolar disorder). In real-world settings, patients currently present in the primary care setting with a wide range of diagnoses and receive bridging care until transition to the specialty psychiatric clinic if it is indicated. The collaborative care model is also being considered for other psychiatric contexts such as for suicide prevention, although there are ongoing questions about scope and effectiveness (Mann et al., 2021).

4.2   Reverse Integrated Care

Reverse integrated care (RIC) models are different from the CCM and other models that bring psychiatric services for patients with depression and anxiety into primary care. The RIC model seeks to bring primary care services into psychiatric settings (Maragakis et al., 2016; McCarron et al., 2015; Ward & Druss, 2017). Such models originated to meet the unique needs of patients suffering from severe mental illness (Gerrity, 2014). Patients with severe mental illness are more likely to experience excess mortality and comorbid medical conditions than the general population (De Hert et al., 2011; Viron & Stern, 2010). Yet patients with psychiatric disorders, particularly psychotic disorders and bipolar disorder, are less likely to access primary care than patients who do not have such disorders (Bradford et al., 2008; Druss et al., 2001a; Olsen et al., 2017). For example, in a large study of Department of Veterans Affairs patients with psychiatric disorders, authors found that patients with psychiatric disorders were less likely to access medical services and that the discrepancy was most profound in young adults with schizophrenia or post-traumatic stress disorder and with all adults with bipolar disorders (Cradock-O'Leary et al., 2002).

Understanding the reasons why patients with severe mental illness are less likely to receive primary care services is important for understanding how RIC models developed. Vanderlip et al. (2016) categorized the factors leading to lack of access to primary care into systemic barriers and barriers related to clinicians and patients. Systemic factors include lack of access to transportation, inability to afford copays, and difficulty managing multiple appointments. Barriers related to clinicians include time limitations, inadequate knowledge of screening practices for patients on psychotropic medications, and the level of comfort of primary care physicians with working with patients with severe mental illness. Patient-specific barriers include low health literacy, cognitive symptoms (apathy, paranoia, anxiety), and not prioritizing physical health (Vanderlip et al., 2016). Stigma has been shown to be another reason why patients with severe mental illness do not seek medical care (Ostrow et al., 2014).

Models that integrate physical healthcare into mental health settings range from enhanced collaboration models that rely on care management to co-located care to fully integrated systems (Gerrity, 2014). Wagner's principles of case/care management and self-management support are often key components of all of these models (Gerrity, 2014; Ward & Druss, 2017). Most existing RIC models—in both integrated systems like the US Veterans Health Administration and free-standing mental health clinics—rely on colocation, in which patients with severe mental illness receive nonpsychiatric medical care in a mental health setting (Errichetti et al., 2020; Gerrity, 2014; Ward & Druss, 2017).

In one of the earliest models of RIC, patients were randomly assigned to a general medical clinic or an RIC clinic, where an on-site family nurse practitioner and family medicine physician provided medical care to patients in a clinic adjacent to the mental health clinic. Additionally, a nurse provided education, collaborated with mental health providers, and managed patients' cases. Patients in this clinic had more primary care visits, were more likely to receive 15 of 17 preventative measures, and had greater overall improved physical health. There was no significant difference in total costs between the RIC clinic and usual care (Druss et al., 2001b).

Even when case management and other core tenets of collaborative care are not provided, the co-location of medical services within mental health clinics has been associated with improved health indicators. One study of veterans with severe mental illness found a significant association between co-location and improved care processes (e.g., diabetic foot exams, colorectal cancer screening, alcohol use screening) and improved outcomes in blood pressure control (Kilbourne et al., 2011).

Despite data that suggests patients with severe mental illness experience improved health outcomes and have positive experiences within an RIC model (Druss et al., 2001a, 2010; Errichetti et al., 2020; Gerrity, 2014; Talley et al., 2019), many settings in which patients with severe mental illness receive psychiatric care are siloed from nonpsychiatric medical care. As a result, it is not uncommon for psychiatrists to be the only medical doctors that patients with severe mental illness see on a regular basis (Sowers et al., 2016; Vanderlip et al., 2016; Ward & Druss, 2017). There is emerging support for psychiatrists to serve an expanded role in managing select aspects of their patients' primary and preventative care. This may represent a distinct arm of RIC interventions (Dixon et al., 2007; Raney, 2013; Sowers et al., 2016; Vanderlip et al., 2016).

The role psychiatrists and other psychiatric care providers can and should play in fulfilling the nonpsychiatric medical care needs of their sickest patients necessarily depends on the setting, the resources within the setting, and the specific needs of the patient population. While collaborative models in which a care manager helps coordinate the various aspects of a patient's care may serve as a gold standard for RIC, such models are likely to be too resource intensive for many psychiatric clinics—particularly mental health clinics that are not tethered to a larger health care system. In such settings, RIC models that empower psychiatrists and other psychiatric care providers to play an expanded role (either independently or in consultation with a primary care physician) may be best suited to meet the needs of a vulnerable patient population. Regardless of the particular mechanism of care delivery, RIC models pose a unique opportunity to address the health of patients with severe mental illness more holistically. Future research is needed to better assess the outcomes for patients receiving nonpsychiatric care in mental health settings in terms of both health status and costs.

5   A Psychiatric Care Model for the Future

Although what we measure and how we deliver care—via CCM, RIC, a hybrid, or some other system—may change, measurement-based care delivery will become routine. As novel therapeutics and neuroscience-informed measures further develop, they may be further integrated into care delivery in an iterative way.

The case of comprehensive assessment and treatment of a first episode of psychosis provides an instructive example. Since psychotic disorders (i.e., schizophrenia, schizoaffective disorder) are associated with profound cognitive impairment, limited psychosocial outcomes, and reduced quality of life (Joshi et al., 2021; Thomas et al., 2017), there is an emphasis on early intervention after the first episode of illness. In 2007, the US National Institute of Mental Health issued a request titled "Recovery After an Initial Schizophrenia Episode (RAISE)" with the goal of developing comprehensive integrated interventions designed to reduce symptoms and disability and enhance vocational, social, and academic outcomes. Additionally, approaches were to be deployed in real-world community treatment settings, and the overall clinical impact was to be compared to treatment as usual. The experimental intervention included personalized medication management, family psychoeducation, resilience-focused individual therapy, and supported education and employment.

In 2016, the first two-year outcomes from the intervention were reported. In 34 clinics in 21 states, over 400 individuals were enrolled, 223 to the comprehensive intervention condition and 181 to treatment as usual (i.e., standard outpatient psychiatric medication management and associated services). Intervention participants reported an improved quality of life and attenuation of symptoms compared with usual care on a clinically meaningful magnitude. The greatest gains were reported by those who experienced a reduced duration of untreated psychosis (Kane et al., 2016).

While this study indirectly highlighted the general need for both collaborative and reverse-integrated care, it also brought to the forefront a series of interrelated questions: (1) How can we predict which individuals will develop psychosis so they may be identified for optimized CCM/RIC through the RAISE model? (2) Once first episode psychosis symptoms emerge, what therapeutic options should be offered aside from usual care?

The first question may be answered by results from the North American Prodrome Longitudinal Study (NAPLS) (Addington et al., 2020). Currently in its third iteration, the NAPLS aims to determine the mechanism of conversion for individuals who are identified as clinically at high risk of developing a chronic psychotic disorder. While many studies have been published on the NAPLS cohort of over 700 clinically high-risk individuals, key findings include a risk calculator designed to determine the risk of psychosis conversion and evidence from neuroimaging (e.g., loss of gray matter) and inflammatory biomarkers (e.g., changes in pro-inflammatory cytokines). Further work to investigate the mechanisms underlying these changes may yield clinically tractable endpoints that are relevant for MBC and psychiatric care delivery.

The answer to the second question has received substantial attention. While we will not summarize the large body of work that informs the answer to date here, we will use cognitive functioning in schizophrenia to highlight the future of biomarker-informed care delivery. As above, while schizophrenia is often thought of as an illness with positive symptoms (i.e., hallucinations, delusions) and negative symptoms (apathy, avolition), cognitive impairment is also widely agreed to be a core dimension of the disease (Green et al., 2000). Currently approved pharmacotherapy treats positive symptoms and to some degree negative symptoms, but it does not affect cognitive symptoms. Interestingly, electroencephalography (EEG) biomarkers have been identified that are tightly linked to cognitive impairment in schizophrenia and to psychosocial disability. Abnormalities in EEG biomarkers have been found in those with chronic psychosis and first-episode psychosis and may predict conversion to first-episode psychosis in those at clinical high risk (Hamilton et al., 2019; Joshi et al., 2018; Light & Braff, 2005; Turetsky et al., 2007). Indeed, EEG biomarker-informed approaches have informed studies of schizophrenia therapeutics and are currently being considered as adjuvant measures relevant for usual care (Joshi & Light, 2018; Joshi et al., 2019; Light et al., 2017).

A biomarker-informed model of psychiatric care delivery for the future could involve multiple components (see Fig. 1). For example, young adults in distress may be screened by primary care providers and referred to psychiatric specialty care providers for further diagnostic and treatment workup. Those who are identified as suffering from major depressive disorder, generalized anxiety disorder, and so forth may be treated and then tracked via MBC, initially with psychiatry specialty care and then eventually primary care via a CCM. For those who are at clinical high risk for psychosis based on symptoms and history, EEG biomarker assessment may be performed to provide additional data related to risk of conversion. For those predicted to be at high risk for symptoms and biomarker screening, further advanced EEG data may be performed to determine whether and which pro-cognitive therapeutics are thought to be helpful. In such a cohort, EEG biomarker data may be routinely tracked to determine therapeutic efficacy. For example, EEG biomarkers predict responsivity to targeted cognitive training for schizophrenia not only after 1 h of training but also after 30 h of training 2 months after initial EEG biomarker collection (Hochberger et al., 2019). For those at low risk for conversion to psychosis based on EEG information or for those where EEG biomarkers do not offer guidance for specific pro-cognitive interventions, CCM or RIC may be deployed. Additionally, psychiatric subspecialty care similar to the RAISE model may be offered to those at high risk for psychosis based on symptoms and/or EEG biomarker data, especially those who are not predicted to highly benefit from pro-cognitive interventions.

While the example above focused on EEG biomarkers, numerous other measures of interest exist. Genetic, imaging, or blood or other biofluid biomarkers are

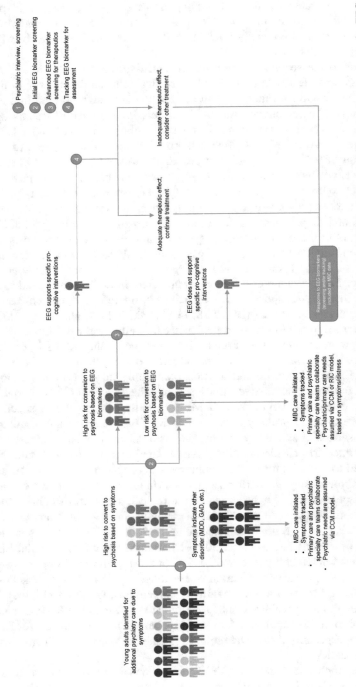

Fig. 1 A future biomarker-informed approach to psychiatric care delivery using young adults at clinically high risk for psychosis as an example. EEG: electroencephalography, CCM: collaborative care model, GAD: generalized anxiety disorder, MBC: measurement-based care, MDD: major depressive disorder, RIC: reverse-integrated care

increasingly being investigated in psychiatry and stand to augment not just the care of patients with psychosis but also the care of patients who suffer from other psychiatric disorders (García-Gutiérrez et al., 2020; Aftab & Sharma, 2021).

6   Conclusions

We have traced the history of the development of the chronic care model for nonpsychiatric medical conditions and the influence of this on the emergence of new models of psychiatric care that use measurement-based care. We have focused on integrated, patient-centric care with improved health outcomes across clinical populations. The development of biomarker-informed care is an exciting measurement tool that can be incorporated in future psychiatric care models.

Advances in medical technology may often occur without attention paid to the potential ethical consequences of implantation in real-world settings. As novel psychiatric care delivery systems begin to emerge in the twenty-first century, questions of justice and particularly just allocation of resources arise. How will these new technologies, including biomarker-informed care, be delivered in a way that values individualized treatment yet also respects resource scarcity relevant to large population-level health? How can emerging models of care be provided to underserved or historically marginalized patients?

Continuing to use applicable metrics of health quality as new care models emerge may serve as a useful framework, especially when the cost of untreated psychiatric disability is included in the equation.

Acknowledgments Dr. Joshi is supported by grants from National Institutes of Health (MH125114; MH123603), the US Department of Veteran's Affairs Rehabilitation Research and Development Service (1IK2RX003395), VISN-22 Mental Illness Research, Education, and Clinical Center (MIRECC), and NARSAD/BBRF (Young Investigator Award).

Dr. Stone is supported by the VISN-22 Mental Illness Research, Education, and Clinical Center (MIRECC).

The contents of this chapter do not represent the views of the University of California, the US Department of Veterans Affairs, or the United States government.

Conflict of Interest   The authors declare no potential conflicts of interest.

References

Aboraya, A., Nasrallah, H. A., Elswick, D. E., Ahmed, E., Estephan, N., Aboraya, D., Berzingi, S., Chumbers, J., Berzingi, S., & Justice, J. (2018). Measurement-based care in psychiatry: Past, present, and future. *Innovations in Clinical Neuroscience, 15*(11–12), 13.
Addington, J., Liu, L., Brummitt, K., Bearden, C. E., Cadenhead, K. S., Cornblatt, B. A., Keshavan, M., Mathalon, D. H., McGlashan, T. H., Perkins, D. O., Seidman, L. J., Stone, W., Tsuang, M. T., Walker, E. F., Woods, S. W., & Cannon, T. D. (2020, April 18). *North American Prodrome Longitudinal Study (NAPLS 3): Methods and baseline description.* Schizophrenia Research. Retrieved from https://www.sciencedirect.com/science/article/pii/S0920996420302176

Aftab, A. & Sharma, M. (2021). How not to think about biomarkers in psychiatry: Challenges and conceptual pitfalls. *Biomarkers in Neuropsychiatry.* Retrieved from https://www.sciencedirect.com/science/article/pii/S2666144621000022

Anderson, L. E., Chen, M. L., Perrin, J. M., & Van Cleave, J. (2015). Outpatient visits and medication prescribing for US children with mental health conditions. *Pediatrics, 136*(5), e1178–e1185.

Berwick, D. M., Nolan, T. W., & Whittington, J. (2008). The triple aim: Care, health, and cost. *Health Affairs (Project Hope), 27*(3), 759–769.

Bradford, D. W., Kim, M. M., Braxton, L. E., Marx, C. E., Butterfield, M., & Elbogen, E. B. (2008). Access to medical care among persons with psychotic and major affective disorders. *Psychiatric Services, 59*(8), 847–852.

Bush, K., Kivlahan, D. R., McDonell, M. B., Fihn, S. D., & Bradley, K. A. (1998). The AUDIT alcohol consumption questions (AUDIT-C): An effective brief screening test for problem drinking. Ambulatory Care Quality Improvement Project (ACQUIP). Alcohol Use Disorders Identification Test. *Archives of Internal Medicine, 158*(16), 1789–1795. https://doi.org/10.1001/archinte.158.16.1789

Coleman, K., Austin, B. T., Brach, C., & Wagner, E. H. (2009). Evidence on the chronic care model in the new millennium. *Health Affairs, 28*(1), 75–85.

Cradock-O'Leary, J., Young, A. S., Yano, E. M., Wang, M., & Lee, M. L. (2002). Use of general medical services by VA patients with psychiatric disorders. *Psychiatric Services, 53*(7), 874–878.

De Hert, M., Correll, C. U., Bobes, J., Cetkovich-Bakmas, M., Cohen, D., Asai, I., Detraux, J., Gautam, S., Möller, H.-J., & Ndetei, D. M. (2011). Physical illness in patients with severe mental disorders. I. Prevalence, impact of medications and disparities in health care. *World Psychiatry, 10*(1), 52.

Dixon, L. B., Adler, D. A., Berlant, J. L., Dulit, R. A., Goldman, B., Hackman, A. L., Oslin, D. W., Siris, S. G., Sonis, W. A., & Valenstein, M. (2007). Best practices: Psychiatrists and primary caring: What are our boundaries of responsibility? *Psychiatric Services, 58*(5), 600–602.

Druss, B. G., Bradford, W. D., Rosenheck, R. A., Radford, M. J., & Krumholz, H. M. (2001a). Quality of medical care and excess mortality in older patients with mental disorders. *Archives of General Psychiatry, 58*(6), 565–572.

Druss, B. G., Rohrbaugh, R. M., Levinson, C. M., & Rosenheck, R. A. (2001b). Integrated medical care for patients with serious psychiatric illness: A randomized trial. *Archives of General Psychiatry, 58*(9), 861–868.

Druss, B. G., von Esenwein, S. A., Compton, M. T., Rask, K. J., Zhao, L., & Parker, R. M. (2010). A randomized trial of medical care management for community mental health settings: The Primary Care Access, Referral, and Evaluation (PCARE) study. *American Journal of Psychiatry, 167*(2), 151–159.

Errichetti, K. S., Flynn, A., Gaitan, E., Ramirez, M. M., Baker, M., & Xuan, Z. (2020). Randomized trial of reverse colocated integrated care on persons with severe, persistent mental illness in southern Texas. *Journal of General Internal Medicine, 35*(7), 2035–2042.

Fortney, J. C., Unützer, J., Wrenn, G., Pyne, J. M., Smith, G. R., Schoenbaum, M., & Harbin, H. T. (2018). A tipping point for measurement-based care. *Focus, 16*(3), 341–350.

García-Gutiérrez, M. S., Navarrete, F., Sala, F., Gasparyan, A., Austrich-Olivares, A., & Manzanares, J. (2020). Biomarkers in psychiatry: Concept, definition, types and relevance to the clinical reality. *Frontiers in Psychiatry, 11*, 432.

Gerrity, M. (2014). *Integrating primary care into behavioral health settings: What works.* Milbank Memorial Fund. Retrieved October 11, 2021, from https://www.milbank.org/wp-content/uploads/2016/04/Integrating-Primary-Care-Report.pdf

Green, M. F., Kern, R. S., Braff, D. L., & Mintz, J. (2000). Neurocognitive deficits and functional outcome in schizophrenia: Are we measuring the "right stuff"? *Schizophrenia Bulletin, 26*(1), 119–136.

Grumbach, K., & Bodenheimer, T. (2002). A primary care home for Americans: Putting the house in order. *JAMA, 288*(7), 889–893. https://doi.org/10.1001/jama.288.7.889

Hamilton, H. K., Roach, B. J., Bachman, P. M., Belger, A., Carrion, R. E., Duncan, E., Johannesen, J. K., Light, G. A., Niznikiewicz, M. A., & Addington, J. (2019). Association between P300 responses to auditory oddball stimuli and clinical outcomes in the psychosis risk syndrome. *JAMA Psychiatry, 76*(11), 1187–1197.

Henke, R. M., Zaslavsky, A. M., McGuire, T. G., Ayanian, J. Z., & Rubenstein, L. V. (2009). Clinical inertia in depression treatment. *Medical Care, 47*(9), 959–967.

Hochberger, W. C., Joshi, Y. B., Thomas, M. L., Zhang, W., Bismark, A. W., Treichler, E. B., Tarasenko, M., Nungaray, J., Sprock, J., & Cardoso, L. (2019). Neurophysiologic measures of target engagement predict response to auditory-based cognitive training in treatment refractory schizophrenia. *Neuropsychopharmacology, 44*(3), 606–612.

Institute of Medicine. (2001). *Crossing the quality chasm: A new health system for the 21st century.* National Academies Press.

Institute of Medicine. (2006). *Improving the quality of health care for mental and substance-use conditions.* National Academies Press.

Joshi, Y. B., & Light, G. A. (2018, November 19). Using EEG-guided basket and umbrella trials in psychiatry: A precision medicine approach for cognitive impairment in schizophrenia [Review]. *Frontiers in Psychiatry, 9*(554). https://doi.org/10.3389/fpsyt.2018.00554

Joshi, Y. B., Breitenstein, B., Tarasenko, M., Thomas, M. L., Chang, W. L., Sprock, J., Sharp, R. F., & Light, G. A. (2018, January). Mismatch negativity impairment is associated with deficits in identifying real-world environmental sounds in schizophrenia. *Schizophrenia Research, 191*, 5–9. https://doi.org/10.1016/j.schres.2017.05.020

Joshi, Y. B., Thomas, M. L., Hochberger, W. C., Bismark, A. W., Treichler, E. B., Molina, J., Nungaray, J., Cardoso, L., Sprock, J., & Swerdlow, N. R. (2019). Verbal learning deficits associated with increased anticholinergic burden are attenuated with targeted cognitive training in treatment refractory schizophrenia patients. *Schizophrenia Research, 208*, 384–389.

Joshi, Y. B., Thomas, M. L., Braff, D. L., Green, M. F., Gur, R. C., Gur, R. E., Nuechterlein, K. H., Stone, W. S., Greenwood, T. A., Lazzeroni, L. C., MacDonald, L. R., Molina, J. L., Nungaray, J. A., Radant, A. D., Silverman, J. M., Sprock, J., Sugar, C. A., Tsuang, D. W., Tsuang, M. T., … Light, G. A. (2021). Anticholinergic medication burden-associated cognitive impairment in schizophrenia. *The American Journal of Psychiatry, 178*(9), 838–847. https://doi.org/10.1176/appi.ajp.2020.20081212

Kane, J. M., Robinson, D. G., Schooler, N. R., Mueser, K. T., Penn, D. L., Rosenheck, R. A., Addington, J., Brunette, M. F., Correll, C. U., & Estroff, S. E. (2016). Comprehensive versus usual community care for first-episode psychosis: 2-year outcomes from the NIMH RAISE early treatment program. *American Journal of Psychiatry, 173*(4), 362–372.

Katon, W. (2012). Collaborative depression care models: From development to dissemination. *American Journal of Preventive Medicine, 42*(5), 550–552.

Kilbourne, A. M., Pirraglia, P. A., Lai, Z., Bauer, M. S., Charns, M. P., Greenwald, D., Welsh, D. E., McCarthy, J. F., & Yano, E. M. (2011). Quality of general medical care among patients with serious mental illness: Does colocation of services matter? *Psychiatric Services, 62*(8), 922–928.

Kroenke, K., & Unutzer, J. (2017). Closing the false divide: Sustainable approaches to integrating mental health services into primary care. *Journal of General Internal Medicine, 32*(4), 404–410.

Kroenke, K., Spitzer, R., & Williams, J. (2001). The PHQ-9: Validity of a brief depression severity measure. *Journal of General Internal Medicine, 16*(9), 606–613.

Lewis, C. C., Boyd, M., Puspitasari, A., Navarro, E., Howard, J., Kassab, H., Hoffman, M., Scott, K., Lyon, A., & Douglas, S. (2019). Implementing measurement-based care in behavioral health: A review. *JAMA Psychiatry, 76*(3), 324–335.

Light, G. A., & Braff, D. L. (2005). Mismatch negativity deficits are associated with poor functioning in schizophrenia patients. *Archives of General Psychiatry, 62*(2), 127–136.

Light, G. A., Zhang, W., Joshi, Y. B., Bhakta, S., Talledo, J. A., & Swerdlow, N. R. (2017). Single-dose memantine improves cortical oscillatory response dynamics in patients with schizophrenia. *Neuropsychopharmacology, 42*(13), 2633–2639.

Mann, J. J., Michel, C. A., & Auerbach, R. P. (2021). Improving suicide prevention through evidence-based strategies: A systematic review. *American Journal of Psychiatry, 178*(7), 611–624.

Maragakis, A., Siddharthan, R., RachBeisel, J., & Snipes, C. (2016, September). Creating a 'reverse' integrated primary and mental healthcare clinic for those with serious mental illness. *Primary Health Care Research and Development, 17*(5), 421–427. https://doi.org/10.1017/s1463423615000523

McCarron, R. M., Bourgeois, J. A., Chwastiak, L. A., Folsom, D., Hales, R. E., Han, J., Rado, J., Rivelli, S., Scher, L., & Yu, A. (2015). Integrated medicine and psychiatry curriculum for psychiatry residency training: A model designed to meet growing mental health workforce needs. *Academic Psychiatry, 39*(4), 461–465. https://doi.org/10.1007/s40596-015-0348-3

Olsen, C. G., Boltri, J. M., Amerine, J., & Clasen, M. E. (2017, December). Lacking a primary care physician is associated with increased suffering in patients with severe mental illness. *Journal of Primary Prevention, 38*(6), 583–596. https://doi.org/10.1007/s10935-017-0490-7

Ostrow, D. L., Manderscheid, D. R., & Mojtabai, D. R. (2014). Stigma and difficulty accessing medical care in a sample of adults with serious mental illness. *Journal of Health Care for the Poor and Underserved, 25*(4), 1956. https://www.ncbi.nlm.nih.gov/pmc/articles/PMC4353597/pdf/nihms666895.pdf

Pincus, H. A., Scholle, S. H., Spaeth-Rublee, B., Hepner, K. A., & Brown, J. (2016). Quality measures for mental health and substance use: Gaps, opportunities, and challenges. *Health Affairs (Project Hope), 35*(6), 1000–1008.

Raney, L. (2013). Integrated care: The evolving role of psychiatry in the era of health care reform. *Psychiatric Services, 64*(11), 1076–1078.

Raney, L. E. (2017). Integrating primary care and behavioral health: The role of the psychiatrist in the Collaborative Care Model. *Focus (American Psychiatric Publishing), 15*(3), 354–360. https://doi.org/10.1176/appi.focus.15305

Sowers, W., Arbuckle, M., & Shoyinka, S. (2016). Recommendations for primary care provided by psychiatrists. *Community Mental Health Journal, 52*(4), 379–386.

Spitzer, R. L., Kroenke, K., Williams, J. B., & Löwe, B. (2006, May 22). A brief measure for assessing generalized anxiety disorder: The GAD-7. *Archives of Internal Medicine, 166*(10), 1092–1097. https://doi.org/10.1001/archinte.166.10.1092

Talley, R. M., Rolin, S. A., Trejo, B. N., Goldman, M. L., Alves-Bradford, J.-M. E., & Dixon, L. B. (2019). Perspectives of individuals with serious mental illness on a reverse–colocated care model: A qualitative study. *Psychiatric Services, 70*(9), 793–800.

Thomas, M. L., Green, M. F., Hellemann, G., Sugar, C. A., Tarasenko, M., Calkins, M. E., Greenwood, T. A., Gur, R. E., Gur, R. C., & Lazzeroni, L. C. (2017). Modeling deficits from early auditory information processing to psychosocial functioning in schizophrenia. *JAMA Psychiatry, 74*(1), 37–46.

Turetsky, B. I., Calkins, M. E., Light, G. A., Olincy, A., Radant, A. D., & Swerdlow, N. R. (2007). Neurophysiological endophenotypes of schizophrenia: The viability of selected candidate measures. *Schizophrenia Bulletin, 33*(1), 69–94.

Unützer, J., Katon, W., Callahan, C. M., Williams, J. W., Jr., Hunkeler, E., Harpole, L., Hoffing, M., Della Penna, R. D., Noël, P. H., & Lin, E. H. (2002). Collaborative care management of late-life depression in the primary care setting: A randomized controlled trial. *JAMA, 288*(22), 2836–2845.

Vanderlip, E. R., Raney, L. E., & Druss, B. G. (2016). A framework for extending psychiatrists' roles in treating general health conditions. *American Journal of Psychiatry, 173*(7), 658–663.

Viron, M. J., & Stern, T. A. (2010). The impact of serious mental illness on health and healthcare. *Psychosomatics: Journal of Consultation and Liaison Psychiatry, 51*(6), 458–465. https://doi.org/10.1016/S0033-3182(10)70737-4

Vos, T., Flaxman, A. D., Naghavi, M., Lozano, R., Michaud, C., Ezzati, M., Shibuya, K., Salomon, J. A., Abdalla, S., Aboyans, V., Abraham, J., Ackerman, I., Aggarwal, R., Ahn, S. Y., Ali, M. K., Alvarado, M., Anderson, H. R., Anderson, L. M., Kathryn, G., … Memish, Z. A. (2012).

Years lived with disability (YLDs) for 1,160 sequelae of 289 diseases and injuries 1990–2010: A systematic analysis for the Global Burden of Disease Study 2010. *Lancet, 380*, 2163–2196.

Wagner, E. (1998). Chronic disease management: What will it take to improve care for chronic illness? *Effective Clinical Practice: ECP, 1*(1), 2–4.

Wagner, E., Austin, B., & Von Korff, M. (1996). Organizing care for patients with chronic illness. *The Milbank Quarterly, 74*(4), 511–544.

Wang, P. S., Lane, M., Olfson, M., Pincus, H. A., Wells, K. B., & Kessler, R. C. (2005). Twelve-month use of mental health services in the United States: Results from the National Comorbidity Survey Replication. *Archives of General Psychiatry, 62*(6), 629–640.

Ward, M. C., & Druss, B. G. (2017). Reverse integration initiatives for individuals with serious mental illness. *Focus, 15*(3), 271–278.

Mobile Sensors in Healthcare: Technical, Ethical, and Medical Aspects

Jens Eckstein

Abstract

Mobile sensors play an increasing role in healthcare, although it is not always clear yet what they can reliably be used for. While some specialties in medicine like cardiology have already integrated apps and smartwatches in their international guidelines, others are still struggling to find infrastructures that are compliant with healthcare standards. The main concerns are data quality and data privacy, which are both handled with different requirements in the consumer market than they are in healthcare. Specific adjustments will make mobile sensors an important part of future healthcare.

1 Mobile Sensors in Healthcare

Over the past 10 years, the use of mobile sensors for private use has been a tremendous success story (Gartner.com, 2021). An increasing number of individuals are following the self-tracking trend that enables them to not only document steps and sleep but also measure temperature, blood pressure, oxygen saturation, and ECGs (Kent, 2020). Most of these procedures were formerly limited to the healthcare environment and its very specific set of rules.

Today we are witnessing the long-predicted emancipation of both patients and healthy individuals who now control their healthcare data and its interpretation. Appointments with healthcare professionals tend to begin with the patient presenting the results of their self-investigation and asking the healthcare professional for their opinion on the data instead of beginning with the statement that they have "not

J. Eckstein (✉)
University Hospital Basel, Basel, Switzerland
e-mail: jens.eckstein@usb.ch

felt very well for some time." While this can be a significant advantage in terms of patient involvement and the patient's future compliance with therapeutic decisions, it can weaken efforts to treat the patient if the professional diagnosis deviates from the one predicted by the patient or by public symptom tracker algorithms (Miller et al., 2020). Thus, the challenge for healthcare professionals is to use these data and tools in a way that creates additional value without sacrificing the high standards of healthcare.

Every piece of information that triggers therapeutic decision-making, including apps used as digital therapeutics, has to be validated and approved according to present legal frameworks, comparable to the standards of pharmacological trials. Patients trust the healthcare system in general, and it is crucial that future diagnostic tools and digital therapeutics adhere to the same high-quality requirements that apply for drugs and diagnostic tests (Gille et al., 2015).

There are several reasons why such rules are still a matter of discussion. One likely reason is that most physicians lack specific technical knowledge. Healthcare professionals have not been trained to use or develop sensor technology, data formats, encryption, algorithms, and databases. This is changing slowly, but for obvious reasons, healthcare professionals do not have the same expertise as IT specialists. Therefore, a medical device certification that healthcare professionals can rely on without having the specific knowledge to understand all the technical details is needed.

A second reason is the power that most companies that produce wearable devices have in the field of marketing and sales. The "traditional" healthcare system cannot, and most likely does not, want to match this. This leads to individuals being more convinced by the results of a smartwatch than by a physician's diagnosis that is based on "old" methods. In the end, health is probably the most relevant topic for most people, and they will choose the safest and most effective approach, which in some instances will involve digital therapeutics and mobile sensors.

Thirdly, the involvement of commercial wearables from the consumer market in healthcare areas reflects a merge between "lifestyle" and healthcare. At first, individuals get used to trust their devices, navigating them from A to B and providing them with important information 24/7. Subsequently, they expect that the information about their health status will be as accurate as their navigation data. To address this assumption, more prominent disclaimers on devices and apps not suitable for healthcare should be mandatory.

For these reasons it is crucial that the healthcare system and its representatives work to create a framework for the responsible use of wearables in healthcare. This framework must be fortified by published data and a strong set of rules, as is the case in a first version of the European medical device regulation of 2021 (European Parliament and Council of the European Union, 2017).

2   Technical Aspects

This chapter will not focus on technical standards and details but will rather address a number of simple technical questions that are often missed when plans are made to move mobile sensors from the consumer into the healthcare market.

Some of the best-selling wearable devices in the consumer market have a battery life of less than 24 h (Apple Watch battery, 2021). People charge them every night and hopefully do not forget to put them on in the morning. This means that their high-tech sensor is not monitoring vital signs during a significant part of the day. Taking into account that sleep is a highly interesting condition and, for example, sleep apnea is an important diagnostic target, this technical shortcoming hinders diagnostics.

In a hospital setting, such a short run time would require nurses to remove the device once a day, charge it, and reinstall it on the patient. In times when human resources are scarce, this is not an option. That is why a sensor designed for healthcare purposes should run at least 7 days in any mode that is available for the device.

Charging has to be as simple as possible and easy to handle even for individuals with poor sight or restrictions on movement. This is why many companies went from systems with miniaturized plugs to wireless charging cradles that can be handled by most user error-free. Magnetic connections to support the correct positioning of plugs or wireless cradles became a widespread standard too.

If such a sensor is carried continuously, it must be waterproof because showering will be necessary during intervals of 7 days, and it should not be destroyed by water if the individual has forgotten to take it off.

Wearing such a sensor device continuously is realistic only if it is very comfortable. This applies to hearables (in-ear sensors) as much as to bracelets or patches. Bracelets might have an advantage in this respect, because with very soft silicone or comparable materials, there is a chance that most people would indeed accept a device on their wrist (Larsen et al., 2020).

This is already the case with watches. But if the device is intended to be worn at night, it should not make any sounds or vibrating alerts or emit light signals. Everything that potentially interrupts sleep will sooner or later trigger the individual to take off the device.

A final aspect related to design is somewhat trivial but can make the difference between highly compliant individuals and a great sensor that is not acquiring data because the device is not on the person who is supposed to wear it: It should be "cool"! At least it should not stigmatize people by showing that they have health problems. Instead it should signal that they are being supported with most up-to-date methods of staying fit and healthy. The reaction of others has to be "Hey, how can I get this service?" rather than "Oh, I feel sorry for you, your condition must be severe" (Ahmad et al., 2020).

The success of such devices will also depend on marketing, even though this is not the focus of science and healthcare. But if we look at the pharmaceutical industry, we see that drugs are sold and effectively applied only if healthcare professionals are familiar with them and patients really take them in the intended way.

Once the design aspects are successfully taken care of and patients are wearing their device continuously to address a specific healthcare question or just to record baseline data, connectivity arises as the next big challenge. Most consumer devices are linked to a specific app provided by the company that built the device. This environment provides users with conveniently visualized information about their health status. Irrespective of the quality of this information, it is generated within the commercial system of a commercial company that needs the consumer's data to improve their own algorithms. This system is perfectly fine for the consumer market if individuals consent to share their data, but it is not acceptable for healthcare, where an individual's data is highly protected (Yue et al., 2016). Therefore, hospitals should host an infrastructure that enables them to link wearable devices and store the data on designated servers for their healthcare data. If the data is analyzed externally, it has to be de-identified, exported, and then reimported and re-identified. Simple analytics can easily be handled on hospital premises (Brasier et al., 2020).

A similar infrastructure is required for outpatients. A number of specific technical solutions are already in place for these patients One of the earliest drivers was the field of cardiology, which began providing "home monitoring" of implanted devices in the early 2000s. Data was transferred to the referring cardiologist via specific Bluetooth access points that connect to the device when it was close. These devices transmitted the data to a central hub and routed it to the responsible site. Most of the time this meant that the access point was located next to the patient's bed (Wilkoff et al., 2008). Other devices that are primarily used at home, such as scales or resting blood pressure monitors, are equipped with modules that transfer the data by the Global System for Mobile Communications (GSM) standard via a hub to the healthcare facility.

The most common setting at present is a link between the sensor and a smart device equipped with GSM and Bluetooth connectivity (most often a smartphone) that is running a specific app designed for this purpose. For healthcare applications, it is crucial that the data be transferred in a safe and reliable way to the healthcare infrastructure without being decrypted and processed by third-party servers. Alternatively, the data can stay on the individual smart device until it is exported and sent to a specific recipient. This is frequently the case with glucose measurements or blood pressure monitors (Funtanilla et al., 2019).

In any of these solutions it is crucial that data privacy is ensured and that the system is certified for healthcare use. It has to be taken into account that medical sensors will not only record a person's medical data, but inadvertently private, nonmedical data too. Therefore patients need certainty that this data will exclusively be used in a medical context or remain inaccessible for any other purposes. Further, it should not be the responsibility of the patient to read through extensive legal documents about the potential use of their data and then click on "accept," hoping that they have made the right choice.

Finally, even with the highest data safety and quality, physicians rely on algorithms to visualize and sometimes interpret the data before they can draw meaningful conclusions. It is not possible to transfer achievements from the consumer market to healthcare without further adaptation because often the ground truth for algorithms developed for the consumer market is based on healthy persons. Data is repeatedly collected, while healthy people are counting steps, climbing stairs, running, and swimming until the algorithm is able to identify the activity and then recognize and quantify it autonomously. But patients most often differ from healthy persons. They walk slower (e.g., if they have heart failure), their gait is less smooth (e.g., if they have hip problems), or their steps are much smaller (e.g., if they have Parkinson's disease) (Patel et al., 2009; Moayedi et al., 2017). Heart rate variability, an important parameter for calculating respiration based on pulse wave signals, becomes less pronounced as people age or if they develop cardiovascular, infectious, or psychiatric diseases (Umetani et al., 1998; Ahmad et al., 2009; Gorman & Sloan, 2000). Unfortunately, many patients are burdened with one or more of these circumstances. This is why the available algorithms have to be tested and validated for the intended use with real patients and not in labs with healthy people. As a result, information about the sensitivity and specificity of the measurements has to be made available with a specific focus on false negative results that would indicate that a person is healthy when in fact they are not. Again, this is not so relevant for consumer market use, when a device indicates that the heart rate while running is 65 beats per minute although it is actually 155 beats per minute. But if a patient has a heart rate of 155 beats per minute and the device calculates only 65 beats per minute, that could lead to delayed diagnostics and therapy, potentially putting a patient's life at risk.

An important question for many developers in this field concerns the threshold that defines whether an algorithm or a device is considered a medical device according to the present regulations. Certification might appear to be a significant hurdle to go through, but it can also help position the product in the long run.

It is important to understand that both algorithms and hardware can be certified medical devices. For example, most blood pressure monitors are certified devices that include both hardware and software. However, the situation is different for algorithms that screen for atrial fibrillation using smartphones or smartwatches. In that case, the algorithm analyzing the video signal of the sensor is certified. This means that it can run on a number of smart devices and still be considered a certified medical device. This approach can use the omnipresence of smartphones and make possible a low-level approach to medical services that would not have been possible without the presence of smartphones almost everywhere in the world.

3   Ethical Aspects

Because of technological change, unforeseen amounts of health-related data are being generated continuously, and we as a society and as healthcare professionals must reach agreements about standards for data privacy and quality, data ownership, and aspects of data exploitation.

Data usage is not only driven by scientific interests but also by commercial interests (EY, 2019). Well-annotated healthcare records and raw data from specific patient groups are needed to feed machine-learning algorithms and neural networks that are programmed to provide shortcuts to the right diagnosis, choose the right treatment, or even prevent disease.

Differences exist in how different national societies view the potential uses of patient data. Currently, the European rules are the most restrictive and protective (Pernot-Leplay, 2020). But of course this topic is a global one and needs to be addressed as such. The baseline of a potential global agreement should be a careful balance between the privacy of the individual and the value added to the global society if the data were to be used for research and development purposes. Another important issue is how the individual donating their data will be rewarded for doing so. For example, they could receive free diagnostics and treatment or financial compensation if the resulting product is commercially successful.

A second question concerns who is liable for the consequences of digital healthcare solutions. While this topic is well regulated within the pharmaceutical industry, it is not yet well defined for digital solutions. As a simple example, consider the decision support systems that are on their way into routine healthcare. If such a system does not recognize the correct diagnosis or, even more problematically, leads the wrong way and causes unnecessary tests with adverse events, who is the responsible party? The IT specialists who programmed the algorithm? The data providers who did not annotate well enough? The company that sells the algorithm? The body that certified it as a medical device? Or the physician in charge of the patient? But how can a physician be responsible for an algorithm that they are unable to control or even understand? In accordance with the procedures established for the pharmaceutical industry, companies producing software should be liable for adverse events if they could have been prevented. Experts in the field are discussing the idea of a Hippocratic Oath for software engineers in healthcare (Kostkova et al., 2016; Grote & Berens, 2020).

Interestingly enough, there is no general agreement on who owns healthcare data. A dominant opinion is that this data belongs to the individual patients and can only be used with their consent (MIDATA, n.d.). On the other hand, data that was acquired in past decades could be used to develop strategies that will help large numbers of future patients if it were available for research and development. A third group of potential data owners are healthcare professionals and insurance companies. This argument partly dates from the time when health records and results belonged to the physician and the patient had to ask if they could have access to it. But nowadays, as patients are increasingly storing their health data in personal accounts, this system appears to be more and more obsolete.

Data cooperatives are an interesting approach that provide individual ownership at the same time that they provide access to datasets. There are different models in the current market. Some cooperatives provide a financial benefit for their members if they sell their data and others finance their organization with the revenue they earn from sharing data and providing it for public research (MIDATA, n.d.; HealthBank, n.d.).

In the end, the ethical dilemma is the possibility that data privacy will become something that only wealthy people can afford while others are forced to sell their data to finance their individual healthcare.

4   Medical Aspects

The unprecedented granularity of healthcare data will change our approach to many diseases because it is likely that, for example, simultaneous recordings of several vital signs will indicate pathological changes much earlier than traditional diagnostics. Now that low-cost mobile devices are available, this will be possible even in middle- and low-income countries. The first potential smartphone-based digital diagnostic tools are already well established and are recommended by international guidelines. For example, apps to screen for atrial fibrillation have been used for years now. They help detect unknown atrial fibrillation, and if oral anticoagulants are indicated, they prevent strokes (Hindricks et al., 2021).

The possibilities and the expected added value that derives from continuous monitoring are immense. Most likely, AI-driven algorithms will be able to identify not only that something is wrong but also come up with a potential diagnosis.

For example, with a regular pneumonia, an increase in heart rate and respiration rate would be expected, as would lower oxygen saturation and blood pressure. However, in patients with COVID-19, interestingly enough, a decrease in heart rate (instead of an increase) has been observed (Capoferri et al., 2020). Together with other typical clinical and imaging findings, this formed a specific pattern for the diagnosis of COVID-19.

It is expected that devices that obtain more specific disease patterns and more data during healthy episodes of individuals will be able to detect deviations from an individual's baseline earlier and prevent diseases or at least chronic damage. Once we can combine the kind of sensor data that is already available and familiar with additional data like lab values from sweat samples or other biofluids, we might better understand the course of some diseases.

At the same time, references for some of our vital signs will have to be adapted because new measurement techniques will allow much more insight. For example, once blood pressure can be measured continuously from photoplethysmography signals, we will not be limited to 24 h of intermittent measurements taken by an inflating cuff. By combining this data on blood pressure with simultaneously recorded other vital signs, we will be able to see a much more detailed picture of an individual's physiology.

5 Conclusions

Wearables will change our view of diseases, our role as healthcare professionals, and our therapeutic standards. The transformation of devices from the consumer market to medical grade devices requires adaptation of multiple parameters, ranging from software and algorithms to hardware and images. An adapted Hippocratic Oath for software developers and medical technology IT specialists is being discussed that should address shared responsibility for the intended use.

Acknowledgments The author likes to acknowledge the contribution of the University Hospital Basel and his entire research team, who helped to create and develop the environment they are now able to use for their patients. Explicitly to be named Bianca Hölz, who is the project lead for mobile sensors of his team and their long-standing cooperation with Leitwert, who provided the device management system that enabled his team to keep their patients data within hospital premises.

Many thoughts and ideas in this review are the result of discussions and lectures of the yearly *Basler Digital Ehtics Symposium* (unispital-basel/digital-ethics). This is why the speakers of this symposium, explicitly to be named Martin Hirsch and Stefan Heinemann, have to be acknowledged here.

The author further has to declare a conflict of interest, owning 0.5% virtual shares of Preventicus, the company with which he developed the first smartphone-based AF detection algorithm.

References

Ahmad, S., Tejuja, A., Newman, K. D., Zarychanski, R., & Seely, A. J. (2009). Clinical review: A review and analysis of heart rate variability and the diagnosis and prognosis of infection. *Critical Care, 13*(6), 232. https://doi.org/10.1186/cc8132

Ahmad, A., Rasul, T., Yousaf, A., & Zaman, U. (2020). Understanding factors influencing elderly diabetic patients' continuance intention to use digital health wearables: Extending the technology acceptance model (TAM). *Journal of Open Innovation: Technology, Market, and Complexity, 6*(3), 81. https://doi.org/10.3390/joitmc6030081

Apple Watch battery. (2021). *Apple Watch Series 7 Battery Information*. Retrieved from https://www.apple.com/watch/battery

Brasier, N., Geissmann, L., Käch, M., Mutke, M., Hoelz, B., De Ieso, F., & Eckstein, J. (2020). Device- and analytics-agnostic infrastructure for continuous inpatient monitoring: A technical note. *Digit Biomark., 4*(2), 62–68. https://doi.org/10.1159/000509279

Capoferri, G., Osthoff, M., Egli, A., Stoeckle, M., & Bassetti, S. (2020). Relative bradycardia in patients with COVID-19. *Clinical Microbiology and Infection, 27*(2), 295–296. https://doi.org/10.1016/j.cmi.2020.08.013

European Parliament and Council of the European Union. (2017, 5 April). *European Regulation (EU) 2017/745 of the European Parliament and of the Council of 5 April 2017 on medical devices, amending Directive 2001/83/EC, Regulation (EC) No 178/2002 and Regulation (EC) No 1223/2009 and repealing Council Directives 90/385/EEC and 93/42/EEC.* Retrieved from https://eur-lex.europa.eu/eli/reg/2017/745/2017-05-05

EY. (2019). *Realising the value of healthcare data: A framework for the future.* Retrieved from https://assets.ey.com/content/dam/ey-sites/ey-com/en_gl/topics/life-sciences/life-sciences-pdfs/ey-value-of-health-care-data-v20-final.pdf

Funtanilla, V. D., Candidate, P., Caliendo, T., & Hilas, O. (2019). Continuous glucose monitoring: A review of available systems. *P T., 44*(9), 550–553.

Gartner.com. (2021, January 12). *Gartner forecasts global spending on wearable devices to total $81.5 billion in 2021 [Press Release]*. Retrieved from https://www.gartner.com/en/newsroom/press-releases/2021-01-11-gartner-forecasts-global-spending-on-wearable-devices-to-total-81-5-billion-in-2021

Gille, F., Smith, S., & Mays, N. (2015). Why public trust in health care systems matters and deserves greater research attention. *Journal of Health Services Research & Policy, 20*(1), 62–64. https://doi.org/10.1177/1355819614543161

Gorman, J. M., & Sloan, R. P. (2000). Heart rate variability in depressive and anxiety disorders. *American Heart Journal, 140*(4), S77–S83. https://doi.org/10.1067/mhj.2000.109981

Grote, T., & Berens, P. (2020). On the ethics of algorithmic decision-making in healthcare. *Journal of Medical Ethics, 46*, 205–211.

HealthBank. (n.d.). *Introducing healthbank: Take control of your health.* Retrieved from https://www.healthbank.coop

Hindricks, G., Potpara, T., Dagres, N., Arbelo, E., Bax, J. J., Blomström-Lundqvist, C., Boriani, G., Castella, M., Dan, G.-A., Dilaveris, P. E., Fauchier, L., Filippatos, G., Kalman, J. M., La Meir, M., Lane, D. A., Lebeau, J.-P., Lettino, M., Lip, G. Y. H., Pinto, F. J., ... ESC Scientific Document Group. (2021). ESC guidelines for the diagnosis and management of atrial fibrillation developed in collaboration with the European Association for Cardio-Thoracic Surgery (EACTS): The task force for the diagnosis and management of atrial fibrillation of the European Society of Cardiology (ESC) developed with the special contribution of the European heart rhythm association (EHRA) of the ESC. *European Heart Journal, 42*(5), 373–498. https://doi.org/10.1093/eurheartj/ehaa612

Kent, R. (2020). Self-tracking health over time: From the use of Instagram to perform optimal health to the protective shield of the digital detox. *Social Media + Society, 6*(3). https://doi.org/10.1177/2056305120940694

Kostkova, P., Brewer, H., de Lusignan, S., Fottrell, E., Goldacre, B., Hart, G., Koczan, P., Knight, P., Marsolier, C., McKendry, R. A., Ross, E., Sasse, A., Sullivan, R., Chaytor, S., Stevenson, O., Velho, R., & Tooke, J. (2016). Who owns the data? Open data for healthcare. *Frontiers in Public Health, 4*, 7. https://doi.org/10.3389/fpubh.2016.00007

Larsen, L., Lauritzen, M., Gangstad, S., & Kjaer, T. (2020). The usages of small electronic devices and health: A feasibility study. *JMIR Formative Research, 5*(1), e20410.

MIDATA. (n.d.). *My data—Our health.* Retrieved from https://www.midata.coop

Miller, S., Gilbert, S., Virani, V., & Wicks, P. (2020). Patients' utilization and perception of an artificial intelligence-based symptom assessment and advice technology in a British Primary Care Waiting Room: Exploratory pilot study. *JMIR Human Factors, 7*(3), e19713.

Moayedi, Y., Abdulmajeed, R., Duero Posada, J., Foroutan, F., Alba, A. C., Cafazzo, J., & Ross, H. J. (2017). Assessing the use of wrist-worn devices in patients with heart failure: Feasibility study. *JMIR Cardio, 1*(2), e8.

Patel, S., Lorincz, K., Hughes, R., Huggins, N., Growdon, J., Standaert, D., Akay, M., Dy, J., & Bonato, P. (2009). Monitoring motor fluctuations in patients with Parkinson's disease using wearable sensors. *IEEE Transactions on Information Technology in Biomedicine, 13*(6), 864–873. https://doi.org/10.1109/TITB.2009.2033471

Pernot-Leplay, E. (2020). China's approach on data privacy law: A third way between the U.S. and the EU? *Penn State Journal of Law & International Affairs, 8*(1).

Umetani, K., Singer, D. H., McCraty, R., & Atkinson, M. (1998). Twenty-four hour time domain heart rate variability and heart rate: Relations to age and gender over nine decades. *Journal of the American College of Cardiology, 31*(3), 593–601. https://doi.org/10.1016/s0735-1097(97)00554-8

Wilkoff, B. L., Angelo Auricchio, A., Brugada, J., Cowie, M., Ellenbogen, K. A., Gillis, A. M., Hayes, D. L., Howlett, J. G., Kautzner, J., Love, C. J., Morgan, J. M., Priori, S. G., Reynolds, D. W., Schoenfeld, M. H., & Vardas, P. E. (2008). Expert consensus on the monitoring of cardiovascular implantable electronic devices (CIEDs): Description of techniques, indications, personnel, frequency and ethical considerations: Developed in partnership with the Heart Rhythm Society (HRS) and the European Heart Rhythm Association (EHRA); and in collaboration with the American College of Cardiology (ACC), the American Heart Association (AHA), the European

Society of Cardiology (ESC), the Heart Failure Association of ESC (HFA), and the Heart Failure Society of America (HFSA). Endorsed by the Heart Rhythm Society, the European Heart Rhythm Association (a registered branch of the ESC), the American College of Cardiology, the American Heart Association. *EP Europace, 10*(6), 707–725. https://doi.org/10.1093/europace/eun122

Yue, X., Wang, H., & Jin, D. (2016). Healthcare data gateways: Found healthcare intelligence on blockchain with novel privacy risk control. *Journal of Medical Systems, 40*, 218. https://doi.org/10.1007/s10916-016-0574-6

New Horizons in Studying the Cellular Mechanisms of Alzheimer's Disease

Sepehr Ehsani

Abstract

Following an analysis of the state of investigations and clinical outcomes in the Alzheimer's research field, I argue that the widely accepted 'amyloid cascade' mechanistic explanation of Alzheimer's disease appears to be fundamentally incomplete. In this context, I propose that a framework termed 'principled mechanism' (PM) can help remedy this problem. First, using a series of five 'tests', PM systematically compares different components of a given mechanistic explanation against a paradigmatic set of criteria and hints at various ways of making the mechanistic explanation more 'complete'. I will demonstrate these steps using the amyloid explanation, highlighting its missing or problematic mechanistic elements. Second, PM makes an appeal for the discovery and application of 'biological principles' that approximate ceteris paribus generalisations or laws and are operative at the level of a biological cell. Although thermodynamic, evolutionary, ecological and other laws or principles from chemistry and the broader life sciences could inform them, biological principles should be considered ontologically unique. These principles could augment different facets of the mechanistic explanation but also allow further *independent* nomological explanation of the phenomenon. Whilst this overall strategy can be complementary to certain 'new mechanist' approaches, an important distinction of the PM framework is its equal attention to the explanatory utility of biological principles. Lastly, I detail two hypothetical biological principles and show how they could each inform and improve the potentially incomplete mechanistic

S. Ehsani (✉)
Theoretical and Philosophical Biology, Department of Philosophy, University College London, Bloomsbury, London, UK

Ronin Institute for Independent Scholarship, Montclair, NJ, USA
e-mail: ehsani@uclmail.net

© The Author(s) 2022
S. Ehsani et al. (eds.), *The Future Circle of Healthcare*, Future of Business and Finance, https://doi.org/10.1007/978-3-030-99838-7_4

aspects of the amyloid explanation and how they could provide independent explanations for the cellular features associated with Alzheimer's disease.

1   Introduction

This chapter aims to show the practical utility of the 'principled mechanism' (PM) account on a current case in biomedicine, namely, on the field of Alzheimer's disease (AD) research. As will be detailed throughout the chapter, PM is a model of biological explanation that supplements mechanistic elements with 'principles', or non-accidental generalisations that may nevertheless fall short of full-blown lawhood. AD studies represent an active area of investigation that has clear clinical and biological implications. In the philosophy of biology literature, there are (to the extent of what the research for this chapter has revealed) no examples of a thorough analysis of AD research, and the few AD-focused accounts that do exist concern, for instance, the idea of a 'genetic cause' using the example of AD (Dekkers & Rikkert, 2006; Nordenfelt, 2006), the subject of selfhood in AD patients (Kontos, 2004), or the concepts of person essentialism and psychological continuity (Olson & Witt, 2020).[1]

The chapter is structured to provide a philosophical case study of the disease, centred on three questions: (i) What is the current problem with AD research and why do we face this problem? (Sect. 3); (ii) why might contemporary philosophical accounts of mechanism in biology not offer tractable solutions to adequately confront this challenge? (Sect. 4); and (iii) what can the PM framework offer instead to move us in a more productive direction (Sects. 5–7)?

The AD field is broad and varied, and I have tried, to the extent possible, to sufficiently represent the current breadth of research whilst also staying on point. I aim to explicate the following answers to the above questions. First, a large segment of the AD field has been, for the most part, of one voice when it comes to the central elements of a mechanistic explanation that has motivated research in the field for the past three decades. The AD mechanistic model and the resultant explanation are greatly detailed (and increasingly so by the day). However, the explanation – despite immense effort – has not translated into the clinic for patients, and many clinical trials have been unsuccessful. I argue that this is not due to challenges in clinical 'translations' of the explanation's predictions, but rather to a fundamental problem with how mechanistic explanations are approached in the field.

Second, I argue that the solution to this problem is not to simply do away with mechanistic explanations, for there is no serious replacement for this explanatory type in biomedicine. The solution should build on the existing mechanistic explanations. Moreover, whilst I am sympathetic to the 'new mechanist' (NM) project

---

[1] Of note, a relevant recent philosophical work presents a framework called 'MecCog' that builds mechanism schemas for diseases including AD (Kundu et al., 2021).

in the philosophy of scientific explanation, I provide several strands of argument to the effect that existing NM accounts, to the extent that they go beyond reflecting current biological practice, may not be sufficiently critical of that practice to be used to help resolve the problem set out in this chapter. Third, I will propose that a series of 'paradigmatic' tests can, as an initial strategy, point to elements within a given mechanistic explanation that could make it more comprehensive and generate new empirical questions. As a next step, I will argue that the addition of biological principles that could *explain* (and help augment our understanding of) the elements highlighted in the tests can make the overall explanation richer and our potential understanding of AD pathobiology more fundamental.

Before proceeding further, I will address two important concerns in Sect. 2, namely, what range of mechanistic concepts the chapter makes use of and why AD is well suited for the purpose of this case study.

2   Usage of Mechanistic Concepts and Context of AD Research in Biology

Perusing current biomedical journals would leave little doubt that the search for 'mechanisms' forms the basis of a great proportion of the research effort. However, there is much ambiguity in the intended meaning of mechanistic concepts and terms in the biological literature (Marder, 2020). This might partly be attributable to the impression that 'mechanism' could be said to be taken as a *primitive* concept in biology (much like 'point' or 'line' in geometry; Pearl & Mackenzie, 2018, p. 373) – a notion on which much else relies but one that is refractory to a simple and universal definition. It goes without saying that philosophers of mechanism have studied these topics extensively, but this literature has not yet found its way into mainstream biomedical research. For our purposes here, however, the intended terminological meanings should be crystallised.

2.1   Actual Mechanisms, Mechanistic Models and Mechanistic Explanations

Consider the statement 'the bacterium *Helicobacter pylori* can lead to (or cause) peptic ulcers'. Here, 'peptic ulcer' is the *phenomenon to be explained* (henceforth the 'phenomenon'). Moreover, *H. pylori* is a putative cause, or a causative agent. One could then ask why *H. pylori* causes peptic ulcers. Perhaps because this is its function in the gastrointestinal environment. The question could be rephrased as: how or by what means does *H. pylori* cause peptic ulcers? The 'how' or the 'means' with which a putative causative agent leads to a phenomenon can be called the *actual mechanism* by which the phenomenon arises (henceforth the 'mechanism').[2] To avoid confusion, I use the word 'mechanism' to indicate an assumption about the work that causes or produces a phenomenon.[3]

We can model a mechanism. One can understand a model to be some representation of reality (or a phenomenon), and it can be used as a heuristic or thinking tool, or as part of a broader explanation, or perhaps as a way to simplify the complexity of the phenomenon. There are different accounts of how a model does the 'representing', but I will not expand on them here.[4] In molecular biology, cellular processes are often represented using a network of parts (e.g. proteins, genes, RNAs), indications of change and movement (e.g. of a protein from one location to another), interactions (e.g. protein–protein, protein–DNA, protein–lipid) and so on. Therefore, we can define a *mechanistic model* as a representation of a mechanism. It follows that a given mechanism could have multiple different representations.

Mechanistic models can subsequently be used as part of a statement or a description to detail and give reasons for a phenomenon (see, e.g. Brini et al., 2020). Let us call this the *mechanistic account* or *mechanistic explanation*. A mechanistic model could give rise to several explanations that investigators can use to make predictions, molecular interventions and so forth (Lombrozo, 2011).

Three caveats are necessary: First, some studies in cellular biology may stop at the stage of detailing certain elements of a model and not progress to a full-fledged mechanistic explanation. For our purposes here, however, the explanatory stage is key. Second, biologists investigating a cellular phenomenon may at times feel it is sufficient to provide an analysis of the putative function of a 'part', such as a protein, and provide only a version of a 'functional' explanation. As will also be seen later in the context of AD, this should indeed be viewed as complementary to mechanistic explanations (see also Theurer, 2018). And third, I am not claiming that all explanations require a model; I am arguing that mechanistic explanations typically use at least some elements of mechanistic models.

2.2 AD Research as a Quintessential Mechanistic Research Programme

AD imposes a huge burden on patients and their families. Worldwide, the projected number of dementia cases (a majority of which is thought to be AD) is estimated to

---

[2] There are distinctions to be made between mechanistic and 'difference-making' accounts of causation, but I will not delve into the topic here.

[3] The reason why this assumption may not apply across the board is that in some cases using 'mechanism' as a stand-in for 'means' may strike as odd. For example, when referring to the means with which a magnetic pole attracts a pole of opposite polarity, talking about 'mechanism' is unusual. Rather, we could talk of magnetic 'fields' and 'forces'.

[4] As an example, a candidate for how models represent has been called the 'DEKI' account (denotation, exemplification, keying up of properties, and imputation) (Frigg & Nguyen, 2016).

reach over 131.5 million individuals by 2050 (PLOS Medicine Editors, 2016). Why is AD a suitable research field for studying the theoretical basis behind mechanistic explanations? First, there has now been more than 50 years of systematic research on AD, and a vast portion of the published works refer to 'disease mechanism', 'mechanistic understanding', 'mechanistic pathways' and many other related concepts. The current cellular understanding of AD is complex to the point that a lot can be said about its various facets, strengths and shortcomings. Furthermore, a well-accepted and overarching mechanistic explanation has been the mainstay of the field for several decades, and, importantly, it has been tested in different lights, for example, in countless laboratory-based assays all the way to many clinical trials. So what exactly is the problem?

3 Problems for the Mainstream Biomedical Research Approach to AD

In 1907, Alois Alzheimer (1864–1915) provided two pathological hallmarks for the disease in the brain, which are now widely known as *amyloid plaques* and *neurofibrillary tangles* (Alzheimer et al., 1995) (these two terms will be referred to repeatedly). The hallmarks are now known to be due to the aggregation of two main types of 'sticky' proteins: the plaques are formed of *amyloid beta (Aβ) peptide* (mostly outside affected neurons) and the neurofibrillary tangles (NFTs) of *tau protein* (inside affected neurons). Focused investigations of Aβ three decades ago are what started the extensive and what one could call the 'mainstream' molecular research effort on AD. What has resulted is a working explanation called the *amyloid cascade hypothesis/mechanistic explanation* (Beyreuther & Masters, 1991; Hardy & Allsop, 1991; Selkoe, 1991), henceforth the 'amyloid explanation'. Although many additional genes and cellular pathways have since been associated to varying degrees with some manifestations of the disease (see Liu et al., 2019), almost all findings in AD are usually interpreted via and/or placed within the amyloid explanation.

3.1 The Amyloid Cascade Mechanistic Explanation

To analyse the amyloid explanation, it would help to choose an illustrative schematic that depicts both processes of amyloid plaque formation by Aβ and NFT formation by tau. However, note that technically the amyloid cascade hypothesis usually only refers to the amyloid plaque formation process in AD and does not include the NFT formation arm. To simplify subsequent references to these two defining lesions of AD, I will use the umbrella term of 'amyloid explanation' to refer to both processes.

Of the available choices, a summarising figure from a review article by Panza and colleagues (Panza et al., 2019) is shown in Fig. 1 and will be used as a reference visual for the amyloid mechanistic model. Also, to simplify the depicted illustration

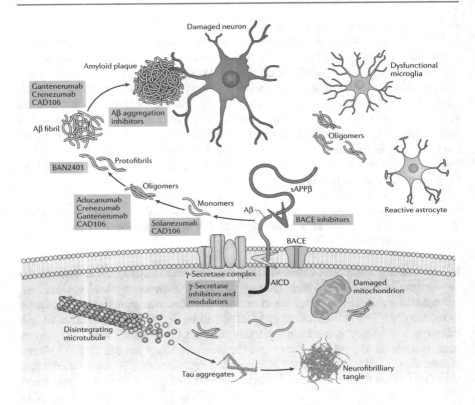

Fig. 1 Putative pathobiological mechanistic model of Alzheimer's disease (Panza et al., 2019). Here the authors show the process of amyloid plaque formation outside the neuronal cell, and the generation of neurofibrillary tangles inside the cell, along with "mechanisms of action of the main anti-amyloid-β (Aβ) drugs that are currently [early 2019] in phase III clinical development for the treatment of Alzheimer disease" (Panza et al., 2019, p. 75). The intracellular endpoint depicted is mitochondrial damage, whereas the extracellular endpoints shown are neuronal damage, microglial dysfunction and reactive astrocytes. Abbreviations, as per the original caption, are: AICD, amyloid precursor protein intracellular domain; BACE, β-secretase; sAPPβ, soluble amyloid precursor protein-β. Reproduced with permission from Panza et al., 2019; copyright Springer Nature

using text, three salient processes in the figure are summarised in Table 1. These are as follows:

1. The *amyloidogenic* amyloid precursor protein (APP) processing pathway. This process *increases* the production of Aβ and the formation of amyloid plaque.
2. The *non-amyloidogenic* APP processing pathway. This process *decreases* the production of Aβ and the formation of amyloid plaque.
3. The NFT formation pathway. This process leads to the aggregation of tau.

Table 1 Three pathways in the AD pathogenesis mechanism (details adapted from Panza et al., 2019). The steps in Table 1 are greatly simplified, given that for each step multiple details and subtleties have been reported. One such important detail, for example, is the varying clearance of Aβ by 'apolipoprotein E' (APOE) proteins (Yamazaki et al., 2019). In fact, variants of APOE are genetic risk factors for late-onset sporadic AD (Ishii & Iadecola, 2020), and there is ongoing extensive research on APOE in the context of AD in general (Li & Zhao, 2021; Lu et al., 2021). However, the point of this chapter is not to analyse AD mechanisms exhaustively but rather to scrutinise the theoretical basis of a typical cellular mechanistic explanation

Amyloidogenic APP processing	Non-amyloidogenic APP processing	Neurofibrillary tangle formation
Increased in AD	*Reduced* in AD	*Increased* in AD
Start • Amyloid precursor protein (APP) **Process** 1. Cleavage by protease β-secretase 1 (BACE1) **Products** • Soluble extracellular fragment, sAPPβ • Cell-membrane-bound fragment, C99 **Process** 2. Cleavage of C99 by protease γ-secretase **Products** • Release of Aβ peptide (40- or 42-amino-acid length) • Aggregation of Aβ to form oligomers, protofibrils, fibrils and plaques	**Start** • Amyloid precursor protein (APP) **Process** 1. Cleavage by extracellular protease α-secretase **Product** • Soluble extracellular fragment, sAPPα	**Start** • Microtubule-associated tau protein **Process** 1. Hyperphosphorylation of tau **Products** • Aggregation of hyperphosphorylated tau • NFT formation
Endpoint • Synapse loss and neuronal death mediated by Aβ oligomers		**Endpoints** • Cytoskeletal changes and disruption of axonal transport • Spread of misfolded/aggregated tau to other cells

In the figure, the lipid membrane of a neuronal cell is shown as a bilayer (two lines of circles with lines in between, like a horizontal ladder). The cytoplasm or intracellular space is the area below the membrane, shown in beige. All the area above the membrane is the extracellular space, and one more neuron and two other cell types in the brain (astrocytes and microglial immune cells, which act to support neurons)[5] are illustrated at a much smaller size. Pathways 1 and 2, which have to do with amyloid plaque formation, both start with the APP protein, which in the figure is shown as a twisting 'tube' that has been cut by two pairs of scissors. The reason for the three colours of the tube (red, orange and blue) is to show the three fragments (or 'peptides') of APP that form when it is cleaved by a number of other proteins (enzymes).

In the *amyloidogenic pathway*, APP is cleaved by an enzyme ('β-secretase' or BACE, depicted as a pair of purple scissors above the membrane) to produce two fragments, namely, 'sAPPβ' (in blue) and 'C99' (the part of APP that remains). The C99 fragment is then cleaved by another enzyme, 'γ-secretase' (depicted as a pair of yellow scissors within the membrane), yielding the Aβ peptide (orange fragment). Aβ 'monomers' start to aggregate to form oligomers, fibrils and plaques (shown sequentially in the extracellular space). Over the past decade, attention has shifted from the insoluble fibrils and plaques to the soluble oligomers as the toxic Aβ form in neurons (Dear et al., 2020). These steps are summarised in the first column of Table 1.

Concomitant with Pathway 1, the *non-amyloidogenic pathway* is also proposed to be taking place on the cell membrane with respect to APP. Specifically, in this pathway, rather than initially being cleaved by β-secretase, APP is cleaved by 'α-secretase' at a different site, leading to the production of a soluble fragment called 'sAPPα' and *preventing* Aβ peptide production. Because this pathway is supposed to be a 'physiological' process that happens normally in the brain, it is not shown in the figure. However, the steps are summarised in the second column of Table 1. In AD, the *balance* between these two pathways is thought to be skewed toward the amyloidogenic route. In other words, more of process 1 and less of process 2 takes place.

Pathway 3 concerns the intracellular formation of NFT, where the central player is the tau protein. Tau is mainly found in the axons (long projections) of neurons and is physiologically associated with promoting the assembly of microtubules. Microtubules are polymers of 'tubulin' proteins and form part of the cytoskeleton; they provide structure to the cell and aid in other functions. In Fig. 1, a microtubule is depicted as a purple cylinder (formed of many tubulin 'spheres') below the membrane, and tau proteins can be seen as blue objects wrapping around the microtubule. In the AD amyloid explanation (and indeed in explanations of other neurodegenerative conditions involving tau),[6] the tau protein, which is modified in the cell by the attachment of a 'phosphoryl' chemical group (i.e. is said to be 'phosphorylated') to a number of its amino acids, becomes *hyper*phosphorylated; that is, multiple sites on the protein become saturated with phosphorylation. It is thought that tau hyperphosphorylation leads to its dissociation from microtubules, which in turn leads to microtubule disintegration and the formation of tau aggregates

---

[5] Indeed, these glial cell types are thought to have crucial involvements in the pathogenesis of AD. See, for example, Da Mesquita et al. (2021), Guttenplan et al. (2021), and Ulrich and Holtzman (2021).

[6] 'Tauopathies' include a broad range of conditions (Shi et al., 2021; Stahlberg & Riek, 2021).

(both depicted in the figure). These aggregates can turn into NFTs and may even spread to other neurons (not shown in the figure), causing further NFTs to form in a given brain region. The steps in this pathway are summarised in the last column of Table 1.

The amyloid explanation centres on these protein aggregation events, the end result of which is neuronal loss and cognitive impairment. What happens in the brain at a cortical level (i.e. populations of neurons and brain regions) is beyond the current discussion, as we are concerned with the more immediate task of accounting for processes at the cellular level. Nonetheless, attention in the field has been directed for more than a decade now toward a region of the brain called the entorhinal cortex as perhaps the first part of the brain that suffers from the loss of its neurons (NTNU, 2020; Shugart, 2020).[7]

The elucidation of each of these three pathways has been a major advance in the field. For instance, research on the mechanistic details of tau aggregation was featured on the cover of *Nature* as recently as November 2019 and October 2021. This shows how important not just the AD research field but also the broader scientific community judges deciphering AD's pathobiology to be.

What might now be apparent is that conceptual gaps exist that the amyloid explanation needs to address: it does not explain, for example, how pathways 1 and 2 interact and influence pathway 3. The non-amyloidogenic pathway is supposedly a normal physiological process, whereas the amyloidogenic pathway is pronounced in disease. Yet to a certain extent, both are taking place in health *and* in disease. Moreover, pathway 3 (involving tau aggregates) has been identified to also have non-neurodegenerative manifestations (Park et al., 2020) and to also participate in normal physiological processes in, for example, hibernating animals (Arendt et al., 2003). The picture is therefore complicated in various ways. Having said that, this is not a complication that would, at least conceptually, pose a problem that current frameworks in the philosophy of biology could not address. For us, the nub of the problem is more fundamental than how the various pathways may interact.

3.2 Capturing the Full Complexity of the Disease

Up to this day, the amyloid explanation has actually been quite *successful* in a certain sense. Details of various aspects of the underlying working model continue to be worked out by different groups, clinical trials are designed based on the explanation and the 'tenet' of the explanation (i.e. the theme of protein aggregation inside and outside neurons) remains quite intact. As mentioned earlier, even when alternative explanations are proposed for AD, they are often pinned to the amyloid explanation. As a case in point, there has been ongoing interest in the possibility of a microbial link to AD (Cairns et al., 2020) and whether Aβ has antimicrobial properties (Pastore et al., 2020). But when an 'antimicrobial protection hypothesis'

---

[7] The locus coeruleus has also been investigated as the site of tau aggregation (Jacobs et al., 2021).

was proposed to account for these possibilities, the authors commented that "the new model extends but remains broadly consistent with the Amyloid Cascade Hypothesis and overwhelming data showing the primacy of Aβ in AD pathology" (Moir et al., 2018, p. 1602). It might be safe to say that the amyloid explanation has, in a way, stood the test of time. Furthermore, it is hard to imagine a *radically different* mechanistic explanation that could circumvent the current one, and the AD hallmarks, altogether.

Nonetheless, there is in fact a fundamental and consequential problem with the amyloid explanation: the explanation has not led to genuine clinical improvement in patients. This reality is highlighted when we consider the many clinical trials that have tested what were meant to be 'disease-modifying' therapeutics validated in the laboratory based on the amyloid account. In an opinion piece titled "we need to radically rethink our approach to Alzheimer's research", Mark Hammond and Tim Newton wrote that "over the past decade we've seen failure after failure in clinical trials for neurodegenerative disease [and] despite over 200 clinical trials, we still don't have any meaningful therapeutics for Alzheimer's" (Hammond & Newton, 2020).[8] This does not stem from the way that the mechanistic explanation is being *translated* from 'bench to bedside'. Practicable strategies already exist in biology to deal with the problem of translation (see, e.g. Henderson et al., 2020).

In fact, many of the AD therapies tested have been produced to *match* the understanding and prediction afforded by the amyloid explanation in remarkably precise ways. In other words, if the explanation suggests that protein 'X' should be lowered in patients (and this has been borne out in laboratory and animal experiments), the therapeutics being tested *are* indeed lowering that protein in patients being tested (see, e.g. Mintun et al., 2021). Hence, the explanation's predictions/demands are being *translated* all the way to patients in a strictly biological sense but are still not successful in halting AD. Therefore, something might be amiss with the explanation itself, in that it is not capturing the full complexity of AD and is somehow seriously incomplete.

It is important to note here that such problems could in fact generalise to – and are typical of – any other mechanistic explanation in biomedicine. In cases such as certain rare monogenic diseases, the explanation might have fewer identified components relative to the amyloid explanation of AD and a more delineated causal chain, whereas in other complex cases, such as various types of cancer, the mechanistic explanation might be much more multifaceted than that of AD. There might also not be a general consensus in the respective research field on a unified mechanistic explanation. That being said, this chapter's analysis could just as easily be applied to the mechanistic explanation of any pathobiological condition.

How should the challenge with the amyloid explanation be approached? I will outline two possibilities, calling them the 'incremental' and the 'non-mechanistic'

---

[8] Of relevance also to this discussion is the multitude of commentaries in the latter half of 2021 and early 2022 on the anti-Aβ monoclonal antibody Aducanumab (Aduhelm) (Dunn et al., 2021; Mullard, 2021; Rogers, 2022; Selkoe, 2021).

options, and then point out that I advocate for a middle ground. To begin with, solutions proposed by some AD investigators appear to argue for staying within the confines of the current mechanistic framework, whilst attempting to increase our understanding of certain details and gaps in our knowledge of the workings of the model, or the timeline of clinical trials and interventions (Aisen, 2019; Petsko, 2018). I call this the incremental approach. Important details that require resolution, for instance, concern clarifying how levels of Aβ in patients are correlated with the stage of the disease (Masters, 2019) or whether it is causative of AD or a by-product of other processes (Panza et al., 2019).

The focus on details might also lead to the addition of new molecules to the explanation that may eventually become therapeutic 'targets'. However, given the long history of AD research, it is quite unlikely that one or more hitherto undiscovered targets waiting to be added to the mechanistic model would suddenly change everything. I cannot 'prove' this, for such an outcome is theoretically possible, although, as I have emphasised, all new details that have thus far been discovered have in one way or another revolved around the amyloid explanation.

The incremental approach might also reveal new knowledge about the existing molecular parts of the amyloid explanation. This is important because the evolutionary history behind the function of each protein stretches back hundreds of millions of years, and any key protein identified in the AD explanation (e.g. APP) very likely also functions in various other cellular processes that might have little to do with AD per se, therefore making molecular interventions on it risky. Additionally, when investigators focus on one mechanism, a general problem of 'masking' may be encountered, whereby "the operation of one mechanism might *mask* or hide the operation" of other mechanisms (Illari, 2011, p. 146; original emphasis). For example, the secretase enzymes might function in as-yet-unidentified processes in neurons that are critical for normal cognition. If that is so, the amyloid explanation must also be able to capture these important aspects of its key protein players. However, there is no obvious path as to how the amyloid explanation can connect with other cellular mechanisms. The incremental approach can in principle reveal insights toward this issue, but it is not clear how exactly this would be achieved.

An opposing option is to look for completely non-mechanistic explanations for AD, but such a suggestion would be received as outlandish in cellular biology. It is inconceivable for anyone in biomedicine to advocate giving up the entire 'mechanistic enterprise' (i.e. the creation of mechanistic models and provision of mechanistic explanations), for there is no viable alternative to such an approach. If someone proposed a completely non-mechanistic approach to studying AD's cellular phenomena – it is hard to imagine what this would look like, for even a purely mathematical approach would have to rely upon some 'platform' in the form of a mechanistic model – it could not realistically inform current research because it would simply not 'connect with' anything that investigators are pursuing. Consider also that even network-based or topological explanations in molecular biology are often used to search for mechanistic elements within them (see Yadav et al., 2020). What is more, the mechanistic enterprise appears to connect with at least some of our intuitive insights about how nature works (Spelke & Kinzler, 2007).

I argue for a middle way, such that the meticulous mechanistic understanding centred on protein aggregation is preserved but also augmented with a 'novel' non-mechanistic approach so that new experiments would not merely bring about 'more of the same', but would rather constitute genuine steps forward in our understanding of the complexity of the disease. This is the ultimate aim of the PM framework, to help show how exactly the amyloid explanation might be 'incomplete' and how one might go about improving it. One can then reasonably hope that the explanation would have a better chance of actually halting the disease.

But first, before outlining the PM approach, I will look for insights toward improving the amyloid explanation in work by contemporary philosophers concerned with mechanistic theory.

4   'New Mechanism' and Clues for Moving Past the Explanatory Problem

Beginning in the 1990s, a renewed interest in mechanisms began to take shape primarily within the philosophy of biology. This strand of investigation is termed 'new mechanism' (NM) to distinguish it from research on the history of mechanical philosophy. NM was a welcome development, for it aimed to systematise – and provide the underlying theory for – mechanistic concepts and usages that were (and for the most part still are) treated superficially in biomedical practice.

A reminder of the context within which NM arose is important here. Many philosophers of science in the mid-twentieth century were pursuing a nomological tradition (i.e. based on natural laws) that is best exemplified by Carl Hempel's (1905–1997) deductive-nomological (DN) model of scientific explanation (Hempel, 1965). The zeitgeist of this approach can perhaps be said to have been "experiment as the source of knowledge, mathematical formulation as the descriptive medium [and] mathematical deduction as the guiding principle in the search for new phenomena to be verified by experimentation" (Dijksterhuis, 1961, p. 3). This also instilled a sense of valuing "rigor, precision, and generality" in scientific theorising (Bogen, 2020, §11).

But the DN approach was problematic, even in the seemingly compatible subfields of physics. As early as the same period as the peak of logical empiricism, Thomas Kuhn (1922–1996) was questioning the highly formal and axiomatic approaches to scientific theories (Kuhn, 1962), and, in the words of Simon Blackburn, advocated a "less formal and more contextualized approach [. . . which] stressed the open-endedness of scientific activity [and] the heuristic value of analogies and models" (Blackburn, 2016, p. 475). Philosophers of biology also took note of such problems. William Wimsatt, who with a group of students and collaborators set the stage for the NM approach, writes that in 1974, he argued that "discovering a mechanism as a relatively stable and manipulable articulation of causal factors better fit the activity of biologists than a search for laws" (Wimsatt, 2017, p. xv).

Over the past 30 years, NM philosophers have provided influential accounts with which to systematically conceive of mechanisms and mechanistic explanations. For example, in 1993, William Bechtel and Robert Richardson wrote that mechanistic research results in "a detailed account of the parts and operations of a mechanism and how they are organized and orchestrated in a specific model system" (Bechtel & Richardson, 2010, p. xli).[9] Peter Machamer, Lindley Darden and Carl Craver defined mechanisms as "entities and activities organized such that they are productive of regular changes from start or set-up to finish or termination conditions" (Machamer et al., 2000, p. 3). Along the same lines, Bechtel and Adele Abrahamsen defined a mechanism as "a structure performing a function in virtue of its component parts, component operations, and their organization [where] the orchestrated functioning of the mechanism is responsible for one or more phenomena" (Bechtel & Abrahamsen, 2005, p. 423). Stuart Glennan and Phyllis Illari have written about the concept of a 'minimal mechanism', whereby "a mechanism for a phenomenon consists of entities (or parts) whose activities and interactions are organized so as to be responsible for the phenomenon" (Glennan, 2017, p. 17; Glennan & Illari, 2017, p. 92).

Without going into the specifics, how biologists think about the AD mechanism arguably matches the accounts above. Moreover, the amyloid explanation itself is attuned to the way that Bechtel and Richardson, for example, defined mechanistic accounts. However, it is not immediately clear based on these accounts how the amyloid explanation might be incomplete and how it could be improved. Depending on the context, the NM accounts require much more expansion to function as a critiquing framework. One could, for example, 'read into' the accounts or find elements that could be useful for our problem, but they do not provide explicit details for us to use. Part of the reason for this might be that many NM philosophers and philosophers of biology in general might not have concentrated on the *failures* present in modern cell biology. Laura Franklin-Hall similarly suggests that "a too-successful enculturation of philosophers into the scientific mindset [makes] it difficult to achieve the critical distance needed to philosophize *about* science" (Franklin-Hall, 2016, p. 71; original emphasis).

Notwithstanding these concerns, what *hints* could one distil from the NM approach about what the amyloid explanation might be lacking? I believe such hints might become apparent when one considers how the NM and related approaches have dealt with ideas concerning the introduction of laws into mechanistic explanations. Craver and James Tabery maintain that mechanisms "seem to play the role of laws in the biological sciences: we seek mechanisms to explain, predict, and control phenomena in nature even if mechanisms lack many of the characteristics definitive of laws in the logical empiricist framework (such as universality, inviolable necessity, or unrestricted scope)" (Craver & Tabery, 2019, §4.1). In another take, Craver and Marie Kaiser write that "mechanists *decenter* laws in their thinking about

---

[9] This is a reprint of the 1993 edition. The quoted text is from the introduction to the original edition.

science because the old paradigm, centering laws, has become mired in debates that are inconsequential and, as a result, have *stopped generating new questions* and producing new results" (Craver & Kaiser, 2013, p. 144; my italics). Whilst a goal of this chapter is to put laws back in the centre of discussion,[10] I share the view of Craver and Kaiser in emphasising the importance of generating new empirical questions as a key criterion of a framework's success. Let us call this hint #1.

The view of Bechtel and Richardson is more compatible with the view on laws I argue for here. They also considered the place of laws or "general and abstract explanatory principles" (Bechtel & Richardson, 2010, p. 232) in mechanistic accounts. Their main motivation was to "question the hegemony of laws in explanation [but] not their existence" (Bechtel & Richardson, 2010, p. 256). In more recent work, Bechtel comments that "laws may be invoked to characterize the overall functioning of the mechanism or some of its operations, but it is the discovery that particular operations are being performed that is required to specify the mechanism" (Bechtel, 2011, p. 537). Congruent with this description, Nancy Cartwright, John Pemberton and Sarah Wieten (whose work is not usually considered part of the NM tradition) have proposed that "when a mechanism M gives rise to a regular behavior RB that is described in a cp [ceteris paribus] law, RB is what it takes for some set of principles that govern the features of M's parts in their arrangement in M all to be instanced together" (Cartwright et al., 2020, p. 18). I will say more on ceteris paribus laws in Sect. 7.

In recent work analysing examples from chronobiology (the biology of time in terms of an organism's 24-hour circadian rhythm), Bechtel mentions "principles of organization (design principles)" which "assert that any system implementing the organization will exhibit the specified behavior" (Bechtel, 2017, p. 19). Relatedly, Sara Green has investigated the idea of design principles in the context of 'systems biology' and introduced the idea of "constraint-based generality" (Green, 2015; Green & Jones, 2016). Whilst the thesis of this chapter is sympathetic to these accounts, they do not explicitly show how the amyloid explanation should be overhauled, and the role and discovery of principles (non-accidental generalisations that may nevertheless fall short of full-blown lawhood) come across as peripheral to the specification and operations of a mechanism. I state this because, for instance, an AD investigator might just assume that the current amyloid explanation is *already* serving the purpose of 'organising' the components of the underlying model by accounting for the temporal cascade of events both inside and outside the cell. Thus, the investigator needs a convincing reason to invoke an extra concept, such as a 'principle'. Nonetheless, the NM works cited in this and the preceding paragraph hint at an explanatory role that principles of organisation could play, at least in a qualitative sense. Let us consider this hint #2.

As might be expected from the often-cyclical nature of the history of ideas, as the NM approach began to become dominant in the philosophy of biology, a small

---

[10] Others, for example Bert Leuridan (2010), have also argued that laws cannot be supplanted by mechanisms in scientific explanations.

but steady wave of proposals reintroduced or amalgamated certain elements of the pre-NM nomological approaches. For example, José Díez has proposed a 'neo-Hempelian' account of scientific explanation, whereby "to explain a phenomenon is to make it expectable by introducing new conceptual/ontological machinery and using special, and non-ad hoc, non-accidental regularities" (Díez, 2014, p. 1413). 'Expectability' is a key notion in Díez's account.[11] Roger Deulofeu and Javier Suárez pick up on this notion in their paper on "when mechanisms are not enough" and write that in their analysis, "the use of scientific laws is supposed to be a minimal *requirement* of all scientific explanations, since the purpose of a scientific explanation is to make phenomena expectable" (Deulofeu & Suárez, 2018, p. 95; my italics).

In this body of literature, one of the closest approaches to the one in this chapter is an account by Alleva et al. (2017) on a problem in biochemistry. The authors are concerned with the mechanistic description of the conformational changes in a protein upon the binding of another molecule ('allosteric' regulation). What they propose "essentially contains nonaccidental, nomological regularities that can properly be considered as laws in a relevant, though minimal, sense of lawhood" (Alleva et al., 2017, p. 12). Importantly, they say that "we do not believe that the mechanistic and our model-theoretic accounts are in opposition" (Alleva et al., 2017, p. 12), but rather "we advocate a plural, syncretic perspective in which every relevant aspect is explicated according to its specific nature" (Alleva et al., 2017, p. 13). This "plural, syncretic perspective" and the notion of 'expectability', even though they originated in works that one might say are 'reacting' to the NM tradition, could still be our hint #3.

The confluence of these three hints – that is, a framework's ability to generate new empirical questions, an explanatory role for principles and generalisations, and an explanation's drive toward expectability – is a niche where the 'principled mechanistic' (PM) explanation can fit. As I shall argue, PM's strength lies first and foremost in generating questions that current mechanistic explanations are not poised to produce. Furthermore, I will argue for an independent and critical explanatory role for 'biological principles'. And, lastly, PM pushes for *quantitative* expectability of the phenomenon being studied.

Beyond these three hints, there are also other intersections between PM and NM. For instance, part of the PM framework involves creating a series of 'tests' to detail what a 'paradigmatic' PM explanation would look like (Sect. 5). For this, concepts developed in the NM literature about mechanistic elements such as decomposable parts, organisation and levels will be of great utility. This is why I consider the PM project to be complementary to NM, yet more prescriptive of what investigators 'ought' to be doing compared to NM when it comes to existing problems in biology.

In closing this section, I should emphasise that my intention is not to imply that all open problems related to current AD research require PM, or some other

---

[11] The notion of 'expectability' recalls what Hempel termed the "nomic expectability of a phenomenon" (Hempel, 1968, p. 119).

augmented mechanistic framework. The purpose of PM is to improve the overall explanation of AD. Nonetheless, recalling the final paragraph of Sect. 3.1, I noted that there are open challenges pertaining to the amyloid explanation that are separate from what I argue to be its 'foundational' shortcomings. One such challenge had to do with how one could reconcile the involvement of pathways 1, 2 and 3 in both physiological and disease processes. Would, for instance, disease in such cases be a matter of imbalance? Accounts in NM, such as those explicating how operations within a mechanism might be organised or what different levels and lines of feedback might exist in a particular mechanistic explanation of a phenomenon, would be well placed to tackle such questions.

5   Toward an Ideal 'Principled Mechanistic' Explanation in the Context of AD

The chapter thus far has indicated that the PM approach aims to strike a middle way between purely mechanistic and non-mechanistic options. Taking a cue from NM philosophers, on the mechanistic side, PM aims for some systematisation of the elements of mechanistic explanations. On the non-mechanistic side, the goal is to adapt hypothesised 'biological principles' to mechanistic explanations, where the resultant PM explanation would be an augmented but still coherent whole.

To begin to demonstrate that satisfactory explanations in biology are liable to require an appeal to principles as well as mechanisms, it might be useful to mention an analogy with 'reaction mechanisms' and thermodynamic laws in chemistry. When a chemist sets out to explain the reaction between some molecules, they detail the reaction mechanism; that is, the sequence of molecular/atomic steps leading to an overall chemical change. But they do not stop there, for they also appeal to thermodynamic laws that further explain the steps.

In fact, thermodynamics (e.g. the second law) has been highly formalised in chemistry in the form of the notion of change in 'Gibbs free energy' (ΔG), "whose sign predicts the direction of reaction, and whose magnitude indicates the maximum amount of work realizable from the reaction" (Feinman & Fine, 2004, p. 2). As such, thermodynamics can help (i) *predict* something about the reaction (recall the notion of 'expectability' from hint #3) and (ii) provide some sort of *quantification* for the yield of the reaction. These could arguably be achieved without necessarily appealing to the mechanistic details of the reaction. However, the notion of ΔG can also (iii) be applied to the details of the reaction mechanism itself to reveal new insights. As an example, chemists have used thermodynamic notions of molecules' lowest free-energy states to study the immensely complex mechanism of hydrogen bond formation amongst clusters of water molecules (Richardson et al., 2016), allowing them to reveal how the bond formation mechanism *itself* might be operating (see also Llored, 2011).

In today's cell biology, we have the equivalent of intricate 'reaction mechanisms' for phenomena such as AD (although perhaps not as systematised as in chemistry), but what is largely missing is the cell biology equivalent of thermodynamic laws.

This, in essence, is the framework that a PM explanation aims to achieve. The tasks at hand are to describe a way to systematise mechanistic explanations and to show how an appeal to principles can augment the power of cell biological explanations. I embark on the first task in this section and look at the second task in Sects. 6 and 7.

Here, based on different NM-related accounts (Bechtel & Abrahamsen, 2005; Bechtel & Richardson, 2010; Cartwright et al., 2020; Glennan & Illari, 2017), earlier approaches to naturalistic explanations and research on AD and non-AD mechanistic explanations in the cell biology literature, I propose to develop a concise series of criteria for a *paradigmatically* 'good' mechanistic explanation. These criteria could be thought of as candidate determinants of the 'good-making features' (borrowing from Newton-Smith, 1981) of a mechanistic explanation. The idea is not to say that fulfilling all the criteria would arrive at an ideal or complete explanation *in an absolute sense*. I only claim that moving toward fulfilling these criteria, if we can, would produce better mechanistic explanations than what we already have. Furthermore, the criteria can be presented in the format of a series of 'tests' to help us determine whether an explanation meets the criteria.

- *TEST #1:* The phenomenon to be explained is set out as unambiguously as possible.

  This first test concerns the explanandum. It is only referring to the phenomenon and is not yet concerned with the explanation per se and is simply appealing to a goal of clearly stipulating what a biologist is to investigate. There is often much work to be done prior to setting out to explain a phenomenon in clarifying the biological problem at hand. Such an aim not only helps avoid explanatory irrelevance but could also facilitate consistency amongst investigators and the ease of communicating different explanatory angles of the phenomenon. For example, setting out to explain 'cell death' (e.g. apoptosis) is clearer than setting out to explain 'cellular dysfunction', without stipulating what the 'dysfunction' implies. In a sense, an investigator wants to pre-empt the question 'But what exactly *are* we explaining?'

- *TEST #2:* The explanation sets out an environment to situate the mechanism leading to the phenomenon and refers to decomposable and detectable parts that constitute the mechanism.

  This test narrows in on two basic epistemic criteria of a mechanistic explanation, namely, the context and the parts. It starts by locating the environment within which the phenomenon and the putative mechanism underlying it occur. Stipulating the environment should be an easy task because it directly corresponds to the cellular location that researchers choose to study. Furthermore, there are not many choices when it comes to the cell: it consists of the intracellular space (i.e. the cytoplasm), the membrane, the extracellular space and 'sub-environments' relevant to the explanation, for example an organelle such as the mitochondrion inside the cytoplasm.

  The explanation should then stipulate the parts (or entities) of interest. The parts can be detected and measured in the stipulated environment(s). Much of cell biology revolves around molecular parts such as DNAs, RNAs and proteins, which are themselves composed of smaller subparts in the form of nucleic acids, amino acids and so forth. There is a reductionist undercurrent in cell biology's reliance on molecular parts for its explanations. The biologist E. O. Wilson explained this as a "search strategy employed to find points of entry into otherwise impenetrably complex systems" (Wilson, 1998, p. 59). Indeed, as already detailed, much of the AD amyloid explanation relies upon a cast of molecular parts in the form of proteins.

- *TEST #3:* The parts represented in the mechanistic model on which the explanation relies are organised and have some form of interaction.

   This test concerns quantitative associations amongst the parts. Once the key parts of a mechanism have been detected, determining how they are spatiotemporally organised relative to each other and interact amongst each other is a rational next step. In the cell, one could have protein–protein, protein–lipid, protein–DNA and many other types of interactions. Investigating such interactions could be done at a small scale or using what are called 'interactome' approaches, which are aimed at providing a quantifiable snapshot of the interaction of a greater number of molecules. Determining interactions between key parts in a mechanistic model and the resulting explanation may also hint at potential interactions with parts in other (ostensibly unrelated) cellular processes, hence aiding in dealing with the possible masking effect of parallel mechanisms mentioned in Sect. 3.2.

   As a lead-up to the next section, consider that if a category of biological principles could be hypothesised that might possibly explain spatiotemporal interactions in the cell, this could have an augmenting role in a PM explanation. More on this later.

- *TEST #4:* The relevant interacting parts described in the explanation exert some form of change on each other via some intermediate means.

   This test stays on the theme of interaction amongst parts but is concerned with the nature of the interactions and the changes they bring about. Put differently, it is essentially about the *consequences* of the associations amongst parts, particularly proteins. Why is this important? A cell's behaviour is ultimately mediated through its plethora of proteins, hence the physicochemical changes that proteins exert on each other are crucial. It might often turn out that the mere fact that two proteins interact could be discovered relatively easily, but the biological significance and change(s) brought about by the interaction would take many years to unravel.[12] What also complicates the understanding of the biological significance of protein–protein interactions is that evolution has created a reality whereby most proteins associate with only a specific subset of other proteins and are relatively inert in terms of interactions with others.[13]

---

[12] This is not restricted to proteins only but could also figure in genomics, where, for example, "activity-by-contact" models have been applied to map the significance of interactions between different genomic elements (Fulco et al., 2019; Gaffney, 2019; Nasser et al., 2021).

[13] I am grateful to Gerold Schmitt-Ulms (University of Toronto) for bringing this point to my attention. See also Schmitt-Ulms et al. (2021).

What could help us establish the nature of the changes exerted by molecular parts on each other is to analyse the intermediate means of their interactions, which could themselves be other mechanisms (composed of parts, etc.) or things that are not standardly classed as mechanisms, such as physicochemical forces. Proteins are thought to interact with each other via various modes of electrostatic attraction resulting in changes in protein conformation and/or the addition of chemical groups (recall the 'hyperphosphorylation' of tau). In this context, a hypothesised category of biological principles that explain macromolecular interactions could inform the test's criteria in a PM explanation.

- *TEST #5:* The explanation can accurately account for the sequence of cellular changes leading to detectable variation in the phenomenon.

Whilst Tests #2 to #4 focus on changes effected on/by individual parts, this test attempts to bridge the parts to the phenomenon by highlighting how a *series* of changes (effected on/by individual parts) may be temporally and causally connected to lead to quantifiable variations in the phenomenon. Indeed, a cornerstone of biological investigations is studying natural or artificial variation/change in a phenomenon as a crucial way of gleaning details about its underlying mechanism.

To help fulfil this explanatory criterion, one or some cellular part(s) should in principle be manipulated (by the investigator or by nature itself in the case of 'natural experiments'), altering the phenomenon and/or effecting changes on other parts and paving the way to determining causal relations amongst the parts in the mechanism underlying the phenomenon. Philosophers of science are well familiar with James Woodward's work on 'interventions' (Woodward, 2016). Whilst interventions in cell biology certainly have to adhere to various methodological standards, the use of 'manipulability' and 'intervention' here is not necessarily committing to the formal constraints of what would count as interventions by Woodward's account.

As a case in point, suppose that in a cell culture dish of dying neurons, the neurons begin to recover under certain natural conditions, thus hinting that halting neuronal death in cell culture is possible. Hence, we have a variation in the cell death phenomenon. Let us then assume that an investigator's quantifiable overexpression of a certain protein in dying neurons recapitulates the said variation in the phenomenon; that is, it halts neuronal death to a certain degree. This now sets the course for researching how and in what causal sequence of resultant changes the intervention on (i.e. overexpression of) the protein ultimately leads to the variation in the phenomenon.

These five tests should not be thought of as individually necessary conditions for a productive research programme leading to a successful mechanistic explanation. Collectively, they are not exhaustive stipulations for a paradigmatic mechanistic explanation. There could surely be further criteria or more exact stipulations for the framework, but the current ones are meant as starting points. Additionally, the tests should not be construed as true-or-false propositions. Even when an explanation fulfils the criteria of a test to a certain degree, the granularity or depth with which those criteria are fulfilled could always be improved upon with refined theoretical work and new empirical findings, and newer questions to investigate could be proposed.

The tests are also not necessarily meant to be hierarchical, but it makes sense for some of them to build on each other. Moreover, a given phenomenon might be explained at least in a rudimentary way even when most of these tests are answered in the negative, that is, if the mechanistic model being investigated is at an early stage of development. But in the case of AD, the mechanistic model and explanation have enough detail to be able to engage with the criteria of each test at an appreciable richness.

Below, each of the tests is applied to the amyloid explanation, marking out specific strengths and shortcomings. The point is to systematically ascertain what the explanation might be missing and how to make it more complete. Furthermore, as introduced above, some of the tests might benefit heuristically from a biological principle that is relevant to their criteria. These opportunities will be highlighted.

- *TEST #1: Is the AD phenomenon set out as unambiguously as possible?*

    The amyloid explanation has, as one of its endpoints, neuronal damage and cell death (beginning in certain parts of the brain, such as the entorhinal cortex). A number of cellular processes leading to Aβ aggregation and NFT formation have been postulated as the cause of such changes. As far as one could tell, the AD field takes *cellular damage* as the reference phenomenon to investigate the disease. This cellular manifestation of AD is, at the very least, defined in relatively unambiguous terms and communicated as such by investigators in the field. One can therefore tentatively say that, for the most part, the answer to this test is *affirmative*.

    Having said that, what the amyloid explanation is currently missing is an exact account of how neuronal death at a single-cell level connects with brain-region-specific damage and how that precisely leads to AD's behavioural symptoms. Thus, there is much work to be done, even though this test is being marked as affirmative.

- *TEST #2: Does the amyloid explanation set out an environment to situate the underlying AD mechanism and refer to decomposable and detectable parts that constitute the mechanism?*

    The amyloid explanation deals within the confines of the environments inside and immediately surrounding single neurons and glial cells. Furthermore, the explanation rests on a number of key protein players such as APP and tau, which are detectable in experimental settings and whose amino acid sequences are known. Therefore, the answer here is also *affirmative*.

    Recall, however, that these tests should not be thought of as true-or-false propositions. For example, what is still missing in the explanation is some account of how, within the densely crowded and highly viscous intracellular environment of the cell, large aggregates of, for instance, tau proteins can even *begin* to form and take up significant intracellular volume. This is not a mere data gap in the explanation; it is a *conceptual* gap that the explanation should cover.

Thus, here again there is much work to be done, even though I have marked the test as affirmative.[14]

- *TEST #3: Are the parts represented in the model the amyloid explanation relies on organised and are they in some form of interaction?*

  Neurons (which are the 'environment' of the amyloid explanation) are quintessential examples of vastly complex network arrangements of proteins, nucleic acids, lipids and other molecular 'parts'. Moreover, the protein players in the explanation are organised into pathways, as outlined in Table 1. Additionally, the chain of direct interactions amongst the parts in either of the (extracellular) Aβ and (intracellular) tau arms of the explanation is clear and is known in some depth. However, the interaction of the parts *between* the two arms of the underlying model is much less clear in the explanation (Bloom, 2014; Love, 2001; Rudenko et al., 2019; Tapia-Rojas et al., 2019). Given that both the extracellular and intracellular pathways are implicated in the pathobiology of the disease, there is strong reason based on the existing model to believe there to be important cross-interactions (Busche & Hyman, 2020; Pascoal et al., 2021),[15] but there is no firm indication yet as to their nature. Hence, the tentative answer here for the amyloid explanation is *negative*. The obvious barrier, and perhaps connection, between the two arms is the *cell membrane*, which spatially separates the internal and external cellular milieus. This possibility will be explored in Sect. 6.

- *TEST #4: Do the relevant interacting parts described in the amyloid explanation exert some form of change on each other via some intermediate means?*

  The question of this test, it may seem, can easily be answered in the affirmative for the cascade of steps that generate the Aβ peptide. For, as detailed in Sect. 3, the very production of the peptide involves changes exerted by one part (one of the 'secretase' enzymes) on another part (the APP protein), for example. But what are the intermediate means? The protein structures and 'active sites' (e.g. of the secretase enzymes that cleave APP) are known and have been the subject of many studies (Dehury et al., 2019; Seegar et al., 2017), and yet, in terms of exactly how the interaction takes place, we have not progressed much beyond relatively basic appeals to electrostatic interactions and hydrogen bonds. Whilst

---

[14] With respect to the properties of the intracellular environment, in the past several years there has been much activity concerning the application of a chemical process called 'phase transition' (i.e. a transition between different states of matter) to neurodegenerative disease research, including AD. The idea behind this application is that protein aggregates found in AD neurons can "form via liquid-to-solid phase transitions" (Mathieu et al., 2020, p. 56). Meanwhile, however, there is no consensus or obvious concern in the AD field as to whether liquid-to-solid phase transitions are governed by a specific biological principle operative in the cell, or if such phase transitions can merely be explained mechanistically without specifying one or more biological principles. This is opportune ground to ask if phase transitions in the cell could actually be explained by a specific hypothesised cellular principle of organisation, and if so, how this would compare with other principles of organisation and provide an independent explanatory window.

[15] Thanks to Lindley Darden (University of Maryland) for bringing this paper to my attention.

we can detect a change exerted upon a protein by another, the means with which the change is exerted is nowhere as intelligible as, for example, detecting the parts themselves, their arrangement and so forth, and much ground needs to be covered to determine exactly how *chemical* principles, such as electrostatic attraction, actually operate at the *protein* and *cellular* scales (see, e.g. Matta, 2006; Zhai et al., 2019). I will therefore mark the answer here as *negative*. As hinted at earlier, it would be immensely useful if chemical principles of interaction could be transformed into a category of principles that would specifically account for *biological* macromolecular interactions. More on this in Sect. 6.

- *TEST #5: Can the amyloid explanation accurately account for the sequence of cellular changes that lead to detectable variation in the AD cellular phenomenon?*

Accounting for detectable variation in the sense of increased protein cleavage, fibrillation and aggregation certainly occupies a central place within the amyloid explanation. Such variations have been painstakingly studied by using, for example, interventions that increase Aβ or tau levels in cultured neurons or in mice and detecting resultant changes in other elements of the presumed underlying mechanism (i.e. parts, interactions, etc.). In addition, certain familial genetic mutations provide *natural* cases of variability of the implicated protein levels. What is still unclear, however, is the certainty and order with which each episode of change can be pinned onto the disease's timeline. As already noted, one of the key open questions in AD research is whether (and to what extent) Aβ aggregation is causative of the disease phenomenon or is protective (Huang et al., 2021; Panza et al., 2019; Sturchio et al., 2021); that is, whether neuronal cell death starts to happen before or after Aβ aggregation begins in any appreciable manner. The same goes for NFT formation by tau: does it happen before, concomitant with, or after plaque formation? Therefore, the sequence of changes (i.e. what happens first, what comes next, etc.) cannot be definitively assigned as of yet. Hence the answer here is *negative*.

These tests applied in the context of the amyloid explanation do two things: first, independent of the issue of biological principles, they can systematically help prioritise which underexplored or missing mechanistic element(s) within the explanation should be investigated and how their discovery could fit into the broader picture of understanding the phenomenon of interest. Second, regardless of the negative or positive assessment of the mechanistic criteria, at least some of the tests could inspire or hint at biological principles or generalisations that could be discovered, adapted or hypothesised to enrich the overall explanation (i.e. the PM explanation) and lead to new research questions. Moreover, a given biological principle might feed back into a particular test that inspired its discovery and help resolve the mechanistic gaps that were identified. How principles might achieve these is the topic of the remaining two sections.

6 Two Biological Principles Relevant to AD

I will begin by describing two hypothetical biological principles that could be candidates for inclusion in a PM investigation of AD. These example principles will help with the discussion in Sect. 7, where more abstract and general aspects of biological principles will be the focus. I should note that proposing and investigating even one novel biological principle and determining its empirical impact requires a dedicated research programme.

I will use two of the paradigmatic tests as a springboard here: Test #3, which had to do with the arrangement and interaction of parts, and Test #4, which was centred on interacting parts exerting some form of change on each other via intermediate means. I argued that a category of biological principles that explain spatiotemporal interactions in the cell and another category that accounts for biological macromolecular interactions could augment our understanding of the criteria picked out in the two tests. To that end, I will propose two principles that I have provisionally termed the 'principle of cellular synchrony' and the 'principle of generative protein domains'. Each falls under one of the two categories.

6.1 Principle of Cellular Synchrony

A few years ago I suggested that the collective vibrations of 'phospholipids' (a class of lipid molecules) that form the cell membrane may act as a *pacemaker* or timekeeping source for cellular processes at a frequency in the picosecond range (i.e. one-trillionth $[10^{-12}]$ of a second) (Ehsani, 2012). Incidentally, this timekeeping proposal bears similarities to observations that physicists studying biological systems made (Adair, 2002; Fröhlich, 1968), an indication that the focus on vibrational behaviour has a clear lineage in biophysics. I should emphasise that this proposal is *not* related to the circadian rhythm (discussed earlier relating to Bechtel, 2017), which pertains to the 24-h timekeeping that happens at an *organism* level and regulates the sleep–wake cycle. Cell membrane vibrations concern an individual cell and at a time regime that is orders of magnitude faster than 1 s. Additionally, there is no connection between this proposal and the pacemaker cells of the heart, which are a group of cells that form an electrical conduction system to control the rate of heart muscle contractions in the order of a few seconds.

There are various methods of attempting to validate the link between cell membrane vibrations and timekeeping in the cell. As the evidence stands to date, the possibility of such a function of the membrane is relatively strong (not discussed further). Building on this possibility, one could posit a *principle of cellular synchrony* that entails that all processes within a cell (e.g. the activity of proteins, intracellular transport, DNA transcription, etc.) happen in a synchronised manner and are cyclically coordinated based on a subsecond vibrational frequency. This further entails that unsynchronised processes may lead to cell death. Such a principle and the notion of a common timing regime answer to the fact that cellular processes have a mind-boggling level of coordination and interdependence (recall, for example, the earlier discussion of mechanisms 'masking' each other; Illari, 2011). Moreover, because membranes are a universal feature of cells from all domains of life (Jekely, 2006), this principle would be expected to be operative in any cell. This is my first example of a 'biological principle'.

Why is this a 'biological' rather than a 'chemical' principle? To be sure, the inherent vibrations of every single phospholipid derive from the molecule's *chemistry*. However, when countless phospholipids come together in a membrane, encapsulate the contents of the cell and produce physical vibrations in unison and that vibrational frequency is transferred across the volume of the cell to affect all the biochemical processes within it, these collectively make the proposed principle a uniquely *biological* one that is operative at a cellular level. Moreover, the principle could be expanded to entail that in a tissue such as the brain, all adjacent cells might potentially have their cellular processes synchronised as well because of direct or indirect membrane contact. This could be an important consequence of the principle because just as processes in individual cells are intricately coordinated, a collection of neurons and other brain cells also need to be 'in sync' in terms of their synaptic communication, production of action potential and many other functions. In AD, for example, the loss of synaptic communication (and consequently coordination) between neurons is thought to be a key pathological step as the disease progresses (Edwards, 2019).

Also, in virtue of the above, no *cellular mechanism*[16] could be said to underlie the principle of cellular synchrony. That is, cell membrane vibrations are not the result of a network of interacting proteins and other molecules in the cell. They essentially happen 'automatically' and 'on their own' because an empty shell of just cell membrane would still have the vibrations. However, the vibrations of *each* phospholipid in the membrane could perhaps be explained with a *chemical* or *molecular* mechanistic explanation along with thermodynamic laws, for example. Thus, even if this principle does admit of further explanation, the explanation is unlikely to be a purely mechanistic one – appealing as it presumably will to thermodynamic laws – and any mechanistic component of the explanation is likely to be at the chemical rather than the biological level.

On the basis of the temporal synchrony that this principle could entail across cellular processes, we might consider it as a member of potential principles of *spatiotemporal interactions*. Going back to Test #3 on how the membrane could bridge the extracellular and intracellular facets of the AD amyloid explanation, a hypothesis that the principle of synchrony brings forth is that both the Aβ peptide and hyperphosphorylated tau might interfere in tandem with the vibrations of the membrane. We know, for example, that extracellular Aβ oligomers "destabilize the [...] membrane's structure, induce a generalized increase in membrane permeability, and insert themselves into the membrane to form cation-conducting pores" (Wang et al., 2016, p. 1914; see also Wang et al., 2021). It has also been reported

---

[16] Here I intend for 'cellular' mechanisms to be distinct from physical or chemical mechanisms.

that the tau protein forms complexes with phospholipids (Ait-Bouziad et al., 2017). And Aβ might in fact directly interact with and facilitate the fibrilization of tau (Vasconcelos et al., 2016).

The interplay of unsynchronised cellular processes and AD pathology, mediated by the membrane and both Aβ and tau, would be a possible new path of investigation. This could lead to novel insights about (i) how the main parts and pathways of the AD mechanistic model could be explained to be connected and (ii) how the pathways interact with and influence each other. This is one scenario in which a new biological principle could *heuristically apply to the elements of a mechanistic explanation*, in this case showing one way of allowing the AD explanation to satisfy the conditions of Test #3. Furthermore, the principle can *independently* (and without necessarily invoking the mechanistic elements) raise the explanatory possibility that AD could, for instance, signal an overall unsynchronised timing amongst cellular processes in a given region of the brain. If such a line of investigation were to be pursued, *quantifications* of the unsynchronised timing of cellular processes might also be studied. For instance, in light of the loss of synaptic communication and coordination, an AD researcher could investigate how long certain cellular processes might be 'off' relative to each other and if this timing difference would increase as the disease progresses.

6.2   Principle of Generative Protein Domains

A second hypothetical biological principle could relate to the geometry and three-dimensional conformation of proteins such as Aβ and tau. In this subsection, I would like to specifically focus on tau, which is taken to be an 'intrinsically disordered' protein (Sabbagh & Dickey, 2016).

Since the 1950s, protein structure has been defined in terms of *domains* or segments that may be of (roughly) three flavours: 'alpha-helical', 'beta-sheet' and 'disordered'. Approximately a third of human proteins are thought to contain disordered segments, and these segments contribute significantly to protein–protein interactions and therefore to protein function (Kim & Chung, 2020).[17] A visual representation of how ordered versus disordered protein domains can be thought of is presented in Fig. 2. A persistent challenge, however, has been that there is no overarching explanatory theory of what a disordered domain is and how it could systematically be conceptualised.

But what if disordered proteins are not really 'disordered' after all? Commentators on the physics of 'order' and 'chaos', or 'patterned' and 'patternless'

---

[17] A helpful overview of this topic is provided in Schmid and Hugel (2020, p. 2) as follows: "proteins are often flexible and will change shape, much like a tree in the wind. Nevertheless, for some of the activities that it performs, a protein must adopt one specific shape. Therefore, the likelihood that the protein will take on this specific shape directly determines how efficiently that protein can perform a specific job". See also Aprile et al. (2021) and Yeates (2019).

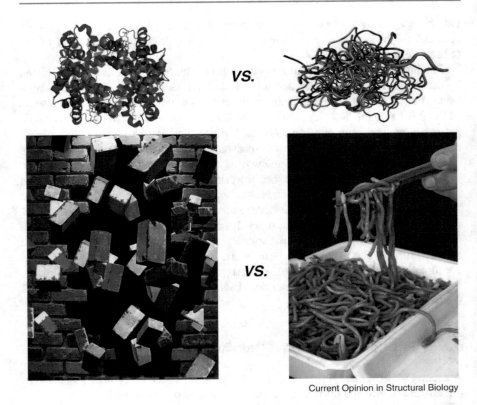

Current Opinion in Structural Biology

Fig. 2 Representations of ordered and disordered proteins. This figure from Uversky (2017) depicts a multidomain ordered protein (an alpha-helical protein) (top left) and a disordered protein (top right). The structural and conformational rigidities of the *domains* within these two types of protein structure are compared to bricks versus noodles. However, is a protein that contains a disordered domain – such as the tau protein (which is actually entirely disordered) – really without any particularly constant shape (like a strand of noodle) or is it perhaps 'structured' in some other way? Related to this discussion, as shown in the figure, are also the notions of stability and resilience: "taking a few or even just one brick can lead to the collapse of the wall, whereas a bowl of noodles remains a bowl of noodles even after many noodles are eaten" (Uversky, 2017, p. 26). Reproduced with permission from Uversky, 2017; copyright Elsevier

phenomena, do not usually entertain a *third* possibility, one that would in principle be neither ordered nor disordered (Crutchfield, 2012).[18] Truly envisioning what a third possibility could be may perhaps be beyond human cognitive capacity, but there have been attempts toward such a goal (see, e.g. Clouser et al., 2019; Sormanni et al., 2017).

---

[18] Guttinger (2021) discusses a process ontology of intrinsically disordered proteins.

Within this context, one could propose a *principle of generative protein domains* that states that so-called disordered protein domains might be 'generative' domains in that they can assume *multiple* precise structures that are appropriate to their immediate cellular environment and interacting partners. The possible structures that a disordered domain could assume might be dependent on the complex balance of a number of factors, including (i) the *chemical* interactions (electrostatic and non-electrostatic) within the protein domain itself (amongst its different amino acids) and between different domains of the same or another protein; (ii) the *geometrical* constraints of the protein (e.g. some structural configurations might simply be geometrically impossible for the protein macromolecule); and (iii) the *physicochemical* properties of the cellular fluid or medium surrounding the protein (its composition, viscosity, etc.) and those properties' effects on the domain's structure.

The factors stipulated for this principle could potentially be operative on any protein domain, regardless of its 'orderedness'. However, it is reasonable to assume that for ordered domains (alpha-helical and beta-sheet), the influence of the first factor (i.e. chemical interactions amongst a domain's amino acids) might be so overwhelming that it outweighs the contributions of the other two factors. This is due to the prevailing notion that the single (albeit dynamic) structure of ordered domains can be entirely explained by chemical properties at the protein sequence level (Söding, 2017) and that these domains assume the same 'constant' structure in most cellular contexts. The principle of generative protein domains can be assigned to the *biological macromolecular interactions* category, and since it is wholly concerned with proteins in cells, it is unambiguously a *biological* principle that is operative at a cellular level.

Could this principle, similar to the principle of cellular synchrony, also be counted as ontologically distinct from cellular mechanistic explanations? I argue that it can, given that it fundamentally concerns the internal and external *chemistry* of proteins. Because of this, it might only be possible to posit *chemical* mechanisms underwriting it, if at all. Consider that we are not dealing with a small molecule interacting with its surrounding medium in the cytoplasm or the geometrical constraints of a few atoms. A protein is a *macro*molecule with potentially many properties that cannot entirely be explained by chemical mechanisms and thermo-dynamic laws (Jiang et al., 2018).

Taking the principle of generative protein domains as *explaining* the structure of disordered protein domains, one could posit that in *certain cellular milieus*, the tau protein may indeed have a precise and constant structure (i.e. a constrained structure without any significant variance), albeit not alpha-helical or beta-sheet ordered. One implication is that the tau protein sequence might be able to 'generate' different three-dimensional structures depending on its hyperphosphorylation status (a geometric and chemical change), and/or on whether it is in the intracellular fluid or interacting with the membrane (a change of medium). This could actually also go some way toward accounting for the *multiple roles* that a disordered protein could have in the cell (see, e.g. Olivieri et al., 2020). The generative protein domains principle could thus help *explain facets of the behaviour of tau in AD neurons independent of the amyloid explanation.*

At the same time, however, the potential implications of this principle could inform the problem highlighted in Test #4. There, a problem was that the current conception of how two proteins interact is tenuous: "in terms of exactly how the interaction takes place, we have not progressed much beyond relatively basic appeals to electrostatic interactions and hydrogen bonds" (Sect. 5). Obtaining new insights on the dynamics of tau's structure could lead to clues about its interaction with other 'ordered' and 'disordered' proteins. The principle might also eventually lead to *quantifications* of the extent to which the interaction between such proteins is dictated by electrostatic forces and hydrogen bonds, and how much – as suggested by the principle's stipulations – is shaped by the medium surrounding the proteins and the mutual geometrical constraints of their interacting domains. We might thus be able to quantify the *strength* of tau's interaction with its key interacting protein partners in the AD amyloid explanation.

The principles of cellular synchrony and generative protein domains are just two examples of potential biological principles that could be hypothesised based on the problems at hand. For each of these principles, one could ask what *parameters* (i.e. context-dependent and changeable factors similar to a temperature variable in a thermodynamic law) could fine-tune the principle. In the case of the cellular synchrony principle, the 'rigidity' of the cell membrane could be a possible parameter, whereby the more rigid the membrane, the lower its vibrational frequency might be expected to be. The rigidity could be dictated by, for instance, how tightly packed the membrane is of phospholipids. In the case of the generative domains principle, potential parameters are indeed stipulated in the principle itself, such as the composition or the viscosity of the medium surrounding the protein. All such parameters need to be validated experimentally.

In all, the examples in this section were meant to demonstrate how the discovery of biological principles could go hand in hand with the elucidation of the mechanistic elements of a mechanistic explanation brought about by the paradigmatic tests. Moreover, the two hypothesised principles showed how biological principles might have both non-mechanistic and mechanistic effects on the overall explanation: They might do independent explanatory work, and they might also act as heuristics for making mechanistic explanations more 'complete'. The next section moves away from the specifics of the examples in this section to draw more general claims about the place of biological principles in a PM explanation.

7   Biological Principles and Mechanistic Explanations

The examples of the principles of cellular synchrony and generative protein domains can help crystallise some general properties about biological principles. Starting with their non-mechanistic effects on the overall explanation, one might initially ask how biological principles would fit into the broader notion of scientific laws. Indeed, in the special sciences (basically any natural science other than fundamental physics), it is hard to come by generalisations that can act as almost universal laws that, as noted previously, are characterised by "universality, inviolable necessity, or unrestricted scope" (Craver & Tabery, 2019, §4.1).[19]

Philosophers of science usually discuss patterns and generalisations in fields like biology under the framework of ceteris paribus laws – that is, laws that hold when *other things are (held) equal*. These laws are essentially generalisations that admit of various context-dependent exceptions and therefore can be thought of as a category of non-exceptionless generalisations – that is, generalisations that include exceptions (Fenton-Glynn, 2016). The discussion of ceteris paribus laws traces its history to the economic sciences but has been applied and critiqued in all branches of the special sciences. For reasons that will be discussed in future work (Ehsani, 2022), in this chapter, the generalisations concerning cell biology that I call 'principles' approximate what some philosophers of science mean by ceteris paribus laws or 'invariant generalisations'.

Some further points also need to be made about the word 'biological' in 'biological principles'. First, principles or laws from the broader *life sciences* could be applied to cell biology. Foremost amongst these are evolutionary principles (Linquist et al., 2016), which generally apply at a *cell population* level. Indeed, many forms of generalisations that cell biologists may know as 'principles' or 'laws' fall within the purview of observational patterns or conjectures in (i) evolution (e.g. concerning genetic plasticity; Hannan, 2018), (ii) zoology (e.g. concerning tissue patterning; Barkai & Shilo, 2020), (iii) ecology or (iv) biogeography and can often have a mathematical form. Second, a motivation for the PM framework is to argue that biological principles for cellular phenomena should be recognised as being distinct from – but connected to – the laws and principles of thermodynamics, evolution, ecology and other related fields.[20]

With these distinctions in mind, how could biological principles deliver independent explanatory work? To begin with, consider, for example, that the principle of cellular synchrony could potentially account for the collective unsynchronised behaviour of a group of adjacent neurons in AD patients without referencing any particular mechanistic explanation, such as the amyloid explanation. The

---

[19] An example is Newton's law of universal gravitation. Even then, however, one needs to be cognisant of the effect of electrical force between charged bodies (see Elgin, 2017, p. 25).

[20] Arguments regarding the distinctiveness of biological principles could be varied and draw from many sources. As a case in point, Marc Lange, in a chapter on "what would natural laws in the life sciences be", writes that "a biological generalization can possess a distinctive variety of necessity – can be a biological law. Associated with this distinctive necessity is a range of invariance under counterfactual antecedents that is broader in some respects than the range of invariance exhibited by the fundamental physical laws" (Lange, 2013, p. 83). Beyond broadness, the distinctiveness of biological principles can also stem from the uniqueness of *cellular* phenomena compared to physical and chemical phenomena. Of note, the discussion of biological principles could just as well cover *organism*-level phenomena, but an in-depth explanation of such phenomena (bearing in mind that an organism is made up of a vast number of different cells) would necessarily be much more complex. Here I have restricted the scope of biological principles only to the phenomena of the cell, which is biology's basic unit of study.

principle could stipulate a common reaction timing regime for some number of cells and, if an investigator so chooses, 'explain' AD cellular phenomena completely non-mechanistically. This line of study could also facilitate the prediction and 'expectability' (Deulofeu & Suárez, 2018) of what might happen in the brain as the disease progresses.[21]

This brings to mind how thermodynamic laws allow a chemist to feel confident, to a certain extent, about what to expect before a reaction is initiated. This does not mean that thermodynamic laws would necessarily lead to the exact prediction of a reaction's outcome (although that is certainly an ultimate goal); instead, it means whether to simply expect the reaction to be endothermic or not, for example. Importantly, the predictive power biological principles facilitate might additionally make the explanation more quantitative, as was described for the two examples: the principle on cellular timekeeping could lead to measurements of the differences in cellular process times, and the principle on disordered protein domains could lead to better quantifications of the strength of protein–protein interactions.

Moving next to the mechanistic explanatory effects of biological principles, recall from Sect. 5 that at least some of the mechanistic criteria the paradigmatic tests picked out could in theory be explained by one or more hypothesised biological principles. The principles could help bring general information to bear on the mechanistic explanation and thus be utilised to (i) understand its various facets, such as the nature of the parts or their interactions (as the generative protein domains principle did for protein structure), and (ii) move toward the resolution of the potentially missing elements of the mechanistic explanation (as the cellular synchrony principle did to bridge the extracellular and intracellular facets of the amyloid explanation).

The mechanistic explanatory effects of principles, I would argue, might complement and fit into at least a segment of current NM investigations, such as the principles of organisation (or design principles) that were alluded to earlier (Bechtel, 2017). However, to what extent this generalises across NM-related investigations is a matter of debate. As quoted in Sect. 4, Cartwright and colleagues are of the opinion that a mechanism's 'regular behaviour' "is what it takes for some set of principles that govern the features of M's parts in their arrangement in M all to be instanced together" (Cartwright et al., 2020, p. 18). On the other hand, Beate Krickel argues that "the new mechanists could in principle accept that [. . .] the interactions between mechanistic components are governed by laws (which they usually do not) but that it does not follow that laws or expectability adds any explanatory power to a mechanistic explanation" (Krickel, 2020, p. 8). This chapter's arguments, however, suggest that biological principles have the potential to increase the explanatory power of mechanistic explanations of cellular phenomena in a heuristic manner. Furthermore, the principles themselves might independently explain certain facets

---

[21] There is pertinent discussion to be had about the independent explanatory work of biological principles and the literature on 'grounding' (e.g. Trogdon, 2018) that I shall postpone to future work.

of the target phenomenon, thereby increasing the explanatory power of the *overall* explanation (which I have called the PM explanation).

To recap, the goal of the PM framework is to discover and apply biological principles or generalisations that are operative in a biological cell. The principles could have independent explanatory power that would aid in prediction and expectability. Biological principles could also make various components of the mechanistic explanation more complete, thereby also increasing the depth of the mechanistic share of the overall explanation.

8   Conclusions

In this chapter, I argued that various strands of clinical evidence point to the conclusion that the existing and widely accepted amyloid cascade mechanistic explanation of Alzheimer's disease (AD) appears to be fundamentally incomplete. I proposed that a 'principled mechanism' (PM) theoretical framework has the potential to inspire new sets of empirical questions and novel avenues of investigation that can take a given mechanistic explanation at any stage of development as its starting point. PM is a two-pronged framework. First, using a short series of 'tests', it systematically compares different components of the mechanistic explanation against a paradigmatic set of criteria and hints at various ways to make the mechanistic explanation more complete. Second, it makes an appeal for the discovery and application of 'biological principles' relevant to the phenomenon being explained. Next, I detailed two hypothetical biological principles, one having to do with 'time' at the cellular level and the other concerning the structure of 'disordered' protein domains, and how they could each inform and improve different aspects of the amyloid explanation of AD. Using these examples, I argued that biological principles are 'principles' because they approximate what some philosophers mean by ceteris paribus laws or 'invariant generalisations', and they are 'biological' because they operate at and are specific to the level of a biological cell. Such principles could aid in several ways, such as augmenting different facets of the mechanistic explanation but also allowing further independent nomological explanation of the phenomenon. Whilst this strategy can be complementary to certain New Mechanist approaches, an important distinction of the PM framework is its equal attention to the explanatory utility of biological principles.

Overall, PM can help move cell biological investigations from what might be called a generally 'mechanistic-descriptive' state (the status quo) to a 'mechanistic-nomological' paradigm, entailing theoretical biological generalisations alongside mechanistic accounts. If the purpose of an AD research programme is to arrive at a deeper form of biological explanation that would enable researchers to move toward finding effective treatments, and in doing so introduce the field to hitherto uninvestigated paths of enquiry, then the PM approach can be useful by making the current AD amyloid model and resultant explanation much more adequate for purpose (see Parker, 2020). Moreover, the PM framework could just as easily be applied to other biomedical domains, such as mechanistic explanations in research about cancer, diabetes or cardiovascular disease, and to explanations for physiological cellular phenomena.

Ultimately, a broader goal of the case study in this chapter is to show that what is perceived by some to be a fragmentation between analytic philosophy and biomedicine is artificial and unhelpful, and that progress can be made when philosophical approaches are directed at open and neglected problems concerning the biological cell (see Ehsani, 2020).

Acknowledgments I would like to convey my many thanks to Luke Fenton-Glynn (UCL Philosophy) and Phyllis Illari (UCL Science and Technology Studies) for their careful reading of and very helpful comments on this manuscript. An earlier draft of the chapter was posted on 30 May 2021 on the *PhilSci-Archive* preprint server (http://philsci-archive.pitt.edu/19123/). This chapter is dedicated to the memory of Eshrat Khazaeinejad.

References

Adair, R. K. (2002). Vibrational resonances in biological systems at microwave frequencies. *Biophysical Journal, 82*(3), 1147–1152.

Aisen, P. (2019). Comment on "End of the BACE inhibitors? Elenbecestat trials halted amid safety concerns" by J. Shugart. *Alzforum*. Retrieved from https://www.alzforum.org/news/research-news/end-bace-inhibitors-elenbecestat-trials-halted-amid-safety-concerns#comment-32966

Ait-Bouziad, N., Lv, G., Mahul-Mellier, A. L., Xiao, S., Zorludemir, G., Eliezer, D., Walz, D., & Lashuel, H. A. (2017). Discovery and characterization of stable and toxic Tau/phospholipid oligomeric complexes. *Nature Communications, 8*(1), 1678.

Alleva, K., Diez, J., & Federico, L. (2017). Models, theory structure and mechanisms in biochemistry: The case of allosterism. *Studies in History and Philosophy of Biological and Biomedical Sciences, 63*, 1–14.

Alzheimer, A., Stelzmann, R. A., Schnitzlein, H. N., & Murtagh, F. R. (1995). An English translation of Alzheimer's 1907 paper, "Uber eine eigenartige Erkankung der Hirnrinde". *Clinical Anatomy, 8*(6), 429–431.

Aprile, F. A., Temussi, P. A., & Pastore, A. (2021). Man does not live by intrinsically unstructured proteins alone: The role of structured regions in aggregation. *BioEssays, 43*(11), e2100178.

Arendt, T., Stieler, J., Strijkstra, A. M., Hut, R. A., Rudiger, J., Van der Zee, E. A., Harkany, T., Holzer, M., & Hartig, W. (2003). Reversible paired helical filament-like phosphorylation of tau is an adaptive process associated with neuronal plasticity in hibernating animals. *The Journal of Neuroscience, 23*(18), 6972–6981.

Barkai, N., & Shilo, B. Z. (2020). Reconstituting tissue patterning. *Science, 370*(6514), 292–293.

Bechtel, W. (2011). Mechanism and biological explanation. *Philosophy of Science, 78*(4), 533–557.

Bechtel, W. (2017). Explaining features of fine-grained phenomena using abstract analyses of phenomena and mechanisms: Two examples from chronobiology. *Synthese(S.I.: Abstraction and Idealization in Scientific Modelling), 2017*, 1–23.

Bechtel, W., & Abrahamsen, A. (2005). Explanation: A mechanist alternative. *Studies in History and Philosophy of Biological and Biomedical Sciences, 36*(2), 421–441.

Bechtel, W., & Richardson, R. C. (2010). *Discovering complexity: Decomposition and localization as strategies in scientific research.* MIT Press.

Beyreuther, K., & Masters, C. L. (1991). Amyloid precursor protein (APP) and beta A4 amyloid in the etiology of Alzheimer's disease: Precursor-product relationships in the derangement of neuronal function. *Brain Pathology, 1*(4), 241–251.

Blackburn, S. (2016). *The Oxford Dictionary of Philosophy* (3rd ed.). Oxford University Press.

Bloom, G. S. (2014). Amyloid-beta and tau: the trigger and bullet in Alzheimer disease pathogenesis. *JAMA Neurology, 71*(4), 505–508.

Bogen, J. (2020). Theory and observation in science. In E. N. Zalta (Ed.), *The Stanford Encyclopedia of Philosophy*. Stanford University.

Brini, E., Simmerling, C., & Dill, K. (2020). Protein storytelling through physics. *Science, 370*(6520), eaaz3041.

Busche, M. A., & Hyman, B. T. (2020). Synergy between amyloid-beta and tau in Alzheimer's disease. *Nature Neuroscience, 23*(10), 1183–1193.

Cairns, D. M., Rouleau, N., Parker, R. N., Walsh, K. G., Gehrke, L., & Kaplan, D. L. (2020). A 3D human brain-like tissue model of herpes-induced Alzheimer's disease. *Science Advances, 6*(19), eaay8828.

Cartwright, N., Pemberton, J., & Wieten, S. (2020). Mechanisms, laws and explanation. *European Journal for Philosophy of Science, 10*(25).

Clouser, A. F., Baughman, H. E., Basanta, B., Guttman, M., Nath, A., & Klevit, R. E. (2019). Interplay of disordered and ordered regions of a human small heat shock protein yields an ensemble of 'quasi-ordered' states. *Elife, 8*, e50259.

Craver, C. F., & Kaiser, M. I. (2013). Mechanisms and laws: Clarifying the debate. In H.-K. Chao, S.-T. Chen, & R. L. Millstein (Eds.), *Mechanism and causality in biology and economics* (pp. 125–145). Springer.

Craver, C. F., & Tabery, J. (2019). Mechanisms in science. In E. N. Zalta (Ed.), *The Stanford Encyclopedia of Philosophy*. Stanford University.

Crutchfield, J. P. (2012). Between order and chaos. *Nature Physics, 8*, 17–24.

Da Mesquita, S., Papadopoulos, Z., Dykstra, T., Brase, L., Farias, F. G., Wall, M., Jiang, H., Kodira, C. D., de Lima, K. A., Herz, J., Louveau, A., Goldman, D. H., Salvador, A. F., Onengut-Gumuscu, S., Farber, E., Dabhi, N., Kennedy, T., Milam, M. G., Baker, W., . . . Kipnis, J. (2021). Meningeal lymphatics affect microglia responses and anti-Aβ immunotherapy. *Nature, 593*(7858), 255–260.

Dear, A. J., Michaels, T. C. T., Meisl, G., Klenerman, D., Wu, S., Perrett, S., Linse, S., Dobson, C. M., & Knowles, T. P. J. (2020). Kinetic diversity of amyloid oligomers. *Proceedings of the National Academy of Sciences of the United States of America, 117*(22), 12087–12094.

Dehury, B., Tang, N., & Kepp, K. P. (2019). Molecular dynamics of C99-bound gamma-secretase reveal two binding modes with distinct compactness, stability, and active-site retention: Implications for Abeta production. *The Biochemical Journal, 476*(7), 1173–1189.

Dekkers, W., & Rikkert, M. O. (2006). What is a genetic cause? The example of Alzheimer's Disease. *Medicine, Health Care, and Philosophy, 9*(3), 273–284.

Deulofeu, R., & Suárez, J. (2018). When mechanisms are not enough: The origin of eukaryotes and scientific explanation. In A. Christian, D. Hommen, N. Retzlaff, & G. Schurz (Eds.), *Philosophy of science: Between the natural sciences, the social sciences, and the humanities* (pp. 95–115). Springer.

Díez, J. (2014). Scientific w-explanation as ampliative, specialized embedding: A neo-hempelian account. *Erkenntnis, 79*, 1413–1443.

Dijksterhuis, E. J. (1961). *The mechanization of the world picture* (C. Dikshoorn, Trans.). Oxford University Press.

Dunn, B., Stein, P., Temple, R., & Cavazzoni, P. (2021). An appropriate use of accelerated approval - Aducanumab for Alzheimer's disease. *The New England Journal of Medicine, 385*(9), 856–857.

Edwards, F. A. (2019). A unifying hypothesis for Alzheimer's disease: From plaques to neurodegeneration. *Trends in Neurosciences, 42*(5), 310–322.

Ehsani, S. (2012). Time in the cell: a plausible role for the plasma membrane. arXiv: 1210.0168.

Ehsani, S. (2020). Analytic philosophy for biomedical research: The imperative of applying yesterday's timeless messages to today's impasses. In P. Glauner & P. Plugmann (Eds.), *Innovative technologies for market leadership: Investing in the future* (pp. 167–200). Springer.

Ehsani, S. (2022). Generalizations for cell biological explanations: distinguishing between principles and laws. *In preparation*.

Elgin, C. Z. (2017). *True enough.* MIT Press.

Feinman, R. D., & Fine, E. J. (2004). "A calorie is a calorie" violates the second law of thermodynamics. *Nutrition Journal, 3*, 9.

Fenton-Glynn, L. (2016). *Ceteris paribus* laws and *minutis rectis* laws. *Philosophy and Phenomenological Research, 93*(2), 274–305.

Franklin-Hall, L. R. (2016). New mechanistic explanation and the need for explanatory constraints. In K. Aizawa & C. Gillett (Eds.), *Scientific composition and metaphysical ground* (pp. 41–74). Palgrave Macmillan.

Frigg, R., & Nguyen, J. (2016). The fiction view of models reloaded. *The Monist, 99*(3), 225–242.

Fröhlich, H. (1968). Long-range coherence and energy storage in biological systems. *International Journal of Quantum Chemistry, 2*(5), 641–649.

Fulco, C. P., Nasser, J., Jones, T. R., Munson, G., Bergman, D. T., Subramanian, V., Grossman, S. R., Anyoha, R., Doughty, B. R., Patwardhan, T. A., Nguyen, T. H., Kane, M., Perez, E. M., Durand, N. C., Lareau, C. A., Stamenova, E. K., Aiden, E. L., Lander, E. S., & Engreitz, J. M. (2019). Activity-by-contact model of enhancer-promoter regulation from thousands of CRISPR perturbations. *Nature Genetics, 51*(12), 1664–1669.

Gaffney, D. J. (2019). Mapping and predicting gene-enhancer interactions. *Nature Genetics, 51*(12), 1662–1663.

Glennan, S. (2017). *The new mechanical philosophy.* Oxford University Press.

Glennan, S., & Illari, P. (2017). Varieties of mechanisms. In S. Glennan & P. Illari (Eds.), *The Routledge handbook of mechanisms and mechanical philosophy* (pp. 91–103). Routledge.

Green, S. (2015). Revisiting generality in biology: Systems biology and the quest for design principles. *Biology & Philosophy, 30*, 629–652.

Green, S., & Jones, N. (2016). Constraint-based reasoning for search and explanation: Strategies for understanding variation and patterns in biology. *Dialectica, 70*(3), 343–374.

Guttenplan, K. A., Weigel, M. K., Prakash, P., Wijewardhane, P. R., Hasel, P., Rufen-Blanchette, U., Münch, A. E., Blum, J. A., Fine, J., Neal, M. C., Bruce, K. D., Gitler, A. D., Chopra, G., Liddelow, S. A., & Barres, B. A. (2021). Neurotoxic reactive astrocytes induce cell death via saturated lipids. *Nature, 599*(7883), 102–107.

Guttinger, S. (2021). Process and practice: Understanding the nature of molecules. *HYLE, 27*, 47–66.

Hammond, M., & Newton, T. (2020). We need to radically rethink our approach to Alzheimer's research. *Wired UK.* Retrieved from https://www.wired.co.uk/article/alzheimers-research

Hannan, A. J. (2018). Tandem repeats mediating genetic plasticity in health and disease. *Nature Reviews Genetics, 19*(5), 286–298.

Hardy, J., & Allsop, D. (1991). Amyloid deposition as the central event in the aetiology of Alzheimer's disease. *Trends in Pharmacological Sciences, 12*(10), 383–388.

Hempel, C. G. (1965). *Aspects of scientific explanation and other essays in the philosophy of science* (pp. 331–496). Free Press.

Hempel, C. G. (1968). Maximal specificity and lawlikeness in probabilistic explanation. *Philosophy of Science, 35*(2), 116–133.

Henderson, N. C., Rieder, F., & Wynn, T. A. (2020). Fibrosis: From mechanisms to medicines. *Nature, 587*(7835), 555–566.

Huang, Y., Happonen, K. E., Burrola, P. G., O'Connor, C., Hah, N., Huang, L., Nimmerjahn, A., & Lemke, G. (2021). Microglia use TAM receptors to detect and engulf amyloid beta plaques. *Nature Immunology, 22*(5), 586–594.

Illari, P. (2011). Mechanistic evidence: Disambiguating the Russo-Williamson thesis. *International Studies in the Philosophy of Science, 25*(2), 139–157.

Ishii, M., & Iadecola, C. (2020). Risk factor for Alzheimer's disease breaks the blood-brain barrier. *Nature, 581*(7806), 31–32.

Jacobs, H. I. L., Becker, J. A., Kwong, K., Engels-Dominguez, N., Prokopiou, P. C., Papp, K. V., Properzi, M., Hampton, O. L., d'Oleire Uquillas, F., Sanchez, J. S., Rentz, D. M., El Fakhri, G., Normandin, M. D., Price, J. C., Bennett, D. A., Sperling, R. A., & Johnson, K. A. (2021).

In vivo and neuropathology data support locus coeruleus integrity as indicator of Alzheimer's disease pathology and cognitive decline. *Science Translational Medicine, 13*(612), eabj2511.

Jekely, G. (2006). Did the last common ancestor have a biological membrane? *Biology Direct, 1*, 35.

Jiang, Q., Teufel, A. I., Jackson, E. L., & Wilke, C. O. (2018). Beyond thermodynamic constraints: Evolutionary sampling generates realistic protein sequence variation. *Genetics, 208*(4), 1387–1395.

Kim, J. Y., & Chung, H. S. (2020). Disordered proteins follow diverse transition paths as they fold and bind to a partner. *Science, 368*(6496), 1253–1257.

Kontos, P. C. (2004). Ethnographic reflections on selfhood, embodiment and Alzheimer's disease. *Ageing & Society, 24*, 829–849.

Krickel, B. (2020). Reply to Cartwright, Pemberton, Wieten: "Mechanisms, laws and explanation". *European Journal for Philosophy of Science, 10*(43), 1–9.

Kuhn, T. S. (1962). *The structure of scientific revolutions*. The University of Chicago Press.

Kundu, K., Darden, L., & Moult, J. (2021). MecCog: A knowledge representation framework for genetic disease mechanism. *Bioinformatics, 37*(22), 4180–4186.

Lange, M. (2013). What would natural laws in the life sciences be? In K. Kampourakis (Ed.), *The philosophy of biology: A companion for educators* (pp. 67–85). Springer.

Leuridan, B. (2010). Can mechanisms really replace laws of nature? *Philosophy of Science, 77*(3), 317–340.

Li, Z., & Zhao, N. (2021). A water pill against Alzheimer's disease. *Nature Aging, 1*(10), 868–869.

Linquist, S., Gregory, T. R., Elliott, T. A., Saylor, B., Kremer, S. C., & Cottenie, K. (2016). Yes! There are resilient generalizations (or "laws") in ecology. *The Quarterly Review of Biology, 91*(2), 119–131.

Liu, P. P., Xie, Y., Meng, X. Y., & Kang, J. S. (2019). History and progress of hypotheses and clinical trials for Alzheimer's disease. *Signal Transduction and Targeted Therapy, 4*, 29.

Llored, J.-P. (2011). The role and the status of thermodynamics in quantum chemistry calculations. In J. C. Moreno-Piraján (Ed.), *Thermodynamics: Interaction studies – Solids, liquids and gases* (pp. 469–490). IntechOpen.

Lombrozo, T. (2011). The instrumental value of explanations. *Philosophy Compass, 6*(8), 539–551.

Love, R. (2001). Untangling the relation between beta-amyloid and tau. *Lancet, 358*(9282), 645.

Lu, K., Nicholas, J. M., Pertzov, Y., Grogan, J., Husain, M., Pavisic, I. M., James, S.-N., Parker, T. D., Lane, C. A., Keshavan, A., Keuss, S. E., Buchanan, S. M., Murray-Smith, H., Cash, D. M., Malone, I. B., Sudre, C. H., Coath, W., Wong, A., Henley, S. M. D., . . . Crutch, S. J. (2021). Dissociable effects of APOE ε4 and β-amyloid pathology on visual working memory. *Nature Aging, 1*, 1002–1009.

Machamer, P., Darden, L., & Craver, C. F. (2000). Thinking about mechanisms. *Philosophy of Science, 67*(1), 1–25.

Marder, E. (2020). Words without meaning. *Elife, 9*, e54867.

Masters, C. L. (2019). Comment on "Electrode detects Aβ aggregates in Alzheimer's plasma" by G. D. Zakaib. *Alzforum*. Retrieved from https://www.alzforum.org/news/research-news/electrode-detects-av-aggregates-alzheimers-plasma#comment-31421

Mathieu, C., Pappu, R. V., & Taylor, J. P. (2020). Beyond aggregation: Pathological phase transitions in neurodegenerative disease. *Science, 370*(6512), 56–60.

Matta, C. F. (2006). Hydrogen-hydrogen bonding: The non-electrostatic limit of closed-shell interaction between two hydrogen atoms. A critical review. In S. J. Grabowski (Ed.), *Hydrogen bonding - New insights* (pp. 337–375). Springer.

Mintun, M. A., Lo, A. C., Duggan Evans, C., Wessels, A. M., Ardayfio, P. A., Andersen, S. W., Shcherbinin, S., Sparks, J. D., Sims, J. R., Brys, M., Apostolova, L. G., Salloway, S. P., & Skovronsky, D. M. (2021). Donanemab in early Alzheimer's disease. *The New England Journal of Medicine, 384*(18), 1691–1704.

Moir, R. D., Lathe, R., & Tanzi, R. E. (2018). The antimicrobial protection hypothesis of Alzheimer's disease. *Alzheimer's & Dementia, 14*(12), 1602–1614.

Mullard, A. (2021). Landmark Alzheimer's drug approval confounds research community. *Nature, 594*(7863), 309–310.

Nasser, J., Bergman, D. T., Fulco, C. P., Guckelberger, P., Doughty, B. R., Patwardhan, T. A., Jones, T. R., Nguyen, T. H., Ulirsch, J. C., Lekschas, F., Mualim, K., Natri, H. M., Weeks, E. M., Munson, G., Kane, M., Kang, H. Y., Cui, A., Ray, J. P., Eisenhaure, T. M., . . . Dey, K. (2021). Genome-wide enhancer maps link risk variants to disease genes. *Nature, 593*(7858), 238–243.

Newton-Smith, W. H. (1981). *The rationality of science*. Routledge & Kegan Paul.

Nordenfelt, L. (2006). Commentary on Wim Dekkers's and Marcel Olde Rikkert's: "What is a genetic disease? The example of Alzheimer's Disease", and Stephen Tyreman's: "Causes of illness in clinical practice: a conceptual exploration". *Medicine, Health Care, and Philosophy, 9*(3), 317–319.

NTNU. (2020). Norway's Nobel laureates take up the fight against Alzheimer's. *EurekAlert*. Retrieved from https://www.eurekalert.org/news-releases/568016

Olivieri, C., Wang, Y., Li, G. C., Manu, V. S., Kim, J., Stultz, B. R., Neibergall, M., Porcelli, F., Muretta, J. M., Thomas, D. D., Gao, J., Blumenthal, D. K., Taylor, S. S., & Veglia, G. (2020). Multi-state recognition pathway of the intrinsically disordered protein kinase inhibitor by protein kinase A. *Elife, 9*, e55607.

Olson, E. T., & Witt, K. (2020). Against person essentialism. *Mind, 129*(515), 715–735.

Panza, F., Lozupone, M., Logroscino, G., & Imbimbo, B. P. (2019). A critical appraisal of amyloid-beta-targeting therapies for Alzheimer disease. *Nature Reviews Neurology, 15*(2), 73–88.

Park, L., Hochrainer, K., Hattori, Y., Ahn, S. J., Anfray, A., Wang, G., Uekawa, K., Seo, J., Palfini, V., Blanco, I., Acosta, D., Eliezer, D., Zhou, P., Anrather, J., & Iadecola, C. (2020). Tau induces PSD95-neuronal NOS uncoupling and neurovascular dysfunction independent of neurodegeneration. *Nature Neuroscience, 23*(9), 1079–1089.

Parker, W. S. (2020). Model evaluation: An adequacy-for-purpose view. *Philosophy of Science, 87*(3), 457–477.

Pascoal, T. A., Benedet, A. L., Ashton, N. J., Kang, M. S., Therriault, J., Chamoun, M., Savard, M., Lussier, F. Z., Tissot, C., Karikari, T. K., Ottoy, J., Mathotaarachchi, S., Stevenson, J., Massarweh, G., Schöll, M., de Leon, M. J., Soucy, J.-P., Edison, P., Blennow, K., . . . Rosa-Neto, P. (2021). Microglial activation and tau propagate jointly across Braak stages. *Nature Medicine, 27*(9), 1592–1599.

Pastore, A., Raimondi, F., Rajendran, L., & Temussi, P. A. (2020). Why does the Abeta peptide of Alzheimer share structural similarity with antimicrobial peptides? *Communications Biology, 3*(1), 135.

Pearl, J., & Mackenzie, D. (2018). *The book of why: The new science of cause and effect*. Basic Books.

Petsko, G. A. (2018). Comment on "Crystal structure of Aβ and proposed receptor solved" by G. D. Zakaib. *Alzforum*. Retrieved from https://www.alzforum.org/news/research-news/crystal-structure-av-and-proposed-receptor-solved#comment-29171

PLOS Medicine Editors. (2016). Dementia across the lifespan and around the globe-pathophysiology, prevention, treatment, and societal impact: A call for papers. *PLoS Medicine, 13*(8), e1002117.

Richardson, J. O., Perez, C., Lobsiger, S., Reid, A. A., Temelso, B., Shields, G. C., Kisiel, Z., Wales, D. J., Pate, B. H., & Althorpe, S. C. (2016). Concerted hydrogen-bond breaking by quantum tunneling in the water hexamer prism. *Science, 351*(6279), 1310–1313.

Rogers, M. B. (2022). CMS plans to limit Aduhelm coverage to clinical trials. *Alzforum*. Retrieved from https://www.alzforum.org/news/research-news/cms-plans-limit-aduhelm-coverage-clinical-trials

Rudenko, L. K., Wallrabe, H., Periasamy, A., Siller, K. H., Svindrych, Z., Seward, M. E., Best, M. N., & Bloom, G. S. (2019). Intraneuronal tau misfolding induced by extracellular amyloid-beta oligomers. *Journal of Alzheimer's Disease, 71*(4), 1125–1138.

Sabbagh, J. J., & Dickey, C. A. (2016). The metamorphic nature of the tau protein: Dynamic flexibility comes at a cost. *Frontiers in Neuroscience, 10*, 3.

Schmid, S., & Hugel, T. (2020). Controlling protein function by fine-tuning conformational flexibility. *Elife, 9*, e57180.

Schmitt-Ulms, G., Mehrabian, M., Williams, D., & Ehsani, S. (2021). The IDIP framework for assessing protein function and its application to the prion protein. *Biological Reviews, 96*(5), 1907–1932.

Seegar, T. C. M., Killingsworth, L. B., Saha, N., Meyer, P. A., Patra, D., Zimmerman, B., Janes, P. W., Rubinstein, E., Nikolov, D. B., Skiniotis, G., Kruse, A. C., & Blacklow, S. C. (2017). Structural basis for regulated proteolysis by the alpha-secretase ADAM10. *Cell, 171*(7), 1638–1648.e7.

Selkoe, D. J. (1991). The molecular pathology of Alzheimer's disease. *Neuron, 6*(4), 487–498.

Selkoe, D. J. (2021). Treatments for Alzheimer's disease emerge. *Science, 373*(6555), 624–626.

Shi, Y., Zhang, W., Yang, Y., Murzin, A. G., Falcon, B., Kotecha, A., van Beers, M., Tarutani, A., Kametani, F., Garringer, H. J., Vidal, R., Hallinan, G. I., Lashley, T., Saito, Y., Murayama, S., Yoshida, M., Tanaka, H., Kakita, A., Ikeuchi, T., ... Scheres, S. H. W. (2021). Structure-based classification of tauopathies. *Nature, 598*(7880), 359–363.

Shugart, J. (2020). In APP knock-in mice, spatial mapping circuitry crumbles. *Alzforum*. Retrieved from https://www.alzforum.org/news/research-news/app-knock-mice-spatial-mapping-circuitry-crumbles

Söding, J. (2017). Big-data approaches to protein structure prediction. *Science, 355*(6322), 248–249.

Sormanni, P., Piovesan, D., Heller, G. T., Bonomi, M., Kukic, P., Camilloni, C., Fuxreiter, M., Dosztanyi, Z., Pappu, R. V., Madan Babu, M., Longhi, S., Peter Tompa, A., Dunker, K., Uversky, V. N., Tosatto, S. C. E., & Vendruscolo, M. (2017). Simultaneous quantification of protein order and disorder. *Nature Chemical Biology, 13*(4), 339–342.

Spelke, E. S., & Kinzler, K. D. (2007). Core knowledge. *Developmental Science, 10*(1), 89–96.

Stahlberg, H., & Riek, R. (2021). Structural strains of misfolded tau protein define different diseases. *Nature, 598*(7880), 264–265.

Sturchio, A., Dwivedi, A. K., Young, C. B., Malm, T., Marsili, L., Sharma, J. S., Mahajan, A., Hill, E. J., El Andaloussi, S., Poston, K. L., Manfredsson, F. P., Schneider, L. S., Ezzat, K., & Espay, A. J. (2021). High cerebrospinal amyloid-beta 42 is associated with normal cognition in individuals with brain amyloidosis. *EClinicalMedicine, 38*, 100988.

Tapia-Rojas, C., Cabezas-Opazo, F., Deaton, C. A., Vergara, E. H., Johnson, G. V. W., & Quintanilla, R. A. (2019). It's all about tau. *Progress in Neurobiology, 175*, 54–76.

Theurer, K. L. (2018). 'Looking up' and 'looking down': On the dual character of mechanistic explanations. *Journal for General Philosophy of Science, 49*, 371–392.

Trogdon, K. (2018). Grounding-mechanical explanation. *Philosophical Studies, 175*, 1289–1309.

Ulrich, J., & Holtzman, D. M. (2021). Immune cells suggest new Alzheimer's treatment possibilities. *Scientific American, 325*(2), 34–39.

Uversky, V. N. (2017). Intrinsically disordered proteins in overcrowded milieu: Membrane-less organelles, phase separation, and intrinsic disorder. *Current Opinion in Structural Biology, 44*, 18–30.

Vasconcelos, B., Stancu, I. C., Buist, A., Bird, M., Wang, P., Vanoosthuyse, A., Van Kolen, K., Verheyen, A., Kienlen-Campard, P., Octave, J.-N., Baatsen, P., Moechars, D., & Dewachter, I. (2016). Heterotypic seeding of Tau fibrillization by pre-aggregated Aβ provides potent seeds for prion-like seeding and propagation of Tau-pathology in vivo. *Acta Neuropathologica, 131*(4), 549–569.

Wang, Z. X., Tan, L., Liu, J., & Yu, J. T. (2016). The essential role of soluble Aβ oligomers in Alzheimer's disease. *Molecular Neurobiology, 53*(3), 1905–1924.

Wang, H., Kulas, J. A., Wang, C., Holtzman, D. M., Ferris, H. A., & Hansen, S. B. (2021). Regulation of beta-amyloid production in neurons by astrocyte-derived cholesterol. *Proceedings of the National Academy of Sciences of the United States of America, 118*(33), e2102191118.

Wilson, E. O. (1998). *Consilience: The unity of knowledge*. Alfred A. Knopf.

Wimsatt, W. C. (2017). Foreword. In S. Glennan & P. Illari (Eds.), *The Routledge handbook of mechanisms and mechanical philosophy* (pp. xiv–xvi). Routledge.

Woodward, J. (2016). Causation and manipulability. In E. N. Zalta (Ed.), *The Stanford Encyclopedia of Philosophy*. Stanford University.

Yadav, A., Vidal, M., & Luck, K. (2020). Precision medicine - networks to the rescue. *Current Opinion in Biotechnology, 63*, 177–189.

Yamazaki, Y., Zhao, N., Caulfield, T. R., Liu, C. C., & Bu, G. (2019). Apolipoprotein E and Alzheimer disease: Pathobiology and targeting strategies. *Nature Reviews Neurology, 15*(9), 501–518.

Yeates, T. O. (2019). Protein assembles into Archimedean geometry. *Nature, 569*(7756), 340–342.

Zhai, L., Otani, Y., & Ohwada, T. (2019). Uncovering the networks of topological neighborhoods in β-strand and amyloid β-sheet structures. *Scientific Reports, 9*(1), 10737.

Harnessing AI and Genomics to Accelerate Drug Discovery

Amir Feizi and Jahir M. Gutierrez

Abstract

Drug development is a laborious and increasingly costly process with an arguably minuscule success rate. Identifying the right target and designing an effective drug candidate are regarded as the most critical steps needed to increase the probability of success of any drug development program. The advent of large-scale genomics datasets and powerful AI algorithms is moving toward addressing these challenges at an unprecedented speed. This chapter will discuss and review recent examples of using AI and genomics to accelerate important aspects of early-stage phases in drug discovery.

1 Introduction

Drug discovery is the earliest stage in pharmaceutical research and development (R&D). In this stage, new candidate molecules are initially screened and validated for therapeutic potential. In the past, drug discovery relied on empirical evidence gained through trial and error, analytical chemistry, and even serendipity. Today, large-scale screenings and powerful computational chemistry tools have greatly enhanced our ability to generate and analyze massive amounts of biochemical data for drug discovery. Despite these important technological advancements, however, drug discovery is becoming significantly more expensive and laborious over time.

A. Feizi (✉)
OMass Therapeutics, Oxford, UK
e-mail: amir.feizi@omass.com

J. M. Gutierrez
Absci Corporation, Vancouver, WA, USA
e-mail: jmgutierrez@absci.com

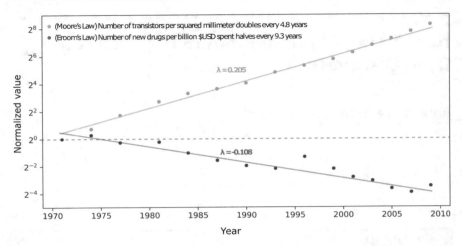

Fig. 1 Comparison of drug discovery (Eroom's law) and transistor integration (Moore's law) rates using data (https://en.wikipedia.org/wiki/List_of_semiconductor_scale_examples) from 1971 through 2010

This apparent paradox results from Eroom's law, a term that refers to a reverse analog of Moore's law in the semiconductor industry, which states that the number of transistors on a microchip doubles approximately every 4 years (Moore, 1998). According to Eroom's law, the number of new drugs developed per $USD billion invested in R&D halves every 9 years after adjusting for inflation (Scannell et al., 2012). Figure 1 shows a comparison of Moore's and Eroom's laws using data from transistor integration and R&D efficiency in the pharmaceutical industry in the period 1971 to 2010. Values are normalized by the initial rate each series had in 1971 (100 transistors per mm^2, 6.24 new drugs per billion dollars spent). The values of lambda (λ) represent the slope of the line of best fit and are equivalent to the inverse doubling and halving times of Moore's law (4.8 years) and Eroom's law (9.3 years), respectively.

At least three main factors contribute to Eroom's law: (1) the decreasing tolerance of risk on the part of regulatory agencies, which makes clinical trials more difficult and more expensive; (2) the small increments of benefit of investigational drugs over already successful drugs, which demand larger clinical trials; (3) the tendency to overestimate the effectiveness of screening methods and underestimate the complexity of the disease in question, which leads to excessive allocation of resources to research and development (Scannell et al., 2012).

In response to these challenges, the British-Swedish pharmaceutical company AstraZeneca developed a drug discovery framework called "5R" (Right target, Right tissue, Right safety, Right patient, and Right commercial potential). Although this framework was developed in 2010, it was not until 2018 that the company published a landmark paper outlining the cornerstones of 5R (Morgan et al., 2018). According to AstraZeneca, the implementation of the 5R framework has resulted in higher

Fig. 2 The major steps in early-stage drug discovery facilitated by AI and genomics. Source: Authors

success rates (from 4% to 19%) at nominating candidate drugs for Phase III clinical trials.

Nowadays, it is recognized that more emphasis should be placed on the early stages of drug development: identifying the right target, identifying the right candidate molecules, and validating these in vitro before testing candidate molecules in animal models (Morgan et al., 2018). This is because getting these early stages right can significantly increase the probability of success in the later stages. Nevertheless, early-stage drug discovery faces important challenges due to the complexity of the biology underlying each disease and the need to run ever-larger screenings. With the advent of high-throughput technologies in biology, and the emergence of powerful and novel artificial intelligence (AI) algorithms, it is now possible to emulate many of these screenings in silico with unprecedented complexity and speed (Fig. 2).

In fact, the application of AI in biology is not new. Artificial neural networks were used to predict the structures of RNA and proteins in the late 1980s (Turner et al., 1988; Holley & Karplus, 1989). However, the computational power and algorithms available at the time hindered the accuracy of predictions, which made it impossible for these early applications to contribute significantly to target discovery and drug design. Today, many companies and institutions around the world have embraced the novel datasets and AI techniques at our disposal with demonstrable success.

There has been a fundamental shift in perception from skepticism and cautious interest to a realization of the strategic role that AI and high-throughput biology must play in the emerging data-centric model of drug discovery (Smalley, 2017).

In this chapter, we will outline the critical roles that AI and genomics play in the early stages of today's drug development process and how they are helping uncover novel drug targets and molecules. Many of the use cases presented here demonstrate the potential of AI to tackle some of the challenges Eroom's law poses to develop new drugs more effectively.

2 Target Identification in the Era of Genomics and AI

Target identification is the most critical step in drug development. A substantial fraction of attrition rate in drug candidate trials is due to poor understanding of the underlying disease biology, which significantly increases the probability of failure to demonstrate efficacy in phase II clinical trials. In this section, we will discuss how target discovery led by genomics and aided by AI techniques is helping drug hunters in their search for the "right" disease targets and is increasing the probability of success in clinical trials.

2.1   Genomics Data as a Key Source of Potential Drug Targets

Many human diseases are linked to genetic variations in the genome. Whereas some diseases have very simple genetic causes (e.g., sickle cell anemia), others can be understood only in terms of complex interactions among several genetic factors. The main goal of genomic medicine is to identify DNA sequence variants that either cause a disease or predispose an individual to developing it. Thus, whole-genome and exome sequencing has been essential tools for identifying fundamental processes of disease pathogenesis and to find novel targets for drug development (Claussnitzer et al., 2020).

Almost 20 years ago, the Human Genome Project announced the completion of the first high-quality version of the human genome. The enterprise involved hundreds of scientists from 20 research institutions around the world and had an approximate total cost of USD $2.7 billion. Today, it is possible to sequence a human genome within 24 h for USD $300. The steep decline in sequencing costs and the sharp increase in sequencing speeds have enabled the creation of vast genomics datasets and population-level studies. In particular, the approach known as Genome-Wide Association Study (GWAS) has emerged as one of the pillars of genomics research, and it is responsible for the recent deluge of diagnostic and therapeutic discoveries in the field.

Briefly, a GWAS is an observational study designed to statistically assess associations between genetic markers and disease. Multiple GWASs allow for the analysis of tens of millions of genome-wide genetic variants across large samples of the population (Uffelmann et al., 2021). These results have substantially improved the identification of many causal genes and variants in over 10,000 rare diseases and have enabled a systematic dissection of the genetic basis underlying common multifactorial diseases (e.g. cancer, diabetes), paving the way for novel preventative and therapeutic strategies (Claussnitzer et al., 2020). In fact, it was recently reported that candidate drug targets with genetic evidence of disease association are twice as likely to lead to approved drugs than targets without such evidence (Nelson et al., 2015; King et al., 2019).

The pace at which genomics data are generated far exceeds the prediction of Moore's law; the amount of genomics data doubles every 7 months (Stephens et al., 2015). This has been accompanied by the development of new statistical and computational methods and data management systems for retrieving, exploring, and analyzing these big data. Today, it is increasingly difficult for scientists to handle large genomic datasets with the conventional hardware and software available for everyday use. This motivated institutions in the public and private sectors to launch projects with the aim of facilitating collaborative access and exploration of genomic data. For instance, the UK Biobank[1] is a pioneering initiative that has built a large-scale database of genomic and health information from half a million individuals in the United Kingdom (Bycroft et al., 2018). The data matrix included in the UK Biobank includes ~40,000 phenotypic data (including medical images and other omics data) associated with ~5 million genomic mutations (Backman et al., 2021). Today, statistical and machine learning techniques are essential for the analysis pipelines in genomics that query and filter these massive variant data tables. However, due to the sensitive nature of these data and the difficulty of handling them, the UK Biobank has recently partnered with DNAnexus (a cloud-based genomics data management company) to develop the Research Analysis Platform[2] (RAP), a system that facilitates the retrieval and analysis of the available data.

The Genome Aggregation Database[3] (gnomAD) is another landmark effort that has aggregated 15,708 whole genomes and 125,748 exomes (the protein-coding part of the genome) from a wide variety of projects (Karczewski et al., 2020). The initiative's goal is to catalog the diversity in exome and genome sequencing data from large-scale sequencing projects. Summarizing these data across diverse human populations could make it easier to analyze genomic variants and their potential role as disease drivers or as drug targets. Figure 3 summarizes the volume and scale of the UK Biobank and gnomAD projects and other important genomics datasets.

In the private sector, AstraZeneca is working on sequencing the full genomes of 2 million individuals to identify new drug targets and enable personalized care based on genetic markers of disease (Claussnitzer et al., 2020). In 2014, Regeneron Pharmaceuticals and Geisinger Health System in the United States announced a strategic collaboration to use large-scale exome sequencing for target discovery. By sequencing the exomes of 60,000 patients, they have highlighted the potential role of angiopoietin-related protein 3 (ANGPTL3) inactivation to protect against cardiovascular disease. In August 2020, Regeneron Pharmaceuticals received FDA approval for evinacumab (a blocker of ANGPTL3) in patients with homozygous familial hypercholesterolemia after completing clinical trials successfully (Raal et al., 2020). This collaboration has given rise to the Regeneron Genetics Center, which has recently discovered a rare coding variant of the GPR75 gene, which is associated with protecting against obesity. This discovery was the result of sequencing and analyzing exomes of 645,000 volunteers from the United Kingdom, the United States, and Mexico (Parsa et al., 2021). It is estimated that more than 1 billion people will be suffering from severe obesity (body mass index > 35) by 2030. Therefore, this discovery could entail a potentially transformative therapy for obesity. In summary, leveraging large-scale genomics datasets and AI models has proven to be a fruitful avenue for analyzing, identifying, and predicting new disease targets for drug development.

---

[1] https://www.ukbiobank.ac.uk

[2] https://www.ukbiobank.ac.uk/enable-your-research/research-analysis-platform

[3] https://gnomad.broadinstitute.org/

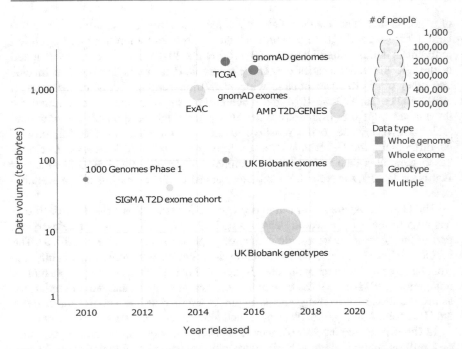

Fig. 3 A sample of large genomics datasets. The scatterplot shows the volume of data (terabytes) of publicly available genomics datasets by the year they were released. Source: Tom Ulrich, Broad Communications.

2.2   AI to Prioritize Drug Targets with a Genetic Basis

In the previous section we discussed how the inefficiencies of drug discovery largely reflect our limited understanding of disease biology, and therefore it is critical to incorporate genetic evidence of potential drug targets to increase the probability of success in drug development. Collectively, GWASs have reported over 60,000 genetic associations across thousands of human diseases and traits (Claussnitzer et al., 2020), but finding the causal variants and prioritizing targets are still major bottlenecks in leveraging genetics data. Most common disease-risk variants map to noncoding sequences and overlap with regulatory regions that multiple genes share. This makes it difficult to identify the causal link and therefore to interpret their functional impact. To address this, an initiative called Open Targets Genetics has been developed with the goal of using AI models to analyze massive amounts of GWAS signals and other functional genomics datasets and make it easier to identify and prioritize drug targets for a given disease (Mountjoy et al., 2021). Open Targets Genetics[4] is an online platform that allows for exploration of prioritized associations between genetic markers and diseases from multiple GWAS databases (including

---

[4] https://genetics.opentargets.org/

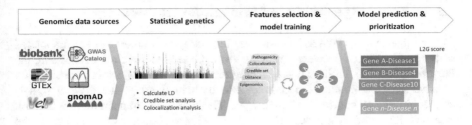

Fig. 4 The Open Targets Genetics AI-enabled pipeline for target prioritization

the UK Biobank). At its core, the AI model is trained on genetic and functional genomic features (e.g., chromatin interaction, colocalization of quantitative trait loci) of 445 gold-standard drug targets. Figure 4 summarizes the Open Targets Genetics pipeline used to associate and prioritize gene variants with traits or diseases using genomics data from the UK Biobank, FinnGen,[5] and the GWAS Catalog.[6] Open Targets Genetics is a spin-off from the Open Target Platform,[7] which was founded in 2014 as a multiyear academic-private partnership. Open Target is a comprehensive tool that supports the systematic identification and prioritization of potential therapeutic drug targets. This platform integrates domain expertise such as genomics, proteomics, chemistry, and disease biology from public institutions such as the Sanger Institute and EMBL-EBI with the drug discovery capability of partners in the pharmaceutical industry.

The gnomAD database discussed earlier is also becoming an invaluable resource for target discovery efforts in the AI space. In fact, a special issue in the prestigious journal *Nature* (May 2020) highlighted several studies that have leveraged data from genomAD for various applications, including detection of predicted loss-of-function genetic variants and evaluating drug targets through functional variation (Minikel et al., 2020).

Recently, there have been further studies that have used AI to understand how variations in regulatory elements of the genome modulate expression of nearby protein-coding genes (Pei et al., 2021). These analyses in combination with the gnomAD database, which includes 241 million variants, will shed light on how variations in the noncoding part of our DNA can influence predisposition through the effects on transcriptional regulation in common diseases with unmet needs.

---

[5] https://www.finngen.fi/en

[6] https://www.ebi.ac.uk/gwas/

[7] https://www.opentargets.org/

2.3   Knowledge Graphs in AI-Driven Target Discovery

As described above, GWASs have successfully mapped thousands of loci associated with complex traits. However, moving from GWAS to function is challenging. Besides genomics, additional sequencing technologies allow for the construction of other omics datasets of high relevance to help interpret the GWAS signals in the biological context and pathways. These include transcriptomics (which measures levels of transcribed RNA molecules), proteomics (which measures the identity and abundance of proteins in a cell), metabolomics (which measures the levels of metabolites), and epigenomics (which measures the presence of chemical modifications in DNA). Quantitative trait locus (QTL) analysis is a statistical method that has been developed to fill this gap by associating each of the omics data types with genotypic data and then identify biological processes involved in diseases (Liu, 2017). However, given the interconnected nature of biology, it remains a challenge to integrate multiple genetic and omics datasets in an objective and unbiased way. Recently, graph theory and knowledge graphs have gained attention in this regard for their ability to accommodate a rich and diverse set of data types that can be queried and analyzed to predict latent relationships between observed values. Google implemented the knowledge graphs in 2012 as a core technology for storing, searching within, and retrieving an immense amount of semantic information. In biology, adoption of knowledge graphs for integrating multi-omics disease data is a natural step forward in target discovery.

Reconstructing a knowledge graph for human diseases involves representing genes and disease as nodes on a graph and representing their relationships as the edges connecting them. These gene-disease relationships are derived from a multitude of sources, including natural language processing and the mining of biomedical texts, GWAS datasets, quantitative trait locus databases, clinical trials, and high-throughput screenings. Since a graph can be represented numerically as an adjacency matrix, the knowledge graph is machine readable, and one can compute the properties of each node based on their context in the graph. This makes knowledge graphs suitable for specialized AI models such as graph convolutional networks (Fig. 5), which can reveal nonobvious associations between genes and drugs and even identify novel targets for existing drugs (Gaudelet et al., 2021).

A recent and interesting example of applying this method is that of Benevolent AI, a UK-based AI-driven drug discovery company that used knowledge graphs to repurpose existing drugs for the treatment of COVID-19. For this, they used a massive knowledge graph of drugs and protein targets and analyzed it with a proprietary AI algorithm. As a result, an oral Janus kinase (JAK)1/JAK2 inhibitor called baricitinib (originally approved for the treatment of rheumatoid arthritis) was identified as a potential treatment for COVID-19 infection. In a partnership with Eli Lilly, Benevolent AI took baricitinib through three phases of clinical trials that showed a moderate reduction in all-cause mortality risk (Marconi et al., 2021).

In addition to this, the company identified a potential target for treating ulcerative colitis that is expected to enter the clinic in early 2023. This target was identified

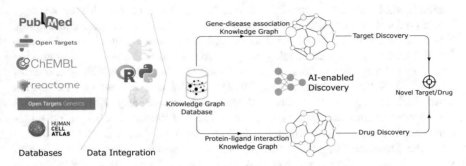

Fig. 5 Data-driven target discovery powered by knowledge graphs and AI

and validated by making extensive use of knowledge graphs and machine learning. Interestingly, no prior reference in the published literature or patents linking the identified target to ulcerative colitis existed at the time of discovery. Thus, knowledge graphs coupled with AI algorithms enable in-depth and complex hypothesis generation for drug development.

3 AI to Accelerate Drug Discovery

Given an identified "right" target, the next step is to design an effective drug candidate. In an excellent recent review, Schneider et al. (2020) discuss the challenges of drug design with AI and classify these challenges into five main areas: (1) preparing relevant datasets with accurate labels (e.g., drug properties versus binding affinities), (2) advancing new algorithms to generating new design ideas, (3) implementing and improving multi-objective optimization algorithms, (4) reducing cycle times of drug design using automation or AI, and (5) changing the research culture and creating an appropriate mindset (Schneider et al., 2020). The latter two challenges are about the impact of automation in reducing the design-make-test-analyze (DMTA) cycle time and the importance of navigating the cultural impact of the AI revolution in accordance with all stakeholders to ensure a productive transformation. In this section, we will discuss the first three challenges in more detail. These relate to which AI technologies have the most impact on drug discovery. We will also discuss DeepMind's AlphaFold 2.0 and how this breakthrough deep learning technology for predicting protein 3D structures could transform de novo drug design.

3.1 Data Are Key

Appropriately labeled data are key for training any AI model and predicting a sensible outcome. The success of deep learning models in traditional applications like image analysis and natural language processing (NLP) has benefitted from the availability of rich and accurate labeled datasets. However, building an accurate labeled dataset to train AI models for drug design is significantly more challenging. The goal of a trained model for drug design is to predict new chemical entities (NCEs) that have the pharmacological properties for the disease or target at hand and that can be synthesized and screened effectively. Publicly available data sources such as ChEMBL (Mendez et al., 2019) or PubChem (including 111 million compounds from 62 million literature and patent documents) (Kim et al., 2021) can be used to construct training datasets but have a limited number of molecules and amount of assay information. Furthermore, as these data sources are collected from the literature, the assays that measured the various aspects of the ligand-target pair use different experimental setups and units and thus are inherently noisy and prone to error. In addition, research articles tend to report only positive data and neglect negative interactions. On the other hand, although pharmaceutical companies generate large proprietary datasets in house, those datasets often do not meet the quality standards needed for AI and require substantial preprocessing. For example, high-throughput screening (HTS) datasets are usually biased toward compounds with desirable pharmacological properties. Furthermore, assays that measure the activity of compounds in vitro or in vivo do not correlate with the endpoint results during clinical trials due to the biological differences between animal models and human subjects. Therefore, the scope and limitations of these datasets need to be carefully assessed before using them as training datasets. The challenge of building appropriate training data for AI in drug design can be tackled using different approaches. In fact, AI itself can aid in the process of curating training data by detecting anomalies, outliers, sparse features, or features with skewed distributions. Finally, AI can also be used to extract useful metadata and ontology information to expand the features in the training datasets and ease data curation by human experts.

3.2   Deep Learning and De Novo Drug Design

The core of drug discovery is screening for compounds with a high binding affinity toward the target of interest and then using medical chemistry for lead optimization before clinical trials. Although advances in HTS have made drug discovery more systematic, the estimated hit rate from such large screenings is between 0% and 0.01%, depending on the target complexity and the throughput and type of the designed assay. In addition, a full-deck HTS assay is time-consuming and expensive and allows for exploration of only a small chemical space.

To reduce the number of HTS assays used, in silico docking software packages can be used to perform virtual screenings and hit identification. However, even the largest virtual screening to date, which included 170 million compounds, fell short of exploring the 10^{18}–10^{20} molecules in the estimated chemical space (Lyu et al., 2019). Although the iterative process of using in vitro or in silico screenings and de novo drug design software can help medicinal chemists identify potential leads, recent advances in deep learning have been shown to be faster and more accurate

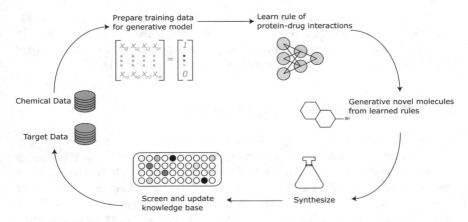

Fig. 6 Data-driven drug discovery powered by knowledge graphs and AI. Source: Authors

alternatives. Whereas de novo drug design software is programmed based on hard-coded rules from medicinal chemistry, deep learning algorithms use neural networks to learn latent representations of these rules. These trained neural networks are then used to run virtual screenings, generate, or "hallucinate" new molecules and even "evolve" molecules from the ground up using genetic algorithms (Baskin, 2020). Numerous neural network architectures are used in deep learning for de novo drug design, including deep multilayer networks, adversarial generative networks, deep recurrent networks, deep convolutional networks, and deep autoencoder networks. For example, deep convolutional neural networks can derive properties of NCEs directly from raw descriptions of their chemical structures and use them to predict the target properties of chemical compounds, while deep multilayer networks are able to map the input molecular descriptors to predict those with the desired properties. Furthermore, autoencoders have been used in combination with recurrent networks to predict NCEs with desired chemical properties. Finally, generative networks have recently gained attention in drug discovery for their ability to "imagine" or "hallucinate" novel molecules that have not been synthesized before (Fig. 6).

The critical advantage of neural networks over previous rule-based models is that by an iterative DMTA process and retraining on new readouts, the models' predictions can reach very high accuracies. Although identifying hits can be facilitated through HTS and deep learning, designing a successful drug is a complex process to optimize for several molecular properties simultaneously (potency, selectivity, clearance, and permeability) and yield a compound that meets the endpoint of clinical trials.

Traditionally, multi-objective optimization techniques and machine learning were used in combination with quantitative structure-activity relationship (QSAR) models to extract features that can be used to optimize a candidate compound. However, as discussed in the previous section, with the advent of deep learning techniques to predict NCEs, it is now possible to combine these algorithms with a QSAR model and rank the predicted NCEs by their QSAR scores. However, the outcome of this type of optimization needs to be supervised with domain expert knowledge, and thus it remains an iterative human-in-loop process.

3.3 AlphaFold 2.0 and Drug Discovery

One of the major long-standing bottlenecks of drug discovery has been the lack of precise three-dimensional structures. To target a protein of interest, having its structure is necessary for identifying or designing a chemical compound with a desirable binding affinity. Furthermore, none of the advanced algorithms discussed in the previous sections would be able to predict binding affinities for a list of hits. Thus, drug developers prefer to work on targets that either have a solved structure or are simple enough to characterize their structure internally. On November 30, 2020, DeepMind,[8] Alphabet's London-based AI subsidiary, astonished the scientific community by reporting that for the first time, a deep learning model called AlphaFold 2.0 could predict protein structures from their sequence alone with a record accuracy that outperformed 100 other teams at the CASP14 competition. The CASP (Critical Assessment of Structure Prediction) competition was co-founded in 1994 by John Moult, a computational biologist at the University of Maryland in College Park, to motivate the improvement of computational methods to accurately predict protein structures. For many years of CASP, no new algorithms had achieved significant accuracy improvements until AlphaFold 2.0 marked a huge leap in prediction accuracy. Experts in the field immediately recognized it as a game-changing and breakthrough technology with the potential to transform biology, medicine, and drug discovery forever. Remarkably, AlphaFold 2.0 structure predictions at CASP14 were indistinguishable from those determined using gold-standard experimental methods such as X-ray crystallography and cryo-electron microscopy (Jumper et al., 2021).

DeepMind published the details of the AlphaFold 2.0 algorithm and released all the underlying code on GitHub as an open-source project. Furthermore, in a collaboration with EMBL,[9] AlphaFold DB provides open access to protein structure predictions for about 350,000 proteins (including the human proteome). AlphaFold 2.0 has been used to predict 75% of the human proteins with a high confidence level and reduced the number of proteins with unknown structural information from 4832 to 1336 or 29, depending on the confidence threshold considered.

Despite these impressive feats, however, drug developers have raised two immediate and critical questions. First, how precise are the prediction qualities for active and allosteric sites within the protein structure? Second, what conformational states are calculated in the predictions? Briefly, AlphaFold 2.0's accuracy for important

---

[8] https://deepmind.com/

[9] AlphaFold Protein Structure Database, https://alphafold.ebi.ac.uk/, accessed November 9, 2021.

functional sites is on average poor compared to other regions in the proteins. This may be because these functional sites have evolved to be flexible and thus do not follow the same folding rules as the rest of the protein. Furthermore, as AlphaFold 2.0 was trained on data from the Protein Data Bank, a repository for experimentally solved structures, the predictions are an inactive state (empty active site) of the proteins, which is not favorable for in silico docking analysis. While AlphaFold 2.0's predictions now provide a reasonable starting point for resolving target protein structures, cryo-electron microscopy and X-ray crystallography will continue to be essential for drug design for years to come. To address AlphaFold 2.0's prediction inaccuracies at the active sites, its model would need to be retrained on a dataset with experimentally solved protein-ligand pairs. Building this type of dataset requires active engagement from and collaboration across pharmaceutical companies, as generating these structural datasets is extremely costly and a wealth of protein-ligand data is already locked in proprietary databases.

Nevertheless, AlphaFold 2.0 is a paradigm-shift solution to a 50-year-old grand challenge in biology, and the research community has already embarked on many innovative projects to expand its core algorithm. AlphaFold 2.0 has been trained specifically on multi-subunit protein structures of known stoichiometry. The resulting model, dubbed AlphaFold-Multimer, significantly improves the accuracy of predicted multimeric interfaces over input-adapted single-chain AlphaFold 2.0 while maintaining high intrachain accuracy (Jumper et al., 2021). Another interesting recent improvement is AlphaFill, an algorithm based on sequence and structure similarity that "transplants" missing ligands, cofactors, and (metal) ions to the AlphaFold models (Hekkelman et al., 2021). Thus, DeepMind's AlphaFold has opened the path to an exciting area of research that combines advances in computing power with algorithm design to advance the field of structural biology. This field is in its infancy but is growing fast, and it is just a matter of time before we begin to see more complex uses of deep learning to tackle more complex problems such as protein-protein, protein-DNA, and protein-RNA complexes. With further improvements to AlphaFold 2.0, the predicted structures could be used as input to the deep learning algorithms for the de novo drug design discussed in the previous sections. This means that one could screen billions of synthetic compounds and identify hits via an automated DMTA process and even run an optimization of ADMET (absorption, distribution, metabolism, excretion, and toxicity) profiles completely in silico. Finally, NCEs identified and optimized over the structures predicted by AlphaFold 2.0 will eventually lead to a reduction of drug discovery time cycle by providing narrower lists of initial compounds that can increase the success rate and efficiency of HTS. However, the speed of optimization and automation of these processes, particularly the synthesis of predicted de novo compounds, could be limited depending on the complexity of the chemical structures. Thus, deep learning has the capacity to transform the laborious and data-intensive process of drug discovery to an active learning process with leaner HTS and a higher hit rate.

4   Future Directions and Challenges Ahead

We have highlighted the importance of genetic evidence in identifying and validating targets and how omics data, in combination with AI technology and knowledge graphs, help find the "right" target and effective biomarkers. Yet the synergistic link between these novel genomics datasets and AI is in its infancy. A key fact to keep in mind is that pharma initially understood AI as an "oracle" capable of predicting the next blockbuster drug rather than just another computational tool with its own limitations. Perceiving AI as a tool (rather powerful one) than a magic solution is critical for ensuring the successful integration of AI into the drug discovery process. Both Big Pharma and AI-tech giants need to understand the collateral constraints. DeepMind's Alpha Fold 2.0 algorithm is an impressive success story of applying deep learning toward solving an extremely difficult and important challenge in computational biology.

A key factor that contributed to AlphaFold success is the collection of high-quality 3D structures generated over several decades. However, as mentioned in Sect. 3.1, preparing an accurately labeled dataset for training AI models remains a key challenge in drug development. In fact, labeling of chemical compounds against a target as "active" or "not active" has been challenging. Recently, the top ten world class pharmaceutical companies have launched the MELLODDY consortium, which aims to use privacy-preserving multitask federated learning to foster data sharing and collaboration for developing better predictive models than predictions arrived at using traditional efforts (Pejó & Biczók, 2020). The MELLODDY project will leverage the world's largest collection of small molecules with known biochemical or cellular activity, and it will increase the efficiency of drug discovery.

When it comes to the AI application in target identification, a large proportion of publications focus on a relatively limited set of diseases. This causes the overrepresentation of the certain indications in knowledge graphs and consequently biased predictions of new drug-target associations. In addition, reporting negative results has been traditionally discouraged in both the academic and private sectors. Thus, AI models and knowledge graphs applied in biology need to account for this important source of bias and information asymmetry. CytoReason is an AI-driven company that is trying to address this challenge by collaborating with pharmaceutical companies to harness negative data and results from clinical trials with the goal of turning them into actionable biological insights for drug discovery. Recently, the scientific community has begun to value the importance of negative data by the introduction of journals specifically dedicated to negative results[10,11]

Putting the trouble of preparing training data and developing novel algorithms aside, another interesting challenge is most AI-driven startups in the drug discovery space have limited experience in pharmaceutical sciences. Therefore, often these startups design their business model around offering specific solutions that tackle a small fraction of the value chain. On the other hand, large, established pharma-

---

[10] https://www.nature.com/collections/gcifjebabg/

[11] https://jnrbm.biomedcentral.com/

ceutical companies find it challenging to incorporate AI into their processes and restructure their organization. This gap is being addressed by the appearance of drug discovery startups that offer end-to-end AI platforms with a clear goal of attaining experience in drug discovery know-how through their partnerships with Big Pharma. As an example of a successful case study, Exscientia, a pioneering AI-driven drug discovery company, has developed an end-to-end solution with the goal of radically transforming the traditional pharmacoeconomic model. The company calls their strategy "shifting the curve" which consists of improving the probability of success and reducing the time and cost required to create a new medicine.[12] Exscientia's end-to-end AI-driven platform includes a learning loop for R&D based on a comprehensive and iterative machine learning system that encompasses target generation, molecular design, and extensive experimental testing (Fig. 6).

Finally, the advent of single-cell sequencing is transforming the genomics and omics to single cell level. This allows researchers to study biological processes at the resolution of single cells. The Human Cell Atlas, a multinational effort that includes 1000 institutes in 75 countries led by scientists at the Broad Institute, has created a comprehensive reference map of all human cells with the mission of transforming the understanding of biology, which could lead to major advances in the way diseases are diagnosed and treated (Regev et al., 2017). As an early adopter, Exscientia combines its AI algorithms with high-resolution single-cell analyses of tissue material from individual patients as differentiator asset to develop more precise medicines that are optimized for patients. Their patient tissue screening platform is used to validate targets by testing the activity of known compounds in primary tissue samples.

Altogether, the area of genomics and multi-omics biology at the single-cell level is emerging as a data-intensive and promising platform for tackling the complexity of human diseases with the aid of AI for identifying new pathways for therapeutic intervention.

5   Conclusion

To address key inefficiencies of drug discovery and the challenges posed by Eroom's law, pharmaceutical companies have embraced AI and genomics as essential components of their early-stage R&D processes. This has given place to important initiatives, international partnerships, and ambitious research programs among key players in the industry. Although several examples of successful applications of these technologies can be found today, ensuring the long-term success of integrating AI and genomics into drug discovery will require continuous innovation and collaboration across the field. Reducing the time cycle and the up-front costs of drug development is just the tip of the iceberg. A long-term vision for AI-enabled

---

[12] From Exscientia's Form F-1, as filed with the United States Securities and Exchange Commission on September 10, 2021.

drug discovery requires us to solve challenges such as reducing the limitations of training datasets and developing new algorithms that match the endpoint objectives in drug design. As these technologies mature and datasets expand in size and scope, AI and genomics will circumvent other important challenges in later stages of drug development.

Acknowledgments The views expressed in this chapter do not reflect those of the authors' organizations. The authors declare no past or present connection(s) with the companies and organizations mentioned in this chapter.

References

Backman, J. D., Li, A. H., Marcketta, A., Sun, D., Mbatchou, J., Kessler, M. D., Benner, C., Liu, D., Locke, A. E., Balasubramanian, S., Yadav, A., Banerjee, N., Gillies, C. E., Damask, A., Liu, S., Bai, X., Hawes, A., Maxwell, E., Gurski, L., ... Ferreira, M. A. R. (2021). Exome sequencing and analysis of 454,787 UK Biobank participants. *Nature, 599*, 628–634. https://doi.org/10.1038/s41586-021-04103-z

Baskin, I. I. (2020). The power of deep learning to ligand-based novel drug discovery. *Expert Opinion on Drug Discovery, 15*, 755–764. https://doi.org/10.1080/17460441.2020.1745183

Bycroft, C., Freeman, C., Petkova, D., Band, G., Elliott, L. T., Sharp, K., Motyer, A., Vukcevic, D., Delaneau, O., O'Connell, J., Cortes, A., Welsh, S., Young, A., Effingham, M., McVean, G., Leslie, S., Allen, N., Donnelly, P., & Marchini, J. (2018). The UK Biobank resource with deep phenotyping and genomic data. *Nature, 562*, 203–209. https://doi.org/10.1038/s41586-018-0579-z

Claussnitzer, M., Cho, J. H., Collins, R., Cox, N. J., Dermitzakis, E. T., Hurles, M. E., Kathiresan, S., Kenny, E. E., Lindgren, C. M., MacArthur, D. G., North, K. N., Plon, S. E., Rehm, H. L., Risch, N., Rotimi, C. N., Shendure, J., Soranzo, N., & McCarthy, M. I. (2020). A brief history of human disease genetics. *Nature, 577*, 179–189. https://doi.org/10.1038/s41586-019-1879-7

Gaudelet, T., Day, B., Jamasb, A. R., Soman, J., Regep, C., Liu, G., Hayter, J. B. R., Vickers, R., Roberts, C., Tang, J., Roblin, D., Blundell, T. L., Bronstein, M. M., & Taylor-King, J. P. (2021, May 19). Utilizing graph machine learning within drug discovery and development. *Briefings in Bioinformatics*. https://doi.org/10.1093/bib/bbab159

Hekkelman, M. L., Vries, I., Joosten, R. P., & Perrakis, A. (2021). AlphaFill: Enriching the AlphaFold models with ligands and co-factors. *bioRxiv*. https://doi.org/10.1101/2021.11.26.470110

Holley, L. H., & Karplus, M. (1989). Protein secondary structure prediction with a neural network. *Proceedings of the National Academy of Sciences, 86*, 152–156.

Jumper, J., Evans, R., Pritzel, A., Green, T., Figurnov, M., Ronneberger, O., Tunyasuvunakool, K., Bates, R., Žídek, A., Potapenko, A., Bridgland, A., Meyer, C., Kohl, S. A. A., Ballard, A. J., Cowie, A., Romera-Paredes, B., Nikolov, S., Jain, R., Adler, J., ... Hassabis, D. (2021). Highly accurate protein structure prediction with AlphaFold. *Nature, 596*, 583–589. https://doi.org/10.1038/s41586-021-03819-2

Karczewski, K. J., Francioli, L. C., Tiao, G., Cummings, B. B., Alföldi, J., Wang, Q., Collins, R. L., Laricchia, K. M., Ganna, A., Birnbaum, D. P., Gauthier, L. D., Brand, H., Solomonson, M., Watts, N. A., Rhodes, D., Singer-Berk, M., England, E. M., Seaby, E. G., Kosmicki, J. A., ... MacArthur, D. G. (2020). The mutational constraint spectrum quantified from variation in 141,456 humans. *Nature, 581*, 434–443. https://doi.org/10.1038/s41586-020-2308-7

Kim, S., Chen, J., Cheng, T., Kim, S., Chen, J., Cheng, T., Gindulyte, A., He, J., He, S., Li, Q., Shoemaker, B. A., Thiessen, P. A., Yu, B., Zaslavsky, L., Zhang, J., & Bolton, E. E. (2021). PubChem in 2021: New data content and improved web interfaces. *Nucleic Acids Research, 49*, D1388–D1395. https://doi.org/10.1093/nar/gkaa971

King, E. A., Davis, J. W., & Degner, J. F. (2019). Are drug targets with genetic support twice as likely to be approved? Revised estimates of the impact of genetic support for drug mechanisms on the probability of drug approval. *PLoS Genetics, 15*, e1008489.

Liu, B. H. (2017). *Statistical genomics: Linkage, mapping, and QTL analysis.* CRC Press.

Lyu, J., Wang, S., Balius, T. E., Singh, I., Levit, A., Moroz, Y. S., O'Meara, M. J., Che, T., Algaa, E., Tolmachova, K., Tolmachev, A. A., Shoichet, B. K., Roth, B. L., & Irwin, J. J. (2019). Ultra-large library docking for discovering new chemotypes. *Nature, 566*, 224–229. https://doi.org/10.1038/s41586-019-0917-9

Marconi, V. C., Ramanan, A. V., de Bono, S., Kartman, C. E., Krishnan, V., Liao, R., Piruzeli, M. C. B., Goldman, J. D., Alatorre-Alexander, J., de Pellegrini, R. C., Estrada, V., Som, M., Cardoso, A., Chakladar, S., Crowe, B., Reis, P., Zhang, X., Adams, D. H., Ely, E. W., & on behalf of the COV-BARRIER Study Group. (2021, September 1). Efficacy and safety of baricitinib for the treatment of hospitalised adults with COVID-19 (COV-BARRIER): A randomised, double-blind, parallel-group, placebo-controlled phase 3 trial. *The Lancet Respiratory Medicine*.https://doi.org/10.1016/S2213-2600(21)00331-3

Mendez, D., Gaulton, A., Bento, A. P., Chambers, J., De Veij, M., Félix, E., Magariños, M. P., Mosquera, J. F., Mutowo, P., Nowotka, M., Gordillo-Marañón, M., Hunter, F., Junco, L., Mugumbate, G., Rodriguez-Lopez, M., Atkinson, F., Bosc, N., Radoux, C. J., Segura-Cabrera, A., ... Leach, A. R. (2019). ChEMBL: Towards direct deposition of bioassay data. *Nucleic Acids Research, 47*, D930–D940. https://doi.org/10.1093/nar/gky1075

Minikel, E. V., Karczewski, K. J., Martin, H. C., Cummings, B. B., Whiffin, N., Rhodes, D., Alföldi, J., Trembath, R. C., van Heel, D. A., Daly, M. J., Genome Aggregation Database Production Team; Genome Aggregation Database Consortium, Schreiber, S. L., & MacArthur, D. G. (2020). Evaluating drug targets through human loss-of-function genetic variation. *Nature, 581*, 459–464. https://doi.org/10.1038/s41586-020-2267-z

Moore, G. E. (1998). Cramming more components onto integrated circuits. *Proceedings of the IEEE, 86*(1), 82–85.

Morgan, P., Brown, D. G., Lennard, S., Anderton, M. J., Barrett, J. C., Eriksson, U., Fidock, M., Hamren, B., Johnson, A., March, R. E., Matcham, J., Mettetal, J., Nicholls, D. J., Platz, S., Rees, S., Snowden, M. A., & Pangalos, M. N. (2018). Impact of a five-dimensional framework on R&D productivity at AstraZeneca. *Nature Reviews Drug Discovery, 17*, 167–181. https://doi.org/10.1038/nrd.2017.244

Mountjoy, E., Schmidt, E. M., Carmona, M., Schwartzentruber, J., Peat, G., Miranda, A., Fumis, L., Hayhurst, J., Buniello, A., Karim, M. A., Wright, D., Hercules, A., Papa, E., Fauman, E. B., Barrett, J. C., Todd, J. A., Ochoa, D., Dunham, I., & Ghoussaini, M. (2021). An open approach to systematically prioritize causal variants and genes at all published human GWAS trait-associated loci. *Nature Genetics, 53*. https://doi.org/10.1038/s41588-021-00945-5

Nelson, M. R., Tipney, H., Painter, J. L., Shen, J., Nicoletti, P., Shen, Y., Floratos, A., Sham, P. C., Li, M. J., Wang, J., Cardon, L. R., Whittaker, J. C., & Sanseau, P. (2015). The support of human genetic evidence for approved drug indications. *Nature Genetics, 47*, 856–860.

Parsa, A., Ankit, G., Sosina, O., Kosmicki, J. A., Khrimian, L., Fang, Y. Y., Persaud, T., Garcia, V., Sun, D., Li, A., Mbatchou, J., Locke, A. E., Benner, C., Verweij, N., Lin, N., Hossain, S., Agostinucci, K., Pascale, J. V., Dirice, E., ... Lotta, L. A. (2021, July 2). Sequencing of 640,000 exomes identifies GPR75 variants associated with protection from obesity. *Science, 373*(6550), eabf8683. https://doi.org/10.1126/science.abf8683

Pei, G., Hu, R., Jia, P., & Zhao, Z. (2021). DeepFun: A deep learning sequence-based model to decipher non-coding variant effect in a tissue-and cell type-specific manner. *Nucleic Acids Research, 49*(W1), W131–W139.

Pejó, B., & Biczók, G. (2020). *Quality inference in federated learning with secure aggregation.* arXiv e-prints arXiv-2007. Unpublished paper. Retrieved from https://arxiv.org/abs/2007.06236

Raal, F. J., Rosenson, R. S., Reeskamp, L. F., Hovingh, G. K., Kastelein, J. J. P., Rubba, P., Ali, S., Banerjee, P., Chan, K.-C., Gipe, D. A., Khilla, N., Pordy, R., Weinreich, D. M., Yancopoulos, G. D., Zhang, Y., Gaudet, D., & ELIPSE HoFH Investigators. (2020). Evinacumab for homozygous familial hypercholesterolemia. *New England Journal of Medicine, 383*, 711–720. https://doi.org/10.1056/NEJMoa2004215

Regev, A., Teichmann, S. A., Lander, E. S., Ido, A., Christophe, B., Ewan, B., Bernd, B., Peter, C., Piero, C., Menna, C., Hans, C., Deplancke, B., Dunham, I., Eberwine, J., Eils, R., Enard, W., Farmer, A., Fugger, L., Göttgens, B., ... Yosef, N. (2017). The human cell Atlas. *eLife, 6,* e27041. https://doi.org/10.7554/eLife.27041

Scannell, J., Blanckley, A., Boldon, H., & Warrington, B. (2012). Diagnosing the decline in pharmaceutical R&D efficiency. *Nature Reviews. Drug Discovery, 11,* 191–200. https://doi.org/10.1038/nrd3681

Schneider, P., Walters, W. P., Plowright, A. T., Sieroka, N., Listgarten, J., Goodnow, R. A., Fisher, J., Jansen, J. M., Duca, J. S., Rush, T. S., Zentgraf, M., Hill, J. E., Krutoholow, E., Kohler, M., Blaney, J., Funatsu, K., Luebkemann, C., & Schneider, G. (2020). Rethinking drug design in the artificial intelligence era. *Nature Reviews Drug Discovery, 19,* 353–364.

Smalley, E. (2017). AI-powered drug discovery captures pharma interest. *Nature Biotechnology, 35,* 604–606.

Stephens, Z. D., Lee, S. Y., Faghri, F., Campbell, R. H., Zhai, C., Efron, M. J., Iyer, R., Schatz, M. C., Sinha, S., & Robinson, G. E. (2015). Big data: Astronomical or genomical? *PLoS Biology, 13*(7), e1002195. https://doi.org/10.1371/journal.pbio.1002195

Turner, D. H., Sugimoto, N., & Freier, S. M. (1988). RNA structure prediction. *Annual Review of Biophysics and Biophysical Chemistry, 17,* 167–192.

Uffelmann, E., Huang, Q. Q., Munung, N. S., de Vries, J., Okada, Y., Martin, A. R., Martin, H. C., Lappalainen, T., & Posthuma, D. (2021). Genome-wide association studies. *Nature Reviews Methods Primers, 1,* 59. https://doi.org/10.1038/s43586-021-00056-9

Ethical Challenges in Applying New Technologies in Orthopedic Surgery

Masoud Ghalambor

Abstract

Technological advances have revolutionized virtually every aspect of healthcare, from research to patient access and from diagnosis and treatment to delivery. However, the use of technology in medicine has also brought about new challenges. Although this chapter focuses on ethical challenges associated with technological advances in orthopedic surgery, the concepts presented are not unique to this field. By shedding light on these challenges, I hope to encourage advances in medicine while encouraging fellow practitioners to keep sight of our primary mission of patient care.

1 Introduction

One of the principles of medical ethics is that physicians should continue to study, apply, and advance scientific knowledge (American Medical Association, 2001). Because of this ethic, the practice of orthopedic surgery has dramatically changed in recent years. Digitization has made the communication and documentation of healthcare data easier. That data can now be mined for analysis and research purposes in ways that were not possible before. Telehealth technologies have made healthcare more accessible for patients and enabled us to reach remote locations. The COVID-19 pandemic has forced physicians to sharpen their virtual examination skills and revealed the need for validated techniques and new technology in order to provide better interactive physical examinations (Tanaka et al., 2020). Advances in laboratory science and diagnostic imaging have enabled us to diagnose disease rapidly and more accurately. Finally, all the advancements in pharmaceutical,

M. Ghalambor (✉)
El Dorado Hills, CA, USA

© The Author(s), under exclusive license to Springer Nature Switzerland AG 2022
S. Ehsani et al. (eds.), *The Future Circle of Healthcare*, Future of Business
and Finance, https://doi.org/10.1007/978-3-030-99838-7_6

orthobiologics, and surgical treatments have helped us solve previously unsolved problems.

This chapter focuses on the ethical issues practitioners should consider when they introduce new technology into their practice. Some of the key issues include safety, efficacy, and proficiency when applying the new technology, monitoring outcomes of procedures that involve new technology, how the industry influences the decisions physicians make about technology, how the marketing of physicians influences the introduction of new technology, and the cost of new technology.

2   Non-Maleficence and Beneficence

"First, do no harm" (non-maleficence) is one of the most fundamental ethical principles in medicine. In the context of application of new technology, adhering to this principle requires the surgeon to be aware of the safety and efficacy of the new device or technique. The proficiency and skill set of the surgeon are even greater concerns when embracing new technology. Ultimately, to ensure that we act for the good of our patients (beneficence) and work to improve their function, we are ethically obligated to monitor and improve the outcome after we introduce a new technology into our practice.

2.1   Safety

As Capozzi and Rhodes (2015) so eloquently explain, because new technology is untested and unproven in large patient groups, potential complications may not be recognized for years. How do we justify the risk of these unforeseen events when we subject our patients to new technology? Does the new technology solve a problem that cannot be solved with our available tools? Are we solving a problem more effectively? Offering the new technology because the patient heard about it and asked for it, because we had a role to play in the development of the product and want to test or promote it, or simply because we want to be on the cutting edge of technology are not appropriate reasons.

Every orthopedic surgeon has witnessed the catastrophic outcomes that can occur when new devices are introduced or applied improperly. My own experience involves the application of a porcine dermal xenograft to augment a revision rotator cuff repair on my left shoulder. A clinical study of 35 patients by Castagna et al. (2018) showed that treating chronic and retracted rotator cuff tears with arthroscopic repair augmented with porcine dermal xenograft was safe and effective and yielded higher functional scores than arthroscopic repair alone. I remember the conversation I had with the surgeon before the operation; he assured me that he had not had any significant complications with this new implant and that he had been quite successful in repairing the more chronic and extensive rotator cuff tears he had seen. In essence, he was solving a previously unsolved problem.

Although the surgical procedure was flawless and there was no infection afterward, I developed a chronic inflammatory response that resulted in extensive extra-articular scarring that required a third surgery and extended time off from work. Looking back, I cannot help but wonder whether the surgeon (and I) were too eager to adopt the new implant. Should there have been more scrutiny about how chronic or how extensive rotator cuff damage should be to justify the risks of augmenting the repair? Since then, my surgeon has continued to perform this operation, has helped many other patients, and has not seen the same complication again.

This personal example highlights the key challenges and concerns regarding the safety of new devices. Given that new technology is introduced after limited testing (by virtue of any clinical trial having to rely on a sample of the overall population) and that adverse outcomes are inevitable, perhaps we should adopt it more cautiously and with a more limited scope of indications.

2.2   Efficacy

Quite often, patients today present with their own diagnosis and treatment plan. They have Googled their symptoms, have made a presumptive diagnosis, and then have consulted websites that offer them surgical solutions. Having a patient who is well informed and willing to take ownership of their condition is a blessing. However, I often find myself spending a considerable amount of time undoing misinformation. The problem is not always as complicated as the results of their internet search might indicate. Quite often the patient may not even need surgery.

Many patients equate new technology with better technology. Direct-to-consumer marketing of new medical technologies helps create this perception. It is important for the patient to recognize that the new product may not solve the problem any better than the old product, may in fact carry increased risks, and more likely than not will cost more.

Orthopedic surgeons are also influenced by the prospects of new gadgets and new methods. We have an obligation to ensure that new devices are safe and to avoid getting caught up in the hype surrounding new and exciting technology. It is not enough that we simply do no harm; we are also obligated to do good through our actions. Consider the following example. At one time, platelet-rich plasma (PRP) was heavily advocated as an adjunct to rotator cuff repairs. Most insurance companies refused to pay for this adjunct procedure, yet many surgeons routinely recommended PRP injections for every rotator cuff repair. This practice still continues (although to a lesser degree) despite multiple studies including a meta-analysis by Xu and Xue (2021) that show that PRP injections do not affect the re-tear rate in patients with small- and medium-sized tears. It is true that PRP injections carry minimal risk of morbidity (they do no harm). But PRP injections beyond the reported indications are of no benefit to the patient and are an unethical source of income for physicians and the industry that promotes it.

The orthopedic community has recognized that misinformation from direct-to-consumer marketing of largely unproven biologic treatments such as PRP and cell-based therapies may erode public trust and the responsible investment needed to bring legitimate biological therapies to patients (Chu et al., 2019). Physicians cannot afford to lose the trust that is at the core of the physician-patient relationship. The global and catastrophic effects of such mistrust and misinformation are unfolding in front of our eyes right now: a significant portion of the population may view COVID-19 vaccination as an experiment that is not backed with long-term data and as a way for physicians and pharmaceutical companies to make money (see e.g., Loomba et al., 2021; Machingaidze & Wiysonge, 2021).

2.3 Proficiency

The field of orthopedic surgery is unique in its extensive use of implants, orthobiologics, and diagnostic procedures (e.g., X-ray, CT, MRI, fluoroscopy, ultrasound, arthroscopy). As is the case in other fields of medicine, advances in orthopedic technology are often evolutionary and are very seldom revolutionary. The distinction is important because with evolutionary advances, one may simply substitute one technique or orthopedic implant with a new, "upgraded" model. In contrast, revolutionary advances are far more challenging to incorporate into a practice and require time and training (see Fig. 1).

Take the example of total ankle arthroplasty as a substitute for an ankle fusion procedure for terminal ankle arthritis. One might think that because the principles of joint replacement are similar whether it is a shoulder, hip, knee, or an ankle joint that

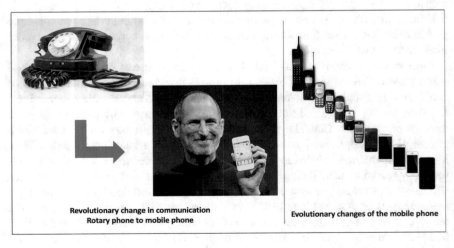

Revolutionary change in communication
Rotary phone to mobile phone

Evolutionary changes of the mobile phone

Fig. 1 Evolutionary versus revolutionary advances. Images obtained from Wikimedia Commons under Creative Commons public license

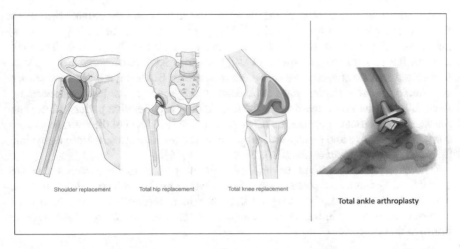

Fig. 2 Schematic diagrams of shoulder, hip, knee, and ankle arthroplasty. Images obtained from Wikimedia Commons under Creative Commons public license

a total ankle replacement is simply an extension of a knee replacement, a surgery that has been successfully performed for over 50 years (see Fig. 2). That is simply not the case. The learning curve associated with performing an ankle replacement properly is steep, even for a surgeon who is proficient with knee replacements. Studies have shown that the learning curve is significant with respect to time to perform the surgery, patient outcomes, and radiographic parameters (Maccario et al., 2021).

There are no general guidelines for achieving the necessary competence in applying new technology. Whether this happens through obtaining hands-on training, watching technique videos, or reading self-instruction articles obviously depends on the details of the new technique or device and the experience level of the surgeon. In addition, a surgeon's proficiency in performing such an operation is highly influenced by how often they will perform the surgery in their practice. This finding is supported by numerous studies and meta-analyses (Bauer & Honselmann, 2017).

Ultimately, what governs a physician's use of new technologies is their ethic, the care they give to making certain that they have the requisite training and experience to use the modality, and their confidence that the intervention is safe for their patients (Iserson & Chiasson, 2002). The old adage of "do it right or don't do it at all" will keep us bound to the ethical principle of doing no harm.

2.4   Monitoring Outcomes

When new technology is released for general use, the outcomes reported are based on limited data and the experience of one or a few investigating surgeons.

Frequently, those outcomes cannot be duplicated by other surgeons who adopt this new technology in their practice. Also, as the use of the technology expands, new complications may surface that have not been previously reported. The skill level of the physician and number of surgeries they have performed with the new technology can be potential causes of complications. However, studies have shown that outcomes of complex joint replacement surgeries are highly influenced by the quality of the entire team or process, including preoperative patient education, preoperative medical optimization of the patient, the skill level of the operating room staff, intraoperative and postoperative pain management, and postoperative physical therapy (see e.g., Bozic et al., 2010; Feng et al., 2018).

The safety and functional advancement of the patient is the ultimate measure of success. Given the complexity and interrelationship of various factors that can alter the final outcome of the surgery, it is our ethical responsibility to monitor our *own* outcomes as we introduce new technology into our practice and take steps to improve that outcome.

3   The Relationship Between the Physician and the Industry

Innovation in orthopedic technology is typically the result of collaboration between orthopedic surgeons and the industry. Orthopedic surgeons are best qualified to provide innovative ideas and feedback, conduct research trials, serve on scientific advisory boards, and serve as faculty to teach the use of new technology. The industry has the engineering and manufacturing know-how, the sales network, and the support structure to bring the product to fruition. It is necessary for physicians to establish a proper relationship with the industry for the purposes of patenting the invention, developing and marketing the product, and eventually collecting royalties or other forms of compensation. However, such relationships should be closely scrutinized. The American Academy of Orthopedic Surgeons has developed guidelines to govern such symbiotic relationships (AAOS, 1998b) to ensure that the best interest of the patient is prioritized above everything else and that the process does not erode the reputation of the medical community and the trust between the physician and patient.

The industry generally rewards the principle investigators with gifts or royalties for the extensive time and effort they devote to the development of a new technology that becomes profitable. When the industry offers physicians indirect or direct rewards for using their product, physicians may be tempted to stretch the indications for using it. Orthopedic surgeons have an ethical obligation to ensure that any gift from the industry does not influence their decision-making about the best treatment for the patient.

Once the new technology becomes available, other surgeons may see an opportunity to market themselves by adopting the new technology and presenting themselves as on the cutting edge. Device manufacturers have also recognized an opportunity to promote their product by directly advertising to the patient. Once they have convinced the patient that the product is the latest and greatest solution to their problem, they will refer the patient to the physicians who have adopted the device. The surgeon is now in an awkward position in that this stream of patients (and a new stream of income) is tied to their willingness to promote a particular product. The ethical responsibilities of the surgeon and the industry with respect to advertising are clearly outlined in the American Academy of Orthopedic Surgeons' position statements and opinions on ethics and professionalism (AAOS, 2004, 2016).

4   Cost Considerations

The steady increase in the cost of healthcare in the United States is partly attributable to the introduction of new technologies that tend to be more expensive than previous solutions (AAOS, 2009). Higher costs for healthcare have resulted in an increase in the number of uninsured and underinsured people in the United States. Therein lies an ethical dilemma. According to the AMA's code of medical ethics (American Medical Association, 2001), physicians need to advance scientific knowledge, but they also need to support access to medical care for all people.

The issue of universal healthcare and debates about the pros and cons of policies that have led to increases in the cost of healthcare are beyond the scope of this chapter. However, it is important to have a good sense of the magnitude of the problem of increased costs for medical care.

4.1   The Cost of Healthcare and Health Outcomes

Figure 3 shows the total expenditure for healthcare in the period 1970 to 2019, adjusted to 2019 US dollars. After adjusting for inflation, the cost of healthcare per capita has increased sixfold in the past half-century. In the past 20 years, the Consumer Price Index (CPI)—the average change in prices that urban consumers pay for various goods and services—has grown annually at an average of 2.1%, while the CPI for medical care has grown at an average rate of 3.5% per year.

Higher healthcare spending is a public good only if it leads to better health outcomes. That is not the case in the United States. The United States lags behind other countries in common measures of health even though healthcare costs more there than elsewhere. According to an Organization for Economic Cooperation and Development report (OECD, 2019), even though the United States spends much more on healthcare than all other OECD countries, it has a lower life expectancy and a higher avoidable mortality rate than the corresponding average values for all other OECD countries (see Fig. 4).

The rising cost of healthcare prohibits a sector of the population from purchasing any healthcare. This is not a problem in countries with universal healthcare, but universal healthcare is not always the best care either. In some countries and/or in certain contexts, "better" healthcare might arguably have to be purchased privately (Horton & Clark, 2016).

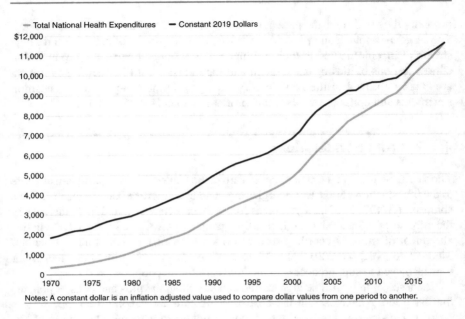

Fig. 3 Total national expenditures for healthcare, United States, 1970–2019. Reproduced from Kamal et al. (2020) under a Creative Commons license

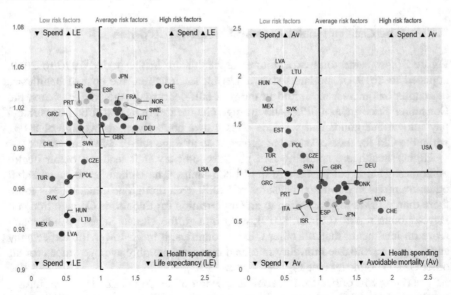

Fig. 4 Life expectancy (left) and avoidable mortality (right) in relation to overall healthcare expenditure, OECD member countries, 2019. Reproduced from (OECD, 2019)

To address this gap in access to healthcare, physicians in the United States devote a considerable amount of time caring for the medically underserved. The American Association of Orthopedic Surgeons considers this to be our moral and ethical obligation (AAOS, 1998a). But we are losing the battle to close this gap. It is constantly increasing, and the capacity of physicians to provide free or reduced-fee care is limited.

4.2   Containing Cost

The American Academy of Orthopedic Surgeons urges its members to act responsibly when they select implants that are more expensive but bring improved outcomes for the patient. The decision about what is best for the patient always lies with the treating physician but cannot be made in complete isolation from cost considerations. As noted above, stretching the indications for a new implant can increase risk to the patient without increasing quality of care. Because new implants are generally more expensive, stretching the indications will also result in an unnecessary increase in cost. Consider the following example of the most basic implant.

The screw is the most commonly used implant in orthopedics for fracture fixation, osteotomies, and arthrodesis. After properly aligning the bones, Kirschner wires and guide wires are used to maintain the position of the bones prior to placing screws. Cannulated screws can be placed across the guide wires and have been touted as more accurate and less time consuming than solid screws. However, they are weaker than solid screws and can be up to ten times more expensive, primarily due to lack of competition and the protection their patent offers (Fig. 5).

For these reasons, cannulated screws should be used only for select cases. Even though techniques for placing solid screws with the same precision as cannulated screws were published almost two decades ago (Motley et al., 2004), many surgeons routinely use cannulated screws. In 2009, the large cannulated screw market in the United States was estimated to be $186 million dollars (Althausen et al., 2014), and the market has been steadily growing. To that effect, considerable savings can be achieved by using solid screws where applicable and switching to generic versions of cannulated screws when their patent expires.

Orthobiologics are another emerging market in orthopedics and routinely used for arthrodesis and to enhance fracture healing. The global market for bone graft and orthobiologic products is over USD 3 billion. A recent survey of orthopedic surgeons (Niedermeier et al., 2014) has shown that over 80% are using orthobiologic products. The same report indicates that orthopedic surgeons do not have an accurate perception of the cost of the products. Historically, autologous bone graft (ABG) has been used because of its osteo-conductive, osteo-inductive, and osteogenic properties. However, there are limitations with regard to the quality and quantity of bone graft and donor site morbidity. A range of products are now available to serve as a substitute for ABG, from synthetic bone grafts such as calcium phosphate or calcium sulfate to simple allografts such as demineralized bone matrix

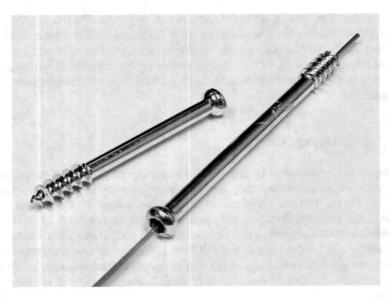

Fig. 5 Solid screw (left) and cannulated screw with guide wire (right)

(DBM) to more complex formulations containing pro-osteogenic cytokines such as recombinant human bone morphogenetic protein (rhBMP-2). Naturally, the latter are far more expensive and more heavily marketed. In one study looking at the cost of bone grafting in instrumented lumbar fusions (Eleswarapu et al., 2021), the average cost per level of fusion using DBM was USD 1522 versus USD 3505 for rhBMP-2. The same study showed that rhBMP-2 was associated with a higher number of radiographic complications. Considering that a single application can add thousands of dollars to the cost of a surgery, these adjuvant treatments should be applied more judiciously and with far more scrutiny.

5   Conclusion

Technological advances have touched every aspect of medicine, enabling us to solve previously unsolved problems. New challenges have emerged as a result of this expansion in knowledge that require us to maintain our focus on our primary mission of caring for the patient, doing no harm, and acting for the good of the patient and the society. This chapter has presented some of the more significant ethical challenges from the point of view of an orthopedic surgeon. New technology must be applied appropriately and efficaciously. The safety and well-being of the patient must be the first concern of any practitioner who adopts it. The indications for using it must be clear, and the surgeons who use it must be proficient and have sufficient experience with it. The choice of treatment should not be influenced by personal gain and can no longer be made in complete isolation from considerations of cost, as increasing costs result in disparities in the quality and availability of healthcare. These basic principles are not unique to orthopedic surgery. Following them will enable us to continue advancing the field of medicine without compromising our values, eroding the public trust, or disrupting the sacred physician-patient relationship.

Acknowledgments The author specializes in arthroscopic and reconstructive surgery of the foot and ankle at the Orthopedic Specialists of Sacramento (Sacramento, California). The views expressed here do not necessarily reflect those of the author's organization. The author declares no potential conflicts of interest.

References

AAOS. (1998a, May). *Care and treatment of the medically underserved.* AAOS Opinion on Ethics and Professionalism 1210. Retrieved May 2002, from https://www.aaos.org/contentassets/6507ec63e5ac4ea48375ad96d154daac/1210-care-and-treatment-of-the-medically-underserved.pdf

AAOS. (1998b, December). *The orthopedic surgeon's relationship with industry.* Opinion on Ethics and Professionalism no. 1204. Retrieved June 2016, from https://www.aaos.org/contentassets/6507ec63e5ac4ea48375ad96d154daac/1204-theorthopaedicsurgeonsrelationshipwithindustry.pdf

AAOS. (2004, October). *Pharmaceutical and device company direct to consumer advertising.* AAOS Position Statement no. 1162. Retrieved from https://aaos.org/globalassets/about/position-statements/1162-pharmaceutical-and-device-company-direct-to-consumer-advertising.pdf

AAOS. (2009, February). *Value-driven use of orthopaedic implants.* Position Statement no. 1104. Retrieved December 2014, from https://aaos.org/contentassets/1cd7f41417ec4dd4b5c4c48532183b96/1104-value-driven-use-of-orthopaedic-implants1.pdf

AAOS. (2016, June). *Advertising by orthopedic surgeons.* AAOS Opinion on Ethics and Professionalism no. 1205. Retrieved from https://www.aaos.org/contentassets/6507ec63e5ac4ea48375ad96d154daac/1205-advertisingopiniononethicsbodapprovedjune2016.pdf

Althausen, P. L., Kurnik, C. G., Shields, T., Anderson, S., Gurnea, T. P., Coll, D., & Lu, M. (2014). Clinical and economic impact of using generic 7.3-mm cannulated screws at a level II trauma center. *The American Journal of Orthopedics, 43*(9), 405–410.

American Medical Association. (2001). *AMA principles of medical ethics.* American Medical Association. Retrieved June 2001, from https://www.ama-assn.org/about/publications-newsletters/ama-principles-medical-ethics

Bauer, H., & Honselmann, K. C. (2017). Minimum volume standards in surgery: Are we there yet? *Visc Med, 33*(2), 106–116.

Bozic, K. J., Maselli, J., Pekow, P. S., Lindenauer, P. K., Vail, T. P., & Auerbach, A. D. (2010). The influence of procedure volumes and standardization of care on quality and efficiency in total joint replacement surgery. *The Journal of Bone and Joint Surgery. American Volume, 92*(16), 2643–2652.

Capozzi, J. D., & Rhodes, R. (2015). Ethical challenges in orthopedic surgery. *Current Reviews in Musculoskeletal Medicine, 8*(2), 139–144.

Castagna, A., Cesari, E., Di Matteo, B., Osimani, M., Garofalo, R., Don, E., Marcacci, M., & Chillemi, C. (2018). Porcine dermal xenograft as augmentation in the treatment of large rotator cuff tears: Clinical and magnetic resonance results at 2-year follow-up. *Joints, 6*(3), 135–140.

Chu, C. R., Rodeo, S., Bhutani, N., Goodrich, L. R., Huard, J., Irrgang, J., LaPrade, R. F., Lettermann, C., Lu, Y., Mandelbaum, B., et al. (2019). Optimizing clinical use of biologics in orthopaedic surgery: Consensus recommendations from the 2018 AAOS/NIH U-13 conference. *The Journal of the American Academy of Orthopaedic Surgeons, 27*(2), e50–e63.

Eleswarapu, A., Rowan, F. A., Le, H., Wick, J. B., Roberto, R. F., Javidan, Y., & Klineberg, E. O. (2021). Efficacy, cost, and complications of demineralized bone matrix in instrumented lumbar fusion: Comparison with rhBMP-2. *Global Spine J, 11*(8), 1223–1229.

Feng, J. E., Novikov, D., Anoushiravani, A. A., Wasterlain, A. S., Lofton, H. F., Oswald, W., Nazemzadeh, M., Weiser, S., Berger, J. S., & Iorio, R. (2018). Team approach: Perioperative optimization for total joint arthroplasty. *JBJS Rev, 6*(10), e4.

Horton, R., & Clark, S. (2016). The perils and possibilities of the private health sector. *Lancet, 388*(10044), 540–541.

Iserson, K. V., & Chiasson, P. M. (2002). The ethics of applying new medical technologies. *Seminars in Laparoscopic Surgery, 9*(4), 222–229.

Kamal, R., McDermott, D., Ramirez, G., & Cox, C. (2020, December 3). *How has US spending on healthcare changed over time?* Peterson KFF Health System Tracker. Retrieved from https://www.healthsystemtracker.org/chart-collection/u-s-spending-healthcare-changed-time/

Loomba, S., de Figueiredo, A., Piatek, S. J., de Graaf, K., & Larson, H. J. (2021). Measuring the impact of COVID-19 vaccine misinformation on vaccination intent in the UK and USA. *Nature Human Behaviour, 5*(3), 337–348.

Maccario, C., Tan, E. W., Di Silvestri, C. A., Indino, C., Kang, H. P., & Usuelli, F. G. (2021). Learning curve assessment for total ankle replacement using the transfibular approach. *Foot and Ankle Surgery, 27*(2), 129–137.

Machingaidze, S., & Wiysonge, C. S. (2021). Understanding COVID-19 vaccine hesitancy. *Nature Medicine, 27*(8), 1338–1339.

Motley, T., Perry, M. D., & Manoli, A., II. (2004). Placement of solid screws with cannulated precision. *Journal of Surgical Orthopaedic Advances, 13*(3), 177–179.

Niedermeier, S. R., Apostel, A., Bhatia, S., & Khan, S. N. (2014). Cost estimates of biologic implants among orthopedic surgeons. *The American Journal of Orthopedics, 43*(1), 25–28.

OECD (Organization for Economic Cooperation and Development). (2019). *Health at a glance 2019: OECD indicators.* OECD Publishing. https://doi.org/10.1787/4dd50c09-en

Tanaka, M. J., Oh, L. S., Martin, S. D., & Berkson, E. M. (2020). Telemedicine in the era of COVID-19. The virtual orthopaedic examination. *Journal of Bone & Joint Surgery, 102*(12), e57.

Xu, W., & Xue, Q. (2021). Application of platelet-rich plasma in arthroscopic rotator cuff repair: A systematic review and meta-analysis. *Orthopaedic Journal of Sports Medicine, 9*(7). https://doi.org/10.1177/23259671211016847

An Assessment of the AI Regulation Proposed by the European Commission

Patrick Glauner

Abstract

In April 2021, the European Commission published a proposed regulation to create a uniform legal framework for AI within the European Union (EU). In this chapter, we analyze and assess the proposal. We show that the proposed regulation is actually not needed due to regulations that already exist. We also argue that the proposal clearly poses the risk of overregulation. As a consequence, this would make the use or development of AI applications in safety-critical application areas, such as in healthcare, almost impossible in the EU. This would also likely further strengthen the technology leadership of Chinese and US corporations. That appears risky from a European perspective. Our assessment is based on the oral evidence we gave in May 2021 to the joint session of the European Union affairs committees of the German federal parliament and the French National Assembly.

1   Introduction

Artificial intelligence (AI) aims to automate human decision-making behavior and is therefore also considered the next phase of the industrial revolution. We have previously reviewed the state of the art and challenges of AI applications in healthcare (Glauner, 2021a). This book provides a forecast of how AI and other technologies are likely to skyrocket healthcare in the foreseeable future. The European Commission published a proposed regulation in April 2021 (European

P. Glauner (✉)
Deggendorf Institute of Technology, Deggendorf, Germany

Woxsen University, Hyderabad, India
e-mail: patrick@glauner.info

EUROPEAN
COMMISSION

Brussels, 21.4.2021
COM(2021) 206 final

2021/0106 (COD)

Proposal for a

REGULATION OF THE EUROPEAN PARLIAMENT AND OF THE COUNCIL

**LAYING DOWN HARMONISED RULES ON ARTIFICIAL INTELLIGENCE
(ARTIFICIAL INTELLIGENCE ACT) AND AMENDING CERTAIN UNION
LEGISLATIVE ACTS**

{SEC(2021) 167 final} - {SWD(2021) 84 final} - {SWD(2021) 85 final}

Fig. 1 EU proposal for a regulation laying down harmonized rules on artificial intelligence (artificial intelligence act). Source: European Commission (2021)

Commission, 2021) that intends to create a uniform legal framework for AI within the European Union (EU). It is therefore sometimes also referred to as the "AI Act." The proposal particularly addresses safety-critical applications, a category that also includes most healthcare applications of AI. The proposal's cover page is depicted in Fig. 1.

It is the first-ever legal framework on AI worldwide. It is currently being debated at various levels, and potential amendments or additions are expected to be published in the course of 2022.

Prior to that, the European Commission published an AI white paper in February 2020 (European Commission, 2020). The white paper intends to be an initial step toward an AI strategy for the EU. However, the white paper lacks crucial points: For example, it does not contrast its proposed actions to those of the contemporary AI leaders. The term "China" does not appear in the white paper at all. Furthermore, the proposed investments appear to be negligible compared to the Chinese investment.

In this chapter, we provide an assessment[1] of the EU Commission's AI regulation proposal. Our assessment is based on the oral evidence we gave to the joint session[2] of the European Union affairs committees of the German federal parliament and the French National Assembly on May 6, 2021. We also submitted written evidence to the committees (Glauner, 2021b). Concretely, we show that the proposed regulation poses the risk of overregulation. This would make the use or development of AI applications in safety-critical application areas, such as in healthcare, in the EU almost impossible. We furthermore provide concrete recommendations that the EU should implement in order to foster a sustainable ecosystem that allows European companies to thrive.

2   Analysis and Assessment

In this section, we provide an analysis of the proposal and assess its most critical parts. We also argue that a number of critical points have not been addressed at all in the proposal.

2.1   The Definition of AI Is Too Broad

There is currently no exact and generally accepted definition of AI—in science or in industry—because of its intersections with other fields, such as statistics and signal processing.[3] This shortcoming fundamentally complicates any kind of AI regulation.

The proposed regulation contains its own definition of AI in *Article 3 (Definitions)*:

> [...]
> (1)"artificial intelligence system" (AI system) means software that is developed with one or more of the techniques and approaches listed in Annex I and can, for a given set of human-defined objectives, generate outputs such as content, predictions, recommendations, or decisions influencing the environments they interact with;
> [...],

---

[1] Our professional background: At Deggendorf Institute of Technology, we teach and conduct research on AI. In addition, we advise companies on the use of AI. That activity includes the definition and implementation of AI strategies, the implementation of AI applications, their operation as well as running training courses.

[2] See video: http://videos.assemblee-nationale.fr/video.10738054_6093a70d0eb8d.commission-des-affaires-europeennes--reunion-commune-avec-la-commission-des-affaires-europeennes-du-6-mai-2021 (in French).

[3] Many popular AI methods also fall into the field of signal processing. However, there have been no correspondingly broad use-case independent regulation attempts in the history of signal processing.

with reference to *Annex I*:

(a) Machine learning approaches, including supervised, unsupervised, and reinforcement learning, using a wide variety of methods including deep learning
(b) Logic- and knowledge-based approaches, including knowledge representation, inductive (logic) programming, knowledge bases, inference and deductive engines, (symbolic) reasoning and expert systems
(c) Statistical approaches, Bayesian estimation, search and optimization methods

In summary, it includes any software[4] that uses machine learning methods or logic-based procedures. However, it also includes any software that uses statistical methods or search and optimization methods. This classifies almost all existing and future software that is not actually AI-related as "AI."

> **Example**
> Any software that computes the mean of numbers uses a "statistical procedure." As a consequence, the proposal classifies it as "AI."

Since almost all software is covered by that set of rules, unforeseeable risks would arise for every company as soon as it uses or develops any kind of software.

2.2   There Is No Need for AI-Specific Regulation

The existing regulations, laws, standards, norms, etc. of technologies are in most cases vertically structured. They generally consider systems that address certain safety-critical use cases, such as in healthcare, aviation, or nuclear power. Also, they typically pay little to no attention to the concrete implementation of these systems through hardware, software or a combination thereof.

AI applications are usually only a small part of larger software/hardware systems. The proposed regulation attempts to regulate this proportion horizontally—and thus independently of use cases. This approach appears to be impractical due to the overall mostly uncritical AI use cases. It can be assumed that additional horizontal regulation would also lead to unclear responsibilities and disputes over responsibilities. Additional regulations should therefore only address novel use cases that are not yet covered by the existing regulations.

The German AI Association is in favor of applying the existing use-case-specific regulations and adapting them to AI-specific requirements if necessary (KI Bundesverband, 2021). Bitkom, the federation of German digital companies,

---

[4] Note that AI can in principle also be implemented through purely hardware-based approaches without software. The proposed regulation ignores this and would not regulate such AI implementations at all.

is also of the opinion that even a more general horizontal regulation of "algorithmic systems" is not practicable (Bitkom, 2020).

2.3   A Lack of Delimitation from the Existing Regulations

The application areas prohibited in *Article 5* of the proposed regulation are very broadly defined and lead to uncertainties for all stakeholders due to the correspondingly wide scope for interpretation.[5] Instead, the definition of specifically prohibited use cases would be much more effective. It should also be examined whether these would have to be explicitly prohibited at all or whether this is already the case today under other laws, such as criminal codes or the General Data Protection Regulation (GDPR) (European Commission, 2016). New prohibitions should also address the relevant use cases in general, and without any reference to AI, as they could (in the future) possibly be implemented without the explicit use of AI methods.

For the same reasons, the definition of concrete use cases without explicit reference to AI would therefore also be helpful in *Article 6 (Classification rules for high-risk AI systems)* for a more precise definition of "high-risk applications" (Heikkilä, 2021). It is also unclear in the proposed regulation what the European Commission specifically means by "safe" applications. Furthermore, the proposed regulations do not define how "safety" could be established in individual use cases at all, especially since many machine learning methods have statistical uncertainty embedded in their definition.

In conjunction with the existing regulations, the proposed regulation also poses the risk of contradictory and twofold requirements, for example, in automated lending (Herwartz, 2021).

2.4   The Proposal Includes Unfulfillable Requirements for "High-Risk Applications"

In addition to the very broad definition of "high-risk applications"[6] in *Article 6*, the proposed regulation provides for corresponding documentation requirements in *Article 11 (technical documentation)*, registration requirements in *Article 60 (EU database for stand-alone high-risk AI systems)*, and reporting requirements in *Article 62 (reporting of serious incidents and of malfunctioning)*. These requirements for the development or use of AI in safety-critical application areas are comparable to the operation of nuclear power plants or the development of aircraft. They therefore will likely inhibit innovation and are thus disproportionate.

---

[5] For example, even operating a search engine on a potentially unrepresentative database could be prohibited by *Article 5(a)* due to the potential impact of the search results.

[6] I would like to thank in particular Tobias Manthey of EvoTegra GmbH for our extensive discussions on the topic of "high-risk applications."

To implement the procedures described in *Article 64 (access to data and documentation)*, the European Commission would practically have to bundle the EU-wide AI expertise of all companies, universities, and experts in the relevant authorities and invest hundreds of billions of euros in its own infrastructure. The requirements for the sandbox tests described in *Article 53 (AI regulatory sandboxes)* state that the entire intellectual property consisting of data and AI would have to be shared with the relevant authorities. This seems disproportionate and unfeasible. In addition, there are open questions about liability should third parties gain access to the intellectual property through sandbox testing.

For these reasons, the proposed regulation would make the development or deployment of relevant safety-critical AI applications, such as any safety-critical assistance systems in healthcare, nearly impossible in the European Union.

2.5 Overregulation Would Strengthen Chinese and US Corporations

One of the goals of the GDPR that the EU passed in 2016 was to limit the power of US cloud providers and strengthen European companies. In the meantime, however, it has become clear that exactly the opposite has occurred (Bershidsky, 2021). In particular, the large US cloud providers have the human and financial resources to implement GDPR-compliant services. They also have the financial resources to settle any fines or avoid them by entering complex and lengthy trials.

The proposed regulation would therefore result in European companies being unable to reach or hold a leadership position in international competition in the future due to overregulation. Chinese and US providers of AI-based services and products would be strengthened by this regulation. As a result, Chinese corporations in particular could squeeze European companies out of the market or take them over in every sector in the medium term (Lee, 2018). From a European perspective, that is undesirable.

2.6 Missing Points

While the proposal is very broad, a number of critical points, including but not limited to the following, have not been (adequately) addressed in it:

- Liability
- Grandfathering and transitional arrangements
- Military applications

We would also like to highlight that the proposed regulation has been significantly toned down compared to the previous drafts with regard to the use of AI in social networks. It no longer specifically addresses social networks, even though that is precisely where there is a realistic danger of AI influencing our society (Evans, 2020).

These points need to be discussed in greater detail by the European Commission when revising the proposal.

3   Recommendations

The European Commission should focus its work on the added value of AI for citizens—especially from the perspective of the anticipated increase in prosperity and quality of life. In doing so, it should refrain from overregulating AI.

Broad AI qualification measures should be created across Europe through a European Hightech Agenda. This would make citizens much more shapers of the digital transformation than being shaped by it. In addition, transfer projects between universities and industry partners should be funded in a more targeted and effective manner. Also, a top European AI research institution should be established along the lines of the European Organization for Nuclear Research (CERN) (Kelly, 2021).

The Bavarian Hightech Agenda[7] should serve as a positive role model. Through this, a variety of AI measures are currently being implemented to strengthen Bavaria-wide competitiveness, such as:

- AI courses and degree programs[8]
- Social projects, such as DeinHaus 4.0[9] for longer and healthier living at home
- Transfer projects between universities and start-ups, such as between Deggendorf Institute of Technology and EVOMECS GmbH for AI-based production planning[10]
- AI transfer centers in rural areas, including the AI center in the Denkwelt Oberpfalz of the LUCE Foundation[11]

4   Conclusions

The proposed regulation published by the European Commission in April 2021 intends to create a uniform legal framework for artificial intelligence (AI) within the European Union (EU). The very broad definition of "AI" contained therein classifies almost any existing and future software as "AI" and would then be covered by this regulatory framework. However, there is no need for AI-specific regulation

---

[7] http://www.bayern.de/politik/hightech-agenda/

[8] http://idw-online.de/de/news765811

[9] http://deinhaus4-0.de/

[10] http://www.evomecs.com/wp-content/uploads/2020/10/131020-Presse_Final_GER.pdf

[11] http://www.luce-stiftung.de/kooperationsvertrag-zwischen-oth-amberg-weiden-und-der-luce-stiftung/

due to the existing regulations—apart from possibly a few novel use cases. The proposed regulation poses the risk of overregulation, which would make the use or development of AI applications in safety-critical application areas, such as in healthcare, almost impossible in the EU. This would also likely further strengthen Chinese and US corporations in their technology leadership.

Acknowledgement The author declares no conflicts of interest.

References

Bershidsky, L. (2021). *Europe's Privacy Rules are Having Unintended Consequences*. http://www.bloomberg.com/opinion/articles/2018-11-14/facebook-and-google-aren-t-hurt-by-gdpr-but-smaller-firms-are. Online Accessed May 17, 2021.

Bitkom. (2020). *Stellungnahme zum Abschlussbericht der DEK: Kurzfassung Bitkom Stellungnahme zum Gutachten und den Empfehlungen der Datenethikkommission*. http://www.bitkom.org/sites/default/files/2020-04/20200402_kurzfassung-bitkom-stellungnahme-zum-abschlussbericht-der-dek.pdf. Online Accessed May 17, 2021.

European Commission. (2016). *The General Data Protection Regulation (GDPR)*. http://ec.europa.eu/info/law/law-topic/data-protection/data-protection-eu_en. Online Accessed May 24, 2021.

European Commission. (2020). *White Paper on Artificial Intelligence: Public Consultation towards a European Approach for Excellence and Trusts*. http://ec.europa.eu/digital-single-market/en/news/white-paper-artificial-intelligence-public-consultation-towards-european-approach-excellence. Online Accessed May 24, 2021.

European Commission. (2021). *Proposal for a Regulation of the European Parliament and the Council: Laying Down Harmonised Rules on Artificial Intelligence (Artificial Intelligence Act) and Amending Certain Union Legislative Acts*. http://digital-strategy.ec.europa.eu/en/library/proposal-regulation-laying-down-harmonised-rules-artificial-intelligence-artificial-intelligence. Online Accessed May 17, 2021.

Evans, D. (2020). *Facebook is still struggling with election manipulation*. http://www.cnbc.com/2020/09/19/2020-presidential-election-facebook-and-information-manipulation.html. Online Accessed May 17, 2021.

Glauner, P. (2021a). Artificial intelligence in healthcare: Foundations, opportunities and challenges. In *Digitalization in healthcare: Implementing innovation and artificial intelligence* (pp. 1–15). Springer.

Glauner, P. (2021b). Schriftliche Stellungnahme für das am 06.05.2021 stattfindende gemeinsame Fachgespräch der Ausschüsse für die Angelegenheiten der Europäischen Union des Deutschen Bundestages und der französischen Assemblée nationale zur Politik der EU im Bereich der Künstlichen Intelligenz (KI) und insbesondere dem Verordnungsvorschlag der Europäischen Kommission zu KI (COM(2021) 206 final). http://www.glauner.info/expert-evidence. Online Accessed May 17, 2021.

Heikkilä, M. (2021). *6 key battles ahead for Europe's AI law*. http://www.politico.eu/article/6-key-battles-europes-ai-law-artificial-intelligence-act/. Online Accessed May 17, 2021.

Herwartz, C. (2021). *Neue EU-Regeln für KI könnten für Europa zum Nachteil werden – Sorge über ausbleibende Investitionen*. http://amp2.handelsblatt.com/politik/international/kuenstliche-intelligenz-neue-eu-regeln-fuer-ki-koennten-fuer-europa-zum-nachteil-werden-sorge-ueber-ausbleibende-investitionen/27113210.html. Online Accessed May 17, 2021.

Kelly, É. (2021). *Call for a "CERN" for AI as parliament hears warnings on risk of killing the sector with over-regulation*. http://sciencebusiness.net/news/call-cern-ai-parliament-hears-warnings-risk-killing-sector-over-regulation. Online Accessed May 17, 2021.

KI Bundesverband. (2021). *Position Paper on EU-Regulation of Artificial Intelligence by the German AI Association.* http://ki-verband.de/wp-content/uploads/2021/03/Final_Regulierung_compressed-1-1.pdf. Online Accessed May 17, 2021.

Lee, K.-F. (2018). *AI superpowers: China, silicon valley, and the nEW wORLD oRDER.* Houghton Mifflin Harcourt.

Post-Truth Implications for COVID-Era Healthcare: Verification, Trust, and Vaccine Skepticism

Aaron James Goldman

Abstract

Why, in the midst of the global Coronavirus pandemic, do so many people seem resistant to the recommendations of established medical experts? In this chapter, I explore possible structural causes of this resistance in the US context. I argue that in the "post-truth" era, attempts to encourage people to wear face masks and get vaccinated confront challenges pertaining to how scientific knowledge is verified and disseminated. Public health interventions that fail to account for the reduction of trust in established healthcare institutions risk reinscribing a dynamic that contributes to the further inefficacy of those interventions.

1 Introduction

Against the backdrop of the COVID-19 pandemic, this chapter offers an overview of the interface between healthcare and the dissemination of knowledge in the "post-truth" era. I will focus on dimensions of post-truth social epistemology associated with Coronavirus skepticism, vaccine hesitancy, anti-vaccinationism, and related movements in the context of the political environment and healthcare system of the United States. My argument, however, gestures to the significance of a more general conflict between healthcare consumers and established scientific, media, political, and healthcare institutions about the epistemic authority of these institutions, a conflict that manifests in various ways throughout the world alongside the increasing visibility of so-called populist movements.

A. J. Goldman (✉)
Lund University, Lund, Sweden
e-mail: aaron.goldman@ctr.lu.se

S. Ehsani et al. (eds.), *The Future Circle of Healthcare*, Future of Business and Finance, https://doi.org/10.1007/978-3-030-99838-7_8

I will argue that interventions by established institutions to persuade healthcare consumers to take certain voluntary measures in order to achieve public health outcomes—for example, vaccination or donning face masks in public spaces with the goal of reducing the spread and severity of COVID-19 cases—can fail to account for the reasons why some populations of healthcare consumers do not trust those institutions. This lack of trust is emblematic of the post-truth era, and it demands responses that are attentive to ongoing societal shifts pertaining to who has authority to determine what constitutes knowledge. Although no individual entity is wholly responsible for such failures, contradictions embedded within the fabric of institutionalized healthcare and its methods of communicating medical knowledge to the public have contributed to an often-justifiable skepticism about the competence, benevolence, efficacy, and honesty of established healthcare institutions. Healthcare interventions must account for the sources of this skepticism lest they risk reinscribing the disconnect.

I want to be clear: I have no interest in making the case that vaccine skeptics and anti-vaccinationists are *correct* to resist public health interventions such as vaccines or face masks, nor do I have any desire to defend the integrity or goals of these (and similar) movements. But at the same time, I contend that attempts to counter these movements with efforts such as improving knowledge about science, cultivating data literacy, or increasing the accessibility of information—regardless of how laudable these goals are in general—evidence a misdiagnosis of the problem. The problem is one of trust, not of ignorance or stupidity, and there are reasons this mistrust exists. It did not originate with the COVID-19 pandemic, although the pandemic has indeed exacerbated it and shone a spotlight on it.

The chapter will proceed as follows: In the next section, I will unpack several key concepts I use, including established institution, epistemology (and epistemic authority), and post-truth. In the third section, drawing on philosopher William James's 1907 *Pragmatism*, I offer an account of the relationship between scientific knowledge, authority, and verification. Here I highlight *trust* as a crucial element in disseminating scientific knowledge. In the fourth section, I argue—in light of my account in the chapter's third section—that established political, scientific, media, and healthcare institutions have not adapted their persuasive techniques to societal shifts in how people access, learn, and appropriate information. The contradictions resulting from this inflexibility prompt populations who perceive themselves as disenfranchised by these institutions to reject their epistemic authority, which ultimately results in their dismissal (as untrustworthy) of these institutions' attempts at persuasion. In the fifth section, I review some ways that established public health institutions could respond to resistance to COVID interventions, and I provide a limited recommendation for how individual healthcare providers might persuade skeptics of the importance of such health interventions, particularly vaccines, when those patients may be disinclined to follow the recommendations of established institutions or credentialed experts.

2 Key Concepts

When I use terms such as "established institution," "epistemic," and "post-truth," what do I mean? To whom or what am I referring? In this section of the chapter, I clarify.

2.1 Established Institutions

I have been using the term "institution" as a shorthand way of referring to any organization and to any set of common, socially significant behaviors or practices that recur in cultures or communities. In this first, more obvious sense, institutions include entities such as the CDC (the United States Centers for Disease Control and Prevention), Oxford University, the United States Democratic and Republican Parties, and CNN and Fox News. In the second sense, I follow in the intellectual tradition of Émile Durkheim, who writes, "without doing violence to the meaning of the word, one may term an *institution* all the beliefs and modes of behaviour instituted by the collectivity" (1901/2013, p. 15). According to this broader definition, examples of institutions include marriage, the prison system, the US hospital system, and the modern university.

I refer to institutions as "established" to highlight those that are often accepted as culturally influential and are widely invested with authority, even if not all populations trust or support those institutions. I have selected this term because it implies a historical foothold, in the sense that such an institution is *already established* by the time its influence or authority is felt. Moreover, the term alludes to the notion of the Establishment, the set of interconnected political, financial, social, and patronage relationships (both official and unofficial) that reinforce structures of power (Fairlie, 1955). (So-called populist political movements tend to rouse support against the Establishment.) The *New York Times*, insofar as it is a newspaper of record, is one example of an established institution, even though many people with left-wing or right-wing political commitments may not trust it to disseminate unadulterated truth.

2.2 Epistemology/Epistemic

Epistemology is a technical term in philosophy that refers broadly to the study of knowledge, including what constitutes knowledge and how knowledge is acquired. In this chapter, I use the term "epistemic authority" to refer to the quality of being believed or trusted as a source of knowledge or to an institution that has this quality. Some people may, for example, view the *New York Times* as an institution with epistemic authority, insofar as they perceive its reporting to reflect what is true. Therefore, for them, it serves as a source of knowledge. Others may view it as lacking epistemic authority, referring to its reporting as "Fake News from a biased newspaper" and dubbing it a "Fake Newspaper" (Trump, 2018, 2020). Some may find public school science class textbooks to be epistemically authoritative; others may find these books to have authority that is secondary to that of certain religious doctrines. Some may take Dr. Anthony S. Fauci, the current director of the United States National Institute of Allergy and Infectious Diseases and the chief medical advisor to the United States president, to be an epistemic authority about the Coronavirus pandemic; others, quite publicly, do not (Enserink & Cohen, 2020).

I have found inspiration in the work of David G. Robertson, a religious studies scholar who researches New Age movements and conspiracisms, for using the term "epistemic authority" to refer to arrangements of social relationships involving trust or distrust that reflect avenues through which knowledge is dispensed (2016, p. 33). Many religious communities and new religious movements invest authority in some texts, charismatic figures, or organizations as opposed to others. Movements such as anti-vaccinationism may work similarly. Such movements coalesce around counter-authorities, including media networks and online communities that challenge the epistemic authority of established institutions in order to position themselves against those institutions.

2.3   Post-Truth

The term "post-truth" refers to a variety of features of present-day culture involving the contested significance of objectivity and shared truth as criteria for politics, ethics, and other aspects of human life. Although the concept itself may not be radically novel (and there are perhaps precedents in the thought of Friedrich Nietzsche and earlier authors), characterizations of our current historical period as a "post-truth period" or "post-truth age" suggest burgeoning patterns (or at least a new awareness of preexisting trends) that involve a diminishing social import of truth (Fuller, 2018). Among other trends, the term "post-truth" points toward ongoing challenges to the epistemic authority of established institutions, shifts in how information is received and digested in general (such as by sharing and consuming stories on social media in the interest of acquiring prestige rather than in the interest of teaching or learning), and political strategies that take advantage of these trends (i.e., "post-truth politics"). As ideas about the nature of knowledge and authority are questioned, access to information and consumption of information have simultaneously become "flattened" (Friedman, 2007; Subramony, 2014). For many, knowledge about the world is not delivered primarily vertically (such as downward from a master craftsperson, a church official, a political leader, a scientist, or a librarian) but is assembled through a combination of widely accessible, often digital sources that demand little investment or commitment from an individual learner. For example, some research has suggested that young people, who are willing to seek out information relating to their health via the web, are more likely to bypass physicians and diagnose themselves (Lowrey & Anderson, 2006). To cite another example, the formation of the right-wing conspiracist movement QAnon—which, despite persistent deviations in authority among some members of its (largely online) community, almost seems to have self-organized into existence via social media—similarly evidences this kind of flattening of access to knowledge.

Though "post-truth politics" can refer to specific tactics politicians use to manipulate an audience based on disinformation that takes advantage of the flattening of knowledge dissemination, it also gestures to the changing significance of expertise as an epistemically and politically important form of authority. Tom Nichols has lamented this trend, noting that "Americans have reached a point where ignorance—at least regarding what is generally considered established knowledge in public policy—is seen as an actual virtue" (2017, p. 61). According to Nichols, it is not that expertise is nonexistent, but rather that it is neither idealized nor invested with authority in the way that it needs to be for an adequate "social division of labor" (p. 62).

But Nichols's claims should raise questions for us: What kind of expertise is no longer idealized? For Nichols, it is that of the institutionally credentialed expert, someone who has obtained legitimacy as an epistemic authority through established institutions (such as respected universities or medical schools or through patronage networks that include the economic and social elite). Who benefits from the preservation of the current social division of labor? Likely the institutionally credentialed expert, someone whose connections to established institutions reinforce a position with social (and often economic) capital. Here, the very idea of expertise is based on a viewpoint that is unwilling to dip its toes too deeply into "post-truth" waters, as if Nichols fears, for example, that fake experts in the Trump administration supplanted true experts (who indeed exist by means of credentialing by established institutions but have lost power in the post-truth age).

When the crass but insightful politics and true-crime podcast host Brace Belden claims that "The notion of the expert was thoroughly discredited during the Trump years," his point serves as a corrective to positions like Nichols's (Beldon & Franczak, 2021, 38:18). Belden's implication is not that Americans (and others) have per se surrendered the *ideal* of expertise, but rather that institutionally credentialed experts associated with both the Trump administration and its political opposition revealed themselves—in the midst of myriad controversies and the Coronavirus pandemic—to be nonexperts, or at least as ineffectual as nonexperts would be, despite their claims to expertise. Perhaps the ideal of expertise is somewhere preserved (or perhaps not), but genuine experts may not be among those with actual power.

3   Truth and Authority in Scientific Knowledge

3.1   Knowledge, Truth, Verification

What do I know about the world? At least according to a commonsense conception of knowledge, I know many things. For instance, I know that atoms exist or at least that there are extremely small particles we call "atoms" that constitute almost every object I might encounter. How do I know this? I have never seen an atom up close, of course, but I have experienced the following. First, I have seen images in textbooks that were produced using scanning probe microscopes, and the captions for those images claim that they depict the outlines of atoms. Second, I have witnessed and participated in small-scale experiments in high school and at university that involve chemical reactions, explanations for which are conditioned upon the existence of atoms and molecules. Third, I have taken medications whose chemical formulae I can read and comprehend, and these medications seem to successfully alleviate symptoms such as headaches or a stuffy nose. Fourth, I have read a paper arguing that the phenomenon of Brownian motion of fluids is likely attributable to the interactions of incredibly small objects (i.e., molecules and the atoms they comprise) that constitute the fluid (Einstein, 1905). Yes, these are the reasons why *I* know that there are atoms.

One might say that insofar as I believe atoms exist, I am a believer in science. Perhaps. But the reasons that I know that atoms exist do not really require that I have conducted research that deploys the scientific method, at least not in the most straightforward sense. I have myself experimentally verified very few of the scientific theories I know. A better account might be that I am a believer in *scientists*.

American pragmatist philosopher William James offers an explanation for this feature of scientific knowledge. In James's account of truth in *Pragmatism*, he describes truth as a process; ideas become true through the process of verification (1907/1975, p. 97). While this may sound esoteric, it captures the practice of empirical investigation and its formalization in the scientific method: When I hypothesize, I must then test or verify my hypothesis. The hypothesis is *made* true (veri-*fied*) to the extent that it passes the test and to the extent that no competing hypothesis passes the test better. A scientist may accomplish this through some form of experiential encounter with the process of an experiment and its results.

But this is not the only way: "Take, for instance, yonder object on the wall," writes James (p. 99). "You and I consider it to be a 'clock,' altho no one of us has seen the hidden works that make it one. We let our notion pass for true without attempting to verify. If truths mean verification-process essentially, ought we then to call such unverified truths as this abortive? No, for they form the overwhelmingly large number of truths we live by." At this point, James differentiates between "indirect" and "direct verifications" (ibid.). For example, the verification of Japan's existence that I perform when I consult a textbook that refers to Japan is indirect. If I visit Japan to confirm its existence, the verification is direct. Both types work together to constitute what we call scientific knowledge. I may not directly verify that an object is a clock, but I use it to determine the time and presume that someone else has verified or could verify that it is a clock: "Verifi*ability* of wheels and weights and pendulum is as good as verification" (ibid., James's italics).

Crucially, the way a culture develops a body of knowledge, a requirement for the existence of professions whose continued success involves the cultivation of cumulative theoretical and practical knowledge from the past (including, but not limited to, biology, medicine, midwifery, and nursing), is by inscribing a canon of direct and indirect verifications and presenting them to initiates for the purpose of offering further (indirect) verifications. Medical and nursing students learn theoretical knowledge (e.g., by reading in a textbook or listening to a lecture) corresponding to hypotheses that other parties directly verified in the past before contributing to the profession themselves. They continue doing so as long as what they learn continues to *work* for them. As James puts it, "Truth lives, in fact, for the most part on a credit system. Our thoughts and beliefs 'pass,' so long as nothing challenges them, just as banknotes pass so long as nobody refuses them. But this all points to direct face-to-face verifications somewhere, without which the fabric of truth collapses . . . We trade on each other's truth" (p. 100). I offload responsibility for verification onto others until I need to check for myself.

In my own life, I am confident that the earth is round, that van Gogh painted *The Starry Night*, that human activity has played a key role in the set of phenomena called "climate change," and that mRNA vaccines like those used against COVID-19 are effective and safe. Some of these claims I am more confident in than others. But I do not know any of them indubitably, nor am I confident because I have directly verified them. They are indirectly verified for me in the sense that they are in principle verifiable directly and generate neither contradictions with my other knowledge (so far as I am aware) nor conflicts in the course of my life.

3.2   Trust

James's comparison of scientific knowledge to banknotes raises the question: When do banknotes get refused? Put differently, when does a challenge or conflict arise that requires me to *re*-verify (directly or indirectly)?

Potential contradictions and conflicts occur often in day-to-day life. I may recall an event happening in a way that another witness disputes, causing me to question the details of my, the witness's, or both of our memories. In most cases, this concerns me very little. Perhaps it may concern me more if I must testify about it in court. Another example: I have often come across conflicting reports of and opinions about celebrities when watching television. This is not unusual. But most of the time I can remain in the tension of uncertainty given the distance between my life and whatever gossip is unfolding. On social media, I am exposed to even more opinions. Again, most of the time the deviations between them do not bother me. But sometimes the matter is pressing (such as how to respond to a pandemic, which may threaten my life or the lives of loved ones), and sometimes there are discrepancies between how much I trust two sources of information.

And here is the crux: trust. Trust—a commitment of some kind, sometimes personal, often emotional—may be the deciding factor. Moreover, a lack of trust in some indirect verification does not necessarily cause me to seek direct verification. In many cases, I personally would have difficulty accomplishing a direct verification, even if it is in principle possible. Instead, I seek an alternative indirect verification from a more trustworthy (to me) source. Given the aforementioned flattening of information access, there are plenty of options to choose from.

In the case of why I know (or think I know) that atoms exist, I know because I trust reports by those who attest (indirectly) to the direct verification of these claims. Even when I see images apparently of atoms or participate in experiments that attest to the existence of atoms, I am trusting a textbook or a teacher or another intermediary to explain how these encounters with phenomena should be interpreted as evidence of atoms. Likewise, when I observe visual evidence of the curvature of the earth, I do not magically intuit the knowledge that the earth is roughly a sphere but must first draw the conclusion that what I observe is indeed evidence of the earth's curvature and then, based on that evidence, synthesize it with further indirectly verified evidence that the earth is not flat. Rarely do I have a reason *not* to trust these sources, and when I do trust public school textbooks and teachers, these instances of trust often reinforce one another because the indirectly verified conclusions also usually corroborate each other.

The case of medical knowledge is not remarkably different, although—especially in the context of a pandemic—it is obviously pressing in a way that the existence of atoms is not. As with atoms, it involves knowledge that many people lack and that most have not directly verified. But has every healthcare provider directly verified everything they have learned in their anatomy classes? Of course not. Perhaps they have verified some of it themselves, but most of these first-person verifications also presume other premises and knowledge they have not directly verified. So why do I believe—and why does my reader (likely) believe—that the Coronavirus pandemic is real and that vaccines are helpful for reducing the spread and severity of cases?

For me, it is because my knowledge of medicine—even though it is not that of a medical professional or medical scientist—is based on indirect verifications from medical professionals in my life to whom I am close and whom I trust. How do I know COVID vaccines work and are safe? I suppose I do not know it without doubt. But I am confident because I am confident in the people who are confident in it, and they are confident because of their confidence in others and (in the case of medical professionals) because of their direct experiences that attest to the suffering of the unvaccinated. These forms of trust form a thick web with other trustworthy (for me) sources of indirect verification: I have had science teachers I trust and I have accrued knowledge of biology that lends me credibility when I speak with medical professionals. This creates a feedback loop where medical professionals I already trust are open to speaking with me, further solidifying my trust in their verifications and recommendations. (As for my reader, I suspect you also have a preexisting investment—including similar relationships of trust—in the epistemic authority of medical scientists, a trust that also deeply informs your opinions about the efficacy and social import of vaccines.)

4 When Banknotes Are Refused

Not everyone is predisposed to trust medical professionals. Still, is there not sufficient evidence in most people's lives—at least in the United States and other developed nations—to convince people to follow recommendations by established authorities such as medical scientists, especially in the midst of a pandemic?

Research conducted on the population of the United States has found that COVID-19 vaccine hesitancy decreased overall during the first half of 2021, but not enough to meet targets of vaccinating 70–90% of the population (King et al., 2021). Among the surveyed population, over half claim not to trust COVID-19 vaccines specifically, compared with only 15% that reported they do not trust vaccines in general, suggesting that causes of resistance to COVID-19 vaccines may be distinct and specific to the pandemic and related circumstances (ibid.). (There is a long history of general vaccine hesitancy that dates back to the establishment of the vaccine paradigm by Edward Jenner in 1796 (Marshall, 2019; Dubé et al., 2015). Historically, vaccines have been divisive even among the educated and scientifically informed.) Among a group of employed people hesitant to take COVID-19 vaccines, about 45% report not trusting the government as a key reason; among healthcare practitioners and technicians, this number is lower (about 35%) but still perhaps higher than many would expect (King et al., 2021).

In this section, I unpack possible reasons why many might find epistemic authorities that compete with established political, medical, and scientific institutions to be more trustworthy. Why might a lack of trust (in the vaccine, in the government) keep someone from doing what established institutions recommend? I hope to suggest that—even if they can be dangerous—movements involving suspicion of attempts at healthcare interventions by established institutions cannot simply be dismissed as ignorance, stupidity, or mental illness. I then investigate how some attempted interventions by public health officials have responded to this dynamic inadequately.

4.1 Sources of Mistrust

4.1.1 Established Institutions (such as the US Government) Do Bad Things

One major reason that trust in established institutions may falter—particularly governments of countries such as the United States or institutions associated therewith—is because of a history of perceived and actual harms perpetrated by those institutions. Though the results by King et al. (2021) are not so granular as to permit drawing conclusions about *why* vaccine skeptics and others might express a lack of trust in the government, notable acts committed by the US government provide some clues.

Political scientist Aaron Good has written of a "pattern of sustained influence that can be detected throughout the post-World War II historical record. Key events bear the imprint of the nascent and/or emergent 'deep state'" (2018, p. 24). What follows in Good's piece is a list of efforts (some well documented, others debated) by the United States to exert foreign and domestic influence outside the channels of traditional democratic governance, including the removal of elected foreign leaders, the Gulf of Tonkin incident, Iran–Contra, pre-Iraq War intelligence activities, and the 2008 financial collapse (pp. 24–25). By the term "deep state," Good does not require the existence of a fantastical cabal of vampiric puppet masters, such as what is posited by reactionary conspiracists, including adherents to the recent Trump-supporting QAnon movement. The term should be understood more broadly as "an obscured, dominant, supra-national source of antidemocratic power" (p. 22). Indeed, the possible existence of a deep state implies powerful forces capable of wielding violence, economic coercion, and other questionable methods to achieve ends beyond the democratic will of the population, but it is not necessarily unified in its means, constitution, or purposes, nor must it even be completely hidden.

Although some skepticism about whether elements of the US government and affiliated entities (including other states) perpetrated all of these alleged actions—and in cases when US involvement is publicly known, whether the particular actors in question are best classified as a "deep state"—is common and reasonable, what is important for the present work is the possibility of a growing public perception of the state's lack of concern for (if not harmful treatment of) human beings (including its own citizens), from both left-wing and right-wing perspectives. Whether or not a "deep state" is responsible, the Wall Street bailout after the 2008 financial crisis, the increasing unaffordability of healthcare in the United States, and even the much-publicized criminal activities and eventual death (officially determined a suicide) of Jeffrey Epstein have all contributed to a growing suspicion and resentment of established institutions by segments of the population. Testifying to this resentment was the (ultimately unsuccessful) insurgency of Bernie Sanders within the context of Democratic Party politics in the primary seasons of the 2016 and 2020 US presidential elections and, more obviously, the victory of Donald Trump in 2016.

I have not even yet mentioned documented cases of abuse in the name of medical science or medical care. Though the 40-year-long Tuskegee Syphilis Study is perhaps one of the most well-known and egregious (Washington, 2006), continued abuses have occurred, including—as reported by the *Guardian*—a CIA-organized effort to acquire DNA from the family of Osama bin Laden under the guise of a (fake) Pakistani vaccine program (Shah, 2011; Robbins, 2012; Siddiqui, 2021). In the context of COVID-19, New York governor Andrew Cuomo, at first widely lauded for his response to the pandemic, has since been accused of misrepresenting nursing home deaths caused by the virus (Gold & Shanahan, 2021).

Even for those who are inclined to trust established institutions, the history of violent and otherwise unscrupulous actions taken by the US government—some documented, some only alleged—provides a basis for understanding why many might not trust institutions associated with that government or trust similar institutions. Resentment or suspicion of an institution based on its likely malevolence may be exactly the sort of thing that introduces a conflict in a chain of verifications, that makes a piece of knowledge no longer *work*, and that prompts someone to refuse a banknote. (After all, in light of the trend toward flattening knowledge dissemination, the threshold for finding another bank, and other banknotes, is quite low.)

With respect to forms of anti-COVID-vaccinationism, it begins to seem less absurd for someone to believe, for example, that Bill Gates has inserted microchip trackers into COVID vaccines, even though unsurprisingly, according to reporting by the BBC, "The Bill and Melinda Gates Foundation told the BBC the claim was 'false'" (Goodman & Carmichael, 2020). If one is already disinclined to trust the

BBC and disinclined to trust Gates, do these denials (a type of attempted indirect verification) *work*? Do the banknotes pass?

4.1.2   A Class Division

Another possible explanation for the increasing mistrust of established healthcare institutions relates to the association of medical researchers, hospital administrators, and physicians with the social and economic elite. Requirements for increasing specialization and more complicated research and medical technology have demanded longer periods of education to achieve the standards of expertise. Because of urbanization and the demand that providing healthcare be cost efficient, the need to centralize caregivers, technicians, and technology in hospitals has distanced physicians from small communities. Moreover, the increasing costs of healthcare and many pharmaceuticals, related to healthcare privatization in the United States, have likely resulted in more extreme class disparities between some healthcare providers and healthcare consumers. (Even the term "healthcare consumer" reinforces the notion of a marketplace exchange rather than a relationship of caregiving.) Put bluntly, the stereotype of the physician or medical scientist in the United States is of someone who spent years studying and now earns enough money to spend most weekends playing golf—things that many US residents are disincentivized from doing or outright unable to do, given economic and social realities.

4.2   "The Science Says . . . "

Consider the following recent article titles in *Nature* related to vaccines against COVID-19: "Should Children Get COVID Vaccines? What the Science Says" (Ledford, 2021) and "How Do Vaccinated People Spread Delta? What the Science Says" (Subbaraman, 2021). Consider also the title of a recent statement by the US Food and Drug Administration: "FDA Will Follow the Science on COVID-19 Vaccines for Young Children" (Woodcock & Marks, 2021).

What is *the* science?

Scientific knowledge (including medical knowledge), as I have argued, requires a network of trust relationships through which instances of direct and indirect verification can be collected and connected to one another. This process both involves and results in the formation of consensus among scientists and the history of scientific research. However, given the nature of empirical investigation, there is never a single *indubitable* canon of collected, certain empirical knowledge.

While headlines and article titles that refer to "the science" certainly do not intend to reflect a form of truth arrived at by means outside the scientific method, the very verbal formulation (i.e., "the science") is antithetical to the process of arriving at scientific consensus. If the consensus were universal, then there would be no one to dispute it. While it is possible for there to be wide consensus, it will be neither universal nor a consensus that necessarily reflects an independent truth about the world. We indeed observe contestations to the results of studies such as these and to the content of statements by established institutions (such as the FDA), which is what prompts such articles to be written in the first place. As King et al. (2021) have noted, these results (and statements) are sometimes—and often enough to be worrisome for the goal of widespread vaccination—dismissed as untrustworthy. Therefore, *the science* does not articulate any one position univocally. This style of communication is, I suspect, geared less toward conveying actual increasing consensus among scientists than it is toward signaling confidence in current research about COVID vaccines (including their efficacy and safety) and attempting to establish an authoritative position about this knowledge. But this technique is unlikely to instill such confidence for those who are already apt to be skeptical.

I am suggesting that these attempts by established scientific, media, and governmental institutions to respond to COVID vaccine hesitancy contain an internal contradiction, namely, a contradiction between the content they explicitly communicate and the style and form of that communication. They communicate scientific findings from a position of self-proclaimed epistemic authority. In doing so, they play the part of trusted, benevolent agencies with certain knowledge about the health of healthcare consumers, yet they simultaneously deny the inherent messiness of scientific research. This is a contradiction that can be detected by their audience, especially when some among the audience are predisposed to mistrust established institutions.

Shifting or uncertain recommendations from US government agencies during the early months of the COVID-19 pandemic in the United States—particularly surrounding questions of the efficacy of medical masks—may have exacerbated the issue. Early in 2020, mask usage was more tepidly recommended than it would be later that year. Most prominently, Trump has pointed to the changing stance on masks as an error by US health officials, particularly Fauci, a leader and public figurehead of the US government pandemic response. Trump, as reported by CNN, said, "But Anthony [Fauci] said, 'Don't wear masks.' Now he wants to wear masks. Anthony also said, if you look back, exact words, here's his exact words: 'This is no problem. This is going to go away soon.' So he's allowed to make mistakes. He happens to be a good person" (CNNpolitics, 2021).

Fauci responded to the charge of "flip-flopping" about mask recommendations during a *New York Times* podcast interview in the summer of 2021:

> The people who are giving the *ad hominem*s are saying, "Ah, Fauci misled us. First he said no masks, then he said masks." Well, let me give you a flash. That's the way science works. You work with the data you have at the time. It is essential as a scientist that you evolve your opinion and your recommendations based on the data as it evolves. That is the nature of science. It is a self-correcting process. And that's the reason why I say people who then criticize me about that are actually criticizing science. It was not a change because I felt like flip-flopping. It was a change because the evidence changed, the data changed. (Swisher, 2021, 17:47)

Based on this interview, Fauci exhibits clear awareness of and sensitivity to the provisional and evolving nature of empirical medical research. However, despite this, his remarks underplay his visible confidence in his initial non-recommendation of masks. A March 2020 interview on *60 Minutes* shows Fauci say the following: "Right now in the United States, people should not be walking around with masks"

(60 Minutes, 2020, 0:20). When the interviewer replies, "You're sure of it? Because people are listening really closely to this," Fauci reaffirms his earlier remark: "Right now there's no reason to be walking around with a mask" (0:25). Later it emerged that a reason for discouraging widespread mask usage in March 2020 was a supply shortage of face masks and other protective equipment for healthcare workers (CNNpolitics, 2021; Ross, 2020). On this reasoning, recommending medical masks for everyone would have resulted in widespread purchasing and hoarding of masks, absorbing some of the supply needed more acutely by healthcare workers, who were exposed more frequently as they attempted to treat infected patients.

What can we learn from all of this? My intention is neither to question nor defend Fauci's competence or leadership during the early pandemic. (Though it is a separate question altogether, one might ask whether it is useful for an individual medical expert such as Fauci to be made into an authoritative figure— even if largely a figurehead—by political and media authorities in the first place, given the expansive and patchwork nature of the US healthcare system.) Originally discouraging widespread use of masks to preserve the supply for healthcare workers may very well have been the correct strategic move, given the available information. (I simply do not know.) Moreover, the research into COVID-19 transmission was still early at the time, making uncertainty understandable. For what it is worth, each seems like a plausible explanation for the confusing, shifting recommendations about masks, even if simultaneously maintaining both explanations as the rationale for these shifts would be unlikely to quell suspicion in the government's healthcare recommendations.

My intention is, instead, to identify aspects of this dynamic that play into the growing distrust of established healthcare (and government) institutions among segments of the public. With Fauci, we have a medical professional credentialed by established institutions making a confident proclamation as an expert (in March 2020). This is amid the chaos of the early pandemic in the United States and the muddled Trump administration's response. Later this recommendation is reversed, and the initial confident presentation (which may have been strategically feigned to achieve the outcome of preserving a mask supply for healthcare workers) is downplayed. Fauci's appeal to the evolving nature of science certainly reflects the process of ongoing medical research, but it does not wholly address the form and style of the original claim about face masks, which was largely to express confidence as an expert representative of an established institution. As in the case of ascriptions of authority to "the science," Fauci's method of communicating medical knowledge constitutes an attempt to double down on a vertical model of dissemination during an era when elites and experts are perceived as untrustworthy and when their recommendations may be met with suspicion. As a result, some of Fauci's audience, suspicious already of established institutions, detect the internal contradiction, which pushes them to seek alternative views from a host of alternative sources, many with their own claims to epistemic authority. To each such audience (those predisposed to trust a representative of an established institution as an epistemic authority and those predisposed not to trust one), Fauci performs the very role they expect.

In this subsection, I have tried to show how attempts by established institutions to respond to the pandemic by reclaiming their status as epistemic authorities can reinscribe a dynamic that prompts the rejection of those attempts at intervention as untrustworthy.

5   Prognostications and Recommendations

5.1   Options for Established Public Health Institutions

I foresee five possible avenues forward for established public health institutions in the aftermath of the COVID-19 pandemic. First, established institutions could embrace coercive methods to achieve health outcomes. One strategy already undertaken has been to issue an executive order requiring vaccination for federal employees (Biden, 2021). Parallel strategies (some more drastic) have been implemented in other countries, involving vaccine passports, requirements to show evidence of vaccination or negative COVID tests when shopping or dining out, and widespread lockdowns (Horowitz & Eddy, 2021). Effectively, this is to wield the power of established institutions to increase rates of vaccination by enforcing political, social, and economic consequences for refusing vaccination. How these consequences are enforced would serve as criteria both for how efficacious they are and for whether they are ethical. Measures that require individuals to get vaccinated or provide evidence of a negative COVID test in order to participate in the consumption of treats and fast food are likely justifiable and may be effective if they are equitably enforced.

Second, established healthcare institutions could attempt to adapt to the post-truth era by developing strategies to disguise their activities amid other dimensions of the social milieu. What I have in mind is a strategy akin to what Matt Christman has imagined, namely, integrating vaccines into the market economy in a way that conceals their origin in the efforts of an established institution (Biederman et al., 2021, 11:10). A government agency could, for example, provide the vaccine to retailers or online marketplaces—where it could be sold for a small amount under a label such as "Trump Miracle Elixir" (ibid.)—in recognition of both the public's association of personal liberty with purchasing power and their weary unfamiliarity (in the context of the US healthcare system) with receiving free care. In the interest of increasing vaccination rates, such a strategy would be tantamount to parasitizing the networks of epistemic counter-authorities who disseminate vaccine skepticism, in order to distribute the vaccine. (Such networks have demonstrated success promoting the use of Ivermectin, a medical treatment not recommended by established institutions.) Though such methods are morally dubious (they arguably violate a duty to ensure informed consent), they do not seem radically distinct from propagandistic marketing and PR techniques already widely used by US agencies.

Third, established institutions could try to rebuild trust by establishing a precedent for communicating the often-messy realities of policy decision-making and medical research. This would avoid the problems that arise from attempts to conceal information, feign confidence, and manipulate the public. Though it is likely that the problematic histories of established institutions have soured most future attempts to gain trust by demonstrating transparency, it is in principle possible to develop a shared, fertile soil in which the seeds of fruitful persuasion may be sown. Whether such a process might work, and what conditions would undergird the possibility of genuine persuasion, are questions for future research.

Fourth, established institutions could voluntarily dismantle and surrender domestic and foreign interests associated with public's distrust. This sort of strategy would require a broader distribution of wealth and power away from the economic and social elite and toward the wider populace. It would constitute more than a reconfiguration of healthcare interventions; it would require a deeper social and political reckoning. It is unlikely that established institutions will pursue this strategy; they would likely fight against it tooth and claw.

A final non-strategy, and perhaps the most likely course to be pursued: change nothing. Continue a top-down method of disseminating information to populations that reject this approach; shame those who resist, as did Macron recently for "yellow vests" protesters (Jeudy, 2021) or as comedy-news outlets often do for political subcultures that already lack social and epistemic capital (The Daily Show with Trevor Noah, 2021); and wait to see what will happen. If this is indeed the path taken, I suspect that communities skeptical of established authorities will simply cling tighter to alternatives, even as new viral variants emerge around the world.

5.2 A Tentative Recommendation for Individual Healthcare Providers

What can individual healthcare workers do, if anything? If my position about the significance of trust in establishing the authority of indirect verifications is largely correct, the most important thing an individual health provider can likely do to encourage hesitant patients to vaccinate is to connect with them about personal experiences pertaining to the Coronavirus and to COVID vaccines instead of relying primarily on disembodied data. Statistics collected from researchers and presented by established institutions may already be untrustworthy to someone who is skeptical about masks or vaccines. This is not necessarily because of data illiteracy, but it could be because of—as I have argued—deeply embedded social and cultural relationships on a societal level that render these sources less than universally authoritative. Recall that even as a healthcare professional, you may not have directly verified the efficacy of vaccines either and that, like your patient, you rely on other sources you trust. These sources may differ from the sources the patient is apt to trust. What may be, to you, the "awe-inspiring" results of applied medical science must be understood in light of the realities of social epistemology; hence, scolding and condescension are likely to be unhelpful (Anonymous, 2021). Instead of appeals to institutional research, relaying information based in a first-person standpoint might generate trust more effectively. Instead of referring to a graph displaying the research of others, consider narrating your own experience or the experiences of a close friend or colleague whose work in emergency rooms has, for example, shown them so many more needless deaths of unvaccinated persons than of those who are vaccinated. This sort of appeal is potentially more useful because instead of presenting information as an abstract truth generated by a distant and supposedly authoritative institution, it accounts honestly for a universal feature of scientific knowledge, namely, that it involves trust of someone else's verifications.

6   Conclusion

In this chapter, I have attempted to situate movements in opposition to mainstream public health interventions during the COVID-19 pandemic in the broader social and cultural context of post-truth. I have argued that there are explanations for distrust of established political, scientific, and healthcare institutions that go beyond ascriptions of data illiteracy or ignorance to those hesitant about vaccines or skeptical of COVID. Finally, I have suggested—in broad form—several possible avenues forward for public health institutions.

To close, I want to linger for a moment on the question of what may be startling to scientists and healthcare professionals about the persistence of anti-vaccinationism and related movements: Is it surprising that so many, seemingly so suddenly, became willing to put themselves and others at risk based on false information, mistrust of credentialed authorities, and other commitments that seem irrational? Perhaps we should instead be surprised that we were inclined to think, in the first place, that most would fall in line. (This observation might also apply to the phenomenon of political inaction against climate change.) It may be a feature specific to a recent historical period—let us call it "modernity"—that a structure existed (or perhaps only ever *seemed* to exist) through which truth could be dispensed legitimately and a diverse populace could be governed accordingly. To be sure, there is an element of utopian fantasy in the vision of a society universally, or even broadly, governed democratically, rationally, and benevolently. Indeed, even insofar as it is a fantasy, it is one that corresponds with some of the highest ideals ever to develop in human beings (altruism, justice, reason, equality). But to believe that such a fantasy can be implemented straightforwardly, that it is anything but fragile, that it is resistant to perversion or corruption (even from within, *especially* from within), and that the invisible hands of a specious meritocracy hold it perpetually aloft rather than rip the rivets from its trusses are fever dreams of a modernity sick unto death.

Acknowledgments Funding from the Crafoord Foundation enabled my research for this piece. I am also grateful for engaging conversations I had with Charlie Carstens, Aron Engberg, Patrik Fridlund, Mitchell Goldman, David Lamberth, Julia M. Reed, Becky Revalk, Dan Snowden, and Brian M. White that deepened my thinking about this topic. All mistakes, lapses in clarity, and opinions are my own.

References

Anonymous. (2021, November 21). ICU is full of the unvaccinated – My patience with them is wearing thin. *The Guardian*. https://www.theguardian.com/world/2021/nov/21/icu-is-full-of-the-unvaccinated-my-patience-with-them-is-wearing-thin

Beldon, B., & Franczak, L. (2021, September 25). Delta male. (No. 186) [Audio podcast episode]. In *TrueAnon*. https://www.patreon.com/posts/episode-186-male-56579098

Biden, J. R. (2021, September 9). *Executive order on requiring coronavirus disease 2019 vaccination for federal employees*. The White House. https://www.whitehouse.gov/briefing-room/presidential-actions/2021/09/09/executive-order-on-requiring-coronavirus-disease-2019-vaccination-for-federal-employees/

Biederman, F., Christman, M., & Menaker, W. (2021, July 22). Cuck Rifle Coffee. (No. 543) [Audio podcast episode]. In *Chapo Trap House*. https://www.patreon.com/posts/543-cuck-rifle-7-54010875

CNNpolitics. (2021). *Facts first: Did Fauci say not to wear masks?* CNN. https://edition.cnn.com/factsfirst/politics/factcheck_e58c20c6-8735-4022-a1f5-1580bc732c45

Dubé, E., Vivion, M., & MacDonald, N. E. (2015). Vaccine hesitancy, vaccine refusal and the anti-vaccine movement: influence, impact and implications. *Expert Review of Vaccines, 14*(1), 99–117. https://doi.org/10.1586/14760584.2015.964212

Durkheim, É. (2013). Preface to the second edition of *The rules of sociological method* (W. D. Halls, Trans.). In S. Lukes (Ed.), *The rules of sociological method and selected texts on sociology and its method* (2nd ed., pp. 6–17). Palgrave Macmillan. (Original work published 1901).

Einstein, A. (1905). Über die von der molekularkinetischen Theorie der Wärme geforderte Bewegung von in ruhenden Flüssigkeiten suspendierten Teilchen. *Annalen der Physik, 322*(8), 549–560.

Enserink, M., & Cohen, J. (2020, May 8). Fact-checking Judy Mikovits, the controversial virologist attacking Anthony Fauci in a viral conspiracy video. *Science*. https://www.science.org/content/article/fact-checking-judy-mikovits-controversial-virologist-attacking-anthony-fauci-viral

Fairlie, H. (1955, September 23). Political commentary. *The Spectator, 6639*, 5–7.

Friedman, T. (2007). *The world is flat: A brief history of the twenty-first century* (3rd ed.). Farrar, Straus and Giroux.

Fuller, S. (2018). *Post-truth: Knowledge as a power game*. Anthem.

Gold, M, & Shanahan, E. (2021, August 4). What we know about Cuomo's Nursing Home Scandal. *New York Times*. https://www.nytimes.com/article/andrew-cuomo-nursing-home-deaths.html

Good, A. (2018). American exception: Hegemony and the dissimulation of the state. *Administration and Society, 50*(1), 4–29. https://doi.org/10.1177/0095399715581042

Goodman, J., & Carmichael, F. (2020, May 30). Coronavirus: Bill Gates 'microchip' conspiracy theory and other vaccine claims fact-checked. *BBC News*. https://www.bbc.com/news/52847648

Horowitz, J, & Eddy, M. (2021, November 29). Austria announces covid vaccine mandate, crossing a threshold for Europe. *New York Times*. https://www.nytimes.com/2021/11/19/world/europe/austria-covid-vaccine-mandate-lockdown.html

James, W. (1975). *Pragmatism* (F. Bowers & I. K. Skrupskelis, Eds.). Harvard University Press. (Original work published 1907).

Jeudy, B. (2021, August 4). *Antivax, présidentielle .... Les confidences polynésiennes de Macron*. Paris Match. https://www.parismatch.com/Actu/Politique/Antivax-presidentielle-Les-confidences-polynesiennes-de-Macron-1751603

King, W. C., Rubinstein, M., Reinhart, A., & Mejia, R. (2021). COVID-19 vaccine hesitancy January-May 2021 among 18–64 year old US adults by employment and occupation. *Preventive Medicine Reports, 24*(4), 101569–101569. https://doi.org/10.1016/j.pmedr.2021.101569

Ledford, H. (2021, July 29). Should children get COVID vaccines? What the science says. *Nature, 595*(7896), 638–639. https://doi.org/10.1038/d41586-021-01898-9

Lowrey, W., & Anderson, W. B. (2006, March). The impact of Internet use on the public perception of physicians: A perspective from the sociology of professions literature. *Health Communication, 19*(2), 125–131. https://doi.org/10.1207/s15327027hc1902_4

Marshall, G. S. (2019). Vaccine hesitancy, history, and human nature: The 2018 Stanley A. Plotkin Lecture. *Journal of the Pediatric Infectious Diseases Society, 8*(1), 1–8. https://doi.org/10.1093/jpids/piy082

60 Minutes. (2020, March 8). *March 2020: Dr. Anthony Fauci talks with Dr Jon LaPook about Covid-19* [Video]. YouTube. https://youtu.be/PRa6t_e7dgI

Nichols, T. (2017, March/April). How America lost faith in expertise: And why that's a giant problem. *Foreign Affairs, 96*(2), 60–73.

Robbins, A. (2012, November). The CIA's vaccination ruse. *Journal of Public Health Policy, 33*(4), 387–389. https://doi.org/10.1057/jphp.2012.37

Robertson, D. G. (2016). *UFOs, conspiracy theories and the New Age: Millennial conspiracism.* Bloomsbury.

Ross, K. (2020, June 12). Why weren't we wearing masks from the beginning? Dr. Fauci explains. *TheStreet.* https://www.thestreet.com/video/dr-fauci-masks-changing-directive-coronavirus

Shah, S. (2011, July 11). CIA organised fake vaccination drive to get Osama bin Laden's family DNA. *The Guardian.* https://www.theguardian.com/world/2011/jul/11/cia-fake-vaccinations-osama-bin-ladens-dna

Siddiqui, Z. (2021, March 9). In Pakistan, Legacy of Fake CIA Vaccination Programs Leads to Vaccine Hesitancy. *Vice.* https://www.vice.com/en/article/5dpvkd/in-pakistan-legacy-of-fake-cia-vaccination-programs-leads-to-vaccine-hesitancy

Subbaraman, N. (2021, August 19). How do vaccinated people spread Delta? What the science says. *Nature, 596*(7872), 327–328. https://doi.org/10.1038/d41586-021-02187-1

Subramony, D. P. (2014, March/April). Revisiting the digital divide in the context of a 'flattening' world. *Educational Technology, 54*(2): 3–9.

Swisher, K. (2021, June 21). Anthony Fauci on the Lab Leak Theory and emailing Mark Zuckerberg: America's chief immunologist claps back. [Audio podcast episode.] In Sway. *New York Times.* https://www.nytimes.com/2021/06/21/opinion/sway-kara-swisher-anthony-fauci.html

The Daily Show with Trevor Noah. (2021, August 24). *Jordan Klepper Debates Anti-Vax Mandate Protesters in NYC* [Video]. YouTube. https://youtu.be/rIhOPOzlvTA

Trump, D. J. [as @realDonaldTrump]. (2018, April 12). *If I wanted to fire Robert Mueller in December, as reported by the Failing New York Times, I would have fired him. Just more Fake News from a biased newspaper!* [Tweet]. Twitter. https://twitter.com/realdonaldtrump/status/984371491277099010 [Accessed 31 October 2021 on Trump Twitter Archive: https://www.thetrumparchive.com/].

Trump, D. J. [as @realDonaldTrump]. (2020, June 4). *The Fake Newspaper!* https://t.co/X6LEqpQeBc [Tweet]. Twitter. https://twitter.com/realdonaldtrump/status/1268497297702367235 [Accessed 31 October 2021 on Trump Twitter Archive: https://www.thetrumparchive.com/].

Washington, H. A. (2006). *Medical apartheid: The dark history of medical experimentation on Black Americans from colonial times to the present.* Doubleday.

Woodcock, J., & Marks, P. (2021, September 10). *Statement: FDA will follow the science on Covid-19 vaccines for young children.* U.S. FDA [United States Food & Drug Administration]. https://www.fda.gov/news-events/press-announcements/fda-will-follow-science-covid-19-vaccines-young-children

Patents on Inventions Involving AI in the Life Sciences and Healthcare

Anna Katharina Heide

Abstract

In recent years, the relevance of artificial intelligence (AI) and its potential applications in various technical areas of the life sciences and healthcare have increased. The accumulation of big data, the development of algorithms, and improvements in computer processing capacity have made possible the integration of AI in the life sciences and healthcare. Some examples of AI applications in these fields are drug and molecular design, the prediction of disease risk, diagnosis of diseases, detection of cancerous cells and tumors, genomics, the monitoring of therapeutic progress, the adjustment of therapeutic treatment, and improvements in manufacturing processes. Such applications change the mode of work in hospitals and for doctors and give rise to interdisciplinary products for which a company seeks a monopoly under patent law. A patented technical monopoly may facilitate a company a dominant market position and a return on investment. However, a patent monopoly is subject to legal regulations that define the preconditions for a patent grant as well as exclusion criteria. These may vary in the particular country for which a patent is sought. This chapter is based on the European Patent Convention (EPC) and the case law of the Boards of Appeal of the European Patent Office (EPO). The examples of granted or refused patents presented here may be assessed differently by other jurisdictions [e.g., the United States Patent and Trademark Office (USPTO), Japan Patent Office (JPO), China National Intellectual Property Administration (CNIPA)].

A. K. Heide (✉)
German and European Patent Attorney, Ruhr-IP Patent Attorneys, Essen, Germany
e-mail: heide@ruhr-ip.com

© The Author(s), under exclusive license to Springer Nature Switzerland AG 2022
S. Ehsani et al. (eds.), *The Future Circle of Healthcare*, Future of Business and Finance, https://doi.org/10.1007/978-3-030-99838-7_9

1   Introduction

Intellectual property (IP) protection deals with various property rights. A distinction is made between technical IP rights, such as patents and utility models, and nontechnical IP rights, such as trademarks and designs. While patents and utility models protect technologies, trademarks have the purpose of protecting the name of the product, for example, and designs have the purpose of protecting the external (aesthetic) appearance of the product or its packaging. While trademarks and designs are perceived by consumers, they often do not know whether the product is protected by a patent. However, patents are of particular importance for those who finance the technology in order to protect their investments through legal monopoly.

The scope of protection and many procedures for the aforementioned IP rights are based on the Paris Convention of 1883, which continues to apply in its adapted version of 1979.[1] This is the basis for most national as well as regional patent systems, such as EPC. This chapter deals exclusively with the technical protection right "patent." Utility models are very similar in many respects, but there are many variations in different jurisdictions, whereas patent law is largely harmonized. Trademarks and designs are valuable IP rights that, together with patents, can establish a valuable product IP strategy for a company. However, the technical monopoly of a company in competition is primarily protected by patents. Therefore, companies from the life sciences and healthcare try to protect their AI-implemented products through patents.

This chapter will not advise the reader about how to write AI patents. Instead, it provides an overview of the relevant legal regulations and some examples of potentially patentable AI inventions. It will provide a better understanding of how AI patents are examined by patent offices, in particular the EPO, and give some practical advice about whether certain AI-implemented inventions in the life sciences and healthcare fields should be filed or kept confidential as trade secrets.

The term AI includes machine learning (ML), support vector machines (SVM), random forest (RF) algorithms, and Bayesian modeling. The terms "life sciences" and "healthcare" within the scope of this chapter include biotechnological, pharmaceutical, biochemical, therapeutic, and diagnostic applications and the respective medical devices, compositions, and compounds used in these fields.

2   Patent Basics

2.1   Definition of a Patent

The term "patent" originates from the Latin term "littera patens," which roughly translates to "open letter." In the seventeenth century, sovereigns used patents to

---

[1] The official English translation of the Paris Convention for the Protection of Industrial Property is available at the URL: https://wipolex.wipo.int/en/text/288514

grant exclusive rights, like the mining rights, to persons or companies. Today different legal provisions define certain aspects of a patent and the extent to which it grants a right to prohibit others from using the patented invention.

2.1.1 Who Is Entitled to Apply for a Patent?

Any natural or legal person may file a patent application with the respective national (the German Patent and Trademark Office, GTMA, the United States Patent and Trademark Office, USPTO, etc.) or multinational patent office (the European Patent Office, EPO) to request the grant of a patent.[2] A patent application may also be filed by a group of persons called joint applicants. Joint applicants may be several natural persons, two or more cooperating companies, or a combination of natural and legal persons. This applies not only for German or European patents but also for US patents and other patent law systems.

The right to a patent belongs to the inventor(s) or their legal successor.[3] The successor in title is usually the inventor's employer, who files the patent application in their own name. By filing the patent application, the applicant requests the grant of the patent. The transfer of the right to the patent from the inventor to the employer is subject to national law and in most cases is initiated by an invention disclosure that the inventor makes to the employer.

2.1.2 The Inventors' Right

The inventor has the right to be named as such with any patent office.[4] This right remains regardless of whether the right to the patent has been transferred to the employer or a third party. If the inventor(s) files the patent application, they are also named as applicant.

2.1.3 Duration of a Patent

The term of a European patent is 20 years from the date of filing of the patent application.[5] The same applies for most patent systems. An exception applies to patents for pharmaceutical products. The proprietor of these products can apply for a supplementary protection certificate (SPC)[6] that extends the term of protection of the granted patent by up to 5 years.

---

[2] For the EPO, see EPC, Article 58, Entitlement to file a European patent application, https://www.epo.org/law-practice/legal-texts/html/epc/2016/e/ar58.html

[3] EPC, Article 60, Right to a European patent, https://www.epo.org/law-practice/legal-texts/html/epc/2020/e/ar60.html

[4] EPC, Article 62 and Article 81, Right of the inventor to be mentioned and Designation of the inventor, https://www.epo.org/law-practice/legal-texts/html/epc/2016/e/ar62.html and https://www.epo.org/law-practice/legal-texts/html/epc/2020/e/ar81.html

[5] EPC, Article 63, Term of the European patent, https://www.epo.org/law-practice/legal-texts/html/epc/2016/e/ar63.html

[6] For further information: https://ec.europa.eu/growth/industry/strategy/intellectual-property/patent-protection-eu/supplementary-protection-certificates-pharmaceutical-and-plant-protection-products_en

2.1.4   Scope of Protection of a Patent

The scope (extent) of protection conferred by a patent shall be determined by the claims, which shall be interpreted according to the description and the drawings of the patent.[7] The claims define the protected invention. The patent claims must therefore be clearly formulated.[8] Any person skilled in the technical field of the invention protected by the patent must be able to understand which combination of technical features is covered by the respective patent. The requirements for clarity are elaborated later in this chapter.

2.1.5   Rights Conferred by a Patent

The patent prohibits any third party from using a product or process that is the subject matter (content) of the patent without the consent of the patent owner.[9] Use is defined as manufacturing, offering for sale, putting on the market, and use or importing or possessing for the said purposes.

On the basis of a patent, the patent holders obtain an exclusive right for the technical solution defined in the patent claims, which constitutes the invention. The idea behind the exclusive right is to ensure incentives for innovation through a time-limited monopolization in order to promote the further development of the monopolized technology. In return, the patent holder must disclose their invention 18 months after the filing date. On the one hand, this disclosure serves to inform everyone about the latest state of development and thus spur further development.

On the other hand, the disclosure serves to inform third parties of which technical solution the company (applicant) has filed an application for the granting of a patent. In the official examination procedure, it is analyzed whether the invention meets the criteria for a grant. The criteria are technicality of the invention, clarity in the definition of the invention, feasibility of the claimed technical solution, and novelty and inventive step. In the following, these criteria that are generally applicable internationally are discussed in particular in the field of AI-implemented inventions in the life sciences and healthcare.

2.2   Patentable Inventions

A patent shall be granted for any invention in all fields of technology that is novel and inventive and has industrial applications.[10] The invention has to be disclosed

---

[7] EPC, Article 69, Extent of protection, https://www.epo.org/law-practice/legal-texts/html/epc/2016/e/ar69.html

[8] EPC, Article 84, Claims, https://www.epo.org/law-practice/legal-texts/html/epc/2016/e/ar84.html

[9] EPC, Article 64, Rights conferred by a European patent, https://www.epo.org/law-practice/legal-texts/html/epc/2020/e/ar64.html; and national patent law.

[10] EPC: Article 52 (Patentable inventions, https://www.epo.org/law-practice/legal-texts/html/epc/2016/e/ar52.html), Article 54 (Novelty, https://www.epo.org/law-practice/legal-texts/html/epc/2020/e/ar54.html), Article 56 (Inventive step, https://www.epo.org/law-practice/legal-texts/html/epc/2020/e/ar56.html), and Article 57 (Industrial application, https://www.epo.org/law-practice/legal-texts/html/epc/2016/e/ar57.html)

in a manner that is sufficiently clear and complete for it to be carried out by a skilled person in the technical field of the claimed invention. Thus, it is not sufficient to define the technical features in the claims; it must be explained in the entire description how the invention can be realized. The entire description comprises the written description, examples, and figures as filed at the filing date of the patent application. Any skilled person in the relevant field must be enabled to repeat the invention. This requirement is satisfied if the patent contains clear instructions for producing the invention.[11]

2.3 Exclusions from Patentability

Against the background of ethical issues, specific objects were excluded from patentability. "Plant or animal varieties or essentially biological processes for the production of plants or animals" are excluded from patentability. Provided that a plant or animal is produced by means of an artificial gene editing process, it is patentable. Microbiological processes, such as microbial fermentation, and the products derived therefrom are also patentable. In addition, diagnostic, therapeutic, and invasive methods applied to the human or animal body, such as injections or surgery, are not patentable. However, it is possible to obtain a patent for products used in these methods, such as surgical instruments, diagnostic devices, and substances.[12] The reason is that physicians must not be prevented from freely deciding on the best treatment for their patient, following their oath. Here, the patent monopoly does not apply, and physicians are free to use any treatment they deem appropriate without being guilty of patent infringement.

In most patent systems, discoveries, scientific theories, and mathematical methods, schemes, rules and methods for performing mental acts, programs for computers, and presentations of information are not regarded as inventions.[13]

As AI and machine learning are based generally on computational models and mathematical methods, one would expect that AI would be excluded from patentability. But AI is more complex, and such technologies are treated differently by patent offices in different regions of the world. Therefore, what follows represents only the policies of the EPO.

---

[11] EPC, Article 83, Disclosure of the invention, https://www.epo.org/law-practice/legal-texts/html/epc/2016/e/ar83.html

[12] EPC, Article 53, Exceptions to patentability, https://www.epo.org//law-practice/legal-texts/html/epc/2020/e/ar53.html

[13] EPC, Article 52, Patentable inventions, https://www.epo.org/law-practice/legal-texts/html/epc/2016/e/ar52.html

3   AI in the Context of Patent Law

3.1   Definition of AI in the Context of Patent Law

Different definitions have been given for AI. In 2004, John McCarthy offered the following definition: "It is the science and engineering of making intelligent machines, especially intelligent computer programs. It is related to the similar task of using computers to understand human intelligence, but AI does not have to confine itself to methods that are biologically observable" (McCarthy, 2004, p. 2). But as early as 1950, Alan Turing asked whether machines can think and offered a test where a human interrogator would try to distinguish between a computer and human text response. Turing's paper "Computing Machinery and Intelligence" (Turing, 1950) is recognized as the origin of the conversation about artificial intelligence.

The EPO has defined artificial intelligence as "the ability of computers and machines to perform mental tasks commonly associated with humans, such as learning, reasoning, and solving problems."[14] "Artificial intelligence and machine learning are based on computational models and algorithms for classification, clustering, regression, and dimensionality reduction such as neural networks, genetic algorithms, support vector machines, k-means, kernel regression, and discriminant analysis."[15] Even if training data reflecting technical information is used for training such computer models and algorithms, its abstract mathematical nature remains (see Sect. 2.3). The potential technical character of inventions implementing computer models and algorithms is discussed below.

3.2   Categories of Inventions

In general, there are two categories of inventions: products and methods. Products consist of chemical or biological compounds and compositions, cells, proteins and molecular sequences, mechanical tools, devices and components thereof, implants, biomaterials, chips, arrays, computers, programmable apparatuses, and more. Methods include, for example, the manufacture of the aforementioned products and analysis of a product but also the use of a product for a specific purpose such as an antibody (product) for use in the therapy of cancer or for diagnosis of a disease (method).

Artificial intelligence and neural networks can be applied to or used in a product or process in any area of technology. A neural network can be used in products such as a heart monitoring device or in a blood glucose level diagnostic device. Another example is the use of a neural network *to classify* and *analyze* images (e.g., of skin,

---

[14] https://www.epo.org/news-events/in-focus/ict/artificial-intelligence.html

[15] EPO, Guidelines for Examination, Part G, Chap. II, Sect. 3.3.1, Discoveries, https://www.epo.org/law-practice/legal-texts/html/guidelines/e/g_ii_3_1.htm

brain, bones, eyes, or motion). AI and neural networks can control *manufacturing processes* for chemical or biological products and can *drive identification* of products such as compounds that may be pharmaceutically active. Consequently, in these examples AI is a feature of a method. Provided the AI-implemented method has identified (via screening) a new product (e.g., a new antibody), the product itself must meet all patentability requirements. Another method could be directed to its manufacture which again may involve AI for the control of the manufacturing. Each of the aforementioned subject matters—screening method for a product, its manufacturing process, and the product itself—has to be novel, inventive, and sufficiently and clearly disclosed to qualify for a patent. Thus, it is important to distinguish the categories of invention in order to identify whether AI is involved in a patentable subject matter—the product and/or the method—or not. This is important for a clear definition of the respective invention. If AI is not a feature of the product (e.g., a new pharmaceutically active compound defined by its chemical properties and its biological activity), there is no need to integrate features of the process that involve AI into claims directed to the product. The AI-driven identification and synthesis of the product may be patentable as "a screening method" or "a method for the manufacture of the product." However, it should be evaluated whether the patent application seeking protection for the method should be filed or kept confidential as trade secrets.

An AI system may also control a medical device or a part of a medical device. In cases where AI contributes to a medical device, the patent claim for the device must include the definition of the AI system. In addition, the method—that is, the steps performed by the developed AI and neuronal network—should be claimed independently. Some examples are described below.

3.3   Computer-Implemented Inventions (CII)

As AI is considered a branch of computer science, inventions involving AI are considered "computer-implemented inventions" (CII). Because of industry demands for access to patents on computer-implemented inventions, the case law of the EPO Boards of Appeal has established a stable and predictable framework for the patentability of computer-implemented inventions. The EPO does not exclude inventions involving computational models and mathematical methods from patentability as long as they have a technical character and the claimed AI contributes to a technical effect.

The EPO's Guidelines for Examination contain a definition of the term CII.[16] Part G, Chapter II, Sect. 3.3, explains how the EPO deals with artificial intelligence and machine learning (Sect. 3.3.1) and simulation, design, or modeling (Sect.

---

[16] EPO, Guidelines for Examination, Part F, Chap. IV, Sect. 3.9, Claims directed to computer-implemented inventions, https://www.epo.org/law-practice/legal-texts/html/guidelines/e/f_iv_3_9.htm

3.3.2).[17] Hence, the guidance provided in Part G, Chapter II, Sect. 3.3, generally applies to computational models and algorithms.

3.4   Technical Character of Inventions Involving AI

Although mathematical methods may contribute substantially to appropriate solutions to technical problems in all fields of technology, they are excluded from patentability as such (see Sect. 2.3). However, this exclusion does not pertain when the AI-implemented invention has a technical character and the AI contributes to the claimed technical solution. The AI-implemented invention must not be used in a purely abstract mathematical method.

Thus, "if a claim [of a patent application] is directed either to a method involving the use of technical means (e.g. a computer) or to a device, its subject-matter has a technical character as a whole and is thus not excluded from patentability" (Guidelines for Examination, part G, Chapter II, Sect. 3.3).[18] For example, it is not sufficient to specify the technical nature of the data or the parameters of the mathematical model, such as heart rate or blood glucose concentration (e.g., calculation of the individual dosage regime of insulin) for an invention to qualify as patentable.

When assessing the contribution a mathematical method makes to the technical character of an invention, it must be taken into account whether the method serves a technical purpose. For the technical field outside healthcare, case laws discuss the legal interpretation of a technical purpose (e.g., T 1227/05,[19] T 1358/09[20]). The EPO examination guidelines also provide examples of technical effects of CII and exclusions (part G, Chapter II, Sects. 3.6.1–3.6.3). Some examples of a technical effect of a computer program are controlling an antilock braking system in a car, determining emissions using an X-ray device, compressing video, restoring a distorted digital image, and encrypting electronic communications.

Examples of technical functions in the life sciences and healthcare that may be served by a mathematical method include[21]:

---

[17] EPO, Guidelines for Examination, Part G, Chap. II, Sect. 3.3.1 (Artificial intelligence and machine learning, https://www.epo.org/law-practice/legal-texts/html/guidelines/e/g_ii_3_3_1.htm) and 3.3.2 (Simulation, design or modeling, https://www.epo.org/law-practice/legal-texts/html/guidelines/e/g_ii_3_3_2.htm)

[18] EPO, Guidelines for Examination, Part G, Chap. II, Sect. 3.3, Mathematical models, https://www.epo.org/law-practice/legal-texts/html/guidelines/e/g_ii_3_3.htm

[19] EPO, T 1227/05 (Circuit simulation I/Infineon Technologies) of 13.12.2006, https://www.epo.org/law-practice/case-law-appeals/recent/t051227ep1.html

[20] EPO, T 1358/09 (Classification/BDGB ENTERPRISE SOFTWARE) of 21.11.2014, https://www.epo.org/law-practice/case-law-appeals/recent/t091358eu1.html

[21] https://www.epo.org/law-practice/legal-texts/html/guidelines/e/g_ii_3_3.htm

- Controlling a specific technical system or process, such as an X-ray apparatus, an insulin pump, or a pacemaker.
- Enhancing or analyzing digital audio or images, for example, denoising within a hearing device or detecting cancerous cells or tumors in a digital image.
- Separating sources in speech signals; speech recognition, for example mapping speech input to text output (e.g., for a hearing device or a device that diagnoses linguistic deficits).
- Encrypting/decrypting or signing electronic communications or generating keys in an RSA cryptographic system; for example, sensor-recorded data in an implant that is encrypted and transmitted to the responsible doctor.
- Determining the energy expenditure of an individual by processing data obtained from physiological sensors, such as deriving the body temperature of a subject from data obtained from an ear temperature detector.
- Providing a genotype estimate based on an analysis of DNA samples and providing a confidence interval for this estimate to quantify its reliability.
- Providing a medical diagnosis using an automated system that processes physiological measurements.
- Simulating the behavior of an adequately defined class of technical items or specific technical processes under technically relevant conditions, for example, simulating molecular interactions that identify potential compounds.

The technical character of AI-implemented inventions arises in the field of life sciences, and healthcare must be sought independently of the applied mathematical laws and in the technical fields of the particular application. Whether or not such AI-implemented inventions are patentable is determined by whether the mathematical laws contribute to a technical aspect of the technical problem in the fields of technology, such as chemistry, biochemistry, pharmacy, and biotechnology. The technical effect of AI must contribute to the specific purpose of the invention, for example, the detection of cardiac arrhythmias, the monitoring of insulin levels, or the release of the suitable insulin dosage. If the technical effect of the AI contributes to the specific purpose of the invention, the AI-implemented invention that relates to a product or a method is patentable.

4 Patentability of AI-Implemented Inventions

4.1 Clarity of the Claims that Define an AI-Implemented Invention

Provided that the invention involving AI meets the EPO's definition of solving a technical problem, the patent claim must define the essential features of the invention in a way that is unambiguous and clear to a person skilled in the art.

As mentioned above (Sect. 2.1.4), the description serves as a basis for the interpretation of the claims, but a person skilled in the art must be able to understand what the essential features of the invention are. That person must be able to recognize when or whether they are operating within the claimed scope of the invention. The patent wording must provide clarity about when one is infringing the patent.

In the context of patent law, a person skilled in the art is considered to be a scientist with sound experience in the relevant technical field of the invention or an interdisciplinary team that includes, for example, someone with knowledge of AI systems and someone with knowledge of the relevant technical field of life sciences and healthcare in which the AI-implemented invention is to be applied. If the terms used to describe the technical features of the invention are not clear and if the description of the patent does not provide an explanation and basis for interpreting the terms in the claims, the patent will be rejected for lack of clarity.[22]

For example, the decision T 1285/10 of the Boards of Appeal of the EPO discusses the clarity of the invention of patent EP1222602B1 filed by the US company Iris Biotechnologies Inc. The patent claims "a method for diagnosing and recommending treatment for a physiological condition, comprising (i) collecting hybridization information of an array of peptide nucleic acid probes …; (ii) transmitting said hybridization information into a central data processing facility, where the hybridization information transmission includes gene expression data …; (iii) analyzing said hybridization information to generate a hybridization profile, and comparing said hybridization profile to hybridization profiles stored in an updateable database …; (iv) determining the most likely pathological or physiological conditions suggested by the comparative analysis of hybridization profiles, using artificial intelligence routines along with suggested methods of treatment for the conditions, to a user; and (v) recommending methods of treatment".[23]

During examination of this patent application, the examination division objected to the expressions "updateable database," "hybridization profile," and "artificial intelligence routines" among others, because they were not clear enough to the skilled person. As a result, the examination division refused the patent. However, when the applicant appealed the decision, the Board decided that these expressions are sufficiently clear for skilled person, especially in the context of the description as a whole.

The Board argued that the database that stores the hybridization profiles is part of the artificial intelligence system and architecture, as the detailed description in the patent showed (see Fig. 1, page 22, EP1222602B1).[24] In the context of the whole disclosure, it is clear that this database may be updated. The update may comprise the hybridization profiles of new patients or new hybridization profiles of existing patients. The Board also judged that the term "hybridization

---

[22] EPC, Article 84, Claims, https://www.epo.org/law-practice/legal-texts/html/epc/2020/e/ar84.html

[23] EPO, T 1285/10 (Genetic analysis computing system/Iris Biotechnologies) of 23.5.2014, https://www.epo.org/law-practice/case-law-appeals/recent/t101285eu1.html

[24] Figure 1 on page 22 is available online: https://worldwide.espacenet.com/patent/search/family/022537965/publication/EP1222602B1?q=EP1222602B1

profile" was clear because the description disclosed "that the term 'hybridization profile' designates the information related to a patient, including the hybridization information collected from the patient and stored in the system database." This language left no room for a skilled person to make another (or wrong) interpretation of the term. The Board also ruled that the expression "artificial intelligence routines" has a well-known meaning. Additionally, the description of the patent gives two examples of such routines, a rule-based expert system and a neural network. Therefore, the Board ruled that this expression was not too broad, contrary to what the examination division had argued in its decision.

The EPO accepted that the independent claim of EP1222602B1 clearly defined the invention in a way that enabled a skilled person to understand the invention and to recognize whether they were practicing within the granted scope of protection of the patent.

This example shows that appropriate wording of terms that define the essential features of the patent and thus the scope of protection is crucial. It may be necessary to introduce new terms in order to define the claimed invention adequately and comprehensibly. If the language goes beyond the technical terms that are proven as part of general knowledge in the respective technical field, the description of the patent must include an unambiguous and clear definition of the newly introduced terms; in the case of the patent claim of Iris Biotechnologies, the new term was "hybridization profile." Technical terms that demonstrably belong to general knowledge in the respective technical field (e.g., "artificial intelligence routines") do not necessarily have to be defined in the description. However, it must be taken into account that technical terms can become more differentiated depending on the technical development. Even experts may disagree about what such technical terms mean or interpret them differently. Therefore, the respective technical knowledge at the filing date of the patent must be taken into account. If the examination division objects to a term within the claim because it is unclear, it must be made clear based on the *original* disclosure of the patent application. At a later stage of examination, it is not possible to add a comprehensive definition of the objected term. It is therefore advisable to introduce further explanations and a few concrete examples as a basis for interpreting technical terms at the filing date.

4.2   Sufficiency of Disclosure of an AI-Implemented Invention

The claims that define the invention must be sufficiently clear and complete to enable a person skilled in the art to carry it out.[25] The disclosure of the invention in the patent application must enable a person skilled in the art to understand and to reproduce the technical innovation by following the language in the claimed invention and, if necessary, by drawing on their general technical knowledge.

---

[25] EPC, Article 83, Disclosure of the invention, https://www.epo.org/law-practice/legal-texts/html/epc/2020/e/ar83.html

This requirement defined in patent law for a patentable invention conflicts with the interest of the patentee to make it difficult for a competitor to rework the invention and to identify ways to circumvent the patent. The balancing act between disclosing as little as possible and as much as necessary to fulfill the requirement of sufficiency of disclosure requires close interaction with a patent attorney in order to avoid the unwilling and possibly unnecessary disclosure of too fine details. On the other hand, the requirement of sufficient disclosure must be met at the filing date of the patent application in order to obtain the grant of a patent.

It is important to note that a lack of sufficient disclosure is usually impossible to cure afterward, and if it is possible, it can be done only with the greatest difficulty. In the fields of the life sciences and healthcare, overcoming this hurdle can be a major problem, especially if the invention is defined by functional features, such as a certain activity or a certain technical effect. Such functional features are often used in the fields of immunology and cell and gene therapy, for example, to define the specificity of an antibody, receptor, or cell. In principle, patentees are not allowed to improve technical details or to submit experiments that are essential for the realization of the invention and that provide proof of the technical effect for the first time.

The examination of sufficient disclosure is always done on a case-by-case basis. The examination division considers two aspects. One is whether at least one way that the technical solution has been disclosed is reproducible, and the other is whether this one way is sufficient for the skilled person to reproduce the invention "without undue burden." An undue burden exists if the invention cannot be reproduced using general expertise and routine experiments and the person skilled in the art would have to carry out experiments on the scale of a research project for this purpose.

4.2.1   Example of a Sufficient Disclosure

In decision T 0466/09, the EPO Boards of Appeal denied sufficiency of disclosure of the invention of the patent EP0883371B1 filed by Nokia Corporation. After the patent was granted, two competitors, Novo Nordisk A/S and Roche Diagnostics GmbH, attacked it with an opposition, arguing that disclosure was insufficient, among other reasons. Below, a comparison of the granted claim 1 (directed to the method) and granted claim 2 (directed to the respective equipment) of EP0883371B1 is provided. Both claims have been amended by incorporating further and more detailed descriptions of features of the mathematical method. In this case, the board confirmed that the more specific claims define a sufficiently disclosed invention but not the originally granted claims. The patent was maintained in amended form as EP0883371B2.[26]

---

[26] B1 represents the granted patent as decided by the examination division and B2 represented the patent maintained as amended during an opposition filed by a third party, The detailed proceedings of T 0466/09 are available under the following URL: https://register.epo.org/application?number= EP97904470

The Boards of Appeal considered that the whole disclosure of the patent provided sufficient information in a manner that sufficiently clear and complete for it to be carried out by a person skilled in the art. The competitors had argued that the mathematical model was not sufficiently disclosed, but the Board ruled that it was sufficient to mention Widrow's adaptive LMS algorithm as an example of the mathematical model to be used. As this algorithm is further described in detail in the well-known technical literature that is part of the common general knowledge of the skilled person in this technical field, the Board rejected this objection. It judged that with regard to the mathematical model to be used (for obtaining measurable blood probe), at least one way of reproducing the technology is indicated clearly enough to enable a person skilled in the art to carry out the invention.

Thus, the Board accepted that a person skilled in the art would know how to quantify the input parameters of "basic data X" of the mathematical model (the patient's diet, medication regime, and physical strain), but Nokia Corporation was required to specify the formulae for this purpose after its competitors objected to its original description.

4.2.2   Example of Insufficient Disclosure

Another relevant decision is T 0161/18, in which the Boards of Appeal judged that the invention was not sufficiently disclosed. The patent application, EP1955228A2,[27] was filed by ARC Seibersdorf Research GmbH. The patent application uses an artificial neural network to transform the blood pressure curve measured at the periphery into the equivalent aortic pressure. The independent claim 1 regarding the method read as follows[28]:

> Method for determining the cardiac output from an arterial blood pressure curve measured at the periphery, in which the blood pressure curve measured at the periphery is transformed by calculation into the corresponding central blood pressure curve and the cardiac output is calculated from the central blood pressure curve, characterized in that the transformation of the blood pressure curve measured at the periphery into the corresponding central blood pressure curve is carried out with the aid of an artificial neural network whose weighting values are determined by learning.

The description of the training of the neural network disclosed only that the input data should cover a wide range of patients of different ages, genders, constitution types, health conditions, and the like. There was no specific information about the network (see page 5, last paragraph to page 6, first paragraph of the description).[29] The description also did not specify which input data are suitable for training. The

---

[27] A1, A2, or A3 at the end of a patent number represents a published patent application, for detailed explanation see URL: https://www.epo.org/searching-for-patents/helpful-resources/first-time-here/definitions.html

[28] https://worldwide.espacenet.com/patent/search/family/038023611/publication/EP1955228A2? q=EP1955228; The original German wording of the patent application has been translated into English.

[29] The references refers to the downloaded document which is available under the following URL: https://worldwide.espacenet.com/patent/search/family/038023611/publication/ EP1955228A2?q=EP1955228

examination division decided that the description did not give enough information to enable a person skilled in the art to reproduce the training of the artificial neural network. It refused the application because the claimed machine learning invention was not sufficiently disclosed, in particular with regard to the artificial neural network.

Meanwhile, the above-mentioned decision T 0161/18[30] was confirmed in decision T 1191/19 of 1 April 2022 wherein the proprietor appealed the refusal of the patent application EP2351523A1 (applicant Fundació Institut Guttmann, Spain). The examining division decided that the claims do not meet the requirements of clear wording of the claims and that the claimed method is not inventive. The boards of appeal confirmed the decision and further denied sufficiency of disclosure.

The underlying invention was directed to *"A computer-implemented method for optimizing predictions for personalized interventions for a determined user in processes the substrate of which is the neuronal plasticity, including one of a neurorehabilitation process, a neuroeducation/neurolearning process and a cognitive neurostimulation process, where said interventions comprise at least cognitive and/or functional tasks to be performed by said determined user or subject of said neurorehabilitation, of said neuroeducation/neurolearning or of said cognitive neurostimulation,"* wherein the method comprises a detailed order of steps.[31] The applicant defended that claim 1 clearly defines a "meta-learning scheme" and cited a list of supporting prior art documents. However, without deciding on (the lack of) clarity of claim 1 (see point 2 of the Reasons, T 1191/19), the board came to the conclusion that the application does not disclose <u>how</u> the meta-learning scheme was applied. Even when taking into account *"the terminology in Figure 1 and the description, the application <u>does not disclose any example set of training data</u> ('database with information regarding a plurality of users at least in relation to interventions to be performed' in claim 1) and <u>validation data</u> (also 'validation data' in claim 1), which the meta-learning scheme requires as input."*[32] Moreover, the minimum number of patients from which training data should be achieved for a meaningful prediction and the set of relevant parameters are not disclosed. Similarly, relevant information for training Classifiers A and B (step a1 of claim 1) or the relevant information for training the Meta Classifier (step c of claim 1) were not disclosed. Furthermore, the structure of the artificial neural networks used as classifiers, their topology, activation functions, end conditions, or learning mechanism were also not included. With reference to the above-mentioned decision T 161/18 (point 2 of the Reasons), the content of the patent application "is more like an invitation to a research programme."[33]

---

[30] The decision is available only in German under URL: https://www.epo.org/law-practice/case-law-appeals/recent/t180161du1.html, the following references are made based on the available online version.

[31] The complete claim URL: https://www.epo.org/law-practice/case-law-appeals/recent/t191191eu1.html

[32] Fig. 1, page 13, paras [0055] and [0056] of EP2351523A1, https://worldwide.espacenet.com/patent/search/family/042128288/publication/EP2351523A1?q=EP2351523A1

4.2.3   Important Aspects of Sufficient Disclosure

It was already mentioned, but it is important to emphasize that a lack of sufficient disclosure is usually impossible to cure after a patent claim has been filed, and if so, then only with the greatest difficulty. The examination of sufficient disclosure is always done on a case-by-case basis. At least one way of reproducing the technical solution of the claimed invention has to be disclosed. In claims covering a broad range of embodiments of the invention, this one way has to be described in enough detail that a skilled person can reproduce the invention over the entire claimed scope "without undue burden." Different embodiments of an invention result if the invention—for example, the product—is defined by several features, and for each feature not only a concrete value but ranges are defined (e.g., concentration ranges, variables for nucleotides, amino acids, different combinations). Thus, the "one way" must be sufficient to enable the skilled person to reproduce the encompassed individual embodiments by the generic definition of the invention. Special attention must be paid to this requirement during the drafting of the patent application. The specifics of both technical and patent law within the relevant jurisdiction have to be taken into account. Two issues are especially important to consider.

First, sufficiency of disclosure of a claimed invention can be argued only on the basis of the originally filed description and on the basis of the common general knowledge at the filing date. Common general knowledge has to be proven by the patent owner. Reference books in the relevant technical field and review articles are accepted as proof provided that they were published prior the filing date of the patent. If such proof can be provided, it is accepted that a skilled person will be able to complete the teaching of the claimed invention and follow the instruction of the patent to realize the claimed invention.

Second, the underlying formula of the mathematical model that provides the technical results responsible for the technical solution of the claimed invention has to be defined in the claims. It is not enough to define the technical problem in the claims. For patent EP0883371B1 (mentioned above), the purpose of the invention was to improve the treatment of patients with diabetes and to enable them to care for themselves more effectively. This problem was formulated in granted claim 1 (left-hand column of Table 1) as follows: "so that the patient can himself monitor and predict the effect of the treatment," but the claim did not define how patients could monitor their blood glucose level or how they could improve the protocol for treating their disease. The technical solution was measuring the glucose concentration at predetermined moments. This was defined in the amended patent after competitors challenged the patent (right-hand column of Table 1). Based on the predictive blood glucose level, the patient is guided to inject the correct insulin dosage at the correct time. The same level of detail is required for patents related to neuronal networks that have to be trained for the technical purpose. In order to fulfill the requirement of sufficient disclosure, the claim must specify which input data is appropriate for training the neuronal network.

---

[33] Reason 4.1 of T 161/18 https://www.epo.org/law-practice/case-law-appeals/recent/t191191eu1.html

Table 1 Original sclaim of EP0883371B1 and amended claim of Patent EP0883371B2

The granted patent claimed[a]	Amended patent after opposition[b]
Claim 1. A method of predicting the glucose level $g(t_i)$ in a patient's blood, comprising:	Claim 1. A method of predicting the glucose level $g(t_i)$ in a patient's blood, comprising:
formulating an adaptive mathematical model (H) about the behavior of the patient's blood glucose level, the model taking into account at least the patient's diet, medication and physical strain and comprising comparing predictive values $\hat{g}(t_i)$, provided by the model, to measured glucose levels $g(t_i)$ and correcting the mathematical model (H) on the basis of the result of said comparison, and	formulating an adaptive mathematical model (H) about the behavior of the patient's blood glucose level, the model taking into account at least the patient's diet, medication and physical strain and comprising comparing predictive values $\hat{g}(t_i)$, provided by the model, to measured glucose levels $g(t_i)$ and correcting the mathematical model (H) on the basis of the result of said comparison, and
providing the patient with means for utilizing said mathematical model (H), so that the patient can himself monitor and predict the effect of the treatment he is to follow on the behavior of his blood glucose level.	providing the patient with means for utilizing said mathematical model (H), so that the patient can himself monitor and predict the effect of the treatment he is to follow on the behavior of his blood glucose level, *the means comprising a mobile phone of a cellular radio system or to a two-way pager connected to a measuring unit, the measuring unit and the mobile phone or to a two-way pager constituting a combined element, wherein a battery of the mobile phone or two-way pager and the measuring unit are integrated into one component (14′) that fits into the battery space of the mobile phone or two-way pager, the method further comprising:*
	...
	measuring the glucose level of a patient's blood sample by the measuring unit and storing the data indicating the moment of measurement of the first measurement result in first memory means (10′),
	transmitting the data stored in the first memory means (10′) via a data transmission link to a data processing system that is available to a person treating the patient,
	calculating a predictive value $\hat{g}(t_i)$ on the basis of the data stored in the first memory means (10, 10′), the predictive value indicating the patient's predicted blood glucose level at a predetermined moment,
	calculating the difference between the calculated predictive value $\hat{g}(t_i)$ and the patient's actual blood glucose level $g(t_i)$ calculated at said predetermined moment, and correcting the mathematical model to calculate a predictive value in order to take into account said difference in subsequent calculations of predictive values.

(continued)

Table 1 (continued)

The granted patent claimed[a]	Amended patent after opposition[b]
Claim 2. Monitoring equipment for predicting the glucose level in a patient's blood comprising:	Claim 2. Monitoring equipment for predicting the glucose level in a patient's blood, comprising:
means (15, 15′) for receiving a measurement result indicating the glucose level in the patient's blood sample and for storing it in a first memory means (10, 10′) together with data indicating the moment of the measurement, wherein the monitoring equipment comprises means (15, 15′) for receiving data concerning at least the patient's diet, medication and physical strain and for storing the data in the first memory means (10, 10′),	means (15, 15′) for receiving a measurement result indicating the glucose level in the patient's blood sample and for storing it in a first memory means (10, 10′) together with data indicating the moment of the measurement, wherein the monitoring equipment comprises means (15, 15′) for receiving data concerning at least the patient's diet, medication and physical strain and for storing the data in the first memory means (10, 10′),
data processing means (11, 12, 11′, 12′) for calculating a predictive value $\hat{g}(t_i)$ on the basis of the data stored in the first memory means (10, 10′), the predictive value indicating the patient's predicted blood glucose level at a predetermined moment, and	data processing means (11, 12, 11′, 12′) for calculating a predictive value $\hat{g}(t_i)$ on the basis of the data stored in the first memory means (10, 10′), the predictive value indicating the patient's predicted blood glucose level at a predetermined moment, and
corrector means (13, 13′) for calculating the difference between the calculated predictive value $\hat{g}(t_i)$ and the patient's actual blood glucose level $g(t_i)$ calculated at said predetermined moment, and for correcting the mathematical model utilized by the data processing means (11, 12, 11′, 12′) to calculate a predictive value in order to take into account said difference in the subsequent calculations of predictive values.	corrector means (13, 13′) for calculating the difference between the calculated predictive value $\hat{g}(t_i)$ and the patient's actual blood glucose level $g(t_i)$ calculated at said predetermined moment, and for correcting the mathematical model utilized by the data processing means (11, 12, 11′, 12′) to calculate a predictive value in order to take into account said difference in the subsequent calculations of predictive values, *a measuring unit for measuring the glucose level of a patient's blood sample, and for storing the data indicating the moment of measurement of the first measurement result in the first memory means (10′), a communications device (MS) connected to the measuring unit, the communications device (MS) comprising a mobile phone of a cellular radio system or to a two-way pager, and means for transmitting the data stored in the first memory means (10′) via data transmission link to a data processing system that is available to a person treating the patient, the measuring unit and the communications device constituting a combined element, wherein a battery of the mobile phone or two-way pager and the measuring unit are integrated into one component (14′) that fits into the battery space of the mobile phone or two-way pager*

[a]https://worldwide.espacenet.com/patent/search/family/008545439/publication/EP0883371B1?q=pn%3DEP0883371B1
[b]https://worldwide.espacenet.com/patent/search/family/008545439/publication/EP0883371B2?q=pn%3DEP0883371B2

4.3   Novelty of an Invention

As mentioned above (Sect. 2.2), a patent is granted if the claimed technical solution is new and inventive. Novelty is acknowledged if prior art does not disclose the invention.[34] Prior art includes any disclosure—oral, written, or video—that was available to the public before the date the patent application was filed with a patent office. It can be disclosed in any language, and it does not matter if a skilled person from the public cannot read or understand the language used. It was made available to the public, and the skilled person can translate it into a desired language. Prior art was made available to the public if a person can request access to the disclosure, even if they have to pay for it.

This results in an absolute concept of novelty. The content of a document is relevant from the day it becomes accessible to the public. For this reason, it is always necessary to identify the earliest publication date. This day is indicated on patent literature. For reference books, it is the printed publication date. In the case of scientific publications, it must be checked whether the article was published earlier in another journal, if applicable, and the earliest online publication date must always be taken into account.

Oral presentations at conferences that are recorded or whose summaries are printed in conference books merit special attention. Very often, parts of the invention are published carelessly by the applicant or the individual inventor and are later painfully held against them as prior art in the examination procedure. To avoid this, the planned presentation or any other planned publication should always be checked internally and coordinated with a patent attorney.

Another problem that should not be underestimated, especially when working with researchers from academia, is that they want to publish about technical progress as quickly as possible because scientific publications are proof of their reputation. Even if this desire is understandable, it conflicts with the patent law requirement of absolute novelty.

However, both are possible if all parties involved agree on a timetable with their patent attorney, so that a patent application is filed first, before the scientific publication. If this order of events is observed, the inventor has the advantage of the double designation.

4.4   Inventive Step of an Invention

Provided that technical solution is patentable, the patent claim has clear wording, the description discloses sufficient information for making the invention and meets the requirement for novelty, and the last hurdle is providing evidence that the novel technical solution would not be obvious to a skilled person.[35] If a skilled

---

[34] EPC, Article 54, Novelty.

[35] EPC, Article 56, Inventive step, https://www.epo.org/law-practice/legal-texts/html/epc/2020/e/ar56.html

person would not arrive at the proposed solution by combining different teachings or common general knowledge, the invention involves an inventive step, and a patent will be granted. What follows briefly describes the so-called problem-solution approach the EPO uses to assess the inventive step by EPO.

The examination division will determine what the relevant prior art is based on the concept of the invention. After it has identified the closest prior art (first document), which often deals with the same technical problem or a similar technical solution for a similar problem in the same or in an adjacent technical field, it identifies the differentiating technical feature(s) of the claimed invention (which is not disclosed in the first document) to the closest prior art.

Starting from the identified differentiating technical feature(s), it is assessed which technical effect is achieved and is disclosed in the patent application for the differentiating technical feature. If the technical feature and its effect are disclosed in another document (second document), the examination division analyses whether said document includes any indication that would motivate the skilled person to adapt the teaching of the first document. If a person skilled in the art of the relevant technical field would be motivated to combine the first and the second document in order to arrive at the claimed invention the examination division evaluates the invention as obvious in view of the prior art. If the problem-solving approach reveals that the combination of the prior art does not lead the person skilled in the art to the claimed solution, the invention is considered inventive, and a patent is granted.

4.4.1 An Example of a Patent Was Revoked Because It Did Not Include an Inventive Step

In the patent EP1247229B1,[36] Koninklijke Philips N.V. claimed it is a "wireless health-monitoring system for monitoring a state or condition of a patient comprising: a wireless health monitoring apparatus (10) that is linked in a wireless fashion, said apparatus (10) including: a health monitoring device (11) ...." additional components and "a server application (62), residing on a computer readable medium and disposed on a server (22) in communication with the wireless network, for causing the server (22) to receive the determined health parameter (122), to calculate a response based in part on the determined health parameter (126); and to provide the response" to an internet-enabled wireless web device. Dependent claim 19 further specified the health monitoring device (11) relies on "a system selected from the group consisting of: an algorithm, an artificial intelligence system, an expert system, a rules-based system, a case-based reasoning system, and combinations thereof." However, Fresenius Medical Care Deutschland GmbH, Garmin Deutschland GmbH, and Fitbit filed oppositions against the granted patent. The opponents identified and submitted additional documents from the prior art disclosing a personal computer with the function of a health-monitoring system

---

[36] The wording of the claims is available under the URL and the numbers are explained in the description of the patent application: https://worldwide.espacenet.com/patent/search/family/022627891/publication/EP1247229B1?q=EP1247229b1

for the individual patient. Finally, in decision T 0927/14, the Boards of Appeal revoked the patent because the invention did not involve an inventive step.[37] In view of the cited prior art, it was considered to be an obvious technical solution to transfer the prior art health-monitoring system to a mobile phone having web-browsing capability on its display in order to provide a wireless health-monitoring system.[38]

4.4.2 Example of a Nonobvious Invention

Another example is patent EP3261024B1 of Siemens Healthcare GmbH, which was granted 14 on May 2021 without being contested by an opposition. The patent relates to a method for the detection of vascular diseases and characterization in medical images using recurrent neural networks. This patent was selected because it is an example of claims with very detailed wording (Table 2).

4.5 Summary of the Patentability of AI-Implemented Inventions

Under the EPC discoveries; scientific theories and mathematical methods; schemes, rules, and methods for performing mental acts; programs for computers; and presentations of information are not considered as inventions. AI and machine learning are typically based on mathematical or computation models and are implemented by programs for computers. However, the EPO considers inventions involving AI to be computer-implemented inventions (CII) with a technical character if the AI contributes to a claimed technical solution in any field of technology such as the life sciences and healthcare.

Such AI inventions must also meet all further requirements of patent law to obtain a patent grant, including proof of novelty, proof of an inventive step, clear language in the claims that define the technical AI-implemented invention, and sufficiency of disclosure in a way that enables a person skilled in the art to carry out and reproduce the invention over the entire claimed scope.

It can be seen in Table 2 that claim 1 was amended by adding restrictions into the step "detecting vascular abnormalities." Due to the specification of encoding each of the image patches into a respective feature vector and following classification based on said feature vectors using a trained recurrent neural network (RNN) or a trained bi-directional RNN, the applicant introduced the differentiating feature over the prior art cited during examination. By doing so, the examiner accepted that by means of the defined RNNs, the technical effect was the detection and achieved classification of vascular abnormalities.

---

[37] EPO, decision T 0927/14, T 0927/14 (Wireless patient monitoring/Philips) of 20.2.2019, https://www.epo.org/law-practice/case-law-appeals/recent/t140927eu1.html

[38] See Reason 7.4 and 8. of the decision: https://www.epo.org/law-practice/case-law-appeals/recent/t140927eu1.html

Table 2 Wording of the patent application and the granted patent

Patent application EP3261024A2[a]	Granted patent EP3261024B1[b]
1. A method for vascular disease detection using a recurrent neural network, comprising:	1. A method for vascular disease detection using a recurrent neural network, comprising:
extracting a plurality of 2D cross-section image patches from a 3D computed tomography angiography (CTA) image, wherein each of 2D cross-section image patches is extracted at a respective one of a plurality of sampling points along a vessel centerline of a vessel of interest in the 3D CTA image; and	extracting a plurality of 2D cross-section image patches from a 3D computed tomography angiography, CTA, image, wherein each of 2D cross-section image patches is extracted at a respective one of a plurality of sampling points along a vessel centerline of a vessel of interest in the 3D CTA image; and
detecting vascular abnormalities in the vessel of interest by classifying each of the plurality of sampling points along the vessel centerline based on the plurality of 2D cross-section image patches using a trained recurrent neural network (RNN).	detecting vascular abnormalities in the vessel of interest by classifying each of the plurality of sampling points along the vessel centerline based on the plurality of 2D cross-section image patches using a trained recurrent neural network, RNN, wherein detecting vascular abnormalities in the vessel of interest by classifying each of the plurality of sampling points along the vessel centerline based on the plurality of 2D cross-section image patches using a trained recurrent neural network, RNN, comprises: encoding each of the 2D cross-section image patches into a respective feature vector using a trained convolutional neural network, CNN; and classifying each of the plurality of sampling points along the vessel centerline based on the feature vectors corresponding to the plurality of 2D cross-section image patches using a trained bi-directional RNN.
10. An apparatus for vascular disease detection using a recurrent neural network, comprising:	9. An apparatus for vascular disease detection using a recurrent neural network, comprising:
means for extracting a plurality of 2D cross-section image patches from a 3D computed tomography angiography (CTA) image, wherein each of 2D cross-section image patches is extracted at a respective one of a plurality of sampling points along a vessel centerline of a vessel of interest in the 3D CTA image; and	means for extracting a plurality of 2D cross-section image patches from a 3D computed tomography angiography, CTA, image, wherein each of 2D cross-section image patches is extracted at a respective one of a plurality of sampling points along a vessel centerline of a vessel of interest in the 3D CTA image; and

(continued)

Table 2 (continued)

Patent application EP3261024A2[a]	Granted patent EP3261024B1[b]
means for detecting vascular abnormalities in the vessel of interest by classifying each of the plurality of sampling points along the vessel centerline based on the plurality of 2D cross-section image patches using a trained recurrent neural network (RNN).	means for detecting vascular abnormalities in the vessel of interest by classifying each of the plurality of sampling points along the vessel centerline based on the plurality of 2D cross-section image patches using a trained recurrent neural network, RNN, wherein the means for detecting vascular abnormalities in the vessel of interest by classifying each of the plurality of sampling points along the vessel centerline based on the plurality of 2D cross-section image patches using a trained recurrent neural network, RNN, comprises: means for encoding each of the 2D cross-section image patches into a respective feature vector using a trained convolutional neural network, CNN; and means for classifying each of the plurality of sampling points along the vessel centerline based on the feature vectors corresponding to the plurality of 2D cross-section image patches using a trained bi-directional RNN.

[a] All claims of the patent application are available under the URL: https://worldwide.espacenet.com/patent/search/family/059828800/publication/EP3261024A2?q=pn%3DEP3261024A2
[b] All granted claims are available under the UL: https://worldwide.espacenet.com/patent/search/family/059828800/publication/EP3261024B1?q=pn%3DEP3261024B1

5   Examples of Patentable Inventions Involving AI in the Life Sciences and Healthcare

A few more examples are summarized below to illustrate inventions involving AI in the life sciences and healthcare. The following patent applications or patents are still under examination, have not yet been granted, or are still vulnerable to third-party opposition. Therefore, the following examples are not legally binding or examples of best practices.[39]

Example 1
EP3759240A1 (under examination at the EPO, granted in the United States)
    Applicant: Recursion Pharmaceuticals, Inc. (United States)
    Title: Systems and Methods for Discriminating Effects on Targets

---

[39] All of the EP patents and applications mentioned in this section can be viewed online at Espacenet (https://worldwide.espacenet.com/patent/), as can any patent application from non-European countries. For that purpose, please, just copy in the cited number.

This patent application relates to systems and methods for identifying a set of perturbations that have an on-target effect against a selected target. The independent claim 1 defines a method for determining whether a set of test perturbations discriminates over a null distribution for an on-target effect against one or more first genetic components of a cell, wherein the set of test perturbations comprises a plurality of test perturbations against the one or more first genetic components and the cell comprises a plurality of genetic components, including the first one or more genetic components. The method is further defined by a computer system. The underlying computational models and mathematical methods would fill at least two pages of this chapter.

It will have to be seen whether and to what extent the invention will be recognized as clear, practicable, novel, and inventive.

Example 2

EP3004892B1 (granted by the EPO and in the United States, Japan, and China)
Proprietor: Nestec S.A. (China)
Title: Method for Diagnosing Irritable Bowel Syndrome

The granted patent relates to a method for aiding in the diagnosis of irritable bowel syndrome (IBS) and/or a clinical subtype thereof in a patient. Independent claim 1 reads as follows:

A method for aiding in the diagnosis of irritable bowel syndrome (IBS) and/or a clinical subtype thereof in a subject, said method comprising obtaining at least two of the following (a) through (f) scores:

(a) detecting in a sample obtained from said subject the level of at least one bacterial antigen antibody marker to obtain a microbiome score;
(b) detecting in said sample the level of at least one mast cell marker to obtain a mast cell score;
(c) detecting in said sample the level of at least one inflammatory cell marker to obtain an inflammatory score;
(d) detecting in said sample the level of at least one bile acid malabsorption (BAM) marker to obtain a BAM score;
(e) detecting in said sample the level of at least one kynurenine marker to obtain an oxidative stress score;
(f) detecting in said sample the level of at least one serotonin marker to obtain a serotonin score;
(g) applying a statistical algorithm to the at least two of said microbiome score, said mast cell score, said inflammatory score, said BAM score, said oxidative stress score, and said serotonin score to obtain a disease score; and
(h) determining a diagnosis of IBS in said subject based on a statistical algorithm that generates a probability of having IBS based on the disease score and a diagnostic model comprising at least two of a microbiome score, a mast cell score, an inflammatory score, a bile acid malabsorption score, an oxidative stress score, a serotonin score and combinations thereof from a retrospective cohort.

Example 3

EP2994159B1 (granted by the EPO and in Japan and China)
    Proprietor: BioNTech RNA Pharmaceuticals GmbH
    Title: Predicting Immunogenicity of T cell epitopes

This granted patent relates to a method for predicting T-cell epitopes and whether modifications in peptides or polypeptides such as tumor-associated neoantigens are immunogenic or not. Independent claim 1 reads as follows:

A computer-implemented method for predicting immunogenic modified peptides comprising amino acid modifications, said modifications being substitutions, the method comprising the steps:

(a) ascertaining a score for binding of a modified peptide to one or more MHC molecules,
(b) ascertaining a score for binding of the non-modified peptide to the one or more MHC molecules,
(c) ascertaining a score for binding of the modified peptide when present in a MHC-peptide complex to one or more T cell receptors, which comprises ascertaining a score for the chemical and physical similarities between the non-modified and modified amino acids, wherein the score for the chemical and physical similarities is ascertained on the basis of the probability of amino acids being interchanged in nature, wherein the more frequently amino acids are interchanged in nature the more similar the amino acids are considered, wherein the chemical and physical similarities are determined using substitution matrices,
    wherein the non-modified peptide and modified peptide are identical but for the modification(s),
    wherein the non-modified peptide and modified peptide are 8 to 15 amino acids in length, and wherein the modified peptide is predicted to be immunogenic if (i) the non-modified peptide has a score for binding to the one or more MHC molecules satisfying a threshold indicating binding to the one or more MHC molecules and (ii) the modified peptide has a score for binding to the one or more MHC molecules satisfying a threshold indicating binding to the one or more MHC molecules and (iii) the non-modified and modified amino acids have a score for the chemical and physical similarities satisfying a threshold indicating chemical and physical dissimilarity.

Example 4

WO2021170179A1
    Applicant: Robert Bosch GmbH
    Title: Method and Device for Carrying Out a QPCR Process

This international patent application relates to a method for carrying out a quantitative polymerase chain reaction (qPCR) process comprising cyclically executing qPCR cycle measurements (S11) of an intensity value after every qPCR cycle in order to obtain a qPCR curve of intensity values after a particular minimum number of qPCR cycles (S12) estimating (S13) the further progression of the qPCR curve with the aid of a data-based trainable qPCR model and carrying out (S15, S17) the qPCR method dependent on the further progression of the qPCR curve.

It remains to be seen whether and to what extent the invention will be recognized as clear, practicable, novel, and inventive.

Example 5: AlphaFold
EP3821433, EP3821434 and EP3821435 (under examination at the EPO)
    Applicant: DeepMind Technologies Ltd
    Title: Machine Learning for Determining Protein Structures

These relate to methods, systems, and apparatus, including computer programs that are encoded to predict protein structure. The method comprises generating a distance map for a given protein, wherein the given protein is defined by a sequence of amino acid residues in a determined structure. The distance map characterizes estimated distances between the amino acid residues in the structure. The method includes 1) generating a plurality of distance map crops wherein each distance map crop characterizes estimated distances between (i) amino acid residues in each of one or more respective first positions in the sequence and (ii) amino acid residues in each of one or more respective second positions in the sequence in the structure of the protein, wherein the first positions are a proper subset of the sequence; and 2) generating the distance map for the given protein using the plurality of distance map crops. The claims define a neuronal network for processing the protein structure prediction. The patent application also includes claims defining a system for performing the operations of the method.

It remains to be seen whether and to what extent the invention will be recognized as clear, practicable, novel, and inventive.

---

6   Ethics of Patents

6.1   Directive 98/44/EC

As mentioned earlier in Sect. 2.3, there are some exclusions from patentability for ethical reasons. These are based on the directive 98/44/EC of the EU[40] wherein it is stated in reasons 16 and 17:

> Whereas *patent law* must be applied so as *to respect the fundamental principles safeguarding the dignity and integrity of the person*; whereas it is important to assert the principle that the *human body*, at any stage in its formation or development, including *germ cells*, and the simple discovery of one of its elements or one of its products, including the *sequence or partial sequence* of a human gene, *cannot be patented;*

> Whereas significant progress in the treatment of diseases has already been made thanks to the existence of *medicinal products derived from elements isolated from the human body* and/or otherwise produced, such medicinal products resulting from technical processes

---

[40] Directive 98/44/EC of the European Parliament and of the Council of 6 July 1998 on the legal protection of biotechnological inventions: https://eur-lex.europa.eu/legal-content/EN/TXT/HTML/?uri=CELEX:31998L0044

aimed at obtaining elements similar in structure to those existing naturally in the human body and whereas, consequently, research aimed at obtaining and isolating such elements valuable to medicinal production *should be encouraged by means of the patent system*;

Therefore, it was decided that an invention directed to an isolated element from the human body or that has been produced in a lab and which can be commercialized ("susceptible of industrial application") is patentable. But the commercialization of the inventions must not be contrary to "ordre public" or morality. Otherwise, it is considered unpatentable. "However, exploitation shall not be deemed to be so contrary merely because it is prohibited by law or regulation."[41] Consequently, it is allowed to seek a patent directed at isolated stem cells with concrete properties or T cells (product) and to direct their use in a therapy to treat, for instance, an autoimmune disease or a particular cancer. However, it depends on national laws whether such products and methods are allowed.

The element—sequences of DNA, RNA, amino acids, polypeptide, protein, antigen, antibody—may be different from or identical to the structure of natural (human) origin, "given that the rights conferred by the patent do not extend to the human body and its elements in their natural environment" (Directive 98/44/EC, reason 20). Furthermore, it is required to explain in the patent application for which purpose said element is used and that said element is identified, purified, and classified. The aforementioned Directive has been integrated into the EPC[42] and must be taken into account ex officio in the examination procedure of biotechnological inventions.

Thus, the foregoing shows that ethics is not foreign to the patent system. The health of the human being is in focus, doctors must be free in their activity, and the human being is protected. Particularly in the life sciences and the healthcare sector, everyone should bear in mind that a granted patent is not a permission to use the invention. The permission for the introduction into the market for applications on humans depends solely on national laws.

6.2   In View of the Pandemic

In the last 2 years, patent law has received new attention. As explained at the beginning, the patent holder obtains a timely and territorially limited monopoly for their invention. This also applies to vaccines, test kits, respiratory equipment, and many other means used to combat the pandemic. For some time now, many organizations have been calling for patent protection to be suspended, especially for vaccines. This requirement goes back to the desire to help all people as quickly as possible with sufficient medicines. This desire is undoubtedly understandable. Therefore, the idea appears that without an existing patent protection and by dissolving the monopoly for the patent holder, the accessibility to the medicines and

---

[41] Article 6 of Directive 98/44/EC.

[42] EPC, Rule 28, Exceptions to patentability, https://www.epo.org/law-practice/legal-texts/html/epc/2020/e/r28.html

the availability for the public could be achieved faster. Therefore, for the common good, the suspension of patent protection has been called for by international aid organizations and the WHO. But is this for the good of all if those who shoulder the entrepreneurial risk and liability for the products are dispossessed of their earned intellectual property (Heide & Bendele, 2021)?

It should not be forgotten that it is precisely thanks to the willingness to take risks on the part of private industry, private investors, and the responsible persons in the respective companies that such drugs are developed at all. This requires a high tolerance for frustration, strong stamina, self-motivation, the ability to deal with defeat, fundamental conviction and, in general, staying power. Anyone who has struggled through a scientific doctoral thesis can understand this. In the entrepreneurial environment, there is also the pressure and impatience of the financial backers. Of course, priority is given to the development of drugs for which there is a high demand and where the return on investment can be maximized. This cannot be denied and is currently the case in connection with COVID-19. However, the rapid availability of a vaccine or therapeutic against COVID-19 is not hindered by patent-protected monopolies, but by the lack of availability of raw materials, production capacities, and logistics.

If patent protections were to be suspended, every third party could use the technology as it is disclosed in the patent without being sued for patent infringement. That would solve the problem, would it not? Anyone could make the necessary vaccine or pharmaceutical for treatment of the infection. This view fails to recognize that the production of vaccines requires highly complex know-how that goes beyond patents. Only the combination of proprietary technology and know-how guarantees the required quality, effectiveness, and product safety of the vaccines. As already discussed above with regard to feasibility, if possible, only as much as necessary and as little as possible is written into a patent application in order to get it granted. It is often not a voluntary decision to formulate patents so "thin" but rather a necessary evil in order to prevent the competitor from registering his patent more quickly. The detailed manifestation of the invention and the necessary know-how is not in the patent. Manufacturing processes in particular are covered by trade secrets. The know-how of the developer and the manufacturer is required. Not everyone who has previously made a headache remedy can easily make a vaccine.

Some opinions point out that many inventions, especially those related to RNA, are based on publicly funded research. A far-reaching comparison of third-party funding in different countries and regions—for example, the United States, the EU, and Germany—would now be required in order to formulate a robust comparison and resilient criticism about the influence of public funds on research. Independent of this, inventions from public institutions, such as universities and research institutes, are—as far as possible—licensed out. The licensees are companies that turn these inventions into products. To this end, public institutions and companies enter into binding license agreements. The public investments are to be (or will be) recouped through contractually fixed license fees. The company receives the right to exploit the invention. If patents were now declared invalid, the basis for such contracts would be withdrawn. This would require a separate discussion from a contract law perspective. In any case, the public institutions would logically also lose the licensing income, and thus public investments would not be recovered.

Should there be a central company that has a dominant position and hinders other companies, there are patent law tools, such as compulsory licenses, to force the company to share the technology. There are different legal bases for this at the national level. Consequently, it is arguably not patent protection that hinders the sufficient availability of the necessary medicines and vaccines, but the lack of competent specialists and the raw materials required for production.

Notwithstanding the statutory options for granting compulsory licenses or "governmental use orders in the interest of the public welfare,"[43] every patent owner is free to make their invention available to third parties. By a waiver, the patentee—a private company or public institution—may declare that it waives the enforcement of its COVID-related patents,[44] or it may terminate patent protection by non-payment of the annually required maintenance fees. Whereby, non-payment of the annual fees terminates patent protection permanently. However, the patent owner can also grant reduced fee or free licenses. These would have the advantage that the patent holder still has some control under the license agreements over who works with the monopolized technology and whether the licensees comply with the quality standards. Patent protection remains in place and the duration of the free license agreement can be limited to the duration of the pandemic. In this way, it is also possible to prevent product pirates from entering the market and inferior and possibly harmful products—presumably based on the protected technology—from damaging the reputation of the originator.

Therefore, the call for compulsory licensing and suspension of patent protection cannot be the means of choice if the development of new cures is also desired in the future (Heide & Bendele, 2021). Proprietary intellectual property, not open sources, is the basis for collaborations, and it is through such collaborations—between different companies but also between public institutions and the industry—that new medicines will continue to be developed in the future. Valid intellectual property rights of the respective contracting parties remain the prerequisite for engaging in risky developments such as drug development, especially in the field of biopharmaceuticals (Max Planck Institute, 2021).

However, on 17 June 2022, the so-called Geneva Package was decided by WTO members,[45] which contains a series of unprecedented decisions such as a

---

[43] For example, in Germany, paragraph 13 sec. 1 of the German Patent Act stipulates that (English translation) "The patent shall not take effect if the Federal Government orders that the invention be used in the interest of public welfare. Furthermore, it shall not extend to a use of the invention ordered in the interest of federal security by the competent supreme federal authority or by a subordinate agency on its behalf."

[44] Statement by Moderna on Intellectual Property Matters during the COVID-19 Pandemic (10/08/2020); available under the URL: https://investors.modernatx.com/Statements%2D%2DPerspectives/Statements%2D%2DPerspectives-Details/2020/Statement-by-Moderna-on-Intellectual-Property-Matters-during-the-COVID-19-Pandemic/default.aspx

[45] Press release: https://www.wto.org/english/news_e/news22_e/mc12_17jun22_e.htm

"Ministerial Declaration on the WTO Response to the COVID-19 Pandemic and Preparedness for Future Pandemics" deciding "a waiver of certain requirements concerning compulsory licensing for COVID-19 vaccines." This decision caused a series of reactions such as the press release of Oliver Schacht, CEO of BIO Deutschland, who said that the decided suspension of patents covering COVID-19 vaccines will not make them available more quickly. Similar to the earlier discussion, he argues that "production of the vaccines is complex, needs a lot of know-how and stable supply chains. In order to achieve a high vaccination rate locally, an appropriate infrastructure and a high level of acceptance among the population are also necessary." The above presented opinion that innovation is driven by patents is recognized in his statement that "[t]he suspension of patent protection, on the other hand, is a fatal signal for innovative companies and their investors."[46] Another reaction is based on the analysis of the content of the waiver.[47] The regulation allows a WTO member to initiate an accelerated procedure to request a compulsory license. The obtained compulsory license is accessible for patents protecting technologies linked to a COVID-19 vaccine and allows WTO members to use such technologies without the consent of the right holder. The amount of a potential license fee has to be orientated on the WHO/United Nations Development Programme (UNDP) guidelines. As a consequence, the waiver as such is not new but important for corporates in the field of COVID-19 vaccines, COVID-19 diagnostics, and COVID-19 therapeutics, as it can be a restriction on return-on-investment strategies in the future. However, Matthieu Dhenne writes in an opinion piece that "it is more like a sign of political goodwill towards developing countries, intended to facilitate their access to the production of 'Covid-19' vaccines, although the success of the initiative will probably rest, in the end, more on the willingness of the rights holders to transfer their know-how."

6.3   Ethics and AI Inventions in Life Sciences and Healthcare

Since this book is about AI-implemented inventions, I would also like to discuss the ethics of such inventions. I would like to refer to two examples. One is from the area of "digital health" in which the personal physician is—largely—replaced by a computer, thus minimising personal contact (e.g. Dermanostic). The other area is drug development, which requires extensive animal testing.

Dermanostic[48] is a dermatologist app that, based on images of a skin change in the affected area and a questionnaire, makes a diagnosis, recommends a therapy

---

[46] Press release: https://www.biodeutschland.org/en/press-releases/biotechnology-industry-regrets-wto-decision-on-patent-suspensions.html

[47] Kluwer Patent Blog "Covid-19 'Patent Waiver': revolution or tempest in a glass of water?", Matthieu Dhenne, http://patentblog.kluweriplaw.com/2022/06/22/covid-19-patent-waiver-revolution-or-storm-in-a-glass-of-water/

[48] https://dermanostic.com/

and, if necessary, issues a prescription. Additionally, if necessary, personal contact is made with the patient. The advantage is that one saves the waiting time for an appointment, overcrowded waiting rooms and gets certainty quickly. The decision about the choice of dermatologist, digital or in person, is a purely personal and voluntary one and therefore not ethically questionable. The question is whether a diagnostic method for detecting a skin disease based on images and utilising AI technology is ethically questionable from a patent law perspective. The diagnostic procedure is not carried out on the patient's body, but using the digital image files. The image files are analysed by the AI in the app and therefore the AI does not intervene on the body. Thus, since there is no harmful intervention on the human body, there is no exclusion from patentability. The handling of image data and personal data is a question of data protection and not a question of patent law. So there is no ethical question to consider here.

Some of the examples of AI implemented inventions discussed above are for simulating molecules and molecular interactions. Screening for drugs using AI is steadily increasing. In this way, further drug candidates are analysed on the basis of previous results and theoretical calculations. If a calculated molecule meets the predefined criteria, it can be recognised by the AI algorithm as a promising molecule. Such criteria not only include effectiveness, but can also be criteria that can relate to toxicity, side effects, bioavailability, dosage and much more. In particular, these are properties that would otherwise have to be determined in animal experiments. Such AI methods could substantially reduce experiments done on animals. Therefore, I consider AI-implemented inventions for drug development to be ethically desirable and to have the potential to make a significant contribution to reducing animal harm and deaths. Furthermore, AI enables the optimization of manufacturing processes by optimizing the required substances and reactants. This can lead to an AI-supported conservation of resources and a reduction in manufacturing waste. AI can thus contribute to the protection of our environment and the future of our children. Patent law concerns do not exist. Instead, patent law can promote such AI-based innovations.

7   The Future

AI-implemented inventions are patentable if the AI contributes to the technical character of the invention and if that technical character is essential for the inventiveness of the proposed technical solution. In the healthcare sector, whether or not an AI contributes to the technical of the invention depends on the field in which the invention will be used (e. g., diagnosis, therapy, drug discovery). In 2019, the World Intellectual Property Organization (WIPO) described AI as "shifting from theory to commercial application" (WIPO, 2019). In 2019, bio-inspired approaches to AI were represented three times more frequently in scientific publications than in patents (WIPO, 2019, Fig. 3.7, p. 44). However, in the future this trend will change because of increased investments in products and technologies that combine AI and biology, such as biological circuits, products for diagnosis, and more efficient drug discovery, and because of the wish of companies and inventors for a return on their investments. Xin et al. 2021, Tables 2, 5, and 6), a recent study of patent databases from the academic and industrial sectors, found that the most patent applications are in the technical fields of "medical image recognition, computer-aided diagnosis, disease monitoring, disease prediction, bioinformatics, and drug development." As patent offices have recognized the demands of the industrial sector, they will continue to establish guiding case law on the patentability of AI, particularly in the life sciences and healthcare.

One example for potential patentable inventions involving AI may emerge from the EU-funded project AIDPATH (AI powered, Decentralized Production for Advanced Therapies in the Hospital). The project aims to develop a system or platform for the manufacture of CAR-T cells[49] for individualized oncological therapy. AI is used to improve the quality control and the whole process. The aim is to make it possible to produce CAR-T cells close to the patient (point of care) and to provide treatments specifically individualized to each patient's needs much more quickly.[50]

Drafting a patent application for inventions involving AI requires technical knowledge about the respective field of application. The author of such a patent application needs knowledge of biological processes, patient physiology, pharmaceutical activities, and chemicals in order to write clear and feasible definition of the technical character of any invention involving AI. A patent application that lacks a proper description of the technical purpose of an invention, in particular an AI-implemented invention, will be refused at a very early stage of examination In addition, competences in the field of AI are required to define the AI part validly. Since these are rarely combined in one person, such patent applications should be prepared in an interdisciplinary manner.

It must be taken into account that every patent application is published 18 months after its filing date. This means that the public will be informed about the new invention/technology long before the applicant is certain about the scope of a legally valid patent. Once a method involving AI is published, any competitor will be motivated to identify a workaround of the patented monopoly in order to avoid dependencies and license fees (provided the inventor can obtain a license), avoid patent infringement, and achieve freedom to operate.

Therefore, the applicant should consider additional and alternative strategies for protecting an invention involving AI and/or consider whether it might be advantageous not to file a patent application and instead treat such AI methods as trade secrets.

This is a strategic decision that depends, among other things, on the inventor's particular business model and the product or method they have invented. In order to identify the right intellectual property strategy for the company and the specific invention, a close and iterative exchange should take place with a patent attorney, the

---

[49] CAR = chimeric antigen receptor; CAR T-cells = T immune cells expressing a CAR.

[50] For more details, see AIDPATH (https://www.sciencrew.com/c/6499?title=AIDPATH)

developers, and the persons responsible for corporate strategy. After all, the decision against a patent and in favor of a trade secret requires internal measures to prevent know-how from migrating to competitors.

Acknowledgments Many thanks to my colleague and friend, Benjamin Petri, who is a German and European Patent Attorney with profound experiences on computer implemented inventions for discussions on AI definitions. The author declares no potential conflicts of interest. The views expressed in this chapter do not necessarily reflect those of the author's organization.

References

Heide, A. K., & Bendele, T. (2021). *Covid-19 – kein Patentschutz in der Pandemie?* CHEM-anager. Retrieved from https://www.chemanager-online.com/news/covid-19-kein-patentschutz-der-pandemie

Max Planck Institute. (2021). *Covid-19 and the Role of Intellectual Property: Position Statement of the Max Planck Institute for Innovation and Competition of 7 May 2021.* Retrieved from https://www.ip.mpg.de/de/forschung/meldungen-aus-der-forschung/covid-19-and-the-role-of-intellectual-property-list-of-supporters.html

McCarthy, J. (2004, November 24). *What is artificial intelligence?* Unpublished paper. Computer Science Department, Stanford University.

Turing, A. M. (1950). Computing machinery and intelligence. *Mind, 59*(236), 433–460. https://doi.org/10.1093/mind/LIX.236.433

WIPO (World Intellectual Property Organization). (2019). *World technology trends 2019 – Artificial intelligence.* https://www.wipo.int/publications/en/details.jsp?id=4386

Xin, Y., Man, W., & Yi, Z. (2021). The development trend of artificial intelligence in medical: A patentometric analysis. *Artificial Intelligence in the Life Sciences, 1*(2021), 100006. https://doi.org/10.1016/j.ailsci.2021.100006

Redesigning Relations: Coordinating Machine Learning Variables and Sociobuilt Contexts in COVID-19 and Beyond

Hannah Howland, Vadim Keyser, and Farzad Mahootian

Each author contributed expertise to the broad range of conceptual developments within this discussion. Hannah Howland drives interdisciplinary and transdisciplinary research by developing new conceptual frameworks that synthesize systems biology and evidence-based design. Howland's criticism of machine learning parameterization in representing the causal topography of "sociobuilt contexts" draws conceptual focus to the interactions between social and built processes that occur on many scales. Howland's conceptual developments in multi-scale dynamical processes, combined with Vadim Keyser's technoscientific work in robustness analysis, culminate in the proposed relation of "iterative entanglement." This includes suggestions to re-parameterize AI systems based on a key understanding of the causal complexities of sociobuilt contexts. Keyser contributes scientific and ethical relations relevant for autonomy in data practices and decision-making. In line with the evidence-based design approach of Sect. 3, Howland and Keyser describe how immersive relationships between affected populations, healthcare providers, and medical researchers occur on multiple scales across overlapping sociobuilt contexts. To highlight the importance of scale and address epistemic responsibility for the health of communities shaped by environmental injustice and

H. Howland
PYATOK | architecture + urban design, Oakland, CA, USA
e-mail: hhowland@pyatok.com

V. Keyser
California State University, Fresno, CA, USA
e-mail: vkeyser@csufresno.edu

F. Mahootian (✉)
New York University, New York City, NY, USA
e-mail: fm57@nyu.edu

*harm, Farzad Mahootian intertwines methodological and
ethical approaches. Mahootian suggests that optimal ethical
and medical outcomes could result from coordinated
interdisciplinary attention to the cross-scale coupling of
biochemical, environmental, social, and institutional dynamics.*

Abstract

We explore multi-scale relations in artificial intelligence (AI) use in order to
identify difficulties with coordinating relations between users, machine learning (ML) processes, and "sociobuilt contexts"—specifically in terms of their
applications to medical technologies and decisions. We begin by analyzing a
recent COVID-19 machine learning case study in order to present the difficulty
of traversing the detailed causal topography of "sociobuilt contexts." We propose
that the adequate representation of the *interactions* between social and built
processes that occur on many scales ought to drive interdisciplinary approaches
for ML modification. Next, we describe ML algorithm development as a process
that is partly dependent on methodological stabilization for reliability and partly
on coordinating relations. In the coordination between user, ML process, and
sociobuilt contexts, we propose that new methods can be explored that promote
the inclusion of patients and communities for the purpose of cross-checking
portions of the ML process. Finally, we suggest that the advantages of responsible
innovation emerge through the iterative entanglement of ethical, methodological,
and ontological considerations within the broader conceptual infrastructure of
epistemic responsibility.

1   Prequel

The relationship between technology and ethics is more complicated than any brief
introduction could provide. It is noteworthy that the best work in this genre is
neither alarmist nor overcredulous about technological trends. The most useful and
thoughtful approach, in our opinion, has been to examine *responsibilities* that arise
when specific technologies are put to *use* in actual practice. Moral reflection on
specific technologies can predate its actual use and subsequent proliferation. But
the use and proliferation within industry can skew moral relations. The historic
Pugwash Conferences on Science and World Affairs, whose charter boasted ten
Nobel laureate signatories including Einstein, took direct aim at limiting nuclear
weapons and caught the world's attention. Both academics and laypersons became
aware, if not always keenly, that there are ethical questions *specific* to science
and technology that require reflection on how the cost of knowledge increases
exponentially along with the rate of destruction. In industry, accelerating rates of
production, destruction, and consumption quickly outstripped moral imagination
over a century ago and continue to do so. About three-quarters of a century after the
nuclear devastation of Nagasaki and Hiroshima and the resulting shift in geopolitics,

it is puzzling that the outdated idea of science and technology as value neutral persists among educated laypersons, scientists, and engineers. Nevertheless, this period saw the rise of the Union of Concerned Scientists and similar organizations in the 1970s as the Radical Science Movement gained momentum (Cutliffe, 2000). In universities, this kind of activism emerged as a number of interrelated interdisciplinary fields (such as science and technology studies or STS) that are devoted to explicating novel issues arising from interrelations between science, technology, and society and values. Sismondo (2009) concisely states some general assumptions behind STS:

> Science and Technology Studies (STS) starts from an assumption that science and technology are thoroughly social activities. They are social in that scientists and engineers are always members of communities . . . These communities set standards for inquiry and evaluate knowledge claims. There is no abstract and logical scientific method apart from evolving community norms . . . The actors in science and technology are also not mere logical operators, but instead have investments in skills, prestige, knowledge, and specific theories and practices. Even conflicts in a wider society may be mirrored by and connected to conflicts within science and technology; for example, splits along gender, race, class, and national lines can occur both within science and in the relations between scientists and non-scientists. (p. 11)

The emergence of a commitment to morally and socially responsible research and innovation (RRI) in science and technology first appears as a core feature of the European Commission's heavily-funded "Horizon 2020" program.[1] The RRI approach first crystallized out of ELSI (the United States) and ELSA (EU) programs of the late 1980s, which were designed to address the ethical, legal, and social implications/aspects of newly emerging technosciences at the time: genomics (specifically the Human Genome Project) and nanotechnology. Since then, the EU's commitment to RRI has generated a variety of research products and programs relevant to our discussion.

We conclude this section with a summary statement of the general features of RRI that are of special relevance to medical contexts. Demers-Payette et al. (2016) applied the Stilgoe et al. (2013) four-dimensional model of cooperative and interacting areas of concern for RRI's general goals of preventing undesirable consequences in the pursuit of effective technological innovation: *anticipation, reflexivity, inclusion,* and *responsiveness.* Though the present case study was not designed with Demers-Payette's work in mind, our findings align generally with aspects of theirs. The key difference is that we highlight what Stilgoe calls reflexivity (attention to local social values at sites of medical intervention) and inclusion (sharing the process, products, roles, and responsibilities for technological choices). Specifically, we propose that *attention to local value systems, social practices, life spaces and histories—relevant to social and built contexts—ought to drive interdisciplinary approaches for implementing medical technology.* This is especially important wherever artificial intelligence (AI) and machine learning (ML) are involved in medical decision-making. Our approach represents a shift of

---

[1] https://ec.europa.eu/programmes/horizon2020/

emphasis that compensates for the near total neglect of social factors in current and past responses to public health needs.

In what follows, we take a "technoscience' approach to examine relations between ethics, technology, and the scientific method where the focus is on how to *apply* technology to uncertain contexts. Our methodological precedent is that by examining the details of how to *use* a specific technological advancement, we can reveal the scientific and ethical consequences. We can then incorporate that information to redesign the technology. The technoscience framework sets the stage for *iterative correction of technology relative to ethical concerns*. This stands in contrast to an approach that is merely alarmist or overcredulous when applied to a given technology. We also take an "evidence-based design" (EBD) approach to understanding social and built contexts. EBD focuses on the analysis of "interactions" between built environments, technologies, organizational systems, and multiple social layers (Elf et al., 2020). With that said, our philosophical ground is set, and now we find ourselves *in medias res* of a particular technological process, currently unfolding: the use of AI in COVID-19.

2   Introduction: Process and Use of AI in Decision-Making

Much work has been done on the incorporation of AI into medical decision-making (Yu et al., 2018; Rajkomar et al., 2019; Topol, 2019; Cutillo et al., 2020). There are numerous AI uses pertaining to overlapping aspects of decision-making. For instance, AI can promote precision and accuracy in information interpretation, reduce medical errors, and accelerate workflow. It can even promote patient control over data (Topol, 2019). Note that here, we can distinguish the use of AI for different aspects of decision-making: decisions about *reliability*, decisions about *workflow*, and decisions relevant for *autonomy*. Of course, the multifaceted use of AI technology depends on its optimal functioning. Even though research supports the accuracy of certain AI technologies for detection and classification of disease (Gulshan et al., 2016; Esteva et al., 2017; Attia et al., 2019; Chen et al., 2020a, b), AI technologies have also demonstrated instability, amalgamation difficulty, limited evidence for accuracy, and evidence of inaccuracy (Yang et al., 2020; Voter et al., 2021).

One consequence of this complicated picture is that AI technological development can be viewed as a *process*. This process depends partly on methodological stabilization for reliability and partly on coordinating multiple relations between user, technology, social contexts, and complex systems. On the side of methodological stabilization, there is the obvious "correspondence relation" between AI data and a complex system (in that AI represents key system properties and it aids in the prediction and explanation of system dynamics). But such simple correspondence relations conceal deeper relations of epistemic commitment. That is, the use of AI is not just based on its reliability. In fact, epistemological trustworthiness, or the acceptance of a given AI technology, does *not* depend on its reliability. Even when there is lack of transparency about AI algorithms, there is a puzzlingly high attribution of algorithm reliability. For instance, recent work has detailed reliability judgments about blackboxed algorithms—specifically the preferential treatment of algorithms ("algorithm appreciation") over predictions made by people (Logg et al., 2019). Algorithm appreciation has also been shown to apply to physicians with less task expertise; when AI conclusions are erroneous, it throws a wrench into the process of diagnostic decision-making (Gaube et al., 2021).

It is frightening to consider that the use of AI for complex data organization, prediction, and medical decision-making can occur without detailed consideration of the methodology behind the particular AI technology as well as its application to complex medical environments. This constitutes a relation of one-directional use that ignores the complex relations behind AI parameterization and implementation in real-life contexts—namely, dynamically changing social and built contexts. Our goal in this discussion is to explore our relations to AI by identifying the difficulties of *coordinating relations between user, ML process, and "sociobuilt contexts,"* *specifically as these apply to medical technologies and decisions.*[2] In Sect. 3, we use a recent COVID-19 machine learning case study in order to present the difficulty of traversing the detailed causal topography of complex systems or "sociobuilt contexts." The reason why we use the term "sociobuilt context" is because the conceptual focal point falls on the interactions between social and built processes. In Sect. 4, we make suggestions about how to change our relation to AI into one that goes beyond simplistic epistemic trust, focusing instead on immersive relations (e.g., "iterative entanglement") and their advantages over typically unreflective uses of AI in medical practice.

3   Representing Sociobuilt Contexts: Problems in Parameterization

Some AI applications require limited parametrization, such as using machine learning to classify SARS-CoV-2 serological rapid diagnostic test results for the purpose of reducing visible "band" reading ambiguities (Mendels et al., 2021). Others involve more complex parameterization that, we argue, necessitates a deeper understanding of social and built processes.

Research is attempting to characterize the role of biases in AI data inputs from imaging and electronic health records (EHR) (Crawford and Calo, 2016; Chen et al., 2019; Ghassemi et al., 2020). Particularly important for our discussion is the presence of EHR data biases (Chen et al., 2018, 2019). For instance, Chen et al.

---

[2] In our case study, we will focus on a specific application of machine learning medical technologies. This is for the purpose of methodological precision about parameterization. While we think that many of our conclusions about parameterization in data analysis can extend to other subfields of AI research, such a discussion is beyond the scope of this paper. Partly, such a discussion depends on the classification of ML relative to AI. Such classificatory work can be accomplished by specifying subfields in AI, but it can also be accomplished through methodological comparison. For a detailed account of the methodological relations between ML and AI, see Emmert-Streib et al. (2020).

(2019) present the view that limited representation in data samples go hand in hand with encoded bias and inequitable medical treatment based on race, ethnicity, gender, and socioeconomic status. Zou and Schiebinger (2018) describe how ML program optimization is heavily dependent on overrepresentation of "White" individuals within training and test data, such that the program optimizes for overrepresented groups in order to boost accuracy. This can have consequences, such as prediction error disparities between races (Chen et al., 2018). The general methodological suggestion in the literature is the need for more and better data in an effort to eliminate bias and refine prediction. For example, the Chen et al. (2018) study uses EHR data from 25,879 intensive care unit admissions from a single medical center and would likely benefit from independent data. But we make the point that even a *predictively useful algorithm can present alternative limitations and biases relevant to AI medical use*. By discussing a recent COVID-19 EHR case study, we describe health properties that are heavily embedded in social-built contexts in order to present the difficulty of representing the detailed causal topography of a complex system.

The recent development of the COVID Inpatient Risk Calculator (CIRC) uses hospital admission factors to predict the likelihood that a patient with COVID-19 will progress to severe disease.[3] Blauer and Garibaldi (2021) write about CIRC and its transformation into SCARP, the Severe COVID-19 Adaptive Risk Predictor, as follows:

> This machine learning process measured the historical effects of readily accessible patient data (demographics, vital signs, lab results, etc.) on their COVID-19 outcomes. The results were then assembled in a calculator that could compute the probability of a given patient progressing to severe disease once that individual's data were inputted. Armed with support from the tool, medical teams could then help make critical decisions about where and how to treat patients. (p. 1)

CIRC has since been transformed into SCARP, which uses real-time data to make patient predictions (Wongvibulsin et al., 2021). The continuing development of CIRC and SCARP extends beyond useful classification and constitutes a flexible predictive tool for medical decisions that can be integrated with EHR data methods and the development of future ML algorithms. Our point of focus for the discussion is on the development and refinement of ML technologies for new territories in EHR data methods. As Blauer and Garibaldi (2021) state,

> None of this data would exist without the sacrifices of frontline healthcare providers, patients, and their families. And, Hopkins researchers plan to continue working with these data to determine how the lessons learned from CIRC and SCARP might apply to diseases other than COVID-19. Researchers are adapting the risk evaluation methods established by CIRC and SCARP to similar respiratory diseases, such as influenza and pneumonia. The ultimate goal is for medical providers to walk into a patient's room armed with data about everything that has happened to the patient up to that moment, gather additional information, and then use all available data to make the next decision. That is the promise

---

[3] CIRC can be found here: https://rsconnect.biostat.jhsph.edu/covid_predict/. Note the warning about model use for purposes of internal and external validity.

of true precision medicine, and a bounty of skills that decision makers across the board should understand and begin to hone. (pp. 2–3).

This passage provides a vision, consisting of at least two notable features: the thoroughness of time-dependent data about "everything that has happened to the patient up to that moment" and *interrelations* between healthcare providers, patients, and families. We agree that both multidimensional data (Sects. 3.1 and 3.2) and patient- and community-focused interrelations (Sect. 3.3) are necessary for rigorous ML methodological development. We discuss each sequentially below.

3.1   New Directions in Variable Choice

Relevant to the point about multidimensional data, we focus on the initial parameterization used by CIRC and SCARP, generated from an existing EHR classificatory scheme, which depends on variable choice.[4] We argue that while the use of statistically significant variables in the model provides predictive utility, CIRC and SCARP also ignore key variables that correspond to intricate social and built contexts, relevant for COVID-19 health outcomes and future patient medical decision-making. While our concerns may not be important for the expeditious implementation of CIRC and SCARP during the early pandemic context, they point to issues with the future development of EHR data and improvement of ML processes. By speedily endorsing useful prediction, we may miss the sociobuilt landscape for the impressive algorithmic trees.

A bit of background about CIRC and SCARP development is in order. Garibaldi et al. (2021) used EHR data from five hospitals within one system in order to create CIRC. As a result of its predictive success, the methodological progress of CIRC seems to be its generalizability and integration with further EHR measures. It is this flexible transition from *useful predictive tool* to *integration within EHR measures* that requires analysis. But before we proceed to generalize the application of a given ML program to decision-making contexts, we set the stage with an epistemic question: Do the variables used in model construction capture key properties of complex systems? Additionally, an accompanying methodological question: What epistemic and non-epistemic considerations are involved in the choices to include,

---

[4] We use "parameters" to refer to elements of a system that characterize the system. The use of "parameter" will sometimes overlap with the traditional use of "variable" as well as the use of "variable" in the development of CIRC and SCARP from EHR data. It is important to note that in scientific practice, traditionally, there is a difference between the use of "parameters" and "variables." The former refers to constants (either universal constants or invariants in the modeling setup under consideration), while the latter defines characteristics of a system with changing values within a modeling setup. In coordination with the literature, we will use "variables" to describe the EHR classificatory categories used for the ML process in CIRC and SCARP. Where necessary, we will also refer to decision-tree parameters such as minimum node size. Note that we will not reference the "hyperparameters" used in the ML process, which are parameters whose values dictate the learning process (e.g., the number of iterations in training).

exclude, or consolidate variables? CIRC and SCARP ML development use a number of EHR variables. For instance,

> Candidate variables present in the data source included demographic and anthropomorphic features, social history, admission source, comorbidities, vital signs, and lab measurements. Available demographic features included age, gender, race, ethnicity, and locality. *Race and ethnicity were consolidated to a single variable and locality was not considered* as a candidate variable due to limitations on generalizing it beyond the region of study. Available anthropomorphic measurements included height, weight, and body mass index, but only body mass index was chosen for generalizability. Elements of social history including smoking status, alcohol status, and drug use present as structured data in the electronic medical record were included as candidate variables. (Wongvibulsin et al., 2021, Supplementary Material, p. 3; our emphasis)

In SCARP, even though the algorithm is provided with 105 candidate variables, on average, each tree only uses 8.69 (SD: 1.80) and 8.00 (SD: 1.27) variables for the 1- and 7-day random forests (Wongvibulsin et al., 2021). This is, of course, due to the success of a limited number of variables in the direct path from the start of a given tree to its terminal leaf in generating associated predicted risk. Such a method provides numerous practical advantages in medical contexts. For instance, medical professionals and patients can input a limited number of variables and still benefit from the predictive power of the 105 variable-incorporated random forest (Wongvibulsin et al., 2021). Also, SCARP takes into account the predictive potential of time-dependent covariates, thereby including updated measurement values (Wongvibulsin et al., 2021). By providing risk calculations for progression to severe COVID-19, appropriate medical decisions (such as quick decisions about patient transfer to other hospitals) can be made (Wongvibulsin et al., 2021). The researchers also consider the future development of SCARP:

> As treatment options for COVID-19 expand and outcomes improve, the risk probabilities reported here may overstate the risk for progression to severe disease or death in future patients. We are committed to preserving the long-term utility of this risk calculator by continuously updating the tool and reporting its prospective performance as treatment options for COVID-19 expand and clinical outcomes improve. (Wongvibulsin et al., 2021, p. 8)

Our reason for describing programs like CIRC and SCARP is for the purpose of understanding deeper relations in technology. Beyond the impressive small-window predictive capacity that is currently being used in clinical EHR settings, there are methodological considerations relevant to tool development in future medical decision-making when assessing "risk." ML use for a 7-day window in severe COVID-19 progression may differ drastically from ML use for long-term risk assessment based on built environment factors. However, both types of ML development may suffer from the same EHR limitations in parameterization and overfitting. Likewise, revision of EHR limitations can benefit the use of ML for both quick prediction and deeper causal tracking.

We begin with variable choice in EHR. In addition to model validation methods that weigh variable importance for prediction, the reasoning behind variable choice is supported by robust clinical research: "... the variables that are used by the majority of trees in the forest are *consistent with clinical knowledge* regarding the importance of these variables in COVID-19 disease progression" (Wongvibulsin et al., 2021, Supplementary Material, p. 4, our emphasis). However, we point out that variable choice is a process, dictated by multiple considerations. Choices could involve the inclusion of certain social determinants of health and not others,[5] the exclusion of built environments relevant to health, and the problematic consolidation of race and ethnicity to a single variable. These are important to consider in the context of independent interdisciplinary research about social and built environment factors in COVID-19 when addressing our initially stated question: Do the variables used in model construction capture key complex system properties? Furthermore, what is the conceptual infrastructure behind those variables (e.g., what is the causal relevance of social determinants of health, and how are they connected to built environments)?

By integrating independent research, we can see that biomarker representation could be improved in CIRC. Furthermore, the methodological focus on particular downstream biomarkers can determine the choice to include or to ignore relevant upstream causal factors in future EHR classification and algorithm development. The case of the biomarker interleukin-8 (IL-8) is especially illustrative of this potential. Early in the pandemic, IL-8 was shown to be useful for predicting the prognosis of COVID-19 disease; furthermore, IL-8 can be even more useful in comparative interleukin evaluation (Li et al., 2021). By itself, a small biomarker revision in an ML process could benefit from the incorporation of other research. It is noteworthy that SCARP uses IL-6 (Wongvibulsin et al., 2021). According to Li et al. (2021), "while IL-6 was an available indicator in severe COVID-19 patients, IL-8 performed better in indicating the progress of COVID-19 disease status from mild to severe" (p. 2). Additionally, in comparison to IL-6, IL-8 levels were better correlated with the "overall clinical disease scores at the *different time points* in the same COVID-19 patients," making it better equipped as a disease prognosis biomarker (Li et al., 2021, p. 6, our emphasis). This latter point is important given that SCARP's RF-SLAM offers continuous-time analysis by tracking how predictor variables change over time (Wongvibulsin et al., 2019; Wongvibulsin et

---

[5] SCARP tracks "behavioral risk factors" like alcohol and tobacco use; CIRC tracks similar factors. Both have limited social determinants of health categories. Since both studies use the Johns Hopkins Medicine healthcare system, a few details are important about the JH-CROWN registry. The JH-CROWN registry, which is hosted on the Precision Medicine Analytic Platform, constitutes a collection of information from multiple data sources: Johns Hopkins' EMR, "Epic," Research Electronic Data Capture, and biospecimen repositories. The registry partitions "elements" based on a number of categories. The JH-CROWN registry notes the following "social history factors": "smoking status, alcohol and illicit drug use" (https://ictr.johnshopkins.edu/coronavirus/jh-crown/). The "social history" category contains an addendum of changes to "social determinants of health" questions/categories. In addition to questions about smoking and alcohol use, new categories about social stress, frequency of religious and social events, food scarcity, history of abuse, transportation, exercise, and education are listed in the addendum. Additionally, the registry provides "geocode" information about patient location and visit. This point will become relevant in Sect. 3.3, where we discuss GIS-EHR integration.

al., 2021). Complementary to continuous-time analysis, Li et al. (2021)suggest that IL-6 and IL-8 can be used in different disease stages of COVID-19. Ma et al. (2021) have noted that while IL-6 is useful for the prediction of COVID-19 severity and survival, it is not "significantly associated with the duration of illness" (p. 6). Their finding is that IL-8 is associated with the duration of illness in patients with severe COVID-19 (Ma et al., 2021). The empirical implication is that comparative interleukin evaluation[6] can be informative about severity, survival, and duration. The methodological implication is to consider the combined use of IL-6 and IL-8 in continuous-time analysis, given the suitability of IL-8 for RF-SLAM.

We caution that the mere improvement in single factor biomarker measures can hide the more significant general problem of *causal representation*. Indeed, the general and particular are interdependent as a focus on selective downstream biomarkers—especially successful ones—can determine the choice to include or to ignore upstream causal factors.[7] For instance, it turns out that due to its multi-scale associations, IL-8 can operate as a pivotal variable that promotes the representation of complex social determinants of health in EHR and algorithm use. If we follow IL-8 cascading causal factors, the relevance of environmentally-modulated molecular processes emerges. Research on molecular mechanisms in IL-8 signaling pathways shows how social and environmental factors overexpress at least seven molecular pathways, leading to disparate health outcomes (Gaye et al., 2017). An explanatorily and predictively clearer picture thus emerges by tracking the connection between social determinants of health, environmental factors, molecular mechanisms, proinflammatory interleukin biomarkers, and disease progression. In our discussion of representing complex systems in Sect. 4.2, we detail that as a pivotal biomarker, IL-8 can be used as a lever that opens information pathways about the progress of a disease across a variety of scales and with reference to physiological, built environment, and sociological interactions. Note that we are oversimplifying the causal web here because phenomena such as environmental racism[8] can create multiple branching causal pathways with concomitant effects, which require adequate scientific representation in theoretical and measurement practices (Keyser and Howland, 2021). Representing such causal complexity is necessary for adequate measurement practices in general and requires *large-scale methodological modifications* (Keyser and Howland, 2021).[9] Moreover, the choice

---

[6] This is consistent with the comparative interleukin evaluation posited by Li et al. (2020).

[7] For a detailed analysis of methodological issues in tracking upstream and downstream processes in biomarkers, see Keyser and Sarry's (2020) discussion of Alzheimer's biomarkers.

[8] For a thorough account of this term and recent case study, see Seamster and Purifoy (2021).

[9] As Keyser and Howland (2021) argue, COVID-19 measurement practices have shown severe limitations in the types of representation involved in tracking complex processes. For instance, measurement practices are just beginning to "...unravel the relationship between COVID-19 outcomes, built environment factors (e.g., pollution exposure), resource access, various forms of systemic racism, and countless causal connections between biotic, built, social, and health processes—but with *severely limited measurement focus on interactions*, like how systemic racism influences health outcomes within the context of the pandemic" (Keyser and Howland, 2021,

of methodological approaches in data practices (e.g., distribution-based approaches vs. risk-based approaches) can hide or reveal the causal processes of various forms of structural racism (Zalla et al., 2021; Kalewold, 2020).[10]

3.2   Sociobuilt Contexts

We propose that effective causal tracking should, in fact, go deeper into the *relations* between social determinants of health and built environments. CIRC and SCARP do not track built environment pollution exposure, for instance, even though the causal importance of pollution is crucial in COVID-19 mortality rate evaluation (e.g., 8% COVID-19 mortality increases associated with 1 $\mu g/m^3$ increase in chronic $PM_{2.5}$ exposure; Wu et al., 2020). Additionally, CIRC only classifies race and ethnicity with a simple *binary* infrastructure: "White" vs. "non-White." This type of classificatory scheme constitutes a frame of reference bias discussed by Zou and Schiebinger (2018), limited categories and data points create self-sustaining validation loops such that data about White individuals becomes the frame of reference used to refine the ML algorithm, while other races and ethnicities are homogenized into the "non-White" category. Independent epidemiological research warns against generalizing data about race and ethnicity, thereby losing detail about, for instance, how various forms of structural racism are producing disproportionate COVID-19 outcomes experienced by Black and Latinx populations (Washington, 2020; Brandt et al., 2020). We suggest the incorporation of independent research to shape the ML process. This might require simple modifications, such as changes in biomarker variables, built environment factors, social determinants of health, and adequate self-representation based on race, ethnicity, and gender. But it also requires a push for interdisciplinary collaboration among natural and social scientists to seek out new variables, relations, and scales.

Yet the social determinants of health *as a function* of the built environment are seldom discussed, especially in COVID-19. It is noteworthy that some researchers have discussed the relation between structural racism and built environment pollu-

---

p. 22). They present a process-view theory of measurement for the purpose of creating more robust measurement practices that capture the complex interactions between biotic, social, built, and health conditions; they also discuss the relations between measurement practices and theory building.

[10] Zalla et al. (2021) argue that distribution-based approaches hide the history of structural racism and the mechanisms through which racism operates. Relevant to the distribution-based approach and the discussion of the mechanisms through which racism operates, Kalewold (2020) presents the Mechanism Discovery Approach that emphasizes "the role of racism in mechanisms producing racial disparities":

I argue that the Mechanism Discovery Approach (MDA) provides heretofore neglected philosophical tools for explanations of [epidemiological racial disparities] ERDs. MDA goes beyond the statistical approach by showing how particular disparities come to be through description of the mechanism that produced them. MDA avoids the pitfalls of race-based studies by accounting for the role of racism in mechanisms producing racial disparities. (Kalewold, 2020, p. 41)

tion exposure relevant for COVID-19 morbidity and mortality (Brandt et al., 2020). Others have warned against the data homogenization of built environments, which is relevant for health data (Terrell and James, 2020). The case of air pollution is instructive in this regard. During the COVID-19 pandemic, general car emission pollution seemed to have decreased on countrywide and worldwide scales. Studies report decreased global pollution levels and improved mortality benefits due to air pollution reduction (Venter et al., 2020; Chen et al., 2020a, b). The data *seems* reassuring about decreases in pollution-related health outcomes and offers hope about short-term pollution health benefits. But if we take a broadscope data approach *only*, car emission decreases can mask increases in industrial pollution, which have a disproportionate effect on long-term $PM_{2.5}$ exposure in Black communities in the United States (Terrell and James, 2020).

This implies that EHR data classificatory schemes, relevant for the ML process, require at least two points of attention. First, the incorporation of interdisciplinary research can co-determine the external validity of variables as well as the modification of relevant variables used in the ML process. This can apply to something as simple as the choice of biomarker measure or something as complex as the interaction between social determinants of health and built environment factors in a region plagued by environmental racism. Second, attention should be paid not only to variable choice in EHR and ML use but also to the *scale* of that data. Actively seeking new methods of parameterization based on diverse variables and interactions, and thus avoiding homogenization, reveals patterns in the data that can improve the ML process. Notice here that modification of variables and scales requires collaborative and interdisciplinary examination of causal relationships.

We propose that ML parameterization requires new methods of capturing complexities, such as specific, relevant characteristics of a patient's dwelling or phenomena like the "pollution burden," where the focus is on interactions between social and built processes (Terrell and James, 2020). To understand such complexities, it is necessary to create an ML infrastructure precise enough to account for *how* an industrialized built context can be parameterized with multiple regulatory roles pertaining to public health burdens. To make the causal language precise, a given sociobuilt context can moderate multiple health burdens at many scales, such as built environment moderation of both environmental pollutants and other social determinants of health that promote multiple proinflammatory mechanisms, for example, via IL-8 signaling and NF-κB signaling (Gaye et al., 2017). The reason why we refer to this as a "sociobuilt context" is because the focus is on the *interactions* between numerous social and built processes.

The representational challenge would be deciding which variables and interactions are relevant for data foundations in the ML process in order to adequately capture social and built processes. This requires detailed scientific classificatory work. Determination of the relevant variable interactions might be fully outside of the epistemological and disciplinary considerations of the AI technology—much like our discussion of key social determinants of health and built environment factors being outside the boundaries of current CIRC and SCARP parameterization. Successful ML integration would require associating key built variables with multiple social determinants of health and COVID-19 variables provided by

EHR data. The methodological suggestion is that whenever the sociobuilt context constitutes key causal roles in COVID-19, it could be beneficial to seek out new EHR and ML frameworks that incorporate such factors. But retraining ML, using broader or more balanced data sets, misses the issue. It does not just amount to a failure in parametrization but *a failure to continuously re-parameterize based on a key understanding of shifts in sociobuilt contexts*. Indeed, this failure seems to indicate the pressing need for shifts of understanding about human-technology and especially human-AI relations, which we discuss in Sect. 4.

The simple, practical objection is, Why would any of this be useful for quick prediction? In fact, it might stall the development of new methods for prediction. The best method would be to choose a series of key variables for disease progression—exactly the random forest approach afforded by RF-SLAM, which identifies a smaller set of important predictor variables from a large set of candidate predictors without the use of a formal variable selection method (Wongvibulsin et al., Supplementary Material, 2021).[11] But as we note in the introduction, the development of ML is a *process*. The use of tools, such as CIRC and SCARP, will be further refined for future EHR and medical decision-making development. Emergency COVID-19 progression prediction is just one aspect of this process. After all, the purpose of ML diagnostic programs can extend beyond predicting the likelihood of COVID-19 mortality within a 7-day period. They can be used in combination with other EHR data for the purpose of physician suggestions about patient risk of future morbidity and mortality as a function of key sociobuilt health factors. Questions about social stressors that moderate NF-κB signaling and industrial pollution that moderates long-term $PM_{2.5}$ exposure are relevant for long-term patient risk evaluation. Such detailed questions can benefit patient autonomy in the EHR process, which is afforded by the availability of multifactor information—a point we discuss in Sects. 3.3 and 4.

Another objection is that in an EHR context, detailed questions about lifetime pollution exposure and sociobuilt factors might prove to be pragmatically difficult. This is where ML integration is important. Built environment GIS data can be easily integrated into EHR records. GIS-EHR integration has been reliably used in medicine (Laranjo et al., 2016). However, proper coordination between multiple programs first requires a key understanding of the causal relevance of sociobuilt interactions, as well as how the relevance of those variables can change over contexts and time. There are numerous integration tools available that can be adapted to represent time-dependent movements through built environments (Kamel Boulos et al., 2019).

It is worth noting that the pursuit of "small data" for causal conclusions might appease our worries about variable choice as well as integration of external research and technology. That is, one might argue AI methods that intersect small data with

---

[11] Notably, RF-SLAM offers many methodological benefits—for instance, by offering continuous-time analysis, it can track how predictor variables change relative to time intervals, thus being useful for "piecewise-constant hazard rates" (Wongvibulsin et al., 2019).

big data could solve the bias of context homogeneity, such as in the use of transfer learning, or "fine-tuning", in medicine. Transfer learning constitutes training ML with a big data set and subsequently refining a solution to a related problem with a small data set. But if the task specification, data sets/sizes, or features are drastically different for the small data application, then transfer learning in medicine proves ineffective (Raghu et al., 2019). Parameterization needs in medicine can also differ from successful parameterization in other transfer learning technologies, with over-parameterization being an issue in transfer-learning models (Raghu et al., 2019). We think that transfer learning would likely demonstrate difficulty in nonhomogeneous sociobuilt contexts. The issue is that if relevant social determinants of health closely entangled with built environments are fully ignored for big data processing, then small data will not produce more causal resolution.

To summarize, we present the difficulty of coordinating relations between ML processes and sociobuilt contexts. The key point is that figuring out something as seemingly simple as variable relevance depends on an understanding of context changes. It is not enough to posit the generalized need for prediction or the simple avenue of transfer learning. Rather, it requires detailed scientific classificatory work that is actively interdisciplinary—a point that we turn to next.

3.3 Evidence-Based Design and Transdisciplinary Research

As noted in the previous section, relevant variable interactions might be fully outside of the epistemological and disciplinary considerations of AI technology (e.g., the exploration of key social determinants of health and built environment factors, relevant for COVID-19 morbidity and mortality). In fact, our suggestion of continuous re-parameterization based on a key understanding of shifts in sociobuilt contexts would greatly benefit from interdisciplinary and transdisciplinary approaches by integrating considerations from non-AI and nonmedical disciplines such as architecture and design. A relevant example of a transdisciplinary field is evidence-based design (EBD), which uses research planning to understand and design resilient healthcare environments. Notably, EBD focuses on analysis of interactions between built environments, technologies, organizational systems, and multiple layers of users, such as staff and patients who are embedded within social networks (Elf et al., 2020). EBD can serve as a mediator between AI technology development and clinical implementation. A team consisting of designers, programmers, and medical health professionals, for example, could schematize methods for improving ML practices to adequately track dynamic sociobuilt contexts. But as "person-centered" and "shared decision-making" relative to EBD is associated with the quality of patient experience (Elf et al., 2020), a given transdisciplinary team should actively involve patient and community relations.

The purpose of our discussion of missing EHR variables that are causally relevant to social determinants and inequitable built environments is to explore new variables that can be utilized to improve EHR classification. As noted earlier, AI can promote patient control over data (Topol, 2019). One potential method for increasing patient control is to give them a say about which data variables are used for EHR records. Recent work urges community involvement and autonomy in scientific data gathering and interpretation (Keyser and Howland, 2021). Coordinating relations between user, ML process, and sociobuilt context can implement new methods of inclusion for patients and communities for the purpose of cross-checking portions of the ML process. For instance, what is the classificatory scheme of EHR data? How is small data coordinated with big data in order to develop nuanced causal information about various forms of structural racism? How is a given ML process validated, and is there a risk for biased validation loops? These are all questions that could give patients a channel for direct causal input into the ML process. We will leave the design of collaborative methods for another discussion. However, it is important to make the methodological suggestion that if the sociobuilt context constitutes key causal roles in COVID-19, then we should seek out new EHR and ML frameworks to incorporate such factors, whether inter- or transdisciplinarily.

4   Reassessment of Relations

We began this discussion with the notion of "epistemic trust" by presenting the fact that even when there is lack of transparency about AI algorithms, there is high attribution of algorithm reliability – specifically the preferential treatment of algorithms ("algorithm appreciation") over predictions made by people (Logg et al., 2019). Such epistemic trust is particularly problematic for diagnostic decision-making when AI conclusions are erroneous (Gaube et al., 2021). It is puzzling how the potentially rich process of building a relation to AI for complex data organization, prediction, and medical decision-making can be reduced to the one-dimensional attitude of algorithm appreciation. That is, algorithm appreciation can occur without detailed consideration of the methodological choices behind the particular AI technology, including the variables used to capture complex sociobuilt contexts. Given lack of transparency, algorithm appreciation constitutes a relation of one-directional *use* that ignores the complex relations behind AI parameterization and implementation in real-life contexts. In this section, we make suggestions about how to change our relation to AI to go beyond one-dimensional use relations. We present the view that fine-tuning AI requires an "iterative entanglement" that consists of constant reassessment of our relation to the AI.

The relation of "use" can constitute one-dimensional epistemic trust, but it can also constitute more detailed relations. We briefly apply Ihde's numerous views on relations in order to discuss the following: "embodiment" and "hermeneutic" relations, representations of complex systems, and ethical relations.

4.1   "Embodiment" and "Hermeneutic" Relations

For Don Ihde (1990, 1991, 1993, 2011), relations can constitute the human use of a technology for the purpose of extending capacity. In Ihde's case, the focus is on perceptual capacity either through direct sensing ("embodiment") or through representation ("hermeneutic"). A key marker of "embodiment relation[s]" is that we often forget that a given technology serves as a mediator in our relation to the world (Ihde, 1990). But in "hermeneutic relations," the technology requires interpretation in order to be useful in representing the world (Ihde, 1990). This is applicable to the aforementioned epistemic trust of using ML programs for the purpose of extending diagnostic capacity. The decision to use blackboxed AI processing over human processing implies not only the *uncritical use* of technology as extension but also a lack of interpretation. Yet in Ihde's account, technology requires functionality or serviceability as well as expertise in use in order for the technology to be "transparent" and work seamlessly (Ihde, 1990). Compare this with the uncritical and unreliable use of AI, for example, by providing unreliable information that doctors might utilize to make erroneous medical decisions (Gaube et al., 2021). In this type of relation, there is neither serviceability nor skill in the process of using the technology. There is also a lack of critical interpretation in the representational results of the technology. We suggest that more attention is required to understand use relations as part of the AI development process. One prerequisite for the use of SCARP, for instance, could be a detailed understanding of *how* the EHR-variable selection process feeds into ML design and produces model parameters. This would constitute teaching a user, a medical health professional, the necessary skill to use the technology.

4.2   Representations of Complex Systems

Ihde's (1990) view is also notable in terms of the relation between "microperceptions" and "macroperceptions." The former is a sensory perception, while the latter requires locating meaning within a complex sociocultural context. According to Ihde (1990), micro- and macroperceptions are codependent. Importantly, technology can dramatically alter macroperceptions because the design of the technology funnels what features to focus on in the world. Embodiment relations can be designed to ignore sensory pathways, while hermeneutic relations can be designed to represent selective parts of the world. This is complementary to our discussion about ignoring variables. A given ML technology can selectively engage parts of a complex system while ignoring other parts of that system. So how we use the technology requires understanding what kind of "macroperceptions" it produces. COVID-19 SCARP outputs are not merely technologically mediated predictions; they also operationalize and institutionalize representations of a complex system composed of biological and sociobuilt processes. As Ihde (2011) points out, even an autonomic computing system that is self-aware, context aware, and anticipatory will still have parameter limits and will depend on its deep relations to human tinkering.[12] A useful extension of this view is that clarifying relations to technology will inform how we tinker with the technology and vice versa.

As an extension of the point on deep relations and tinkering, Peter-Paul Verbeek (2011) focuses on the entanglement and causal interactions between humans and technology in the form of "immersive relations." Humans and technology are not simply metaphysically entangled within "immersive relations." As observable and coupled systems, their feedback loops ensure each has causal import and impact on physical and normative processes. This is an extension of Ihde's (2011) relation-focused concepts. Technologies are extensions of human causal processes. But interactions between humans and technology also become a continuous process such that e.g., technological development and medical decision-making are co-determining (Verbeek, 2011). Verbeek calls for a critical refocusing on the "quality of interaction" between humans and technology. We made a similar point in Sect. 3, where we discussed that understanding complicated sociobuilt contexts requires constantly fine-tuning AI. We discussed this in terms of reassessing relevant variables relative to nonhomogeneous contexts. But fine-tuning AI requires an "iterative entanglement," which effectively makes Verbeek's account consistent with a generally process-relational view of technology. In the medical context, this consists of constant reassessment of relations between healthcare practitioners and the AI system. Reassessment necessitates the emergence of a set of second-order practices with respect to AI operations. These practices partly pertain to periodic monitoring of the relevant variables used by AI in risk assessment protocols, such as CIRC. They also depend on balancing EHR data considerations for fine-tuning and accuracy checking. Finally, they depend on assessing our epistemic and ethical stance. Understanding contexts that are changing and complex requires treating AI development dynamically rather than expecting it to autonomously run to completion and generate a reliable result.

Verbeek's account may be further articulated by thinking about the relationship between human and artificial intelligence as a coupled system. By taking a deeper dive into Verbeek's metaphors of immersion, entanglement, and fine-tuning, we may move this conception a step closer to operationalizing "iterative entanglement." In this context, consider the simplest relevant complex system, the coupled system: two individual systems, A and B, whose cycles are bound by exchanging one or more components (i.e., matter, energy, information) required by both within their shared environment, thus rendering them codependent. The dynamics of A are inextricably bound to those of B, such that changes of reaction rates in A will alter those of B. So together, they form a coupled system thus adding quantitative precision to Verbeek's sense of "entanglement." Their relationship is constitutive of each of them, and of the coupled system they compose, so long as these systems are open to the flow of matter, energy and information. This is immersion in the flow. Earley (2013) argues

---

[12] As a physicist, Andrew Pickering arrived at a similar concept (Pickering, 1984). He argues that this tinkering is how all science functions in actual practice—what he refers to as "the mangle of practice" (Pickering, 1995).

that because it assumes events and relations (not substances and properties) as the ultimate units of reality, process ontology is particularly well suited to analyzing open chemical systems.[13] If the heart as a living organ had to choose just one ontology, it would certainly choose process ontology (as illustrated by Winfree's pioneering chronobiological coronary research) for the heart is all about keeping time and timing, which geometrizes time.[14]

The importance of tracking the temporal dimension of such systems is that it throws timing into high relief. Winfree's experimental work on hearts and fruit flies demonstrated that timing is a sort of Archimedean lever for moving the world of a living being by resetting—and even stopping—certain metabolic cycles. This model supports the arguments made in the previous section about the potential benefit of designing protocols to track specific flows of material and information through sociobuilt systems. As relations between social and technological systems are diachronic, a study of their temporal profiles (with special attention to spatiotemporal scales, junctures, and cascades) could be especially useful. This seems to be why and how IL-8 is such a pivotal biomarker: It can serve as a lever that opens information pathways about the progress of a disease across a variety of spatiotemporal scales and with reference to physiological, built environment, and sociological interactions. Because IL-8 can indicate key interactions at multiple scales, as mentioned earlier, it can be used to track causal factors across spatiotemporal scales. Given that both the COVID-19 pandemic and social response constitute a complex system that occupies several orders of magnitude from nanometers to acres, time series graphs could be of great potential use. The interactions of a single biomarker such as IL-8 across several orders of magnitude, for example, could have the potential to reveal hitherto unobserved aspects of the system. Such information could justify the construction of new interventions based on hitherto uncollected data and may even indicate new parameters for improving ML and AI algorithms.[15]

Winfree demonstrated the usefulness of timing for intervening in the dynamics of complex systems, an approach that has found general application in chronobiology across a variety of scales. Chronobiology predates Winfree, but his work initiated its modern conceptual and mathematical development.[16] "Chronomics" is a promising

---

[13] Joseph Earley has demonstrated how process ontology makes sense of the dynamics of nonequilibrium systems. His detailed treatment of dissipative structures adapted ontological features of Whitehead's process philosophy to Nobel laureate Ilya Prigogine's treatment of the nonlinear dynamics of urban traffic.

[14] Winfree's applied mathematical studies of heart disease and other biological phenomena produced two volumes: *When time breaks down* (1987) and *The geometry of biological time* (2001).

[15] Winfree strikes a similar note: "We are not talking about a mere reconceptualization of known biology, or worse, just redescribing it in fancy language. Rather, *these concepts exposed errors of fact and pointed to unforeseen facts that no one believed on occasions when they were encountered by accident*, facts that no one would have ever considered looking for. They present a way of thinking geometrically about biological dynamics, and about the laboratory experiments implemented to check its counter-intuitive implications" (Winfree, 2001, preface, emphasis added).

[16] Review article, Rensing et al., (2001).

way of mapping relationships between individuals, populations, and environments that is consistent with the coupled systems and time series approach discussed above:

> Chronobiology is the study of mechanisms underlying *chronomes, structures in time, found in organisms, in populations, and in the environment.* The development of chronomics from chronobiology can be compared with that of genomics from genetics. Genetic focus on factors underlying inter-organismic diversity in space needs the complementary chronobiologic realization of intra-individual and intra-population diversity in time. Genetics led to genomics, the mapping of genomes; *chronobiology led to chronomics, the mapping of chronomes that were found to be near matches of environmental chronomes near and far.* (Halberg, et al., 2013, emphasis added)

4.3   Ethical Relations

Questions of ethical relations are deeply embedded in healthcare. Insurers, administrators, government officials, hospital ethicists, designers, and AI programmers are as entangled as patients and clinicians. Less visible but equally important is the focus on relations pertaining to the lived experience of patients in their communities and the settings in which public healthcare is researched and delivered. Knowledge about such experiential relations cannot be adequately produced in laboratory settings; it requires paying close attention to the histories of those who have suffered multigenerational, multidimensional discrimination. This discrimination includes (but is not limited to) a lack of access to clean, healthy, and safe living environments to capacious and well-provisioned healthcare facilities to educational and social services and further contextual factors that require attention and community insight. The sociobuilt environment is the immediate context for the entire discussion. One of the key strategies of a process-ontological approach to such problems is to shift focus away from thinglike objects and onto processual relations. One immediate result is that context becomes crucial. This is because it conditions the formation, maintenance, disruption, and dissolution of relations.

The shift from things to relations reorients inquiry to seek persistent patterns of interaction. The value of this shift in focus is that it facilitates the transition of awareness from a complex collection of individual things to the systems in which they are embedded – this is akin to Ihde's micro- and macroperceptions. During the height of the COVID-19 pandemic, for example, everyone's attention was forcibly made bifocal; one eye fell to individual care for self and loved ones, while the other eye was acutely aware of the existence (but not the shape) of distributed systems of interaction that make everyday life possible. So while disease vectors are most definitely and persistently thinglike, and while we benefit from standard biochemical analyses of such things, there are challenges facing public health officials that are decidedly *not* thinglike. They require a new focus on persistent patterns in human-technology interactions.

According to Ihde (2011), our relations with technology see human agency sometimes maintained and other times violated. For instance, humans keep machines operating within parameters while machines automate by feeding off of human information, such as by profiling (Ihde, 2011). We propose that keeping ethical relations in mind in the ML process is essential. In order for the ML process to become collaborative and to include medical health professionals, interdisciplinary researchers, and patient communities, data use considerations ought to be explored. There are trade-offs in the specificity of data variables and violations of privacy. Detailed information pertaining to social determinants of health or built environment factors can compromise access, information, and decision-making privacy. It can also contribute to paternalism in medical professional-to-patient interactions based on overly specific EHR information. So re-parameterization in ML requires careful balancing between causal resolution and patient privacy and autonomy.

Still, there are limits on the extent to which upstream modulation of any technology can sufficiently anticipate and prevent unwanted or harmful effects. There are limits to the downstream mitigation of harmful or ineffective technological outcomes as well. Fisher et al. (2006) articulated a third alternative within the STS context: midstream modulation. This approach to examining and intervening in the normative dimensions of technological progress is precisely consistent with the iterative entanglement and fine-tuning discussed above. These are related modes of responsible research and innovation. Midstream modulation has been applied beyond academic research laboratories to technological development in medical and industrial settings (Pronk, 2018). The dynamism of innovation is preserved in and through the intertwined processes of anticipation, reflexivity, inclusion, and responsiveness,[17] which co-define ethical standards emphasizing the responsibility that comes with the power of knowing.

In the context of human-technology systems, as is the case with all coupled systems, both members are modified by their nested relationship. In an ideal scenario, responsible technology development continuously updates based on ethical standards, and there is reciprocal, though not symmetrical, updating. Both technology development and ethical standards are responsive to mitigating risk and promoting autonomy. Both technological and ethical standards are extended, articulated, and developed in response to the emergence of unanticipated choices that weren't even possibilities prior to the emergence of new technologies and new diseases. The historical notes of the Prequel section of this paper recount the gradual responsiveness to epistemic responsibilities that gave rise to the field of science and technology studies and related interdisciplinary work.

Interactions between ethical standards, methodologies, and ontologies are bidirectional and iteratively entangled. Synergism among such considerations can be fostered to compensate for the relative neglect of ethical standards and the restriction of scientific ontologies to the biochemical scale, as illustrated in Fig. 1.

Figure 1a simplistically represents the primary relationship shaping medical AI development as only the relation between methodologies (M) and the operative ontology (O), which includes only biomedical entities and processes. 1b adds ethical

---

[17] See discussion of RRI in Sect. 1. Prequel, above.

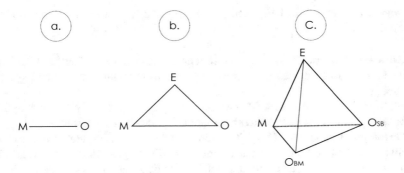

Fig. 1 Key factors shaping medical AI and ML algorithm development. Relations between the methodological (M), ontological (O), and ethical (E) are iteratively entangled and operate reciprocally. The simplistic relationship in (**a**) progresses to the more complex but vague relationships of (**b**). Finally, (**c**) presents a more adequate set of relations wherein the tetrahedral arrangement represents the ongoing *iterative engagement* among the ethical, methodological, and ontological factors: **Ethical concerns, E**: Issues raised in medical ethics, now expanded to consider health disparities due to various forms of environmental injustice and systemic racism. **Methodological concerns, M**: Issues of analyzing variables of interest, applicable statistical techniques, and other matters in algorithm development. **Ontological concerns, O_{BM}**: The standard set of considerations that together shape medical AI approaches to the COVID-19 pandemic. These include relevant entities of the ontology of the life sciences – from compact entities (e.g., biomolecules) to more diffuse reaction networks (e.g., metabolic cycles) and up to organismic and ecological networks. "O_{BM}" designates a *biomedical ontology*. **Ontological concerns, O_{SB}**: The hitherto missing fourth piece that, we propose, can and should be introduced as an additional area of ontological concern that pays more detailed attention to "sociobuilt contexts," which consist of *interactions* between built and social processes. Accordingly, "O_{SB}" designates a *sociobuilt ontology*

considerations (E) to the relationship between M and O. However, E's impact on changes in methodology as well as on the operative ontology is addressed in general terms; it is largely post hoc and too often ad hoc. This illustrates approaches where ethical considerations are discussed side by side with methodological and ontological considerations, but the moderating role is insufficiently developed. In Fig. 1c, the addition of previously unrepresented sociobuilt variables (O_{SB}) to existing biomedical ones (O_{BM}) brings a new dimension to the design of medical AI and ML algorithms. We use a tetrahedral arrangement to illustrate ongoing iterative engagement among the ethical, methodological, and ontological factors discussed above.[18] The simplistic relationship in Fig. 1a progresses to the more complex

---

[18] The tetrahedral graphic model was previously used by Mahootian and Eastman (2009) to explicate a functionally similar set of relationships embedded in NASA's "knowledge discovery in databases" within initiatives, such as the National Virtual Telescope program. Referring specifically to relationships between space science data, sensors, high performance computing, and modeling, we noted that "[c]ontinued optimal development of any of these new technical applications depends on the development of the others" (Mahootian and Eastman, 2009, p. 71). Similarly, Borne notes that emerging technologies and approaches produced a "Data-Sensor-Computing-Model synergism" (Borne, 2009, p. 1).

but vague relationships of Fig. 1b. Finally, Fig. 1c presents a more adequate set of relations wherein we have:

- **Ethical concerns, E**: Issues raised in medical ethics, now expanded to consider health disparities due to various forms of environmental injustice and systemic racism.
- **Methodological concerns, M**: Issues of analyzing variables of interest, applicable statistical techniques, and other matters in algorithm development.
- **Ontological concerns, O_{BM}**: The standard set of considerations that together shape medical AI approaches to the COVID-19 pandemic, as discussed in previous sections. These include relevant entities of the ontology of the life sciences—from compact entities (e.g., biomolecules) to more diffuse reaction networks (e.g., metabolic cycles) and up to organismic and ecological networks. O_{BM} designates a *biomedical ontology*.
- **Ontological concerns, O_{SB}**: The hitherto missing fourth piece that, we propose, can and should be introduced as an additional area of ontological concern that comprises the daily lives of persons in communities. It pays more detailed ontological attention to sociobuilt contexts, which consist of interactions between built and social processes. Accordingly, O_{SB} designates a *sociobuilt ontology*.[19]

5   Conclusion

Philosopher of science Lorraine Code (2020) notes that "it is instructive, for epistemological purposes, to focus upon the assumed or alleged knowledge itself, to consider what is involved in the contention that there is often a responsibility to know, or at least to know better than one does" (p. 2). We have attempted to do just that in the present discussion. We have brought evidence and inference in support of the claim that we have "a responsibility to know, or at least to know better" than we currently do and furthermore, "that knowing well is a matter of considerable moral significance" (Code, 2020, p. 2). We have made specific recommendations

---

[19] Wilfrid Sellars' (1963) distinction between "scientific" and "manifest" seems pertinent here with regard to our pairing of biomedical and sociobuilt considerations. While our discussion cannot be reduced to this work, it is important to note that Sellars presents a way to combine the two views:

Thus the conceptual framework of persons is the framework in which we think of one another as sharing the community intentions which provide the ambience of principles and standards (above all, those which make meaningful discourse and rationality itself possible) within which we live our own individual lives. A person can almost be defined as a being that has intentions. Thus the conceptual framework of persons is not something that needs to be reconciled with the scientific image, but rather something to be joined to it. Thus, to complete the scientific image we need to enrich it not with more ways of saying what is the case, but with the language of community and individual intentions, so that by construing the actions we intend to do and the circumstances in which we intend to do them in scientific terms, we directly relate the world as conceived by scientific theory to our purposes, and make it our world and no longer an alien appendage to the world in which we do our living (Sellars, 1963, p. 40).

about ML use in a medical context and with regard to the public health response to COVID-19. Though our recommendations arise from this rather specific context, they embody certain understandings that apply more generally. We recur to Code (2020) for a pointed statement about this, namely, that "the *Lebenswelt*, the world in which human cognitive agents live and experience and know, is in every way as real as (and indeed in many ways more real for human beings than) the world described . . ." (p. 10). In this vein, John Monberg (2006) made two interesting observations at the beginning of the era of "social computing." First, "AI theorists ignore the social ground of intelligence, the connection between their computers and the world, and most importantly, the connection between society and their own work" (Monberg, 2006, p. 15). Second, "that intelligence only emerges in a social setting [that] holds for computers as well as humans" (Monberg, 2006, p. 17). It is interesting to note that Monberg's article was published in 2006, around the dawn of social networking platforms such as Facebook and Twitter. At the time, few anticipated the extent of social facilitation that computers are now capable of. Fewer still anticipated the commercial value and sheer quantity of the data generated by our personal lives.

The present state of affairs might further incline our convictions toward technological determinism. Such fatalistic conclusions depend upon the abdication of an epistemic responsibility. We have a moral and epistemic obligation to "know better" in this respect. Just as AI technologies are not *actually* intelligent, do not *know* anything, and only mechanically perform the tasks assigned to them, medical AI technologies can—at best—perform the tasks we set for them. In delivering on tasks, they are as deficient as the scope of our understanding. The community-based participatory research approach has long been recognized as a beneficial model for research by the US National Institutes of Health. The general features of such a model, suitably adapted, would be ideal for addressing the multi-scalar concerns and methods suggested above. By expanding the scope of the problem to cover larger sociobuilt contexts and then incorporating these factors in midstream strategies to evaluate, recalibrate, and re-parameterize medical AI, we may move public health approaches toward more effective and epistemically responsible systemic relations with affected populations than we have at present.

Acknowledgments The views presented in this chapter do not necessarily represent the views of the author(s)' organization(s). The authors declare no potential conflicts of interest.

References

Attia, Z. I., Kapa, S., Lopez-Jimenez, F., McKie, P. M., Ladewig, D. J., Satam, G., Pellikka, P. A., Enriquez-Sarano, M., Noseworthy, P. A., Munger, T. M., Asirvatham, S. J., Scott, C. G., Carter, R. E., & Friedman, P. A. (2019). Screening for cardiac contractile dysfunction using an artificial intelligence-enabled electrocardiogram. *Nature Medicine, 25*(1), 70–74. https://doi.org/10.1038/s41591-018-0240-2

Blauer, B., & Garibaldi, B. T. (2021). *New data method drives hospital care for COVID-19 patients.* Johns Hopkins University Pandemic Data Initiative. https://coronavirus.jhu.edu/pandemic-data-initiative/data-outlook/new-data-method-drives-hospital-care-for-covid-19-patients

Borne, K. (2009). *Astro2010: State of the Profession Position Paper (March 2009)*. https://www.academia.edu/55636155/Astroinformatics_A_21st_Century_Approach_to_Astronomy

Brandt, E. B., Beck, A. F., & Mersha, T. B. (2020). Air pollution, racial disparities, and COVID-19 mortality. *The Journal of Allergy and Clinical Immunology, 146*(1), 61–63. https://doi.org/10.1016/j.jaci.2020.04.035

Chen, I. Y., Johansson, F. D., & Sontag, D. (2018). Why is my classifier discriminatory? *Proceedings of the 32nd International Conference on Neural Information Processing Systems* (pp. 3543–3554).

Chen, I. Y., Szolovits, P., & Ghassemi, M. (2019). Can AI help reduce disparities in general medical and mental health care? *AMA Journal of Ethics, 21*(2), E167–E179. https://doi.org/10.1001/amajethics.2019.167

Chen, K.-C., Yu, H.-R., Chen, W.-S., Lin, W.-C., Lee, Y.-C., Chen, H.-H., Jiang, J.-H., Su, T.-Y., Tsai, C.-K., Tsai, T.-A., Tsai, C.-M., & Lu, H. H.-S. (2020a). Diagnosis of common pulmonary diseases in children by X-ray images and deep learning. *Scientific Reports, 10*(1), 17374. https://doi.org/10.1038/s41598-020-73831-5

Chen, K., Wang, M., Huang, C., Kinney, P. L., & Anastas, P. T. (2020b). Air pollution reduction and mortality benefit during the COVID-19 outbreak in China. *The Lancet Planetary Health, 4*(6), e210–e212. https://doi.org/10.1016/S2542-5196(20)30107-8

Code, L. (2020). *Epistemic Responsibility*, State University of New York Press.

Crawford, K., & Calo, R. (2016). There is a blind spot in AI research. *Nature, 538*(7625), 311–313. https://doi.org/10.1038/538311a

Cutillo, C. M., Sharma, K. R., Foschini, L., Kundu, S., Mackintosh, M., Mandl, K. D., Beck, T., Collier, E., Colvis, C., Gersing, K., Gordon, V., Jensen, R., Shabestari, B., Southall, N., & MI in Healthcare Workshop Working Group. (2020). Machine intelligence in healthcare – Perspectives on trustworthiness, explainability, usability, and transparency. *npj Digital Medicine, 3*(1), 47. https://doi.org/10.1038/s41746-020-0254-2

Cutliffe, Stephen H. (2000) Ideas, Machines, and Values: An Introduction to Science, Technology, and Society Studies. Lanham, MD: Rowman & Littlefield.

Demers-Payette, O., Lehoux, P., & Daudelin, G. (2016). Responsible research and innovation: a productive model for the future of medical innovation. *Journal of Responsible Innovation, 3*(3), 188–208. https://doi.org/10.1080/23299460.2016.1256659

Earley, J. E., Sr. (2013). An invitation to chemical process philosophy. In J.-P. Llored (Ed.), *The philosophy of chemistry: Practices, methodologies, and concepts*. Cambridge Scholars Publisher.

Elf, M., Anåker, A., Marcheschi, E., Sigurjónsson, Á., & Ulrich, R. S. (2020). The built environment and its impact on health outcomes and experiences of patients, significant others and staff – A protocol for a systematic review. *Nursing Open, 7*(3), 895–899. https://doi.org/10.1002/nop2.452

Emmert-Streib, F., Yli-Harja, O., & Dehmer, M. (2020). Artificial Intelligence: a clarification of misconceptions, myths and desired status. *Front Artificial Intelligence, 3*, 524339. https://doi.org/10.3389/frai.2020.524339

Esteva, A., Kuprel, B., Novoa, R. A., Ko, J., Swetter, S. M., Blau, H. M., & Thrun, S. (2017). Dermatologist-level classification of skin cancer with deep neural networks. *Nature, 542*(7639), 115–118. https://doi.org/10.1038/nature21056

Fisher, E., Mahajan, R. L., & Mitcham, C. (2006). Midstream modulation of technology: Governance from within. *Bulletin of Science, Technology and Society, 26*(6), 485–496. https://doi.org/10.1177/0270467606295402

Garibaldi, B. T., Fiksel, J., Muschelli, J., Robinson, M. L., Rouhizadeh, M., Perin, J., Schumock, G., Nagy, P., Gray, J. H., Malapati, H., Ghobadi-Krueger, M., Niessen, T. M., Kim, B. S., Hill, P. M., Ahmed, M. S., Dobkin, E. D., Blanding, R., Abele, J., Woods, B., et al. (2021). Patient trajectories among persons hospitalized for COVID-19: a cohort study. *Annals of Internal Medicine, 174*(1), 33–41. https://doi.org/10.7326/m20-3905

Gaye, A., Gibbons, G. H., Barry, C., Quarells, R., & Davis, S. K. (2017). Influence of socioeconomic status on the whole blood transcriptome in African Americans. *PLoS One, 12*(12), e0187290. https://doi.org/10.1371/journal.pone.0187290

Gaube, S., Suresh, H., Raue, M., Merritt, A., Berkowitz, S. J., Lermer, E., & Ghassemi, M. (2021). Do as AI say: susceptibility in deployment of clinical decision-aids. *npj Digital Medicine, 4*(1), 31.

Ghassemi, M., Naumann, T., Schulam, P., Beam, A. L., Chen, I. Y., & Ranganath, R. (2020). A review of challenges and opportunities in machine learning for health. *AMIA Joint Summits on Translational Science Proceedings. AMIA Joint Summits on Translational Science, 2020*, 191–200.

Gulshan, V., Peng, L., Coram, M., Stumpe, M. C., Wu, D., Narayanaswamy, A., Venugopalan, S., Widner, K., Madams, T., Cuadros, J., Kim, R., Raman, R., Nelson, P. C., Mega, J. L., & Webster, D. R. (2016). Development and validation of a deep learning algorithm for detection of diabetic retinopathy in retinal fundus photographs. *JAMA, 316*(22), 2402–2410. https://doi.org/10.1001/jama.2016.17216

Halberg, F., Pan, W., Bakken, E. E., & Cornélissen, G. (2013). Peptide chronomics. In A. J. Kastin (Ed.), *Handbook of biologically active peptides* (2nd ed.). Academic. https://doi.org/10.1016/B978-0-12-385095-9.02001-7

Ihde, D. (1990). *Technology and the lifeworld: From garden to earth*. Indiana University Press.

Ihde, D. (1991). *Instrumental realism: The interface between philosophy of science and philosophy of technology*. Indiana University Press.

Ihde, D. (1993). *Philosophy of technology: An introduction*. Paragon Press.

Ihde, D. (2011). Smart: Amsterdam urinals and autonomic computing. In M. Hildebrandt & A. Rouvroy (Eds.), *The philosophy of law meets the philosophy of technology: Autonomic computing and transformations of human agency*. Routledge.

Kalewold, K. (2020). Race and medicine in light of the new mechanistic philosophy of science. *Biology & Philosophy, 35*. https://doi.org/10.1007/s10539-020-09759-x

Kamel Boulos, M. N., Peng, G., & VoPham, T. (2019). An overview of GeoAI applications in health and healthcare. *International Journal of Health Geographics, 18*(1), 7. https://doi.org/10.1186/s12942-019-0171-2

Keyser, V., & Howland, H. (2021). Measurement perspective, process, and the pandemic. *European Journal for Philosophy of Science, 11*(1), 13. https://doi.org/10.1007/s13194-020-00326-5

Keyser, V., & Sarry, L. (2020). Robust biomarkers: Causally tracking Alzheimer's. In A. LaCaze & B. Osimani (Eds.), *Uncertainty in pharmacology, Boston studies in the philosophy and history of science 338*. Springer Nature Switzerland AG. https://doi.org/10.1007/978-3-030-29179-2_13

Laranjo, L., Rodrigues, D., Pereira, A. M., Ribeiro, R. T., & Boavida, J. M. (2016). Use of electronic health records and geographic information systems in public health surveillance of Type 2 Diabetes: A feasibility study. *JMIR Public Health and Surveillance, 2*(1), e12. https://doi.org/10.2196/publichealth.4319

Li, L., Li, J., Gao, M., Fan, H., Wang, Y., Xu, X., Chen, C., Liu, J., Kim, J., Aliyari, R., Zhang, J., Jin, Y., Li, X., Ma, F., Shi, M., Cheng, G., & Yang, H. (2021). Interleukin-8 as a biomarker for disease prognosis of coronavirus disease-2019 patients. *Frontiers in Immunology, 11*, 3432. https://doi.org/10.3389/fimmu.2020.602395

Logg, J. M., Minson, J. A., & Moore, D. A. (2019). Algorithm appreciation: People prefer algorithmic to human judgment. *Organizational Behavior and Human Decision Processes, 151*, 90–103. https://doi.org/10.1016/j.obhdp.2018.12.005

Ma, A., Zhang, L., Ye, X., Chen, J., Yu, J., Zhuang, L., Weng, C., Petersen, F., Wang, Z., & Yu, X. (2021). High levels of circulating IL-8 and soluble IL-2R are associated with prolonged illness in patients with severe COVID-19. *Frontiers in Immunology, 12*. https://doi.org/10.3389/fimmu.2021.626235

Mahootian, F., & Eastman, T. (2009). Complementary frameworks of scientific inquiry: hypothetico-deductive, hypothetico-inductive, and observational-inductive, with eastman, T., world futures. *Journal of Genenral Evolutionary, 65*, 61–75.

Mendels, D.-A., Dortet, L., Emeraud, C., Oueslati, S., Girlich, D., Ronat, J.-B., Bernabeu, S., Bahi, S., Atkinson, G. J. H., & Naas, T. (2021). Using artificial intelligence to improve COVID-19 rapid diagnostic test result interpretation. *Proceedings of the National Academy of Sciences, 118*(12), e2019893118. https://doi.org/10.1073/pnas.2019893118

Monberg, J. (2006) Conceptions of the social that stand behind artificial intelligence decision making. *The Journal of Technology Studies, Winter/Spring, 32*(1/2), 15–22.

Pickering, A. (1984). *Constructing quarks: A sociological history of particle physics.* University of Chicago Press.

Pickering, A. (1995). *The mangle of practice: Time, agency, and science.* University of Chicago Press.

Pronk, R. (2018). *Modelling midstream modulation in medical technology.* Masters Thesis, University of Twente. Twente.

Raghu, M., Zhang, C., Kleinberg, J., & Bengio, S. (2019). Transfusion: Understanding transfer learning with applications to medical imaging. *NeurIPS.* https://arxiv.org/abs/1902.07208

Rajkomar, A., Dean, J., & Kohane, I. (2019). Machine learning in medicine. *New England Journal of Medicine, 380*(14), 1347–1358. https://doi.org/10.1056/NEJMra1814259

Rensing, L., Meyer-Grahle, U., & Ruoff, P. (2001). Biological timing and the clock metaphor: Oscillatory and hourglass mechanisms. *Chronobiology International, 18*(3), 329–369.

Seamster, L., & Purifoy, D. (2021). What is environmental racism for? Place-based harm and relational development. *Environmental Sociology, 7*(2), 110–112. https://doi.org/10.1080/23251042.2020.1790331

Sellars, W. (1963). *Science, perception and reality.* Routledge & K. Paul.

Sismondo, S. (2009) An introduction to science and technology studies, John Wiley & Sons, Incorporated.

Stilgoe, J., Watson, M., & Kuo, K. (2013). Public engagement with biotechnologies offers lessons for the governance of geoengineering research and beyond. *PLoS Biology, 11*(11), e1001707.

Terrell, K. A., & James, W. (2020). Racial disparities in air pollution burden and COVID-19 deaths in Louisiana, USA, in the context of long-term changes in fine particulate pollution. *Environmental Justice.* https://doi.org/10.1089/env.2020.0021

Topol, E. J. (2019). High-performance medicine: The convergence of human and artificial intelligence. *Nature Medicine, 25*(1), 44–56. https://doi.org/10.1038/s41591-018-0300-7

Venter, Z. S., Aunan, K., Chowdhury, S., & Lelieveld, J. (2020). COVID-19 lockdowns cause global air pollution declines. *Proceedings of the National Academy of Sciences, 117*(32), 18984. https://doi.org/10.1073/pnas.2006853117

Verbeek, P.-P. (2011). Subject to technology on autonomic computing and human autonomy. In M. Hildebrandt & A. Rouvroy (Eds.), *The philosophy of law meets the philosophy of technology: Autonomic computing and transformations of human agency.* Routledge.

Voter, A. F., Larson, M. E., Garrett, J. W., & Yu, J.-P. J. (2021). Diagnostic accuracy and failure mode analysis of a deep learning algorithm for the detection of cervical spine fractures. *American Journal of Neuroradiology.* https://doi.org/10.3174/ajnr.A7179

Washington, H. (2020). How environmental racism is fuelling the coronavirus pandemic. *Nature, 581*(7808), 241. https://doi.org/10.1038/d41586-020-01453-y

Winfree, A. T. (1987). *When time breaks down: The 3-dimensional dynamics of electrochemical waves and cardiac arrhythmias.* Princeton University Press.

Winfree, A. T. (2001). *The geometry of biological time* (2nd ed.). Springer.

Wongvibulsin, S., Wu, K. C., & Zeger, S. L. (2019). Clinical risk prediction with random forests for survival, longitudinal, and multivariate (RF-SLAM) data analysis. *BMC Medical Research Methodology, 20*(1), 1. https://doi.org/10.1186/s12874-019-0863-0

Wongvibulsin, S., Garibaldi, B. T., Antar, A. A. R., Wen, J., Wang, M.-C., Gupta, A., Bollinger, R., Xu, Y., Wang, K., Betz, J. F., Muschelli, J., Bandeen-Roche, K., Zeger, S. L., & Robinson, M. L. (2021). Development of Severe COVID-19 Adaptive Risk Predictor (SCARP), a calculator to predict severe disease or death in hospitalized patients with COVID-19. *Annals of Internal Medicine, 174*(6), 777–785. https://doi.org/10.7326/M20-6754

Wu, X., Nethery, R. C., Sabath, B. M., Braun, D., & Dominici, F. (2020). Exposure to air pollution and COVID-19 mortality in the United States: A nationwide cross-sectional study. *medRxiv : the preprint server for health sciences*, 2020.04.05.20054502. https://doi.org/10.1101/2020.04.05.20054502

Yang, Y., Jin, G., Pang, Y., Wang, W., Zhang, H., Tuo, G., Wu, P., Wang, Z., & Zhu, Z. (2020). The diagnostic accuracy of artificial intelligence in thoracic diseases: A protocol for systematic review and meta-analysis. *Medicine, 99*(7), e19114–e19114. https://doi.org/10.1097/MD.0000000000019114

Yu, K.-H., Beam, A. L., & Kohane, I. S. (2018). Artificial intelligence in healthcare. *Nature Biomedical Engineering, 2*(10), 719–731. https://doi.org/10.1038/s41551-018-0305-z

Zalla, L. C., Martin, C. L., Edwards, J. K., Gartner, D. R., & Noppert, G. A. (2021). A geography of risk: Structural racism and coronavirus disease 2019 mortality in the united states. *American Journal of Epidemiology, 190*(8), 1439–1446. https://doi.org/10.1093/aje/kwab059

Zou, J., & Schiebinger, L. (2018). AI can be sexist and racist – it's time to make it fair. *Nature, 559*(7714), 324–326. https://doi.org/10.1038/d41586-018-05707-8

Sensor Devices, the Source of Innovative Therapy and Prevention

Anna Kasparbauer, Veronika Reisner, Cosima Schenk, Anna Glas,
Helana Lutfi, Oscar Blanco, and Thomas Spittler

Abstract

Sensor or sensing devices in the form of wearables have drawn a lot of attention
in the past few years. Technologies such as fitness trackers and smartwatches
allow controlled insight on heart rate, body fat, or sleep quality. However, sensing
technology is not limited to wearable devices. Especially in the healthcare sector,
utilization of multiple sensor types and systems shows promise. This chapter
provides an overview of existing sensor elements and measurable parameters
and demonstrates healthcare applications in prevention, diagnostics, and therapy.
Current trends integrate biomedical sensing with feedback systems that actively
engage and influence patient movement and behavior. These advances come with
challenges and raise questions for future implementation of sensor systems in
therapy.

1   Introduction

The estimated fiscal value of sensor technology in the world market has doubled
from 102 billion US dollars in 2010 to 205 billion US dollars and is expected
to reach 411 billion US dollars by 2026. This increase represents a compound
annual growth rate of 12–15%. Production technologies, modern vehicles, and smart

A. Kasparbauer · V. Reisner · H. Lutfi · O. Blanco · T. Spittler (✉)
Deggendorf Institute of Technology, Pfarrkirchen, Germany
e-mail: t.spittler@th-deg.de

C. Schenk
Ludwig-Maximilians-Universität, Munich, Germany

A. Glas
Akademie der Bildenden Künste, Munich, Germany

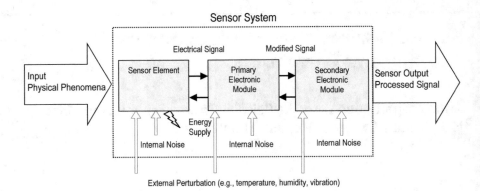

Fig. 1 Functional elements of a sensor system

power supply systems are nowadays inconceivable without sensors. Next to vehicle industry, information and communication technologies, and the building sector, the medical and healthcare sector is among the top five industries that hold the sensor market share. In the medical sector, the demand differs from that of industrial branches in that quantities are low but the products are adaptive, precise, and highly specialized. Sensors continue to improve in quality, they are more specific and robust, and they have become smarter and manufacturing costs are decreasing. In general, sensor systems convert a measured quantity (an input) into a signal (an output) by using a functional relation (Bumberger et al., 2015). A simplified explanation is that a sensor receives a desired parameter and follows the principle of measurement. The parameter value is often a change in physical phenomena, which is first converted into an electrical signal with primary electronic modules (e.g., a change in voltage, current, or frequency). Secondary electronic processes allow the conversion to a digital signal, which enables digital signal processing, such as error correction, filtering, automatic adaptation, or automatic monitoring. Therefore, sensor devices are also referred to as sensor systems, which consist of a sensor element and primary and secondary electronic modules (Fig. 1). Today myriad parameters can be obtained from various sensor devices, and the definition of sensor incorporates the functions of a converter, a detector, a transducer, a transmitter, and/or a gauge.

In the medical sector, there are three distinguishable application areas for sensor systems: prevention, diagnostics/monitoring, and therapeutic interventions.

Prevention relates to products that capture, store, and transmit health data, for example, lifestyle apps and fitness trackers but also telehealth platforms, health information technology, and general consumer health information. These technologies do not require clinical evidence and are hallmarked by ease of access through wearable devices or use of mobile devices (mHealth, eHealth devices). The use of sensor devices in diagnostics and monitoring includes digital diagnostics tools, remote patient monitoring, ingestible sensors, and drug delivery devices.

These aim to support the decision-making processes of clinicians and care providers. In contrast, sensor technology as part of therapeutic intervention feeds information directly to patients. Furthermore, this technology adapts to therapy progress and provides assistance for the therapist's tasks. The application range includes health sensors, home medical assistance systems, continuous health monitoring systems, and sensor systems in physical rehabilitation and assistive systems. It is worth differentiating here between therapy devices and assistive devices. Assistive devices generally aim to compensate for lost functions, whereas therapy devices support the therapeutic progress, for example, by actively engaging the patient in muscular training after a stroke.

This chapter aims to broaden the perspective on available sensor devices and discuss their application in therapy and rehabilitation. The beginning of the chapter provides a brief introduction to the classification of sensors and its common uses in healthcare. Next, it discusses the value of artificial intelligence in the interpretation of sensor data and provides several examples of sensor systems in diagnostics, monitoring, and therapeutic applications. The discussion considers cutting-edge technology in stroke rehabilitation and recent advances in the integration of biosensors.

2 Sensors

Sensors measure or detect a wide variety of physical, chemical, and biological entities, including proteins, bacteria, chemicals, gas, light intensity, motion, position, sound, and temperature (Table 1). Sensor types can be classified in various ways. The following section gives a brief overview of distinguishable types. A sensor is active or passive depending on its external excitation signal or power signal. Sensors are also classified by their input parameter or means of detection (electric, biological, chemical, radioactive, etc.). A further classification approach is based on conversion phenomena, for example, photoelectric, thermoelectric, electrochemical, and electromagnetic, describing the change from input to output signal. Sensors are also categorized as digital or analogue, another classification that derives from the output. Furthermore, sensors are labeled according to their field of application, for example, healthcare, military, vehicle industry, and electronics. Additionally, specific features and physical properties are used to categorize a sensor system, for example, temperature sensors, proximity sensors, or infrared sensors. Finally, some types of sensors are hallmarked by their ability to detect input in real time, for example, acoustics, pollution, brightness, and other real-time changes in the environment (Shinde et al., 2014). This latter category includes intelligent sensor systems used in olfactory biosensing, biomimetic taste sensors, visual sensors, tactile sensors, and cochlear implants. The following sections give examples of commonly used sensor types and their applications in the healthcare sector.

Table 1 Overview of different measuring parameters

Mechanical parameters: Solid state

Distance	Form	Vibration	Denseness
Length	Position	Acceleration	Rotation speed
Thickness	Motion	Mass	Torque
Proximity	Surface texture	Weight	Hardness
Angle	Motion	Pressure	Coefficient of elasticity
Inclination	Velocity	Momentum	Expansion
Plane	Mass flow rate	Height	

Mechanical parameters: Fluids and gas

Flow rate	Flow direction	Fill level	Vacuum
Volumetric flow	Viscosity	Pressure	Volume

Thermal parameters

Temperature	Radiance temperature	Conductance	Entropy
Infrared radiation	Thermal capacity	Comfort	

Optical parameters

Light intensity	Wavelength	Polarization	Light density
Color	Refractivity		

Acoustic parameters

Intensity	Frequency	Velocity	Polarization
Pressure			

Radiation parameters

Flow	Type	Energy	Intensity

Chemical parameters

Concentration	pH value	Ice	Dust concentration
Composition	Redox potential	Pollution	Electrical conductivity
Reaction rate	Humidity	Particle size	Thermal conductivity
Molecular weight	Water content		

Magnetic and electronic parameters

Electricity	Phase	Power	Capacitance
Voltage	Electrical field	Resistance	Dielectric constant
Charge	Magnetic field	Inductance	Electrical polarization
Frequency			

Others

Time	Frequency	Amount	Pulse length

2.1   Active Versus Passive Sensors

An active (also known as parametric) sensor is a sensing device that requires an external source of power to operate. In active sensing, transmitters send out signals, such as light wavelengths or electrons that bounce off a target, which causes a sensor to detect their reflection. Examples of active sensing include capacitive and inductive sensors (Iqbal et al., 2020).

In contrast, passive-sensing (also known as self-generating) sensors are able to generate electrical signals by themselves and are not dependent on an external power supply. For instance, a piezoelectric sensor is a self-generating sensor. Piezoelectric sensors are based on the principle of transforming a physical dimension into force and act on the opposite faces of the sensing element that forms the piezoelectric effect, which is related to the production of electric charge in crystalline material through the consequence of applied mechanical stress. Specifically in the field of monitoring and detection of health-promoting behavior, passive sensing plays a pivotal role. The convenience of using personal smartphone devices enables sensing during daily habits without the restriction of mobility or self-conscious feelings of being under observation (Trifan et al., 2019).

2.2 Physical Sensors

Sensors that use physical properties such as radiation, light, flow, heat, pressure, magnetic field, and parameters related to mass or energy to generate signals for quantification are categorized as physical sensors. These sensors operate based on relative output signal variations in their electrical parameters. A classification of physical sensors is presented in Table 1. These sensors detect and quantify the different physical nature or phenomenon or physical system (Ahmad & Salama, 2018).

2.2.1 Mechanical Sensors

Mechanical sensors are based on the principle of measuring variations in a device or a material according to an input such as motion, velocity, and accelerometer that causes the mechanical deformation of that device or material. When this input is converted into an electrical output, the sensor is defined as electromechanical. In addition to electrical output, output signals can be magnetic, optical, and thermal (McGrath & Scanaill, 2013). Accelerometers and gyroscopes are the most widely used forms of microelectromechanical systems (MEMS) sensors. MEMS consist of mechanical microstructures, microsensors, microactuators, and microelectronics, all integrated into one silicon chip. These sensors are ideal for challenging demands related to the measurement of mass flow and are therefore suitable for medical devices such as blood pressure monitors, pacemakers, ventilators, and respirators (Cornet & Holden, 2018).

2.2.2 Radiation Sensors

Radiation-sensing technologies measure the flow, type, energy, and dosage of radioactive rays. Because the effects of ionizing radiation on the human body are very critical, detectors are used in high-risk environments and fields such as mining, avionics, nuclear, high-energy physics, space, and healthcare. Additionally, functional failures in electronics and erroneous outcomes can be a consequence of continuous exposure to radiation. Knowing that a dose rate is accurate and the cumulative dose are central for assessing system performance and health risks in this field of application (Karmakar et al., 2021). In the medical field, imaging techniques either use X-rays as an external beam source or a radiation source (using an isotope as radiotracer) internal to body. Advances in medical imaging combine techniques such as positron emission tomography and single photon emission tomography. This benefits localization accuracy however comes with high costs.

2.2.3 Thermal Sensors

Temperature is the degree of the collective kinetic energy of a material's molecules. Thermal sensors measure on-body temperature, which is a vital indicator for physical health. Common examples of thermal sensors are mercury or alcohol thermometers, which depend on a quantity of mercury or dyed ethanol that expands as temperature increases. Thermal sensors include thermocouples, resistance thermometers, silicon sensors, and infrared radiation thermometers (Jha, 2015).

2.2.4 Optical Sensors

Optical sensors measure a change in light intensity related to the emission or absorption of light. They detect waves or photons in different forms of light, including visible, infrared, and ultraviolet regions of the spectrum. Optical sensors can be classified into photodetectors, infrared sensors, fiber-optic sensors, and interferometers. These sensors are highly sensitive, small, and lightweight. They are immune to electromagnetic interference and are suitable for remote sensing. They have a wide dynamic range, are highly reliable, and have the capacity to monitor a wide range of chemical and physical parameters. Because of these qualities, optical sensors are widely used in applications that require position sensing and encoding. However, they are expensive and are vulnerable to environmental and physical damage (McGrath & Scanaill, 2013). Recent advances in clinical practice use optical pressure sensors to assist the diagnosis of coronary microvascular dysfunction by assessing intravascular blood flow (Mackle et al., 2021).

2.2.5 Magnetic Sensors

A magnetic sensor is mainly used to monitor the variations in a magnetic field caused by mechanical stress or magnetic moment. A variety of target tissues may be used, such as blood, cerebrospinal fluid, and a culture medium. Magnetic sensors are used in various biomedical applications such as testing the degree of blood coagulation and blood flow, early detection of heart valve prosthetic failure, treatment of cancer cells with MnO_2 nanoparticles coated with silica, and in endoluminal artificial urinary sphincters (Ahmad & Salama, 2018) and more recently respiratory rhythm (Hwang et al., 2021).

2.3 Chemical Sensors

Chemical sensors consist of a sensing layer and a transducer that translates interaction between target compound also referred to as analyte and the sensing layer into a measurable signal. Based on the compound to be detected, chemical sensors are classified in gas sensors and biosensors (Wen, 2016).

Common gas sensor technologies are electrochemical sensors, metal oxide sensors, catalytic sensors, infrared gas sensors, and photoionization detectors (Nazemi et al., 2019). Electrochemical gas sensors assess the electrochemical reaction between an electrode and an analyte. The shift in resistance, frequency, current, or voltage is proportional to the analyte concentration. Metal oxide gas sensing works on the principle of change in conductivity in the sensing layer due to contact with the analyte. Concentration of analyte is proportional to the change in conductance of the metal oxide used as sensing layer. Catalytic gas sensors use the temperature increase during oxidation processes and translates the change in temperature to a signal that is proportional to the analyte concentration. Infrared gas sensors detect variation in wavelengths caused by hazardous gases, and photoionization detectors use ultraviolet light to detect volatile organic compounds.

Gas sensors play a pivotal role in environment monitoring. However, several limitations such as high production costs and safety issues restrict application in wearable systems. Among gas sensors, electrochemical and metal oxide sensors are promising candidates for future health application (Li et al., 2014; Yang et al., 2021).

In biosensing technology, commonly used sensing layers are molecular recognition elements, such as animal or plant cells, protein receptors, organelles, antibodies, tissues, microbes, enzymes, molecularly imprinted polymers, and nucleic acids (Bhalla et al., 2016). An electrochemical biosensor consists of a biological sensing element that converts the response to an analyte into an electrical signal. The magnitude of the signal depends on the concentration of the measured chemical. Recent advances have focused on bioresorbable sensors that make surgical removal obsolete since the components dissolve in biofluids. These types of sensors are suitable for measuring temperature, pressure, motion, flow rate, and different types of biomarkers. The sensor is protected by a coat of silicon dioxide, which has a slow dissolution rate that ranges from several weeks to several months (for a detailed review of recent developments in biosensors, see Mohankumar et al., 2021). Table 2 provides an overview of applied chemical sensors and their field of use.

Important performance parameters for such sensors include selectivity, reproducibility, stability, sensitivity, and linearity. In addition, the size of the device and power consumption, cost-efficiency, lifetime, and integration into wireless network are inevitable factors for the implementation in various fields of application (Bhalla et al., 2016).

3   Innovative Applications

The human body sends electrical, mechanical, thermal, and biochemical signals indicating physical health, emotion, and behavior. Innovative technologies in healthcare call for continuously monitoring and collecting these biosignals from human body with the aim to recognize and promote physical and psychological health. Sunwoo et al. (2021) provide an extensive overview of current trends in wearable and implantable bioelectronics. The authors discuss recent developments in electrical, mechanical, and chemical sensing. The advantages of simultaneous and high-quality

Table 2 Subtypes of chemical sensors and application

Category	Subtype	Application
Biosensors	Bioresorbable	Pressure and temperature sensing
	Flexible and wearable	Monitoring of neurological function
	Electrochemical	Rehabilitation and physical therapy
	Enzymatic	Cardiopulmonary and vascular monitoring
	Field-effect transistor	Glucose monitoring
	Graphene	Humidity sensing
	Polymer	Detection of biomarkers, proteins, neurotransmitter, DNA, and drugs
Gas sensors	Electrochemical	Detection of hazardous gases
	Metal oxide	Breath analysis
	Catalytic	Air quality
	Infrared	Monitoring oxygen and carbon dioxide levels
	Photoionization	Specific sector-relevant gas detection

recording with bioelectronics are expanded by recent advances in design aspects of the sensing material. This includes *stretchability*, the adaptation of sensing material to flexible bio-tissue surfaces; *conformability*, the increase of adhesion at device-tissue interface; and *deployability*, the level of integration without interference with tissue integrity. Promising candidates meeting these criteria include liquid metals, conductive nanomaterials, polymer, hydrogel composites, and elastomeric nanocomposites. However, some challenges need to be resolved regarding loss of electrical conductivity, fabrication techniques, compatibility with existing fabrication techniques, inflammatory reactions, and optimization for integration of device systems (Jayaram et al., 2022; Ohayon & Inal, 2020; Sunwoo et al., 2021).

The integration of unit devices, such as a sensor within a system, requires advanced interconnection and thorough processing and analysis of the information they provide. This can be a demanding task (Ha et al., 2020). Conventional sensor systems may be challenged when there is a high throughput of data that can lead to an overload of the system and result in erroneous output (Ha et al., 2020).

One solution to this problem is using machine learning algorithms, particularly deep learning algorithms and neural networks. Machine learning is a subfield of artificial intelligence that has generated a lot of interest in recent years. The number of scientific publications on artificial intelligence related to healthcare has experienced a steep increase since 2014. About 70% of papers published in this field were conducted between 2014 and 2019. This trend illustrates the dynamic adaptation of machine learning and deep learning algorithms to solve health problems most notably in research fields, such as cancer, depression, Alzheimer disease, heart failure, and diabetes (Guo et al., 2020).

Machine learning and deep learning make accurate analysis of new data possible by generating mathematical and statistical models based on existing data (El Naqa & Murphy, 2015). While traditional sensor systems compare input information with a threshold and react according to that comparison, smart sensor systems that use artificial intelligence analyze the data in two steps. First, they preprocess it to analyze relevant features. Then they pass the relevant data to a smart model that has been trained with a machine learning algorithm and is able to analyze the data and solve the specific regression or classification problem of the application (Ha et al., 2020).

The combination of sensors and artificial intelligence can lead to applications that are able to analyze large amounts of data accurately and interconnect with other devices as well, as one can see in smart environments (Shanthamallu et al., 2018). Using smart sensors can be very beneficial in the context of healthcare since they optimize the acquisition and analysis of patients' health data. There are multiple applications, and new sensing technologies are being developed that aim at improving healthcare services for patients with acute and chronic conditions (Formica & Schena, 2021).

Sensors allow more complex digital devices to collect specific types of data from a wide variety of sources. On their own, however, sensors provide very little benefit. While bioresorbable sensors have not become common in standard clinical practice, flexible and wearable biosensor systems have found general acceptance in the areas of health prevention, monitoring, and rehabilitation. Body sensors are usually wearable devices that are attached to clothes or worn on the body. Results from a recent review that investigated incidence rates of sensors in the field of rehabilitation and care for disabled patients indicate that electrocardiograms (14%), wearable sensors (14%), inertial measurement units (13%), and temperature sensors (11%) represent half of the applied sensor types. Other forms of sensors were present in low rates (<4%), including pressure, vibration, chemical, electrochemical, piezoelectric, flexible, smartphone, capacitive, resistive, force, optical, and touch sensors (do Nascimento et al., 2020).

Sensors are the foundation for many of the innovative therapies and prevention methods that have been developed in modern healthcare. Sensor devices in the healthcare context require meaningful processing and analysis of the information obtained. The value of sensors comes from how the collected data is used and transformed into informative patterns. Smart sensors use built-in computing resources and pass them on to a centralized hub, creating, for example, a wireless sensor network whose nodes are connected with other sensors and centralized hubs.

The hardware that sensors are built from is a set of physical circuits and controllers that perform a set of activities. They are able to perform these activities using instructions that come from the controller. In most sensor systems, the data is converted to a digital form and passed through a controller to an interface. The controller contains customized software that provides instructions to the various parts of the hardware. The interface connects the sensor with a software platform or device that can connect with the sensor, such as a smartphone or a computer that can present the sensor data using a variety of tools and applications (McGrath & Scanaill, 2013).

Although device software follows a similar structure, the software can be highly variable depending on the intended use. All device software includes analysis that uses an algorithm that can interpret the different variables and data the sensor collects. The algorithm then produces an output. This output is what the remaining software uses for a variety of functions depending on the use case. In healthcare, sensor-based devices are used for diagnosis, monitoring, and therapy.

3.1   Diagnosis

Diagnostic sensor devices are essential for preventative health programs and techniques. For example, sensor technologies can be used as *single shot* analysis tools that detect presence or absence of risk factors for disease or as *long-term monitoring* analysis tools that collect data over a longer period of time (Bhalla et al., 2016). For example, cancer research uses electrochemical biosensing for the detection of biomarkers (Crulhas et al., 2021). In addition, a current example for long-term monitoring as a noninvasive diagnostic tool is the application of magnetic sensors for the detection of respiratory virus infections (Hwang et al., 2021).

Some of the most recent innovations in sensor devices use advanced analytics that combine several streams of sensor data. One such example is the use of artificial intelligence during a clinical interview to diagnose major depressive disorder. This solution combines various sensor data from a recorded clinical interview. The artificial intelligence algorithms combine analysis of visual information from facial expression, the pitch of the voice from audio records, and speech from transcripts (Haque et al., 2018). The software for this solution is significantly more complex because each of these streams of sensory information are analyzed with several algorithms separately and another algorithm combines the results of each individual analysis to generate a score that determines the likelihood of major depressive disorder diagnosis.

Due to the strict diagnostic criteria, the sensitivity needed to collect data, and the potentially high volume of data analysis required, diagnostic sensor devices are often the most complex sensor-based use cases in healthcare. Other use cases have different software requirements.

3.2   Monitoring and Prevention

Using sensor-based devices for monitoring typically requires less algorithmic analysis and handles a higher volume of data over a longer period of time. Unlike diagnostic solutions, innovative monitoring solutions are more focused on utility and practicality than on computational accuracy. These solutions often monitor a combination of vital signs such as heart rate, blood pressure, temperature, respiration rate, and blood oxygenation (McGrath & Scanaill, 2013). Wearable devices, for example, monitor the patients' health status without requiring the patient to interact with the device (Luxton & Riek, 2019). By embedding these technologies in day-to-day life, the process of monitoring a person's health status can prevent major implications in the case of illness and inform care providers and therapists about an individual's health issues.

One main application of wearable devices is fall detection. Since the applied machine learning algorithms are able to distinguish between inconspicuous data and data that indicates a potentially dangerous incident, wearable devices are able to detect falls and alert healthcare providers or family members (Luxton & Riek, 2019). These devices use inertial sensors that detect motion acceleration (Pierleoni et al., 2015). Wearable devices can also be used to remind patients of their treatment regime, for example, physical exercises that are an important part of rehabilitation (Greiwe & Nyenhuis, 2020).

With an aging population on the one hand and a reduced number of young workers to provide care and assistance on the other hand, modern societies are facing the challenge of how to provide adequate care to elderly people and ensure their well-being. Wearable devices offer the opportunity to ease the burden (Chan et al., 2012).

Apart from wearable devices, there is also the possibility of embedding sensors in the environment of the patient to identify a patient's needs and assist them in their everyday life. The term "smart home healthcare" is used for such technologies (Bennett et al., 2017) based on the concept of smart homes or a network of technological devices that connect services by monitoring home attributes (Jiang et al. 2004). Both concepts are also closely related to the "Internet of Things," which connects different monitoring devices in the environment and communicates via the Internet (Stojkoska & Trivodaliev, 2017).

Smart home healthcare provides care for patients by using sensors that are embedded in their home (including infrared sensors, light sensors, temperature sensors, or sensors used for video surveillance or movement detection). Because these technologies often seem to blend in with the natural environment, the sensors are referred to as ambient sensors. Similar to wearable devices, these sensors analyze the data they collect and support therapeutic processes such as reporting difficulties or making an emergency call (Bennett et al., 2017). Ambient assisted living technologies help take care of patients or elderly people by monitoring their health state and enabling them to live more independently (Kleinberger et al., 2007).

3.3   Therapy

Sensors can be particularly powerful in therapeutic interventions because solutions can provide feedback based on the underlying physiological signals instead of waiting for individuals to experience symptoms. For example, self-tracking with smart watches positively affects physical activity level in patients with cardio-vascular disease (Vogel et al., 2017). Self-monitoring is facilitated with passive collection of data and can be used to actively remind the user by noticing deviation from set goals or habits (Cornet & Holden, 2018). Self-monitoring is a common strategy in behavioral psychotherapy; however, it suffers from inconsistencies and subjective bias. Objective measurement of physical stress response combined with deep learning and machine learning algorithms have the potential to create patient-centered therapy interventions (Giannakakis et al., 2019). Some nonclinical sensor technologies advertise stress release and improved sleep by combining biosignals and artificial intelligence techniques, as, for example, *Welltiss Mind PEMF Wearable - SleepGadgets* (Celje, Slovenia) (n.d.).[1] The company manufactures a pulsed electromagnetic field (PEMF) wearable circlet. The associated app is designed to help individuals relax and improve sleep using EEG sensors that are attached to the skin to measure the electrical activity of the brain. The PEMF generates a specific frequency signal designed to replicate brain wave activity at a relaxed state to help individuals relax. The EEG sensor measures this signal to ensure that it maintains consistent frequency and adapts to the different app functions. Recent systemic reviews of PEMF have pointed out potential effects of the method on some human cell types (Mansourian & Shanei, 2021) and in pain treatment of patients with osteoarthritis (Yang et al., 2020); however, underlying working principles remain unclear and optimal application parameters are unknown. Under precaution, PEMFs are considered to be safe; nonetheless, exposure to electromagnetic fields potentially leads to adverse effects on physical and mental health (Hu et al., 2020). Further clinical investigation with high-quality, large-scale randomized control trials is inevitable for the method to become an efficient standard therapy procedure.

4   Recent Advances

The applications of smart sensors in healthcare offer new methods of measuring important health data and have great potential to improve therapy and rehabilitation and prevent medical conditions. Because of technological progress in the past few years (including new developments in areas such as the Internet of Things, ubiquitous computing, and the miniaturization of sensors), many new applications have been developed that have brought revolutionary change to the healthcare industry (Formica & Schena, 2021; Pramanik et al., 2019). In general, new technologies that use smart sensors might change healthcare services significantly by providing individualized information to healthcare providers and thus improving the patient's treatment. It has been suggested that these technologies might also facilitate the transition from hospital care to home rehabilitation and make possible a longer-lasting therapy that has positive long-term effects for the patient's well-being (O'Neill et al., 2020). It has been reported that the transition to at-home rehabilitation can often be experienced as problematic or that the patient's health status decreases after returning home (Markiewicz et al., 2020). By using sensors to monitor health status, remind patients about continuing their treatment, or even provide support for physical exercises, healthcare providers could continue to accompany the patient on their way to recovery.

---

[1] https://www.welltiss.com/

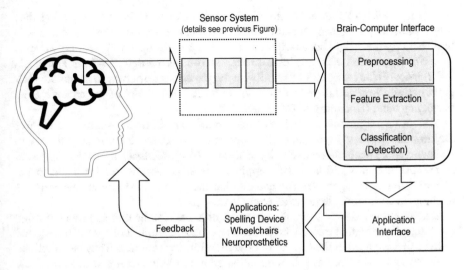

Fig. 2 Components of a brain-computer interface

While in-home monitor sensor technology holds great potential for early detection of physical and cognitive decline and timely intervention, it is also noteworthy that these systems can be perceived as burdensome and intrusive to some users. In addition, there are concerns about data privacy and the neglect of real-life contact between caregiver and patient. Moreover, today, limited evidence supports the effectiveness of home care systems, and further research is needed to distinguish positive factors of home care treatment systems (Ho, 2020; Lussier et al., 2019).

Another development are neural sensors that track brain activity and enable interaction with the environment. Examples of technologies that use neural sensors include brain-computer interfaces or neurofeedback (Fig. 2). The term brain-computer interface (BCI) refers to a human-machine interaction that enables patients to communicate with assistive technologies, such as wheelchairs or prosthetic limbs, just by thought. They are especially useful in helping patients who suffer from partial or total paralysis due to conditions that impair the neural pathways responsible for motor control (Diez, 2018).

BCIs use information from sensors that measure brain activity. Most of them use EEG data. While some BCI applications record brain activity using different methods, such as sensors based on neuroimaging or implanted intracortical electrodes (Martini et al., 2020), EEG is used most frequently since it is the most practical for clinical use (Graimann et al., 2010).

The measured signals are processed in three steps. First, all data is preprocessed to reduce background noise; then a set of relevant features is extracted from the data, and the information is classified and translated into computer-generated output data (Diez, 2018). This output is then transformed into a device command that leads to an action of the technological device, which also provides feedback to the patient (see Fig. 2; Pfurtscheller et al., 2004). One key characteristic of BCIs is that they rely on intentional control, meaning that they do not passively analyze changes in brain activity that might occur without intent. Instead, the user must willingly decide to perform a mental task that leads to the reaction of the device (Graimann et al., 2010). Most BCIs using EEG data rely on the patient to learn how to modulate their brain activity in a certain way that leads to a modified signal of the specific EEG frequency band (Hochberg & Donoghue, 2006).

Recent developments in BCI research include hybrid BCI systems that involve multimodal sensory inputs and the application of deep learning algorithms to achieve a more accurate analysis of the signals. Neurofeedback has been suggested as another useful addition to BCI applications since it provides feedback to the patient about their cognitive effort and thus has the potential to facilitate the patient's attempts to communicate (Martini et al., 2020).

Recent studies demonstrate the potential of exoskeletons that can be controlled by using sensors that record brain activity. Exoskeletons are wearable robotic devices that are used in the context of rehabilitation, for example. They can facilitate or assist movement for patients with impaired motor skills after a stroke and show the same efficacy as conventional therapy approaches of gait training (Louie & Eng, 2016). Machine learning algorithms are trained to detect brain activity that predicts intended action. The device reacts to the brain signal of intended action and executes the movement. Patients who are paralyzed thus share the feeling of having executed the movement themselves. The advantages here are the detection of motor planning within the sensorimotor cortex and immediate feedback with the robotic device. Near-simultaneous reaction of the robotic device to brain activity stimulates neuroplastic processes and has the potential to emulate the disrupted neural motor pathway (Kirchner et al., 2019).

Another innovative field of application is biofeedback, a therapeutic intervention that involves measuring physiological signals and providing real-time feedback. These physiological signals may contain information about the arousal or stress level of the person, for example, by measuring the heart rate or respiration rate (Giannakakis et al., 2019; McKee, 2008). A recent study shows that using sensors to measure changes in heartbeat helped children and teens regulate emotions such as anxiety or anger in stressful situations. The children and teenagers in the study played a video game that could be manipulated by the heartbeat. The study participants who learned to regulate their heartbeats through gameplay experienced a reduced expression of negative emotions such as anger (Ducharme et al., 2021).

A recent study in mice used a sensor to study serotonin neurotransmission under natural conditions. Treatment of affective disorders benefits from using pharmaceuticals to increase serotonin levels. Using serotonin sensors has the potential to inform pharmaceutical treatment of mental health disorders and enable practitioners to monitor changes in neurotransmitter levels in relation to symptom expression (Unger et al., 2020).

Novel design and materials introduced in the field of bioelectronics continuously offer new opportunities of sensing and stimulation. Prospective research fields include electrical potential sensing, controlled drug delivery, optical stimulation, and electrical stimulation (Sunwoo et al., 2021). Listing current promising devices is beyond the scope of this chapter; therefore, only few examples from the excellent review by Sunwoo et al. (2021) are mentioned here: electrooculogram sensor around the human eye to steer a drone, pressure-sensitive organic transistors over radial artery, wearable thermal stimulators for articular thermotherapy, sweat sensors detecting vitamin levels, and smart wristbands for drug administration. Implantable bioelectronics include deep-brain electrodes and bioresorbable electronic patches to deliver drugs while bypassing blood-brain barrier (Supplementary Material, Sunwoo et al., 2021).

5 Challenges

Sensing from individuals in real time faces several challenges and significantly differs from classical methods of sensor technology in terms of reproducibility, measuring time, and possibilities of methods. The acceptability and tolerability of such products is crucial for effective and measurable treatment outcomes. This chapter has presented only a few use cases in the biomedical area, focusing on rehabilitation and health monitoring. The use of these wearable sensors has become very popular, especially since a healthy lifestyle is increasingly being discussed (Greiwe & Nyenhuis, 2020). Many of these technologies are already implemented in diagnostics and monitoring systems in the forms of home medical assistance, continuous health monitoring, physical rehabilitation, and assistive systems (for a detailed review, see do Nascimento et al., 2020).

However, current approaches have yet to tap into the full potential of biosensing technologies by integrating bioacoustic, biochemical, bioelectrical, biomagnetic, bio-optical, and biothermal information in meaningful and supportive therapeutic interventions. Tremendous advancements have been made in recent years in the development of hardware and software for sensors. Recent advancements in microsensors and biomedicine, specifically neurosensors and biosensing technology, will contribute to the growth of sensing applications in the healthcare sector. However, since the manufacturing of the technology can be cumbersome, economic aspects along with inquisitiveness are the driving forces of prospective trends. Therefore, the right market for specific analyte plays a role (e.g., glucose detection for diabetes) as well as the clear-cut advantages over existing methods of measuring. Furthermore, prerequisites for successful productions of technology include performance stability over time, which is specifically a challenge for sensors with organic sensing material (Bhalla et al., 2016). The trend is toward more reliable, more sensitive, and more selective sensor systems at a lower cost and needs to strike a balance between research progress and profit (Werthschützky, 2018).

The neurofeedback approaches, as illustrated in the use case of exoskeletons for stroke rehabilitation and biofeedback technologies, have gone beyond the stages of pure data acquisition, analysis, and decision-making. Now sensing devices help prevent illness, diagnose disease, and monitor the health status of individuals and play an active role in their therapeutic progress. These systems are based on feedback loops. However, this raises issues for the design of smart sensor systems in the context of more complex therapeutic interventions. What is the desired state or outcome? The fact that the desired outcome of therapy is not easily quantified in measurable terms makes real-time feedback less useful. Sensors apply the conversion principle by comparing data input to standards. If this is not possible, the output cannot be interpreted in meaningful ways. Is the system's output interpretable? If not, the measured error cannot be calculated and cannot inform the caregiver or patient how to adapt or make decisions. Moreover, the collection of big data within a sensor network raises several challenges in regard to networking, interoperability, security, and privacy (Stojkoska & Trivodaliev, 2017). While data transmission is addressed via secure encryption methods, privacy issues and data ownership are not transparent. Prospective research must develop data privacy protocols and unveil third-party use of personal data or storage in order. Sharing data with physicians or within a group of people is accepted if the goal is clear; however, this should not commence without permission of the user, and accessibility needs to be limited and traceable (Trifan et al., 2019).

6   Conclusion

Recent advances in sensor technology include devices that help practitioners make diagnoses, monitor the health of patients, and provide therapeutic interventions. Innovative approaches use advanced smart sensor technology to execute actions and provide real-time feedback interaction with the patient. Future devices continue the advancement from single detection devices to interactive components in the treatment of health problems. Challenges remain in optimization of single sensors for system integration and meaningful interpretation of signal patterns with artificial intelligence methods. Once data ownership and security concerns in regard to technical devices and data storage are addressed, sensor technologies hold great potential to revolutionize individualized diagnostic, preventive, and therapeutic intervention.

Acknowledgments The authors declare no potential conflicts of interest.

References

Ahmad, R., & Salama, K. N. (2018). Physical sensors for biomedical applications. *Proceedings of IEEE Sensors*, 12–14. https://doi.org/10.1109/ICSENS.2018.8589646

Bennett, J., Rokas, O., & Chen, L. (2017). Healthcare in the Smart Home: A study of past, present and future. *Sustainability (Switzerland), 9*(5), 1–23. https://doi.org/10.3390/su9050840

Bhalla, N., Jolly, P., Formisano, N., & Estrela, P. (2016). Introduction to biosensors. *Essays in Biochemistry, 60*(1), 1–8. https://doi.org/10.1042/EBC20150001

Bumberger, J., Paasche, H., & Dietrich, P. (2015). Systematic description of direct push sensor systems: A conceptual framework for system decomposition as a basis for the optimal sensor system design. *Journal of Applied Geophysics, 122*, 210–217. https://doi.org/10.1016/j.jappgeo.2015.06.003

Chan, M., Estève, D., Fourniols, J. Y., Escriba, C., & Campo, E. (2012). Smart wearable systems: Current status and future challenges. *Artificial Intelligence in Medicine, 56*(3), 137–156. https://doi.org/10.1016/j.artmed.2012.09.003

Cornet, V. P., & Holden, R. J. (2018). Systematic review of smartphone-based passive sensing for health and wellbeing. *Journal of Biomedical Informatics, 77*(July 2017), 120–132. https://doi.org/10.1016/j.jbi.2017.12.008

Crulhas, B. P., Basso, C. R., Castro, G. R., & Pedrosa, V. A. (2021). Review—Recent advances based on a sensor for cancer biomarker detection. *ECS Journal of Solid State Science and Technology, 10*(4), 047004. https://doi.org/10.1149/2162-8777/abf757

Diez, P. (2018). Smart wheelchairs and brain-computer interfaces. In P. Diez (Ed.), *Smart wheelchairs and brain-computer interfaces: Mobile assistive technologies*. Academic Press. https://doi.org/10.1016/C2016-0-04336-X

do Nascimento, L. M. S., Bonfati, L. V., Freitas, M. L. B., Mendes Junior, J. J. A., Siqueira, H. V., & Stevan, S. L. (2020). Sensors and systems for physical rehabilitation and health monitoring—A review. *Sensors, 20*(15), 4063. https://doi.org/10.3390/s20154063

Ducharme, P., Kahn, J., Vaudreuil, C., Gusman, M., Waber, D., Ross, A., Rotenberg, A., Rober, A., Kimball, K., Peechatka, A. L., & Gonzalez-Heydrich, J. (2021). A "proof of concept" randomized controlled trial of a video game requiring emotional regulation to augment anger control training. *Frontiers in Psychiatry, 12*, 1–12. https://doi.org/10.3389/fpsyt.2021.591906

El Naqa, I., & Murphy, M. J. (2015). What is machine learning? In M. Murphy (Ed.), *Machine learning in radiation oncology* (pp. 3–11). Springer. https://doi.org/10.1007/978-3-319-18305-3_1

Formica, D., & Schena, E. (2021). Smart sensors for healthcare and medical applications. *Sensors (Switzerland), 21*(2), 1–5. https://doi.org/10.3390/s21020543

Giannakakis, G., Grigoriadis, D., Giannakaki, K., Simantiraki, O., Roniotis, A., & Tsiknakis, M. (2019). Review on psychological stress detection using biosignals. *IEEE Transactions on Affective Computing, 1*, 1949–3045. https://doi.org/10.1109/TAFFC.2019.2927337

Graimann, B., Pfurtscheller, G., & Allison, B. (Eds.). (2010). *Brain-computer interfaces*. Springer, Berlin. https://doi.org/10.1007/978-3-642-02091-9

Greiwe, J., & Nyenhuis, S. M. (2020). Wearable technology and how this can be implemented into clinical practice. *Current Allergy and Asthma Reports, 20*(8), 36. https://doi.org/10.1007/s11882-020-00927-3

Guo, Y., Hao, Z., Zhao, S., Gong, J., & Yang, F. (2020). Artificial intelligence in health care: bibliometric analysis. *Journal of Medical Internet Research, 22*(7), e18228. https://doi.org/10.2196/18228

Ha, N., Xu, K., Ren, G., Mitchell, A., & Ou, J. Z. (2020). Machine learning-enabled smart sensor systems. *Advanced Intelligent Systems, 2*(9), 2000063. https://doi.org/10.1002/aisy.202000063

Haque, A., Guo, M., Miner, A. S., & Fei-Fei, L. (2018). *Measuring depression symptom severity from spoken language and 3D facial expressions* (pp. 1–7). http://arxiv.org/abs/1811.08592

Ho, A. (2020). Are we ready for artificial intelligence health monitoring in elder care? *BMC Geriatrics, 20*(1), 1–7. https://doi.org/10.1186/s12877-020-01764-9

Hochberg, L. R., & Donoghue, J. P. (2006). Sensors for brain-computer interfaces: Options for turning thought into action. *IEEE Engineering in Medicine and Biology Magazine, 25*(5), 32–38. https://doi.org/10.1109/MEMB.2006.1705745

Hu, H., Yang, W., Zeng, Q., Chen, W., Zhu, Y. B., Liu, W., Wang, S., Wang, B., Shao, Z., & Zhang, Y. (2020). Promising application of Pulsed Electromagnetic Fields (PEMFs) in musculoskeletal disorders. *Biomedicine and Pharmacotherapy, 131*, 110767. https://doi.org/10.1016/J.BIOPHA.2020.110767

Hwang, K. Y., Jimenez, V. O., Muchharla, B., Eggers, T., Le, A. T., Lam, V. D., & Phan, M. H. (2021). A novel magnetic respiratory sensor for human healthcare. *Applied Sciences (Switzerland), 11*(8), 1–10. https://doi.org/10.3390/app11083585

Iqbal, M. A., Hussain, S., Xing, H., & Imran, M. A. (2020). *Enabling the Internet of Things: Fundamentals, Design and Applications: Wiley.*

Jayaram, A. K., Pappa, A. M., Ghosh, S., Manzer, Z. A., Traberg, W. C., Knowles, T. P. J., Daniel, S., & Owens, R. M. (2022). Biomembranes in bioelectronic sensing. *Trends in Biotechnology, 40*(1), 107–123. https://doi.org/10.1016/j.tibtech.2021.06.001

Jha, C. M. (2015). Thermal sensors. In C. M. Jha (Ed.), Springer. https://doi.org/10.1007/978-1-4939-2581-0

Jiang, L., Liu, D. Y., & Yang, B. (2004). Smart home research. In *Proceedings of 2004 international conference on machine learning and cybernetics, 2,* 659–663. IEEE

Karmakar, A., Wang, J., Prinzie, J., De Smedt, V., & Leroux, P. (2021). A review of semiconductor based ionising radiation sensors used in harsh radiation environments and their applications. *Radiation, 1*(3), 194–217. https://doi.org/10.3390/radiation1030018

Kirchner, E. A., Will, N., Simnofske, M., Kampmann, P., Benitez, L. M. V., de Gea Fernández, J., & Kirchner, F. (2019). Exoskelette und künstliche Intelligenz in der klinischen rehabilitation. In M. Pfannstiel, P. Da-Cruz, & H. Mehlich (Eds.), *Digitale Transformation von Dienstleistungen im Gesundheitswesen V* (pp. 413–435). Springer Fachmedien Wiesbaden. https://doi.org/10.1007/978-3-658-23987-9_21

Kleinberger, T., Becker, M., Ras, E., Holzinger, A., & Müller, P. (2007). Ambient intelligence in assisted living: Enable elderly people to handle future interfaces. In C. Stephanidis (Ed.), *Universal access in human-computer interaction. Ambient interaction. UAHCI 2007* (Vol. 4555, pp. 103–112). Springer. https://doi.org/10.1007/978-3-540-73281-5_11

Li, H., Mu, X., Yang, Y., & Mason, A. J. (2014). Low power multimode electrochemical gas sensor array system for wearable health and safety monitoring. *IEEE Sensors Journal, 14*(10), 3391–3399. https://doi.org/10.1109/JSEN.2014.2332278

Louie, D. R., & Eng, J. J. (2016). Powered robotic exoskeletons in post-stroke rehabilitation of gait: A scoping review. *Journal of Neuro Engineering and Rehabilitation, 13*(1), 1–10. https://doi.org/10.1186/s12984-016-0162-5

Lussier, M., Lavoie, M., Giroux, S., Consel, C., Guay, M., Macoir, J., Hudon, C., Lorrain, D., Talbot, L., Langlois, F., Pigot, H., & Bier, N. (2019). Early detection of mild cognitive impairment with in-home monitoring sensor technologies using functional measures: A systematic review. *IEEE Journal of Biomedical and Health Informatics, 23*(2), 838–847. https://doi.org/10.1109/JBHI.2018.2834317

Luxton, D. D., & Riek, L. D. (2019). Artificial intelligence and robotics in rehabilitation. In *Handbook of rehabilitation psychology* (3rd ed., pp. 507–520). American Psychological Association. https://doi.org/10.1037/0000129-031

Mackle, E. C., Coote, J. M., Carr, E., Little, C. D., van Soest, G., & Desjardins, A. E. (2021). Fibre optic intravascular measurements of blood flow: A review. *Sensors and Actuators A: Physical, 332,* 113162. https://doi.org/10.1016/j.sna.2021.113162

Mansourian, M., & Shanei, A. (2021). Evaluation of pulsed electromagnetic field effects: A systematic review and meta-analysis on highlights of two decades of research in vitro studies. *Bio Med Research International, 2021,* 1–22. https://doi.org/10.1155/2021/6647497

Markiewicz, O., Lavelle, M., Lorencatto, F., Judah, G., Ashrafian, H., & Darzi, A. (2020). Threats to safe transitions from hospital to home: A consensus study in North West London primary care. *British Journal of General Practice, 70*(690), e9–e19. https://doi.org/10.3399/bjgp19X707105

Martini, M. L., Oermann, E. K., Opie, N. L., Panov, F., Oxley, T., & Yaeger, K. (2020). Sensor modalities for brain-computer interface technology: A comprehensive literature review. *Neurosurgery, 86*(2), E108–E117. https://doi.org/10.1093/NEUROS/NYZ286

McGrath, M. J., & Scanaill, C. N. (2013). Sensor Technologies. In *Sensor technologies: Healthcare, wellness, and environmental applications* (1st ed.). Apress. https://doi.org/10.1007/978-1-4302-6014-1

McKee, M. G. (2008). Biofeedback: An overview in the context of heart-brain medicine. *Cleveland Clinic Journal of Medicine, 75*(Suppl. 2), 31–34. https://doi.org/10.3949/ccjm.75.Suppl_2.S31

Mohankumar, P., Ajayan, J., Mohanraj, T., & Yasodharan, R. (2021). Recent developments in biosensors for healthcare and biomedical applications: A review. *Measurement: Journal of the International Measurement Confederation, 167*(May 2020), 108293. https://doi.org/10.1016/j.measurement.2020.108293

Nazemi, H., Joseph, A., Park, J., & Emadi, A. (2019). Advanced micro-and nano-gas sensor technology: A review. *Sensors (Switzerland), 19*(6). https://doi.org/10.3390/s19061285

O'Neill, C., Proietti, T., Nuckols, K., Clarke, M. E., Hohimer, C. J., Cloutier, A., Lin, D. J., & Walsh, C. J. (2020). Inflatable soft wearable robot for reducing therapist fatigue during upper extremity rehabilitation in severe stroke. *IEEE Robotics and Automation Letters, 5*(3), 3899–3906. https://doi.org/10.1109/LRA.2020.2982861

Ohayon, D., & Inal, S. (2020). Organic bioelectronics: from functional materials to next-generation devices and power sources. *Advanced Materials, 32*(36), 2001439. https://doi.org/10.1002/ADMA.202001439

Pfurtscheller, G., Neuper, C., & Birbaumer, N. (2004). Human brain-computer interface. In *Motor cortex in voluntary movements: A distributed system for distributed functions*. https://doi.org/10.1201/9780203503584.ch14

Pierleoni, P., Belli, A., Palma, L., Pellegrini, M., Pernini, L., & Valenti, S. (2015). A high reliability wearable device for elderly fall detection. *IEEE Sensors Journal, 15*(8), 4544–4553. https://doi.org/10.1109/JSEN.2015.2423562

Pramanik, P. K. D., Upadhyaya, B. K., Pal, S., & Pal, T. (2019). Internet of things, smart sensors, and pervasive systems: Enabling connected and pervasive healthcare. In *Healthcare data analytics and management* (pp. 1–58). Elsevier. https://doi.org/10.1016/b978-0-12-815368-0.00001-4

Shanthamallu, U. S., Spanias, A., Tepedelenlioglu, C., & Stanley, M. (2018). A brief survey of machine learning methods and their sensor and IoT applications. *8th International Conference on Information, Intelligence, Systems and Applications*, 1–8. https://doi.org/10.1109/IISA.2017.8316459

Shinde, M., Gupta, M., & Gawade, S. (2014). Overview of different types of sensors used in eHealth environment. *International Journal of Infinite Innovations in Technology*, 2278–9057.

Stojkoska, B. L. R., & Trivodaliev, K. V. (2017). A review of Internet of Things for smart home: Challenges and solutions. *Journal of Cleaner Production, 140*, 1454–1464. https://doi.org/10.1016/j.jclepro.2016.10.006

Sunwoo, S.-H., Ha, K.-H., Lee, S., Lu, N., & Kim, D.-H. (2021). Wearable and implantable soft bioelectronics: Device designs and material strategies. *Annual Review of Chemical and Biomolecular Engineering, 12*(1), 359–391. https://doi.org/10.1146/annurev-chembioeng-101420-024336

Trifan, A., Oliveira, M., & Oliveira, J. L. (2019). Passive sensing of health outcomes through smartphones: Systematic review of current solutions and possible limitations. *JMIR mHealth and uHealth, 7*(8), e12649. https://doi.org/10.2196/12649

Unger, E. K., Keller, J. P., Altermatt, M., Liang, R., Matsui, A., Dong, C., Hon, O. J., Yao, Z., Sun, J., Banala, S., Flanigan, M. E., Jaffe, D. A., Hartanto, S., Carlen, J., Mizuno, G. O., Borden, P. M., Shivange, A. V., Cameron, L. P., Sinning, S., ... Tian, L. (2020). Directed evolution of a selective and sensitive serotonin sensor via machine learning. *Cell, 183*(7), 1986–2002.e26. https://doi.org/10.1016/j.cell.2020.11.040

Vogel, J., Auinger, A., Riedl, R., Kindermann, H., Helfert, M., & Ocenasek, H. (2017). Digitally enhanced recovery: Investigating the use of digital self-tracking for monitoring leisure time physical activity of cardiovascular disease (CVD) patients undergoing cardiac rehabilitation. *PLoS One, 12*(10), e0186261. https://doi.org/10.1371/journal.pone.0186261

Welltiss Mind PEMF wearable - SleepGadgets.io. (n.d.). Retrieved December 10, 2021, from https://sleepgadgets.io/welltiss-mind-pemf-wearable/

Wen, W. (2016). Introductory chapter: What is chemical sensor? In W. Wen (Ed.), *Progresses in chemical sensor*. IntechOpen. https://doi.org/10.5772/64626

Werthschützky, R. (2018). *Sensor Technologien 2022*. AMA Verband für Sensorik und Messtechnik e.V. https://ama-sensorik.de/fileadmin/Pubikationen/180601-AMA-Studie-online-final.pdf

Yang, X., He, H., Ye, W., Perry, T. A., & He, C. (2020). Effects of pulsed electromagnetic field therapy on pain, stiffness, physical function, and quality of life in patients with osteoarthritis: A systematic review and meta-analysis of randomized placebo-controlled trials. *Physical Therapy, 100*(7), 1118–1131. https://doi.org/10.1093/ptj/pzaa054

Yang, D., Gopal, R. A., Lkhagvaa, T., & Choi, D. (2021). Metal-oxide gas sensors for exhaled-breath analysis: A review. *Measurement Science and Technology, 32*(10), 102004. https://doi.org/10.1088/1361-6501/AC03E3

Digital and Computational Pathology: A Specialty Reimagined

Tim-Rasmus Kiehl

Abstract

The field of pathology, which provides tissue diagnoses for clinical and research purposes, is at the heart of medical decision-making. The current move to digital pathology (DP) is a fundamental change in how primary diagnostic work, consultations, education, and multidisciplinary conferences are performed. DP is the prerequisite for computational pathology (CPATH), the big-data approach to pathology that extracts information from images, typically using artificial intelligence (AI) methods. While CPATH offers significant new capabilities and workflows, it also brings new challenges. There will be knock-on effects on other specialties and in teaching and research. The emerging next-generation pathology will be more quantitative, will have more diagnostic consistency, and will be more connected to its medical peers.

1   Transformations of the Past

Pathology, the study of the causes and effects of disease, has gone through several transformations in its history (Fig. 1). Nothing has changed about the basic goal of rendering a tissue diagnosis from the interpretation of macroscopic and especially microscopic morphology. The introduction of microscopy in the 1850s–1870s (van den Tweel & Taylor, 2010) brought about a modern, histology-based understanding of disease (i.e., histopathology) and revolutionized medicine. In the 1980s, immunohistochemistry, which uses antibodies to highlight specific antigens

T.-R. Kiehl (✉)
Charité–Universitätsmedizin Berlin, corporate member of Freie Universität Berlin and Humboldt Universität zu Berlin, Institut für Pathologie, Charitéplatz 1, Berlin, Germany
e-mail: rasmus.kiehl@charite.de

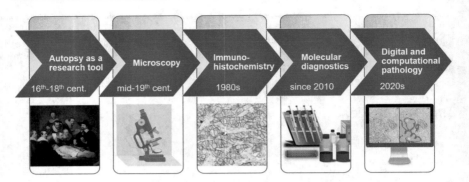

Fig. 1 A history of transformations in pathology. The specialty is again on the verge of major changes from a new convergence of technologies

in tissue, entered clinical practice (Gatter et al., 1985; Taylor, 1986). Molecular pathology, which was widely adopted in the 2010s and is still a developing field, goes beyond the microscope with a broad array of methods for analyzing nucleic acids in particular.

Among the many challenges in the specialty are an aging workforce (Colgan & Geldenhuys, 2012; Metter et al., 2019; Robboy et al., 2013), an insufficient number of trainees to match future demands, and rising workloads (Metter et al., 2019; Märkl et al., 2021; Bonert et al., 2021). The complexity of case assessment is increasing in tandem with the demands of precision medicine, adding further to the workload (Warth et al., 2016). A trend toward subspecialization is related to the growing complexity of the specialty (Sarewitz, 2014; Ohori et al., 2016; Conant et al., 2017), as is the case in internal medicine, surgery, and radiology. However, the required subspecialty expertise is not always available. In addition, there are external pressures. As life expectancy continues to rise, so does the prevalence of chronic illnesses and neoplasms (Halaweish & Alam, 2015).

New technologies are now converging to reshape the specialty once again. DP makes possible novel use cases and innovative workflows. DP is also the foundation for CPATH (Louis et al., 2014; Abels et al., 2019), which is based on machine learning. Together, DP and CPATH will create many effective responses to the challenges pathology faces. CPATH will bring many new capabilities in classifying lesions, segmenting tissue elements, discovering biomarkers, and using image features to predict therapy and outcome. These developments will require new ways of training medical students and trainees in various specialties. DP will make the wealth of information in pathology much more accessible to colleagues in other specialties. An opportunity is emerging to rebrand a specialty that contributes much to medical decision-making yet is poorly understood by the public and colleagues in other specialties. The chapter concludes with an attempt to envision an age when the changes CPATH offers have become routine practices.

2 Digital Pathology

The current practice of pathology still centers on conventional microscopes and glass slides for the most part, but this is changing. The digital transformation has gone much more slowly than initially expected due to high up-front costs, an unclear business case, insufficient standardization, as well as regulatory issues. Comparisons have been made to radiology (Montalto, 2008; Cornish et al., 2012; Hipp et al., 2011; Patterson et al., 2011), which went digital decades ago, but there are fundamental differences. Microscopic images are at least $10\times$, sometimes $100\times$ larger than black-and-white radiology images and require more resources. Workflow in radiology was simplified with the elimination of films, which cut costs. In contrast, pathologists still have to generate glass slides as before, but now they must also scan them and manage the data, which adds expenses. Radiology adopted an image standard long ago (i.e., DICOM, digital imaging and communications in medicine), while proprietary standards are still the rule in pathology. DICOM for pathology is under development (Herrmann et al., 2018; Clunie, 2021). It appears that digitization in pathology presents greater challenges than in other areas of medical imaging.

DP is the practice of pathology using digital imaging technology. It "includes the acquisition, management, sharing and interpretation of pathology information—including slides and data—in a digital environment" (Royal College of Pathologists, 2021). The definition of DP should not be limited to microscopy since pathology also involves macroscopic and molecular information. The laboratory information system (LIS) has interfaces to laboratory equipment, sample archiving, and more. DP has its roots in virtual microscopy (i.e., viewing microscopic images with a computer) and telepathology (i.e., pathology over a distance) (Weinstein, 1986). A significant catalyst for the field was whole slide imaging (WSI) (Farahani et al., 2015; Pantanowitz et al., 2018) in which a specialized robotic microscope scans an entire histologic slide rapidly and at high resolution. Most digital microscopy involves bright-field images, but fluorescent images (fluorescent immunohistochemistry, fluorescence in situ hybridization) and multispectral images (information across the spectrum of light) can also be scanned. After over two decades of technological innovation (high-throughput WSI scanners, LIS interfaces, storage, networks, etc.), DP appears sufficiently robust and affordable for deployment in clinical use. A vibrant DP commercial sector has emerged for hardware (scanners, servers, storage, communication) and software (LISs, WSI viewers, image analysis). Regulatory approval by the US Food and Drug Administration of WSI scanners for primary diagnosis (Evans et al., 2018) was an important milestone. Vendor neutral archives can manage images from different sources. An exemplary DP cockpit is shown in Fig. 2a. The workflows of conventional pathology, DP, and CPATH are shown in Fig. 2b–d.

DP has many advantages over glass-and-microscope pathology. Workflow improvements include faster case delivery from the lab, leading to shorter turnaround times (Hanna et al., 2019b). For urgent cases, multiple colleagues

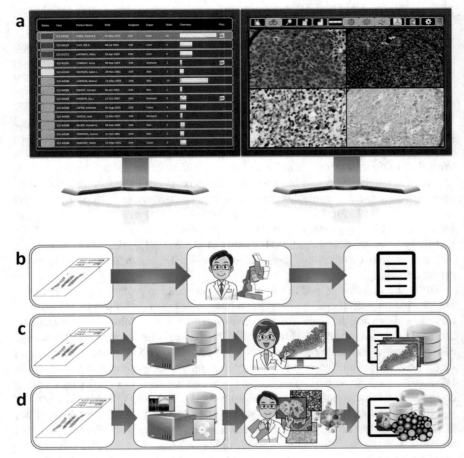

Fig. 2 (**a**) A digital pathology "cockpit": The laboratory information system (LIS) (left screen) shows a list of patients and case overview while the WSI viewer (right screen) displays the corresponding histologic images in slide-by-slide mode. (**b–d**) Comparison of workflows: (**b**) In conventional (analog) pathology, glass slides are delivered from the lab to the pathologist, who reads them with a conventional light microscope and reports the findings in the LIS. (**c**) In DP, the slide is digitized with a WSI scanner and stored locally. The pathologist reviews the case on a monitor and reports it in the LIS, and WSIs are subsequently available for easy retrieval and sharing. (**d**) In CPATH, after digitization, the WSI undergoes preanalytical quality control and extensive precomputing. The pathologist reviews the case on a CPATH workstation and runs additional computational tools. The case is stored locally and in cloud-based services and may also be submitted to a repository for research

can view a case simultaneously. The pathologist can annotate directly in the slide for diagnostic documentation, education, and research. Access to a patient's prior cases is easier and faster. Information storage is more reliable with no degradation of tissue over time (i.e., fading) or breakage of glass. The retrieval of similar cases for comparison and research is also easier. Images can be transmitted quickly over vast distances for applications such as telepathology, teleconsultation, education, and clinical trials. The recent COVID-19 pandemic was an important catalyst for DP as it suddenly made remote viewing, reporting, and teaching necessary in many centers (Hanna et al., 2020; Stathonikos et al., 2020; Williams et al., 2020; Araújo et al., 2021; Browning et al., 2021). For multidisciplinary tumor boards, WSI has advantages over static images (because it is interactive) and multiheaded microscopes (because it accommodates remote participants). The possible disadvantages of DP include the initial cost, data storage requirements, insufficient LIS integration, lack of Z-stacking in most scanners, and the risk of workload increases (e.g., expansion of second opinions) (Farahani et al., 2015; Jahn et al., 2020).

A number of use cases for DP exist, including clinical and nonclinical applications (Dash et al., 2021). For primary diagnosis (Volynskaya et al., 2018; Asa & Evans, 2020; Retamero et al., 2020; Schüffler et al., 2021; Borowsky et al., 2020), many validation studies indicate high concordance between glass slides and DP (Snead et al., 2016; Hanna et al., 2019a, 2020; Mukhopadhyay et al., 2018; Azam et al., 2021). In case review (e.g., internal or external review, consultation, and second opinions, including telepathology and remote work) (Zhao et al., 2015; Chong et al., 2019), DP is faster, safer, and often cheaper than sending slides by mail, as was done previously. These review capabilities will make it easier to generate consensus diagnoses among pathologists, thereby helping to reduce diagnostic variability and diagnostic errors. A long-established use case is intraoperative consultation (e.g., frozen or "quick" sections) that can be performed by telepathology (Horbinski et al., 2007; Evans et al., 2009; Ribback et al., 2014; Dietz et al., 2020) and is therefore appealing for multisite hospitals or those without sufficient subspecialty expertise. Multidisciplinary tumor boards benefit from DP because it eliminates much preparation work and enables presentations from WSI, which greatly improves their quality (Krupinski et al., 2018). Digital microscopy has been used in teaching for many years (Mea et al., 2017; Rodrigues-Fernandes et al., 2020; Hassell et al., 2021; Evans et al., 2021) and has proven to be an effective learning tool (Ordi et al., 2015; Saco et al., 2016) that high proportions of trainees accept. DP also brings new opportunities in quality assurance and quality control (QA/QC) (Janowczyk et al., 2019; Wright et al., 2020; Chen et al., 2021).

The business case for DP is improving. As initially mentioned, DP adoption by mainstream pathologists has been slow. One reason was that the business case was still challenging. However, this is now changing, and many centers have reported productivity gains from DP adoption (Baidoshvili et al., 2018; Hanna et al., 2019b; Retamero et al., 2020). In addition, new long-term revenue opportunities are opening up in the areas of telepathology and clinical trials (Barisoni & Hodgin, 2017; Pell et al., 2019). Several studies have examined the business case to provide guidance (Lujan et al., 2021; Williams et al., 2019). CPATH enables new use cases in image analysis that are impossible with conventional microscopes, further improving the economic case for DP adoption. Indeed, comparisons are sometimes made between the iPhone, which created the basis for apps, and WSI scanners that make pathology AI applications possible.

DP will likely lead to profound changes in workflows in ways that are difficult to predict. The DP environment is not simply a new user interface (i.e., a modernized version of the conventional microscope) but a foundation for a very different way to practice that opens up entirely new capabilities, such as CPATH and biomarker analysis.

3   Computational Pathology

3.1   Background and Definitions

A discussion of the new capabilities and use cases enabled by CPATH should be prefaced by a reminder that definitions in this area are still evolving. Experts from the Digital Pathology Association define CPATH broadly as "a branch of pathology that involves computational analysis of a broad array of methods to analyze patient specimens for the study of disease" (Abels et al., 2019, p. 287). They point out that definitions of CPATH may be affected by the context in which they are presented, which may sometimes lead to confusion. A more comprehensive earlier description of CPATH (Louis et al., 2014, p. 1133) stated that it "incorporates multiple sources of raw data (e.g., clinical and laboratory data, imaging); extracts biologically and clinically relevant information; uses mathematical models at the levels of molecules, individuals, and populations for diagnostic inferences and predictions; and presents that clinically actionable knowledge to customers." Important foundational technologies for CPATH are machine learning (a type of AI that learns from examples of measurements and can generalize them after a learning phase to predict a variable of interest) and especially deep learning (i.e., a type of machine learning that is based on artificial neural networks that contain many intermediate, hidden layers of increasing complexity). In supervised machine learning, a label (ground truth) is attached to the data. In contrast, unsupervised machine learning does not use such assigned labels and is instead based on clustering and principal component analysis. In end-to-end deep learning (i.e., the model learns to connect initial input data and the final output result), images are the input and a corresponding clinical variable or molecular data is used for training. The output may be a therapy prediction or a prognostic assessment directly from raw images. A term that is sometimes used interchangeably with CPATH is "pathomics" (Saltz et al., 2017), also called "histomics" or "tissue phenomics." It is the "pieces and parts" approach to pathology data. A WSI is broken down into very small units for further integration with molecular data, omics data, or other biomedical imaging data. Features are then extracted from tissue with the help of computational algorithms and are subsequently used to create prediction models. Pathomics enables reproducible and quantitative data mining for histology. The parallel field in radiology is called radiomics (Mayerhoefer et al., 2020; Yip & Aerts, 2016). The AI revolution in pathology is connected to and influenced by other fields of AI research, including other medical imaging and developments in more distant fields, such as autonomous vehicles.

3.2 Applications of CPATH

When machine learning methods were first introduced to the field, the goal was often to recapitulate the pathologist's approach (e.g., automate tumor grading in a way that a human would proceed). As machine learning and deep learning methods have evolved, they have become increasingly able to perform tasks that are beyond the capabilities of a pathologist. Histopathologic image analysis, whether based on machine learning or deep learning techniques or more conventional methods, falls into several general categories. Segmentation is the precise delineation of the borders of one particular tissue element from its surroundings. Examples of frequently segmented objects are epithelia, glands, stroma, cells, or nuclei. In order to obtain sufficient training and validation data for segmentation, large numbers of manual annotations by pathologists are often required—a time-consuming and expensive step. Classification is often based on various clustering methods, such as supervised clustering (when labeled or annotated data are available) or unsupervised clustering (label scarcity). Images are grouped into categories, such as tumor vs. non-tumor, tumor subtypes, or grades of tumors.

There is more information in histopathology images than meets the human eye. However, with machine learning and deep learning methods, these "subvisual" features may be used for tasks such as classification or predicting molecular findings from hematoxylin and eosin (H&E) images. Certain histomorphologic features correlate with molecular features, and given sufficient training data, a prediction of molecular signatures from WSIs may be possible (Coudray et al., 2018; Yamashita et al., 2021). Advanced deep learning-based approaches make it possible to infer molecular features and therapy responses from tissue biomarkers (Krause et al., 2021; Echle et al., 2021). In the workflow of the future, diagnostic images could be prescreened for molecular predictions to flag those with a high likelihood of a negative result. Subsequent molecular testing may then not be necessary on these cases. Some mutations are mutually exclusive, and the availability of such image-based preliminary testing could allow for better triage of molecular testing. Much actual testing would still have to be done, but this approach may help cut costs (Kacew et al., 2021). Similarly, information about prognosis may also be obtained in this way although it requires training with clinical outcome data (Bychkov et al., 2018; Kather et al., 2019).

Numerous specific CPATH use cases have emerged. Some of them are depicted in a hypothetical app store shown in Fig. 3. They include QA/QC tools, detection and segmentation tools, diagnostic assistance for common tasks such as finding mitotic figures, predictive tools, grading tools, and more advanced analysis tools.

Fig. 3   (A humorous take on a) hypothetical CPATH app store

Also included is the ability to find matching cases in large databases with image search (see below). Some of the tools in Fig. 3 are tongue-in-cheek, hinting at the hype surrounding AI.

3.3   AI Applications Beyond Histopathologic Analysis

Interest in applying AI to anatomic pathology has largely been focused on histologic image analysis, mostly tasks related to visual recognition and understanding. Many other potential uses have not been studied as thoroughly. Among them is the extraction of a patient's relevant clinical history from various sources and automated writing and standardization of pathology reports (e.g., automated generation of synoptic reports for cancer cases). For patient engagement, automated reports in a language patients can understand could be accessed through a patient portal (Krasowski et al., 2017). Another area is laboratory automation (Naugler & Church, 2019) and laboratory QA/QC (Janowczyk et al., 2019). The potential to generate virtual stains has been demonstrated, which may involve scanning unstained paraffin sections and computing staining patterns or transforming one stain into another (de Haan et al., 2021). Other potential applications involve assisting with managing workload, multi-omics (correlation, integration), and multimodal data fusion (e.g., radiology-pathology).

3.4   Challenges in Pathology AI

Despite the very impressive progress in pathology AI in recent years, there are many risks and challenges. An immediate problem is the lack of sufficiently large training datasets that represent the extensive variability that exists in clinical data across different institutions (e.g., among institutions, regions, ethnicities). Such datasets are the prerequisite for clinical-grade CPATH (as opposed to research-grade) and will benefit from the establishment of repositories (see below). Low availability of annotations by pathologists for training data has also been a problem. However, this may improve with the wider adoption of automated high-throughput methods that make the annotation process far more efficient (Miao et al., 2021). AI could lead to much larger volumes of data to be extracted from histologic images. This deluge of data could expose the workforce to the risk of information overload. Pathologists may get bogged down in too much data that does not have much benefit for clinical care. There are also concerns related to human/computer interaction, such as decision fatigue (i.e., frequent inappropriate alerts leading the human operator to ignore the signal) (Ancker et al., 2017; Baron et al., 2021). Another potential risk is automation bias; the human operator may become complacent and rely on a machine's output without doing sufficient double-checking (Parasuraman & Riley, 1997). There are concerns that when deep learning algorithms take over some very specialized diagnostic functions, pathologists' skills may fall into disuse and atrophy (Sarwar et al., 2019).

New areas of research and development will certainly emerge from these topics. The topic of AI explainability has received much attention as AI approaches in pathology have become increasingly successful. There are concerns that the models with the best performance are also the least transparent ones. Labels such as "opacity" or "black box" are sometimes used when discussing AI. The field of explainable AI (xAI) in medicine "deals with the implementation of transparency and traceability of statistical black-box machine learning methods, particularly deep learning" (Holzinger et al., 2019, p. 1). In other words, xAI intends to bring transparency to the process by revealing the reasons for the decisions a model makes. When applied to anatomic pathology, xAI mechanisms will likely be embedded in the analysis of WSIs (Tosun et al., 2020) to improve trust in the models and the safety of the CPATH workflow.

3.5   Pathologist vs. AI?

Will AI replace pathologists? There are some concerns in the specialty about the possible elimination of jobs (Sarwar et al., 2019). The threat of automation may discourage potential trainees from choosing the specialty, thus increasing the growing shortage of pathologists. However, it appears unlikely that machines or AI will replace pathologists as the latter are needed to do more integrative tasks, to examine the data products coming from CPATH, and to do new types of research on topics such as biomarkers and pathomics (Saltz et al., 2017). Human pathologists are also needed to detect rare pathologies that the algorithms have not been trained on. For the near future, it seems more likely that pathologists using AI will replace those not using it, creating a combination of human and machine intelligence (augmented intelligence). AI-based diagnostic support systems can help avoid decision fatigue and enable the pathologist to do more work. For the longer term, however, emerging technologies will bring significant changes in workflow. These changes will enable machines to perform diagnostic tasks in ways that are very different from how human pathologists operate.

3.6   Reference Databases, DP Repositories, and Large-Scale Initiatives in CPATH

With image search, a reference database containing tens of thousands of curated and annotated cases can be queried with a current case to identify similar cases. The image search can involve histologic and other features. As a new capability in CPATH, this opens up new opportunities for diagnostic support and may lead to significant changes in workflow. The technologies for reverse image search developed at Google were applied to histologic images; the resulting search tool is called "Similar Medical Images Like Yours," or "SMILY" (Hegde et al., 2019). Another example is "Yottixel," which uses barcoding technology to represent images (Kalra et al., 2020a, b). "Pathobot" implements AI-driven image search and uses social media data for similarity ranking (Schaumberg et al., 2020).

The advances in applying AI technologies to pathology over the last 6–7 years have also spurred investments in large-scale infrastructure projects, such as repositories and large CPATH initiatives. Some of the problems with the robustness of AI applications seem to be primarily problems of data availability. More data from different institutions that represent a larger number of laboratories, staining conditions, scanners, and so forth are likely to improve robustness. The "BIGPIC-TURE" project is a large public-private consortium led by Radboud University in the Netherlands that is funded by the EU Innovative Medicines Initiative. BIGPICTURE is building a central repository of millions of annotated DP slides to support the development of AI models (Moulin et al., 2021). The "EMPAIA" project (EcosysteM for Pathology Diagnostics with AI Assistance), funded by the German Federal Ministry for Economic Affairs and Climate Action (Homeyer et al., 2021), is building a platform for the development and validation of AI services that will include data repositories and a marketplace. Its goal is to support an entire ecosystem of stakeholders, including AI developers, clinical laboratories, research institutions in academia and the private sector, certification bodies, and other participants. Five collaborative committees are working to remove regulatory, legal, technical, and organizational obstacles to pathology AI. The initiative also produces advanced half-day training events called "EMPAIA Academy" for AI skills development. The Pathology Innovation Collaborative Community (PIcc, formerly the Alliance for Digital Pathology) (Marble et al., 2020) is a significant regulatory science initiative where public and private stakeholders work with the US Food and Drug Administration to accelerate advances in the precompetitive phase of DP. Additional large-scale initiatives exist in the UK with funding from UK Research and Innovation (UKRI), including iCAIRD (https://icaird. com), PathLAKE (https://www.pathlake.org), and NPIC (https://npic.ac.uk/). These public-private consortia are building large repositories of annotated and curated WSI data with corresponding clinical information.

4 Broader Effects on Other Specialties, Education, and Research

4.1 Integrative Pathology and Other Specialties

Pathologists have always been integrators of information from different sources, combining their morphologic and molecular findings (morpho-molecular pathology) (Jones et al., 2017) and putting them in the context of clinical practice and basic science. The term "integrative" even became part of the name of a professional society, the European Society of Integrative Digital Pathology (Eloy et al., 2021). As pathology becomes even more data-rich, the role of the integrator will become stronger and will involve combining histomorphology, molecular pathology, omics data, AI-derived data products, clinical information, and other medical imaging modalities, such as radiology.

Significant opportunities are emerging for cross-disciplinary practice. Analogous to the way that radiologic images are now viewed by physicians in many specialties but only formally reported by radiologists, changes will happen with pathology images in the future. Once histologic images are decoupled from the microscope, other specialties can use them in the clinical setting and in teaching and research. Use cases for DP and CPATH are emerging for various specialties. For example, during surgery, when tissue is sent to pathology for an intraoperative consultation ("frozen section"), the surgeon will not just receive a verbal diagnosis but can see the actual histology on screen during the procedure without leaving the operating room. A radiologist can review not just the pathology report but the actual histology images, receiving much more granular feedback on the earlier radiology diagnosis (Lundström et al., 2017; Mun et al., 2020). Diagnosis and therapy will be more closely coupled, following the example of oncologic pathology ("companion diagnostics," "theranostics"). The impact will be significant in dermatology and dermatopathology, fields that are already adopting novel imaging technologies (Glines et al., 2020).

4.2 Education and Outreach

The DP/CPATH revolutions will significantly impact the training of medical students, pathology trainees, and trainees in other specialties. Curricular changes at many medical schools in North America have resulted in the integration of various topics into core curricula. In the process, pathology teaching has often been curtailed or entirely eliminated. As a result, many medical students no longer have adequate exposure to this field and increasingly lack a tissue-based understanding of disease. This is a problem for the future of pathology because it is vitally important to attract good trainees. In response, digital platforms such as PathElective (Lilley et al., 2021) have sprung up that offer high-quality content to those who are willing to invest the time and effort beyond their required curriculum. The COVID-19 pandemic presented additional opportunities to use DP techniques to teach pathology (Hassell et al., 2021; Hassell & Afzal, 2021; Patel et al., 2021).

Whenever new topics emerged in recent decades, the specialty has responded by creating new training programs for pathology postgraduates, such as fellowships in molecular diagnostics (Rosenbaum et al., 2021) and pathology informatics (Levy et al., 2012; Mandelker et al., 2014; Quinn et al., 2014). The introduction of CPATH will necessitate an overhaul of existing anatomic pathology training programs and will lead to the creation of new fellowship programs.

DP/CPATH topics can support outreach. As mentioned earlier, when histologic images are "freed" from the microscope with DP, new ways to use them become possible. One such application is patient education and engagement. In the past, most pathologists have had minimal contact with patients, but this may change as digital technologies allow for much easier dialog. Indeed, the concept of a patient-pathologist consultation program has been presented (Booth et al., 2019; Jug et al., 2021; Lapedis et al., 2020; Shachar et al., 2021). If this becomes popular, it could give much more visibility to pathologists. Also significant for outreach is the small but vibrant presence of pathology on social media (Deeken et al., 2020; El Hussein et al., 2020; Mukhopadhyay et al., 2021). On platforms such as Twitter, Facebook, and LinkedIn, pathologists share educational material, announce events, interact with applicants, and much more. In the future, pathologists will likely move to dedicated, more formal services based on WSIs and CPATH functionality.

The ongoing transformation provides excellent opportunities for rebranding the specialty (El Hussein et al., 2021). Some of the ingredients of rebranding are the capabilities of DP/CPATH, integrative pathology, and improved outreach. Rebranding is essential because the perception of pathology is suboptimal among the general public, where autopsy activities predominate, and among colleagues in other medical specialties, who often have little knowledge about what pathology does.

4.3   Nonclinical Settings: Biobanking, Experimental and Veterinary Pathology, Toxicology, and Pharmaceutical Development

As a translational discipline, pathology is a bridge between basic biomedical science and various clinical fields. The same technologies that underpin the digital and computational pathology revolution are entering all other areas that perform tissue analysis. Because the workflows in those areas can differ significantly from routine clinical workflow, technologies will need to be adapted. For example, slide viewers designed for clinical diagnostic work are often case-centric and may not be suitable for preclinical pharmaceutical development that is more batch-centric.

Biobanking and biospecimen science are closely tied to the clinical diagnostic space and have started to use WSI scans as part of specimen annotation (Hamilton et al., 2014; Wei & Simpson, 2014). There is great potential in incorporating pathologist annotations and CPATH-derived data products and further combining these with molecular data, such as proteomics and methylomics. There is also great potential for robotics in biobanking and basic tissue-based research. For example, combining laser capture microdissection with robotics and AI will make possible new applications that were previously too time-consuming if performed by a human operator. Veterinary medicine has started to integrate DP techniques for teaching and diagnostic use (Bertram & Klopfleisch, 2017; Brown et al., 2016; Jones-Hall et al., 2021). CPATH techniques will be applied to organoids, tumoroids, xenografts, avatars, and other microanatomic models.

In drug discovery and development, DP is already changing the way clinical trials are conducted. Pharmaceutical companies are digitizing central pathology review (Mroz et al., 2013; Barisoni & Hodgin, 2017; Pell et al., 2019), bringing improvements in efficiency and accuracy. Compared to clinical diagnostics, some aspects of applying CPATH to preclinical pharmaceutical development and toxicological pathology may be easier to implement as the analyses are often highly standardized. AI tools are especially well suited for highly repetitive tasks, which will make it possible to expand preclinical development and toxicological pathology activities (Turner et al., 2020).

5 Conclusions and Perspectives

Pathology is entering another transformative phase. The introduction of DP will be the foundation for CPATH. Parallel changes will come from a larger number of additional areas that are beyond the scope of this chapter. Among them are novel imaging and visualization technologies, such as augmented reality, in vivo microscopy, and 3D pathology, as well as multiplexing, multi-omics, and multimodal data fusion. Advances in robotics and laboratory automation will also influence this convergence.

As pathologists reinvent themselves, their task will remain the same: extracting, simplifying, and distilling information. The role of pattern recognition abilities may become somewhat less important as AI-based methods will take over some of these tasks. However, managing complexity and performing integrative tasks will likely become more important. Some of the broader changes that characterize current and future practice are contrasted in Table 1. With AI and multiplexing, pathology will become more quantitative (e.g., tumor markers Ki-67 and PD-L1). Variability of diagnosis and reporting can be reduced significantly. Large reference databases

Table 1 Current pathology characteristics and the trends leading to next-generation pathology

Past/current	Future
Analog (glass slides and microscope)	Digital (WSI)
Morphologic	Morphomolecular
Qualitative and intuitive	Quantitative
Highly variable reporting (poorly structured, difficult to database)	Highly structured reporting (synoptic/structured, easy to database)
High diagnostic variability	High diagnostic consistency (AI-based quantification; ubiquitous "second read")
Decentralized laboratories and practice settings	Increasingly centralized laboratories
Location-dependent practice	Connected, "networked" practice
Case-by-case diagnosis, mostly from one pathologist	Image search using large reference databases and crowd wisdom
Research-grade CPATH (possibly brittle; few and narrow applications)	Clinical-grade CPATH (robust; wide variety of applications)
2D (using conventional histologic images)	3D (from novel image acquisition technologies)
Single-plex	Multiplex
Single parameter analyses	Multi-omics
Pathology or radiology or other imaging	Cross-disciplinary diagnostic imaging
Pathologist remote from patient	Pathologist connecting with patient (e.g., patient-specific reports, patient portals, patient-pathologist consultation)

can support standardization. With CPATH-enabled multimodal data fusion from different imaging sources, diagnostic imaging will become more cross-disciplinary.

What will the practice of pathology look like when this transformation is complete, perhaps 10 years after publication of this book? Workflow will be different in many ways, including AI-based QC in the lab to improve and standardize quality; the routine, automatic preordering of special stains and immunohistochemistry by AI (Chatrian et al., 2021); and the precomputation of diagnostic parameters even before pathologist review. DP will be the norm for primary diagnosis, consultation, teaching, and other functions. Previously unavailable diagnostic tools such as heat maps will be commonplace. The pathologists of the future will be sorting through AI-generated data products. They will be spending more time doing QA/QC. Automated AI-based preliminary diagnoses will be available for most indications. Even sooner, AI-based "second-read" mechanisms could be introduced that work in the background, surfacing only when a discrepancy occurs. Large reference case databases will be available for diagnostic support and standardization. Large image repositories will enhance research. Based on new biomarkers ("pathomics"), a new golden age of tissue-based research is likely. Pathologists will be more connected to each other as telepathology will improve ways to work collaboratively. They will also be communicating more with their patients. These changes also have the potential to address many currently unmet diagnostic needs. There is considerable demand for diagnostic services in developing countries that do not have sufficient numbers of pathologists and very little subspecialization. With telepathology plus automation of some diagnostic tasks, many gaps in service can be closed, even with a stagnating professional workforce.

In summary, major changes are underway and pathology will likely get even more exciting. Machines will take over some functions from pathologists but will also enable them to extract more information. The changes will introduce new workflows and entirely new capabilities. Wide-ranging effects for other specialties and for education and research can be expected.

Acknowledgments Support for the writing of this chapter was provided by the EMPAIA project, which is funded by the German Federal Ministry for Economic Affairs and Climate Action (BMWK) under FKZ 01MK20002A. The author declares no conflicts of interest.

References

Abels, E., Pantanowitz, L., Aeffner, F., Zarella, M. D., van der Laak, J., Bui, M. M., Vemuri, V. N., Parwani, A. V., Gibbs, J., Agosto-Arroyo, E., Beck, A. H., & Kozlowski, C. (2019). Computational pathology definitions, best practices, and recommendations for regulatory guidance: A white paper from the Digital Pathology Association. *The Journal of Pathology, 249*(3), 286–294. https://doi.org/10.1002/path.5331

Ancker, J. S., Edwards, A., Nosal, S., Hauser, D., Mauer, E., Kaushal, R., & HITEC Investigators. (2017). Effects of workload, work complexity, and repeated alerts on alert fatigue in a clinical decision support system. *BMC Medical Informatics and Decision Making, 17*(1), 36. https://doi.org/10.1186/s12911-017-0430-8

Araújo, A. L. D., do Amaral-Silva, G. K., Pérez-de-Oliveira, M. E., Gallagher, K. P. D., López de Cáceres, C. V. B., Roza, A. L. O. C., Leite, A. A., Mariz, B. A. L. A., Rodrigues-Fernandes, C. I., Fonseca, F. P., Lopes, M. A., Speight, P. M., Khurram, S. A., Júnior, J. J., Martins, M. D., de Almeida, O. P., Santos-Silva, A. R., & Vargas, P. A. (2021). Fully digital pathology laboratory routine and remote reporting of oral and maxillofacial diagnosis during the COVID-19 pandemic: A validation study. *Virchows Archiv: An International Journal of Pathology, 479*(3), 585–595. https://doi.org/10.1007/s00428-021-03075-9

Asa, S. L., & Evans, A. (2020). Issues to consider when implementing digital pathology for primary diagnosis. *Archives of Pathology and Laboratory Medicine, 144*(11), 1297. https://doi.org/10.5858/arpa.2020-0168-LE

Azam, A. S., Miligy, I. M., Kimani, P. K.-U., Maqbool, H., Hewitt, K., Rajpoot, N. M., & Snead, D. R. J. (2021). Diagnostic concordance and discordance in digital pathology: A systematic review and meta-analysis. *Journal of Clinical Pathology, 74*(7), 448–455. https://doi.org/10.1136/jclinpath-2020-206764

Baidoshvili, A., Bucur, A., van Leeuwen, J., van der Laak, J., Kluin, P., & van Diest, P. J. (2018). Evaluating the benefits of digital pathology implementation: Time savings in laboratory logistics. *Histopathology, 73*(5), 784–794. https://doi.org/10.1111/his.13691

Barisoni, L., & Hodgin, J. B. (2017). Digital pathology in nephrology clinical trials, research, and pathology practice. *Current Opinion in Nephrology and Hypertension, 26*(6), 450–459. https://doi.org/10.1097/MNH.0000000000000360

Baron, J. M., Huang, R., McEvoy, D., & Dighe, A. S. (2021). Use of machine learning to predict clinical decision support compliance, reduce alert burden, and evaluate duplicate laboratory test ordering alerts. *JAMIA Open, 4*(1), ooab 006. https://doi.org/10.1093/jamiaopen/ooab006

Bertram, C. A., & Klopfleisch, R. (2017). The pathologist 2.0: An update on digital pathology in veterinary medicine. *Veterinary Pathology, 54*(5), 756–766. https://doi.org/10.1177/0300985817709888

Bonert, M., Zafar, U., Maung, R., El-Shinnawy, I., Kak, I., Cutz, J.-C., Naqvi, A., Juergens, R. A., Finley, C., Salama, S., Major, P., & Kapoor, A. (2021). Evolution of anatomic pathology workload from 2011 to 2019 assessed in a regional hospital laboratory via 574,093 pathology reports. *PLoS One, 16*(6), e0253876. https://doi.org/10.1371/journal.pone.0253876

Booth, A. L., Katz, M. S., Misialek, M. J., Allen, T. C., & Joseph, L. (2019). "Please help me see the dragon I am slaying": Implementation of a novel patient-pathologist consultation program and survey of patient experience. *Archives of Pathology and Laboratory Medicine, 143*(7), 852–858. https://doi.org/10.5858/arpa.2018-0379-OA

Borowsky, A., Glassy, E., Wallace, W., Kallichanda, N., Behling, C., Miller, D. V., Oswal, H. N., Feddersen, R., Bakhtar, O. R., Mendoza, A. E., Molden, D., Saffer, H. L., Wixom, C. R., Albro, J. E., Cessna, M. H., Hall, B. J., Lloyd, I. E., Bishop, J., Darrow, M. A., et al. (2020). Digital whole slide imaging compared with light microscopy for primary diagnosis in surgical pathology: A multicenter, double-blinded, randomized study of 2045 cases. *Archives of Pathology and Laboratory Medicine, 144*(10), 1245–1253. https://doi.org/10.5858/arpa.2019-0569-OA

Brown, P. J., Fews, D., & Bell, N. J. (2016). Teaching veterinary histopathology: A comparison of microscopy and digital slides. *Journal of Veterinary Medical Education, 43*(1), 13–20. https://doi.org/10.3138/jvme.0315-035R1

Browning, L., Fryer, E., Roskell, D., White, K., Colling, R., Rittscher, J., & Verrill, C. (2021). Role of digital pathology in diagnostic histopathology in the response to COVID-19: Results from a survey of experience in a UK tertiary referral hospital. *Journal of Clinical Pathology, 74*(2), 129–132. https://doi.org/10.1136/jclinpath-2020-206786

Bychkov, D., Linder, N., Turkki, R., Nordling, S., Kovanen, P. E., Verrill, C., Walliander, M., Lundin, M., Haglund, C., & Lundin, J. (2018). Deep learning based tissue analysis predicts outcome in colorectal cancer. *Scientific Reports, 8*(1), 3395. https://doi.org/10.1038/s41598-018-21758-3

Chatrian, A., Colling, R. T., Browning, L., Alham, N. K., Sirinukunwattana, K., Malacrino, S., Haghighat, M., Aberdeen, A., Monks, A., Moxley-Wyles, B., Rakha, E., Snead, D. R. J., Rittscher, J., & Verrill, C. (2021). Artificial intelligence for advance requesting of immunohistochemistry in diagnostically uncertain prostate biopsies. *Modern Pathology, 34*, 1780–1794. https://doi.org/10.1038/s41379-021-00826-6

Chen, Y., Zee, J., Smith, A., Jayapandian, C., Hodgin, J., Howell, D., Palmer, M., Thomas, D., Cassol, C., Farris, A. B., Perkinson, K., Madabhushi, A., Barisoni, L., & Janowczyk, A. (2021). Assessment of a computerized quantitative quality control tool for whole slide images of kidney biopsies. *The Journal of Pathology, 253*(3), 268–278. https://doi.org/10.1002/path.5590

Chong, T., Palma-Diaz, M. F., Fisher, C., Gui, D., Ostrzega, N. L., Sempa, G., Sisk, A. E., Valasek, M., Wang, B. Y., Zuckerman, J., Khacherian, C., Binder, S., & Wallace, W. D. (2019). The California telepathology service: UCLA's experience in deploying a regional digital pathology subspecialty consultation network. *Journal of Pathology Informatics, 10*, 31. https://doi.org/10.4103/jpi.jpi_22_19

Clunie, D. A. (2021). DICOM format and protocol standardization: A core requirement for digital pathology success. *Toxicologic Pathology, 49*(4), 738–749. https://doi.org/10.1177/0192623320965893

Colgan, T. J., & Geldenhuys, L. (2012). The practice of pathology in Canada: Decreasing pathologist supply and uncertain outcomes. *Archives of Pathology and Laboratory Medicine, 136*(1), 90–94. https://doi.org/10.5858/arpa.2011-0188-OA

Conant, J. L., Gibson, P. C., Bunn, J., & Ambaye, A. B. (2017). Transition to subspecialty sign-out at an academic institution and its advantages. *Academic Pathology, 4*, 2374289517714767. https://doi.org/10.1177/2374289517714767

Cornish, T. C., Swapp, R. E., & Kaplan, K. J. (2012). Whole-slide imaging: Routine pathologic diagnosis. *Advances in Anatomic Pathology, 19*(3), 152–159. https://doi.org/10.1097/PAP.0b013e318253459e

Coudray, N., Ocampo, P. S., Sakellaropoulos, T., Narula, N., Snuderl, M., Fenyö, D., Moreira, A. L., Razavian, N., & Tsirigos, A. (2018). Classification and mutation prediction from non-small cell lung cancer histopathology images using deep learning. *Nature Medicine, 24*(10), 1559–1567. https://doi.org/10.1038/s41591-018-0177-5

Dash, R. C., Jones, N., Merrick, R., Haroske, G., Harrison, J., Sayers, C., Haarselhorst, N., Wintell, M., Herrmann, M. D., & Macary, F. (2021). Integrating the health-care enterprise pathology and laboratory medicine guideline for digital pathology interoperability. *Journal of Pathology Informatics, 12*(1), 16. https://doi.org/10.4103/jpi.jpi_98_20

de Haan, K., Zhang, Y., Zuckerman, J. E., Liu, T., Sisk, A. E., Diaz, M. F. P., Jen, K.-Y., Nobori, A., Liou, S., Zhang, S., Riahi, R., Rivenson, Y., Wallace, W. D., & Ozcan, A. (2021). Deep learning-based transformation of H&E stained tissues into special stains. *Nature Communications, 12*(1), 4884. https://doi.org/10.1038/s41467-021-25221-2

Deeken, A. H., Mukhopadhyay, S., & Jiang, X. (2020). Social media in academics and research: 21st-century tools to turbocharge education, collaboration, and dissemination of research findings. *Histopathology, 77*(5), 688–699. https://doi.org/10.1111/his.14196

Dietz, R. L., Hartman, D. J., & Pantanowitz, L. (2020). Systematic review of the use of telepathology during intraoperative consultation. *American Journal of Clinical Pathology, 153*(2), 198–209. https://doi.org/10.1093/ajcp/aqz155

Echle, A., Rindtorff, N. T., Brinker, T. J., Luedde, T., Pearson, A. T., & Kather, J. N. (2021). Deep learning in cancer pathology: A new generation of clinical biomarkers. *British Journal of Cancer, 124*(4), 686–696. https://doi.org/10.1038/s41416-020-01122-x

El Hussein, S., Lyapichev, K. A., Crane, G. M., Mirza, K. M., Pemmaraju, N., Medeiros, L. J., Khoury, J. D., & Loghavi, S. (2020). Social media for hematopathologists: Medical practice reinvented-#Hemepath. *Current Hematologic Malignancy Reports, 15*(5), 383–390. https://doi.org/10.1007/s11899-020-00600-6

El Hussein, S., Khoury, J. D., Lyapichev, K. A., Tashakori, M., Khanlari, M., Miranda, R. N., Kanagal-Shamanna, R., Wang, S. A., Ahmed, A., Mirza, K. M., Crane, G. M., Medeiros, L. J., & Loghavi, S. (2021). Next-generation scholarship: Rebranding hematopathology using Twitter: The MD Anderson experience. *Modern Pathology, 34*(5), 854–861. https://doi.org/10.1038/s41379-020-00715-4

Eloy, C., Zerbe, N., & Fraggetta, F. (2021). Europe unites for the digital transformation of pathology: The role of the new ESDIP. *Journal of Pathology Informatics, 12*(1), 10. https://doi.org/10.4103/jpi.jpi_80_20

Evans, A. J., Chetty, R., Clarke, B. A., Croul, S., Ghazarian, D. M., Kiehl, T.-R., Perez Ordonez, B., Ilaalagan, S., & Asa, S. L. (2009). Primary frozen section diagnosis by robotic microscopy and virtual slide telepathology: The University Health Network experience. *Human Pathology, 40*(8), 1070–1081. https://doi.org/10.1016/j.humpath.2009.04.012

Evans, A. J., Bauer, T. W., Bui, M. M., Cornish, T. C., Duncan, H., Glassy, E. F., Hipp, J., McGee, R. S., Murphy, D., Myers, C., O'Neill, D. G., Parwani, A. V., Rampy, B. A., Salama, M. E., & Pantanowitz, L. (2018). US Food and Drug Administration approval of whole slide imaging for primary diagnosis: A key milestone is reached and new questions are raised. *Archives of Pathology and Laboratory Medicine, 142*(11), 1383–1387. https://doi.org/10.5858/arpa.2017-0496-CP

Evans, A. J., Depeiza, N., Allen, S.-G., Fraser, K., Shirley, S., & Chetty, R. (2021). Use of whole slide imaging (WSI) for distance teaching. *Journal of Clinical Pathology, 74*(7), 425–428. https://doi.org/10.1136/jclinpath-2020-206763

Farahani, N., Parwani, A. V., & Pantanowitz, L. (2015). Whole slide imaging in pathology: Advantages, limitations, and emerging perspectives. *Pathology and Laboratory Medicine International, 7*, 23–33. https://doi.org/10.2147/PLMI.S59826

Gatter, K. C., Alcock, C., Heryet, A., & Mason, D. Y. (1985). Clinical importance of analysing malignant tumours of uncertain origin with immunohistological techniques. *Lancet, 1*(8441), 1302–1305. https://doi.org/10.1016/s0140-6736(85)92794-1

Glines, K. R., Haidari, W., Ramani, L., Akkurt, Z. M., & Feldman, S. R. (2020). Digital future of dermatology. *Dermatology Online Journal, 26*(10), 13030/qt75p7q57j.

Halaweish, I., & Alam, H. B. (2015). Changing demographics of the American population. *The Surgical Clinics of North America, 95*(1), 1–10. https://doi.org/10.1016/j.suc.2014.09.002

Hamilton, P. W., Bankhead, P., Wang, Y., Hutchinson, R., Kieran, D., McArt, D. G., James, J., & Salto-Tellez, M. (2014). Digital pathology and image analysis in tissue biomarker research. *Methods (San Diego, Calif.), 70*(1), 59–73. https://doi.org/10.1016/j.ymeth.2014.06.015

Hanna, M. G., Reuter, V. E., Hameed, M. R., Tan, L. K., Chiang, S., Sigel, C., Hollmann, T., Giri, D., Samboy, J., Moradel, C., Rosado, A., Otilano, J. R., England, C., Corsale, L., Stamelos, E., Yagi, Y., Schüffler, P. J., Fuchs, T., Klimstra, D. S., & Sirintrapun, S. J. (2019a). Whole slide imaging equivalency and efficiency study: Experience at a large academic center. *Modern Pathology, 32*(7), 916–928. https://doi.org/10.1038/s41379-019-0205-0

Hanna, M. G., Reuter, V. E., Samboy, J., England, C., Corsale, L., Fine, S. W., Agaram, N. P., Stamelos, E., Yagi, Y., Hameed, M., Klimstra, D. S., & Sirintrapun, S. J. (2019b). Implementation of digital pathology offers clinical and operational increase in efficiency and cost savings. *Archives of Pathology and Laboratory Medicine, 143*(12), 1545–1555. https://doi.org/10.5858/arpa.2018-0514-OA

Hanna, M. G., Reuter, V. E., Ardon, O., Kim, D., Sirintrapun, S. J., Schüffler, P. J., Busam, K. J., Sauter, J. L., Brogi, E., Tan, L. K., Xu, B., Bale, T., Agaram, N. P., Tang, L. H., Ellenson, L. H., Philip, J., Corsale, L., Stamelos, E., Friedlander, M. A., et al. (2020). Validation of a digital pathology system including remote review during the COVID-19 pandemic. *Modern Pathology, 33*(11), 2115–2127. https://doi.org/10.1038/s41379-020-0601-5

Hassell, L. A., & Afzal, A. (2021). Flattening the world of pathology education and training and shortening the curve of pathology learning. *American Journal of Clinical Pathology, 156*(2), 176–184. https://doi.org/10.1093/ajcp/aqab034

Hassell, L. A., Peterson, J., & Pantanowitz, L. (2021). Pushed across the digital divide: COVID-19 accelerated pathology training onto a new digital learning curve. *Academic Pathology, 8*, 2374289521994240. https://doi.org/10.1177/2374289521994240

Hegde, N., Hipp, J. D., Liu, Y., Emmert-Buck, M., Reif, E., Smilkov, D., Terry, M., Cai, C. J., Amin, M. B., Mermel, C. H., Nelson, P. Q., Peng, L. H., Corrado, G. S., & Stumpe, M. C. (2019). Similar image search for histopathology: SMILY. *NPJ Digital Medicine, 2*, 56. https://doi.org/10.1038/s41746-019-0131-z

Herrmann, M. D., Clunie, D. A., Fedorov, A., Doyle, S. W., Pieper, S., Klepeis, V., Le, L. P., Mutter, G. L., Milstone, D. S., Schultz, T. J., Kikinis, R., Kotecha, G. K., Hwang, D. H., Andriole, K. P., Iafrate, A. J., Brink, J. A., Boland, G. W., Dreyer, K. J., Michalski, M., et al. (2018). Implementing the DICOM standard for digital pathology. *Journal of Pathology Informatics, 9*, 37. https://doi.org/10.4103/jpi.jpi_42_18

Hipp, J. D., Fernandez, A., Compton, C. C., & Balis, U. J. (2011). Why a pathology image should not be considered as a radiology image. *Journal of Pathology Informatics, 2*, 26. https://doi.org/10.4103/2153-3539.82051

Holzinger, A., Langs, G., Denk, H., Zatloukal, K., & Müller, H. (2019). Causability and explainability of artificial intelligence in medicine. *Wiley Interdisciplinary Reviews. Data Mining and Knowledge Discovery, 9*(4), e1312. https://doi.org/10.1002/widm.1312

Homeyer, A., Lotz, J., Schwen, L. O., Weiss, N., Romberg, D., Höfener, H., Zerbe, N., & Hufnagl, P. (2021). Artificial intelligence in pathology: From prototype to product. *Journal of Pathology Informatics, 12*, 13. https://doi.org/10.4103/jpi.jpi_84_20

Horbinski, C., Fine, J. L., Medina-Flores, R., Yagi, Y., & Wiley, C. A. (2007). Telepathology for intraoperative neuropathologic consultations at an academic medical center: A 5-year report. *Journal of Neuropathology and Experimental Neurology, 66*(8), 750–759. https://doi.org/10.1097/nen.0b013e318126c179

Jahn, S. W., Plass, M., & Moinfar, F. (2020). Digital pathology: Advantages, limitations and emerging perspectives. *Journal of Clinical Medicine, 9*(11), E3697. https://doi.org/10.3390/jcm9113697

Janowczyk, A., Zuo, R., Gilmore, H., Feldman, M., & Madabhushi, A. (2019). HistoQC: An open-source quality control tool for digital pathology slides. *JCO Clinical Cancer Informatics, 3*, 1–7. https://doi.org/10.1200/CCI.18.00157

Jones, J. L., Oien, K. A., Lee, J. L., & Salto-Tellez, M. (2017). Morphomolecular pathology: Setting the framework for a new generation of pathologists. *British Journal of Cancer, 117*(11), 1581–1582. https://doi.org/10.1038/bjc.2017.340

Jones-Hall, Y. L., Skelton, J. M., & Adams, L. G. (2021). Implementing digital pathology into veterinary academics and research. *Journal of Veterinary Medical Education*, e20210068. doi:https://doi.org/10.3138/jvme-2021-0068

Jug, R., Booth, A. L., Buckley, A. F., Newell, J., Kesterson, J., Gardner, J. M., Ozcan, L., Liu, B., Green, C. L., Joseph, L., & Cummings, T. J. (2021). Multisite quality improvement study of a patient-pathologist consultation program. *American Journal of Clinical Pathology, 155*(6), 887–894. https://doi.org/10.1093/ajcp/aqaa202

Kacew, A. J., Strohbehn, G. W., Saulsberry, L., Laiteerapong, N., Cipriani, N. A., Kather, J. N., & Pearson, A. T. (2021). Artificial intelligence can cut costs while maintaining accuracy in colorectal cancer genotyping. *Frontiers in Oncology, 11*, 630953. https://doi.org/10.3389/fonc.2021.630953

Kalra, S., Tizhoosh, H. R., Choi, C., Shah, S., Diamandis, P., Campbell, C. J. V., & Pantanowitz, L. (2020a). Yottixel—An image search engine for large archives of histopathology whole slide images. *Medical Image Analysis, 65*, 101757. https://doi.org/10.1016/j.media.2020.101757

Kalra, S., Tizhoosh, H. R., Shah, S., Choi, C., Damaskinos, S., Safarpoor, A., Shafiei, S., Babaie, M., Diamandis, P., Campbell, C. J. V., & Pantanowitz, L. (2020b). Pan-cancer diagnostic consensus through searching archival histopathology images using artificial intelligence. *NPJ Digital Medicine, 3*, 31. https://doi.org/10.1038/s41746-020-0238-2

Kather, J. N., Krisam, J., Charoentong, P., Luedde, T., Herpel, E., Weis, C.-A., Gaiser, T., Marx, A., Valous, N. A., Ferber, D., Jansen, L., Reyes-Aldasoro, C. C., Zörnig, I., Jäger, D., Brenner, H., Chang-Claude, J., Hoffmeister, M., & Halama, N. (2019). Predicting survival from colorectal cancer histology slides using deep learning: A retrospective multicenter study. *PLoS Medicine, 16*(1), e1002730. https://doi.org/10.1371/journal.pmed.1002730

Krasowski, M. D., Grieme, C. V., Cassady, B., Dreyer, N. R., Wanat, K. A., Hightower, M., & Nepple, K. G. (2017). Variation in results release and patient portal access to diagnostic test results at an academic medical center. *Journal of Pathology Informatics, 8*, 45. https://doi.org/10.4103/jpi.jpi_53_17

Krause, J., Grabsch, H. I., Kloor, M., Jendrusch, M., Echle, A., Buelow, R. D., Boor, P., Luedde, T., Brinker, T. J., Trautwein, C., Pearson, A. T., Quirke, P., Jenniskens, J., Offermans, K., van den Brandt, P. A., & Kather, J. N. (2021). Deep learning detects genetic alterations in cancer histology generated by adversarial networks. *The Journal of Pathology, 254*(1), 70–79. https://doi.org/10.1002/path.5638

Krupinski, E. A., Comas, M., Gallego, L. G., & GISMAR Group. (2018). A new software platform to improve multidisciplinary tumor board workflows and user satisfaction: A pilot study. *Journal of Pathology Informatics, 9*(1), 26. https://doi.org/10.4103/jpi.jpi_16_18

Lapedis, C. J., Horowitz, J. K., Brown, L., Tolle, B. E., Smith, L. B., & Owens, S. R. (2020). The patient-pathologist consultation program: A mixed-methods study of interest and motivations in cancer patients. *Archives of Pathology and Laboratory Medicine, 144*(4), 490–496. https://doi.org/10.5858/arpa.2019-0105-OA

Levy, B. P., McClintock, D. S., Lee, R. E., Lane, W. J., Klepeis, V. E., Baron, J. M., Onozato, M. L., Kim, J., Brodsky, V., Beckwith, B., Kuo, F., & Gilbertson, J. R. (2012). Different tracks for pathology informatics fellowship training: Experiences of and input from trainees in a large multisite fellowship program. *Journal of Pathology Informatics, 3*, 30. https://doi.org/10.4103/2153-3539.100362

Lilley, C. M., Arnold, C. A., Arnold, M., Booth, A. L., Gardner, J. M., Jiang, X. S., Loghavi, S., & Mirza, K. M. (2021). The implementation and effectiveness of PathElective.com. *Academic Pathology, 8*, 23742895211006828. doi:https://doi.org/10.1177/23742895211006829

Louis, D. N., Gerber, G. K., Baron, J. M., Bry, L., Dighe, A. S., Getz, G., Higgins, J. M., Kuo, F. C., Lane, W. J., Michaelson, J. S., Le, L. P., Mermel, C. H., Gilbertson, J. R., & Golden, J. A. (2014). Computational pathology: An emerging definition. *Archives of Pathology and Laboratory Medicine, 138*(9), 1133–1138. https://doi.org/10.5858/arpa.2014-0034-ED

Lujan, G., Quigley, J. C., Hartman, D., Parwani, A., Roehmholdt, B., Meter, B. V., Ardon, O., Hanna, M. G., Kelly, D., Sowards, C., Montalto, M., Bui, M., Zarella, M. D., LaRosa, V., Slootweg, G., Retamero, J. A., Lloyd, M. C., Madory, J., & Bowman, D. (2021). Dissecting the business case for adoption and implementation of digital pathology: A white paper from the Digital Pathology Association. *Journal of Pathology Informatics, 12*, 17. https://doi.org/10.4103/jpi.jpi_67_20

Lundström, C. F., Gilmore, H. L., & Ros, P. R. (2017). Integrated diagnostics: The computational revolution catalyzing cross-disciplinary practices in radiology, pathology, and genomics. *Radiology, 285*(1), 12–15. https://doi.org/10.1148/radiol.2017170062

Mandelker, D., Lee, R. E., Platt, M. Y., Riedlinger, G., Quinn, A., Rao, L. K. F., Klepeis, V. E., Mahowald, M., Lane, W. J., Beckwith, B. A., Baron, J. M., McClintock, D. S., Kuo, F. C., Lebo, M. S., & Gilbertson, J. R. (2014). Pathology informatics fellowship training: Focus on molecular pathology. *Journal of Pathology Informatics, 5*(1), 11. https://doi.org/10.4103/2153-3539.129444

Marble, H. D., Huang, R., Dudgeon, S. N., Lowe, A., Herrmann, M. D., Blakely, S., Leavitt, M. O., Isaacs, M., Hanna, M. G., Sharma, A., Veetil, J., Goldberg, P., Schmid, J. H., Lasiter, L., Gallas, B. D., Abels, E., & Lennerz, J. K. (2020). A regulatory science initiative to harmonize and standardize digital pathology and machine learning processes to speed up clinical innovation to patients. *Journal of Pathology Informatics, 11*, 22. https://doi.org/10.4103/jpi.jpi_27_20

Märkl, B., Füzesi, L., Huss, R., Bauer, S., & Schaller, T. (2021). Number of pathologists in Germany: Comparison with European countries, USA, and Canada. *Virchows Archiv: An International Journal of Pathology, 478*(2), 335–341. https://doi.org/10.1007/s00428-020-02894-6

Mayerhoefer, M. E., Materka, A., Langs, G., Häggström, I., Szczypiński, P., Gibbs, P., & Cook, G. (2020). Introduction to radiomics. *Journal of Nuclear Medicine, 61*(4), 488–495. https://doi.org/10.2967/jnumed.118.222893

Mea, V. D., Carbone, A., Di Loreto, C., Bueno, G., De Paoli, P., García-Rojo, M., de Mena, D., Gloghini, A., Ilyas, M., Laurinavicius, A., Rasmusson, A., Milione, M., Dolcetti, R., Pagani, M., Stoppini, A., Sulfaro, S., Bartolo, M., Mazzon, E., Soyer, H. P., & Pantanowitz, L. (2017). Teaching digital pathology: The International School of Digital Pathology and proposed syllabus. *Journal of Pathology Informatics, 8*, 27. https://doi.org/10.4103/jpi.jpi_17_17

Metter, D. M., Colgan, T. J., Leung, S. T., Timmons, C. F., & Park, J. Y. (2019). Trends in the US and Canadian pathologist workforces from 2007 to 2017. *JAMA Network Open, 2*(5), e194337. https://doi.org/10.1001/jamanetworkopen.2019.4337

Miao, R., Toth, R., Zhou, Y., Madabhushi, A., & Janowczyk, A. (2021). Quick Annotator: An open-source digital pathology based rapid image annotation tool. *ArXiv:2101.02183*. http://arxiv.org/abs/2101.02183

Montalto, M. C. (2008). Pathology RE-imagined: The history of digital radiology and the future of anatomic pathology. *Archives of Pathology and Laboratory Medicine, 132*(5), 764–765. https://doi.org/10.5858/2008-132-764-PRTHOD

Moulin, P., Grünberg, K., Barale-Thomas, E., der Laak, J., & van. (2021). IMI-Bigpicture: A central repository for digital pathology. *Toxicologic Pathology, 49*(4), 711–713. https://doi.org/10.1177/0192623321989644

Mroz, P., Parwani, A. V., & Kulesza, P. (2013). Central pathology review for phase III clinical trials: The enabling effect of virtual microscopy. *Archives of Pathology and Laboratory Medicine, 137*(4), 492–495. https://doi.org/10.5858/arpa.2012-0093-RA

Mukhopadhyay, S., Feldman, M. D., Abels, E., Ashfaq, R., Beltaifa, S., Cacciabeve, N. G., Cathro, H. P., Cheng, L., Cooper, K., Dickey, G. E., Gill, R. M., Heaton, R. P., Kerstens, R., Lindberg, G. M., Malhotra, R. K., Mandell, J. W., Manlucu, E. D., Mills, A. M., Mills, S. E., et al. (2018). Whole slide imaging versus microscopy for primary diagnosis in surgical pathology: A multicenter blinded randomized noninferiority study of 1992 cases (pivotal study). *The American Journal of Surgical Pathology, 42*(1), 39–52. https://doi.org/10.1097/PAS.0000000000000948

Mukhopadhyay, S., Kanakis, C., Golab, K., Hermelin, D., Crane, G. M., & Mirza, K. M. (2021). The network that never sleeps. *Laboratory Medicine, 52*(4), e83–e103. https://doi.org/10.1093/labmed/lmaa113

Mun, S. K., Wong, K. H., Lo, S.-C. B., Li, Y., & Bayarsaikhan, S. (2020). Artificial intelligence for the future radiology diagnostic service. *Frontiers in Molecular Biosciences, 7*, 614258. https://doi.org/10.3389/fmolb.2020.614258

Naugler, C., & Church, D. L. (2019). Automation and artificial intelligence in the clinical laboratory. *Critical Reviews in Clinical Laboratory Sciences, 56*(2), 98–110. https://doi.org/10.1080/10408363.2018.1561640

Ohori, N. P., Radkay, L. A., Macpherson, T. A., Yousem, S. A., & Schoedel, K. E. (2016). Changes in resident graduate characteristics in a large pathology training program, 1994 to 2013. *Academic Pathology, 3*, 2374289516643543. https://doi.org/10.1177/2374289516643543

Ordi, O., Bombí, J. A., Martínez, A., Ramírez, J., Alòs, L., Saco, A., Ribalta, T., Fernández, P. L., Campo, E., & Ordi, J. (2015). Virtual microscopy in the undergraduate teaching of pathology. *Journal of Pathology Informatics, 6*, 1. https://doi.org/10.4103/2153-3539.150246

Pantanowitz, L., Sharma, A., Carter, A. B., Kurc, T., Sussman, A., & Saltz, J. (2018). Twenty years of digital pathology: An overview of the road travelled, what is on the horizon, and the emergence of vendor-neutral archives. *Journal of Pathology Informatics, 9*, 40. https://doi.org/10.4103/jpi.jpi_69_18

Parasuraman, R., & Riley, V. (1997). Humans and automation: Use, misuse, disuse, abuse. *Human Factors, 39*(2), 230–253. https://doi.org/10.1518/001872097778543886

Patel, R., Hoppman, N. L., Gosse, C. M., Hagen-Moe, D. J., Dunemann, S. K., Kreuter, J. D., Preuss, S. A., Winters, J. L., Sturgis, C. D., Maleszewski, J. J., Solanki, M. H., Pritt, B. S., Rivera, M., Mairose, A. M., Nelsen, M. A., Hansing, K. L., Lehman, S. M., Gruhlke, R. C., & Boland, J. M. (2021). Laboratory medicine and pathology education during the COVID-19 Pandemic—Lessons learned. *Academic Pathology, 8*, 23742895211020490. https://doi.org/10.1177/23742895211020487

Patterson, E. S., Rayo, M., Gill, C., & Gurcan, M. N. (2011). Barriers and facilitators to adoption of soft copy interpretation from the user perspective: Lessons learned from filmless radiology for slideless pathology. *Journal of Pathology Informatics, 2*, 1. https://doi.org/10.4103/2153-3539.74940

Pell, R., Oien, K., Robinson, M., Pitman, H., Rajpoot, N., Rittscher, J., Snead, D., Verrill, C., & UK National Cancer Research Institute (NCRI) Cellular-Molecular Pathology (CM-Path) Quality Assurance Working Group. (2019). The use of digital pathology and image analysis in clinical trials. *The Journal of Pathology. Clinical Research, 5*(2), 81–90. https://doi.org/10.1002/cjp2.127

Quinn, A. M., Klepeis, V. E., Mandelker, D. L., Platt, M. Y., Rao, L. K. F., Riedlinger, G., Baron, J. M., Brodsky, V., Kim, J. Y., Lane, W., Lee, R. E., Levy, B. P., McClintock, D. S., Beckwith, B. A., Kuo, F. C., & Gilbertson, J. R. (2014). The ongoing evolution of the core curriculum of a clinical fellowship in pathology informatics. *Journal of Pathology Informatics, 5*(1), 22. https://doi.org/10.4103/2153-3539.137717

Retamero, J. A., Aneiros-Fernandez, J., & Del Moral, R. G. (2020). Complete digital pathology for routine histopathology diagnosis in a multicenter hospital network. *Archives of Pathology and Laboratory Medicine, 144*(2), 221–228. https://doi.org/10.5858/arpa.2018-0541-OA

Ribback, S., Flessa, S., Gromoll-Bergmann, K., Evert, M., & Dombrowski, F. (2014). Virtual slide telepathology with scanner systems for intraoperative frozen-section consultation. *Pathology, Research and Practice, 210*(6), 377–382. https://doi.org/10.1016/j.prp.2014.02.007

Robboy, S. J., Weintraub, S., Horvath, A. E., Jensen, B. W., Alexander, C. B., Fody, E. P., Crawford, J. M., Clark, J. R., Cantor-Weinberg, J., Joshi, M. G., Cohen, M. B., Prystowsky, M. B., Bean, S. M., Gupta, S., Powell, S. Z., Speights, V. O., Gross, D. J., & Black-Schaffer, W. S. (2013). Pathologist workforce in the United States: I. Development of a predictive model to examine factors influencing supply. *Archives of Pathology and Laboratory Medicine, 137*(12), 1723–1732. https://doi.org/10.5858/arpa.2013-0200-OA

Rodrigues-Fernandes, C. I., Speight, P. M., Khurram, S. A., Araújo, A. L. D., da Perez, D. E. C., Fonseca, F. P., Lopes, M. A., de Almeida, O. P., Vargas, P. A., & Santos-Silva, A. R. (2020). The use of digital microscopy as a teaching method for human pathology: A systematic review. *Virchows Archiv, 477*(4), 475–486. https://doi.org/10.1007/s00428-020-02908-3

Rosenbaum, J. N., Berry, A. B., Church, A. J., Crooks, K., Gagan, J. R., López-Terrada, D., Pfeifer, J. D., Rennert, H., Schrijver, I., Snow, A. N., Wu, D., & Ewalt, M. D. (2021). A curriculum for genomic education of molecular genetic pathology fellows: A report of the Association for Molecular Pathology Training and Education Committee. *The Journal of Molecular Diagnostics, 23*(10), 1218–1240. https://doi.org/10.1016/j.jmoldx.2021.07.001

Royal College of Pathologists. (2021). *Digital pathology.* https://www.rcpath.org/profession/digital-pathology.html

Saco, A., Bombi, J. A., Garcia, A., Ramírez, J., & Ordi, J. (2016). Current status of whole-slide imaging in education. *Pathobiology: Journal of Immunopathology, Molecular and Cellular Biology, 83*(2–3), 79–88. https://doi.org/10.1159/000442391

Saltz, J., Almeida, J., Gao, Y., Sharma, A., Bremer, E., DiPrima, T., Saltz, M., Kalpathy-Cramer, J., & Kurc, T. (2017). Towards generation, management, and exploration of combined radiomics and pathomics datasets for cancer research. *AMIA Joint Summits on Translational Science Proceedings. AMIA Joint Summits on Translational Science Proceedings, 2017,* 85–94.

Sarewitz, S. J. (2014). Subspecialization in community pathology practice. *Archives of Pathology and Laboratory Medicine, 138*(7), 871–872. https://doi.org/10.5858/arpa.2014-0084-ED

Sarwar, S., Dent, A., Faust, K., Richer, M., Djuric, U., Van Ommeren, R., & Diamandis, P. (2019). Physician perspectives on integration of artificial intelligence into diagnostic pathology. *NPJ Digital Medicine, 2,* 28. https://doi.org/10.1038/s41746-019-0106-0

Schaumberg, A. J., Juarez-Nicanor, W. C., Choudhury, S. J., Pastrián, L. G., Pritt, B. S., Prieto Pozuelo, M., Sotillo Sánchez, R., Ho, K., Zahra, N., Sener, B. D., Yip, S., Xu, B., Annavarapu, S. R., Morini, A., Jones, K. A., Rosado-Orozco, K., Mukhopadhyay, S., Miguel, C., Yang, H., et al. (2020). Interpretable multimodal deep learning for real-time pan-tissue pan-disease pathology search on social media. *Modern Pathology: An Official Journal of the United States and Canadian Academy of Pathology, Inc, 33*(11), 2169–2185. https://doi.org/10.1038/s41379-020-0540-1

Schüffler, P. J., Geneslaw, L., Yarlagadda, D. V. K., Hanna, M. G., Samboy, J., Stamelos, E., Vanderbilt, C., Philip, J., Jean, M.-H., Corsale, L., Manzo, A., Paramasivam, N. H. G., Ziegler, J. S., Gao, J., Perin, J. C., Kim, Y. S., Bhanot, U. K., Roehrl, M. H. A., Ardon, O., et al. (2021). Integrated digital pathology at scale: A solution for clinical diagnostics and cancer research at a large academic medical center. *Journal of the American Medical Informatics Association,* ocab085. doi:https://doi.org/10.1093/jamia/ocab085

Shachar, E., Hasson, S. P., Fayngor, R., Wolf, I., & Hershkovitz, D. (2021). Pathology consultation clinic for patients with cancer: Meeting the clinician behind the microscope. *JCO Oncology Practice, 17*(10), e1559–e1566. https://doi.org/10.1200/OP.20.00948

Snead, D. R. J., Tsang, Y.-W., Meskiri, A., Kimani, P. K., Crossman, R., Rajpoot, N. M., Blessing, E., Chen, K., Gopalakrishnan, K., Matthews, P., Momtahan, N., Read-Jones, S., Sah, S., Simmons, E., Sinha, B., Suortamo, S., Yeo, Y., El Daly, H., & Cree, I. A. (2016). Validation of digital pathology imaging for primary histopathological diagnosis. *Histopathology, 68*(7), 1063–1072. https://doi.org/10.1111/his.12879

Stathonikos, N., van Varsseveld, N. C., Vink, A., van Dijk, M. R., Nguyen, T. Q., de Leng, W. W. J., Lacle, M. M., Goldschmeding, R., Vreuls, C. P. H., & van Diest, P. J. (2020). Digital pathology in the time of Corona. *Journal of Clinical Pathology, 73*(11), 706–712. https://doi.org/10.1136/jclinpath-2020-206845

Taylor, C. R. (1986). *Immunomicroscopy: A diagnostic tool for the surgical pathologist.* W. B. Saunders.

Tosun, A. B., Pullara, F., Becich, M. J., Taylor, D. L., Fine, J. L., & Chennubhotla, S. C. (2020). Explainable AI (xAI) for Anatomic Pathology. *Advances in Anatomic Pathology, 27*(4), 241–250. https://doi.org/10.1097/PAP.0000000000000264

Turner, O. C., Aeffner, F., Bangari, D. S., High, W., Knight, B., Forest, T., Cossic, B., Himmel, L. E., Rudmann, D. G., Bawa, B., Muthuswamy, A., Aina, O. H., Edmondson, E. F., Saravanan, C., Brown, D. L., Sing, T., & Sebastian, M. M. (2020). Society of Toxicologic Pathology Digital Pathology and Image Analysis Special Interest Group article: Opinion on the application of artificial intelligence and machine learning to digital toxicologic pathology. *Toxicologic Pathology, 48*(2), 277–294. https://doi.org/10.1177/0192623319881401

van den Tweel, J. G., & Taylor, C. R. (2010). A brief history of pathology: Preface to a forthcoming series that highlights milestones in the evolution of pathology as a discipline. *Virchows Archiv: An International Journal of Pathology, 457*(1), 3–10. https://doi.org/10.1007/s00428-010-0934-4

Volynskaya, Z., Chow, H., Evans, A., Wolff, A., Lagmay-Traya, C., & Asa, S. L. (2018). Integrated pathology informatics enables high-quality personalized and precision medicine: Digital pathology and beyond. *Archives of Pathology and Laboratory Medicine, 142*(3), 369–382. https://doi.org/10.5858/arpa.2017-0139-OA

Warth, A., Stenzinger, A., Andrulis, M., Schlake, W., Kempny, G., Schirmacher, P., & Weichert, W. (2016). Individualized medicine and demographic change as determining workload factors in pathology: Quo vadis? *Virchows Archiv: An International Journal of Pathology, 468*(1), 101–108. https://doi.org/10.1007/s00428-015-1869-6

Wei, B.-R., & Simpson, R. M. (2014). Digital pathology and image analysis augment biospecimen annotation and biobank quality assurance harmonization. *Clinical Biochemistry, 47*(4–5), 274–279. https://doi.org/10.1016/j.clinbiochem.2013.12.008

Weinstein, R. S. (1986). Prospects for telepathology. *Human Pathology, 17*(5), 433–434. https://doi.org/10.1016/s0046-8177(86)80028-4

Williams, B. J., Bottoms, D., Clark, D., & Treanor, D. (2019). Future-proofing pathology part 2: Building a business case for digital pathology. *Journal of Clinical Pathology, 72*(3), 198–205. https://doi.org/10.1136/jclinpath-2017-204926

Williams, B. J., Fraggetta, F., Hanna, M. G., Huang, R., Lennerz, J., Salgado, R., Sirintrapun, S. J., Pantanowitz, L., Parwani, A., Zarella, M., & Treanor, D. E. (2020). The future of pathology: What can we learn from the COVID-19 pandemic? *Journal of Pathology Informatics, 11*, 15. https://doi.org/10.4103/jpi.jpi_29_20

Wright, A. I., Clarke, E. L., Dunn, C. M., Williams, B. J., Treanor, D. E., & Brettle, D. S. (2020). A point-of-use quality assurance tool for digital pathology remote working. *Journal of Pathology Informatics, 11*, 17. https://doi.org/10.4103/jpi.jpi_25_20

Yamashita, R., Long, J., Longacre, T., Peng, L., Berry, G., Martin, B., Higgins, J., Rubin, D. L., & Shen, J. (2021). Deep learning model for the prediction of microsatellite instability in colorectal cancer: A diagnostic study. The Lancet. *Oncology, 22*(1), 132–141. https://doi.org/10.1016/S1470-2045(20)30535-0

Yip, S. S. F., & Aerts, H. J. W. L. (2016). Applications and limitations of radiomics. *Physics in Medicine and Biology, 61*(13), R150–R166. https://doi.org/10.1088/0031-9155/61/13/R150

Zhao, C., Wu, T., Ding, X., Parwani, A. V., Chen, H., McHugh, J., Piccoli, A., Xie, Q., Lauro, G. R., Feng, X., Hartman, D. J., Seethala, R. R., Wu, S., Yousem, S., Liang, Y., & Pantanowitz, L. (2015). International telepathology consultation: Three years of experience between the University of Pittsburgh Medical Center and KingMed Diagnostics in China. *Journal of Pathology Informatics, 6*, 63. https://doi.org/10.4103/2153-3539.170650

Modern Home Care: A Glimpse into the Future of Patient-Centered Healthcare Systems

Horst Kunhardt

Abstract

Today, we already have many technologies that could contribute to a sustainably oriented healthcare system in which patients are at the center of the care processes. Advances in human genome sequencing and personalized therapies for serious diseases, AI-based drug development, robotic surgery, and digital networking are already possible and in use today. What is missing so far is a continuum of care that extends from a person's home, place of work, and outdoor time to the doctor's office, clinic, rehabilitation center, and nursing home. Our current healthcare system is still too fragmented and operates in different sectors that are poorly coordinated. Managed care is a methodical and practical approach that could address this lack of interconnectedness and enable a user- or patient-centered system. The first step toward this is continuity of data from the different settings. This chapter will look at a possible future in which networking and data continuity is already a reality and then, starting from that endpoint, show the milestones reached so far and discuss what is still needed to achieve a patient-centered healthcare system that works proactively.

1 A Glimpse into the Future

The year is 2059 and the author of this chapter has celebrated his 100th birthday. Thanks to a healthy lifestyle, regular checkups, vaccinations, and continuous monitoring of his health data with an AI-based health coach, he has largely been able to maintain his independence into this age. The author's home is equipped

H. Kunhardt (✉)
Deggendorf Institute of Technology, Deggendorf, Germany
e-mail: horst.kunhardt@th-deg.de

with networked sensors that continuously cover all safety, health, well-being, and communication concerns and link to a regional community health hub. The AI-based software of the community health hub generates daily health status forecasts and autonomously makes decisions in the event of an emergency by notifying relatives and emergency services. For this purpose, the author created a digital twin that takes into account current data on weather, indoor climate, nutritional status, movement patterns, and communication behavior and uses this data to predict how the state of health will change. The digital twin-based health and support coach also connects to microservices in the region where the author lives to request specific services from craftspeople, provide mobility services, and coordinate deliveries of products and services via autonomous drones. Some of the author's peers live in neighborhood or multigenerational homes. This means that social contact and support are possible at all times. Autonomous robots in households have been available for years and support residents with various service tasks and concierge services.

The healthcare system of 2059 has been transformed through numerous reforms and legislative changes into a salutogenic system that focuses on keeping citizens healthy. Because the system emphasizes health promotion and disease prevention, chronic diseases have been greatly reduced. This also means that the cost of health-care is lower. Doctors' offices, clinics, nursing homes, therapists, and pharmacies are all networked in a digital health ecosystem. As a result, unnecessary multiple examinations are avoided, medications are automatically checked for interactions, and treatment in the event of an illness is coordinated and optimized across the entire supply chain. Healthcare facilities are needed only for emergencies and serious illnesses. Because of this, the population is optimally supported with the available care facilities. Treatment is guideline-oriented on the basis of evidence-based care. The insurance system for all citizens is now oriented toward providing networked, patient-centered care that produces high-quality results.

To prepare for the patient-centered care system, the health education of the population was expanded and the curricula of all schools, training centers, and universities include health promotion and prevention. Businesses and companies consistently run occupational health management programs and put great emphasis on the health and safety of their employees. Experience with teleworking and videoconferencing during earlier pandemics has shown that mobility has also been reduced to what is necessary. With a socially accepted focus on sustainable production, renewable energies, and well-coordinated regional transport systems in smart cities and smart regions, valuable resources are protected.

Internationally active organizations such as the WHO and other UN agencies and aid organizations have been strengthened and have managed to distribute vaccines and medicines fairly worldwide in the event of pandemics. Technologies such as smart farming and smart factories have been able to optimize the production and equitable distribution of food. Quantum computers are used to automatically optimize global supply chains and align them with globally accepted ethical standards. As a pioneer of these developments, a "European Health Data Space" was established as a reference system starting in 2015. It is able to sustainably implement the results from past research programs in the fields of cybersecurity, AI, quantum computing, big data, the human brain, and robotics.

This is what it could look like in 2059. But let's look at where we are in the present.

2   The Situation in 2020

Most of the technologies described above are already available today. In the context of ambient assisted living, sensor technology was developed in 2000 that is used today in smart homes. These sensor and actuator solutions are used largely to control energy systems, such as heating, water, and air-conditioning. Wearables and mobile solutions in the form of apps in the field of health are very popular and are in great demand. Almost every major provider has smartphones and smartwatches on the market. Smart clothing can also be found, but at present, it is more likely to be used in the sports and fitness sector.

Robotics are widely used in the manufacturing industry. So are robot-assisted operations and autonomous robots in the field of logistics. In the home environment, only vacuum robots with a limited range of functions are available, and robots do not yet provide general household support. In the nursing home environment, specialized robotic solutions could be used as lifting aids. Social robots, such as the seal PARO, or robots modeled on pets are also intended to facilitate contact with residents showing signs of dementia (Hung et al., 2019).

Autonomous drones for the transport of medicines or articles of daily use are still in the testing stage but could provide an important supply service in the future, especially in rural regions.

Telemedicine solutions, such as teleconsultation, video consultation, teleradiology, teletherapy, telepathology, second opinion by video, and so forth, are currently in productive use and can provide support for specialists in the field.

The German healthcare system has been prepared for greater IT availability since 2000. In an international comparison of the degree of digitization in healthcare systems, however, the German healthcare system performs poorly. Essentially, an overall strategy is lacking. One area of focus is the implementation of data protection regulations (Thiel et al., 2018).

The Digital Supply Act (Digitales Versorgungsgesetz) and the Digital Supply-Care Modernization Act (Digitale Versorgung-Pflege Modernisierungsgesetz) of 2021 have paved the way for digital health apps and digital nursing applications. App- or Web-based applications must be approved as a medical device in order to be paid for by health insurance or long-term care insurance. The Federal Institute for Drugs and Medical Devices (Bundesinstitut für Arzneimittel und Medizinprodukte, BfArM) provides a directory for this purpose where patients and medical professionals can locate approved digital health applications that can be prescribed.

Service providers such as clinics, doctors, and pharmacies and, in the future, nursing services, therapists, and pharmacies will be interconnected via a telematics infrastructure (TI). The TI offers secure data communication between service providers and provides patients with a digital health record in which prescriptions and data about treatment are stored. Doctors and patients should decide together which data is stored in the digital health record. The aim is to both strengthen patient sovereignty and reduce redundancies in data storage.

In the Home4.0 research project of the Deggendorf Institute of Technology, which is funded by the Bavarian State Ministry of Health and Care for the period 2018 to 2024, a smart home environment is being developed in the district of Lower Bavaria. The aim of the research project is to find out how homes of people over 65 years of age with an emerging need for assistance and care can remain in their familiar social environment for as long as possible with technological-digital support. To answer the research questions, active and passive sensors will be installed in 100 households over a period of 9 months, data on everyday life will be collected, and AI-based algorithms will be used to detect changes. The goal is to obtain assessments of health and care status before falls or changes in health occur. Another goal is to link the continuously collected data with services in a specific region. A data protection impact assessment, a data protection concept, and an ethics vote are available for the research project as it involves personal data from the private sphere (Home4.0, 2021).

Figure 1 shows the IT structure of the Home4.0 research project.

Sensor data from the everyday lives of study participants are sent to a database at the university's computer center where they are examined using data analysis methods and searched for patterns or anomalies. The aim is to check the validity of the data before machine learning algorithms make predictions about health status. This can be used to build an electronic home health record that contains data from the home environment.

At present, however, digital health records offered by health insurers are not networked with all sectors of the healthcare system. For example, the digital health records that insured persons can use voluntarily contain only data from health insurance and must be maintained and expanded by the insured persons themselves. Currently, there is no automatic networking with data from visits to general practitioners and hospital stays.

To ensure continuity of care from the home environment to the doctor's office to the clinic and, if necessary, to the rehabilitation clinic or nursing home, access to all data from the various sectors and, above all, from the home environment is required. Only then can electronic health records develop their full potential and automatically respond to emergencies, recognize interactions in medication prescriptions, and provide information and advice about health problems.

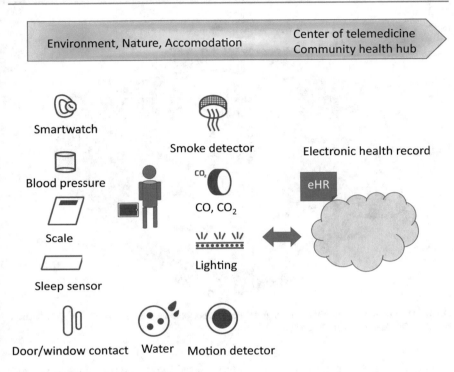

Fig. 1 Data model for the Home4.0 research project

3   What Is Still to Be Done?

Many of the elements of a proactive health system that links vital signs and data from daily life in the home environment with health and disease care data are already available. Smart home solutions, wearables, and health apps are available and already in use.

A 2019 study by the industry association Bitkom on the future of consumer technology indicates that smartwatches and fitness trackers are steadily gaining in popularity. According to the study, approximately one-third of a random sample of 1007 respondents aged 16 and older use smartwatches and fitness trackers (Klöß, 2019).

The number of smartwatch and fitness tracker users declines with age however; only 6% among 1047 respondents aged 18 and older were using them in 2017 (Statista, 2017).

Another issue is a lack of data continuity that links the various levels of health and care delivery in a secured system (see Fig. 2).

While the system of pathogenesis (i.e., the treatment of diseases and care in nursing homes) is strongly regulated by law and is largely evidence based, as in the case of medical devices or recent developments in the field of so-called omics

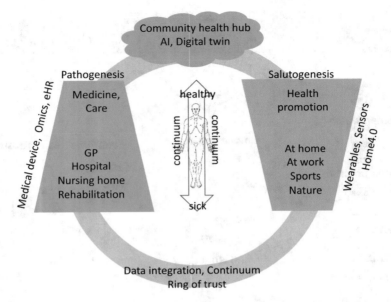

Fig. 2 Data continuity within a ring of trust; EHR: electronic health record. Author's illustration based on Brinkhaus and Esch (2021)

(genomics, proteomics), the field of "salutogenesis" (i.e., health promotion) is less regulated. In the area of salutogenesis, many applications are used in the home environment or in sports that are currently viewed mainly as consumer electronics. These solutions have not been evaluated in systematic, controlled studies.

In Germany, the first developments in the regulation and certification of digital health apps that are prescribed by a doctor have been regulated via the Digital Health Care Act. BfArM tests apps under the Medical Devices Act and grants approval. However, as of November 2021, there are only 23 approved digital health apps in the categories shown in Fig. 3.

Jungmann (2021) shows that physicians in Germany have prescribed digital health apps only 3700 times and that 53% of physicians either do not want to prescribe them or do not yet know what they do. Compared to the 445 million prescriptions issued each year in Germany, digital health apps are still a tiny proportion.

The information digital health apps collect lacks the data continuity shown in Fig. 2, that is, a ring of trust model that connects the various data sources in a secure manner and can thereby deliver the added value of networked, proactive care.

Figure 4 shows how the different settings and environments can be integrated via in the form of a community health hub or a center for telemedicine.

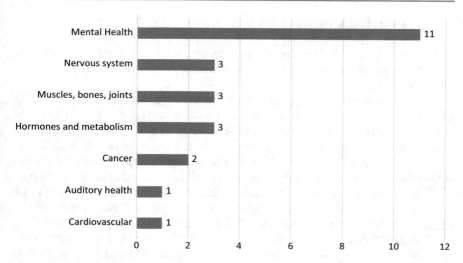

Fig. 3 Number of approved digital health apps (author's chart based on BfArM, 2021)

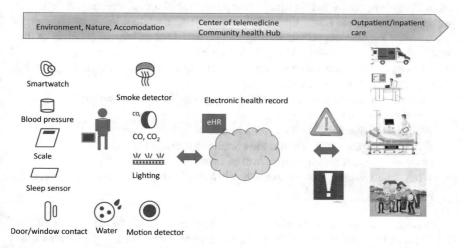

Fig. 4 Model of a community health hub

However, the following questions arise:

- Who should operate the community health hub?
- What geographical area should the community health hub cover?
- How will the community health hub be funded?
- What value would a community heath hub bring to health system users and providers?

4 Social Relevance

In an earlier paper (Kunhardt, 2021), I introduced a model of expanded chronic care. This model would link the services of the healthcare system to the specific resources of a region (Fig. 5).

Experience from the Home4.0 project can be integrated into this model. For example, cloud-based data analysis and AI-based forecasting models can be linked at the individual level with the available services in a region. An integrated health hub can serve as a basis for regional health management (Malachowski et al., 2018).

The fact that healthcare takes place in a predominantly local and regional context is the motivation for community health hub models. In an analysis of 518 million cases of physicians' claims with health insurance companies in 2009 and 2010, Schang et al. (2017) determined the travel times from patients' homes to the offices of general practitioners and specialists. They found that general practitioners could be reached within less than 30 minutes in about 90% of cases. For specialists, travel time was less than 30 minutes in about 60% of the cases. The density of physicians in a region naturally plays a decisive role in achieving short distances. Particularly in rural regions, where public transport is poorly developed, there can be significant deviations from these travel times. This makes it all the more important to provide telemedical support to patients so they can be cared for as long as possible at their place of residence or in their home. During the COVID-19 pandemic, patients used video consultations more frequently. Perhaps the experiences from the pandemic can be transferred to post-pandemic times.

How can the questions from the previous section now be answered?

- Who should operate the community health hub?
- What geographical area should the community health hub cover?
- How will the community health hub be funded?
- What value would a community heath hub bring to health system users and providers?

A community health hub can be operated by a network of physicians or a medical care center. In principle, the coordination of health services in a region is also a task of the public health service or a health department. However, years of cost-cutting measures in this area have weakened existing healthcare structures. In times of a shortage of skilled medical personnel, an additional buildup of skilled personnel is unlikely.

A community health hub can easily cover a county. Projects such as Health Regions Plus of the Bavarian State Ministry of Health and Care could provide coordination and networking for the partners in healthcare. Health Regions Plus cover various fields of action, such as nursing, prevention, and healthcare. Currently, there are 57 Health Regions Plus in Bavaria, which corresponds to 72 out of 96 districts (Health Regions Plus, 2021). However, the Health Regions Plus network has budget for only one full-time position that covers five years of network management.

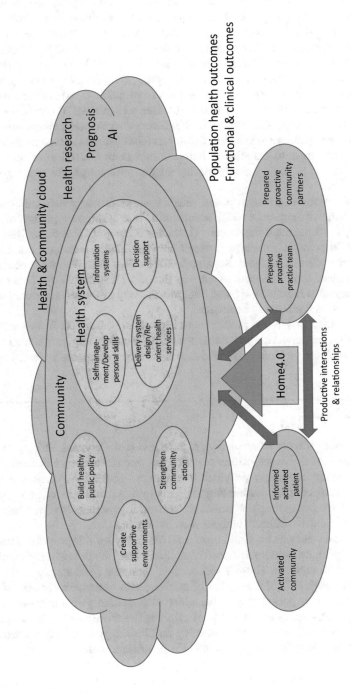

Fig. 5 Expanded chronic care model showing author's adaptation of Home4.0 based on Barr et al. (2003)

The financing of a community health hub can be regulated according to the services it provides. Ideally, health insurers should participate in a community health hub since proactive healthcare, starting in the home environment of the insured, can help avoid higher treatment costs. For example, falls among the elderly could be prevented if initial indications of a possible fall were detected by analyzing movement data. Also, in an emergency, continuous monitoring in the home environment could allow help to be organized quickly and rescue services to be alerted. The care of chronic diseases requires a high level of compliance by patients. Existing resources that promote patient compliance could be improved with the support of apps that promote health literacy, remind patients to take medication, and provide motivation to exercise at home. Rapid communication of questions to healthcare facilities could quickly clarify misunderstandings and mean greater safety for patients.

Networked, coordinated care would mean savings through reduced hospital admissions, better compliance with medication, and a higher quality of life. For example, the integrated care plan "Gesundes Kinzigtal" (based in Hausach, Germany) could provide a savings contract between health insurance companies and service providers (Gesundes Kinzigtal, 2021). But even for this successful networking project, a high amount of start-up financing was necessary. This model project for integrated regional care was comprehensively evaluated and could serve as an example for a community health hub.

With the means of AI-based prediction of individual health data from the home environment and the networking of these data with the other caregivers, added value can be generated for patients and the demands on the healthcare system can be reduced.

5 Conclusion

We live in an aging society in which people have less social contact. Elderly people often live alone in their homes, which are often not free of barriers. Healthcare and nursing care are predominantly provided in a regional context. Although there are various model projects for coordinating and networking care services in a region, these projects have not yet become standard. Networking partners in care who work in different sectors with different budgets is a challenging task.

To date, digital solutions have still been used too rarely for this purpose. There is also a lack of digital networking between smart homes and the provision of medical, nursing, and social services. There is still no data continuity, and supply chains are incomplete. Although a lot of money has been invested in a telematics infrastructure in Germany over a long period of time, the added value is hardly visible to individual patients and physicians. A constant social effort is therefore needed to safeguard what has been achieved so far and to develop an IT strategy that delivers real and perceptible added value from digitization in the healthcare sector.

Acknowledgments The author declares no potential conflicts of interest.

References

Barr, V. J., Robinson, S., Marin-Link, B., Underhill, L., Dotts, A., Ravensdale, D., & Salivaras, S. (2003). The expanded chronic care model: An integration of concepts and strategies from population health promotion and the chronic care model. *Healthcare Quarterly, 7*(1), 73–82. https://doi.org/10.12927/hcq.2003.16763

BfArM (Bundesinstitut für Arzneimittel und Medizinprodukte). (2021) Das DiGA-Verzeichnis: Antworten zur Nutzung von DiGA. Accessed November 5, 2021, from https://diga.bfarm.de/de

Brinkhaus, B., & Esch, T. (Eds.). (2021). *Integrative Medizin und Gesundheit*. Med. wiss. Verlagsgesellschaft.

Gesundes Kinzigtal. (2021). *Krankenkassen: Starke Partner*. Accessed November 6,2021, from https://www.gesundes-kinzigtal.de/krankenkassen/

Health Regions Plus. (2021). Gesundheitsregionen[plus]—Entscheidungen vor Ort treffen. Accessed November 6, 2021, from https://www.gesundheitsregionenplus.bayern.de/

Home4.0. (2021). Project website. Accessed November 1, 2021, from https://www.deinhaus40.de/

Hung, L., Liu, C., Woldum, E., Au-Yeung, A., Berndt, A., Wallsworth, C., . . . Chaudhury, H. (2019). The benefits of and barriers to using a social robot PARO in care settings: A scoping review. *BMC Geriatrics, 19*(1), 232.

Jungmann, S. (2021, 10 June). Warum Ärzte DiGAs nicht verschreiben. *Taggespiegel Background*. Accessed November 5, 2021, from https://background.tagesspiegel.de/gesundheit/warum-aerzte-digas-nicht-verschreiben

Klöß, S. (2019). *Zukunft der Consumer Technology*. Bitkom, Deloitte.

Kunhardt, H. (2021). Home 4.0—With sensor data from everyday life to health and care prognosis. In P. Glauner, P. Plugmann, & G. Lerzynski (Eds.), *Digitalization in healthcare: Implementing innovation and artificial intelligence*. Springer.

Malachowski, C., Skopyk, S., Toth, K., & MacEachen, E. (2018). The integrated health hub (IHH) model: The evolution of a community based primary care and mental health centre. *Community Mental Health Journal, 55*(4), 578–588.

Schang, L., Kopetsch, T., & Sundmacher, L. (2017). Zurückgelegte Wegzeiten in der ambulanten ärztlichen Versorgung in Deutschland. *Bundesgesundheitsblatt, 60*(12), 1383–1392.

Statista. (2017). *Umfrage zur Nutzung von Smartwatches und Fitness-Trackern am Handgelenk in Deutschland nach Alter und Geschlecht im Jahr 2017*. Accessed November 6, 2021, from https://de.statista.com/statistik/daten/studie/454312/umfrage/nutzung-von-smartwatches-und-fitness-trackern-nach-alter-und-geschlecht/

Thiel, R., Deimel, L., Schmidtmann, D., Piesche, K., Hüsing, T., Rennoch, J., . . . Kostera, T. (2018). *#SmartHealthSystems: Digitalisierungsstrategien im internationalen Vergleich*. Bertelsmann Stiftung. Retrieved from https://www.bertelsmann-stiftung.de/en/publications/publication/did/smarthealthsystems

Teledermatology: Current Indications and Future Perspectives

Estefanía Lang, Alice Martin, and Elien Wallaeys

Abstract

Digitalisation is evolving in every aspect of medicine. The use of teledermatology was boosted enormously during the COVID-19 pandemic. Quarantines and sometimes even the closure of doctor's offices made it impossible for some people to get dermatological care. However, during the pandemic, the scepticism about teledermatology declined. It is a welcome and handy tool that extends the provision of medical care. It does not replace traditional dermatology completely, but since both modes of care have benefits and flaws, they can coexist and complement each other. This chapter discusses the opportunities and pitfalls of teledermatology and gives a sneak peek at future possibilities.

1 Introduction

In the past, a doctor's routine was completely analogue. As personal computers became more accessible in the 1980s and the widespread use of the Internet took hold in the late 1990s, digitalisation in medicine became an exciting opportunity. It offers the possibility to get rapid access to files, to store information more efficiently and accurately, and to easily share information with other healthcare practitioners. As technology has evolved, it now offers a chance for patients to get treated more quickly and even serves patients who would otherwise not have an easy access to a healthcare practitioner, for example, because of immobility or distance.

E. Lang (✉) · A. Martin · E. Wallaeys
Dermanostic GmbH, Düsseldorf, Germany
e-mail: e.lang@dermanostic.com

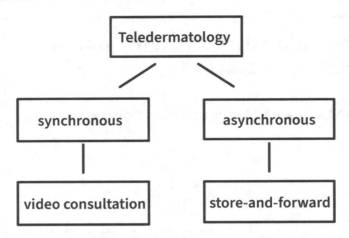

Fig. 1 Overview of the different communication methods in teledermatology

The COVID-19 pandemic accelerated the evolution of telemedicine in a variety of medical domains. All of a sudden, there was a huge need to be able to deliver medical care from a distance.

Digitalisation initially met with scepticism. People are often not open to change because the established methods are well known and familiar. However, when they realise that this new method can help by improving the quality and efficiency of healthcare, they tend to accept this new path, albeit sometimes slowly.

Currently, there are two ways of practicing teledermatology: video consultation or the store-and-forward method. Video consultation is synchronic consultation and communication in which the patient and the doctor are in direct contact via video camera. In the store-and-forward method, the patient sends pictures and case history information about their health status that the dermatologist analyses in an asynchronous way (Fig. 1). This way of communicating offers the advantage of having a higher image quality and does not require any special camera device or the need for simultaneous Internet access.

Video consultation, on the other hand, makes it easier to communicate with the patient, explain the diagnosis and treatment, and respond more directly to the needs and questions of the patient (Lang et al., 2021). Empathy, which is as important as a correct diagnosis, is much more difficult to conduct through the store-and-forward method. Information about serious diseases such as cancer, or conditions such as sexually transmitted diseases, is not always easy to convey through this method. In these cases, a lot of care is needed in choosing the right words to convey information without making a patient overly anxious or insecure. A phone call can help as an add-on to overcome this problem.

2   Practical Examples

Traditionally, dermatology involved the documentation of patient records, which were kept handwritten in patients' files, and, for example, birthmark diagnostics using a dermatoscope (a reflected light microscope). When malignancy was suspected, many birthmarks could be clarified only by surgical removal.

The 'hit rate' for a melanoma (a type of skin cancer that develops from the pigment-producing cells) varies from a positive finding among a few moles removed (by very experienced dermatologists) to one in many moles removed (in young dermatology residents). Nowadays, there are programs that use an algorithm that may arguably surpass the world's best dermatologists in diagnosing moles (Haenssle et al., 2018). When the dermatoscopic image is analysed, the program assesses whether it is a benign mole or skin cancer. This program is used, for instance, in FotoFinder's 'Moleanalyzer pro' skin-imaging system (FotoFinder Systems GmbH, Bad Birnbach, Germany). The program works using a 'deep learning system' and continuously improves the reliability of its diagnoses.

Digitalisation offers great potential in dermatology as the diagnosis is made on the basis of patient questionnaires and photos of the skin lesion. Currently, the patient's appearance and information provided by the patient can usually lead to a result. The dermatologist's experience enables them to compare the patient's case with known or stored information. This practice is to a certain extent digitisable.

Algorithms already exist that categorise the skin changes and partially diagnose skin changes on the basis of two-dimensional images. Using a deep learning system, a team at Google has developed a program that can correctly diagnose 26 skin conditions (Liu et al., 2020) (see also Kelly et al., 2019). This is possible because of pattern analysis of changes in the skin. These changes can be extensive and flat or grouped and raised, they may or may not include scaling, and the colour may be distributed in circular, linear, or cockade-shaped patterns. Each skin change shows pathognomonic changes and its own characteristics. Due to the two-dimensional representation, some important information is lost. Therefore, it is important to get images from a wider perspective in order to get three dimensions. Standardised testing and quality management are also important for building artificial intelligence. In dermatology, there are well over 500 different skin diseases (WHO, 2016) and many manifest in very different ways. High data volumes and continuous development in all ethnic groups is essential so that future AI can recognise skin changes in all people. For example, dermatitis (inflammation of the skin) may manifest differently depending on skin tone. Such important considerations are not yet taken into account and require further development (see also Adelekun et al., 2021; Faye et al., 2020).

Fungal diseases offer another example of how digitalisation can improve diagnosis. In the past, the infected skin, hair, or nail scales were inoculated onto an agar plate, where the fungus would grow for 2 to 4 weeks. The final diagnosis would be made when the fungus could be completely identified on the agar plate. Nowadays, the PCR diagnostic method detects the DNA of the fungus. The result is

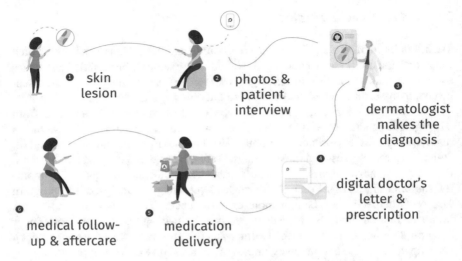

Fig. 2 In the store-and-forward method, the patient identifies a skin lesion (1) and takes a photo and answers a questionnaire (2) so the physician can make a diagnosis (3) and send the patient a digital letter and prescription (4). Thus, the medication can be delivered to the patient (5), and the patient keeps in contact with the doctor through digital aftercare (6)

available in the laboratory within a few hours and is digitally transmitted to the attending physician. PCR detection can be performed under local and systemic medical treatment, which is not possible with the agar culture method. As a rule, PCR is superior to the culture diagnostic method. It is easy to use and will be the gold standard in the near future.

Digitalisation also offers great advantages in follow-up with patients. In the past, patients received treatment for the skin disease and presented for follow-up examinations at intervals of several months. Now photo documentation can enable a practitioner to determine whether the therapy should stay the same or change. Photo documentation on site is already an established control and evaluation method and is part of digitalisation. The next stage is asynchronous documentation by the patient themselves using the store-and-forward method. This enables the patient to obtain a dermatological assessment and professional aftercare remotely (Fig. 2).

Telemedical documentation is also being used in other disciplines that closely monitor parameters (such as blood pressure or blood sugar) during treatment (Treskes et al., 2020).

3   Chances

Digitalisation offers many advantages. First and foremost, it provides increased speed and scaling because many steps can be automated and now require less time. Teledermatology enables dermatologists to see many more patients daily than they could see during normal consultations. Since the undressing of the patient, which takes time on site, is skipped in this process, dermatological care can be provided to a larger group of patients with fewer healthcare professionals. Hence, medical knowledge is provided more efficiently.

Digitalisation also deals with the evolving problem of huge waiting lists. Through teledermatology, patients can be helped almost immediately without having to wait for weeks or even months to get a proper appointment (Lang et al., 2020).

Moreover, it helps overcome issues of anxiety or embarrassment related to consulting a doctor. Especially for sexually transmitted diseases or skin lesions in the genital area, teledermatology lowers the threshold of anxiety related to seeking medical care.

Digitalisation can also standardise care since automation means that processes are consistent. This makes it possible to measure quality and minimises diagnostic and treatment errors. For example, the algorithm may be able to classify suspicious birthmarks with a higher level of diagnostic certainty than the average dermatologist can provide. However, this is true only in the case of non-overlapped lesions. In a context 'with clinical close-up images, dermoscopic images, and textual case information for review, the management decisions of most dermatologists were either on or slightly above the level' of the AI algorithm (Haenssle et al., 2020, p. 142).

Apps already exist that make it possible to check moles with the patient's smartphone (e.g., SkinVision (Amsterdam, the Netherlands)). Through this, the patient can learn the status of a birthmark that is suspicious without having to make a dermatology appointment. This is a double-edged sword, however, because the patient can only photograph the moles that they can see. During an on-site full-body examination, all areas of the skin and mucous membranes are examined so that the dermatologist can detect moles that are not accessible to the patient.

Another opportunity in digitalisation is increased access to medical care. Through time-independent treatment in asynchronous telemedicine, even areas with a weak infrastructure can be reached. Immobile patients can be treated comfortably from home, and family members can introduce young children and digitally less savvy patients to digitalisation. Therefore, teledermatology has an intergenerational effect.

Increased speed and scaling and the broader access to medical care will significantly reduce the cost of healthcare. In addition to broader access to medicine, digitalisation also makes individualised treatment possible. Systems can be trained with high volumes of data and can record and recognise exceptions. The data-based programs can then draw the attention of the treating doctor to rare diseases in a patient. One example is erythroderma, a reddening that affects more than 90% of the skin that can hide a variety of skin diseases. These include both common dermatological diseases (e.g., neurodermatitis or psoriasis) and rare diseases (lymphoma, blood cancer, or syphilis). As a rule, doctors in private practice see some diseases very rarely in their clinical career. Today, medical students are taught to think in terms of the most likely diagnosis. However, this can be the undoing of patients with rare diseases if rare diseases are recognised too late or are not even recognised.

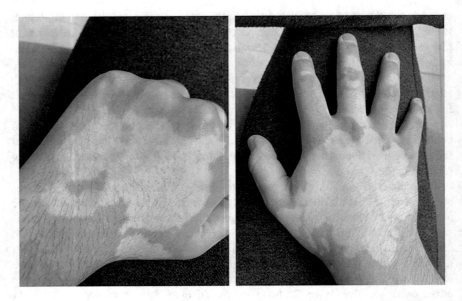

Fig. 3 A patient consults via teledermatology because of a sudden hypopigmentation of his hands. The diagnosis of vitiligo was made. Image courtesy of dermanostic

Digitalisation means that a diagnosis will be reached not by a human who systematically excludes diseases but by an artificial intelligence that draws from its knowledge of every disease in a database. Access to many digital images in the form of a digital atlas already helps medical colleagues in training every day as well as colleagues who use one of the largest digital libraries for further training. Especially in dermatology, the saying 'learning by doing' or, better, 'learning by seeing' is applicable. Since healthcare providers see way more patients in a teledermatological setting, their learning curve tends to grow much faster. A digital atlas offers them the opportunity to learn about rare diagnoses that they would almost never encounter in a daily practice setting. The teledermatological approach also makes it much easier to consult certain experts, which not only contributes to the learning curve of the dermatologist but also increases the quality of healthcare that is available. Any patient can in theory get access to the best expert healthcare at any time (assuming, of course, the availability of physicians, etc.) even from home (Fig. 3).

In addition, teledermatology connects generations of practitioners with each other so that knowledge is retained even when colleagues retire because digitisation means that they can continue to work from home. Digitalisation also reduces our ecological footprint, not only because it saves paper but also because teledermatology enables people to seek healthcare without having to travel for kilometers. Especially in areas with a low number of healthcare professionals per square kilometer, carbon dioxide emissions can be reduced dramatically.

4   Limits

At the present time, digitisation has limitations and dangers if sufficient education is not provided. Digitalisation and telemedicine are a supplement to established procedures, not a replacement for them. As described in the example with the fungal skin disease, digitisation should not be used without the expertise of a dermatologist so that gaps will be closed. In addition, birthmark assessment via an app can be dangerous if it replaces the recommended mole screening at the local dermatologist.

As mentioned, the dermatologist looks at all areas of the skin and can detect skin lesions that the patient may not have noticed. In addition, when the patient is the one who decides which birthmark is suspicious, they may exclude a nonpigmented birthmark that can hide the dangerous amelanotic melanoma.

Diagnostic uncertainty is complex in teledermatology. Dermatology offers the opportunity to diagnose many skin diseases without any further investigation, but in certain cases, a full investigation that includes bloodwork and a biopsy is needed in order to make a correct diagnosis. In those cases, one needs to rely on the patients' sense of responsibility to seek this extra care. If further treatment is needed, for example, in the case of skin cancer, which needs to be removed surgically, the dermatologist needs to trust that the patient will return for additional care. Follow-up can also be difficult because of the distance between doctor and patient, not only in space but also emotionally.

Teledermatology stands or falls with the quality of the image. Bad images equal bad diagnostics. Thanks to the evolving technology, smartphone cameras have become more sophisticated and now produce more detailed pictures. But even with a good camera, bad pictures can be taken due to a patient's inexperience. Requesting better pictures over and over again can irritate the patient, hampering the doctor-patient relationship. Because patients are not always aware of what is considered to be a good picture, it may be necessary to educate them about how to take good quality pictures. Certain areas are particularly difficult to photograph (e.g., the back, skinfolds, scalp lesions). Mucosal lesions can also be difficult to photograph or interpret. Due to their wet appearance, flash photography can cause reflection, leaving white spots on the picture that could resemble some skin lesions, for example, in candida (yeast) infections or lichen ruber mucosae (a.k.a. lichen planus mucosae), a chronic inflammatory disease.

A huge limitation in teledermatology is that it does not evaluate three dimensions. Only two-dimensional imagery is possible with pictures or videos. This makes the evaluation of tumorous lesions especially challenging. Pictures at different angles are the minimum requirement for addressing this problem, but they are not always sufficient.

Furthermore, the impossibility of a tactile approach can also bring some diagnostic uncertainty. The actinic keratosis, a precancerous lesion, for example, is mostly diagnosed on site by feeling the lesion and experiencing that it is rough to touch. This sense of touch cannot be transmitted through pictures. Asking the patient about the tactile aspect of the lesion only offers added value if the patient is educated enough to understand and correctly interpret this question.

Diagnosing a lesion without sufficient image quality can lead to misdiagnosis. Although in certain cases the pressure is high to provide a diagnosis, the dermatologist should not step into this pitfall. Instead, they should leave the lesion undiagnosed and refer the patient to an on-site dermatologist.

Programs such as the previously mentioned FotoFinder's Molefinder pro make the work of dermatologists easier, but relying on them solely is dangerous. Since these programs are trained to track patterns, they can overlook some small subtle changes that are indicative of a melanoma or produce a false positive that leads to unnecessary treatment.

Miscommunication and lack of empathy can also be hurdles to overcome. If patients only send pictures, it can be challenging to accurately guess what they are concerned about and how to deal or respond to their concerns. As mentioned earlier, showing empathy is not easy in a teledermatological setting (especially with the store-and-forward method) since it excludes non-verbal communication. Moreover, the subtleties of verbal communication (intonation, pronunciation) and non-verbal communication (gestures with hands and eyes) cannot be submitted through written language, which is often interpreted as more distant or harsh. Especially with cancer diagnoses, it is important to take great care to choose the right phrasing to communicate information.

This challenge is also present in on-site consultations. Because of time pressures, a consultation with an on-site dermatologist can be short. And even on-site, people are often misunderstood. In the digital world, good communication can happen if the dermatologist provides an extensive response to every concern and question of the patient.

Furthermore, an important limitation is an overall scepticism about digitalised medical care. To address this, digital medicine should be combined with personal contact: a mixture of 'digitech' and 'digitouch' (see Park & Kressel, 2018). Patients should receive human care from dermatologists and not receive a written diagnosis, such as a diagnosis of skin cancer, without being offered the psychological support they may need ('digitouch'). Ethics plays a major role here; patients with worries and fears need a supportive telephone call, for example.

Digitalisation should always be checked for its usefulness. An example is birthmark diagnostics. In the early days of digitalisation, it was possible to prove that the algorithm initially classified moles as dangerous if they were circled in blue. This was due to the fact that doctors had marked suspicious birthmarks for the surgeon shortly before the operation and the circled birthmark was photographed and introduced into the database. This taught the algorithm that circled moles were often more malignant, but it 'learned' this on a completely wrong basis.

This illustrates that digitalisation should be actively questioned and continuously optimised. Otherwise, false connections can arise that have far-reaching consequences.

5 The Future of Teledermatology

Digitalisation will continue to expand. In the next few years, personal contact with the dermatologist will not necessarily have to take place. Diagnostic methods will also continue to develop, and AI will offer an established advantage not only in birthmark diagnostics but also in the case of other diseases.

A big step in the evolution of teledermatology would be the development of certain apps or camera devices that make it possible for patients to take dermatoscopy pictures. Assessing pigmented skin lesions without dermatoscopy is practically impossible, so dermatoscopic imaging is needed to close this telediagnostic gap.

In addition to telemedicine, laboratory diagnostics can be combined with dermatology in the future. This means that the patient will receive a diagnosis telemedically, and, for example, laboratory specimen collection material could be sent to the patient's home. This would eliminate the need to take samples on site, and the patient could take a few drops of blood (similar to blood sugar control) or a skin lesion sample with a swab and send the sample to the laboratory. The results could be sent to the dermatologist, and the therapy could be approved. Such scenarios can already be envisaged and make sense for both the patient and the doctor. In today's scenario, the patient had to make three visits to a healthcare facility: first, the patient receives a diagnosis from a dermatologist, then a general practitioner or a lab takes a blood sample, and finally, the patient receives a prescription after the dermatologist has all the test results.

6 Conclusion

Digitalisation and teledermatology are evolving and will become more vital in the future. It offers many advantages, such as serving a larger number of patients with fewer healthcare professionals, overcoming the problem of waiting lists, reducing error, reducing healthcare costs, and increasing healthcare quality. The biggest limitations of teledermatology, however, are the absence of three-dimensionality and the use of touch to diagnose lesions, the need for outstanding image quality, and the difficulties related to building an empathic patient-doctor relationship. Thus, teledermatology will complement on-site dermatology as the need for medical care grows.

Acknowledgements We would like to acknowledge the expert contributions of Prof. Dr. med. Jorge Frank, Dr. med. Barbara Meyer-Lehmann, Prof. Dr. med. Percy Lehmann, Dr. Klaus-Werner Schulte, and Dr. med. Norbert J. Neumann over the last years. The authors declare no potential conflicts of interest.

References

Adelekun, A., Onyekaba, G., & Lipoff, J. B. (2021). Skin color in dermatology textbooks: An updated evaluation and analysis. *Journal of the American Academy of Dermatology, 84*(1), 194–196.

Faye, O., Meledie N'Djong, A. P., Diadie, S., Coniquet, S., Niamba, P. A., Atadokpede, F., . . . Delarue, A. (2020). Validation of the patient-oriented SCORing for atopic dermatitis tool for black skin. Journal of the European Academy of Dermatology and Venereology, 34(4), 795–799.

Haenssle, H. A., Fink, C., Schneiderbauer, R., Toberer, F., Buhl, T., Blum, A., . . . Zalaudek, I. (2018). Man against machine: Diagnostic performance of a deep learning convolutional neural network for dermoscopic melanoma recognition in comparison to 58 dermatologists. Annals of Oncology, 29(8), 1836–1842.

Haenssle, H. A., Fink, C., Toberer, F., Winkler, J., Stolz, W., Deinlein, T., . . . Level, I. I. G. (2020). Man against machine reloaded: Performance of a market-approved convolutional neural network in classifying a broad spectrum of skin lesions in comparison with 96 dermatologists working under less artificial conditions. Annals of Oncology, 31(1), 137–143.

Kelly, C. J., Karthikesalingam, A., Suleyman, M., Corrado, G., & King, D. (2019). Key challenges for delivering clinical impact with artificial intelligence. *BMC Medicine, 17*, 195. https://doi.org/10.1186/s12916-019-1426-2

Lang, E., Martin, A., & Frank, J. (2020). Digitalisierung in der Medizin während der COVID-19-Pandemie—Möglichkeiten und Grenzen der Teledermatologie. *Kompass Dermatologie, 8*, 150–152. https://doi.org/10.1159/000512398

Lang, E., Martin, A., & Frank, J. (2021). Teledermatology: Dermatologist-by-app as a chance in rheumatology? *Arthritis and Rheumatism, 41*(3), 191–198. https://doi.org/10.1055/a-1383-2945

Liu, Y., Jain, A., Eng, C., Way, D. H., Lee, K., Bui, P., . . . Coz, D. (2020). A deep learning system for differential diagnosis of skin diseases. Nature Medicine, 26(6), 900–908.

Park, S. H., & Kressel, H. Y. (2018). Connecting technological innovation in artificial intelligence to real-world medical practice through rigorous clinical validation: What peer-reviewed medical journals could do. *Journal of Korean Medical Science, 33*(22), e152. https://doi.org/10.3346/jkms.2018.33.e152

Treskes, R. W., van Winden, L. A. M., van Keulen, N., van der Velde, E. T., Beeres, S., Atsma, D. E., & Schalij, M. J. (2020). Effect of smartphone-enabled health monitoring devices vs regular follow-up on blood pressure control among patients after myocardial infarction: A randomized clinical trial. *JAMA Network Open, 3*(4), e202165.

WHO. (2016). *Diseases of the skin and subcutaneous tissue*. International statistical classification of diseases and related health problems 10th Revision (ICD-10). Retrieved from https://icd.who.int/browse10/2016/en#/XII

Using Artificial Intelligence for the Specification of m-Health and e-Health Systems

Kevin Lano, Sobhan Y. Tehrani, Mohammad Umar, and Lyan Alwakeel

Abstract

Artificial intelligence (AI) techniques such as machine learning (ML) have wide application in medical informatics systems. In this chapter, we employ AI techniques to assist in deriving software specifications of e-Health and m-Health systems from informal requirements statements. We use natural language processing (NLP), optical character recognition (OCR), and machine learning to identify required data and behaviour elements of systems from textual and graphical requirements documents. Heuristic rules are used to extract formal specification models of the systems from these documents. The extracted specifications can then be used as the starting point for automated software production using model-driven engineering (MDE). We illustrate the process using an example of a stroke recovery assistant app and evaluate the techniques on several representative systems.

1 Introduction

Health informatics systems (*e-health systems*) include electronic health record management and analysis, diagnostic tools for clinicians, patient management systems for general practitioners and hospitals, and a wide range of mobile health (*m-health*) apps for general and specific health purposes. Health applications may need to deal

K. Lano · M. Umar · L. Alwakeel
Informatics Department, King's College London, London, UK
e-mail: kevin.lano@kcl.ac.uk; mohammad.umar@kcl.ac.uk; lyan.alwakeel@kcl.ac.uk

S. Y. Tehrani (✉)
Dept. of Computer Science, University College London, London, UK
e-mail: sobhan.tehrani@ucl.ac.uk

© The Author(s), under exclusive license to Springer Nature Switzerland AG 2022
S. Ehsani et al. (eds.), *The Future Circle of Healthcare*, Future of Business
and Finance, https://doi.org/10.1007/978-3-030-99838-7_15

with very large amounts of data, which may include uncertain information, and often involve multiple categories of users and stakeholders. The processed information is usually subject to high confidentiality requirements, e.g., due to GDPR and related legislation.

For each type of health application, software correctness is of high and even critical importance: incorrect patient information or analysis results can impair treatment or lead to incorrect and harmful medical interventions. Apps for patient self-management or health advice must also provide accurate and appropriate information (Public Health England, 2017). The well-publicised problems that arose in the United Kingdom in 2020 with the nationally distributed COVID-19 advisory app highlighted the particular challenges of implementing m-health apps.

Therefore, rigorous requirements analysis is of key importance for e-health and m-health applications. In this chapter, we address this challenge by providing assistance tools to automate the formalisation of software requirements statements, using natural language processing (NLP) and machine learning (ML) techniques. NLP and ML are instances of artificial intelligence (AI) techniques, which are increasingly being applied to support software engineering and development activities, in addition to widespread use in e-health and m-health applications, for example, to perform activity classification of mobile users or deducing calorie counts by image recognition applied to a photograph of a meal.

In an agile development context, parts of a system may be developed in different iterations, and their requirements are analysed using techniques such as interviews and exploratory prototyping in close collaboration with customer representatives. The techniques described in this chapter can be used to support the construction of models and prototypes from requirements and enable customers to quickly see the semantic consequences of different requirements statements. We use the AgileUML toolset (Eclipse, 2021) to visualise and analyse formalised specifications. The toolset can be utilised to synthesise code in several 3GLs, including C, Java, Python, and Swift. Mobile apps for the Android and iOS platforms can also be generated (Lano et al., 2021).

Section 2 describes the stroke recovery assistant case study and highlights some of the aspects of requirements statements that need to be addressed by a requirements formalisation approach.

Section 3 describes our requirements formalisation approach, using the case study to illustrate the process steps. In Sects. 3.1, 3.2 and 3.3, we summarise the application of NLP, ML, and OCR techniques in our process for automated requirements engineering (RE). In Sects. 3.4 and 3.5, we describe specific techniques for the formalisation of data and behavioural requirements from natural language statements and give examples from the case study.

Section 4 describes how automated RE can be used in an overall agile development process.

Section 5 surveys related work, and Sect. 6 gives conclusions.

2   Requirements Statement Example: The Stroke Recovery Assistant Case Study

Requirements statements are typically written in natural language and usually consist of a combination of text and diagrams, with text predominant. Requirements statements may include non-technical issues, such as the roles of stakeholders in the development process (Robertson and Robertson, 2012). In this chapter, we only consider the technical requirements of the data and functionality of the system to be constructed.

We take as a typical example of a health application the stroke recovery assistant of King's Health Partners (2011). This involves both in-hospital systems for doctors and researchers, and a mobile app for patients to track their own progress. The requirements statement consists of:

- One page of text defining:

  1. The high-level goals of the project: "To improve the quality of life of patients who have suffered a stroke"; "To forecast recovery paths based on historical data and prediction algorithms"; "To build a data warehouse of clinical data"
  2. The scope of the system, including "A mobile app and web-based interface for data collection—for use by doctors in hospital"; "A mobile app and web-based interface for doctors to estimate recovery curves"; "A mobile app and web-based interface for patients to access information about recovery exercises, get information about their process, and track their recovery progress"; "An algorithm to compute recovery curves based on historical data"
  3. Security and infrastructure requirements, e.g., the use of secure data connections, and the use of a single database for internal and external use
  4. Some further objectives and success criteria, which are actually user stories, e.g.: "Allow doctors to collect a patient's data while they are in hospital"

- One page of informal diagrams showing the expected user interface behaviour of the doctor's UI, and a mock-up of the mobile UI for doctors (Fig. 1)
- One page of "supplementary requirements" that details the requirements from page 1, and number these as REQ-1 to REQ-10

The document is typical of software requirements documents, in that:

- It is almost completely informal, written at a high level of abstraction.
- Substantial additional background knowledge and information must be obtained before development can begin—such as the precise definition of the recovery prediction algorithm to be encoded in software.
- Conflicts exist between different requirements, e.g., the requirement to have a single database potentially conflicts with the requirements to provide both active

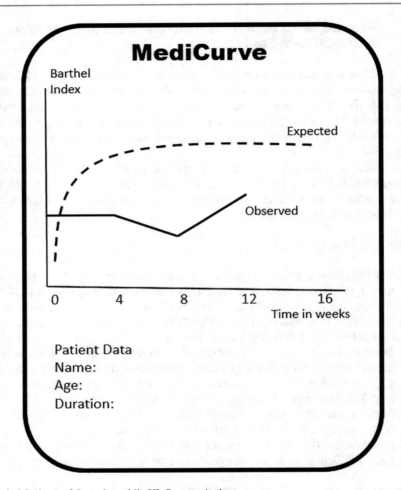

Fig. 1 Mock-up of doctor's mobile UI. Source: Authors

data and research data: for confidentiality purposes, the research data should be separate from active data and anonymised.
- Significant details are omitted, such as the design of the patient's UI, which will require specialised approaches to achieve usability for this group of patients.

Although a requirements engineer will take this requirements statement as their starting point, substantial additional investigation and requirements elicitation from the customer and using background documents are necessary. We will also use supplementary documentation (such as Collin et al., 1988) in our semi-automated RE process applied to this case study.

3   Requirements Formalisation Process and Techniques

There are typically four main stages in any requirements engineering (RE) process (Kotonya & Sommerville, 1996):

1. Domain analysis and requirements elicitation
2. Evaluation and negotiation
3. Requirements specification and formalisation
4. Requirements validation and verification

A wide range of RE techniques can be used at these stages, such as document mining and structured and semi-structured interviews for requirements elicitation, and experimental prototyping and formal reviews for requirements validation.

In our approach, we focus on requirements *formalisation* to support the requirements specification of technical requirements and do not address requirements elicitation. However, the process of formalisation may clarify the understanding of requirements by the customer and developer by providing a formal model and visualisation of requirements statements (e.g., Fig. 5 shows a visualisation of a formal model derived from the stroke recovery assistant requirements). The process could also contribute to requirements evaluation and validation by detecting potential conflicts, redundancy, and omissions in the requirements statements, and by providing a unified technical specification for formal review.

As highlighted above, software requirements statements are typically expressed in a combination of natural language text and informal diagrams, with text as the predominant element. Thus we work with text as the input, which may include text derived from diagrams using OCR. The first stage of requirements formalisation involves extracting sentences from requirements documents and adding linguistic and semantic information as annotations to these sentences. In Sects. 3.1, 3.2, and 3.3, we describe the application of NLP, ML, and OCR for this stage.

Following the extraction of semantic information from requirements statements, the second stage of the formalisation process builds Unified Modelling Language (UML) and Object Constraint Language (OCL) models in two successive steps: extraction of a data model (Sect. 3.4) and extraction of a behavioural model (Sect. 3.5).

3.1   Natural Language Processing

NLP is a collection of techniques for the processing of natural language text, including:

- Part-of-speech (POS) tagging/classification: identifying the linguistic category of words in a text, such as nouns, adjectives, verbs, etc.
- Tokenisation and splitting of text into sentences

- Lemmatisation: identifying the root forms of verbs, nouns, etc.
- Syntax analysis: construction of a parse tree identifying the subclauses of a sentence and their hierarchical relationships
- Dependency analysis: identifying the roles of words in the sentence, i.e., certain nouns are the subjects and others are the objects of the sentence, and the other words act as adjectival modifiers of nouns
- Named entity recognition: identifying known terms such as cities, countries, etc.
- Reference correlation: identifying when the same element is referenced from different sentences.

NLP tools include Stanford NLP (Stanford University, 2020), Apache OpenNLP (Apache Software Foundation, 2019), iOS NLP Framework, and WordNet (Fellbaum, 2010).

The standard parts of speech include (Santorini, 1990):

- Determiners—tagged as $\_DT$, e.g., "a", "the"
- Nouns—$\_NN$ for singular nouns and $\_NNS$ for plural
- Proper nouns—$\_NNP$ and $\_NNPS$
- Adjectives—$\_JJ$, $\_JJR$ for relative adjectives, $\_JJS$ for superlatives
- Possessives—$\_PRP\$$
- Modal verbs—$\_MD$ such as "should", "must"
- Verbs—$\_VB$ for the base form of a verb, $\_VBP$ for present tense except 3rd person singular, $\_VBZ$ for present tense 3rd person singular, $\_VBG$ for gerunds, $\_VBD$ for past tense
- Adverbs—$\_RB$
- Prepositions/subordinating conjunctions—$\_IN$

Figure 2 shows the metamodel of linguistic information that we use in automated RE. The information is obtained using NLP tagging, parsing, and dependency analysis.

NLP techniques are relevant to the automation or semi-automation of requirements engineering activities such as extracting requirements from documentation, or formalisation of requirements as UML models, and they have been used in many works in these areas (Umar, 2020).

However, the trained models available with the existing NLP tools are usually oriented towards general English text, which differs significantly from the subset of English typically used in software requirements statements. In particular, requirements statements do not usually use colloquial or casual English, and they use computing/software terminology. Words such as "track", "security", and "record" are used in a more specific way in software descriptions, compared to their use in general English. The existing models therefore sometimes misclassify words in

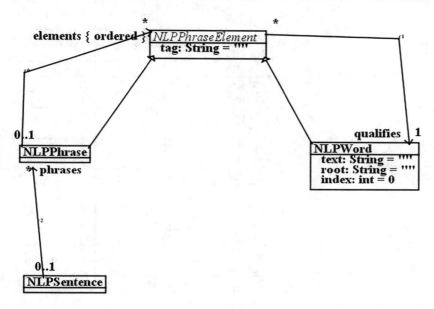

Fig. 2 NLP metamodel. Source: Authors

requirements statements. For this reason, we decided to retrain a POS tagging model using a corpus of requirements statements that we collected for data and behavioural requirements analysis (Sects. 3.4 and 3.5).

Table 1 shows the original POS tagging error rates (for words and for sentences) on the requirements documents used for training, and Table 2 the original and revised error rates on test cases after retraining of the Apache OpenNLP *maxent* POS model with manually corrected versions of the tagging. In the training set, 0.5% of words are misclassified, and 12.9% of sentences contain a misclassified word, which significantly affects the accuracy of our formalisation processes.

Retraining of the tagger reduced the error rates on the test cases from 0.4% per word and 9.4% per sentence to 0.2% per word and 5.6% per sentence (Table 2). This process was effective in removing the more serious errors; however, tagging and syntax analysis errors still arise in some cases (Sect. 4).

Table 1 POS tagger error rates

Case (# sentences)	Tagging word errors	Tagging sentence errors
Stroke assistant (8)	1	1
TrackFormer (4)	2	2
g02 (99)	17	16
g03 (60)	11	7
g04 (51)	7	5
g05 (53)	11	10
g08 (66)	2	2
g10 (98)	15	12
g11 (74)	14	12
g12 (53)	3	2
g13 (53)	12	10
g14 (67)	15	13
g16 (66)	8	7
g17 (64)	9	8
g18 (101)	16	15
g19 (138)	26	24
g21 (73)	12	10
g22 (83)	8	5
g23 (56)	3	3
Error rates	0.5%	12.9%

Table 2 Retrained POS tagger error rates

Case (# sentences)	Original tagging errors (words, sentences)	Retrained tagger errors (words, sentences)
g24 (52)	9, 9	3, 3
g25 (100)	3, 3	3, 2
g26 (100)	13, 13	6, 6
g27 (115)	9, 7	4, 4
g28 (60)	9, 8	10, 10
Error rates	0.4%, 9.4%	0.2%, 5.6%

3.2   Machine Learning

Machine learning covers a wide range of techniques by which knowledge about patterns and relationships between data is gained and represented as implicit or explicit rules in a software system. ML can be used for classification of inputs (e.g., to classify the severity of a patient's condition), translation (as in machine translation of natural language), or prediction. The techniques include K-nearest neighbours (KNN), decision trees, inductive logic programming (ILP), and neural nets. In each case, there is typically a training phase, in which known relationships of the existing data are provided to the ML software and rules expressing these relationships are induced, and a testing phase, to assess the accuracy of the learned rules on new data. The rules are usually embodied in an ML model file. Given a corpus of data with known classifications/results, this corpus is partitioned into a training set and a testing set, normally in a ratio such as 80:20. Only the training set is used to learn rules and construct an ML model. The accuracy of the trained ML model is typically assessed in terms of the level of agreement between its predictions on the test set and the correct results.

Toolsets for ML include Google MLKit, TensorFlow, Keras, ScikitLearn, and Theano.

NLP and ML can be usefully combined in requirements formalisation, whereby detailed linguistic information from NLP analysis can be provided as inputs to an ML process. Additionally, ML can be used to learn specific POS tagging rules for the restricted set of natural language texts that arise in software requirements documents, as described above.

3.3   Requirements Formalisation from Diagrams

Requirements statements often consist of a combination of text and informal diagrams, e.g., King's Health Partners (2011), Robertson and Robertson (2012). Apart from their visual content, such diagrams may also provide additional textual content, which can be used to identify key background terminology, data, and behaviour (e.g., as in Fig. 1).

To extract the textual content of diagrams, we use optical character recognition (OCR). We applied the Google MLKit OCR library to example diagrams including those of King's Health Partners (2011), Robertson and Robertson (2012) and the TS33.102 security standard of 3GPP.[1] While the basic OCR algorithm is able to recognise individual typed words, it is not effective at recognising blocks of text spread over successive lines. For example, 59 of 60 individual words in the road maintenance system context diagram of Robertson and Robertson (2012) are correctly recognised, but only 5 out of 19 blocks of text. To address this issue, we extend the OCR algorithm to consider two text elements as part of a single block if they are (approximately) left-aligned or right-aligned and are vertically immediately adjacent. Text blocks are merged by this process until no further combinations are possible. This increases the number of correct blocks and removes incomplete and incorrect blocks.

Accuracy in this chapter is measured by the standard *F-measure* defined by $F = \frac{2*p*r}{p+r}$, where precision $p = \frac{correct\ identifications}{total\ identified}$ and recall $r = \frac{correct\ identifications}{total\ correct}$. Table 3 shows the F-measure for individual word recognition

---

[1] https://portal.3gpp.org/desktopmodules/Specifications/SpecificationDetails.aspx? specificationId=2262. Retrieved May 15, 2021.

Table 3 Original and enhanced text recognition accuracy

Case	F-measure for word detection	F-measure of block detection	F-measure for merged block detection
1: Road maintenance (Robertson and Robertson, 2012)	0.97	0.38	0.65
2: Stroke assistant (King's Health Partners, 2011)	0.93	0.59	0.83
3: 3GPP TS33.102 (1)	0.9	0.64	0.88
4: 3GPP TS33.102 (2)	0.91	0.41	0.51

and for the original and enhanced text block recognition algorithms. A limitation of this approach is that the basic OCR algorithm sometimes identifies incorrect bounds for text areas, which is a factor in case 4 of Table 3.

Object recognition and OCR need to be coordinated, and text elements derived from a sketch image associated with other visual elements from the image (e.g., class rectangles or association lines) if they satisfy relevant spatial conditions (containment/overlapping or proximity constraints). We provide our enhanced OCR analysis as an Android app (Fig. 3). The app displays the merged text blocks and also records these in a file.

3.4 Deriving Data Model Specifications from Requirements Statements

The data model of an application is the basis for functional and behavioural specifications; thus we formalise this model prior to formalising functionality. As input to this step, we use the explicit requirements statements of the app and any necessary background documents and pre-existing models. In the medical domain, there may already exist detailed specifications of particular hardware to be used. For example, the diffusion pump controller (Campos and Harrison, 2011) is of this kind. Particular medical models may also be assumed, such as the Barthel Index model (Collin et al., 1988) for the performance of daily living activities (ADL), in the case of the stroke recovery assistant app. Our approach accommodates this situation by integrating the requirements formalisation approach with the model editor of AgileUML, so that any prior existing model can be loaded and its elements searched to identify and classify named terms in the analysed requirements statement. We assume that data and behaviour requirements are clearly separated, with global behaviour requirements expressed as user stories.

To assist in statement classification and semantic analysis, we define a knowledge base of software requirements terminology, including parts-of-speech (POS) information on words, synonyms, and semantic properties of terms (e.g., "temperature" is likely to denote a real-valued attribute).

For specific domains such as medicine or telecoms, a domain-specific knowledge base is also necessary, to capture information on terms with a specialised meaning in

Fig. 3 Extended OCR app.
Source: Authors

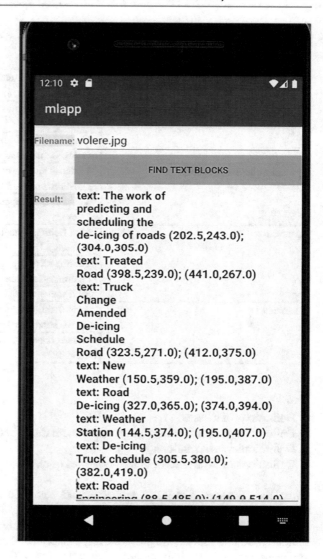

the domain, such as "dysphagia", "intervention", "consultation", and "out-patient" in medicine, and "connection" and "cell" in telecoms. A domain-specific knowledge base will usually take precedence over the general knowledge base.

We use the Stanford NLP toolset (Stanford University, 2020) and Apache OpenNLP (Apache Software Foundation, 2019) to perform part-of-speech tagging of English sentences, to construct syntax trees, and to identify dependencies within sentences. The resulting information is then used as input for a classifier that identifies sentences as either:

Table 4 Variation in requirements statement sentences

Statement type	Examples
Classdefinition	"Each bond has a unique name, a numeric term, a numeric coupon, and whole-number frequency"
	"The app records the weight, age, height and sex of users"
	"The property table holds details of address, price and vendor"
Specialisation/generalisation	"A bond is either a corporate bond or government bond"
	"A customer is a special case of a user"
Associations	"Each Bond is issued by one issuer"
	"The app records a training programme for each user"
	"Each student attends several courses"
Invariants	"Bond durations are never more than the bond term"
	"The sex is either male or female"

1. Definitions of classes
2. Definitions of specialisation/generalisation relations between classes
3. Definitions of associations
4. Definitions of invariants or other properties of classes.

After classification, a detailed syntactic and semantic analysis can be applied to extract model content from the text information. Successive sentences are analysed taking into account of the partial models already obtained from preceding sentences, so that models are progressively elaborated. Contradictions, redundancy, and omissions within requirements statements can also be identified during this process.

The wide variability in expression of data requirements statements in practice can be seen in Table 4.

In order to classify sentences as one of the above four categories, we apply heuristic rules based on a number of factors: (1) the similarity of the main verb to one characteristic of the classification category; (2) occurrences of terminology indicating the classification category; (3) sentence structure and intra-sentence dependencies; and (4) classifications of terms from the general knowledge base.

Characteristic features of class definition sentences are:

- Occurrence of verbs synonymous to "have", "has", "holds", "consists", "specifies", "comprises", "is defined by", "stores", "records", "maintains", etc.
- The class being introduced or further defined is the main noun of the sentence subject, except in cases where the subject denotes the system/app, in which case the class occurs in the object part.
- Terminology such as "each/every X instance …"/"all X instances …"/"An X instance" suggesting that X is a class.
- Terms denoting attributes occur in the object part.

Characteristics of specialisation/generalisation sentences are:

- Occurrence of verbs synonymous to "specialises", "generalises", "inherits", "extends", "abstracts", "classified", "derived", etc., or the sentence structure is similar to forms such as "… is a special case of …"; "… is either an X or …"; "… is an X [with …]".
- Adjectival qualifiers applied to already known classes, suggesting that the qualified term denotes a subclass of the unqualified: "secure channel".
- A conjunctive/disjunctive clause combines two or more known class terms: "patients and caretakers" and "treatments and exercises".
- Usually, the only named elements are classes, not features.
- If the left-hand side (subject) does denote a known feature, then the sentence is instead a constraint defining the permitted values of the feature.

Characteristics of association definition sentences are:

- Occurrence of verbs synonymous to "linked to"/"related to"/"associated with", etc., or the use of an attribution verb ("has", "composed of", etc.) with the object naming classes.
- Alternatively, the main verb may name the association role, with the related class Y in the sentence object: "Each X role [quantifier] Y(s)".
- Usually, the only named elements are role names and classes, not attributes.

Invariants are difficult to characterise, but the occurrence of words synonymous to "is always"/"are never" or of comparatives/superlatives ($\_JJR$, $\_JJS$) is one indicator of this form. The subject may be a feature f of class X in a possessive phrase of the form "The X's f" or equivalent. Comparator and mathematical operators may be used.

In order to detect synonyms, we use a thesaurus and word distance measures of name edit distance (NSS) (Levenshtein, 1966) and name semantic similarity (NMS) (Lano et al., 2020). Users can set a threshold for the level of similarity that is to be regarded as significant. We found that the WordNet thesaurus (Fellbaum, 2010) was too general for practical use since it covers all possible meanings of a word in general English, while requirements statements use a restricted and usually technical vocabulary. Thus we developed our own thesaurus.

We use the standard XML thesaurus format of Rowley (2007) to define this thesaurus and to represent domain and general background knowledge in knowledge bases. An example from the general requirements knowledge base is

```
<CONCEPT>
<DESCRIPTOR>temperature</DESCRIPTOR>
<POS>NN</POS>
<SEM type="double">attribute</SEM>
<PT>temperature</PT>
<NT>heat</NT>
<NT>body-temperature</NT>
<NT>ambient-temperature</NT>
</CONCEPT>
```

Any preferred term (PT) or non-preferred term (NT) in the concept word group will be treated as having the same semantics and part-of-speech classification defined in the SEM and POS clauses. Care should be taken to avoid ambiguity and conflicting definitions of the same word when designing or extending a knowledge base of this form.

Subsequent to classification, detailed semantic analysis takes place in three phases applied over the sequence of sentences in the requirements statement:

1. Recognition of classes:
   (a) Words identical to the names of classes already existing in the software model or recognised from a previous sentence.
   (b) Words denote classes according to background knowledge in the general or specialised knowledge base (e.g., "webpage", "ward").
   (c) Words denote classes according to their role in the sentence (e.g., as the subject of the principal form of class definition sentence).
   (d) Words are proper nouns (tagged as NNP or NNPS)—the singular form of the noun is taken as the class name. A more liberal approach could be to also consider other nouns (NN or NNS) with an initial capital as proper nouns, if they do not appear as the first word of a sentence.
   Inheritance relations are established based on the sentences classified as defining specialisations.
2. Recognition of attributes:
   (a) A word is identical to the name of an attribute already known from the pre-existing software model or from previous sentences.
   (b) A word denotes an attribute according to general or specific background knowledge (e.g., "age", "dose").
   (c) A word is an attribute according to the role of the word in the sentence (e.g., it occurs in the object of class definition sentences, and it is not a class or role).
   The types, multiplicities, and stereotypes of attributes are also extracted.

Table 5 Redundancy/conflicts in data requirements statement sentences

Redundancies	Inconsistencies	Omissions
Two statements both define feature f of class C	Two statements give conflicting types/multiplicities for feature f of C	A class is referenced but not defined
Two statements both express that class D subclasses class C	Two statements express contradictory subclass relationships between classes	A subclass relation is assumed but not declared

3. Reference recognition:
   (a) A word is identical to the name of a reference already known from the pre-existing software model or from previous sentences.
   (b) A word denotes a reference according to background knowledge (e.g., "parent").
   (c) The word is a reference according to the form of the sentence (e.g., "The monitoring equipment includes a set of movement sensors").
   (d) The word has its initial letter in lower case, and the initial uppercased singular form of the word is the name of a known class (e.g., "patients", "ward").
   Reference types, multiplicities, and stereotypes are also extracted (e.g., "series" suggests an $\{ordered\}$ stereotype on a feature).

In order to validate the data formalisation approach, we compared the result of formalisation with models manually created from the same requirements statements by a modelling expert. We used 11 cases, including Lano (1989), King's Health Partners (2011), and three cases from Kaggle (2021). These contain 67 sentences in total. We achieved an average F-measure of 0.91 for the accuracy of sentence classification and 0.84 for the accuracy of models.

The formalisation process can also assist in requirements validation, by detecting redundancy, omissions, or inconsistencies in requirements statements (Table 5).

Possible quality problems with the synthesised model can be identified, such as 1–1 associations and multiple inheritance. Some potential cases of refactoring can also be identified, such as multiple subclasses of the same class all possessing copies of the same feature. Classes that are synonymous or have identical data can be merged.

Traceability of the specification with respect to the requirements is maintained by recording a many–many relation $dependsUpon : ModelElement \leftrightarrow NLPPhraseElement$ that identifies which requirements statement elements contributed to the definition of each derived model element. The originating elements $dependsUpon(\{x\})$ of a class or use case x (for behaviour analysis) are recorded as stereotypes of x.

3.5   Deriving Behavioural Model Specifications from Requirements Statements

Following data formalisation, behavioural formalisation can be applied; this uses the extracted data specification.

We assume that behavioural requirements are of two kinds:

- Expected functionalities/services offered by the system, expressed as user stories. These can be formalised as UML use cases in AgileUML.
- Operation specifications for operations/methods of particular classes, expressed in terms of the expected inputs and outputs of these operations.

In this chapter, we focus upon the first case.

User stories are the principal form of behaviour requirement used in agile methods. They express some unit of functionality which a user of the system expects from the system, in other words, the use cases which the system should support. User stories are typically expressed in the format

$$[actor\ identification]\ goal\ [justification],$$

where the actor identification and justification are optional.

For example:

"As an A, I wish to B, in order to C"

The actor identification defines which system actor the use case is for. The goal describes the intended use case actions, and the justification explains its purpose. These correspond to the graphical use case form of Fig. 4.

Other alternative formats for user stories are

"The A should be able to B, in order to C"
"The A must be able to B, so that C"
"The system must allow A to B"
"The system shall provide B"
"A will be able to B"

Fig. 4 Use case derivation from user stories. Source: Authors

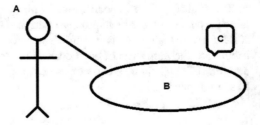

or simply *B* by itself, as in the King's Health Partners (2011) patient analysis behavioural requirements for the doctor's interface:

```
Add new user.

Add new patient.

Add new patient data.

Update existing patient data.

Patient-specific numerics.

Patient-specific graphics.

Group-level graphics.

Group-level numerics.
```

These were extracted from an informal diagram of the system behaviour using the Google MLKit OCR facilities.

In each format, a reference to any actor *A* occurs prior to *B*. A modal verb ("should", "must", etc.) identifies the obligation to provide the functionality *B*. Statements *B* and *C* typically refer to the classes and features recognised in the data formalisation stage. *B* should begin with a verb in infinitive form (the tag *VB*). In the absence of a formalised data model, classes are recognised according to background knowledge and their role in the sentence. For example, *User*, *Patient*, and *Group* are recognised as classes in the above patient analysis requirements.

In addition to the background knowledge file *output/background.txt* on nouns, we also provide a knowledge base *output/verbs.txt* of verbs and their classifications (*read, edit, create, delete, other*). This file is in the same thesaurus format as the background file for nouns and can be edited by the user to provide further information on verbs. An example entry is

```
<CONCEPT>
<DESCRIPTOR>search</DESCRIPTOR>
<POS>VB</POS>
<SEM>read</SEM>
<PT>search</PT>
<NT>find</NT>
<NT>retrieve</NT>
<NT>extract</NT>
<NT>scan</NT>
<NT>inspect</NT>
<NT>identify</NT>
<NT>examine</NT>
</CONCEPT>
```

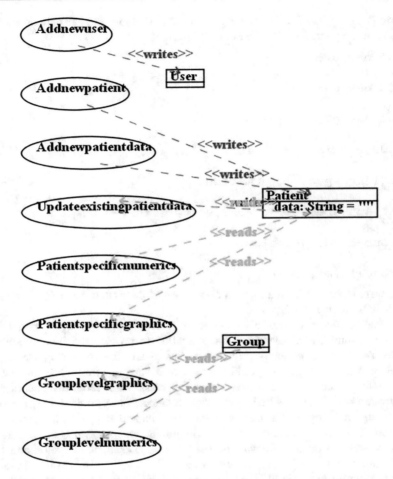

Fig. 5 Formalised model and dependencies of (King's Health Partners, 2011) patient analysis requirements. Source: Authors

User stories that represent standard functionalities such as creating, editing, deleting, and reading instances of a class can be classified into these categories based on the verbs used in the goal part B of the user story. The classified sentence is then formalised as a UML use case. The semantics of the use case depends on the classification of the user story. The actor A of a use case is recorded in a stereotype $actor = \text{"}A\text{"}$ of the formalised use case. If A is a class name, then an instance of the actor becomes the first parameter of the use case.

Data dependencies between classes and use cases can then be computed and shown visually (e.g., Fig. 5).

We validated the behaviour formalisation process using the 22 requirements statements of Mendeley Software Repository (2018), 3 cases from Kaggle (2021), and the stroke recovery assistant case. In total, there are 2218 user stories in these cases. The accuracy of use case classification and the accuracy of the formalised UML models were measured. In computing the F-measure for formalisation, we consider how many synthesised classes and use cases are semantically valid or invalid w.r.t. the requirements. The overall average for classification accuracy was 0.97 and for formalisation 0.94.

The main source of imprecision in behaviour formalisation is due to errors in tagging, e.g., tagging of "And" as a NNP instead of CC. In addition, (i) general concepts such as "Application", "UI", or "System" are incorrectly recognised as classes; (ii) successive nouns in the actor identification part are not combined but become separate classes, e.g., "Attending Physician" is represented as two separate classes.

These issues could be corrected by: (i) defining a separate list of key-words/blocked words, which cannot be used as class names and (ii) automatically combining successive nouns in the actor identification.

We prefer to leave (ii) as a developer choice, so that if they want the combined term to become a class, they can write it as one word "AttendingPhysician", etc.

As with the formalisation of data requirements, possible flaws in user stories can be detected during this analysis process:

- The goal part B does not begin with a verb.
- The formalised use case has multiple possible classifications (e.g., create and delete), indicating a user story that is too complex and should be decomposed.
- A complete requirements statement would be expected to have a $createE$, $editE$, or $readE$ use case for each entity E of the system.

Duplicated requirements sentences and multiple variant versions of the same concept can also be detected by the user story formalisation process. A useful facility that could be added would be to group those use cases with a common actor into separate subsystems. Likewise, it would be useful to be able to group together all use cases that refer to a given class or a subset of classes. The formalised models contain sufficient information to perform such modularisations.

4   Integration of Automated Requirements Engineering into an Agile MDE Process

In an agile method such as Scrum or XP, parts/subsystems of a system are developed and delivered within iterations or "sprints". Lifecycle stages of feasibility analysis, requirements capture, and requirements specification are performed for each system part and themselves may involve iteration. For example, a prototype may be constructed to demonstrate how the developer intends to implement the subsystem requirements. This can then be reviewed by the customer representative in order to check that the intended approach satisfies the customer requirements. Modifications are made if necessary, and the prototype progressed towards a production version.

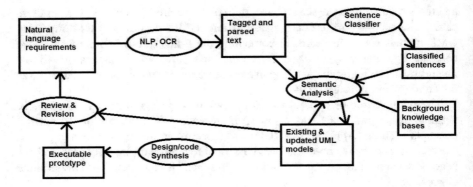

Fig. 6 Automated requirements engineering in the agile MDE process. Source: Authors

The automated RE techniques described in Sects. 3.4 and 3.5 can accelerate this development iteration cycle, by automating model construction and the synthesis of prototypes from these models (Fig. 6). Traceability is a key facility in this situation, enabling the developer and customer to identify which requirements statements contribute to possibly erroneous use cases and executable behaviour.

The requirements of each system part may consist of a group of related user stories. These form a work item that will be listed in the product backlog of the system and in the iteration backlog of the iteration responsible for its development. In an agile MDE process, a common class diagram model is usually shared by all the teams working in an iteration, in order to ensure a consistent data model is used (Lano, 2017). The different groups of use cases will typically form separate work items, but each group depends upon the common data model. Together with the models and requirements statements, a project could also maintain a project-specific knowledge base, which records particular terminologies and word classifications relevant to the project.

As an example of this process, we consider some further data and behaviour requirements from King's Health Partners (2011):

```
For each patient,
record the BarthelIndex.

Each patient has a name, age,
date admitted, and stay duration.

Each patient has measures of diabetes,
incontinence, dysphagia,
visual field and comorbidity.

Each patient has estimates of mortality
risk and disability risk.
```

Patients are either inpatients or outpatients.

Comorbidity is either present or absent or unknown.

As a nurse, I need to process the admission of a patient to a ward.

As a doctor, I wish to assess the condition of a patient.

As a doctor, I need to approve the discharge of a patient from hospital.

Part of the formalised model extracted from the above sentences is

```
package app {
  class BarthelIndex {
  stereotype originator="1";
  }

  class Patient {
  stereotype originator="1";
  stereotype modifiedBy="1";
  stereotype modifiedBy="2";
  stereotype modifiedBy="3";
  stereotype modifiedBy="4";

    attribute name : String;
    attribute age : double;
    attribute date : String;
    attribute duration : double;
    attribute measures : Set(String);
    attribute diabetes : String;
    attribute incontinence : String;
    attribute dysphagia : String;
    attribute visualField : String;
    attribute comorbidity : ComorbidityTYPE;
    attribute estimates : Set(String);
    attribute mortalityRisk : double;
    attribute disabilityRisk : double;
    reference record : BarthelIndex;
  }
```

Review of this model reveals several flaws: "admitted" and "stay" are omitted from the model because they were misclassified by the NLP tagger as verbs. The parse tree of the second sentence is

```
(ROOT
  (S
    (NP (DT Each) (NN patient))
    (VP (VBZ has)
      (NP
        (NP (DT a) (NN name)
          (, ,) (NN age)
          (, ,) (NN date))
        (SBAR
          (S
            (VP
              (VP (VBD admitted))
              (, ,)
              (CC and)
              (VP (VB stay)
                (NP (NN duration)))))))))
    (. .)))
```

To avoid this problem, we can change the text to "Each patient has a name, age, admission date and stay duration".

In addition, spurious attributes *measures* and *estimates* have been derived. This can be remedied by clarifying the third requirements sentence to:

```
Each patient has a diabetes measure,
incontinence measure, dysphagia measure,
visual field measure and comorbidity.
```

and similarly for the fourth sentence. The revised model derived from these improved requirements is shown in Fig. 7.

A quality check of this model gives the warning that all subclasses of *Patient* are empty, so these could be refactored into an enumeration. Again, the requirements could be revised (*stayDuration* could be moved to *Inpatient*, for example). From this model, Java code can be generated for a prototype app implementation (Lano et al., 2021), together with a test suite and test harness (Fig. 8).

5   Related Work

In Alwakeel and Lano (2021), we evaluated 110 m-health apps in the domain of patient self-managed health-care. This survey identified that there has been increasing use of ML techniques in such apps, to perform activity detection and behaviour analysis. However, this evaluation also identified that there is a lack of guidelines for the specification and design of such systems, and in particular for the

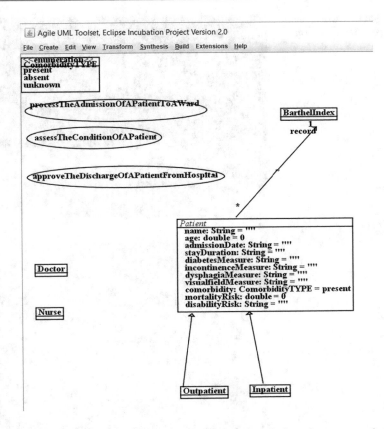

Fig. 7 Formalised requirements of stroke assistant (patient analysis and management). Source: Authors

selection of ML techniques. An MDE-based approach would therefore appear to be beneficial in increasing the rigour of m-health app development.

We also carried out a systematic literature review (SLR) of papers in the field of automated requirements engineering, published between 1996 and 2020 (Umar, 2020). From an original set of 3853 papers, 54 studies were shortlisted and analysed in detail. We found that NLP was the main approach used, with 52% of cases using some NLP techniques, and most approaches were semi-automated rather than fully automated. Of NLP techniques, 13 cases used parsing, 11 used POS, and 3 used dependency analysis. 14 cases used a combination of NLP and ML, with naive Bayes the most common classifier used (4 cases), and neural nets were used in 2 cases.

Subsequent to the SLR, further relevant papers (Saini et al., 2020; Burgueño et al., 2019; Xu et al., 2020) have been published. Compared to Saini et al. (2020), we also use a hybrid NLP/ML approach and a knowledge base; however, we adopt

Fig. 8 Stroke assistant app prototype. Source: Authors

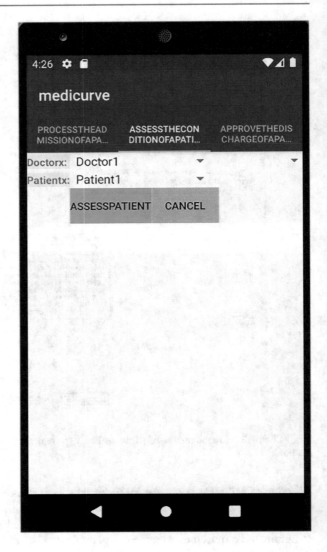

the use of both a general knowledge base and specialised knowledge bases for particular domains (finance and telecoms). Our approach is therefore closer to the framework for using NLP in requirements engineering suggested in Berzins et al. (2007). With regard to datasets, Saini et al. (2020) use a set of student solutions to a particular coursework problem, while we use diverse examples both from student projects and industrial cases, including the large dataset (Mendeley Software Repository, 2018) of user stories. While our accuracy measures are generally lower than those of Saini et al. (2020), this may be due to the higher variability in the form of the requirements in our dataset.

In Xu et al. (2020), a customised NLP approach is applied to formalise statements regarding physical construction layouts from textual requirements and to express these in an extended OCL. The approach could have more general potential for formalising application invariants or standards documentation in OCL; however, our preference is for the use of established NLP tools where possible, with customisation of the language models via retraining to specialised domains.

NLP techniques also have relevance for text mining tasks such as extraction of information from medical reports, to support analysis and prediction processes. In general, text mining is more effectively performed upon more highly structured and semantically coded documentation, rather than upon less structured source material.

National guidelines for health apps have been published in the United Kingdom (Public Health England, 2017). These emphasise the critical importance of the correctness in health apps. Our iterative approach can help to assure correctness by providing a resolution of ambiguities and errors in software requirements at an early development stage.

6   Conclusions

In summary, our requirements formalisation approach for health applications provides an effective means for extracting specifications from natural language requirements. Integration with an existing MDE toolset provides a direct means of visualising, analysing, and prototyping formalised requirements.

In future work, we aim to:

- Extend the data and behaviour requirements formalisation techniques to encompass a wider range of input texts and diagrams, in particular to formalise detailed constraints and operation definitions.
- Investigate the production of other models from formalised requirements, such as activity models/workflows, identify use case relationships, and implement further quality checks/analysis on formalised requirements.
- Investigate the formalisation of models from sketches.

Acknowledgments Lyan Alwakeel acknowledges the funding support of University of Tabuk, Saudi Arabia.

Muhammad Aminu Umar acknowledges the funding support of the Petroleum Technology Development Fund (PTDF), the Federal Government of Nigeria.

The authors declare no potential conflicts of interest.

References

Alwakeel, L., & Lano, K. (2021). *Functional and technical aspects of mobile health applications: A systematic literature review.* King's College London.

Apache Software Foundation. (2019). *Apache OpenNLP Toolkit.* https://opennlp.apache.org/

Berzins, V., Martell, C., & Adams, P. (2007). Innovations in natural language document processing for requirements engineering. In *Monterey workshop* (pp. 125–146). Springer.

Burgueño, L., Cabot, J., & Gérard, S. (2019). An LSTM-based neural network architecture for model transformations. In *2019 ACM/IEEE 22nd International Conference on Model Driven Engineering Languages and Systems (MODELS)* (pp. 294–299). IEEE.

Campos, J. C., & Harrison, M. (2011). Modelling and analysing the interactive behaviour of an infusion pump. *Electronic Communications of the EASST, 45*, 20–45.

Collin, C., Wade, D., Davies, S., & Horne, V. (1988). The Barthel ADL index: A reliability study. *International Disability Studies, 10*(2), 61–63.

Eclipse (2021). *Eclipse AgileUML project.* https://projects.eclipse.org/projects/modeling.agileuml

Fellbaum, C. (2010). WordNet. In *Theory and applications of ontology: Computer applications* (pp. 231–243). Springer.

Kaggle (2021). *Software requirements dataset.* www.kaggle.com/iamsouvik/software-requirements-dataset

King's Health Partners. (2011). *Stroke recovery assistant project brief, version 1.0.*

Kotonya, G., & Sommerville, I. (1996). Requirements engineering with viewpoints. *Software Engineering Journal, 11*(1), 5–18.

Lano, K. (2017). *Agile model-based development using UML-RSDS.* CRC Press.

Lano, K. (1989). The Specification of a Real-Time System in Z. REDO Report 2487-TN-PRG-1015, Oxford University Computing Laboratory, *Programming Research Group*, 11 Keble Rd., Oxford, OX1 3QD, UK.

Lano, K., Alwakeel, L., Rahimi, S. K., & Haughton, H. (2021). Synthesis of mobile applications using AgileUML. In *14th Innovations in Software Engineering Conference (Formerly Known as India Software Engineering Conference)* (pp. 1–10). Association for Computing Machinery.

Lano, K., Fang, S., Umar, M., & Yassipour-Tehrani, S. (2020). Enhancing model transformation synthesis using natural language processing. In *Proceedings of the 23rd ACM/IEEE International Conference on Model Driven Engineering Languages and Systems: Companion Proceedings* (pp. 1–10). Association for Computing Machinery.

Levenshtein, V. I. (1966). Binary codes capable of correcting deletions, insertions, and reversals. In *Soviet physics Doklady* (Vol. 10, pp. 707–710). Soviet Union.

Mendeley Software Repository. (2018). *Mendeley user story dataset.* Accessed January 5, 2021 from https://data.mendeley.com/dataset/7zbk8zsd8y/1

Public Health England. (2017). *Criteria for health app assessment.* Accessed May 20, 2021 from https://www.gov.uk/government/publications/health-app-assessment-criteria

Robertson, S. & Robertson, J. (2012). Mastering the Requirements Process: Getting requirements right, *Addison-Wesley*, 3rd edition, 547 pages.

Rowley, J. (2007). BS 8723 structured vocabularies for information retrieval: Part 1: Definitions, symbols and abbreviations, and part 2: Thesauri. *Journal of Documentation, 63*, 428–443.

Saini, R., Mussbacher, G., Guo, J. L., & Kienzle, J. (2020). DoMoBOT: A bot for automated and interactive domain modelling. In *Proceedings of the 23rd ACM/IEEE International Conference on Model Driven Engineering Languages and Systems: Companion Proceedings* (pp. 1–10).

Santorini, B. (1990). *Part-of-speech tagging guidelines for the Penn Treebank Project.*

Stanford University. (2020). *Stanford NLP*. Accessed May 20, 2021 from https://nlp.stanford.edu/software

Umar, M. A. (2020). Automated requirements engineering framework for agile development. *ICSEA 2020* (p. 157).

Xu, X., Chen, K., & Cai, H. (2020). Automating utility permitting within highway right-of-way via a generic UML/OCL model and natural language processing. *Journal of Construction Engineering and Management, 146*(12), 04020135.

The Outlook for Novel Pharmaceutics

Maryam Parhizkar and Dimitrios Tsaoulidis

Abstract

Recent advances in treatment and prevention using novel approaches are opening the door for a seismic shift in healthcare. In this chapter, we report advances in four key areas of personalised medicine: tissue engineering, regenerative medicine, gene therapy, and nanomedicine. We include examples of products currently in the market, barriers to translating these novel therapies to the clinic, and the outlook for emerging therapies.

1 Introduction

Every year, regulatory bodies around the world approve hundreds of new medications. Most of these are variations of existing products that include new dosages for already approved drugs or cost-saving generics. These products aim to improve the quality of care, provide greater access to medication, and create a competitive marketplace in order to improve both affordability and public health. However, a small number of novel drugs are being approved that provide innovative approaches that are advancing clinical care to a new level.

The pharmaceutical industry is going through a paradigm shift that is catalysed by new and disruptive technologies (such as nanotechnology, additive manufacturing, and artificial intelligence (AI)) that facilitate the development of groundbreak-

M. Parhizkar (✉)
School of Pharmacy, University College London, London, UK
e-mail: maryam.parhizkar@ucl.ac.uk

D. Tsaoulidis
Department of Chemical and Process Engineering, University of Surrey, Guildford, UK
e-mail: d.tsaoulidis@surrey.ac.uk

© The Author(s), under exclusive license to Springer Nature Switzerland AG 2022
S. Ehsani et al. (eds.), *The Future Circle of Healthcare*, Future of Business and Finance, https://doi.org/10.1007/978-3-030-99838-7_16

ing new therapies. These new therapies include innovative solutions involving cell and gene therapies, tissue-engineered products, and nanomedicine. It is expected that these novel therapies will bring important benefits to future healthcare and revolutionise the treatment of diseases such as neurological disorders or cancers. In addition, these therapies, which are often targeted and specific, will offer tailored solutions based on the needs of individual patients that will pave the way for more personalised therapies.

In this chapter, we will review some of the novel approaches that are expected to be adopted in the future, including examples from several clinically approved treatments. We will also discuss the challenges associated with the translation of these novel therapies to the clinic.

2   Personalised Medicine

Personalised medicine is the concept of tailoring healthcare based on a patient's genetics, phenotype, lifestyle, and environment. This strategy could influence the outcome of therapies by enhancing efficacy and increasing the safety of drugs whilst improving patient compliance and reducing costs. Personalised medicine is often intertwined with 'precision medicine', which is the use of data and genomics to tailor interventions to specific patient groups. Precision medicine relies heavily on data, analytics, and information. Rapid advancements in genomic technologies have provided a deeper understanding of pathology and the progression of diseases. This knowledge coupled with emerging methodologies for monitoring treatment responses drives more personalised approaches to the management and treatment of diseases.

The 'one-size-fits-all' model for delivering medicine is a thing of the past, and there is an urgent need to target specific medication to specific patient populations at the best dose and the right time. The introduction of government initiatives has pushed the fields of precision and personalised medicine forward. The '100,000 Genomes Project' in the United Kingdom was completed in 2018. The project aimed to combine genomic sequencing data with National Health Service medical records to sequence 100,000 genomes from around 85,000 patients affected by cancer or rare diseases (Wilson & Nicholls, 2015). The launch of the Precision Medicine Initiative in the United States in 2015 (Sankar & Parker, 2017) to create a centralised database of medical records from a diverse cohort of one million volunteers is another example of government support for developing personalised medicine.

2.1   Personalised Medicine in the Market

Oncology is the field that has been most impacted by the developments in precision medicine. However, personalised therapies in other therapeutic areas, including rare genetic disorders and diseases of the central nervous system, are slowly catching up. Although many of the approved precision treatments for cancer fall short of being tailored to a specific individual, they allow for more detailed stratification of patients based on the oncogenic mutation of their tumours. Some common mutations are the human epidermal growth factor receptor 2 (HER2) in certain breast and stomach cancers and the epidermal growth factor receptor (EGFR) in lung cancer.

Advances in 'omic' technologies have led to the discovery of a variety of molecular-based targeted therapies. Monoclonal antibodies (mAbs), proteins with the ability to bind to a specific molecular target, are promising therapeutic candidates for cancer that offer low toxicity. Therapies based on monoclonal antibodies are the fastest-growing precision medicine. There are currently more than 20 Food and Drug Administration (FDA)-approved mAbs-based drugs in oncology alone (Lu et al., 2020). Some examples are Herceptin (trastuzumab) for HER-2, BRAF inhibitor Zelboraf (vemurafenib) (Plexxikon/Genentech), and EGFR inhibitor Tagrisso (osimertinib) (AstraZeneca Pharmaceuticals) (Schilsky, 2010). Monoclonal antibodies are also used in the treatment of autoimmune diseases (e.g., daclizumab for the treatment of multiple sclerosis or ustekinumab for psoriasis), infections (ibalizumab for HIV), bone loss (denosumab to treat osteoporosis), inflammatory diseases (adalimumab for rheumatoid arthritis), and haematological disorders (eculizumab for the treatment of paroxysmal nocturnal haemoglobinuria).

Next-generation sequencing technologies at the single-cell level have generated more precise information about novel drug targets and have resulted in the development of more personalised approaches. Regulators such as the FDA and the European Medicines Agency (EMA) have approved 'tumour-agonistic' treatments. The first and most famous example is Keytruda (pembrolizumab) (Merck) (Emancipator, 2020), which targets a genetic signature (a biomarker expressed in non-small-cell lung cancer) regardless of the tumour location.

More recently, genetically engineered chimeric antigen receptor (CAR) T-cell therapies have emerged as a promising step towards individualised cancer immunotherapy. The FDA has approved treatments such as Kymriah (Novartis) for children with acute lymphoblastic leukaemia and Yescarta (Kite Pharma) for adults with advanced lymphomas. In these treatment strategies, T cells are removed from the patient's blood and are modified to target tumour cell antigens before they are infused back into the bloodstream (Abreu et al., 2020). CAR T-cell therapies exemplify customised and personalised approaches to treat patients with relapse from malignancies that are resistant to treatment. So far, CAR T-cell therapies have demonstrated more successful responses to treatment compared with conventional therapies.

2.2 The Outlook for Personalised Medicine

The success of personalised medicine will depend on the integrity of data and a high level of understanding of the diseases and individual patients' needs. Data collection and analytics will play a big part in this process. Advances in genomics, diagnostic or predictive AI, genetic sequencing, and imaging data will be essential to gain more insight into disease processes. However, there will be many challenges to protect the integrity of data due to its large volume and complexity. This also includes the transformation of the data that is another hurdle to overcome.

Another barrier in translating personalised therapies in the clinic is the high cost associated with the lengthy procedures of finding and validating specific biomarkers and analysis of vast amounts of data. Innovative trial designs and complex manufacturing processes (e.g., cell and gene therapies) are also very expensive. Promising innovations in CAR T manufacturing and potential 'off-the-shelf' T-cell production methods could help bring down the cost of these therapies in years to come and make them more accessible to a larger population of patients.

Uncertainty about regulation is another key factor that is hindering the translation of personalised medicine. Personalised medicine requires innovative clinical trial design with smaller sample sizes. This leads to difficulties with providing sufficient evidence of safety and efficacy, which limits eligibility for regulatory approval.

Addressing these barriers to personalised medicine, in combination with scientific advances in related fields such as digital health and artificial intelligence, will enable personalised therapies to reach their promised potential and reform the model of healthcare systems globally.

3 Gene Therapy

In the last two decades, cell and gene therapy has come of age, from theoretical conceptual approaches to patient-focused clinical practice. Cell therapy involves the treatment of diseases by modifying certain sets of cells or by transferring cells (either autologous or allogeneic) with a relevant function into the patient's body. Gene therapy involves the treatment of diseases by adding or replacing genes in cells or inactivating genes in cells. In gene therapy, the genetic material is transferred in a carrier or vector into the appropriate cells of the patient's body. Unlike traditional therapeutics, gene therapy assisted by emerging technologies, functional genomics screens, AI, machine learning, and human genetic locus associations can effectively introduce novel recombinant genetic material to increase the capability of cells and the immune system to fight or ameliorate infectious diseases, various types of cancer, and genetic disorders (Lostalé-Seijo & Montenegro, 2018).

Exogenous genetic material can replicate with the cell, and new cells can contain the same genetic material as the parent cell. The genetic material is transfected or transduced into cells via the negatively charged cell membrane. The genetic material may consist of negatively charged nuclei acids such as plasmid DNA to introduce protein expression, short-regulatory RNA or RNA interference to silence or knockout genes, messenger RNA (mRNA) to regulate protein expression, and antisense oligonucleotides to modulate gene expression (Tijsterman et al., 2002).

3.1   Gene Therapy and Gene Delivery

Gene therapy can be classified into two main categories depending on which types of cells are treated: somatic gene therapy, which does not pass the genetic change to the next generations, and germline gene therapy, which does pass the genetic change to the next generations (Tachibana et al., 2013). Although germline gene therapy may have great potential, it is accompanied by many bioethical considerations and its adoption has received criticism from the scientific community (Brokowski & Adli, 2020). At the time of writing, germline gene editing (for reproduction) is not allowed. Although many types of gene therapy are in clinical trials, the main therapeutic strategies that are used to treat several diseases and target specific populations of somatic cells are gene correction, gene addition, and gene silencing (Sung & Kim, 2019). Gene correction involves modifying part of a gene using gene editing technologies (e.g., CRISPR/Cas9) to replace a faulty region of DNA and produce a protein that functions properly. Gene addition can be achieved when a new copy of a gene is carried into the cells by an adeno-associated virus (AAV) to produce a protein. Gene silencing is a mechanism that regulates or prevents the production of a specific protein by degrading mRNA (Manjunath et al., 2013).

Depending on the type of the disease and the cells involved, genetic material can be administered either directly, i.e., in vivo, to the target cells that remain in the body of the patient or indirectly, i.e., ex vivo, where the cells are removed from the body of the patient and genetic material is delivered to the cells in vitro and are then introduced back to the patient (Hernandez-Alcoceba et al., 2016). Selecting the correct gene delivery system is important for the success of the gene therapy and requires an understanding of intracellular delivery, the target mechanism, and the long-term expression between the delivery system and the target cells. Although different types of gene delivery systems (vectors) that can be applied in gene therapy have been developed, all of them have certain limitations and side effects.

Most commonly, gene delivery systems are categorised as viral based, non-viral based, and hybrid (Cevher et al., 2012). Viral vectors have been successfully used over the last 50 years although these systems involve certain shortcomings such as cytotoxicity, immunogenicity, carcinogenicity, large-scale production limitations, and limited carrying capacity. The viruses involved are nonreplicating, meaning that they can induce host immune responses but cannot replicate in normal cells. The most frequently employed forms of viral vectors are retrovirus vectors, adenoviral vectors, lentivirus vectors, AAV vectors, herpes simplex virus vectors, and poxvirus vectors (Nayerossadat et al., 2012). It is worth mentioning that the success of virus vector-based gene therapies has a broader impact on the approval of new therapies that are constantly being proposed and investigated. Most recently, in response to the COVID-19 pandemic, AstraZeneca and Johnson and Johnson developed vaccines that use adenovirus vectors to carry double-stranded DNA to cells for transient spike protein expression (Moore, 2021).

Two gene therapies based on AAV vectors, Luxturna (Spark Therapeutics) (2017) and Zolgensma (Novartis) (2019), have been used to treat retinal dystrophy and spinal muscular atrophy, respectively (Bulaklak & Gersbach, 2020). In Luxturna, a functional copy of the gene RPE65 (which is responsible for producing an enzyme that is necessary for the normal function of retinal cells) is administered in the subretinal space by injecting an AAV vector solution. Zolgensma utilises the novel AAV technology platform NAV AAV9 to deliver functional copies of the *SMN1* gene (which is responsible for producing a protein that is necessary for the normal functioning of the nerves that control muscle movement to neurons). Another example is Strimvelis (GlaxoSmithKline), which is approved in the EU. Strimvelis is indicated for the treatment of patients with adenosine deaminase deficiency and acts by transducing CD34+ cells with a retroviral vector to restore gene function and introducing them back to the patients.

Non-viral vectors have become a realistic alternative to viral vectors since they can effectively improve transfection and exhibit low host immunogenicity. In addition, they can lower the cost of large-scale production. Non-viral systems can be categorised into chemical and physical systems based on the method used to facilitate their uptake into the target cells. Chemical methods, which are more widely used than physical ones, include carriers prepared from natural or synthetic compounds that deliver the genetic material into the cells. This can often be facilitated through nanoparticle delivery using liposomes or cationic polymer complexes. We discuss these delivery systems and present examples of approved non-viral gene delivery products in more detail in the following section.

3.2 The Outlook for Gene Therapy

There are still many technical challenges that surround the global progress of cell and gene therapies as a mainstream clinical application. The primary obstacle to broader application of these therapies is the immune response to gene delivery vectors and transgenic products. It is necessary to further improve gene delivery methods to increase the efficiency and reduce the toxicity before their clinical implications can be realised.

Another challenge in the translation of gene therapy is the difficulty of evaluating these products. Regulatory agencies are still not fully on pace with their rapid development and the associated risks for the assessment of these products. Finally, most protocols developed for cell and gene therapies are specialised and require sophisticated facilities to prepare and administer gene therapies, which hinders their progress. There is an urgent need to review existing protocols with the goal of making cell and gene therapies more accessible to patients.

There will be a genuine attempt to bring curative cell and gene therapies to the market in the next decades. Most notably, the US National Institutes of Health and the Bill and Melinda Gates Foundation have recently committed to invest £160 million on research for advanced gene-based strategies for sickle cell disease and HIV. Using cell- and gene-based therapies to inactivate viruses, eliminate cancers, and treat inherited diseases is more likely than ever to be feasible in the long term.

4   Nanomedicine

Nanomedicine, as the name suggests, is a branch of medicine that uses nanotechnology to diagnose, prevent, and treat diseases. Nanomedicine uses a variety of structures, often referred to as nanocarriers, nanomaterials, nanoparticles, nanodrugs, or nanotherapeutics, that have at least one dimension in nanoscale. By leveraging the unique properties of materials in nanoscale, nanomedicine is offers new platforms in diagnostics and therapy through innovative routes such as targeted nanodrug delivery systems, nanorobots, and biocompatible nanoparticles for diagnosis, sensing, delivery, and actuation in living cells and organs.

Numerous materials compose the nanocarriers that deliver small-molecule drugs and biologics such as lipids, proteins, metals, or polymers. Depending on parameters such as composition, morphology, size, and surface charge, nanomedicine can be broadly categorised into (i) nanoparticles (e.g., lipid, polymeric, or inorganic nanoparticles and liposomes, where the active molecule is physically encapsulated in the delivery system), (ii) nanocrystals (where the active agent is shaped into crystalline nanoparticles in the presence of stabilisers for enhanced solubility and bioavailability of the drug), (iii) drug conjugates (where the active agent is chemically conjugated to the carrier system such as polymer-drug or antibody-drug conjugates), and (iv) polymer-protein conjugates.

Nanoparticles are ideal candidates for detecting and treating many diseases. They have the potential to act as vectors for gene therapy, carriers of multiple drugs, and tracking agents, for example. It has been reported that nanoparticles can improve the solubility and pharmacokinetic profile of drugs and enhance efficacy and reduce toxicity whilst providing enhanced selectivity and delivering lower dosages of drugs. Nanoparticles can also preserve the bioactivity of unstable biomolecules.

4.1   Nanomedicine in the Market

Nanomedicine is at the forefront of future healthcare. More than 50 nanomedicine formulations have been approved, and there is clear evidence of the potential for even more novel therapeutic approaches that can overcome unmet clinical needs, including the treatment of cancer and neurodegenerative and cardiovascular diseases.

Doxil (Padagis), a PEGylated liposome encapsulating doxorubicin (a potent chemotherapy agent), was the first marketed nanomedicine. The FDA approved it in 1995 for the treatment of several cancer types such as metastatic breast cancer and ovarian cancer. This was considered to be the dawn of the application of nanotechnology in medicine. It was followed by the development of other drug nanocarriers such as Myocet (Zeneus), Eligard (Tolmar Pharmaceuticals), Abraxane (Bristol Myers Squibb), and Genexol PM (Samyang Biopharm) (Anselmo & Mitragotri, 2016).

Eligard, which was approved in 2002, is a novel sustained released depot formulation of leuprolide acetate for hormonal therapy in prostate cancer. The formulation consists of a controlled-release (Atrigel: Reckitt Benckiser Pharmaceuticals) drug delivery system that consists of a biodegradable polymer polylactic-*co*-glycolic acid (PLGA) and *N*-methyl-2-pyrrolidone as a biocompatible solvent. It has been reported that this delivery system provides two times higher release rates of the drug than conventional depot formulations (Tombal & Berges, 2006). Abraxane is the first FDA-approved formulation to use nanoparticle-albumin-bound platform technology. Abraxane, a protein-based nanoformulation of paclitaxel, received its initial FDA approval for breast cancer therapy in 2005 (Wagner et al., 2006).

Nanoparticles with layered structures can provide the capacity to incorporate further components to enhance the nanoparticles' viability with different therapeutics and antibodies, including gene delivery systems. Nanoparticles with compartmentalised structures have emerged as an effective strategy for successful delivery of anticancer drugs due to the advantages of high surface area, high fluid permeation, and separation of incompatible drugs into physically distinct environments and the ability to tune drug-release rates via incorporation into controlled release polymers.

In 2017, the FDA approved a liposomal nanomedicine, Vyxeos (Jazz Pharmaceuticals), for the treatment of acute myeloid leukaemia. Vyxeos combines two chemotherapy drugs, cytarabine and daunorubicin, into a single nanoformulation at a synergistic ratio of 5:1 for enhanced efficacy whilst lowering the cumulative dose (Germain et al., 2020). The nanosystem allows for simultaneous and controlled delivery of two drugs with variable pharmacodynamic and biodistribution profiles at an optimal ratio that could not be reached if the two drugs were administered by any other method. It is anticipated that the success of this innovative approach will be reproduced with a variety of other combination therapies. Encapsulation of multiple drugs in nanocarriers could open more avenues in novel treatment for all ages and groups of patients, improve the performance of medicinal therapies already in the market, and reduce overall healthcare costs.

Nanomaterials in the form of nanocrystals can have therapeutic properties on their own without a delivery system. A recent example, Hasinfy, is a crystalline hafnium oxide nanoparticle that is functionalised with negatively charged phosphate coating. Hasinfy, which the FDA approved in 2019, is a new class of radiation-enhancing nanoparticles that represent the next generation of nanotherapeutics that complement and provide synergistic benefits to standard radiotherapy (Anselmo & Mitragotri, 2019).

4.2 Nanomedicine beyond Cancer

Most of the nanomedicine in the market has been approved for cancer treatment. This is due to the favourable passive targeting capability and the accumulation of nanoparticles through the enhanced permeability and retention effect at malignant tumours. However, a variety of other treatments have benefited from recent advancements in the field such as treatments for fungal infections and macular degeneration, iron-replacement therapies, and the treatment of rare genetic diseases (Gadekar et al., 2021).

An early example is AmBisome (Gilead Sciences), a liposomal nanoformulation of amphotericin B for the treatment of fungal infection, which the EMA approved in 1997. In 2000 the FDA and the EMA approved another liposomal nanoformulation for treatment of neovascularisation from age-related macular degeneration, Visudyne (Novartis), encapsulating verteporfin through photodynamic therapy (Bressler & Bressler, 2000).

Onpattro (Alnylam Pharmaceuticals) is the first lipid nanoparticle formulation that contains small interfering ribonucleic acid (siRNA), which the FDA approved in 2018. Onpattro is prescribed for the treatment of a rare disease, hereditary transthyretin amyloidosis-induced polyneuropathy. The approval of this nanoformulation as the first platform technology for delivering nucleic acids is a great accomplishment in the field of nanomedicine for non-viral vector gene therapy (Adams et al., 2018). This nanoformulation and similar approaches could make gene-based therapies readily available to patients if the challenges with their delivery can be addressed.

As mentioned previously, genes and nucleotide-based drugs have great potential in future advanced medicinal therapies. However, they still pose specific limitations in delivery through systemic routes. They rapidly degrade in vivo and cannot reach the target site, whilst their uptake into cells is electrostatically hampered as they are often negatively charged. Hence, they require both protection and stealth carriers in order to enter organs and cells. Onpattro was designed to efficiently encapsulate siRNA in a lipid nanoparticle. Onpattro also prevents in vivo degradation of siRNA and enables it to escape endosomal clearance and delivers it within the cell cytoplasm.

Following the success of the approved nanoformulations currently in the market and the high number of ongoing clinical trials in nucleic acid-based nanomedicine, including mRNAs, it is expected that several new products will reach the market in the coming years. In fact, the COVID-19 pandemic unleashed new possibilities for nanomedicine therapies to be taken more seriously by the pharmaceutical industry and regulatory bodies. Vaccines developed by Moderna and Pfizer-BioNTech using lipid-based nanoparticles as delivery vehicles were given to millions of people around the world as a preventative measure against the infectious SARS-CoV-2 virus (Balkrishna et al., 2021). The development of mRNA-based vaccines at an extraordinary speed highlights the importance of mRNA-based nanomedicine for delivering solutions in a variety of other fields such as regenerative medicine, gene therapy for genetic disorders, cancer vaccines, and protein-replacement therapies.

Nanomedicine is not limited to the delivery of drugs and genes. Many nanomedicine products have been approved and are being developed for early-stage disease diagnosis and imaging. One clinically approved imaging nanomedicine is Magtrace (Mammotome|Danaher Corporation), a non-radioactive magnetic tracer that contains superparamagnetic iron oxide nanoparticles for sentinel lymph node biopsies in breast cancer (Hersi et al., 2019). Other examples for diagnostics such as iron oxide nanoparticles for PET/MRI scans (Thomas et al., 2019) or liposome/nanoparticles containing radiomarkers (e.g., ^{99}Tc and ^{111}In) for single-photon emission computed tomography (SPECT) and PET analysis (Thomas et al., 2019) are currently in clinical trials. It is anticipated that nanomedicine will be a key player in future disease diagnostics.

The landscape of nanomedicine is undergoing a radical change. With more than 30% of the clinical trials under investigation focusing on applications other than cancer, it will not be very long until new nanomedicine products emerge for other diseases such as genetic disorders, central nervous system diseases, and infectious diseases.

The application of nanotechnology in medicine goes beyond therapeutic interventions. The unique properties of nanomaterials (mechanical, electrical, optical, and acoustic) offer cross-disciplinary solutions in healthcare. For instance, nanosensors are currently being developed and approved for diagnosing and controlling diseases (Munawar et al., 2019). Nanosensors have great potential for accurately detecting biomarkers in cancer and infectious diseases (e.g., Zika, Ebola, and COVID-19).

4.3 The Outlook for Nanomedicine

Despite the advances in the field and the recent emergence of nanomedicine products in the market, the uptake of nanomedicine is very slow. This is attributed to many challenges, including safety, regulatory hurdles, cost, reproducibility, and issues with scaling up that need to be resolved before nanomedicine can enter the market on a larger scale.

Synthesizing multifunctional nanoparticles requires several steps that pose challenges for large-scale good manufacturing practice (GMP) production that lead to an increase in the cost of manufacture. Current technologies that process nanoparticles are not automated, and the various stages of the synthesis cannot be isolated. Conventional small-scale batch reactors are utilised for the synthesis of nanoparticles. These reactors are poorly controllable and are not well characterised and suffer from insufficient mixing and low heat and mass transfer rates. This can lead to low reproduction efficiency, upscaling issues, and inability to decouple the manufacturing stages in real time.

The lack of regulatory and safety guidelines is another major hurdle for the translation of nanomedicine. Even though nanomedicine products have been in the market for two decades, the regulations that are used to ensure their quality, safety, and efficacy in clinical use are no longer appropriate. The development of standard protocols for testing complex formulations and a suitable regulatory framework for evaluation are necessary before nanomedicine can be translated to the clinic.

The shorter or alternative treatment schedules, better outcomes, and lower toxicity that nanomedicine offers would have a major impact on the accessibility and delivery of therapy and outcomes. The potentially curative nature of nanomedicine and the breakthroughs in new targeting treatments require the pharmaceutical industry to recalibrate its model for developing therapies and to push the boundaries beyond traditional therapeutic approaches.

5 Tissue Engineering and Regenerative Medicine

One of the global healthcare challenges is improving the quality of life for a diseased and aging population. This can be done through innovative solutions such as tissue engineering and regenerative medicine. Regenerative medicine is an emerging field of medicine aimed at restoring and establishing structure and function of lost or damaged organs and tissues. Current transplantation therapies suffer from lack of donor supplies and from severe immune complications post-transplantation. Regenerative medicine is the next frontier in minimising the risks of organ rejection and accelerating patients' recovery post-transplant.

Regenerative medicine owes its success to the advances in tissue engineering that have led to the discovery of novel biomaterials that can support cell transplantation and proliferation. Tissue-engineered biomaterials combined with cells can mimic the native extracellular matrix of tissues and the in vivo environment of cells, making enhanced cell proliferation and improved differentiation possible. Tissue engineering assembles cells, scaffolds, and biologically active molecules (e.g., growth factors) to regenerate or replace damaged/diseased tissues.

Regenerative medicine combines tissue engineering with other approaches such as immunomodulation, nanomedicine, and gene- and cell-based therapy to induce restoration. It involves interventions that use cells as the central units of reconstruction. The cells used in regenerative medicine are typically differentiated cells that maintain proliferation capacity and are classified as autologous (the patient's own cells) or allogeneic (donor cells). Whilst both therapies use the same common technologies to promote cell growth, the scale is different. Autologous cells are custom products derived from harvested tissue of the patient, and the treatment is often delayed by the cell culture expansion process. Personalised medicine can easily be adapted to this type of cell therapy. Allogeneic cell sources, on the other hand, can be obtained 'off the shelf' and can be mass-produced to treat many patients (Mao & Mooney, 2015). Sufficient amount of time is available to quality control these products prior to administration, and therefore, the risk of an adverse immune reaction is diminished with allogeneic therapies.

5.1 Regenerative Therapies in the Market

Various factors are driving the growth of the regenerative medicine market. The widespread use of organ transplantation and the prevalence of chronic diseases and genetic disorders as well as an increase in the size of a geriatric population with musculoskeletal, dermatological, oncological, and cardiovascular diseases are contributing to the expansion of the market for regenerative medicine.

Carticel (Vericel Corporation) is the first biologic product the FDA has approved in the orthopaedic field. It uses autologous cultured chondrocytes to treat focal articular cartilage defects. The autologous chondrocytes are derived from in vitro expansion of the cells harvested from the patient's normal femoral cartilage. The expanded cells are then implanted at the site of injury, resulting in recovery of tissue that is comparable to results from conventional techniques. This technology was followed by the FDA approval of Maci (Vericel Corporation) in 2016, for the repair of symptomatic cartilage defects of the knee. Maci is the first approved product that utilises tissue-engineering scaffolds to grow cells from healthy cartilage tissue from the patient's own knee. Autologous cultured chondrocytes are implanted on a matrix from biodegradable porcine membrane (Vinatier & Guicheux, 2016).

Apligraf (Organogenesis) is another example of a commercially available advanced tissue-engineering composite. Apligraf is a bioengineered skin substitute for treating chronic wounds, including diabetic foot ulcers and venous leg ulcers. The tissue-engineering graft consists of allogeneic cells and contains a dermal layer of neonatal fibroblasts in a bovine type I collagen lattice and an epidermal layer containing human keratinocytes (Zaulyanov & Kirsner, 2007).

The first FDA approval for regenerative medicine in dental care was Gintuit (Organogenesis). Similar to Apligraf, Gintuit is an allogeneic cellular biodegradable scaffold containing fibroblast/keratinocyte therapy derived from neonatal foreskin that artificially creates a vascular wound bed to treat mucogingival conditions. Clinical data demonstrated that Gintuit regenerates 2 millimetres of gum tissue although the mechanism of action is not clear (Schmidt, 2012).

Benefiting from a 5-year regulatory 'free-for-all' in regenerative medicine in Japan, HeartSheet (Terumo) was conditionally approved in 2015 (McCabe & Sipp, 2016). HeartSheet is an autologous skeletal myoblast product that uses cell sheet technology and has been authorised for use in patients with serious heart failure. HeartSheet was one of the three treatments that received approval under the Pharmaceutical and Medical Devices Act that was introduced in Japan in 2014. The law allows for conditional approval of treatments that have gone through some (limited) clinical testing (Sipp, 2015). This provides the opportunity to market the product nationally under the condition that extra data should be collected over a 7-year time frame.

5.2 The Outlook for Regenerative Medicine

Even though there are various attempts globally to develop stem cell therapies for conditions like heart failure and other chronic diseases (e.g., Parkinson's), no approved therapies for these conditions have garnered widespread adoption. Despite the large research and development funding opportunities and initiatives that governments (e.g., Japan's Pharmaceutical and Medical Devices Act) have introduced that are more lenient towards accelerated regulatory approval, very few products are available to patients. The lack of regenerative medicine products in the market and clinics is a major drawback that is primarily caused by scarcity of data on treatment outcomes and strict regulatory controls by health authorities.

Tissue engineering and regenerative medicine are still in their infancy, and there are numerous fundamental aspects to be addressed such as the selection of cell sources, assembly of complex organs, design of tissue-specific materials, and the development of specialised bioreactors. In addition, manufacturing regenerative medicine products involves multiple challenges that include the high cost of product development, complex and inefficient operations, and difficulty maintaining uniform cell quality. Finally, the mechanisms for forming new tissues or organs with tissue-engineered materials in vivo are still poorly understood. Tissue-engineered materials could reach their full potential in clinical applications if these limitations can be overcome.

The expansion of tissue engineering and the regenerative medicine field can be further supported by combining different disciplinary approaches, including stem cell biology, functional biomaterials, nanotechnology, and, most recently, additive manufacturing (e.g., 3D bioprinting) and by the use of AI. A better understanding of the patient's disease state, age, and microbiome that includes data supported by precision medicine will likely help with the advancement of the field. Finally, 3D cell culture and tissue models of disease and novel organ-on-chip technologies will allow more realistic preclinical testing of regenerative medicine approaches and facilitate the translation of promising approaches to the clinic (Han et al., 2020). Regenerative medicine offers revolutionary therapeutic approaches to treating devastating diseases in cases where a cure is not offered by conventional treatments. Innovations in this field could potentially address chronic diseases and eliminate the ongoing drug therapy demands.

6 Conclusions

Novel therapies such as tissue-engineering products, gene and cell therapies, and nanomedicine are growing rapidly. Targeted therapies and personalised medicine have paved the way for new clinical trial methodologies. Even though these innovative advanced therapy products are still in the early stages of development, it is highly likely that they will reach the market earlier than anticipated. Due to their complex nature, there is a need for extensive and complex preclinical and clinical developments. Regulatory uncertainty, complicated manufacturing processes, and the high cost of manufacture are common barriers for these products reaching the market. However, as these novel interventions offer the potential to cure severe chronic conditions and currently incurable diseases, the processes involved in their translation into the market are also changing and the industry and regulatory bodies are keen to adopt new strategies for their approval. Therefore, it is possible that patients could have access to these alternatives in the near future.

Acknowledgements The authors declare no potential conflicts of interest.

References

Abreu, T. R., Fonseca, N. A., Gonçalves, N., & Moreira, J. N. (2020). Current challenges and emerging opportunities of CAR-T cell therapies. *Journal of Controlled Release, 319,* 246–261.

Adams, D., Gonzalez-Duarte, A., O'Riordan, W. D., Yang, C. C., Ueda, M., Kristen, A. V., Tournev, I., Schmidt, H. H., Coelho, T., Berk, J. L., Lin, K. P., Vita, G., Attarian, S., Planté-Bordeneuve, V., Mezei, M. M., Campistol, J. M., Buades, J., Brannagan, T. H., Kim, B. J., Oh, J., Parman, Y., Sekijima, Y., Hawkins, P. N., Solomon, S. D., Polydefkis, M., Dyck, P. J., Gandhi, P. J., Goyal, S., Chen, J., Strahs, A. L., Nochur, S. V., Sweetser, M. T., Garg, P. P., Vaishnaw, A. K., Gollob, J. A., Suhr, O. B. (2018). Patisiran, an RNAi therapeutic, for hereditary transthyretin amyloidosis. *New England Journal of Medicine, 379*(1), 11–21.

Anselmo, A. C., & Mitragotri, S. (2016). Nanoparticles in the clinic. *Bioengineering and Translation Medicine, 1*(1), 10–29.

Anselmo, A. C., & Mitragotri, S. (2019). Nanoparticles in the clinic: An update. *Bioengineering and Translation Medicine, 4*(3), e10143.

Balkrishna, A., Arya, V., Rohela, A., Kumar, A., Verma, R., Kumar, D., Nepovimova, E., Kuca, K., Thakur, N., Thakur, N., & Kumar, P. (2021). Nanotechnology interventions in the management of COVID-19: Prevention, diagnosis and virus-like particle vaccines. *Vaccine, 9*(10), 1129.

Bressler, N. M., & Bressler, S. B. (2000). Photodynamic therapy with verteporfin (Visudyne): Impact on ophthalmology and visual sciences [Review]. *Investigative Ophthalmology and Visual Science, 41*(3), 624–628.

Brokowski, C., & Adli, M. (2020). Ethical considerations in therapeutic clinical trials involving novel human germline-editing technology. *CRISPR Journal, 3*(1), 18–26.

Bulaklak, K., & Gersbach, C. A. (2020). The once and future gene therapy. *Nature Communications, 11*(1), 5820.

Cevher, E., Sezer, A. D., & Çağlar, E. (2012). Gene delivery systems: Recent progress in viral and non-viral therapy. In A. D. Sezer (Ed.), *Recent advances in novel drug carrier systems* (pp. 437–470). INTECH.

Emancipator, K. (2020). Keytruda and PD-L1: A real-world example of co-development of a drug with a predictive biomarker. *AAPS Journal, 23*(1), 5.

Gadekar, V., Borade, Y., Kannaujia, S., Rajpoot, K., Anup, N., Tambe, V., Kalia, K., & Tekade, R. K. (2021). Nanomedicines accessible in the market for clinical interventions. *Journal of Controlled Release, 330,* 372–397.

Germain, M., Caputo, F., Metcalfe, S., Tosi, G., Spring, K., Åslund, A. K. O., Pottier, A., Schiffelers, R., Ceccaldi, A., & Schmid, R. (2020). Delivering the power of nanomedicine to patients today. *Journal of Controlled Release, 326,* 164–171.

Han, F., Wang, J., Ding, L., Hu, Y., Li, W., Yuan, Z., Guo, Q., Zhu, C., Yu, L., Wang, H., Zhao, Z., Jia, L., Li, J., Yu, Y., Zhang, W., Chu, G., Chen, S., & Li, B. (2020). Tissue engineering and regenerative medicine: Achievements, future, and sustainability in Asia [Review]. *Frontiers in Bioengineering and Biotechnology, 8,* 83.

Hernandez-Alcoceba, R., Poutou, J., Ballesteros-Briones, M. C., & Smerdou, C. (2016). Gene therapy approaches against cancer using in vivo and ex vivo gene transfer of interleukin-12. *Immunotherapy, 8*(2), 179–198.

Hersi, A.-F., Eriksson, S., Ramos, J., Abdsaleh, S., Wärnberg, F., & Karakatsanis, A. (2019). A combined, totally magnetic technique with a magnetic marker for non-palpable tumour localization and superparamagnetic iron oxide nanoparticles for sentinel lymph node detection in breast cancer surgery. *European Journal of Surgical Oncology, 45*(4), 544–549.

Lostalé-Seijo, I., & Montenegro, J. (2018). Synthetic materials at the forefront of gene delivery. *Nature Reviews Chemistry, 2*(10), 258–277.

Lu, R.-M., Hwang, Y.-C., Liu, I. J., Lee, C.-C., Tsai, H.-Z., Li, H.-J., & Wu, H.-C. (2020). Development of therapeutic antibodies for the treatment of diseases. *Journal of Biomedical Science, 27*(1), 1.

Manjunath, N., Yi, G., Dang, Y., & Shankar, P. (2013). Newer gene editing technologies toward HIV gene therapy. *Viruses, 5*(11), 2748–2766.

Mao, A. S., & Mooney, D. J. (2015). Regenerative medicine: Current therapies and future directions. *Proceedings of the National Academy of Sciences, 112*(47), 14452–14459.

McCabe, C., & Sipp, D. (2016). Undertested and overpriced: Japan issues first conditional approval of stem cell product. *Cell Stem Cell, 18*(4), 436–437.

Moore, J. P. (2021). Approaches for optimal use of different COVID-19 vaccines: Issues of viral variants and vaccine efficacy. *JAMA, 325*(13), 1251–1252.

Munawar, A., Ong, Y., Schirhagl, R., Tahir, M. A., Khan, W. S., & Bajwa, S. Z. (2019). Nanosensors for diagnosis with optical, electric and mechanical transducers. *RSC Advances, 9*(12), 6793–6803.

Nayerossadat, N., Maedeh, T., & Ali, P. A. (2012). Viral and nonviral delivery systems for gene delivery. *Advanced Biomedical Research, 1*, 127.

Sankar, P. L., & Parker, L. S. (2017). The precision medicine Initiative's all of us research program: An agenda for research on its ethical, legal, and social issues. *Genetics in Medicine, 19*(7), 743–750.

Schilsky, R. L. (2010). Personalized medicine in oncology: The future is now. *Nature Reviews Drug Discovery, 9*(5), 363–366.

Schmidt, C. (2012). Gintuit cell therapy approval signals shift at US regulator. *Nature Biotechnology, 30*(6), 479.

Sipp, D. (2015). Conditional approval: Japan lowers the bar for regenerative medicine products. *Cell Stem Cell, 16*(4), 353–356.

Sung, Y. K., & Kim, S. W. (2019). Recent advances in the development of gene delivery systems. *Biomaterials Research, 23*(1), 8.

Tachibana, M., Amato, P., Sparman, M., Woodward, J., Sanchis, D. M., Ma, H., Gutierrez, N. M., Tippner-Hedges, R., Kang, E., & Lee, H.-S. (2013). Towards germline gene therapy of inherited mitochondrial diseases. *Nature, 493*(7434), 627–631.

Thomas, G., Boudon, J., Maurizi, L., Moreau, M., Walker, P., Severin, I., Oudot, A., Goze, C., Poty, S., Vrigneaud, J.-M., Demoisson, F., Denat, F., Brunotte, F., & Millot, N. (2019). Innovative magnetic nanoparticles for PET/MRI bimodal imaging. *ACS Omega, 4*(2), 2637–2648.

Tijsterman, M., Ketting, R. F., & Plasterk, R. H. (2002). The genetics of RNA silencing. *Annual Review of Genetics, 36*(1), 489–519.

Tombal, B., & Berges, R. (2006). Eligard®: Advantages for optimal testosterone control. *European Urology Supplements, 5*(18), 900–904.

Vinatier, C., & Guicheux, J. (2016). Cartilage tissue engineering: From biomaterials and stem cells to osteoarthritis treatments. *Annals of Physical and Rehabilitation Medicine, 59*(3), 139–144.

Wagner, V., Dullaart, A., Bock, A.-K., & Zweck, A. (2006). The emerging nanomedicine landscape. *Nature Biotechnology, 24*(10), 1211–1217.

Wilson, B. J., & Nicholls, S. G. (2015). The human genome project, and recent advances in personalized genomics. *Risk Management and Healthcare Policy, 8*, 9–20.

Zaulyanov, L., & Kirsner, R. S. (2007). A review of a bi-layered living cell treatment (Apligraf©) in the treatment of venous leg ulcers and diabetic foot ulcers. *Clinical Interventions in Aging, 2*(1), 93–98.

The Future Open Innovation Approach in Health Care Needs Patients' Support

Julia Plugmann and Philipp Plugmann

Abstract

The COVID-19 pandemic showed that a global health-care crisis can create massive long-term economic, social, and psychological problems. In light of the consequences of COVID-19, which include large numbers of deaths and long-term health problems around the globe, we came to a realization. It is one thing to develop a highly efficient life science industry with better conditions for established companies and start-ups, but there are other important things to consider, such as increasing the speed of data collection in order to reveal what is happening as soon as a local, national, or global health-care crisis starts and increasing the ability of the industry to develop and deliver products to keep the population safe. Epidemiological research institutions, regulatory authorities, and clinical trial hospitals must be prepared to initiate a high-speed response to such crises. Although the morbidity and mortality caused by the current pandemic have been devastating and tragically high, the next potential pandemic could conceivably even be worse. This chapter focuses on the need for the life science industry to provide support to patients as soon as possible. One way to facilitate that process is collecting health-care data from the public using relatively new technology. Owners of smartphones could quickly input their personal health-care data into an open innovation platform with informed

J. Plugmann
Leverkusen, Germany
e-mail: plugmann@gmx.de

P. Plugmann (✉)
SRH University of Applied Health Sciences, Campus Rheinland, Leverkusen, North Rhine-Westphalia, Germany

Woxsen University, Hyderabad, India
e-mail: philipp.plugmann@srh.de

S. Ehsani et al. (eds.), *The Future Circle of Healthcare*, Future of Business and Finance, https://doi.org/10.1007/978-3-030-99838-7_17

consent. This in turn could be used in theories and modeling by life science companies, government institutions, and research groups to drive the research and development of innovative medical treatment drugs and technologies in partnership with AI.

1   Introduction

In light of the ongoing COVID-19 pandemic, now is the time to motivate patients around the globe to act because everyone benefits from rapid data collection when a local, national, or global health-care crisis hits. Worst-case scenarios such as a health-care crisis combined with a blackout or a global stock market crash would bring even more problems. Life scientists and policy makers need to plan for a variety of scenarios in order to prevent the massive conflicts that such situations could cause.

The following two studies were presented at the second Annual World Open Innovation Conference in November 2015, which the Garwood Center for Corporate Innovation organized at the University of California, Berkeley, and at the Artificial Intelligence-Clash of the Deggendorf Institute of Technology in Germany in October 2021, which focus on health-care technologies. The latter conference was based on the monthly meetings of a team of international researchers and expert teams that worked to develop prototypes under the leadership of Patrick Glauner, one of the youngest professors of artificial intelligence in Europe. This team helped us reach a new perspective: an understanding of the need for the population to voluntarily deliver data to an open innovation platform to make rapid solution possible in health-care crisis situations. This requires a media campaign to motivate people to support such data collection systems. In this case, it is the behavior of patients or individuals that is the gatekeeper rather than innovative technologies or drugs. We conducted a research project to determine whether patients would be willing to participate in providing such data.

2   Study 1

Our first study was presented at the second World Open Innovation Conference as "users' (patients') willingness to transfer personal data to a future IT service of open innovation driven IT health care companies to receive an efficient service—a follow-up study." The presentation was in the form of a poster.

Research has shown that technology companies, including in the health-care sector, use a limited open innovation approach (West, 2003) to reduce costs in research and development and to achieve higher profits (Chesbrough, 2006). Integrating information from the public in research and development in health care is seen as essential for the advancement of innovation (Bullinger et al., 2012). From a commercial perspective, the only way to achieve higher profits is through new products and services for the marketplace that meet the needs of users and enter the market ahead of products from competitors. Today, this means mobile health (mHealth) (Estrin & Sim, 2010). Opening up mHealth architecture decreases barriers to entry, and community participation helps researchers develop new tools and design new mHealth apps.

IT and tech companies that embrace mHealth involve users and lead users as innovators (Bogers et al., 2010) as the companies develop new products and services. Lead users especially can help companies create breakthrough products and services that are not on the radar of market researchers or internal innovation teams (von Hippel et al., 1999).

2.1   Theoretical Background

In this paper, we analyze user (patient) willingness to transfer all their data to a future IT service provided by a health-care IT company that embraces open innovation in order to contribute to radical innovation (Lettl et al., 2006). The open innovation approach with users and lead users has been very successful in the past under certain conditions (Baldwin & von Hippel, 2011; van de Vrande et al., 2009). But the open innovation architecture and processes must be redeveloped, and it was not certain that users (patients) would support a future IT service that collects both medical data and nonmedical data. The results of this study can help entrepreneurs in the health-care IT industry to develop a prototype IT service based on an open innovation approach and to decide how open it can become (West, 2003). Our research identified the user requirements for transferring medical and nonmedical data as part of a holistic health-care IT service approach.

2.2   Research Design

This follow-up study is based on the first study, which we presented in 2014 (Plugmann & Plugmann, 2014). The first study analyzed user (patient) willingness to transfer medical data to an innovative health-care app. This follow-up study analyzes the willingness of users to transfer both medical and nonmedical data to an open innovation app.

2.3   First Study

The first study was presented at the 12th Open and User Innovation (OUI) Conference, in July 2014 at the Harvard Business School. It concerned the willingness of users (patients) to transfer medical data to a health-care app. In the future, there will be different interaction scenarios between users (patients) and health-care IT companies and their applications. The future scenarios and prototypes help us understand how to involve users and which new products and services to create (Kanto et al., 2014; Parmentier & Mangematin, 2014; Steen et al., 2014):

First future scenario: The user (patient) decides if the medical doctor or dentist is authorized to input information to this app in addition to the information the patient provides and who is authorized to look at the data and the results of data analysis.

Second future scenario: The health insurance company (or other service delivery company in the health-care industry) offers the app user a discounted monthly premium if they use the company's app.

Third future scenario: The IT development company provides the kind of health-care data app that users want, and the user customizes the features and functions of the app.

We presented these three future scenarios and the results of our study on user (patient) willingness to share their personal health data with an innovative app in July 2014. The data for that study were collected from January to December 2013 in a multicenter study involving four dental clinics in Germany. The study participants were 528 patients with a history of periodontal disease that we interviewed in two groups. In the first group ($n = 244$), no user had a preexisting physical disease (e.g., diabetes, coronary heart disease), and in the second group ($n = 284$), participants had at least one physical disease.

The study results showed that 93% of the second group would share their individual health-care data using such an app ($p < 0.02$). They would allow their doctors and dentists to enter certain medical data and would also input information on a daily or weekly basis (e.g., how they felt, what they ate, and if they still smoked). In the first group, 32% said they would share their individual health data with such an app.

2.4   Follow-Up Study

The first study considered only the flow of health data between patients, doctors, and dentists using an app on a mobile device. After we saw the very high (93%) willingness of patients to share personal health data on an app, the next question was: What if data collection would be expanded to create a holistic approach? A holistic approach to delivering better health care to the user (patient) would require both medical and nonmedical data about the user. The influence of such a future user community and the potential results from research data based on such an IT service could also help researchers develop open innovation processes and drive future research in the open innovation field (Chesbrough & Bogers, 2014).

Research Question We prototyped a future IT health-care service that would be offered by a health-care IT company that embraces open innovation. That IT product (service) would collect all the personal medical and nonmedical data it could get—with the individual's permission—using sensor system technologies. The research question was whether users would be willing to transfer all their medical and nonmedical data to a future IT service provided by a health-care IT company that embraced open innovation. Would such an IT service prototype meet users' needs?

And would it lead to a high level of willingness to transfer all data to a health-care company that offered this service?

Secondary Data From February 2014 to February 2015, we interviewed patients in a multicenter study in Cologne and Bonn (four dental clinics and six medical practices) in Germany and asked them about the importance of several factors. Out of more than 2439 patients, just 821 met the criteria for inclusion: a past history of dental and medical illness, age 20–75 years, at least one chronic medical disease (e.g., diabetes or coronary heart disease), experience with using IT, and a positive attitude to IT services. The definition of data in this study means all data that can be collected in a way that makes sense for a holistic health-care IT service approach. Examples include what food the person eats, how that food is prepared, the weight of the person, whether they participate in sports, health data and history, the stress profile of the person, the individual's genetic risks if testing is available, information about the person's environment, how much sleep the person gets and the quality of their sleep, personal hygiene practices, and how much the person is exposed to the sun and whether they take steps to protect themselves from UV rays. Collecting such data would require the use of various electronic sensors and devices.

In addition, we emailed 67 directors of small and midsized technology companies in the health-care industry in Germany and Belgium to ask for interviews. Just 17 answered and 8 agreed to an interview.

Primary Data For this follow-up study, we chose a multicenter study with two steps. First, we used a qualitative research method; we interviewed eight directors of small and midsized technology companies in the health-care sector in Germany and Belgium. We asked about their views on future scenarios of technological products and services for patients based on present or future technologies and concepts. We also interviewed 16 patients who had a history of dental and medical illness about their expectations about such products in the future and their willingness to transfer their personal data to a health-care company that embraced open innovation. We then grouped the information we obtained in the interviews into three main categories.

Next, we designed a prototype IT model, and in step two of the study, we presented it to patients who met our criteria for inclusion. Using a quantitative research method, we asked them questions from a standardized questionnaire that we had designed based on the information we obtained in the interviews.

Data Analysis After the interviews (step 1), we identified and coded the main subjects discussed. The coding helped us identify patterns and develop a list of standards from the point of view of the industry and of the user.

Finally, we analyzed the users' responses to the standardized questionnaire using statistical analysis software (IBM SPSS 27.0).

2.5   Prototype Model of a Future Health-Care Service Using IT

Our prototype model of a future health-care service combined IT applications that are currently available with sensor systems technology, but this combination itself is not currently on the market and represents a future technology approach. This combination allows users (patients), as the legal owner of their data, to transfer all dental, medical, and other data that they and the company define as relevant to the health-care company (subject to the user's consent) so the user can receive efficient health care. The open innovation process allows every single user to see anonymous data from other customers, to benefit from research results based on outcomes from the common data pool of this specific user community, and to interact directly with the company to communicate their wishes. This data can serve as the basis for an individualized model for meeting user needs that can be developed within a very short time.

2.6   Findings

The study participants identified three factors that they considered to be preconditions before they would be willing to upload their personal data. Ninety-one percent ($n = 748$) of study participants reported that being able to influence future IT service in health care through an open innovation process was important to them. The second most important factor to participants was the security of IT data; 89.4% ($n = 734$) said that this was an important consideration for them. The third most important factor to participants was the ability to benefit from scientific research results based on the data pool of the IT service community; 86.6% ($n = 711$) reported this as important to them. A significant proportion (87.8%; $n = 721$) said that if these three important standards—an open innovation process, IT security, and access to scientific results from the community data pool—were guaranteed, they would be willing to input all their medical and nonmedical data electronically.

2.7   Conclusions

This study showed that patients who satisfied the inclusion criteria identified three important factors as preconditions before they would be willing to transfer their medical and nonmedical data: an open innovation process that integrates users and their ideas, IT security, and the ability to benefit from the data pool (research results) of the users of this service. This empirical study shows an important result: Provided that these three standards are met, user (patient) willingness to transfer personal medical and nonmedical data to a future IT service provided by health-care companies that embrace open innovation is high. For the study participants, the trade-off for sharing their data is that they would receive efficient health care.

This study contributed to our understanding of users' willingness to participate in the open innovation process (von Hippel et al., 1999), what standards users expect in the open innovation process (Chesbrough & Bogers, 2014), and how far companies have to welcome the open innovation process (West, 2003) to succeed in the future health-care services market.

3 Study 2

Based on study 1, we focused our research in the following years on the academics who would possibly be involved in the open innovation process. The study was presented in October 2021 at the Artificial Intelligence-Clash of the Deggendorf Institute of Technology in Germany. Its title was "Academics' willingness to participate in an open innovation ecosystem platform which develops medical technology products."

Building an open innovation ecosystem can involve a local or a global approach (Chesbrough et al., 2014). Knowledge transfer (Bacon et al., 2019), interorganizational relationships (Radziwon & Bogers, 2019), research opportunities (West & Bogers, 2017), the effects of open innovation on entrepreneurship (Nambisan et al., 2018), and connections between corporations and communities (Gupta et al., 2017) can all contribute to the potential for open innovation ecosystem platforms that develop medical technology products.

Our research question for study 2 was, How willing are academics to participate in a project to develop medical technology products? The question is motivated by open innovation platforms in other industries—such as Local Motors in the automotive industry (https://localmotors.com), where projects to build technology products have been marketed with an effective approach that attracts creators and innovators (Local Motors by LMI, 2010). The term "medical technology products" refers to future medical technology that could solve serious health crises such as cancers or trauma injuries in a new way by combining different present and future technologies with AI at the center—like the "Med-Bay" in the movie *Elysium* (Sony Pictures, 2013), for example.

3.1 Theoretical Background

In this study, we analyze academics' willingness to cocreate an open innovation ecosystem platform that features new medical technology products with other individuals, groups, communities, and corporations. The potential of radical innovation through open innovation (Kennedy et al., 2017), the advantages of external knowledge searches (Flor et al., 2018), and the benefits of heterogeneous intellectual capital (Agostini & Nosella, 2017) can all have a significant impact on building new innovative technological devices. Open innovation has the potential to deliver all of these things to small- and medium-sized enterprises and to the global economy (Vanhaverbeke et al., 2018).

There is still a lot of untapped potential in IT as applied to medicine. The participation of academics will determine how far this new technology can go. Barriers to innovation (Smith & Sandberg, 2018), failed implementations (Von Briel & Recker, 2017), and closed social and cultural patterns of companies are just a few of the challenges that an open innovation ecosystem platform has to meet if it is to succeed. The best way forward is to ask academics if they would be willing to participate in developing new IT technology for health care and what factors would increase their willingness to participate.

3.2   Research Design

This study is based on three books published by Springer International: *Innovative Technologies for Market Leadership* (Glauner & Plugmann, 2020), *Creating Innovation Spaces* (Nestle et al., 2021), and *Digitalization in Healthcare* (Glauner et al., 2021). Over 60 coauthors contributed interesting chapters, but would those authors or their colleagues be willing to participate in an open innovation ecosystem platform to develop a new medical technology product? Initial talks with these individuals showed no clear motivation or willingness to participate in such a project, so we decided to ask academics from different disciplines whether they would be willing to participate and what key factors would increase their willingness.

Research Question We expect the results of our study to have a high impact in helping to create open innovation ecosystem platforms to develop radical medical technology products. For such a project, we need highly motivated academics who will persist in the face of failures, barriers to success, and conflicts over a long period of time.

The main questions were:

1. Would you be interested in participating?
2. Would you invest your time and participate for 1 year?
3. Would you invest your time and participate for longer than 1 year?
4. Would language be a barrier if it is not German or English?
5. Could you accept a project leader?
6. Is money a motivating factor for you in this context?
7. Is fun a motivating factor for you in this context?

Primary Data We conducted phone or video interviews over a period of 2 years from February 2019 to February 2021 in North Rhine-Westphalia in Germany. We interviewed 306 academics in Cologne, Bonn, Leverkusen, and Düsseldorf from six disciplines: engineering (50), computational science (52), medicine and biology (51), physics and chemistry (50), design (53), and philosophy (50). The criterion for including these academics was that they had to have worked for more than 3 years after completing their examinations at a university or in a company or a combination of both. Age was not an exclusion criteria. We chose the academics at random from the social media platforms LinkedIn and XING and contacted them by email. If they agreed to speak with us, we contacted them by phone or by video call. In the first round, we contacted 941 academics by email and received 213 responses. After the second round, 4 weeks later, we had 306 academics who participated in the questionnaire.

Before we used a questionnaire as a quantitative empirical tool, we began preliminary investigation to identify some clusters or key factors we should consider before designing the questionnaire. For this exploratory preliminary investigation, we organized seven interviews with experienced academics. They all had more than 15 years of experience in industry or university settings where they participated in scientific and industry projects to develop new technologies and implement innovative products and services. Via email, we asked 42 academics at small and midsized technology companies or universities in North Rhine-Westphalia in Germany for interviews. Of these, 26 answered and 7 agreed to participate in an interview. Those academics came from our personal networks, and each of them had been known to us for longer than 5 years.

In each interview, which took about 30 minutes, we talked in general terms about experiences and key factors that would make academics more willing to participate in an open innovation ecosystem platform to develop medical technology products.

Data Analysis After the interviews (step 1), we identified and coded the main subjects that arose. The coding helped us identify patterns and develop a list of possible factors from the academics' perspective.

The questionnaire that we used with the 306 academics (step 2) was based on the results of the interviews and covered the most important subjects that came out of the interviews. The factors were time, money, and social and cultural requirements. Finally, we analyzed the academics' responses to the standardized questionnaire using statistical software (IBM SPSS 27.0).

3.3   An Open Innovation Ecosystem Platform for Developing Medical Technology Products

This future platform will be a place where academics can cocreate, cooperate, and interact to develop new medical technology products. These products could produce high-quality solutions to the health crises individuals experience—such as cancers or trauma injuries—in a very short time and with a high level of safety and affordability. The products will require interdisciplinary approaches and academics of all ages from all types of disciplines who have different levels of experience. Academics will devote their work and time to these projects on a purely voluntary basis; this is so the participants will not have conflicts of interest with their universities or the companies they work for. The participants will be oriented toward open innovation. They will volunteer their free time, their knowledge, and their commitment with the common goal of developing a radical new medical technology product.

3.4   Findings

The results show how many of all the academics who answered the questionnaire ($n = 306$) answered the seven questions with a "yes":

1. Would you be interested in participating? 85.95% ($n = 263$)
2. Would you invest your time and participate for 1 year? 46.41% ($n = 142$)
3. Would you invest your time and participate for longer than 1 year? 19.93% ($n = 61$)
4. Would language be a barrier if it is not German or English? 59.48% ($n = 182$)
5. Could you accept a project leader? 69.93% ($n = 214$)
6. Is money a motivating factor for you in this context? 18.63% ($n = 57$)
7. Is fun a motivating factor for you in this context? 75.49% ($n = 231$)

Our results showed that 85.95% ($n = 263$) of the asked academics ($n = 306$) would participate in an open innovation ecosystem platform to develop medical technology products; this result was statistically significant ($p < 0.04$).

Less than half (46.41%; $n = 142$) would invest their time for 1 year, and only 19.93% ($n = 61$) would invest their time for longer than 1 year. For 59.48% ($n = 182$), language is a barrier if it is not German or English. Almost three-quarters (69.93%; $n = 214$) could accept a project leader. For only a small proportion (18.63%; $n = 57$), money is a motivating factor. Most (75.49%; $n = 231$) answered that fun was a motivating factor. The cross-tabulations that show the relationships of these answers to the six academic fields are part of the work that is in progress.

4   Conclusions

The results of study 2 showed that academics' willingness to participate in an open innovation ecosystem platform to develop a medical technology product is high but that their willingness will decrease if the project is longer than 1 year. If the project language is not German or English, it could be a barrier for a significant proportion of the study participants. Money is not a key factor for academics, but having fun is.

This study contributes to our understanding of the relevance that the length of a project (time), material incentives (money), and social and cultural factors (fun) can have for the willingness of academics to participate in the open innovation process (von Hippel et al., 1999).

Based on the results and conclusions of these two studies and on our other publications and books that we have coedited, we have arrived at a new understanding of the need for the population to participate voluntarily in delivering personal and health-care data to an open innovation platform to make it possible for medical practitioners to deliver rapid solutions in crisis situations and scenarios that we perhaps cannot imagine today. Such an innovation will require continuous campaign to deliver information about the new technology to the public and investment from the public and private sectors to motivate individuals to support these data collection systems in the future. In this case, individual patients will be part of a big group that delivers big data.

The third study is in progress, and we expect to present preliminary results at the end of 2022 or in early 2023. One of the important next questions that should be carefully studied concerns the pitfalls of the widespread sharing of medical and nonmedical data and their safeguarding, anonymization, and secure analysis. In the future, patient privacy rights will have to focus not just on the perspective of individuals but also on new community-based legislation to address the need for big data to develop high-speed solutions to crises. Developing the new database will take time, but we can hope to gain new ideas for protecting the health of all nations in crisis situations of many types. In closing, and thinking far ahead, whether or not we can develop perennial dreams such as space travel and secure a multiplanetary future for our species depends on our ability to convey the message to global populations that providing data in an open innovation platform will not only define the future of health care but also the probability that our species will survive in different crisis scenarios that no one can imagine today.

Acknowledgments The authors declare no potential conflicts of interest.

References

Agostini, L., & Nosella, A. (2017). Enhancing radical innovation performance through intellectual capital components. *Journal of Intellectual Capital, 18*(4), 789–806.

Bacon, E., Williams, M. D., & Davies, G. H. (2019). Recipes for success: Conditions for knowledge transfer across open innovation ecosystems. *International Journal of Information Management, 49*(December), 377–387.

Baldwin, C., & von Hippel, E. (2011). Modeling a paradigm shift: From producer innovation to user and open collaborative innovation. *Organization Science, 22*(6), 1399–1417.

Bogers, M., Afuah, A., & Bastian, B. (2010). Users as innovators: A review, critique, and future research directions. *Journal of Management, 36*(4), 857–875.

Bullinger, A. C., Rass, M., Adamczyk, S., Moeslein, K., & Sohn, S. (2012). Open innovation in health care: Analysis of an open health platform. *Health Policy, 105*(2), 165–175.

Chesbrough, H. W. (2006). *Open innovation: The new imperative for creating and profiting from technology*. Harvard Business Press.

Chesbrough, H., & Bogers, M. (2014). Explicating open innovation: Clarifying an emerging paradigm for understanding innovation. In H. Chesbrough, W. Vanhaverbeke, & J. West (Eds.), *New frontiers in open innovation* (pp. 3–28). Oxford University Press.

Chesbrough, H., Kim, S., & Agogino, A. (2014). Chez Panisse: Building an open innovation ecosystem. *California Management Review, 56*(4), 144–171.

Estrin, D., & Sim, I. (2010). Open mHealth architecture: An engine for health care innovation. *Science, 330*(6005), 759–760.

Flor, M. L., Cooper, S. Y., & Oltra, M. J. (2018). External knowledge search, absorptive capacity and radical innovation in high-technology firms. *European Management Journal, 36*(2), 183–194.

Glauner, P., & Plugmann, P. (Eds.). (2020). *Innovative technologies for market leadership: Investing in the future*. Springer Nature.

Glauner, P., Plugmann, P., & Lerzynski, G. (Eds.). (2021). *Digitalization in healthcare: Implementing innovation and artificial intelligence*. Springer Nature.

Gupta, A., Dey, A., & Singh, G. (2017). Connecting corporations and communities: Towards a theory of social inclusive open innovation. *Journal of Open Innovation: Technology, Market, and Complexity, 3*, 17.

Illustrated Fiction. (2019, September 12). *The med-bay in Elysium (2013)* [video]. YouTube. https://www.youtube.com/watch?v=ZK1r6VP49qI

Kanto, L., Alahuhta, P., Kukko, K., Pihlajamaa, J., Partanen, J., Vartiainen, M., & Berg, P. (2014). How do customer and user understanding, the use of prototypes and distributed collaboration support rapid innovation activities? In *Proceedings of PICMET '14 conference: Portland International Center for Management of Engineering and Technology;* Infrastructure and Service Integration. IEEE.

Kennedy, S., Whiteman, G., & van den Ende, J. (2017). Radical innovation for sustainability: The power of strategy and open innovation. *Long Range Planning, 50*(6), 712–725.

Lettl, C., Herstatt, C., & Gemuenden, H. G. (2006). Users' contributions to radical innovation: Evidence from four cases in the field of medical equipment technology. *R&D Management, 36*(3), 251–272.

Local Motors by LMI. (2010, June 23). How local motors works. [Video]. YouTube. https://www.youtube.com/watch?v=azCRuwtE_n0

Nambisan, S., Siegel, D., & Kenney, M. (2018). On open innovation, platforms, and entrepreneurship. *Strategic Entrepreneurship Journal, 12*(3), 354–368.

Nestle, V., Glauner, P., & Plugmann, P. (Eds.). (2021). *Creating innovation spaces: Impulses for start-ups and established companies in global competition*. Springer Nature.

Parmentier, G., & Mangematin, V. (2014). Orchestrating innovation with user communities in the creative industries. *Technological Forecasting and Social Change, 83*(March), 40–53.

Plugmann, P., & Plugmann, J. (2014). Users (patients) willingness to open personal health data for an innovative app to receive a more efficient health care service. *12th Annual open and user innovation conference (Harvard Business School)*.

Radziwon, A., & Bogers, M. (2019). Open innovation in SMEs: Exploring inter-organizational relationships in an ecosystem. *Technological Forecasting and Social Change, 146*, 573–587.

Smith, G., & Sandberg, J. (2018). Barriers to innovating with open government data: Exploring experiences across service phases and user types. *Information Polity, 23*(3), 249–265.

Steen, M., Buijs, J., & Williams, D. (2014). The role of scenarios and demonstrators in promoting shared understanding in innovation projects. *International Journal of Innovation and Technology Management, 11*(1), 1440001.

Van de Vrande, V., de Jong, J. P. J., Vanhaverbeke, W., & Rachemont, M. (2009). Open innovation in SMEs: Trends, motives and management challenges. *Technovation, 29*(6), 423–437.

Vanhaverbeke, W., Frattini, F., Roijakkers, N., & Usman, M. (Eds.). (2018). *Researching open innovation in SMEs*. World Scientific.

Von Briel, F., & Recker, J. (2017). Lessons from a failed implementation of an online open innovation community in an innovative organization. *MIS Quarterly Executive, 16*(1), 35–46.

Von Hippel, E., Thomke, S., & Sonnack, M. (1999). Creating breakthroughs at 3M. *Harvard Business Review, 77*(September–October), 47–57.

West, J. (2003). How open is open enough? Melding proprietary and open source platform strategies. *Research Policy, 32*(7), 1259–1285.

West, J., & Bogers, M. (2017). Open innovation: Current status and research opportunities. *Innovations, 19*(1), 43–50.

Uncertainty in Medicine: An Active Definition

Erman Sozudogru

Abstract

This chapter presents an active definition of uncertainty, focusing on the source and nature of the uncertainties in medical practice. This definition moves away from the common notion that equates uncertainty with the gaps in our knowledge. I argue that we must understand it as the subjective experience of the gaps in our knowledge. An important part of this experience is the awareness that our future actions are underdetermined by our current state of knowledge and that we need further judgements to determine the best course of action. The active definition of uncertainty highlights the complex nature of the judgements medical practitioners and researchers must make to resolve uncertainty.

1   Introduction

Uncertainty is endemic in medicine despite the desire for certainty in clinical decision-making. Uncertainties arise when providing a diagnosis, deciding on the best course of treatment, evaluating clinical trial results, and determining public health interventions, among other situations. The drive for certainty in medicine can lead medical practitioners to overlook uncertainty instead of understanding the sources and the nature of that state. This can have grave consequences in medicine because it gives clinicians a false sense of security that overlooks the complexities of the decision-making process. These concerns have been raised in several articles by medical professionals who call for practitioners to acknowledge uncertainty in medicine and develop better ways of dealing with it. Simpkin and

E. Sozudogru (✉)
Department of Science and Technology Studies, University College London, London, UK
e-mail: erman.sozudogru@ucl.ac.uk

Schwartzstein (2016) state that uncertainty is suppressed and ignored because it induces a sense of vulnerability and a sense of fear about what lies ahead. They add that "doctors often fear that by expressing uncertainty, they will project ignorance to patients and colleagues, so they internalize and mask it. We are still strongly influenced by a rationalist tradition that seeks to provide a world of apparent security" (Simpkin & Schwartzstein, 2016, p. 1713). Despite this tendency to suppress or ignore uncertainty, medical professionals continually make decisions based on limited knowledge that results in uncertainty about their decisions. Simpkin and Schwartzstein argue that physicians need to learn how to acknowledge and tolerate uncertainty. In addition, physicians must be able to help their patients manage uncertainty. Hatch (2017) highlights how the tendency to overlook or ignore uncertainty in medicine can lead to overconfidence in the results of medical research, particularly from clinical trials. Hatch emphasises that a well-designed trial obscures uncertainties and communicates that certain results can overturn existing medical practices.

As a philosopher of medicine, my aim in this chapter is to look at some of the characterisations of uncertainty and develop an active definition of uncertainty that can provide a better way to understand and deal with it in medical practice. Defining uncertainty is not an easy task, and I do not claim to provide a universal definition. Instead, I will focus on how medical practitioners, researchers, and philosophers think about uncertainty in order to identify common threads and then provide an active definition for uncertainty that can help medical practitioners better acknowledge the source of uncertainty and develop ways of dealing with it. Uncertainty is often associated with ignorance. Some philosophers have attempted to define uncertainty as the gap between our current state of knowledge and the perfect state of knowledge. For these philosophers, uncertainty can be overcome by filling these gaps. While the gap argument highlights that ignorance is an important aspect of uncertainty, it has several shortcomings. In what follows, I will provide a detailed description of the gap argument and raise two objections. First, building on the philosophy of science literature, I will argue against the idea that there is a single complete and comprehensive account of the world that would provide us with the perfect state of knowledge. Second, I will argue that uncertainty is a subjective experience of an individual's lack of knowledge. This position is built on Paul Han's recent work that defines uncertainty as a metacognitive process where a person or a group actively reflect on their lack of knowledge or understanding.

I introduce another important feature of uncertainty that needs to inform our definition, that is, the fact that we experience uncertainty when our actions are underdetermined by our existing knowledge. Thinking about uncertainty in terms of our actions shifts the focus from the need to gain more knowledge toward a focus on making the best judgement in light of existing knowledge in the context where these judgements address particular medical problem in light of the present state of knowledge and other factors specific to a given context. While we should strive to improve the state of our knowledge, I argue that more information does not provide more certainty in every situation. In addition, there are instances in medicine where we need to act before we can access new information. In such cases, uncertainty must be understood as how our present state of knowledge informs our judgements about possible actions and their consequences. Hence, dealing with uncertainty requires a better understanding of the judgements medics ought to make when facing uncertainty.

2   Philosophical Definition of Uncertainty

There have been few attempts by philosophers to define uncertainty. Djulbegovic et al. (2011) provide a detailed survey of attempts to think about uncertainty in medicine. While many scholars from different disciplines discuss uncertainty, Djulbegovic et al. (2011) is a valuable resource for summarising different positions and relating each attempt to define uncertainty in medicine. Their summary includes statistical, epistemic, and psychological definitions of uncertainty. Here, I will focus on epistemic uncertainty given that uncertainty is often equated to gaps in our knowledge or, generally speaking, to our ignorance.[1] In other words, each attempt to define uncertainty relies on the epistemic notion that uncertainty can be equated to gaps in our knowledge. Here, I will characterise what I call the gap argument, followed by highlighting its shortcomings.

2.1   The Gap Argument

Djulbegovic et al. (2011) provide a survey of different accounts of uncertainty, conceptualised in different ways. They acknowledge that uncertainty can be defined in multiple ways depending on the context. With that in mind, they have defined two types of uncertainties: epistemic uncertainty and statistical uncertainty. While they treat these two separately, the definition of statistical uncertainty relies on the definition of epistemic uncertainty. The statistical definition of uncertainty focuses on the quantification of risk and unpredictability in light of our existing knowledge. However, the cause of statistical uncertainty can be explained by epistemic uncertainty.

Epistemic uncertainty focuses on the relationship between the unknown and existing knowledge. It is defined as the type of uncertainty that is "related to our knowledge of the state of a system, about some underlying fact of matter, typically due to lack of useful or complete information" (Djulbegovic et al., 2011, p. 301). Djulbegovic et al. link epistemic uncertainty to gaps in our existing knowledge or, in their words, "a lack". Similarly, Nikolaidis et al. (2005) define uncertainty as the "gap between certainty and present state of knowledge", and Zimmermann (2000,

---

[1] Here, my aim is not to discuss the construction of ignorance. Thus, my argument does not make use of the agnotology literature. A more systematic study of ignorance calls for a nuanced understanding of what ignorance is and how it can be used to deliberately generate uncertainties. However, this topic is beyond the scope of this chapter.

p. 192) claims that uncertainty "implies that in a certain situation a person does not dispose about information which quantitatively and qualitatively is appropriate to describe, prescribe or predict deterministically and numerically a system, its behavior or other characteristics".

These three definitions all attempt to define uncertainty as a lack of knowledge. They all hold that we can reduce uncertainty by filling the gaps in our current system of knowledge. Djulbegovic et al. argue that uncertainty can be expressed on a scale that has ignorance on one end and certainty on the other. While they acknowledge that we can never be entirely certain due to the problem of induction, they argue that a perfect state of knowledge exists that can be acquired. Thus, the gap between our current state of knowledge and the assumed perfect state of knowledge is the type of epistemic uncertainty we seek to reduce.

Djulbegovic and co-authors claim that scientific methodology is the "primary means" of reducing uncertainty. Citing Popper's work on falsification, they again acknowledge that because scientific knowledge is fallible, we cannot have complete certainty. Nonetheless, they claim that scientific methods are the best way to address uncertainties. It is worth noting that their discussion of scientific methods is relatively quick and does not provide details about what they take to be scientific methodology. However, given that they take uncertainty to be the gap in our scientific knowledge, it follows that we would turn to scientific practices generally to provide us with the information to fill these gaps.

Djulbegovic et al. identify specific forms of uncertainty in medical practice and provide relevant clinical examples and suggestions about how to address or overcome uncertainty in each case. Most of the solutions they provide focus on filling the gaps in our knowledge. For example, in dealing with conflicting evidence, they call for "developing reliable, unbiased, and up-to-date sources of evidence and ensuring its delivery at the right place, for the right patient, at the right time" (Djulbegovic et al., 2011, p. 306). Similarly, in cases of uncertainty related to a lack of information about the effects of treatments and accuracy of diagnosis, authors suggest "obtaining more or better evidence. This can be achieved by conducting research (when the entire medical community needs information) or making existing evidence available when needed, as advocated by the EBM [evidence-based medicine] movement" (ibid.).

Similar to Djulbegovic et al., McNeil (2001) reduces uncertainty to the gaps in our knowledge, arguing that uncertainty is caused by 1) lack of convincing evidence because of delayed or obsolete data from clinical studies, 2) applicability of evidence generated by randomised controlled trials, and 3) uncertainty about the interpretation of data.

The arguments I reviewed so far think of uncertainty as a lack of knowledge or information, hence as a state that can be ameliorated through further research. These accounts are successful in identifying that lack of knowledge is an important feature of uncertainty. However, they are limited because of their overemphasis on the objective gaps in our knowledge.

2.2   Shortcomings of the Gap Argument

I now turn to the two main shortcomings of the gap argument. The first is the reliance on the assumption that a perfect state of knowledge exists that we should strive for. The second is the limited view that uncertainty can be overcome by generating more knowledge.

One can think of a perfect state of knowledge in reductionist terms where we expect our theories at lower, more fundamental levels to inform theories at a higher level. For instance, our knowledge of diseases at the clinical level can be explained by understanding biochemical mechanisms and genetics. As formulated by Nagel (1951), reductionism was part of the broader tradition of logical empiricism, where one of the main aims was the unity of science. Unity of science can be summarised briefly as the philosophical project associated with logical empiricism that aims to connect different scientific language and methods across disciplines. For Nagel, unity of laws and theories were possible given the behaviour of macroscale objects is explained in terms of microscale processes. In other words, our theories about macroscale objects can be derived from theories at microscale.

The logical empiricist project to unify science has been criticised on the grounds that it provides a restrictive and unrealistic characterisation of scientific practices. Patrick Suppes (1978) argues that the subject matters, methods, and languages of different scientific disciplines are not reducible to one unified subject, method, and language. Using case studies from scientific practices (including the medical sciences), Suppes argues that scientific activity is an act of perpetual problem-solving where scientists approach different problems with "a potpourri of scientific methods, techniques, and concepts, which in many cases we have learned to use with great facility" (Suppes, 1978, p. 14). Following Suppes, when we look at biomedical research, we do not see unification methods or accounts produced by different methods that have been reductively unified. For anyone involved in medical practice or research, this is at best a far-fetched idea that is difficult to realise given the complexity of biological systems. Instead, we see a plurality of approaches, each employing different methods, models, and theories. This is particularly evident when we look at research on chronic conditions like heart disease or obesity where we see the same phenomena being studied using multiple approaches that focus on factors ranging from genetics to socio-economics.

Kellert et al. (2006) reject reductionism, and more broadly, they reject the position they describe as monism, which they define as the assumption that the ultimate aim of science is to "establish a single, complete and comprehensive account of the natural world (or the part of the world investigated by the science) based on a single set of fundamental principles" (Kellert et al., 2006, p. x). They reject this position on the grounds that plurality in scientific practices must be considered as evidence that "there are kinds of situations produced by the interaction of factors each of which may be representable in a model or theory, but not all of which are representable in the same model or theory" (Kellert et al., 2006, p. xiv). Kellert et al. suggest that in order to understand and explain different aspects of phenomena, it is necessary to have multiple approaches. Instead of recognising multiplicity as a problem, Kellert et al. argue that plurality is characteristic of scientific inquiry that cannot be eliminated and that our understanding of science should be free of the assumption that there is a complete and coherent account or perfect knowledge that we should aim for. The multiplicity in scientific practices is taken to be evidence that we should not assume that there is a broad perfect state of knowledge that allows us to derive particular knowledge from fundamental principles. They argue that the existence of such an account should be treated as an open-ended empirical question.

Following the pluralist arguments against the unity of science and monism, it is difficult to maintain that there is a perfect state of knowledge in the broader sense. We cannot reduce an array of accounts provided by different disciplines to a single unified account that would make up the perfect state of knowledge. Instead, we must accept the plurality of accounts that we can drive evidence from, each contingent with the aims of the particular research project.

Given the plurality within scientific and medical practices, we must not assume that there is a perfect unified state of knowledge that we must aim to get to. In other words, it is uncertain that a perfect state of knowledge exists that is knowable. Hence, defining uncertainty as the gap between our current state of knowledge and an assumed (but unverified and unknown) perfect state of knowledge is not very useful in the sense that our pursuit of reducing uncertainty will generate further uncertainty because the aims of that pursuit are based on assumptions that themselves are open-ended questions.

We can also think more specifically about the perfect state of knowledge. In medicine, the "best" state of knowledge is often thought as "the best evidence". To be able to define the best evidence, we need to think about qualities that would make a given set of evidence better than others. This is not a trivial task, and it has been discussed in detail by both medical practitioners and philosophers. Using the best evidence of causation is particularly important in the clinic when diagnosing and making decisions about the appropriate treatment or care. Proponents of evidence-based medicine (EBM) have argued for an evidence hierarchy where randomised controlled trials and their meta-analyses would get the top spot in the hierarchy (Evidence-Based Medicine Working Group, 1992; Sackett et al., 1996). They rank other forms of evidence, such as evidence of disease mechanisms, lower in the hierarchy.

Randomised controlled trials (RCTs) measure the strength of correlation between a putative cause and effect. Evidence hierarchies have received a fair share of criticism from philosophers of science. Cartwright (2010), who discusses the various shortcomings of RCTs, identifies one as the problem of extrapolating results from an experimental population to a wider population. Stegenga (2011) highlights how different meta-analyses can contradict one another. Clarke et al. (2013, 2014) focus on the lower end of the evidence hierarchy, arguing that statistical forms of evidence must be accompanied by mechanistic forms of evidence. Parkkinen et al. (2018) developed this idea further to provide procedures for evaluating evidence of mechanisms in medicine. These works have shown that we cannot identify one best form of evidence of causation, be it statistical or mechanistic. Instead, what constitutes the best evidence is contingent on the questions we are asking. We cannot expect statistical evidence to be the best evidence in every situation.

Thus far, I have argued that the perfect state of knowledge is an assumption. Pluralist literature has successfully argued that scientific practices do not fully support this assumption. Instead of a single unified account, scientific practices provide multiple accounts of different aspects of phenomena. Furthermore, what constitutes best evidence cannot be defined independently of the context in which we ask a question. In other words, determining what best evidence is or what is enough knowledge to constitute certainty often requires a series of judgements that are particular to their context. We do not have general criteria for success; that is, we do not know when the gap in knowledge is filled. Therefore, we cannot rely on an objective measure that assumes a perfect state of knowledge to define or measure uncertainty.

My second objection to the gap argument is that it overlooks the subjective nature of uncertainty. Here, I argue that uncertainty is not the objective gaps in our knowledge but the subjective experience of these gaps. This argument is motivated by the position developed by Paul Han (2021), who defines uncertainty as the "self-reflexive awareness of [our] ignorance" (p. 14). This definition is based on Flavell's concept of metacognition, which is the knowledge of one's cognitive processes and the results of this process (Flavell, 1979). Thus, for Han, uncertainty is not about some aspect of reality; it is the subjective experience of our ignorance.

Han further elaborates his description of the uncertainty position by comparing it to William James's description of certainty. For James, certainty is "of somethings we feel that we are certain: when we know, and we know what we do know" (James, 1896, p. 13). Building on James' definition of certainty, Han argues that uncertainty is not the absence of knowing but the *feeling* of the absence of knowing. For Han, there are two important components of uncertainty: the absence of understanding and the presence of conscious awareness. Certainty, on the other hand, is the presence of both understanding *and* presence of conscious awareness. Hence, we cannot merely focus on the gaps in our understanding but must also consider the subjective experience of these gaps. As Han argues, "Metacognition consists of an individual's knowledge about their own cognitive abilities, the strategies and tasks they must employ to think and take action, and the expected outcomes of different courses of action" (p. 19).

For Han, uncertainty is an adaptive form of knowledge of one's ignorance. The agent experiencing uncertainty engages in a deliberative form of thinking that requires a series of judgements. These judgements are informed by the agent's perception of the novelty in light of their prior knowledge and values. In other words, the scale or levels of certainty or uncertainty cannot be understood merely through quantifying how much we do not know. As Han puts it, "The appropriate level of uncertainty or certainty for any given individual or situation is a complex moral judgment that depends on various factors, including personal values, needs, and dispositions, as well as situational demands for certainty versus uncertainty" (Han, 2021, p. 18).

In summary, uncertainty cannot be defined as the gap between the current state of knowledge and the presumed perfect state of knowledge. Our best attempts to define the best state of knowledge or best evidence are not supported by medical and scientific practices. These practices rely on a plurality of approaches to build explanatory models or establish causal claims that are contingent on their particular aims. We need to acknowledge that uncertainty arises from the subjective reflection on our state of knowledge. The subjective nature of uncertainty is very important because the scale and the nature of uncertainty depend on the person or the group's assessment of a given situation.

Our subjective reflection of our ignorance or, more broadly, our state of knowledge is an important element of uncertainty. Nevertheless, a satisfactory definition of uncertainty must be able to differentiate between cases where our conscious reflection of our lack of knowledge leads to uncertainty and cases where it does not. There are many things we do not know, and we are aware of our lack of knowledge. Nevertheless, we are not uncertain every time we acknowledge a gap or a shortcoming in our knowledge. An important aspect of uncertainty that we need to acknowledge is linked to our actions. I will argue that uncertainty arises when we are aware that our future actions are undetermined by our current state of knowledge.

3   Active Definition of Uncertainty

Thus far, I have argued that the best definition of uncertainty is the subjective awareness of our ignorance. However, every awareness of ignorance does not result in uncertainty. Let us consider a clinical scenario where a clinician prescribes a beta-blocker for a patient with frequent migraines. The clinician's decision to prescribe propranolol is backed up by systematic reviews and meta-analyses that show drugs like propranolol are effective in reducing the frequency and the number of migraine attacks (Jackson et al., 2019). However, when asked, she might acknowledge gaps in her knowledge regarding the underlying mechanism of action or acknowledge that her understanding of the systematic reviews may lack detail. Nonetheless, she would not experience uncertainty when prescribing this medicine if she is satisfied that this patient's medical history does not suggest that it would cause any harm. The clinician's state of knowledge is adequate to support her action of prescribing propranolol to her patient even though she has an explicit awareness of the gaps in her understanding of how beta-blockers prevent migraines.

Let us compare this to a similar scenario where a clinician is talking to a similar patient experiencing frequent headaches. During the discussion of different treatment options, the patient shares that they take Truvada daily (emtricitabine/tenofovir) for pre-exposure prophylaxis (PrEP) of HIV. The clinician—who, in this scenario is not familiar with PrEP—experiences uncertainty regarding her actions. Her lack of knowledge of Truvada prevents her from making a quick decision, like suggesting common painkillers to manage the headaches. Here, the uncertainty arises when her current state of knowledge underdetermines her actions.

A quick search will reveal that Truvada used as PrEP might adversely affect glomerular function, and the long-term use can lead to kidney damage (Ascher et al., 2020). Therefore, the current advice by the UK's National Institute of Health and Care Excellence (NICE) cautions pairing Truvada as PrEP with nonsteroidal anti-inflammatory drugs (NSAIDs) that also cause kidney damage (NICE, 2016). Hence, the clinician might rule out the use of NSAIDs that are available as over-the-counter painkillers and start considering alternatives like the aforementioned beta-blockers. This hypothetical interaction shows that the clinician not only has to acknowledge her ignorance but also has to recognise that her lack of knowledge can lead to decisions with undesirable outcomes.

In these circumstances, the concept of metacognition is still an important aspect of defining uncertainty. In both clinical scenarios, I highlighted the importance of the clinicians reflecting on their state of knowledge and ignorance. Such reflection often requires an identification of the different forms of ignorance, like known unknowns (the mechanism of propranolol action in preventing migraines, potential interactions between PrEP and headache medications) and unknown unknowns (information patients choose not to or forgot to disclose). This reflection allows the clinician to assess different treatment options and the expected outcomes and assign relative risk. The key aspect of this consideration is the question, "What is the best way to act?"

I argue that uncertainty is best defined when we think about it in terms of our actions. Defining uncertainty through our actions allows us to think about how we can best deal with it. We experience uncertainty when we are cognizant that our future actions are not determined by our current state of knowledge. Thus, uncertainty leads to a form of inquiry that involves a series of complex judgements. These can be the individual judgements of a clinician or the judgements a larger group makes that aim to reach a consensus through shared values. Moreover, these judgements require inquirers to think about ways to frame the problem that we are feeling uncertain about and determine potential actions and their consequences. The important point here is that these judgements rely on the inquirer's knowledge of the situation, the broader context, and how the inquirer values different possible outcomes.

So far, the examples I have provided are simple clinical scenarios that can be resolved by clinicians seeking more knowledge about something they do not know to inform their decision about how to act. For example, after quick research, the clinician can gain adequate knowledge to be able to make a judgement on how to act: determine whether PrEP is the cause of headaches (as headaches are often associated with Truvada as PrEP) or prescribe alternative pain relief. And in both cases, clinicians can sensibly delay their decisions until they gain more information to help with their judgements. However, we can look at other, more complicated examples that will show the merits of thinking about uncertainty in terms of our actions and their consequences.

In March 2021, Denmark suspended the use of the AstraZeneca vaccine Vaxzevria following the report of rare blood clots and one death (Wise, 2021). Following Denmark, several European countries, as well as Australia and Canada, suspended the use of this vaccine as a precautionary measure (Dyer, 2021). This move was despite the reassurance of the European Medicines Agency (EMA) that "there is currently no indication that vaccination has caused these conditions, which are not listed as side effects with this vaccine. The position of EMA's safety committee PRAC is that the vaccine's benefits continue to outweigh its risks and the vaccine can continue to be administered while investigation of cases of thromboembolic events is ongoing" (EMA, 2021a).

Initially, the reports of patients developing rare blood clots after receiving the vaccine were not greater than the cases of blood clots in general population (Wise, 2021). Nonetheless, sixteen European countries suspended the use of this vaccine, while countries like the UK, Belgium, and Poland carried on with their vaccination programmes. This example shows how uncertainty arising from the reports of rare blood clots led to an inquiry where different public health institutions and scientific bodies made judgements about how to act. The choice between suspending and continuing the use of the AstraZeneca vaccine was subject to a complicated judgement that relied on a small sample of evidence, background knowledge about vaccines, and ethical and social considerations that are specific for each country.

The EMA's position later shifted after further studies acknowledged that "a causal relationship between the vaccination with Vaxzevria and the occurrence of thrombosis in combination with thrombocytopenia is considered plausible" (EMA, 2021b). However, this was accompanied by advice that the AstraZeneca vaccine should be used as the rate of death and suffering caused by COVID-19 is greater than the rate of vaccine-induced prothrombotic immune thrombocytopenia.

While Norway, Denmark, and Sweden chose to use an abundance of caution and suspended the use of the AstraZeneca vaccine, other countries such as Germany and Italy resumed using the AstraZeneca vaccine, restricting its use to people over a certain age. Countries like the UK, which never suspended the use of the vaccine, took similar measures by offering the AZ vaccine to people over 40.

One might argue that the suspension of the AstraZeneca vaccine in Scandinavian countries like Norway and Denmark is contrary to a scientific consensus about the safety of this vaccine. This is particularly striking given the fact that further studies into the link between the AstraZeneca vaccine and the cases of blood clots by Greinacher et al. (2021) provided a mechanistic explanation for vaccine-induced prothrombotic immune thrombocytopenia. However, this case highlights that in dealing with uncertainty, more knowledge does not always lead to the same conclusion. This is because the final judgement relies on several factors, including the number of cases, the number of deaths in each country, and the length and severity of lockdowns. For instance, Steinar Madsen, the medical director of the Norwegian Medicines Agency, has acknowledged that new evidence shows that the AstraZeneca vaccine has a positive risk-benefit ratio overall, but he underlined the fact that Norway only had 650 deaths from COVID-19 at the time, stating that "we are in a totally different situation to the UK, Italy, Germany, France, Czechia. If we had been in a precarious situation like in the UK, the attitude of the Norwegian population would have been different" (Milne et al., 2021). Similarly, Geir Bukholm, director of the Division of Infection Control and Environmental

Health at the Norwegian Institute of Public Health, stated that "since there are few people who die from COVID-19 in Norway, the risk of dying after vaccination with the AstraZeneca vaccine would be higher than the risk of dying from the disease, particularly for younger people" (NIPH, 2021). While new mechanistic information emerged that explained how to avoid vaccine-induced prothrombotic immune thrombocytopenia, this new information was one of the many factors that informed the judgements scientists and medical advisors made.

This case shows that dealing with uncertainty requires a series of complicated judgements and is not necessarily eliminated when we gain more knowledge. If we consider uncertainty to be a gap in our knowledge, that leads us to think that we will have a single answer once the gap is filled. While new knowledge may allow us to resolve uncertainties (which might not always be the case), additional knowledge is considered along with other factors that are unique to the context in which we are experiencing uncertainty. The diverse responses of European countries highlight how the same information can differently inform judgements that are made to resolve uncertainty. Each of these judgements aims to determine the best course of action. The case reports about the consequences of the AstraZeneca vaccine highlighted our ignorance about the link between vaccines and blood clots. The uncertainty increased when we became aware of our ignorance of this link and our consequent inability to determine the best course of action. In other words, reports of rare and unusual blood clots led to a form of reflection on our present state of knowledge that did not present a clear answer about how to proceed with the immunisation programmes. Medical advisors and scientists from each country had to make sets of complex judgements about how to act before they had access to more information. While suspending the use of the AstraZeneca vaccine might have seemed like the safest option in the face of uncertainty, that decision would have had severe downsides: Pausing or slowing immunisation programmes during a pandemic can leave people vulnerable to COVID-19 infection and erode public trust in the vaccine programmes altogether. These judgements are not merely guided by what we know or do not know about vaccines and blood clots but also on factors that are specific to each context where these judgements are made. Decisions about how to act during a pandemic in the face of uncertainty yield different results depending on the rates of transmission, people's risk-taking behaviours, the social and economic impact of lockdowns and social distancing measures, and broader ethical discourses on personal risk versus communal risk. More information may be helpful, but our judgements are contingent on multiple factors, including moral, social, and political values.

4 Conclusion: From Definition to Action

The main motivation behind this chapter is to provide an active definition of uncertainty that can help medical practitioners better acknowledge and address uncertainties in their practice. I demonstrated why we cannot define uncertainty as to the gap between our current state of knowledge and the perfect state of knowledge. I provided a pluralist argument against the idea that there is a perfect state of knowledge. Instead of treating uncertainty as a gap in our knowledge, we must understand it as the subjective experience of these gaps and the awareness that our future actions are not determined by our current state of knowledge. In other words, clinicians will experience uncertainty when they cannot determine the best course of action for their patients based on all the information they have. Similarly, public health officials and medical advisors will face uncertainty when the present state of knowledge underdetermines the appropriate form of action. This active definition serves as a helpful starting point for medical practitioners and researchers in their reflections on the source of uncertainty and their recognition of the complexities of the judgements they must make about how to act in different situations. The active definition also highlights the complexities involved in managing uncertainty, therefore predicting future challenges in applying flowcharts and artificial intelligence to deal with uncertainties. To address the worries expressed in the medical literature and rise to the challenge of acknowledging and dealing with uncertainties, we need to acknowledge the subjective source of uncertainty and recognise the complexities in judgements we need to make to resolve them.

Acknowledgments I want to thank Sepehr Ehsani for inviting me to write this chapter and for his support during the process. I also want to thank Raquel Velho for reading the earlier drafts and the excellent advice and Eilidh Gunn, Rachel Coles, Anna King, and Imogen Bidwell for discussing the clinical scenarios with me.

References

Ascher, S., Scherzer, R., Estrella, M., Shigenaga, J., Spaulding, K., Glidden, D., . . . Jotwani, V. (2020). HIV pre-exposure prophylaxis with tenofovir disoproxil fumarate/emtricitabine and changes in kidney function and tubular health. *AIDS (London), 34*(5), 699–706.

Cartwright, N. (2010). What are randomised controlled trials good for? *Philosophical Studies, 147*(1), 59.

Clarke, B., Gillies, D., Illari, P., Russo, F., & Williamson, J. (2013). The evidence that evidence-based medicine omits. *Preventive Medicine, 57*(6), 745–747.

Clarke, B., Gillies, D., Illari, P., Russo, F., & Williamson, J. (2014). Mechanisms and the evidence hierarchy. *Topoi, 33*(2), 339–360.

Djulbegovic, B., Hozo, I., & Greenland, S. (2011). Uncertainty in clinical medicine. In F. Gifford (Ed.), *Philosophy of medicine* (Vol. 16, pp. 299–356). Elsevier.

Dyer, O. (2021). Covid-19: EMA defends AstraZeneca vaccine as Germany and Canada. *BMJ, 2021*, 373–n883.

EMA (European Medicines Agency). (2021a). *Covid-19 vaccine AstraZeneca: PRAC investigating cases of thromboembolic events—vaccine's benefits currently still outweigh risks: Update.* Accessed October 30, 2021, from https://www.ema.europa.eu/en/news/covid-19-vaccine-astrazeneca-prac-investigating-cases-thromboembolic-events-vaccines-benefits

EMA (European Medicines Agency). (2021b). *Vaxzevria (previously COVID-19 Vaccine AstraZeneca): Link between the vaccine and the occurrence of thrombosis in combination with thrombocytopenia.* Accessed October 30, 2021, from https://www.ema.europa.eu/en/medicines/dhpc/vaxzevria-previously-covid-19-vaccine-astrazeneca-link-between-vaccine-occurrence-thrombosis

Evidence-Based Medicine Working Group. (1992). Evidence-based medicine: A new approach to teaching the practice of medicine. *JAMA, 268*(17), 2420–2425.

Flavell, J. H. (1979). Metacognitive aspects of problem solving. In L. B. Resnick (Ed.), *The nature of intelligence* (pp. 232–906). Lawrence Erlbaum.

Greinacher, A., Thiele, T., Warkentin, T. E., Weisser, K., Kyrle, P., & Eichinger, S. (2021). Thrombotic thrombocytopenia after ChAdOx1 nCov-19 vaccination. *The New England Journal of Medicine, 384*(22), 2092–2101.

Han, P. K. J. (2021). *Uncertainty in medicine: A framework for tolerance.* Oxford University Press.

Hatch, S. (2017). Uncertainty in medicine. *BMJ, 357*, j2180.

Jackson, J. L., Kuriyama, A., Kuwatsuka, Y., Nickoloff, S., Storch, D., Jackson, W., Zhang, Z.-J., & Hayashino, Y. (2019). Beta-blockers for the prevention of headache in adults, a systematic review and meta-analysis. *PLoS One, 14*(3), e0212785.

James, W. (1896). Will to believe.

Kellert, S., Longino, H., & Waters, K. (Eds.). (2006). *Scientific pluralism.* University of Minnesota Press.

McNeil, B. J. (2001). Hidden barriers to improvement in the quality of care. *New England Journal of Medicine, 345*(22), 1612–1620.

Milne R, DP Mancini, & C. Cookson. (2021, March 21). Nordic nations hold off on AstraZeneca jab as scientists' probe safety concerns. *Financial Times.* Accessed October 30, 2021, from https://www.ft.com/content/0ef3a623-f3a2-4e76-afbd-94a915b24ad5

Nagel, E. (1951). *The structure of science.* Harcourt.

NICE. (2016). *Pre-exposure prophylaxis of HIV in adults at high risk: Truvada (emtric-itabine/tenofovir disoproxil).* National Institute of Heath and Care Excellence. Evidence Summary. nice.org.uk/guidance/esnm78

Nikolaidis, E., Ghiocel, D., & Singhla, S. (2005). *Engineering design reliability handbook.* CRC Press.

NIPH. (2021). *Norwegian Institute of Public Health's recommendation about AstraZeneca vaccine.* Norwegian Institute of Public Health. Accessed October 30, 2021, from https://www.fhi.no/en/archive/covid-19-archive/covid-19%2D%2D-archived-news-2021/apr/astrazeneca-vaccine-removed-from-coronavirus-immunisation-programme-in-norw/

Parkkinen, V.-P., Wallmann, C., Wilde, M., Clarke, B., Illari, P., Kelly, M. P., Norell, C., Russo, F., Shaw, B., & Williamson, J. (2018). *Evaluating evidence of mechanisms in medicine: Principles and procedures.* Springer.

Sackett, D. L., Rosenberg, W. M. C., Gray, J. A. M., Haynes, R. B., & Richardson, W. S. (1996). Evidence based medicine: What it is and what it isn't. *BMJ, 312*(7023), 71–72.

Simpkin, A. L., & Schwartzstein, R. M. (2016). Tolerating uncertainty: The next medical revolution? *New England Journal of Medicine, 375*(18), 1713–1715.

Stegenga, J. (2011). Is meta-analysis the platinum standard of evidence? *Studies in History and Philosophy of Science Part C: Studies in History and Philosophy of Biological and Biomedical Sciences, 42*(4), 497–507.

Suppes, P. (1978). The plurality of science. *PSA: Proceedings of the Biennial Meeting of the Philosophy of Science Association, 1978*, 3–16.

Wise, J. (2021). Covid-19: European countries suspend use of Oxford-AstraZeneca vaccine after reports of blood clots. *BMJ, 2021*, 373–n883.

Zimmermann, H. J. (2000). An application-oriented view of modelling uncertainty. *European Journal of Operational Research, 122*(2), 190–198.

Innovations for Sustainable Healthcare

Thomas Spittler and Helana Lutfi

Abstract

Climate change continues to have negative health effects on individuals, such as increasing the chronicity of diseases and the burden of environmental poisons that lead to expensive treatments. Global health organizations believe that medical services entail a responsibility to enact climate neutrality. Climate neutrality would be managed through goals leading toward the achievement of sustainability in hospitals, the environment, and healthcare. The purpose of this chapter is to provide a vision for sustainable healthcare by identifying the features of a sustainable healthcare system and the most important components of sustainability.

1 Introduction

The overall health of a population is attributed to five major factors: genetics, behavioral, environmental, medical, and social ones. Climate change continues to have negative impacts, such as chronic diseases, environmental poisons, and carbon emissions, on individuals in addition to the burden of expensive treatments for illness caused by environmental factors. Although the health sector plays a key role in addressing these issues, it also directly impacts climate change by consuming resources (e.g., medicines, food, natural gas for heating, and petrol for transporting patients). As a result, healthcare is associated with a significant carbon footprint. Global health organizations believe that providing medical services entails a

T. Spittler (✉) · H. Lutfi
Faculty of European Campus Rottal-Inn (ECRI), Deggendorf Institute of Technology, Pfarrkirchen, Germany
e-mail: thomas.spittler@th-deg.de; helana.lutfi@th-deg.de

responsibility to work toward climate neutrality. Innovation and the implementation of technology in healthcare can help alleviate climate change by minimizing the footprint of this industry (Busse et al., 2019).

In order to contribute to green information technology (green IT), manufacturers must focus on producing environmentally friendly medical products. Data centers with green technology, green cloud computing, and green data storage are all major aspects of green IT. To illustrate, cloud computing could be considered a green solution because it provides resource virtualization, improved energy efficiency, and in-depth resource utilization. In cloud computing, resources (computers, network servers, storage, applications, services, etc.) undergo virtualization and utilization to separate computing environments from their physical infrastructure. Separation enables various operating systems and applications to run simultaneously on a single machine. In turn, this allows people in the medical sector to engage more efficiently with the management of product life cycles (or PLMs; Godbole & Lamb, 2018). Notable opportunities for more efficient and green IT practices in healthcare are electronic health records (EHR) and telemedicine, or "medicine at a distance." This allows for data virtualization and a reduction in the number of physical devices (as well as the amount of power consumption and paper usage). The use of virtual collaboration promotes the more efficient practice of medicine at a distance by allowing healthcare providers to share data anywhere at any time (McNickle, 2011). The ecological principles guiding green productivity practices when developing healthcare products are as follows: use resources sustainably, maintain ecological balance, and protect ecological biodiversity throughout the product development process. This means using green design during concept development and design, manufacturing, distribution, and use, the servicing of the product, and recycling (see Fig. 1). Healthcare organizations that implement a green information and communication strategy may improve their productivity, reduce their carbon emissions, and increase their cost savings (Whichello et al., 2020).

The green mission in healthcare aims to transform healthcare across the world through reducing its environmental footprint, establishing policies for healthy products, and building leadership in environmental health. Environmentally friendly healthcare products and the green mission are closely linked to effective healthcare management, social interactions between patients and providers, community-based healthcare approaches, and the use of modern technologies. Technology will play a major role in shaping the future of healthcare because information and telecommunications technologies are advancing rapidly. Next-generation digital technologies will likely be used in new ways and cluster in new activities and practices (Mayer-Foulkes et al., 2021).

The purpose of this chapter is to provide a vision for sustainable healthcare by identifying the features of a sustainable healthcare system and the most important components of sustainability. It also provides insight into global and rural healthcare challenges. Finally, it offers an overview of how environmental healthcare services can bring about solutions to these negative challenges.

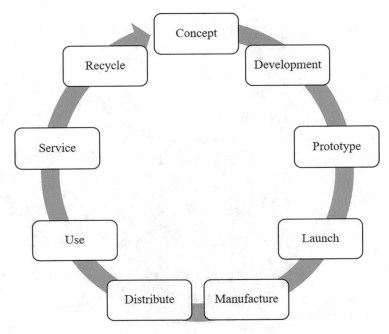

Fig. 1 Green product life cycle management (PLM)

2 Sustainability in Healthcare

Taking into consideration various issues of sustainability in relation to health and well-being is crucial. In the field of sustainable health, individual well-being and disease prevention are emphasized, often before the need for care arises. However, individual health is impacted by the surrounding environment—both indoors and out. Toxic chemicals and heavy metals, for example, have a negative impact on the health of human beings. The implementation of inpatient and outpatient care that aims to achieve sustainable behavior, technologies, and hospitals is known as sustainable healthcare (Eriksson & Turnstedt, 2019).

Sustainable healthcare can be defined as providing care that is living and working within our means with regard to natural resources. It is healthcare that avoids placing detrimental stress on environmental and human systems, thus risking the health of the present and future population (Schroeder et al., 2012). A sustainable healthcare system should focus on saving costs, minimizing waste, and increasing recycling. However, the approach should also achieve quality of life through the maintenance of healthy lifestyles, the extension of equitable access to the health services provided by the system, and a reduction in hospital readmissions (Fischer, 2014). Figure 2 shows the focus features by a sustainable healthcare system.

Figure 3 presents the heart of the sustainability approach to healthcare. It is based on providing universal healthcare by ensuring access to healthcare services,

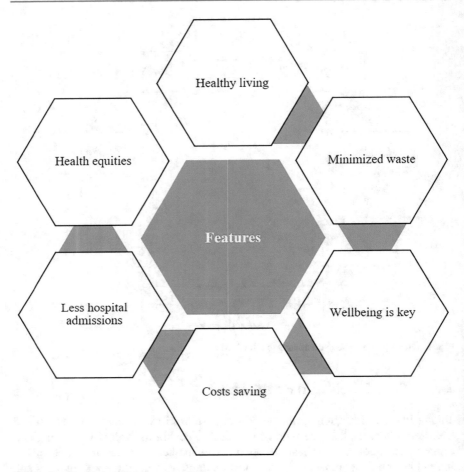

Fig. 2 Sustainable healthcare system features

a connection to human health, environmental protection, and a reduction in climate impact. Building a sustainable healthcare system means constructing a healthcare system that individuals and groups can easily access. Interoperability, for instance, is crucial for achieving transparent, sustainable, and successful healthcare management. Setting sustainable objectives and goals is thus essential to decision-making about future ambitions regarding the creation of smart hospitals (Mulvaney, 2020).

2.1 Building a High-Value Health System

The purpose of a healthcare system is to promote, restore, and maintain the health and well-being of the population in order to achieve social goals. In a well-

Fig. 3 The heart of the
sustainability approach in
healthcare

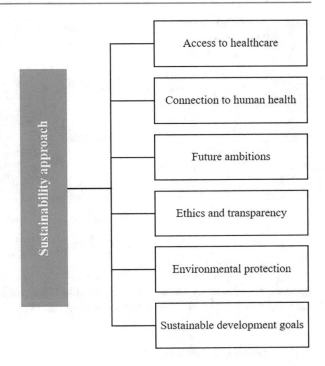

functioning healthcare system, people and institutions collaborate to improve the
quality of care according to established policies and guidelines. In 2018, the World
Health Organization (WHO) published three essential parameters for obtaining
excellence in healthcare around the world. The first parameter is effective delivery of
services by providing evidence-based healthcare to those who need it. The second,
safety, involves avoiding harm to those for whom the care is intended. The third,
people-centeredness, includes providing care tailored to individual preferences,
needs, and values (Atun & Moore, 2021).

Managers of healthcare systems who want to ensure sustainability over the
long term should scrutinize services at two levels. The first is at the level of the
provision of healthcare services, which include preventive, chronic, acute, and
palliative care. There is a growing consensus that quality of care is determined by
the degree to which healthcare is "effective, safe, and people-centered" (Busse et
al., 2019, p. 6). The second is at the level of the entire healthcare system. Healthcare
systems are "high quality" when they meet their overall objectives of better health,
responsiveness, financial security, and efficiency (Busse et al., 2019, p. 12).

International declarations have focused on four targeted goals for healthcare (see
Fig. 4). Those goals are as follows: the provision of affordable healthcare, accessible
services, services that are appropriate for the population being served, and patient
care that meets standards for quality (Busse et al., 2019). Healthcare systems that

embrace sustainability should aim to provide high-quality care that is aware of financial and social constraints (Mortimer et al., 2018).

2.2   Green Hospitals

In Germany in 2013, the Bavarian State Ministry for Health and Care (Bayerisches Staatsministerium für Gesundheit und Pflege, n.d.) implemented the Green Hospital Initiative (GHI). Launched by the Bavarian State Ministry for Environment and Health in 2011, the GHI focuses on energy efficiency as a contribution to the Bavarian energy transition and is based on a holistic approach. As this approach has expanded, the substance of the GHI was adapted to include the social and political elements of a green hospital.

In Germany, green hospitals have taken hold, especially in Bavaria. They promote ecological and sustainable goals through three major pillars: energy, the environment, and people. The energy pillar includes energy efficiency, renewable energy, energy management, and energy conservation measures. The environment pillar includes measures to prevent or reduce pollution, such as reducing resource waste, making better use of space, and implementing environmental management practices within the facility. The human pillar includes paying attention to how a hospital affects people, both within the hospital (e.g., attending to the well-being of employees and patients) and outside it (e.g., ensuring that supply chains use fair labor practices) (Müller, 2020). Hospital's environmental footprint can be drastically reduced by utilizing simple, smart, and sustainable measures (Dhillon & Kaur, 2015).

Figure 5 illustrates the internal and external foci of sustainability in hospitals that implement the Green Hospital Program. A hospital can achieve sustainability

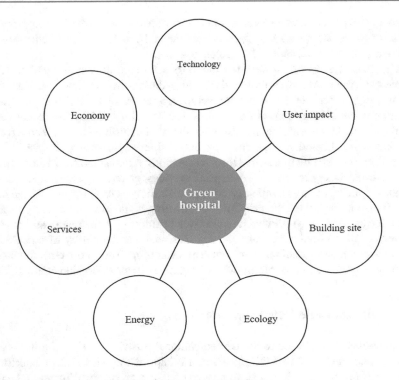

Fig. 5 Internal and external aspects of a Green Hospital Program

in these seven areas through conducting cost-benefit analyses, assessing its environmental impact on users, assessing the risks of the technologies it uses, conserving energy, reducing waste, recycling, and reusing certain healthcare products. The program involves meeting requirements related to the hospital building and its facilities that are determined by both local and state regulations (such as building codes, energy conservation ordinances, and renewable energy heating laws) and laws—particularly laws that prohibit discrimination and regulate healthcare, trade, environmental practices, and labor or collective bargaining laws. Finally, one GHI requirement is a low likelihood that a hospital will close within the next 5 years (Godbole & Lamb, 2018).

2.3   Sustainability and Resilience

The COVID-19 pandemic has significantly contributed to bringing the term "resilience" into the context of global health. The world is recognizing the need for a paradigm shift to ensure a long, sustainable, and resilient future. Resilience can be seen as a descriptive concept that focuses on a system's dynamic features. For instance, early identification and treatment to prevent the further development of illness or comorbidity can help increase resilience by reducing hospitalization and healthcare costs (Ossebaard & Lachman, 2021).

A resilient healthcare system is crucial to achieving universal healthcare. All people have the right to quality healthcare regardless of where they live. Education and prevention are key priorities for achieving universal healthcare. The global community should be focused on the need for flexibility and agility in delivering healthcare and on developing the resilience that will contribute to healthcare for all. That is how sustainability in healthcare can be achieved (Mulvaney, 2020).

Resilience can be distinguished from sustainability. A sustainable healthcare system performs its key functions—delivering services, generating resources, ensuring adequate funding, and providing good administration—continuously. At the same time, it also incorporates the principles of ensuring equitable access and providing efficient care in order to achieve its objectives of improving the health and meeting the needs of the population that it serves. Resilience is the ability of a healthcare system to adapt, learn, and recover from crises emerging from short-term shocks and cumulative tensions in order to limit their negative effects (Corvalan et al., 2020).

2.4   Sustainable Development Goals

Global cooperation has led to the United Nations' Sustainable Development Goals (SDGs) (see Fig. 6). The SDGs provide a blueprint to peace and prosperity for people and the planet. They seek to ensure human dignity, equality, and a healthy environment by ending poverty and hunger in all their forms and dimensions. They also seek to protect the planet by advocating for sustainable consumption, production, and management—and by taking urgent action to address climate change (UN, 2020). The overall goal is for all humans to live prosperous, peaceful, satisfying lives and work toward economic, technological, and social progress in harmony with nature (Mayer-Foulkes et al., 2021).

Some of the SDGs seek to ensure sustainable healthcare by promoting the efficient and sustainable use of natural resources. Relevant practices include preventing waste, reducing consumption, and recycling or reusing products (see Fig. 7). Sustainability is strengthened when countries increase their capacity to adapt to and cope with climate-related hazards. All of these factors are expected to reduce the global maternal mortality ratio. The ratio is targeted to be less than 70 per 100,000 live births (UN, 2020).

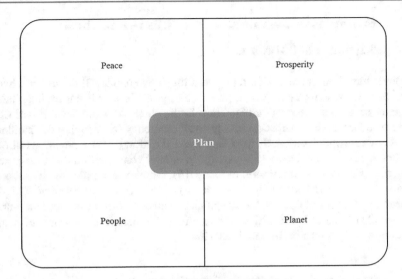

Fig. 6 The Four Ps of the Sustainable Development Goals

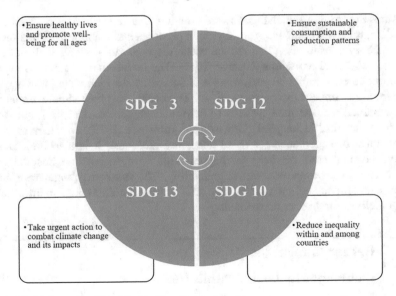

Fig. 7 Healthcare-related Sustainable Development Goals

3   Examples of Sustainable Practices in Healthcare

3.1   Sustainable Buildings

Hospitals based on green design report that they have enhanced the general health status of their patients by improving their quality of life. For instance, hospitals in Denmark created a "healing" architecture in the shape of a four-leaf clover using evidence-based design. This design improved efficiency by reducing the incidence of patient rehospitalization. It also improved the flow of movement within the hospital, leading to an 8% to 15% savings in energy consumption due to increased efficiency (European Commission et al., 2016). Another example involves the use of solar cells on the roof of the hospital to generate power in Sweden. This has reduced the amount of energy that hospitals consume. It further reduces the impact of hospitals on the climate, which in turn affects the health of members of nearby communities (Eriksson & Turnstedt, 2019).

3.2   Sustainable Healthcare Organizations

Hospitals are driving the change toward creating a sustainable society. This could include purchasing policies regarding green products and technologies that tend to lower energy consumption and reduce waste disposal costs, along with pollution and toxic chemical emissions (Gholve, 2015). The inclusion of systems to monitor and improve environmental performance is necessary for identifying how systems and structures impact their surroundings. Therefore, hospitals should implement environmental management systems to help managers make decisions that would lead to a sustainable hospital (Eriksson & Turnstedt, 2019). In order to create a high level of acceptance for these necessary measures, it is also important to involve hospital staff (to help in the transition to a sustainable hospital) and, finally, to raise awareness about sustainability. The measures range from active participation processes, such as "World Café" or "Design Thinking," to information and guidelines for various departments.

4   Recent Challenges

4.1   Challenges for Global Public Health

In 2021, WHO published online key facts reporting that noncommunicable diseases (NCDs) account for 71% of deaths worldwide. Almost 41 million people die every year from preventable NCDs. According to the WHO, these illnesses are often associated with older age groups. Still, there is evidence that more than 15 million people who die from an NCD are in the 30 to 69 age group. Low- and middle-income countries, in particular, bear an especially heavy burden; 80% of all deaths from NCDs each year are in these countries (WHO, 2021). One of the main contributing causes of NCDs is air pollution (Campbell-Lendrum & Prüss-Ustün, 2019), and healthcare facilities worldwide have a heavy carbon footprint. They contribute over 4% to total global emissions of carbon dioxide. Most of this comes from the burning of fossil fuels (Health Care Without Harm, 2019). Air quality is a major concern for both developed and developing countries. Reducing air pollution will reduce the global burden of NCDs. Energy emissions being produced by healthcare facilities include various forms of dioxides, such as sulfur, nitrogen, and carbon dioxide, as well as mercury (WHO, 2019).

4.2 Challenges for Rural Health

Rural areas contend with five specific challenges (see Fig. 8). Addressing the problems of biodiversity loss, economic inequality, climate change, resource depletion, and population loss is necessary in order to achieve healthcare sustainability in rural areas (Schroeder et al., 2012).

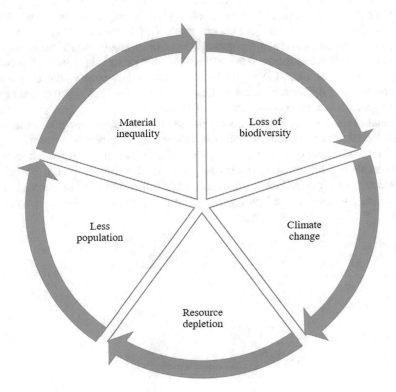

Fig. 8 Five problems that contribute to rural healthcare challenges

5   Research and Innovation

In 2018, Godbole and Lamb identified various methods to connect digital technology with sustainability strategies. One example is increasing the cost of digital innovation in ways that contribute to environmental solutions, such as through carbon pricing and ecological tax reform. Defining clear targets and milestones before building road maps to transform how digitalization relates to energy use, land use, and industries can move markets and planning processes in a sustainable direction.

In the past, healthcare reform has focused predominantly upon the provision of services. However, the concept of healthcare reform has expanded to encompass all aspects of healthcare. These include raising awareness about health and disease prevention through regular health checkups. Today, healthcare providers are focusing on effective monitoring, ways to maintain health, and support for disease management. In addition, new methods and new technology have increased the reach and availability of healthcare services. All healthcare stakeholders, which include doctors, hospitals, insurers, researchers, and government officials, should be seeking novel methods to address the challenges of twenty-first-century healthcare. As providers focus on new healthcare models and practices that can improve the quality of care, device and pharmaceutical manufacturers are pioneering new products to make healthcare more affordable and extend the reach of providers (Eriksson & Turnstedt, 2019). Figure 9 presents the policy areas where governments can provide support for healthcare professionals who are seeking sustainable ways to give patients the best possible care (WHO, 2017).

Potential areas where healthcare can increase sustainability include research and development, human resources, business offices, and commercial enterprise operations that enable organizations to relocate their businesses through growth strategies (thus delivering better care, minimizing risk, and reducing costs). Sustainable healthcare operations further require an equitable distribution of resources in terms of funding for research and programs, employees, and infrastructure (Accenture, n.d.).

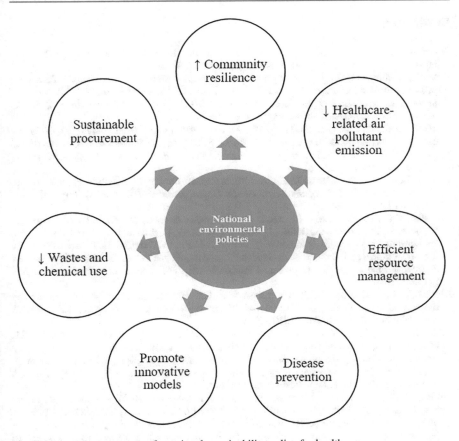

Fig. 9 Potential components of a national sustainability policy for healthcare

6   Conclusion

One of the goals of improving healthcare in the twenty-first century is achieving sustainability. Sustainable healthcare encompasses products, services, and healthcare operations with superior environmental performance. It does so without compromising the quality level of the care itself. Sustainable healthcare is supported by sustainable hospitals, behaviors, and technologies. Although achieving a sustainable healthcare system involves significant challenges, doing so can lead to benefits such as greater employee satisfaction, a reduction in resource waste, the minimization of risk, and lower operating costs. And, of course, the overall goal is to reduce harm to the planet.

Acknowledgments The authors appreciate the guidance, constructive comments, and fruitful discussions from reviewers for coordinating and editing this chapter.

References

Accenture (n.d.). *Health Enterprise operations*. Accenture. Retrieved November 15, 2021, from https://www.accenture.com/us-en/services/health/enterprise-operations

Atun, R., & Moore, G. (2021). *Building a high-value health system*. Oxford University Press.

Bayerisches Staatsministerium für Gesundheit und Pflege (n.d.). *Green Hospital^{PLUS} Bayern-Das nachhaltige Krankenhaus*. Retrieved October 10, 2021, from https://www.stmgp.bayern.de/meine-themen/fuer-krankenhausbetreiber/green-hospital-plus/

Busse, R., Panteli, D., & Quentin, W. (2019). An introduction to healthcare quality: Defining and explaining its role in health systems. In R. Busse, N. Klazinge, D. Panteli, & W. Quentin (Eds.), *Improving healthcare quality in Europe; characteristics, effectiveness and implementation of different strategies* (pp. 3–18). OECD Publishing.

Campbell-Lendrum, D., & Prüss-Ustün, A. (2019). Climate change, air pollution and noncommunicable diseases. *Bulletin of the World Health Organization, 97*(2), 160–161. https://doi.org/10.2471/BLT.18.224295

Corvalan, C., Villalobos Prats, E., Sena, A., Campbell-Lendrum, D., Karliner, J., Risso, A., Wilburn, S., Slotterback, S., Rathi, M., Stringer, R., Berry, P., Edwards, S., Enright, P., Hayter, A., Howard, G., Lapitan, J., Montgomery, M., Prüss-Ustün, A., Varangu, L., & Vinci, S. (2020). Towards climate resilient and environmentally sustainable health care facilities. *International Journal of Environmental Research and Public Health, 17*(23), 8849. https://doi.org/10.3390/ijerph17238849

Dhillon, V. S., & Kaur, D. (2015). Green hospital and climate change: Their interrelationship and the way forward. *Journal of Clinical and Diagnostic Research: JCDR, 9*(12), LE01–LLE5. https://doi.org/10.7860/JCDR/2015/13693.6942

Eriksson, D., & Turnstedt, L. (2019). *Nordic Sustainable Healthcare*. Retrieved November 11, 2021, from http://urn.kb.se/resolve?urn=urn:nbn:se:norden:org:diva-5696

European Commission, Directorate-General for Environment, Debergh, P., Bakas, I., & Greeven, S. (2016). *Study on the energy saving potential of increasing resource efficiency: Final report*. Publications The Office. https://data.europa.eu/doi/10.2779/172229

Fischer, M. (2014). Fit for the future? A new approach in the debate about what makes healthcare systems really sustainable. *Sustainability, 7*(1), 294–312. https://doi.org/10.3390/su7010294

Gholve, S. (2015). Environmental protection by implementation of green purchasing, green productivity, green marketing and green quality management systems. *World Journal of Pharmaceutical Research, 04*(10), 2005–2028.

Godbole, N. S., & Lamb, J. P. (2018). *Making healthcare green; the role of cloud, green IT, and data science to reduce healthcare costs and combat climate change*. Springer International Publishing AG.

Health Care Without Harm. (2019). *Health care's climate footprint: How the health sector contributes to the global climate crisis and opportunities for action*. Health care without Harm and Arup. Retrieved November 14, 2021, from https://noharm-global.org/sites/default/files/documents-files/5961/HealthCaresClimateFootprint_092319.pdf

Mayer-Foulkes, D., Serván-Mori, E., & Nigenda, G. (2021). The sustainable development goals and technological capacity. *Revista Panamericana de Salud Publica (Pan American Journal of Public Health), 45*, e81. https://doi.org/10.26633/RPSP.2021.81

McNickle, M. (2011). 5 most powerful green IT practices. *Healthcare IT News*. https://www.healthcareitnews.com/news/5-most-powerful-green-it-practices

Mortimer, F., Isherwood, J., Wilkinson, A., & Vaux, E. (2018). Sustainability in quality improvement: Redefining value. *Future Healthcare Journal, 5*(2), 88–93. https://doi.org/10.7861/futurehosp.5-2-88

Müller, A. (2020). *Green hospital: not only ecological, but holistic sustainability*. MEDICA. Retrieved November 15, 2021, from https://www.medica-tradefair.com/en/News/Topic_of_the_Month/Older_Topics_of_the_Month/Topics_of_the_Month_2020/Green_Hospital/Green_Hospital_not_only_ecological,_but_holistic_sustainability

Mulvaney, A. (2020). *Why health system resilience is key to a sustainable future.* AstraZeneca. Retrieved October 11, 2021 from https://www.astrazeneca.com/what-science-can-do/stories/why-health-system-resilience-is-key-to-a-sustainable-future.html

Ossebaard, H. C., & Lachman, P. (2021). Climate change, environmental sustainability and health care quality. *International Journal for Quality in Health Care, 33*(1), mzaa036. https://doi.org/10.1093/intqhc/mzaa036

Schroeder, K., Thompson, T., Frith, K., & Pencheon, D. (2012). *Sustainable healthcare.* Wiley.

UN. (2020). *Transforming our world: The 2030 agenda for sustainable development.* United Nations Department of Economic and Social Affairs. Retrieved October 17, 2021, from https://sdgs.un.org/2030agenda

Whichello, C., Bywall, K. S., Mauer, J., Stephen, W., Cleemput, I., Pinto, C. A., van Overbeeke, E., Huys, I., de Bekker-Grob, E. W., Hermann, R., & Veldwijk, J. (2020). An overview of critical decision-points in the medical product lifecycle: Where to include patient preference information in the decision-making process? *Health Policy (Amsterdam, Netherlands), 124*(12), 1325–1332. https://doi.org/10.1016/j.healthpol.2020.07.007

WHO. (2017). *Environmentally sustainable health systems: A strategic document.* Retrieved October 18, 2021, from https://www.euro.who.int/__data/assets/pdf_file/0004/341239/ESHS_Revised_WHO_web.pdf

WHO. (2019). *Noncommunicable diseases and air pollution. WHO European high level conference on communicable diseases.* World Health Organization. Retrieved November 16, 2021, from https://www.euro.who.int/__data/assets/pdf_file/0005/397787/Air-Pollution-and-NCDs.pdf

WHO. (2021). *Noncommunicable diseases.* World Health Organization. Retrieved October 8, 2021, from https://www.who.int/news-room/fact-sheets/detail/noncommunicable-diseases

Medical Additive Manufacturing in Surgery: Translating Innovation to the Point of Care

Florian M. Thieringer, Philipp Honigmann, and Neha Sharma

Abstract

Alongside computed tomography, additive manufacturing (also known as three-dimensional or 3D printing) is a significant MedTech innovation that allows the fabrication of anatomical biomodels, surgical guides, medical/dental devices, and customized implants. Available since the mid-1980s, 3D printing is growing increasingly important in medicine by significantly transforming today's personalized medicine era. 3D printing of biological tissues will provide a future for many patients, eventually leading to the printing of human organs. Unlike subtractive manufacturing (where the material is removed and 3D objects are formed by cutting, drilling, computer numerical control milling, and machining), the critical driver for the exponential growth of 3D printing in medicine has been the ability to create complex geometric shapes with a high degree of functionality. 3D printing also offers the advantage of developing highly customized solutions for patients that cannot be achieved by any other manufacturing technology.

F. M. Thieringer (✉) · N. Sharma
Cranio-Maxillo-Facial Surgery and 3D Print Lab, University Hospital Basel, Basel, Basel-Stadt, Switzerland

Swiss MAM Research Group, Smart Implants – MIRACLE II, Department of Biomedical Engineering, University of Basel, Allschwil, Basel-Landschaft, Switzerland
e-mail: florian.thieringer@usb.ch

P. Honigmann
Hand and Peripheral Nerve Surgery, Department of Orthopaedic Surgery and Traumatology, Kantonsspital Baselland, Bruderholz, Switzerland

Swiss MAM Research Group, Smart Implants - MIRACLE II, Department of Biomedical Engineering, University of Basel, Allschwil, Basel-Landschaft, Switzerland

Department of Biomedical Engineering and Physics, Amsterdam UMC, University of Amsterdam, Amsterdam Movement Sciences, Amsterdam, the Netherlands

© The Author(s) 2022
S. Ehsani et al. (eds.), *The Future Circle of Healthcare*, Future of Business and Finance, https://doi.org/10.1007/978-3-030-99838-7_20

1   Introduction

In the last few years, three-dimensional or 3D printing (also called additive manufacturing or AM as well as rapid prototyping) has experienced a rapid boom in industry—especially in medicine and surgery. However, the technology itself is not new. Stereolithography or SLA, a key technology for 3D printing, was invented more than three decades ago by Charles W. "Chuck" Hull in the United States (Brooks, 2016). The breakthrough in medical and surgical technology was then led by the availability of affordable and user-friendly 3D printers, software solutions, and the continuous improvement of radiological (slice) imaging to produce virtual and highly realistic anatomical models (Hatz et al., 2020). Before, rapid prototyping was complicated, high-priced, and largely unattractive for the average user. Now, inexpensive, user-friendly, and compact 3D printers make it easy to get started with the basics of AM—even in medicine (Hatz et al., 2020; Wegmüller et al., 2021).

Pioneer clinics in high-medical technology enabled a close link between this technology and clinical processes, advancing early translation. For example, they produced stereolithographic models for oral and maxillofacial surgery applications (see Fig. 1). The essential added value of a technological innovation such as 3D printing to the entire treatment chain became apparent alongside the immediate benefits to patients. For the first time, complex human anatomy could become "comprehensible" to clinicians by making complex surgical procedures safer, simpler, and shorter through 3D models and patient-specific or customized implants.

2   Applications in Medicine

Due to the success of medical 3D printing, more and more physicians and engineers in medical fields grew aware of the advantages of its use in the healthcare sector. New treatment methods were developed, enabling therapy options that were hardly conceivable just a few years ago (Honigmann et al., 2017; Honigmann et al., 2018; Meyer et al., 2019; Msallem et al., 2017; Soleman et al., 2015a; Wegmüller et al., 2021).

In modern dentistry and craniomaxillofacial surgery, 3D printing has now become an integral part of the digital medical treatment process. It is commonly utilized in the production of surgical sawing or drilling templates and guides (Soleman et al., 2015a; Sommacal et al., 2018), dental or anatomical bone models (Hatz et al., 2020), active drinking (feeding) plates and dental appliances for pretreatment of cleft lip and palate patients (Beiglboeck et al., 2019; Wegmüller et al., 2021), orthodontic aligners (transparent splints for the computer-planned movement of teeth), and temporary restorations. It is also used for complex prosthetic solutions, including patient-specific implants made of titanium, ceramics, or high-performance polymers making up a "human replacement part" (Han et al., 2019; Honigmann et al., 2017, 2021; Msallem et al., 2017; Schön et al., 2021; Thieringer et al., 2016, 2017).

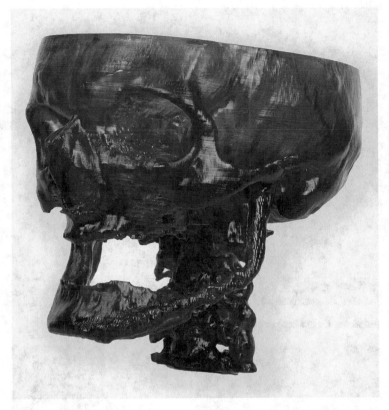

Fig. 1 Stereolithographic model for surgical planning (Zeilhofer, University of Basel)

At present, many 3D printing materials are biocompatible. Some are also certified for medical applications and can therefore be used in contact with the human body or even as a substitute for human tissue (bioprinting) (Cao et al., 2020; Dey & Ozbolat, 2020; Honigmann et al., 2018; Zhang et al., 2021; Zhao et al., 2021). These innovative fabrication processes are currently being explored in several interdisciplinary projects led by research groups at the Department of Biomedical Engineering and the Department of Biomedicine at the University of Basel, Switzerland (Figs. 2 and 3).

2.1   Benefits of Medical 3D Printing

3D printing in medicine and surgery offers engineers, developers, and doctors the advantage of segmenting, designing, and constructing anatomical 3D models on a computer. After a brief wait, they can hold these models in their hands—literally "grasping" the anatomy. Whether directly or indirectly 3D printed, these anatomical

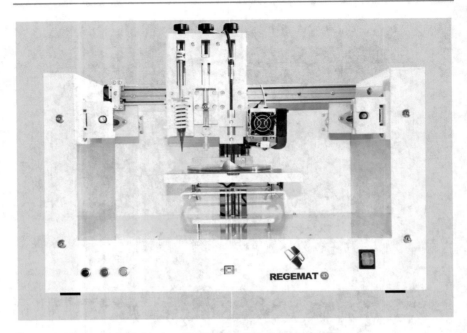

Fig. 2 Bioprinter for bio-ink/gel matrix (Regemat 3D, Granada, Spain)

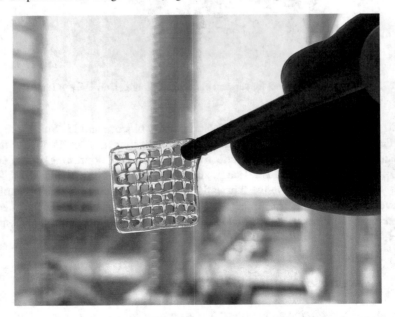

Fig. 3 3D bioprinted bio-ink/gel matrix (Swiss MAM Research Group, Thieringer, DBE)

models and implants allow surgeons to provide highly accurate, patient-specific care that offers numerous benefits at various points in medical and surgical treatment processes (Han et al., 2019; Hatz et al., 2020; Honigmann et al., 2017; Meyer et al., 2019; Sommacal et al., 2018; Wegmüller et al., 2021).

2.2   Popular 3D Printing Technologies in Medicine

In general, the 3D printing processes most widely used in the medical field all apply the raw material (e.g., plastics/polymers, polymer resins, metals, ceramics, and other materials that include biological substances such as body cells) in a layer-by-layer manner—i.e., additively—to a print bed. The material is then cured by either physical or chemical processes. With some 3D printers, these layers are only a few micrometres thin. The printed results are produced to a high resolution, accurately representing the original computer-aided design (CAD) file in all of its geometric dimensions and specifications (Hatz et al., 2020). In addition, 3D printing based on layer-by-layer manufacturing offers almost unlimited freedom in the production of 3D objects. This is a great benefit especially to the production of complex anatomical models or even biomechanically optimized structures with lightweight designs, such as osteosynthesis plates or implants. Layer-by-layer manufacturing enables these products to withstand high loads with low material input (Honigmann et al., 2017, 2018; Thieringer et al., 2016) (Figs. 4 and 5).

2.3   Research Activities in Medical 3D Printing

The research group "Medical Additive Manufacturing" (www.swiss-mam.ch) was founded in 2013 within the Department of Clinical Morphology and Biomedical Engineering. At present, it is firmly integrated into the Department of Biomedical Engineering (DBE) at the University of Basel. There, we deal with all aspects of 3D printing in medicine and surgery. The focus areas of the research projects are:

- Materials and innovative printing processes, including the use of high-performance polymers (such as PEEK) in the manufacture of biocompatible patient-specific implants and various printing processes in medical applications.
- Clinical processes or the integration of medical 3D printing at the point of care.
- Implants or the fabrication of patient-individual, 3D-printed, human "spare parts" from various materials (e.g., PEEK, ceramics, titanium, etc.) and "smart" implants (e.g., with sensor technology in the reconstruction of orbital defects).
- Imaging and planning methods (virtual surgical planning) for the digitalization of the surgical treatment process.
- Software development and surface imaging processes (optical scanning processes in medical use).
- As a new field of research, bioprinting, such as the production of biological, resorbable scaffolds or the combined 3D printing of carrier structures and

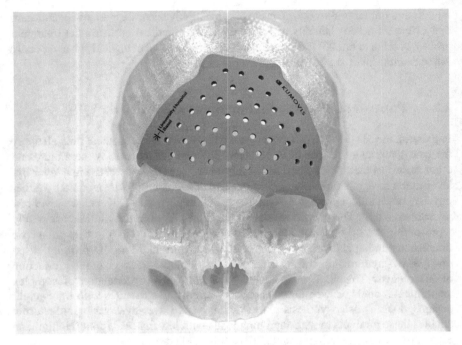

Fig. 4 3D-printed skull implant made of polyetheretherketone (PEEK) (Swiss MAM Research Group, Thieringer, DBE)

biological tissues/cells (e.g., cartilage or bone) as essential steps in the field of regenerative surgery.

Other areas of research include the influence of 3D planning and printing processes on the quality of treatment, as well as

- economic aspects, the optimization of patient treatment by integrating three-dimensional, "tangible" anatomical models into the clinical treatment chain, and the integration and evaluation of digital and,
- virtual reality (VR) and augmented reality (AR) methods along with 3D-printed models in:
- medical teaching, further education, and training focused on surgical disciplines/hand surgery and craniomaxillofacial surgery.

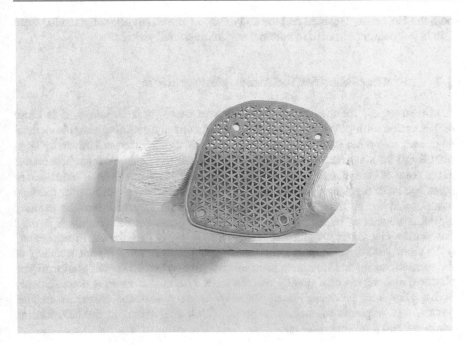

Fig. 5 3D-printed polyetheretherketone (PEEK) shell for guided bone regeneration (Swiss MAM Research Group, Thieringer, DBE)

3 Point-of-Care Manufacturing

As a complement to the research group mentioned above, the 3D Print Lab was established in 2016 at University Hospital Basel by the Department of Craniomaxillofacial Surgery and the Radiology Department to install "medical 3D printing and 3D visualization" technology. The point-of-care-established 3D Print Lab is centrally located and easily accessible to all of the medical and surgical specialties at the university hospital. The 3D Print Lab is an essential and valuable addition to the research group at DBE, enabling translational research close to the clinic. Given its spatial proximity to the treatment centre at the hospital and the rapid acceptance by numerous medical disciplines that resulted, it was possible to establish an innovative 3D research and service lab unique in form in Switzerland and Europe. Numerous clinical and scientific collaborations with national and international partners were quickly initiated to advance research into the field of medical 3D printing from a variety of perspectives in order to optimize patient treatment—especially in terms of oral and craniomaxillofacial surgery. The 3D Print Lab is now listed as an exemplar project for medical innovation and successful translation by government representatives, the board of directors, and hospital management at both the University Hospital and the University of Basel. Additionally, the 3D Print Lab is frequently presented to national and international visitors.

3.1   Prerequisites for Technology Integration

A critical aspect for the clinical translation of these research activities is close collaboration with physicians (particularly surgeons and radiologists), biomedical engineers, and other healthcare stakeholders. This was realized at University Hospital Basel through the provision of a service platform to achieve local acceptance at the point of care. For instance, standard operating procedures were established to meet legal and regulatory requirements. The manufacturing processes for medical models, surgical cutting guides, and implants were all integrated into the existing digital structures of the hospital. The ordering process for 3D models is carried out via the electronic patient file, just as for an X-ray or computed tomography (CT) scan. Additional requirements involve end-to-end, fully digital tracking of the manufacturing and treatment process through a validated digital platform. The platform also serves as a quality management system that ensures a consistently high quality in the products. Finally, these systems enable traceability from models, guides, and implants to medically certified raw materials for the 3D printing workflow and relevant processes.

4   Relevant Studies and Publications for Point-of-Care 3D Printing in Basel

4.1   A Desktop 3D Printer Vs. a Professional Device

Can an entry-level 3D printer create high-quality anatomical models? Assessing the accuracy of mandibular models printed by a desktop 3D printer and a professional device (Hatz et al., 2020).

This study addresses a very clinical question: Can a low-cost, consumer-oriented, Fused Filament Fabrication (FFF) 3D printer produce anatomical mandibular models with a level of precision equal to that of a professional, expensive, industry-oriented, Selective Laser Sintering (SLS) 3D printer? We selected mandibular models as anatomical reference models because they are commonly used in our clinical practice as maxillofacial surgeons to preform (prebend) standard titanium implants (e.g., reconstructive titanium plates) preoperatively—a realistic clinical setup. After comparing the optically scanned 3D-printed exemplary models with the original standard tessellation language (STL) data set, a statistical evaluation of the measurement results revealed that both manufacturing methods showed high accuracy with clinical acceptability. In particular, comparison of the FFF models (the low-cost method) with the original STL files showed a mean difference of -0.055 ± 0.227 mm and a median difference of -0.022 (-0.153 to 0.065) mm. As a

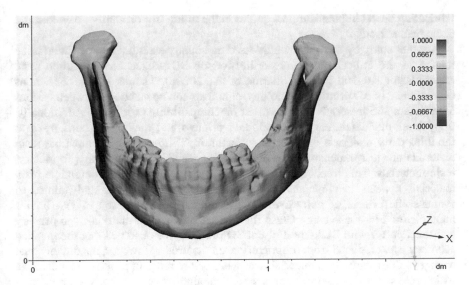

Fig. 6 Part comparison (heat map) analysis of an FFF-printed, low-budget mandibular model (Swiss MAM Research Group, Thieringer, DBE)

result, we demonstrated that mandibular models printed in-house with low-cost FFF 3D printers are serious alternatives to professionally (outsourced and expensive) fabricated 3D models (Fig. 6).

4.2 Evaluation of 3D Printers for Guided Implant Surgery (Wegmüller et al., 2021)

The study addressed a similar question through close cooperation with colleagues from the University Dental Clinics of the University of Basel (Filippi and Kühl). This time, we compared a professional printing process for dental implant surgical guides (digital light processing) to a cost-effective FFF process (see above).

To do so, we produced eight different surgical drill guides using 3D printers. After removal of the support structures, we optically recorded the guides with a surface scanner. Here, too, the STL data from the surgical guides were virtually superimposed in the analysis software to determine deviations; the corresponding measured values were then statistically evaluated. Although the results were promising, the findings contrasted with the previously mentioned study as the manufacturing accuracy of the FFF-printed surgical guides proved unable to meet the requirements of dental implantology (Sommacal et al., 2018). But given the rapid pace of technological advances, especially in FFF printing processes, we can now assume that this technology will be used more and more frequently when fabricating dental implant surgical guides in the future (for primarily economic and ecological reasons).

Another study by the authors addressed an equally essential and pertinent issue related to the effects of steam sterilization on 3D-printed biocompatible resin materials for surgical guides (Sharma et al., 2020b). Thanks to the continuous development of 3D printing technology, clinicians can now choose between various 3D printers and materials with certified biocompatibility properties. Additionally, 3D printer manufacturers are developing printers and making systems open to the third-party materials of other manufacturers. Third-party biocompatible resin materials are less expensive than proprietary (manufacturer-standard/proprietary) resin materials. This freedom to select from various low-cost biocompatible resin materials appeals to clinicians. Considering these aspects, this study aimed to evaluate the effects of autoclaves on the dimensional accuracy of test bodies manufactured in-house using Class IIa biocompatible resin materials (proprietary and third party) with SLA and PolyJet 3D printers. We observed that the greatest accuracy was produced from proprietary resin materials. However, the dimensional change of third-party resin materials was within close range of proprietary materials, which means they can serve as an economical alternative. The off-site production and shipping of 3D-printed surgical guides can be time-consuming and costly. In contrast, the in-house fabrication of surgical guides can be completed quickly and at a much lower cost.

4.3   An Interactive, Fully Digital Design Workflow for a Custom, 3D-Printed, Facial Protection Orthosis (Face Mask) (Sharma et al., 2020c)

In this paper, we integrated the existing tools of medical image processing software, CAD, 3D digitization, and AM to provide a "no-touch", practitioner–/patient-friendly solution for a professional football player who had suffered a cheekbone injury during practice and needed a patient-specific, face-protective orthosis or face mask. The player's 3D face scan and radiological data sets were digitally sent to the authors from our colleague at the University Clinic of Oral and Maxillofacial Surgery in Innsbruck, Austria (Netzer). Design and virtual planning considered which anatomical structures required protection and which rigid anatomical structures could provide support and stability for the face mask. Based on functional and clinical aspects at the fractured site, a virtually designed face mask was fabricated in-house using a carbon-reinforced polylactic acid composite material with an FFF 3D printer. The face mask was tailor-made and fit the player perfectly. The inside of the mask was cushioned by a softer fabric with a high absorption capacity. An elasticated band was used to secure the mask around the player's head.

The lightweight face mask required no alterations. It had a comfortable fit and shortened the convalescence period for the player. Here, we illustrate the potential for the proposed workflow in similar facial fracture situations—thereby providing

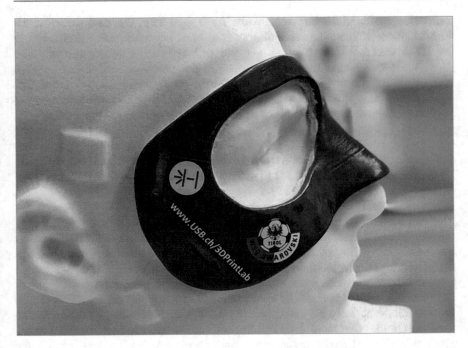

Fig. 7 FFF-printed, carbon-reinforced, polylactide (PLA), custom face mask (Swiss MAM Research Group, Thieringer, DBE)

greater ease of fabrication and cost-effectiveness through an in-house production facility (Fig. 7).

4.4 Computer-Assisted Virtual Planning and Surgical Template Fabrication for Fronto-Orbital Advancement (Soleman et al., 2015b)

In this paper, we described a new digital treatment workflow in the field of cranio-facial surgery through an interdisciplinary research project (maxillofacial surgery and paediatric neurosurgery). The subject of this fully digital, virtual planning procedure, which has been established in our clinic for several years now, is based on a CT data set (digital imaging and communications in medicine or DICOM) of paediatric patients. We used 3D-printed incision and deformation templates for the correction of craniosynostoses and other cranial malformations. After segmentation of the radiological image data, we performed virtual surgical planning on the computer by considering all surgical steps for symmetrization/correction of the deformed paediatric skull. Following the 3D printing of biocompatible and sterilizable plastic moulds in our lab, the virtual computer planning data was transferred to the child intraoperatively. As a final step, the new shape of the "orbital bandeau" and the remaining cranial bone segments were positioned in the 3D-printed moulds and joined together with resorbable osteosynthesis plates (SonicWeld Rx® system), precisely as planned preoperatively. We demonstrated a high predictive and repeatability accuracy for the procedures described above. The application of this procedure, which is now established in our clinics, is simple and very cost-effective due to the in-house planning and production of the guides.

4.5 Craniofacial Reconstruction through a Cost-Efficient, Hybrid Process that Uses 3D Printing and Intraoperative Fabrication (Msallem et al., 2017)

This paper evaluated and described a novel, cost-effective process for the in-house fabrication of patient-specific plastic/polymethyl methacrylate (PMMA) implants for the reconstruction of cranial defects. For the reconstruction of complex cranial defects, patient-specific custom implants (either milled PEEK or 3D-printed titanium) have proven successful. Still, they must be purchased from external companies at high cost and sometimes with a considerable time lag. This can be problematic, especially for clinics in countries with financially weak healthcare systems. On the other hand, PMMA is a bone cement that has been tried and tested for decades. Yet the use of this cement to produce cranial roof implants has decisive disadvantages—not only in the direct adaptation of the material to the patient but also in handling the toxic components of PMMA and curing the material at high temperatures. As proof of concept, we developed a simple manufacturing process based on virtual 3D implant planning, in-house 3D printing, and the fabrication of sterilizable silicone moulds for use in the operating room to produce patient-specific "hybrid" implants. This work has been a cornerstone of successful, intensive cooperation between craniomaxillofacial surgery and neurosurgery departments. More than 30 skullcap reconstruction surgeries (cranioplasty) have now been performed (Schön et al., 2021) and are currently being evaluated in further studies. The easy-to-implement procedure can also be used in clinics with limited financial resources, enabling the production of accurate, precisely fitted (Chamo et al., 2020), 3D print-based, patient-specific "hybrid" implants made of PMMA (Fig. 8).

4.6 "Hybrid" Patient-Specific Implants in Orbital Floor Fractures (Sigron et al., 2020, 2021)

This paper evaluated and described another application for 3D printing involving the in-house fabrication of patient-specific "hybrid" implants to reconstruct orbital floor fractures. To repair orbital floor fractures, titanium meshes are generally bent and adjusted during surgery. These adjustments are based on the size and shape of the fractured orbital floor. Due to the complex 3D anatomy of the orbit

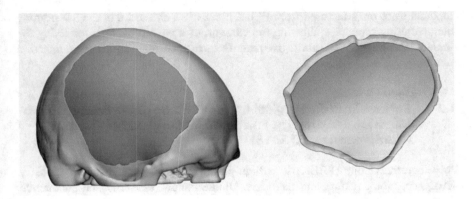

Fig. 8 Design process for a patient-specific skull implant (Swiss MAM Research Group, Thieringer, DBE)

itself, along with limited surgical access, orbital reconstructions continue to be a significant challenge. This leads to increased surgical time and, on occasion, inaccurate results caused by the freehand, manual adaptation of the meshes. In such clinical scenarios, 3D-printed anatomical models can be an asset. So we compared the efficacy of the intraoperative bending of titanium meshes (the conventional approach) with a preformed, patient-specific, "hybrid" titanium mesh implant based on an in-house, 3D-printed, anatomical model. We observed that use of the 3D-printed orbital anatomical model to prebend the plate preoperatively resulted in a considerable reduction to the operation time (by an average of 42.5 mins in our cases). Compared to the conventional approach, the model also provided a more accurate reconstruction of the orbital floor with a better functional outcome.

4.7 A 3D-Printed, Patient-Specific Scaphoid Replacement: A Cadaveric Study (Honigmann et al., 2017)

A close collaboration between our research group and other clinical and research partners, this interdisciplinary study goes a step further in the direction of 3D-printed, patient-specific implants. Within the framework of this research project described in the paper, a novel scaphoid prosthesis was developed based on anatomical data. The prosthesis was then implanted and evaluated at the Institute of Anatomy at the University of Basel within the framework of a cadaver study (static CT motion and dynamic motion analysis/cinematography). An interesting aspect was the innovative design of this implant, which included a curved channel for the passage of the tendon of the M. flexor carpi radialis as well as the evaluation of different manufacturing processes based on material-scientific biomechanical and clinical aspects. For this study, sample scaphoid prostheses were 3D printed from titanium, PEEK, and ceramic and compared. In addition, reference scaphoid implants were manufactured from PEEK blocks. We showed that the 3D printing manufacturing processes allowing the creation of a curved channel for fixing the implant were superior to subtractive manufacturing processes (milling) or injection moulding.

4.8 Patient-Specific Surgical Implants Made of 3D-Printed PEEK: Material, Technology, and Scope of Surgical Application (Honigmann et al., 2018)

Polyetheretherketone (PEEK) is a high-performance polymer used in industry, aerospace, motor racing, and medicine. Unlike metals, PEEK is non-conductive, shows hardly any/no artefacts in radiological imaging examinations, and exhibits excellent tissue compatibility without the classic stress-shielding effect commonly observed in titanium implants. Classical subtractive manufacturing methods for individual implants include the expensive milling process (milling with loss of material). This process cannot produce complex geometric shapes (e.g., hollow bodies, a honeycomb structure, lightweight construction) or the injection moulding of PEEK, which is problematic for individual implants. Until a few years ago, there were no (or only very costly) processes for manufacturing patient-specific implants additively. Our research group recognized the potential application of 3D printing to custom PEEK implants several years ago and has conducted extensive research in this area. Through exclusive cooperation with an industrial partner, we were able to test and evaluate the first industrial 3D PEEK printers within the scope of several studies. In the present paper, aspects of the digital workflow (from the patient's DICOM data set to the material extrusion-based FFF 3D printing of patient-specific PEEK implants in the clinical-medical context) were highlighted and critically evaluated. In another study, we demonstrated the potential for smoother integration and faster implant production (within 2 hours) for the above-mentioned complexly shaped, patented, PEEK, patient-specific scaphoid prosthesis (Honigmann et al., 2021).

Building upon these positive initial findings, we evaluated the performance of in-house, 3D-printed, PEEK cranial implants. We then assessed their clinical applicability in reconstructive surgery applications. We observed that the custom, 3D-printed, cranial implants had high dimensional accuracy, repeatability, and clinically acceptable morphologic similarity in terms of fit and contour continuity. Biomechanically, the tested cranial implants had a mean (SD) peak load of 798.38 ± 211.45 N. In conclusion, the findings from these studies (Sharma et al., 2020a, 2021) revealed the profound effects of bringing in new dimensions to point-of-care manufacturing. Custom implants can be manufactured close to the operating room and directly sterilized, streamlining the entire production workflow. These advancements will result in a paradigm shift that will propel the point-of-care manufacturing digital workflow of customized implants to unprecedented heights. In a nutshell, the addition of in-house 3D printing has brightened the prospects for PEEK, FFF, 3D printing in craniomaxillofacial, trauma, and orthopaedic surgery.

4.9　An in Vitro Study of Osteoblast Response on Fused-Filament Fabrication 3D-Printed PEEK for Dental and Craniomaxillofacial Implants (Han et al., 2019)

Part of an international collaboration, this paper describes the effects of different surface textures of untreated, polished, and sandblasted PEEK test specimens. The specimens were 3D printed by our research group on human osteosarcoma cell lines (cell adhesion, metabolic activity, and proliferation). A fascinating finding from this study is that untreated PEEK surfaces showed a significant increase in cell metabolic activity and proliferation after 5 days, with a higher cell density than in comparison groups. The study promises exciting prospects for possible surface configurations of 3D-printed implants, for example, for use in orthopaedics, spinal surgery, neurosurgery, and, of course, oral and craniomaxillofacial surgery. Our group is already conducting further studies of surface treatment.

4.10　An in Vitro Mechanical and Biological Properties of 3D-Printed Polymer Composite and β-Tricalcium Phosphate Scaffold on Human Dental Pulp Stem Cells (Cao et al., 2020)

As a part of an international collaboration, another paper in the field of regenerative medicine describes the fabrication of a polymer composite with a bone-forming material. We successfully fabricated 3D composite scaffolds with interconnected porous structures made up of poly(lactic-co-glycolic acid) with tricalcium phosphate (3D-PLGA/TCP). We also fabricated native 3D-TCP scaffolds using two relatively different 3D-printing technologies and investigated the mechanical and biological responses of human dental pulp stem cells (hDPSCs). Our findings showed that the native 3D-TCP scaffolds have a higher compressive strength than 3D-PLGA/TCP scaffolds, but the 3D-PLGA/TCP scaffolds were more flexible mechanically. We further showed how the addition of a 3D structure and TCP components to PLGA polymer increased the hDPSCs adhesion and proliferation while also promoting osteogenic differentiation. These findings indicate future potential to repair minor and critical bone defects in oral and maxillofacial surgery. Our group is already conducting additional research in this area.

5　Conclusions

Integration of the additive manufacturing of anatomical patient models, surgical templates, and patient-specific implants into hospital processes offers numerous advantages. These include high-level, interdisciplinary exchange between relevant professional groups, a faster turnaround time for implant manufacturing, support for preoperative and intraoperative planning, improved treatment outcomes, and lower overall healthcare costs in the medium term. We believe that even medical 3D printing of patient-specific implants could become an integral part of larger hospitals, potentially offering numerous applications (especially as relates to reconstructive surgery).

Acknowledgments We would like to thank Professor Hans-Florian Zeilhofer, Emeritus Head of Craniomaxillofacial Surgery at University Hospital Basel and Associate Vice President Innovation at the University of Basel, for his mentoring, inspiration, and endless innovative spirit, which has enabled numerous high-tech applications in clinical use. We thank the Werner Siemens Foundation for generously supporting our research activities, which are part of the MIRACLE (Minimally Invasive Robot-Assisted Computer-guided LaserosteotomE) project. Last but not least, we would like to thank Sepehr Ehsani for making this book possible with his tireless diligence and dedication. The authors declare no potential conflicts of interest.

References

Beiglboeck, F., Thieringer, F. M., Scherrer, G., & Mueller, A. A. (2019). 3D-printing for orthopedic treatment of infants with cleft lips and palate deformities. *International Journal of Oral and Maxillofacial Surgery, 48*, 5.

Brooks, M. (2016). The day the world became 3D. *New Scientist (1971), 232*(3096), 40–41.

Cao, S., Han, J., Sharma, N., Msallem, B., Jeong, W., Son, J., Kunz, C., Kang, H.-W., & Thieringer, F. M. (2020). In vitro mechanical and biological properties of 3D printed polymer composite and β-Tricalcium phosphate scaffold on human dental pulp stem cells. *Materials (Basel, Switzerland), 13*(14), 3057.

Chamo, D., Msallem, B., Sharma, N., Aghlmandi, S., Kunz, C., & Thieringer, F. M. (2020). Accuracy assessment of molded, patient-specific polymethylmethacrylate craniofacial implants compared to their 3D printed originals. *Journal of Clinical Medicine, 9*(3), 832.

Dey, M., & Ozbolat, I. T. (2020). 3D bioprinting of cells, tissues and organs. *Scientific Reports UK, 10*(1), 14023.

Han, X., Sharma, N., Xu, Z., Scheideler, L., Geis-Gerstorfer, J., Rupp, F., Thieringer, F. M., & Spintzyk, S. (2019 Jun). An in vitro study of osteoblast response on fused-filament fabrication 3D printed PEEK for dental and Cranio-maxillofacial implants. *Journal of Clinical Medicine, 8*(6), 771–716.

Hatz, C. R., Msallem, B., Aghlmandi, S., Brantner, P., & Thieringer, F. M. (2020). Can an entry-level 3D printer create high-quality anatomical models? Accuracy assessment of mandibular models printed by a desktop 3D printer and a professional device. *International Journal of Oral and Maxillofacial Surgery, 49*(1), 143–148.

Honigmann, P., Schumacher, R., Marek, R., Büttner, F., Thieringer, F., & Haefeli, M. (2017). A three-dimensional printed patient-specific scaphoid replacement: A cadaveric study. *The Journal of Hand Surgery, 43*(4), 407–412.

Honigmann, P., Sharma, N., Okolo, B., Popp, U., Msallem, B., & Thieringer, F. M. (2018). Patient-specific surgical implants made of 3D printed PEEK: Material, technology, and scope of surgical application. *BioMed Research International, 2018*, 4520636.

Honigmann, P., Sharma, N., Schumacher, R., Rueegg, J., Haefeli, M., & Thieringer, F. (2021). In-hospital 3D printed scaphoid prosthesis using medical-grade polyetheretherketone (PEEK) biomaterial. *BioMed Research International, 2021*, 1301028.

Meyer, S., Hirsch, J.-M., Leiggener, C. S., Zeilhofer, H.-F., & Thieringer, F. M. (2019). A simple, effective, universal, and reusable osteotomy tool for jaw reconstructions with microvascular fibula-transplants. *British Journal of Plastic Surgery., 27*, 1–19.

Msallem, B., Beiglboeck, F., Honigmann, P., Jaquiéry, C., & Thieringer, F. (2017). Craniofacial reconstruction by a cost-efficient template-based process using 3D printing. *Plastic and Reconstructive Surgery—Global Open, 5*(11), e1582.

Schön, S. N., Skalicky, N., Sharma, N., Zumofen, D. W., & Thieringer, F. M. (2021). 3D-printer-assisted patient-specific polymethyl methacrylate cranioplasty: A case series of 16 consecutive patients. *World Neurosurgery, 148,* e356–e362.

Sharma, N., Aghlmandi, S., Cao, S., Kunz, C., Honigmann, P., & Thieringer, F. M. (2020a). Quality characteristics and clinical relevance of in-house 3D-printed customized Polyetheretherketone (PEEK) implants for craniofacial reconstruction. *Journal of Clinical Medicine, 9*(9), 2818.

Sharma, N., Cao, S., Msallem, B., Kunz, C., Brantner, P., Honigmann, P., & Thieringer, F. M. (2020b). Effects of steam sterilization on 3D printed biocompatible resin materials for surgical guides-an accuracy assessment study. *Journal of Clinical Medicine, 9*(5), 1506.

Sharma, N., Welker, D., Cao, S., von Netzer, B., Honigmann, P., & Thieringer, F. (2020c). Industrializing additive manufacturing. *Proceedings of AMPA 2020, 2020,* 26–36.

Sharma, N., Aghlmandi, S., Dalcanale, F., Seiler, D., Zeilhofer, H.-F., Honigmann, P., & Thieringer, F. M. (2021). Quantitative assessment of point-of-care 3D-printed patient-specific polyetheretherketone (PEEK) cranial implants. *International Journal of Molecular Sciences, 22*(16), 8521.

Sigron, G. R., Rüedi, N., Chammartin, F., Meyer, S., Msallem, B., Kunz, C., & Thieringer, F. M. (2020). Three-dimensional analysis of isolated orbital floor fractures pre- and post-reconstruction with standard titanium meshes and "hybrid" patient-specific implants. *Journal of Clinical Medicine, 9*(5), 1579.

Sigron, G. R., Barba, M., Chammartin, F., Msallem, B., Berg, B.-I., & Thieringer, F. M. (2021). Functional and cosmetic outcome after reconstruction of isolated, unilateral orbital floor fractures (blow-out fractures) with and without the support of 3D-printed orbital anatomical models. *Journal of Clinical Medicine, 10*(16), 3509.

Soleman, J., Thieringer, F., Beinemann, J., Kunz, C., & Guzman, R. (2015a). Computer-assisted virtual planning and surgical template fabrication for frontoorbital advancement. *Neurosurgical Focus, 38*(5), E5–E8.

Soleman, J., Thieringer, F., Beinemann, J., Oesch, V., Kunz, C., & Guzman, R. (2015b). Computer-assisted virtual planning and surgical template fabrication for fronto-orbital advancement. *Journal of Neurological Surgery, Part A: Central European Neurosurgery, 76*(S01), 907.

Sommacal, B., Savic, M., Filippi, A., Kühl, S., & Thieringer, F. (2018). Evaluation of two 3D printers for guided implant surgery. *The International Journal of Oral & Maxillofacial Implants [Internet], 33,* 1–4.

Thieringer, F., Popp, U., Okolo, B., Schumacher, R., & Honigmann, P. (2016). Custom implants for humans from a 3-D printer. *Kunststoffe International, 4,* 15–17.

Thieringer, F. M., Sharma, N., Mootien, A., Schumacher, R., & Honigmann, P. (2017). Industrializing additive manufacturing. *Proceedings of Additive Manufacturing in Products and Applications – AMPA, 2017,* 308–315.

Wegmüller, L., Halbeisen, F., Sharma, N., Kühl, S., & Thieringer, F. M. (2021). Consumer vs. high-end 3D printers for guided implant surgery—An in vitro accuracy assessment study of different 3D printing technologies. *Journal of Clinical Medicine, 10*(21), 4894.

Zhang, Y. S., Haghiashtiani, G., Hübscher, T., Kelly, D. J., Lee, J. M., Lutolf, M., McAlpine, M. C., Yeong, W. Y., Zenobi-Wong, M., & Malda, J. (2021). 3D extrusion bioprinting. *Nature Reviews Methods Primers, 1*(1), 75.

Zhao, D.-W., Ren, B., Wang, H.-W., Zhang, X., Yu, M.-Z., Cheng, L., Sang, Y.-H., Cao, S.-S., Thieringer, F. M., Zhang, D., Wan, Y., & Liu, C. (2021). 3D-printed titanium implant combined with interleukin 4 regulates ordered macrophage polarization to promote bone regeneration and angiogenesis. *Bone & Joint Research, 10*(7), 411–424.

The Future of Medical Education

Mark H. Wan and Qiu Ning Lee

Abstract

Changes in medical education have been ongoing throughout the past centuries in order to adapt to new discoveries in medicine and to new changes that physicians face. In this chapter, we will discuss how the content and its delivery have evolved in medical school curricula to allow for the increased knowledge that is now required for the graduating doctor. Next, we will discuss the advancements in technology that have been piloted and will become more mainstream in medical education.

Mark H. Wan and Qiu Ning Lee contributed equally to this work.

M. H. Wan (✉)
Liverpool Hospital, Sydney, NSW, Australia

Faculty of Medicine, Health and Human Sciences, Macquarie University, Macquarie Park, NSW, Australia

Faculty of Medicine, University of New South Wales, Sydney, NSW, Australia
e-mail: mark.wan@health.nsw.gov.au

Q. N. Lee (✉)
The Prince Charles Hospital, Chermside, QLD, Australia

Faculty of Medicine, The University of Queensland, Herston, QLD, Australia
e-mail: qiuning.lee@health.qld.gov.au

© The Author(s), under exclusive license to Springer Nature Switzerland AG 2022
S. Ehsani et al. (eds.), *The Future Circle of Healthcare*, Future of Business
and Finance, https://doi.org/10.1007/978-3-030-99838-7_21

1   Introduction

Medical education has gone through many major changes. Modern medical education, to put it succinctly, arguably began in the Middle Ages, when medical education was relocated to universities. Prior to that, doctors were educated through apprenticeships (Custers & Cate, 2018). At the time, medical education at universities was predominantly for "learned gentlemen" while surgeons generally apprenticed themselves with a seasoned practitioner. The structure of teaching "basic and clinical sciences" (as we would call them today) in the earlier years and providing clinical exposure in the later years was established at universities during this period (Custers & Cate, 2018).

In the twentieth century, a major change in medical education came when Abraham Flexner, an educational reformer, examined medical education in the United States and Canada. His report in 1910 recommended higher admission standards and higher-quality research and teaching (Cooke et al., 2006). This resulted in a much higher-quality and more uniform medical education and the training of more competent doctors. The medical schools that could not meet standards also closed.

Since then, there have been many more changes in medical education. Two examples are the introduction of problem-based learning by McMaster University in Canada (Servant-Miklos, 2019) and the creation of objective structured clinical exams in 1975 at the University of Dundee in Scotland (Harden et al., 1975). Changes are continuing to push medical education into the future. In this discussion, we, as practicing medical doctors with academic roles, will discuss the constant evolution and future of medical education in the areas of curriculum and the implementation of future technologies.

2   Curriculum

As medical science has advanced and knowledge has increased, the need to provide future doctors with a large volume of new and updated information and insights has been a constant challenge. One of the first things that one of our teachers at medical school said was that we were going to learn more scientific content in medical school than he had done only 10 years earlier. This has been made possible especially with advancements in technology. Medical articles and texts are now readily available online. Students can easily access journals through PubMed or electronic versions of their texts, saving the time it would take to search for the content in a library. Having these resources available so readily contributes to learning larger volumes of information.

Another contribution to improving the learning experience is the streaming and recording of lectures. This enables students to attend lectures from the comfort of their homes if they are unable to attend in person or to prioritize their schedule and attend the lecture later. As medical students, we often found it helpful to maximize our productivity by reviewing lectures according to our own schedules and skipping the parts of lectures that covered subjects with which we were already familiar. As medical education continues to advance, remote learning and virtual lectures will become more prominent. The current pandemic has demonstrated that many learning activities can be done remotely. Before the pandemic, while lectures may have been done remotely, tutorials and other group-based sessions were always done face-to-face. Now, as tutorial leaders, we use Zoom or Skype sessions to conduct tutorials effectively. Many laboratory sessions such as pathology and anatomy labs have also been moved to online sessions. While the argument exists that nothing can replace the feeling of touching human tissues and structures in an anatomy laboratory, some medical schools operate their anatomy labs without a cadaver program for financial and/or logistical reasons. These schools rely on models, photographs, and anatomy software that produce 3D models for their anatomy teaching. As medical education moves toward the future, technology will play a larger role in helping medical educators deliver material online for the convenience of both students and teachers and to help students assimilate larger amounts of information.

Furthermore, to help instructors teach larger amounts of information, there has been a shift from passive to more active learning. Some schools have done away with lectures entirely and left it up to the students to learn the material with supplied and supplemental resources. Students who learn in this way solidify their understanding through group discussions and tutorials.

One of the first major shifts from passive to active learning began with the introduction of problem-based learning, also known as case-based learning (Norman et al., 1993). In this learning forum, students discuss a medical case among each other while being supervised by an expert tutor who is also a medical doctor. From our own experiences, we have noticed the many benefits of problem-based learning, such as benefiting from the strengths of colleagues, including the expertise they have derived from life experiences such as previous involvement in research or in other healthcare professions. We have found that case-based learning helps foster teamwork and communication, which are key skills in clinical practice.

Most importantly, case-based learning simulates real-life situations that students will encounter on the wards as the cases are drawn from real clinical cases. However, case-based learning is not without its faults. Certain topics are difficult to grasp through self-learning and case discussions and require a dedicated lecture. We have noticed that this is especially true for topics related to anatomy that cannot be explained in detail in case-based learning due to time constraints and the lack of models or resources. This can also be said for topics involving basic science that can be distracting to explain in group sessions. Case-based learning also depends significantly on student participation, but discussions can often be dominated by more extroverted students and not necessarily by those who have the correct answers. Despite this, the benefits of case-based learning outweigh its deficits. Many studies have shown that case-based learning can be beneficial in multiple areas such as collaboration and problem-solving (Burgess et al., 2021; Cen et al., 2021; Zhao et al., 2020) However, schools should use passive learning such as lectures together with active learning opportunities in order to maximize each student's potential if they want to produce proficient doctors. Indeed, some medical schools have been moving back toward giving more lecture content while still retaining active learning and case-based learning sessions. Some medical schools have created separate streams of learning, which allows students to select the track that best suits their career interests and styles of learning.[1] This will likely become more prominent in the future as more medical schools move toward separate pathways.

While it is true that changes in how content is delivered and changes in the curriculum have made important strides in helping students learn content in the preclinical years of medical school, there have also been changes in what content medical school education emphasizes. Because there has been a heavier emphasis on the ever-evolving science of biomedicine in order to deal with the increasing complexity of health conditions, doctors graduating from medical school today are becoming more and more scientifically sound in their knowledge but also progressively less independent than doctors who graduated in prior years. We distinctly recall that a classmate during the first week of medical school told us that her doctor parents graduated medical school just 30 years earlier equipped with the knowledge to practice independently as general practitioners in a rural area and the ability to perform "minor" surgical procedures such as uncomplicated appendectomies. Today, general practitioners are their own specialty, and the graduating doctor needs to undergo several years of specialty training in order to practice independently in their chosen specialty. Medicine has become more and more specialized. Procedures such as appendectomies, which were once general skills for graduating doctors, are now progressively being taught at the postgraduate level and are firmly in the realm of their own specialties. As medical science evolves, medical education will become more scientifically oriented, and many more procedural skills will be taught at the postgraduate level.

3   Technology and the Future of Medical Education

In addition to distance learning, advancements in simulations and virtual reality can improve the education of future and current doctors.

Medical education has long employed the use of simulated situations and used simulated or actor patients. However, the use of mixed-reality simulations could further aid the integration of formal knowledge and clinical experience. These offer realistic medical scenarios but eliminate patient harm. Users in a controlled

---

[1] As select examples, one could point to the "Pathways MD curriculum" at Harvard Medical School (https://meded.hms.harvard.edu/pathways), the "Distinction Track Program" at the University of Louisville School of Medicine (https://louisville.edu/medicine/distinction/tracks), two different educational tracks at the University of Oklahoma College of Medicine (https://medicine.ouhsc.edu/Prospective-Students/Admissions/Educational-Tracks), or the personalized pathways of the new MD curriculum (launched in 2020) at the University of Sydney School of Medicine (https://www.sydney.edu.au/medicine-health/study-medicine-and-health/postgraduate-courses/doctor-of-medicine.html).

learning environment could observe abnormal pathology that is not otherwise readily available through live patient encounters. This would enable them to practice deliberately and reflect on their performances individually or via team training and could safely learn from their mistakes in order to achieve a well-defined benchmark (Guze, 2015). Medical faculty could review their performance and provide individualized/effective feedback, especially in an exam scenario. Blended learning approaches using virtual worlds and other serious games can provide repeated exposure to meet different students' requirements when combined with face-to-face simulation or clinical placement.

There has also been exploration into using virtual or augmented reality in medical education. This technology has the potential to revolutionize the teaching of anatomy, surgery, and clinical medicine. Augmented reality can provide 3D models that are difficult to visualize in a classroom, allowing users to grasp concepts and visually absorb how those systems work, both independently and with one another. This method of integrating theoretical materials is most effective with visual learners and has proven to improve students' engagement and support self-directed learning (Bogomolova et al., 2020).

The US National Library of Medicine has created the Visible Human Project that involves digitized color photographic slides with 1 mm anatomical sections, allowing users to visualize cross-sectional cryosection, CT, and MRI images obtained from one male cadaver and one female cadaver.[2] Some notable applications or software that provide 3D anatomy images with augmented reality include Complete Anatomy '22 (3D4Medical/Elsevier) and Human Anatomy Atlas (Visible Body). For detailed learning of cardiac anatomy, HeartWorks AR (Intelligent Ultrasound) combines cardiac structure with overlaying transthoracic and transesophageal echocardiogram ultrasound views and can be integrated clinically. HoloHuman (GigXR and Elsevier) is a 3D human anatomy atlas that features full-size immersive holograms that allow instructors to provide students with a holographic learning environment via mixed reality headsets.

Ma et al. (2016) have developed a personalized and interactive augmented reality "magic mirror" system, using a sensor to track the user positions, allowing personalized in situ visualization of anatomy on the user's body. It also shows text information, medical images, and interactive 3D models of organs. One study showed that students who used augmentation of traditional lecture and cadaveric dissection laboratories in conjunction with 3D technologies had significantly higher test scores than those who used two-dimensional pictures, graphs, and text (Peterson & Mlynarczyk, 2016). Another study showed that mobile augmented reality resulted in better test scores, and more permanent learning was achieved in a shorter time as compared to traditional lectures (Küçük et al., 2016). Given that dissection with cadavers is very expensive and time-consuming, the use of such "virtual slides" (at least at the introductory stages of anatomy) can make students' learning more cost-effective and additionally reduce the cost of hiring instructors.

---

[2] The project website is available at https://www.nlm.nih.gov/research/visible/visible_human.html

4 Conclusion

Medical education will continue to grow and evolve as we make advancements in medicine. Continuously adapting curricula and teaching methodologies is necessary in order to meet the needs of educating future doctors and provide them with the latest information and skills they need to be safe practitioners. This will require ongoing use of distance learning and improvements in telecommunications. While the teaching of increasing theoretical information may come at the cost of learning procedural skills at the undergraduate medical education level, this is necessary to deal with the increasing complexity of technical medical knowledge. That being said, advanced skills can be taught at the postgraduate level.

Other developments such as multiple learning streams in medical faculties have also begun to provide students with a tailored experience that best suits their learning styles. Simulations along with virtual and augmented reality have additionally been used at the undergraduate and postgraduate levels of medical education that show promising outcomes. As these technologies grow, they will become more mainstream in the training of the next generation of doctors.

Acknowledgments The authors declare no potential conflicts of interest. The views expressed in this chapter do not necessarily reflect those of the authors' organizations.

References

Bogomolova, K., van der Ham, I. J., Dankbaar, M. E., van den Broek, W. W., Hovius, S. E., van der Hage, J. A., & Hierck, B. P. (2020). The effect of stereoscopic augmented reality visualization on learning anatomy and the modifying effect of visual-spatial abilities: A double-center randomized controlled trial. *Anatomical Sciences Education, 13*(5), 558–567.

Burgess, A., Matar, E., Roberts, C., Haq, I., Wynter, L., Singer, J., Kalman, E., & Bleasel, J. (2021). Scaffolding medical student knowledge and skills: Team-based learning (TBL) and case-based learning (CBL). *BMC Medical Education, 21*(1), 238.

Cen, X. Y., Hua, Y., Niu, S., & Yu, T. (2021). Application of case-based learning in medical student education: A meta-analysis. *European Review for Medical and Pharmacological Sciences, 25*(8), 3173–3181.

Cooke, M., Irby, D. M., Sullivan, W., & Ludmerer, K. M. (2006). American medical education 100 years after the Flexner report. *New England Journal of Medicine, 355*(13), 1339–1344.

Custers, E., & Cate, O. T. (2018). The history of medical education in Europe and the United States, with respect to time and proficiency. *Academic Medicine, 93*. (3S Competency-Based, Time-Variable Education in the Health Professions), S49–S54.

Guze, P. A. (2015). Using technology to meet the challenges of medical education. *Transactions of the American Clinical and Climatological Association, 126*, 260–270.

Harden, R. M., Stevenson, M., Downie, W. W., & Wilson, G. M. (1975). Assessment of clinical competence using objective structured examination. *British Medical Journal, 1*(5955), 447–451. 10.1136/bmj.1.5955.447.

Küçük, S., Kapakin, S., & Göktaş, Y. (2016). Learning anatomy via mobile augmented reality: Effects on achievement and cognitive load. *Anatomical Sciences Education, 9*(5), 411–421.

Ma, M., Fallavollita, P., Seelbach, I., Von Der Heide, A. M., Euler, E., Waschke, J., & Navab, N. (2016). Personalized augmented reality for anatomy education. *Clinical Anatomy, 29*(4), 446–453.

Norman, G. R., Davis, D. A., Lamb, S., Hanna, E., Caulford, P., & Kaigas, T. (1993). Competency assessment of primary care physicians as part of a peer review program. *Journal of the American Medical Association, 270*(9), 1046–1051.

Peterson, D. C., & Mlynarczyk, G. S. (2016). Analysis of traditional versus three-dimensional augmented curriculum on anatomical learning outcome measures. *Anatomical Sciences Education, 9*(6), 529–536.

Servant-Miklos, V. F. C. (2019). Fifty years on: A retrospective on the World's first problem-based learning Programme at McMaster University. *Medical School, Health Professions Education, 5*(1), 3–12.

Zhao, W., He, L., Deng, W., Zhu, J., Su, A., & Zhang, Y. (2020). The effectiveness of the combined problem-based learning (PBL) and case-based learning (CBL) teaching method in the clinical practical teaching of thyroid disease. *BMC Medical Education, 20*(1), 381.

Personalized Dental Medicine with Specific Focus on the Use of Data from Diagnostic Dental Imaging

Andy W. K. Yeung and Michael M. Bornstein

Abstract

Personalized dental medicine considers customized patient care by collecting patient data and relating it to research evidence to facilitate the diagnostic process, treatment planning, and follow-up. This chapter discusses how personalized dental medicine can apply artificial intelligence tools to various dental specialties, specifically focusing on diagnostic dental imaging.

1 General Introduction

Personalized dental medicine is a contemporary approach of modern dentistry that is centered on evidence-based practice such as using artificial intelligence (AI) in the contexts of big data, patient care, and service (Joda et al., 2021). AI applications have gradually begun playing an important role in personalized dental medicine as it relates to patient data, health-care applications, and services (Joda et al., 2021). This approach differs from traditional patient management because it focuses on patient-centered outcomes instead of delivering standardized care to every patient

A. W. K. Yeung
Oral and Maxillofacial Radiology, Applied Oral Sciences and Community Dental Care, Faculty of Dentistry, University of Hong Kong, Hong Kong, China

Department of Oral Health & Medicine, University Center of Dental Medicine Basel UZB, Basel, Switzerland
e-mail: ndyeung@hku.hk

M. M. Bornstein (✉)
Department of Oral Health & Medicine, University Center of Dental Medicine Basel UZB, Basel, Switzerland
e-mail: michael.bornstein@unibas.ch

(Joda et al., 2020). The environment of the oral cavity creates a unique interaction between the patient and their genome and unique microbiome, which consists of the genetic materials that belong to the microorganisms harbored inside that cavity (Chen & Jiang, 2014). As many oral diseases are attributed to oral pathogens and the genetic susceptibility of the patient, personalized dental medicine should consider customized patient care by collecting the patient's data and referring to research evidence to devise the most optimal management strategy for that person.

2   Applicability of Personalized Dental Medicine in Various Specialties

A brief overview of potential applications of personalized dental medicine within each field of dentistry is given in the subsections below. In each section, we discuss some commercially available products. These are summarized in Table 1.

2.1   Implantology/Oral Surgery

AI and personalized dental medicine might be helpful in predicting peri-implantitis and improving the precision of oral surgical interventions such as for the temporomandibular joint (TMJ) and orthognathic surgery.

Personalized dental medicine may be relevant to the diagnosis of peri-implantitis, which is associated with many factors. Gene polymorphism involving interleukin (IL) 1 and 17 was found to be associated with peri-implantitis (Kadkhodazadeh et al., 2013; Laine et al., 2006). The level of a bone turnover marker called receptor activator of nuclear factor kappa-B ligand (RANKL) has been found to be useful for differentiating peri-implant mucositis from peri-implantitis (Rakic et al., 2020). Recently, AI models were shown to predict peri-implantitis onset in 70% of cases by analyzing demographic data such as functional time of an implant, oral hygiene/plaque control record, smoking habits, keratinized mucosal width, and number of occlusal supports (Mameno et al., 2021).

Personalized dental medicine could also be used when planning surgical interventions and prosthesis. For example, a personalized 3D-printed prosthetic TMJ may reduce the risk of nerve damage during surgery and improve clinical and biomechanical performance compared to stock devices in patients with end-stage TMJ osteoarthritis (Ackland et al., 2017). Similarly, personalized 3D-printed titanium plates could be used to guide osteotomy and the repositioning of bone segments during orthognathic surgery, improving their fit and potentially reducing morbidity for the patient (Li et al., 2017).

Table 1 Commercially available tests that could be useful for personalized dental medicine approaches in different fields of dental medicine

Product/test	Function	Purpose/potential clinical impact
Oral tumor/cancer		
OraRisk HPV (OralDNA Labs, Eden Prairie, Minnesota, United States)	Determines an increased risk for HPV-related oral cancer from saliva sample	Risk assessment and deciding on treatment options
OraRisk HSV (OralDNA Labs, Eden Prairie, Minnesota, United States)	Identifies herpes simplex virus (HSV-1 and HSV-2) in the saliva to facilitate differential diagnosis of oral vesicles and ulcers	Disease diagnosis
SaliMark OSCC (PeriRx, Broomall, Pennsylvania, United States)	Tests biomarkers for early OSCC in saliva (genes *DUSP1*, *SAT1*, *OAZ1*, *MT-ATP6*, and *RPL30*)	Disease detection
Periodontology		
MyPerioPath (OralDNA Labs, Eden Prairie, Minnesota, United States)	Identifies periodontal pathogens in saliva. Identifies 10 species-specific bacteria [*Aggregatibacter actinomycetecomitans*, *Porphyromonas gingivalis*, *Tannerella forsythia*, *Treponema denticola*, *Eubacterium nodatum*, *Fusobacterium nucleatum/periodontium*, *Prevotella intermedia*, *Campylobacter rectus*, *Parvimonas micra*, *Eikenella corrodens*] and 1 genus of bacteria [*Capnocytophaga* species (*gingivalis*, *ochracea*, *sputigena*)]	Risk assessment
MyPerioID (OralDNA Labs, Eden Prairie, Minnesota, United States)	Tests for genetic variants of IL-1 gene in saliva	Risk assessment
Cariology		
CariScreen (CariFree, Albany, Oregon, United States)	Tests for cariogenic bacterial load in dental plaque by detecting the amount of adenosine triphosphate (ATP) bioluminescence irrespective of bacteria identity	Risk assessment
Dentocult SM Strip mutans (Orion Diagnostica, Espoo, Finland)	Tests for mutans streptococci in saliva and plaque	Risk assessment
CRT bacteria (Ivoclar Vivadent Inc., Schaan, Liechtenstein)	Tests for mutans streptococci and lactobacilli in saliva and plaque	Risk assessment
Saliva-Check BUFFER (GC Corp., Tokyo, Japan)	Checks salivary resting flow rate and consistency and pH of resting and stimulated saliva	Risk assessment

2.2   Oral Oncology

Personalized dental medicine might be helpful for personalizing the treatment strategy for neoplasms in the oral cavity. For ameloblastoma cases with special gene mutation, oral medications that target the mutation could be provided as an adjunct therapy. For carcinoma cases with human papillomavirus (HPV) positivity, less aggressive treatments might be considered because their survival outcomes are more favorable.

The first therapeutic choice today for ameloblastomas, one of the most common odontogenic tumors, is surgical resection. However, when surgical resection is contraindicated, alternative treatment options have to be considered. For instance, therapy that targets endothelial growth factor receptors has been found to be effective in blocking the proliferation of ameloblastoma cells in vitro, but it has been ineffective against ameloblastoma with B-Raf proto-oncogene serine/threonine kinase (*BRAF*) V600E mutation (Gomes et al., 2014). To block the proliferation of ameloblastoma cells with such mutations, vemurafenib rather than therapy that targets endothelial growth factor receptors has been found to be effective in vitro (González-González et al., 2020). Gültekin et al. (2018) have reported that ameloblastoma with a single *BRAF* mutation usually had a lower risk of relapse, whereas multiple genetic mutations were associated with a higher risk of recurrence. These reports suggested that genotyping ameloblastomas and/or other oral tumors may be useful for devising the best management strategy in the future and may minimize morbidity. Recent case reports have shown that the oral administration of BRAF inhibitors can reduce tumor size and improve the quality of life of patients with a *BRAF*-mutated ameloblastoma with lung metastasis (Broudic-Guibert et al., 2019; Kaye et al., 2015).

Kreimer et al. (2005) have reported that HPV was present in about 26% of patients with head and neck squamous cell carcinoma (SCC). In particular, the figure was 23.5% for oral SCC (OSCC) cases. Therefore, patients who are at high risk due to familial history or who are highly sexually active may consider taking vaccines to protect against carcinogenic, high-risk HPV virus types such as HPV-16/HPV-18, regardless of their sex (Jiang & Dong, 2017; Näsman et al., 2020). It is now recommended that patients diagnosed with oral or oropharyngeal cancer should test for HPV status because HPV positivity affects cancer staging and disease behaviors (e.g., forming smaller primary tumors with potentially more favorable outcomes) (Kato et al., 2020). This might result in individualized and less aggressive treatment approaches for individuals who are HPV positive, such as less invasive surgery, chemoradiation with reduced dose of radiation and chemotherapy, or removal of chemotherapy (Mirghani & Blanchard, 2018).

2.3   Periodontology

AI and personalized dental medicine might be helpful in assessing the risk of periodontal disease, devising tailor-made oral hygiene instructions, and deciding or defining individualized follow-up frequencies.

It is a common practice to give personalized oral hygiene instructions to patients with periodontitis. Instead of the traditional, stereotyped approach where patients are asked to demonstrate their way of toothbrushing on a big, plastic dental model, nowadays dentists can prescribe cleaning tools that are suitable for the particular patient. For example, interdental brushes are available in different sizes, and single-tuft brushes can be used to clean proximal surfaces adjacent to an edentulous ridge. Besides tailoring management strategies based on an individual's oral conditions, dentists can also investigate environmental factors such as lifestyle, use of tobacco and/or alcohol, medication, diabetes, obesity, malnutrition, and psychological stress. All of these can impact the clinical manifestation of periodontitis (Bartold, 2018). These factors may be analyzed by AI models to predict the overall periodontitis risk for the diagnosis and treatment planning stages (Shankarapillai et al., 2010).

The interactions between the host and bacteria also matter. Karimbux et al. (2012) have found that IL-1 gene polymorphisms are associated with increased inflammation and hence increased severity of chronic periodontitis. Pani et al. (2021) have associated the presence of all three red complex bacteria (i.e., *Porphyromonas gingivalis*, *Treponema denticola*, and *Tannerella forsythia*) with higher levels of proinflammatory cytokine IL-1 than the presence of only one or two. When dealing with patients with chronic periodontitis, it may be beneficial to identify the periodontal pathogens in patient's oral cavity (e.g., by MyPerioPath; see the periodontology section of Table 1) in order to better understand the severity of inflammation and define the frequency of recall appointments to monitor the patient's disease status. For example, patients with all three red complex bacteria mentioned above may need more frequent follow-up appointments to ensure good oral hygiene practice to better control inflammation.

2.4   Cariology

AI and personalized dental medicine can help determine the risk of caries.

Tailor-made oral hygiene instructions and dietary analysis are standard practice today. Besides teaching patients about controlling food intake and tooth cleaning behavior, dentists can consider other personal factors that lead to caries. For example, they can check the salivary flow rate, pH, and buffer capacity to see if there are any deficiencies that make the patient vulnerable to developing caries. Multiple genome-wide association studies have been conducted to reveal genetic susceptibility to caries. Some identified genes were associated with cell signaling, tooth development, and immune response to oral pathogens, whereas others had a more unclear role in cariogenesis (Alotaibi et al., 2021; Chisini et al., 2020; Shaffer et al., 2013; Wang et al., 2012). Some genes are responsible for regulating taste and saliva, which are also relevant to caries (Opal et al., 2015). With more scientific evidence, perhaps genetic-based diagnostics could be deployed in the future to assess caries risk.

The oral microbiome can also be checked using dental plaque and saliva samples. A higher proportion of aciduric, saccharolytic bacteria would favor the development of caries (Belibasakis et al., 2019). Salivary biomarkers have also been identified as diagnostic of caries, including IL-4, IL-13, IL-2-RA, and eotaxins (Paqué et al., 2021). These could be checked as part of the caries risk assessment (see the cariology section of Table 1) in order to determine the frequency of follow-up appointments or to make decisions about which restorative materials to use (e.g., glass ionomer releases fluoride) based on the individual's risk. Due to the multifactorial nature of caries etiology, the role of particular bacteria may be affected by a critical threshold, the ecological balance, and the host factors (Banas & Drake, 2018). Perhaps data analysis with the aid of AI may allow us to get a better understanding of it in the future.

2.5   Orthodontics

Orthodontics focuses on aesthetics as well as on masticatory and speech function. Each patient should be treated with a personalized approach instead of simply aligning the teeth in a standardized manner. AI can also annotate anatomical landmarks during cephalometric analysis to help in the initial diagnostic process.

The vertical type of facial growth pattern is commonly known in orthodontics as a major factor that affects facial profile aesthetics and subsequent treatment planning. In cephalometric analysis, other parameters should also be examined carefully for each patient. For example, Derwich et al. (2021) report that the sagittal position of the lower incisors significantly affects the facial profile convexity and that a Z-angle (the angle formed by the intersection of the Frankfort plane and a line connecting the soft tissue of the pogonion and the most protrusive lip point) $\leq 68.0°$ was usually detected for patients with a convex facial profile. Orthodontists deliver personalized care based on an individual's expectations and measurement values based on cephalometric analysis. Silva et al. (2022) found that the landmark annotations and measurement values during cephalometric analysis by AI were reliable. Eventually, facial growth is modulated by hereditary and environmental factors (Carlson, 2015). One obvious example is skeletal class III malocclusion, a polygenic trait that is more prevalent in certain ethnicities (Dehesa-Santos et al., 2021). Knowing the tendency of skeletal growth pattern can enable the clinician to plan the treatment with more confidence. Nieto-Nieto et al. (2017) have suggested that genetic factors could influence external apical root resorption during orthodontic movement, such as IL-1 polymorphisms. However, results were inconsistent, as a recent meta-analysis concluded (Nowrin et al., 2018).

3 Applicability of Personalized Dental Medicine in Diagnostic Dental Imaging

Diagnostic imaging is a vital component of personalized dental medicine because personalized disease prevention often relies on image-based screening such as clinical photos, radiographic images, or intraoral and facial scans. Trabecular thickness and bone volume obtained from cone beam computed tomography (CBCT) scans might serve as bone imaging biomarkers for diagnosis of TMJ osteoarthritis (Ebrahim et al., 2017). Increased local blood flow as observed by ultrasonography at a site of inflammation might also serve as an imaging biomarker for detecting peri-implant diseases (Chan & Kripfgans, 2020).

Personalized optimization of the radiation dose during diagnostic imaging is one of the important goals of modern dentomaxillofacial radiology. Nowadays, the traditional notion of "as low as reasonably achievable" has evolved to "as low as diagnostically acceptable being indication-oriented and patient-specific" (Oenning et al., 2021). The latter dosage has been advocated for pediatric patients in particular (Oenning et al., 2018). Ideally, individual factors in the biologic radiation response, such as age, gender, and other individual factors related to radiosensitivity, should be considered (Belmans et al., 2021). Various manufacturers have implemented personalized radiation doses achieved by automatic exposure control for different imaging modalities, such as for panoramic imaging (Davis et al., 2015) and CBCT (Fig. 1) (Rottke et al., 2019).

The use of AI in 2D and 3D imaging would facilitate a dentist's decisions regarding diagnosis, treatment planning, and follow-up. Some potential clinical examples are listed below.

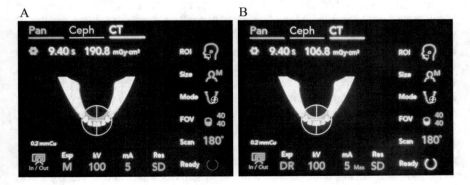

Fig. 1 Reduction of radiation dose of a CBCT scan of the anterior mandible with a field of view (FOV) of 4×4 cm^2 by changing the exposure setting from manual (M; Fig. 1a) mode to dose reduction (DR; Fig. 1b) mode. The tube current was changed from a constant of 5 mA to become dynamic with a maximum of 5 mA. The degree of rotation, kV, exposure time, and voxel size remained unchanged. The radiation dose was thus reduced by 45% (Veraview X800, J. Morita, Japan)

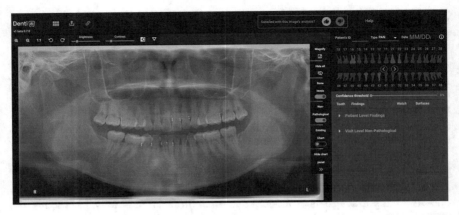

Fig. 2 Automatic tooth detection and numbering by AI. After inputting a panoramic image, the AI software (Denti.AI, Toronto, Canada) has detected the missing teeth and colored them gray in the dental chart on the upper right corner. The teeth that are present are numbered correctly in the chart and are colored in green if they are healthy and in yellow if periodontal bone loss is suspected

AI could analyze radiographic images to provide basic diagnostic tasks such as tooth detection and numbering (Tuzoff et al., 2019) (Fig. 2). AI models can also use clinical photos, periapical radiographs, and bitewing radiographs to diagnose caries (Kühnisch et al., 2022; Schwendicke et al., 2021; Zheng et al., 2021). Similarly, AI can use CBCT and periapical images to diagnose periapical pathosis (Orhan et al., 2020; Pauwels et al., 2021). In particular, AI could differentiate periapical cysts from odontogenic keratocysts using CBCT imaging so that a dentist could choose to refer a patient to an endodontist (in the case of periapical cysts) or a maxillofacial surgeon (in the case of odontogenic keratocysts) (Yilmaz et al., 2017). In addition to identifying dental pathosis, AI models can also analyze imaging to detect nondental pathosis that may be unfamiliar to general dentists. Take panoramic radiography as an example. AI could detect the atherosclerotic carotid plaques that are occasionally found in the field of the carotid artery bifurcation (Kats et al., 2019), osteoporosis based on the shape and relative thickness of the mandibular cortex (Lee et al., 2019), and even maxillary sinusitis (Murata et al., 2019).

One may easily relate imaging (especially 3D imaging) to treatment planning, for example, for wisdom tooth surgery. The main clinical issue is the relationship (proximity) of the mandibular canal to the roots of the lower third molars. For cases where it was necessary to remove lower third molars, surgeons were found to be more confident about making their treatment decisions and opted for fewer coronectomy decisions after seeing CBCT imaging (Szalma et al., 2020). Many surgeons who have access only to panoramic imaging that shows darkening roots and narrowing of the mandibular canal would opt for coronectomy (Szalma et al., 2020). Treatment planning for prosthodontic patients could also be influenced by imaging. For example, AI could classify different types of partially edentulous arches based on clinical photos and facilitate the design of removable partial dentures (Takahashi et al., 2021).

In terms of follow-up, patients with dental implants may pose a challenge to general dentists at the first visit. If the patient does not know about the details of the implants or if such details cannot be retrieved from the surgeon who inserted them, then it would be difficult to help if a fixture is fractured or a screw has become loose. A recent study reported that an AI model could accurately classify the implant identity in test panoramic and periapical images with 95.5% sensitivity and 85.3% specificity (Lee et al., 2020). AI models could also compute peri-implant bone loss ratio from periapical radiographs to assess the severity of peri-implantitis. This information could be helpful when patients came back for a regular (e.g., annual) follow-up (Cha et al., 2021).

There are many more other applications of AI in diagnostic imaging, but the examples listed above seem enough to demonstrate that AI can help general dentists identify potential health concerns and promptly refer the patient to a general physician, an ENT surgeon, or a specialist in the respective field in dental medicine. AI can help dentists practice personalized disease prevention and treatment in diagnostic imaging.

Meanwhile, intraoral scanning should not be neglected as a part of diagnostic imaging because it might replace conventional impression taking for prosthetic purposes. For example, intraoral scanning could capture the edentulous region for rapid prototyping of the polymerized cast to produce a CAD/CAM denture framework for patients with a limited mouth opening who could not undergo conventional impression-taking procedures (Wu et al., 2017). This circumvents the problem of insufficient space for proper tray insertion and alignment. AI can also analyze intraoral scans to detect the margin line of a crown preparation to reduce laboratory time and human error during crown design and fabrication (Lerner et al., 2020). AI algorithms can process data from extraoral scanning (i.e., facial scanning) used to record a patient's facial profile to evaluate changes brought by orthodontic treatment or orthognathic surgery to identify children at risk for autism spectrum disorder (Liu et al., 2016). AI could also analyze the scan data to produce personalized treatment plans and outcome predictions for plastic and reconstructive surgery (Knoops et al., 2019). Intraoral scans, extraoral scans, and other imaging modalities can collectively acquire data to produce a virtual record of a patient. AI could achieve the fusion (or co-registration) of data from these modalities, for example, between CBCT and intraoral scans, without human intervention (Chung et al., 2020).

4   Conclusions and Future Outlook

This brief overview has introduced concepts of personalized dental medicine and discussed how AI can facilitate the practice of personalized dental medicine in the different fields of dentistry. It is applicable for diagnosis, treatment planning, and follow-up. In diagnostic imaging, personalized optimization of radiation dose, personalized diagnosis and prompt referral, and facilitating workflows (such as the use of intraoral scans to replace traditional impression taking) could make diagnosis and treatment more predictable and precise. These tasks could be enhanced and made more efficient with the aid of AI. Many studies have already been done to demonstrate the high potential of AI in image interpretation. With the advancement of science and the accumulation of big data, it is envisioned that personalized dental medicine will become more and more common and will eventually be incorporated into every dental visit. The current hindrance is that few free or commercially available AI products exist in the market, so AI is still seldom implemented in daily practice. Also, many AI models are stand-alone algorithms that require manual data input. Privacy-preserving cloud-based image storage and AI services may be a practical solution and may become the mainstream in the future using AI models that are incorporated in the operating software of radiographic devices and intraoral/extraoral scanners.

Acknowledgments The authors declare no potential conflicts of interest.

References

Ackland, D. C., Robinson, D., Redhead, M., Lee, P. V. S., Moskaljuk, A., & Dimitroulis, G. (2017). A personalized 3D-printed prosthetic joint replacement for the human temporomandibular joint: From implant design to implantation. *Journal of the Mechanical Behavior of Biomedical Materials, 69*, 404–411.

Alotaibi, R. N., Howe, B. J., Chernus, J. M., Mukhopadhyay, N., Sanchez, C., Deleyiannis, F. W., Neiswanger, K., Padilla, C., Poletta, F. A., & Orioli, I. M. (2021). Genome-Wide Association Study (GWAS) of dental caries in diverse populations. *BMC Oral Health, 21*, 377.

Banas, J. A., & Drake, D. R. (2018). Are the mutans streptococci still considered relevant to understanding the microbial etiology of dental caries? *BMC Oral Health, 18*, 129.

Bartold, P. M. (2018). Lifestyle and periodontitis: The emergence of personalized periodontics. *Periodontology 2000, 78*(1), 7–11.

Belibasakis, G. N., Bostanci, N., Marsh, P. D., & Zaura, E. (2019). Applications of the oral microbiome in personalized dentistry. *Archives of Oral Biology, 104*, 7–12.

Belmans, N., Oenning, A. C., Salmon, B., Baselet, B., Tabury, K., Lucas, S., Lambrichts, I., Moreels, M., Jacobs, R., & Baatout, S. (2021). Radiobiological risks following dentomaxillo-facial imaging: Should we be concerned? *Dentomaxillofacial Radiology, 50*(6), 153. https://doi.org/10.1259/dmfr.20210153

Broudic-Guibert, M., Blay, J.-Y., Vazquez, L., Evrard, A., Karanian, M., Taïeb, S., Hoog-Labouret, N., Oukhatar, C. M. A., Boustany-Grenier, R., & Arnaud, A. (2019). Persistent response to vemurafenib in metastatic ameloblastoma with BRAF mutation: A case report. *Journal of Medical Case Reports, 13*(1), 245.

Carlson, D. S. (2015). Evolving concepts of heredity and genetics in orthodontics. *American Journal of Orthodontics and Dentofacial Orthopedics, 148*(6), 922–938.

Cha, J.-Y., Yoon, H.-I., Yeo, I.-S., Huh, K.-H., & Han, J.-S. (2021). Peri-implant bone loss measurement using a region-based convolutional neural network on dental periapical radiographs. *Journal of Clinical Medicine, 10*(5), 1009.

Chan, H.-L., & Kripfgans, O. D. (2020). Ultrasonography for diagnosis of peri-implant diseases and conditions: A detailed scanning protocol and case demonstration. *Dentomaxillofacial Radiology, 49*(7), 1. https://doi.org/10.1259/dmfr.20190445

Chen, H., & Jiang, W. (2014). Application of high-throughput sequencing in understanding human oral microbiome related with health and disease. *Frontiers in Microbiology, 5*, 508.

Chisini, L. A., Cademartori, M. G., Conde, M. C. M., Tovo-Rodrigues, L., & Correa, M. B. (2020). Genes in the pathway of tooth mineral tissues and dental caries risk: A systematic review and meta-analysis. *Clinical Oral Investigations, 24*, 3723–3738.

Chung, M., Lee, J., Song, W., Song, Y., Yang, I.-H., Lee, J., & Shin, Y.-G. (2020). Automatic registration between dental cone-beam CT and scanned surface via deep pose regression neural networks and clustered similarities. *IEEE Transactions on Medical Imaging, 39*(12), 3900–3909.

Davis, A., Safi, H., & Maddison, S. (2015). The reduction of dose in paediatric panoramic radiography: The impact of collimator height and programme selection. *Dentomaxillofacial Radiology, 44*(2), 20140223. https://doi.org/10.1259/dmfr.20140223

Dehesa-Santos, A., Iber-Diaz, P., & Iglesias-Linares, A. (2021). Genetic factors contributing to skeletal class III malocclusion: A systematic review and meta-analysis. *Clinical Oral Investigations, 25*, 1587–1612.

Derwich, M., Minch, L., Mitus-Kenig, M., Zoltowska, A., & Pawlowska, E. (2021). Personalized orthodontics: From the sagittal position of lower incisors to the facial profile esthetics. *Journal of Personalized Medicine, 11*(8), 692.

Ebrahim, F. H., Ruellas, A. C., Paniagua, B., Benavides, E., Jepsen, K., Wolford, L., Goncalves, J. R., & Cevidanes, L. H. (2017). Accuracy of biomarkers obtained from cone beam computed tomography in assessing the internal trabecular structure of the mandibular condyle. *Oral Surgery, Oral Medicine, Oral Pathology and Oral Radiology, 124*(6), 588–599.

Gomes, C. C., Diniz, M. G., & Gomez, R. S. (2014). Progress towards personalized medicine for ameloblastoma. *Journal of Pathology, 232*(5), 488–491.

González-González, R., López-Verdín, S., Lavalle-Carrasco, J., Molina-Frechero, N., Isiordia-Espinoza, M., Carreón-Burciaga, R. G., & Bologna-Molina, R. (2020). Current concepts in ameloblastoma-targeted therapies in B-raf proto-oncogene serine/threonine kinase V600E mutation: Systematic review. *World Journal of Clinical Oncology, 11*(1), 31–42.

Gültekin, S. E., Aziz, R., Heydt, C., Sengüven, B., Zöller, J., Safi, A. F., Kreppel, M., & Buettner, R. (2018). The landscape of genetic alterations in ameloblastomas relates to clinical features. *Virchows Archiv, 472*(5), 807–814.

Jiang, S., & Dong, Y. (2017). Human papillomavirus and oral squamous cell carcinoma: A review of HPV-positive oral squamous cell carcinoma and possible strategies for future. *Current Problems in Cancer, 41*(5), 323–327.

Joda, T., Bornstein, M. M., Jung, R. E., Ferrari, M., Waltimo, T., & Zitzmann, N. U. (2020). Recent trends and future direction of dental research in the digital era. *International Journal of Environmental Research and Public Health, 17*(6), 1987.

Joda, T., Yeung, A., Hung, K., Zitzmann, N., & Bornstein, M. (2021). Disruptive innovation in dentistry: What it is and what could be next. *Journal of Dental Research, 100*(5), 448–453.

Kadkhodazadeh, M., Baghani, Z., Ebadian, A. R., Youssefi, N., Mehdizadeh, A. R., & Azimi, N. (2013). IL-17 gene polymorphism is associated with chronic periodontitis and peri-implantitis in Iranian patients: A cross-sectional study. *Immunological Investigations, 42*(2), 156–163.

Karimbux, N. Y., Saraiya, V. M., Elangovan, S., Allareddy, V., Kinnunen, T., Kornman, K. S., & Duff, G. W. (2012). Interleukin-1 gene polymorphisms and chronic periodontitis in adult whites: A systematic review and meta-analysis. *Journal of Periodontology, 83*(11), 1407–1419.

Kato, M. G., Baek, C.-H., Chaturvedi, P., Gallagher, R., Kowalski, L. P., Leemans, C. R., Warnakulasuriya, S., Nguyen, S. A., & Day, T. A. (2020). Update on oral and oropharyngeal cancer staging: International perspectives. *World Journal of Otorhinolaryngology-Head and Neck Surgery, 6*(1), 66–75.

Kats, L., Vered, M., Zlotogorski-Hurvitz, A., & Harpaz, I. (2019). Atherosclerotic carotid plaque on panoramic radiographs: Neural network detection. *International Journal of Computerized Dentistry, 22*(2), 163–169.

Kaye, F. J., Ivey, A. M., Drane, W. E., Mendenhall, W. M., & Allan, R. W. (2015). Clinical and radiographic response with combined BRAF-targeted therapy in stage 4 ameloblastoma. *Journal of the National Cancer Institute, 107*(1), 378.

Knoops, P. G., Papaioannou, A., Borghi, A., Breakey, R. W., Wilson, A. T., Jeelani, O., Zafeiriou, S., Steinbacher, D., Padwa, B. L., & Dunaway, D. J. (2019). A machine learning framework for automated diagnosis and computer-assisted planning in plastic and reconstructive surgery. *Scientific Reports, 9*(1), 13597.

Kreimer, A. R., Clifford, G. M., Boyle, P., & Franceschi, S. (2005). Human papillomavirus types in head and neck squamous cell carcinomas worldwide: A systematic review. *Cancer Epidemiology and Prevention Biomarkers, 14*(2), 467–475.

Kühnisch, J., Meyer, O., Hesenius, M., Hickel, R., & Gruhn, V. (2022). Caries detection on intraoral images using artificial intelligence. *Journal of Dental Research, 101*(2), 158–165. https://doi.org/10.1177/00220345211032524

Laine, M. L., Leonhardt, Å., Roos-Jansåker, A. M., Peña, A. S., Van Winkelhoff, A. J., Winkel, E. G., & Renvert, S. (2006). IL-1RN gene polymorphism is associated with peri-implantitis. *Clinical Oral Implants Research, 17*(4), 380–385.

Lee, J.-S., Adhikari, S., Liu, L., Jeong, H.-G., Kim, H., & Yoon, S.-J. (2019). Osteoporosis detection in panoramic radiographs using a deep convolutional neural network-based computer-assisted diagnosis system: A preliminary study. *Dentomaxillofacial Radiology, 48*(1), 20170344. https://doi.org/10.1259/dmfr.20170344

Lee, J.-H., Kim, Y.-T., Lee, J.-B., & Jeong, S.-N. (2020). A performance comparison between automated deep learning and dental professionals in classification of dental implant systems from dental imaging: A multi-center study. *Diagnostics, 10*(11), 910.

Lerner, H., Mouhyi, J., Admakin, O., & Mangano, F. (2020). Artificial intelligence in fixed implant prosthodontics: A retrospective study of 106 implant-supported monolithic zirconia crowns inserted in the posterior jaws of 90 patients. *BMC Oral Health, 20*(1), 80.

Li, B., Shen, S., Jiang, W., Li, J., Jiang, T., Xia, J., Shen, S. G., & Wang, X. (2017). A new approach of splint-less orthognathic surgery using a personalized orthognathic surgical guide system: A preliminary study. *International Journal of Oral and Maxillofacial Surgery, 46*(10), 1298–1305.

Liu, W., Li, M., & Yi, L. (2016). Identifying children with autism spectrum disorder based on their face processing abnormality: A machine learning framework. *Autism Research, 9*(8), 888–898.

Mameno, T., Wada, M., Nozaki, K., Takahashi, T., Tsujioka, Y., Akema, S., Hasegawa, D., & Ikebe, K. (2021). Predictive modeling for peri-implantitis by using machine learning techniques. *Scientific Reports, 11*(1), 11090.

Mirghani, H., & Blanchard, P. (2018). Treatment de-escalation for HPV-driven oropharyngeal cancer: Where do we stand? *Clinical and Translational Radiation Oncology, 8*, 4–11.

Murata, M., Ariji, Y., Ohashi, Y., Kawai, T., Fukuda, M., Funakoshi, T., Kise, Y., Nozawa, M., Katsumata, A., & Fujita, H. (2019). Deep-learning classification using convolutional neural network for evaluation of maxillary sinusitis on panoramic radiography. *Oral Radiology, 35*(3), 301–307.

Näsman, A., Du, J., & Dalianis, T. (2020). A global epidemic increase of an HPV-induced tonsil and tongue base cancer-potential benefit from a pan-gender use of HPV vaccine. *Journal of Internal Medicine, 287*(2), 134–152.

Nieto-Nieto, N., Solano, J. E., & Yañez-Vico, R. (2017). External apical root resorption concurrent with orthodontic forces: The genetic influence. *Acta Odontologica Scandinavica, 75*(4), 280–287.

Nowrin, S. A., Jaafar, S., Ab Rahman, N., Basri, R., Alam, M. K., & Shahid, F. (2018). Association between genetic polymorphisms and external apical root resorption: A systematic review and meta-analysis. *Korean Journal of Orthodontics, 48*(6), 395–404.

Oenning, A. C., Jacobs, R., Pauwels, R., Stratis, A., Hedesiu, M., Salmon, B., & DIMITRA Research Group. (2018). Cone-beam CT in paediatric dentistry: DIMITRA project position statement. *Pediatric Radiology, 48*(3), 308–316.

Oenning, A. C., Jacobs, R., & Salmon, B. (2021). ALADAIP, beyond ALARA and towards personalized optimization for paediatric cone beam CT. *International Journal of Paediatric Dentistry, 31*, 676–678.

Opal, S., Garg, S., Jain, J., & Walia, I. (2015). Genetic factors affecting dental caries risk. *Australian Dental Journal, 60*(1), 2–11.

Orhan, K., Bayrakdar, I., Ezhov, M., Kravtsov, A., & Özyürek, T. (2020). Evaluation of artificial intelligence for detecting periapical pathosis on cone-beam computed tomography scans. *International Endodontic Journal, 53*(5), 680–689.

Pani, P., Tsilioni, I., McGlennen, R., Brown, C. A., Hawley, C. E., Theoharides, T. C., & Papathanasiou, E. (2021). IL-1B (3954) polymorphism and red complex bacteria increase IL-1β (GCF) levels in periodontitis. *Journal of Periodontal Research, 56*(3), 501–511.

Paqué, P. N., Herz, C., Wiedemeier, D. B., Mitsakakis, K., Attin, T., Bao, K., Belibasakis, G. N., Hays, J. P., Jenzer, J. S., & Kaman, W. E. (2021). Salivary biomarkers for dental caries detection and personalized monitoring. *Journal of Personalized Medicine, 11*(3), 235.

Pauwels, R., Brasil, D. M., Yamasaki, M. C., Jacobs, R., Bosmans, H., Freitas, D. Q., & Haiter-Neto, F. (2021). Artificial intelligence for detection of periapical lesions on intraoral radiographs: Comparison between convolutional neural networks and human observers. *Oral Surgery, Oral Medicine, Oral Pathology and Oral Radiology, 131*(5), 610–616.

Rakic, M., Monje, A., Radovanovic, S., Petkovic-Curcin, A., Vojvodic, D., & Tatic, Z. (2020). Is the personalized approach the key to improve clinical diagnosis of peri-implant conditions? The role of bone markers. *Journal of Periodontology, 91*(7), 859–869.

Rottke, D., Dreger, J., Sawada, K., Honda, K., & Schulze, D. (2019). Comparison of manual and dose reduction modes of a MORITA R100 CBCT. *Dentomaxillofacial Radiology, 48*(2). https://doi.org/10.1259/dmfr.20180009

Schwendicke, F., Rossi, J., Göstemeyer, G., Elhennawy, K., Cantu, A., Gaudin, R., Chaurasia, A., Gehrung, S., & Krois, J. (2021). Cost-effectiveness of artificial intelligence for proximal caries detection. *Journal of Dental Research, 100*(4), 369–376.

Shaffer, J., Feingold, E., Wang, X., Lee, M., Tcuenco, K., Weeks, D., Weyant, R., Crout, R., McNeil, D., & Marazita, M. (2013). GWAS of dental caries patterns in the permanent dentition. *Journal of Dental Research, 92*(1), 38–44.

Shankarapillai, R., Mathur, L. K., Nair, M. A., Rai, N., & Mathur, A. (2010). Periodontitis risk assessment using two artificial neural networks: A pilot study. *International Journal of Dental Clinics, 2*(4), 36–40.

Silva, T. P., Hughes, M. M., Menezes, L. D. S., de Melo, M. D. F. B., Takeshita, W. M., & Freitas, P. H. L. D. (2022). Artificial intelligence-based cephalometric landmark annotation and measurements according to Arnett's analysis: Can we trust a bot to do that? *Dentomaxillofacial Radiology, 51*(6), 20200548. https://doi.org/10.1259/dmfr.20200548

Szalma, J., Vajta, L., Lovász, B. V., Kiss, C., Soós, B., & Lempel, E. (2020). Identification of specific panoramic high-risk signs in impacted third molar cases in which cone beam computed tomography changes the treatment decision. *Journal of Oral and Maxillofacial Surgery, 78*(7), 1061–1070.

Takahashi, T., Nozaki, K., Gonda, T., & Ikebe, K. (2021). A system for designing removable partial dentures using artificial intelligence. Part 1. Classification of partially edentulous arches using a convolutional neural network. *Journal of Prosthodontic Research, 65*(1), 115–118. https://doi.org/10.2186/jpr.JPOR_2019_354

Tuzoff, D. V., Tuzova, L. N., Bornstein, M. M., Krasnov, A. S., Kharchenko, M. A., Nikolenko, S. I., Sveshnikov, M. M., & Bednenko, G. B. (2019). Tooth detection and numbering in panoramic radiographs using convolutional neural networks. *Dentomaxillofacial Radiology, 48*(4), 20180051.

Wang, X., Shaffer, J. R., Zeng, Z., Begum, F., Vieira, A. R., Noel, J., Anjomshoaa, I., Cuenco, K. T., Lee, M.-K., & Beck, J. (2012). Genome-wide association scan of dental caries in the permanent dentition. *BMC Oral Health, 12*, 57.

Wu, J., Li, Y., & Zhang, Y. (2017). Use of intraoral scanning and 3-dimensional printing in the fabrication of a removable partial denture for a patient with limited mouth opening. *Journal of the American Dental Association, 148*(5), 338–341.

Yilmaz, E., Kayikcioglu, T., & Kayipmaz, S. (2017). Computer-aided diagnosis of periapical cyst and keratocystic odontogenic tumor on cone beam computed tomography. *Computer Methods and Programs in Biomedicine, 146*, 91–100.

Zheng, L., Wang, H., Mei, L., Chen, Q., Zhang, Y., & Zhang, H. (2021). Artificial intelligence in digital cariology: A new tool for the diagnosis of deep caries and pulpitis using convolutional neural networks. *Annals of Translational Medicine, 9*(9), 763.

Index

© The Author(s), under exclusive license to Springer Nature Switzerland AG 2022   399
S. Ehsani et al. (eds.), *The Future Circle of Healthcare*, Future of Business
and Finance, https://doi.org/10.1007/978-3-030-99838-7

Printed in the United States
by Baker & Taylor Publisher Services